England

WORLD BIBLIOGRAPHICAL SERIES

General Editors:
Robert G. Neville (Executive Editor)
John J. Horton

Robert A. Myers   Ian Wallace
Hans H. Wellisch   Ralph Lee Woodward, Jr.

John J. Horton is Deputy Librarian of the University of Bradford and currently Chairman of its Academic Board of Studies in Social Sciences. He has maintained a longstanding interest in the discipline of area studies and its associated bibliographical problems, with special reference to European Studies. In particular he has published in the field of Icelandic and of Yugoslav studies, including the two relevant volumes in the World Bibliographical Series.

Robert A. Myers is Associate Professor of Anthropology in the Division of Social Sciences and Director of Study Abroad Programs at Alfred University, Alfred, New York. He has studied post-colonial island nations of the Caribbean and has spent two years in Nigeria on a Fulbright Lectureship. His interests include international public health, historical anthropology and developing societies. In addition to *Amerindians of the Lesser Antilles: a bibliography* (1981), *A Resource Guide to Dominica, 1493-1986* (1987) and numerous articles, he has compiled the World Bibliographical Series volumes on *Dominica* (1987), *Nigeria* (1989) and *Ghana* (1991).

Ian Wallace is Professor of German at the University of Bath. A graduate of Oxford in French and German, he also studied in Tübingen, Heidelberg and Lausanne before taking teaching posts at universities in the USA, Scotland and England. He specializes in contemporary German affairs, especially literature and culture, on which he has published numerous articles and books. In 1979 he founded the journal *GDR Monitor*, which he continues to edit under its new title *German Monitor*.

Hans H. Wellisch is Professor emeritus at the College of Library and Information Services, University of Maryland. He was President of the American Society of Indexers and was a member of the International Federation for Documentation. He is the author of numerous articles and several books on indexing and abstracting, and has published *The Conversion of Scripts, Indexing and Abstracting: an International Bibliography* and *Indexing from A to Z*. He also contributes frequently to *Journal of the American Society for Information Science*, *The Indexer* and other professional journals.

Ralph Lee Woodward, Jr. is Director of Graduate Studies at Tulane University, New Orleans, where he has been Professor of History since 1970. He is the author of *Central America, a Nation Divided*, 2nd ed. (1985), as well as several monographs and more than sixty scholarly articles on modern Latin America. He has also compiled volumes in the World Bibliographical Series on *Belize* (1980), *Nicaragua* (1983), and *El Salvador* (1988). Dr. Woodward edited the Central American section of the *Research Guide to Central America and the Caribbean* (1985) and is currently editor of the Central American history section of the *Handbook of Latin American Studies*.

VOLUME 160

England

Alan Day

Compiler

CLIO PRESS

OXFORD, ENGLAND · SANTA BARBARA, CALIFORNIA
DENVER, COLORADO

British Library Cataloguing in Publication Data

England. – (World bibliographical series; vol. 160)
I. Day, Alan II. Series
016.9942

ISBN 1-85109-040-1

Clio Press Ltd.,
55 St. Thomas' Street,
Oxford OX1 1JG, England.

ABC-CLIO,
130 Cremona Drive,
Santa Barbara,
CA 93116, USA.

Designed by Bernard Crossland.
Typeset by Columns Design and Production Services Ltd, Reading, England.
Printed and bound in Great Britain by
Bookcraft (Bath) Ltd., Midsomer Norton

1000131 62X

THE WORLD BIBLIOGRAPHICAL SERIES

This series, which is principally designed for the English speaker, will eventually cover every country (and many of the world's principal regions), each in a separate volume comprising annotated entries on works dealing with its history, geography, economy and politics; and with its people, their culture, customs, religion and social organization. Attention will also be paid to current living conditions – housing, education, newspapers, clothing, etc.– that are all too often ignored in standard bibliographies; and to those particular aspects relevant to individual countries. Each volume seeks to achieve, by use of careful selectivity and critical assessment of the literature, an expression of the country and an appreciation of its nature and national aspirations, to guide the reader towards an understanding of its importance. The keynote of the series is to provide, in a uniform format, an interpretation of each country that will express its culture, its place in the world, and the qualities and background that make it unique. The views expressed in individual volumes, however, are not necessarily those of the publisher.

VOLUMES IN THE SERIES

Contents

Contents

Contents

Introduction

A potentially confusing question of nomenclature revolving around
different geographical and political terms should be clarified right
from the start. The British Isles, consisting of two main islands, The
United Kingdom and Ireland, lie off the northwest coast of Europe.
The larger of these islands was known as Britannia in the days of the
Roman Empire. After the Anglo-Saxon invasions in the second half
of the fifth century a period of swift political changes ensued which
eventually resulted in the formation of three independent countries,
the kingdoms of England and Scotland, and a number of small
kingdoms in Wales. A measure of stability was first established in
England and, in the medieval period, successive English kings took
advantage of warring Welsh factions, and by a slow pattern of
attrition, imposed a political settlement when the English monarch's
eldest son was given the title of Prince of Wales in the year 1301, a
title which survives to this day. It may be seen as a measure of poetic
justice that, after a period of civil and dynastic wars in the fifteenth
century, a monarch of Welsh descent, Henry Tudor, ascended the
throne in 1485.

Just over a century later the two kingdoms of England and
Scotland were joined in the person of King James VI of Scotland who
became James I of England by hereditary succession. In 1707 the
English and Scottish parliaments were united and the modern state of
the United Kingdom of Great Britain formally came into existence.
In 1922 Ireland was partitioned: the mainly Protestant province of
Ulster opted for incorporation within the United Kingdom whilst the
remaining Roman Catholic provinces were formed into the Irish Free
State which later became the Republic of Ireland.

England may be regarded as the central country of the United
Kingdom by virtue of the fact that it is the most populated and the
most industrialized of mainland Britain, that London is the capital
city, and that it is the only part which shares a border with the other

two. At this point, to subside the rising hackles of overseas visitors, it should be explained that the term 'Great Britain' is geographical rather than bombastic or chauvinist in intent. Associated World Bibliographical Series volumes already published include Michael Owen Shannon's *Northern Ireland* (1191. No. 129. 1,962 entries) and *Irish Republic* (1986. No. 69. 1,459 entries); Eric G. Grant's *Scotland* (1982. No. 34. 1,408 entries); and Gwilym Huws and Hywel Roberts' *Wales* (1991. No. 122. 876 entries).

Historically the British monarchy was a crucial element in the political stability of Great Britain. Its long history, including its successive dynastic houses, is concisely recorded in Patrick W. Montague-Smith's *The royal line of succession* (London: Pitkin, 1952. 24p.) which contains genealogical tables of all the royal houses from Anglo-Saxon times to the present including the descent of the Royal Family from the Kings of Scotland, the sovereign princes of Wales (from 844 AD), and from the Irish kings (from 1,002 AD).

These expository remarks have a direct bearing on the selection of material for this bibliography. Whenever possible only titles of immediate and exclusive relevance to England are admitted but in many cases this is impracticable. So central is England to Great Britain, politically, geographically, socially, constitutionally, and economically, that a large number of titles are essentially British in scope rather than specifically English. It would be unrealistically pedantic to omit such items and would severely restrict the bibliography's coverage and usefulness. However, in these instances, the annotation is almost entirely limited to their English content.

By the end of the nineteenth century Great Britain had built up a global empire based on trade and the protection of its powerful navy. But, emerging victorious from two cataclysmic World Wars, 1914-18 and 1939-45, it was forced to concentrate on its social and economic problems at home and the colonial empire was dismembered in the 1950s and 1960s. As one of the principal Allies in the Second World War, who established the United Nations Organization in 1945, it retains a permanent seat in the Security Council and is still able to exert a strong diplomatic influence. Today it is struggling to come to terms with its drastically diminished status within the European Community. Even the City of London, whose financial market pre-eminence was once unchallenged, is in danger of losing its former leading role. No attempt is made in these pages to cover Britain's imperial legacy and involvement or its possible political and economic union in Europe since two volumes on the Commonwealth and the European Community are announced in Clio Press' International Organizations series.

If the British *Raj* is dead two aspects of England have pervaded every continent and seem set fair to survive indefinitely: Test Match cricket, a peculiarly English game, now played worldwide, and the English language. Incomparably rich in its sheer number of words, stemming from Celtic, Latin, and Teutonic roots, this hybrid language which was brought into coherent form in the sixteenth century, has indisputably displaced French as the world's *lingua franca*. Although purists may decry the debased forms of English in evidence overseas, the continuing facility of the English language to absorb new words, and even sentence constructions, appears to guarantee its longlasting well-being. Restricted to 'British' English in scope the number of entries in this bibliography dedicated to all its aspects reflects its national importance and international standing. In politically correct terminology this uniquely English manifestation of cultural imperialism has permeated the world's business and finance, trade, science, and diplomacy.

As opposed to Scottish, Welsh, or Cornish nationalism, English nationalism has virtually ceased to exist apart from a strident hard-core hooliganism on the part of football supporters at international soccer matches. Empire Day is no longer celebrated, St. George's Day is better known as Shakespeare's birthday, Armistice Day, when the nation remembers its dead in two World Wars, no longer receives the attention of fifty years ago when traffic would stop for a two minute silence. But, in times of national crisis, such as the war in the South Atlantic after Argentina invaded the Falkland Islands in 1982, probably the last colonial war in English history, a strong sense of national unity is immediately apparent. Elton discerns a submergence of the English identity in a larger national patriotism in the maelstrom of nineteenth-century industrialization and imperialism, but paradoxically sees its possible revival arising from a loss of national sovereignty to a united Europe.

In general the English people have maintained a stoical calm amidst the convulsions of the twentieth century, possibly reaching a peak of social unity when threatened by imminent invasion in 1940. The General Strike of 1926 was never repeated but in recent decades social and political unrest has culminated in militant trade unionism on the streets and in race riots in the inner cities where large communities of immigrants have settled. A pronounced social distrust of the police has recently emerged to an extent which would have seemed unbelievable only a few years ago, not least because of its involvement in suppressing political unrest and its perceived racist prejudices and attitudes.

That this disillusionment with the police has become a matter of deep national concern can perhaps be best understood by reference to Geoffrey Elton's newly published book *The English* (Oxford:

Introduction

Blackwell, 1992. 248p.). In this work he attributes the continuity of English society, which has absorbed a succession of foreign monarchs from Normandy, Wales, Scotland, Holland, and Germany, a successful invasion, the threat of several others, two bitter and destructive civil wars, and a change of the state religion, to two decisive factors. One, an institutional monarchy which has created a central power, and, secondly, dependent on the social order imposed by that central power, a system of law that theoretically preserves individual rights and liberties. In that context the general unease about law enforcement practices is not difficult to understand. Whether the liberties of the subject can continue to be safeguarded when the power of central government is outstripping the restraints of parliamentary scrutiny remains to be seen.

England boasts a highly developed communications industry. Although later than in some other European countries the first printing presses were set up in London, and in other centres, before the end of the fifteenth century. The historical and current output of books – 78,835 titles were published in 1992 alone – ensures that every conceivable subject or academic discipline is plentifully covered by printed material in book form.

Bibliography

A corresponding organized record of these myriads of books has also long been available. The national library, the British Library, was first established as the British Museum in 1753, and there is a flourishing public library system, somewhat in decline in recent years, but still providing reasonably efficient reference and lending services. Biographies, reference and information works abound in all subjects. This has made it possible to select items for this bibliography on merit; with so many titles to choose from, those entered may be considered the most informative and the most comprehensive available.

Most of the items registered are recent publications – the latest editions of standard works, and other new material, are obviously to be preferred for the up-to-date nature of their information. This is not to say that earlier works have been entirely neglected; the oldest title mentioned is *Domesday Book*, compiled nine centuries ago. Because of the vast literature available in book form only a very few periodical articles are included and then only when they make a substantial contribution to the subject in question.

In all cases items are listed under their prime subject. For example, works of population and demographic statistics are entered under Population rather than Statistics which is limited to general statistical titles. Similarly, *Who's who in British Athletics* is to be found under Sport, not biography which, again, is restricted to general biographical dictionaries. Uniformity in the number of entries under each subject heading has not been attempted; some subjects obviously have a more extensive literature than others. The aim throughout has been to present a balanced selection of titles but it would be a false policy to rigidly insist on equality of numbers. Within each subject heading or sub-heading items are arranged alphabetically by author, editor, or compiler, and in their absence by title. To save space entries for individual books included in multi-volumed works like *Oxford history of England*, *Dictionary of national biography*, or the *Victoria county history*, are condensed into a single entry and, occasionally, related or similar titles are subsumed in the annotation of other titles.

Generally, books on individuals, musicians, authors, artists, famous sportsmen, have been excluded. But there are unavoidable exceptions to this rule. King Arthur, or Robin Hood, for instance, could hardly be omitted from Folklore. In Science and Technology books on celebrated English scientists have been included because of their worldwide significance and because of the paucity of other material. For the same reason histories of one or two named industrial firms are incorporated into the Industry section. On similar grounds books on individual newspapers, emplifying the history, progress, and practices of the British press, could not be ignored.

Acknowledgements

In compiling this bibliography my task has been made immeasurably easier by the co-operation of my professional colleagues on the staff of Manchester, Stockport and Trafford Libraries. Access to the collections of the John Rylands University of Manchester Library, and the Metropolitan University of Manchester Library, also proved invaluable. At Clio Press Dr. Robert G. Neville, Executive Editor World Bibliographical Series, was always ready with sympathetic and encouraging advice. Linda Myers typed a difficult script, sometimes in very trying circumstances, with her usual high standard of accuracy and efficiency.

The Country and Its People

1 The character of England.
Edited by Ernest Barker.   Oxford: Clarendon, 1947. 595p.
Very much a *fin de guerre* distillation of the English character, past and present, this
collection of twenty-seven essays by well-known writers and academics (C. T. Onions,
Victoria Sackville-West, Francis Meynell, J. A. Williamson, etc.) ranges over the
English people, their religion, government, law, industry, commerce and finance,
childhood and education, the universities and scholarship, science, language and
literature, thought, humour, press, visual arts, the making of books, music, outdoor
life, homes and habits, and on England at war and England and the sea. Even when
published the essays presented an idealized picture; at the end of the century they
retain some historical value as a record of how some educated people viewed their
history and culture.

2 The English world: history, character and people.
Edited by Robert Blake.   London: Thames & Hudson, 1982. 268p.
bibliog.
In this brightly illustrated volume thirteen writers and scholars attempt to unravel the
English tradition in which is mingled the cultures of various invaders, the ancient
institution of its monarchy, its national Church, the English literary heritage, and the
evolution of the English landscape.

3 Britain 1992: An official handbook.
London: HMSO for Central Office of Information, 1992. 43rd ed. 465p.
14 maps. bibliog.
Designed essentially for overseas use, this attractively produced handbook gives the
latest facts and figures on most aspects of British life. Areas covered include the land
and people; government; overseas relations; defence; justice and law; social welfare;
education; planning, urban regeneration and housing; environmental projection;
religion; the national economy; industry and commerce; energy and natural resources;
agriculture, fisheries and forestry; transport and communications; employment;

finance; overseas trade; science and technology; the arts; the press; television and radio; and sport and recreation. It is open to criticism on the grounds that it presents a too cosy and sanitized picture of contemporary life in Britain for overseas consumption.

4 **The Sunday Times book of the countryside: including one thousand days out in Great Britain and Ireland.**
Edited by Philip Clarke, Brian Jackman, Derrick Mercer.   London: Macdonald, 1980. 350p. bibliog.

This pictorial volume begins with the making of the countryside, shows how the natural landscape was formed and shaped, and demonstrates the part played by man in modelling it to suit his purposes since prehistoric times. There are separate chapters on wildlife, the coast, gardens, weather and climate, leisure and recreational opportunities, and the future of the countryside.

5 **Britons: forging the nation 1707-1837.**
Linda Colley.   London: Yale University Press, 1992. 432p.

Great Britain came into being in 1707 when the English parliament at Westminster passed the Act of Union, joining the two ancient kingdoms of England and Scotland, together with the equally ancient principality of Wales, into one United Kingdom. Its enduring success was by no means apparent: the peoples of the three distinct nations enjoyed different histories, languages, and customs, sharing only mistrust and a history of armed conflict. This work demonstrates how a British identity was superimposed on their chequered history, and eventually forged an overseas empire. Contemporary disruptive influences indicate that the union is not entirely solid even today.

6 **The English.**
Geoffrey Elton.   Oxford: Blackwell, 1992. 256p. 8 maps. bibliog.

Two crucial factors which ensured the continuity of English society for more than a thousand years are distinguished in this single-volume history: the early emergence of a strong institutional monarchy and a consequent system of law that preserved and cherished hard-won rights and liberties. Elton argues that a fiercely renascent Welsh and Scottish nationalism, and a loss of sovereignty to the European Community, could spark off a renewal of the English sense of identity which was submerged in the nineteenth-century establishment of a world empire.

7 **Everyman's England.**
Bryn Frank.   London: Dent, 1984. 296p. 10 maps.

Drawing upon his long experience as editor of the British Tourist Authority's monthly feature magazine, *In Britain*, and his in-depth knowledge of England, the author travels an idiosyncratic, anti-clockwise circular tour, searching for 'odd and unregarded corners . . . that rarely get into the guidebooks'.

8   **The English town.**
Mark Girouard.   New Haven, Connecticut: Yale University Press, 1990.
330p. bibliog.

Every conceivable aspect of English towns and cities is traced in this magnificently illustrated historical, architectural and social panorama. The origins and development of the market place; waterside; castle; church and charities; houses and people; assembly rooms; walks; terraces, squares, and crescents; town hall; High Street; warehouse; works and back streets, suburbs, parks and bright lights, are all described in terms of their functions and their contribution to the townscape as a whole. This is a major book from a leading architectural historian.

9   **Exploring English character.**
Geoffrey Gorer.   London: Cresset, 1955. 483p.

Based on a return of 11,000 questionnaires advertised in *The People*, a popular Sunday newspaper, Gorer examines English homelife, friendships, relations with neighbours, leisure activities, ideas about sex, love and marriage and the upbringing of children, and attitudes towards the law and the police, and to religious and magical beliefs. This work was published in two editions: the complete edition which includes 150 pages of statistical tables, prepared from the returned questionnaires by Oldham Press research section staff, and the standard edition which lacks these tables but which in all other aspects is indistinguishable from the complete edition.

10   **The real counties of Britain.**
Russell Grant.   Oxford: Lennard, 1989. 242p. 3 maps.

Three different types of county are indignantly perceived by the author, geographical, administrative, and postal, which have evolved from the contortions of local government in the modern period and the Royal Mail's efforts to rationalize its postal delivery services. This book reverts to the historical-geographical counties which in many cases date back to Anglo-Saxon times and which lasted for 900 years and still continue regardless of the never-ending bureaucratic changes of local government. For each county a double-page spread outlines its history, past and present industry, topography, famous people and local characters, art and literature, local folklore, and county culinary flavour.

11   **Living and working in Britain: a survival handbook.**
David Hampshire.   Haslemere, England: Survival, 1991. 719p. bibliog.

'Worth its weight in British sausages', according to the *Introduction*, this user-friendly and comprehensive handbook undoubtedly represents the most up-to-date and exhaustive source of practical information about everyday life in Britain currently on the market. Finding a job, work conditions, permits and visas, accommodation, post office services, radio and television, education, public transport, motoring, insurance, finance, sports and leisure, shopping, and a basket of odds and ends, are all covered in detail.

The Country and Its People

12 The Gallup survey of Britain.
Gordon Heald, Robert J. Whybrow.   London: Croom Helm, 1986.
303p.

Gallup has been conducting public opinion polls in Britain for over fifty years. This survey, which was intended to be the first of an annual series, purports to record the British public's views on the economy, the environment, domestic politics, law and order, social issues, and international affairs. Four appendices give an account of how polls are conducted, a diary of events for 1985, Gallup's general election record 1945-1983, and party fortunes 1984-1985. Whybrow's *Britain speaks out 1937-87: a social history as seen through the Gallup data* (London: Macmillan, 1989. 224p.) attempts to create a similar picture of British society over the whole period of Gallup polls.

13 The Domesday Book: England's heritage then and now.
T. Hinde.   London: Hutchinson, 1985. 351p. maps. bibliog.

Produced in conjunction with the English Tourist Board, this sumptuously illustrated volume is essentially a 12,500 entry modern name gazetteer of Domesday Book settlements, in thirty-seven county sections, recording important events since Domesday Book was compiled, and the settlements' present status. What is quite astounding is that most of them still survive in one form or another. Other features include an introduction to Domesday, a glossary, and a list of major Domesday landholders.

14 The Cambridge illustrated dictionary of British heritage.
Edited by Alan Isaacs, Jennifer Monk.   Cambridge, England:
Cambridge University Press, 1986. 484p. bibliog.

For overseas visitors wishing to get beneath the skin of a naturally not very articulate people this illustrated dictionary could well be the answer. Its 1,500 entries capture the essence of British life: its ancient customs and traditions, the monarchy and other institutions, and its language and literature. Quite simply it is an extremely useful one-stop reference guide.

15 Typically British: the Prudential Mori guide.
Eric Jacobs, Robert Worcester.   London: Bloomsbury, 1991. 192p.

Tracing the trends and developments in the British public's views on contemporary topics, this publication intends year by year to report on the public perception of such topics as love, sex, and marriage; its hopes, dreams, and achievements; and Britain's role in the modern world, thus accurately interpreting the mood of the nation by investigating its behaviour, attitudes, and values. From time to time old topics will be revived to note how public opinion has changed.

16 Recording Britain: a pictorial Domesday of pre-war Britain.
David Mellor, Gill Saunders, Patrick Wright.   Newton Abbot,
England: David & Charles, 1990. 160p.

Fearful of what war might bring the Ministry of Labour and the Pilgrim Trust commissioned many of Britain's foremost artists in 1940 to record the nation as it was before enemy action took its toll. This book presents over 100 watercolours depicting market towns, agricultural landscapes, rural industries, city streets, architectural follies, etc. of pre-War England and Wales. Among the artists represented are John

4

Piper, Kenneth Rowntree, Barbara Jones, Rowland Hilder, Michael Rothenstein, and Sir William Russell Flint.

17 **Our village.**
Mary Russell Mitford.   London: Dent; New York: Dutton, 1970. 340p.
(Everyman's Library).
'Our village: sketches of rural character and scenery' was first printed in the *Lady's Magazine* and collected in five volumes from 1824 to 1832. They attempted 'to delineate country scenery and country manners as they exist in a small village in the south of England'. This selection provides an eminently readable slice of early nineteenth-century social history.

18 **The English village.**
Richard Muir.   London: Thames & Hudson, 1980. 208p. bibliog.
The growth and development and, perhaps, the decline of English villages, has a long history. In an age which too often scoffs at or ignores history and tradition, this book is a timely reminder of the people and landscape of rural England and of the villages they built.

19 **The Shell countryside book.**
Richard Muir, Eric Duffy.   London: Dent, 1984. 318p. 15 maps.
bibliog.
Lavishly illustrated, this highly informative and attractive book tells the story of the countryside and explores every aspect of the rural scene. There are chapters on various types of scenery, geological and natural history, and others on country roads, village churches, country cottages, farms, country parks, and conservation issues.

20 **The rise of English nationalism: a cultural history 1740-1830.**
Gerald Newman.   New York: St. Martins Press, 1987. 294p. bibliog.
This convincing and impressive reinterpretation of English history and culture in the era of King George III adduces that England was probably the first country to experience modern nationalism which, in essence, stems from an existing awareness of national land, culture, and people, an instinct to defend these against foreign domination, historic external enemies and wars, and a search for loyalty and self-identification, all of which were in strong evidence in eighteenth-century England. Newman's thoughtful and scholarly work seeks to grasp and identify these elements which have long been obscured by the absence of a well-defined nationalist movement and by the concentration by historians and other commentators on the growth of Britain's imperial power overseas.

21 **An Englishman's home.**
J. H. B. Peel.   Newton Abbot, England: David & Charles, 1978. 207p.
map.
'Neither an essay in history nor a life story of people nor a treatise on architecture', this engaging book casts its eye over manors, cottages, castles, gardens, monasteries, vicarages, ships, town houses, farmhouses, and housing estates, to portray the Englishman's home.

22 **Myths of the English.**
   Edited by Roy Porter.   Oxford: Polity Press, 1992. 250p.
This collection of essays explores the essence of 'Englishness', the images, characters, myths, and peculiarities that have helped form the national identity over the last few centuries. Guy Fawkes, comic opera, English tramps, the English 'Bobby', old wives tales, and the Great War of 1914-1918, are among the topics investigated.

23 **The English.**
   J. B. Priestley.   London: Heinemann; New York: Viking Press, 1973.
   256p.
An intuitive and informal investigation of the English temperament over the last four centuries, searching for individuals whose lives and characteristics exemplify 'the essential Englishness of the English', this book is a perfect present for well disposed foreign visitors, not least for those trying to grapple with the English class system.

24 **The changing anatomy of Britain.**
   Anthony Sampson.   London: Hodder & Stoughton, 1982. 476p.
When Sampson's *Anatomy of Britain* was published in 1962 it immediately established itself as the authoritative guide to the workings of the British state. This completely new work presents a picture of the country's rulers twenty years on and assesses what happened to the hopes and promises of change in the 1970s. It traces the fortunes of the main political parties, narrates the attempts to reform the Civil Service, and examines the defence and secret services in the light of the Falklands crisis. The power of new money is explored, the reality of the City of London's façade is questioned, and the tribal background of the country's leaders, the schools and universities that nurtured them, are critically evaluated in this personal tour of the political and social scene. *The anatomy of Britain 1992* (*Independent On Sunday*, 29 March 1992, 16p.) is in tabloid newspaper format and examines the changes in Britain brought about by the Thatcher and Major administrations since the Labour Party was last in office. *The essential anatomy of Britain: democracy in crisis* (London: Hodder & Stoughton, 1992. 256p.) argues that the rights and liberties of the British citizen are threatened by the insidious centralization of power at Westminster and the corresponding diminishment of the functions and influence of local government, the trade unions, the church, and the universities. More insidious still is the encroaching power of the European community.

25 **Patriotism: the making and unmaking of British national identity**.
   Edited by Raphael Samuel.   London: Routledge, 1989. 3 vols.
With coverage extending from the turbulent years of the thirteenth century to the present day, these three volumes of historical essays (vol. 1, History and politics, 336p.; vol. 2, Minorities and outsiders, 304p.; vol. 3, National fictions, 304p.) explore the changing notions of patriotism in Britain. Collectively they explain how and why a complex sense of national identity emerged from three disparate peoples inhabiting an insignificant island group off continental Europe's northwestern shores.

26 **The English companion: an idiosyncratic A-Z of England and Englishness.**
Godfrey Smith.   London: Pavilion, 1984. 272p.

Described by the author as 'an informal ramble through English things', this witty and stylish book examines anything and everything that takes his fancy. 'Certain English attributes seem never to change: a daunting philistinism, a shaky grip on hygiene, an obsession with animals, a predilection for gambling, a gift with gardens, a passion for sport, an incomprehension of foreigners and a huge sense of humour'.

27 **English nationalism.**
Louis L. Snyder.   In: *Encyclopedia of nationalism*. Louis L. Snyder. London: St. James Press, 1990, p. 88-92.

Quoting from John Milton's *Areopagitica*, published in 1644, Snyder's short study shows how the special character of English nationalism stemmed from a strong adherence to a national church which rebelled against a foreign Pope, and how it developed into a libertarian and humanitarian movement from the mid-seventeenth century onwards. Even at the height of its status as a world power during the Age of Imperialism England was motivated by a strong Christian and liberal moral sense.

28 **Britain besides the sea.**
Christopher Somerville.   London: Grafton, 1989. 284p. 9 maps. bibliog.

The author's aim is 'to highlight the richness of history and strength of character, the enormous variety and vitality of the communities, large and small, around our coastline; also to point to some of the changes that threaten their identities and ways of life as change sweeps over all of them'. Alternatively encouraging and depressing, this affectionate and systematic tour of Britain's coastal communities should be required reading for all local planning authority members.

29 **Studying and living in Britain 1991.**
Compiled by the British Council.   Plymouth, England: Northcote House, 1991. annual.

Completely revised in 1984, and updated with new material annually, this publication is intended for overseas students, tourists, and businessmen visiting Britain for the first time. It offers advice and information on arriving in Britain, how to find accommodation, and on all aspects of the British way of life.

30 **The English and their Englishness: 'a curiously mysterious, elusive and little understood people'.**
Peter J. Taylor.   *Scottish Geographical Magazine*, vol. 107, no. 3. (Dec. 1991), p. 146-59.

Taylor's provocative essay, 'something of a personal odyssey, a trip where my fellow nationals have rarely trod', explores the neglected theme of English/British nationalism from a political-geographical perspective. He finds a curious and not quite credible ambiguity between the English sense of patriotism and a distrust of nationalism which is regarded as a complex, foreign, and none too commendable concept. By dint of an historical analysis and a review of previous commentators' remarks on what distinguishes the English from their Welsh, Scots, and Irish neighbours, he arrives at a spatial hierarchical regionalization of England and perceives a strong possibility that it will eventually divide along political, geographical, and economic lines.

31 Timpson's English eccentrics.

John Timpson. Norwich, England: Jarrold, 1992. 224p.

Eccentricity is fondly regarded as a peculiarly English trait. This entertaining gallimaufry remembers the exploits of over 100 decidedly oddball characters, builders, collectors and inventors.

32 Timpson's England: a look beyond the obvious at the unusual, the eccentric, and the definitely odd.

John Timpson. Norwich, England: Jarrold, 1987. 263p. 11 maps.

For three years in the mid-1980s John Timpson presented the BBC Radio 4 peripatetic political and current affairs programme *Any Questions*. It was his practice to recall little-known stories on the places the programme visited. Over 400 of these are included here under such alliterative and appealing headings as 'Wonderous ways with water' or 'Come tip-toe through the tombstones'. A map section is printed for readers wishing to pin-point specific places mentioned and there is a subject-index cum gazetteer.

33 The English seaside resort: a social history 1750-1914.

John K. Walton. Leicester, England: Leicester University Press; New York: St. Martin's Press, 1983. 265p. 5 maps.

This investigative study, which has emerged from an academic thesis, analyses the social forces at work in the development of seaside resorts, mainly in Victorian and Edwardian England. A relationship between seaside holidays and urban expansion is established, the changes in consumer demand which accelerated the rise of the resorts are described, and various aspects which also exerted an influence, such as landownership, local government, and the provision of entertainment, are thoroughly aired and explored. The interaction of residents and visitors, of all social classes, is also explored.

34 Nationalism in Britain.

Nancy J. Walker, Robert M. Worcester. *Canadian Review of Studies in Nationalism*, vol. 13, no. 2 (fall 1986), p. 249-69.

The authors address the complexities of British nationalism in four categories: attitudes towards Europe; jingoism during the Falklands War; the 'special' relationship with the United States; and the growth of Welsh and Scottish nationalism. From this two conclusions are drawn: that the inhabitants of Great Britain still cling stubbornly to their own insular identity and interests, and that the United Kingdom is splitting apart. The English National Party is brushed aside as 'a harmless group of elderly folklore enthusiasts'.

35 **The English spirit.**
Edited by Anthony Weymouth.   London: Allen & Unwin, 1942. 135p.

Twenty talks broadcast on the BBC's Empire Service are printed in this collection issued in the dark days of the Second World War. The English countryside, Drake's Drum, the rebel in English literature, *Punch*, the village pub, and a village choral festival, are some of the essentially English topics included.

Travellers' Accounts

36   **Bibliography of Domesday Book.**
     David Bates.   Woodbridge, England: Boydell, 1987. 166p.
A total of 4,684 briefly annotated items, identifying place-names, interpreting
terminology and statistics, assessing how the record was compiled, and studying
Domesday Book's administrative and legal significance, are listed under three
headings: general studies, local studies (by historical counties), and a name and subject
index. The bibliography is comprehensive since 1886, the year a brief commemorative
volume was published.

37   **The green bag travellers: Britain's first tourists.**
     Anthony Burton, Pip Burton.   London: Deutsch, 1978. 152p. bibliog.
Travel within the British Isles became highly fashionable in the eighteenth century
when travellers took advantage of the new turnpike roads to visit outstanding beauty
spots. By the end of the century travel books were pouring from the presses as people
recorded their impressions of remote communities, stately homes, and romantic ruins.
This work quotes liberally from contemporary descriptions of a countryside that was
soon to experience dramatic social and physical changes.

38   **The Torrington diaries: a selection from the tours of the Hon. John Byng**
     (later Fifth Viscount Torrington) between the years 1781 and 1794.
     Edited, with an introduction by C. Bruyn Andrews, and abridged into
     one volume by Fanny Andrews. With an introduction to this edition by
     Arthur Bryant.   London: Eyre & Spottiswoode, 1954. 528p.
The complete edition of Torrington's diaries was published in four volumes, between
1934 and 1938, when they were immediately acknowledged as a significant source of
eighteenth century social history, revealing Byng as a talented and entertaining diarist.
It derives its chief value as an eye-witness account of the transformation of England
from a mainly agrarian to a primarily industrial economy. Although from a very
different social class, Byng shared many of the opinions and prejudices of William
Cobbett.

39 **Rural rides.**
William Cobbett.   London: Dent, 1966. 2 vols. (Everyman's Library).
William Cobbett (1763-1835) was unquestionably one of the most literate, radical, and pugnacious of all the English social and political writers. This account of his journeys through England, from October 1821 to October 1832, represents his views on what was happening to the English countryside at a time when it was changing dramatically as a result of the agricultural enclosures and the growth of the industrial towns. It expresses a growing concern at the poverty and misery experienced by the mass of common people who had not shared in the commercial and business wealth generated by the Industrial Revolution. Infused with his own trenchant personality and political beliefs, with snatches of autobiography, *Rural Rides* is a classic piece of reportage, belonging as much to English literary as economic and social history. This Everyman's Library edition follows the text of the 1853 edition with notes added by James Paul Cobbett and carries a perceptive introduction by Asa Briggs.

40 **A tour through the whole island of Great Britain.**
Daniel Defoe, edited and introduced by Pat Rogers.   Exeter, England: Webb & Bower, 1989. 240p. map.
When Defoe's *Tour* first appeared in three volumes, between 1724 and 1726, it was a pioneering achievement. Nothing like it had ever been published before although its form was partly derived from William Camden's *Britannia*, substituting a current review of the state of Britain for Camden's antiquarian approach. Ostensibly Defoe travelled in a series of circuits from London, describing what he saw around him: 'the situation of things is given not as they have been, but as they are; the improvements in the soil, the product of the earth, the labour of the poor, the improvement in manufactures, in merchandises, in navigation, all respects the present time, not the time past'. In fact, some of his material of his purported contemporary journeys was pressed into service from travels of up to twenty years earlier. This edition cuts in half the original third of a million words but successfully retains the flavour of Defoe's vivid and sharply drawn text. Another abridged edition of value, edited by P. N. Furbank, W. R. Owens, and A. J. Coulson (New Haven, Connecticut, Yale University Press, 1991. 300p. 43 colour plates) contains an introduction outlining Defoe's life, places this work in the context of his other books, and reveals the extent of his involvement in the life of early eighteenth-century Britain.

41 **The description of England by William Harrison.**
Edited by George Edelen.   Ithaca, New York: Cornell University Press for The Folger Shakespeare Library, 1968. 512p.
William Harrison (1534-1593) contributed the *Description of England* to Raphael Holinshed's *The chronicles of England* published in 1577. It provides a total portrait of the political scene, and of the living conditions in mid-Elizabethan England, and is especially valuable for its insight into the dramatic social changes of the period.

42 **Letters from England 1813-1844.**
Maria Edgeworth, edited by Christina Colvin.   Oxford: Clarendon Press, 1971. 649p.
Maria Edgeworth, the Irish novelist, enjoyed a wide circle of friends in England, amongst them artists and sculptors, politicians and economists, and Midland industrialists. As a literary 'lion' she was invited to the dinner tables and salons of

Society hostesses. These private letters were never intended for publication although many were inexpertly edited for *A memoir of Maria Edgeworth* privately issued in 1867, two years after her death, and in *The life and letters* published in 1894. This present edition includes over 100 letters not previously published. For readers willing to immerse themselves in Maria Edgeworth's world they provide a striking and vivid impression of English society in the first half of the nineteenth century.

43 Domesday Book: a guide.
Rex Weldon Finn. Chichester, England: Phillimore, 1973. 109p. bibliog.

The Domesday Book, England's oldest and best known public record, is frequently misinterpreted. This guide to its use analyses its compilation and the various methods used in different parts of the country, and interprets the meaning and significance of the terminology employed, to alert the non-specialist reader to the many misunderstandings that can occur.

44 An American Quaker in the British Isles. The travel journals of Jabez Maud Fisher 1775-1779.
Edited by Kenneth Morgan. Oxford: Oxford University Press and the British Academy, 1991. 300p. (Records of Social and Economic History).

Jabez Maud Fisher, a young Philadelphia Quaker, was sent by his father to gather detailed information on business conditions in the British Isles. His travel journals provide a distinctive commentary on the economic and social life of late eighteenth-century Britain.

45 The illustrated journeys of Celia Fiennes c.1682-c.1712.
Edited by Christopher Morris. Exeter, England: Webb & Bower, 1988. 248p. 2 maps.

Celia Fiennes' *Through England on a side saddle in the time of William and Mary* was originally printed in an unsatisfactory edition in 1888. This version, prepared from her original manuscript, and first published by Cresset Press in 1947, is a more reliable account of her travels during which she rode at least once through every county of England. Spa towns, stately homes, local crops, and 'curiosities', particularly attracted her attention in a lively and colourful description of late seventeenth-century English society.

46 Domesday Book.
Edited by John Morris. Chichester, England: Phillimore, 1986. 38 vols.

Domesday Book is the original record of William the Conqueror's survey of his new kingdom compiled in 1086 by seven panels of commissioners of all royal estates or manors and those of the King's tenants-in-chief. *Domesday Book* – the name signifies a record from which there is no appeal – covered every county of England with the exception of Northumberland, Durham, Cumberland, Westmorland, and the northern parts of Lancashire. It forms a starting point for the history of most English towns and villages, although no record survives for London, and provides valuable economic and statistical information on eleventh century England. This edition includes thirty-five county volumes and three index volumes for places, persons, and subjects, and presents parallel Latin/English texts. Each county volume has an introduction, a glossary, maps, and an index.

47 **The King's England.**
   Edited by Arthur Mee.   Barnsley, England: King's England Press,
   1989-90. 41 vols.

First published by Hodder and Stoughton between 1936 and 1953 these county volumes provide a remarkably vivid historical and topographical guide to England in the years prior to the Second World War. In each volume the places described are arranged alphabetically with historical, biographical and architectural notes. *Enchanted land* is an introductory volume. Richard Dalby's 'Arthur Mee's King's England series', *Book and Magazine Collector*, no. 36 (March 1987), gives the full background to this immensely popular series.

48 **I saw two Englands: the record of a journey before the war, and after the outbreak of war, in the year 1939.**
   H. V. Morton.   London: Methuen, 1942. 296p.

It was not unknown in the 1930s for authors, not all of them travel writers, to be commissioned to tour (usually) rural England and set down their observations and reflections. Morton was very experienced in this particular literary genre and his well-turned travelogue may fairly represent how England imagined it was coping with the onset of another major European war.

49 **Travel in England in the seventeenth century.**
   Joan Parkes.   Oxford: Oxford University Press, 1925. 354p. 4 maps.
   bibliog.

Casting a wide net this survey reveals a number of unusual and unexpected aspects of seventeenth-century travel. In addition to discussing the state of the roads and bridges, or the types of conveyances available, the author also focuses on the legal restrictions on travel by Roman Catholic recusants and the perennial trials and tribulations faced by travellers, assaults and abductions, travel in time of war or plague, and the effects of extreme and inclement weather. The progress of the monarch through his dominions, and the royal retinue, and the experiences of all classes of travellers from the nobility to players and mummers, migrant traders, and vagrants, are all clearly expressed in this well-researched panorama.

50 **English journey: being a rambling but truthful account of what one man saw and heard and felt and thought during a journey through England during the autumn of the year 1933.**
   J. B. Priestley.   London: Heinemann, in association with Gollancz,
   1934. 422p.

A classic account of an attempt to discover and describe how the economic depression of the early 1930s had affected England. Three Englands are distinguished: firstly Old England, 'the country of the cathedrals and ministers and manor houses and inns . . . quaint highways and byways'; secondly, nineteenth-century England, 'the industrial England of coal, iron, steel, cotton, wool, railways . . . thousands of rows of houses all alike'; and thirdly, 'the new post-war England, belonging far more to the age itself than to this particular island . . . the England of arterial and by-pass roads, of filling stations and factories . . . giant cinemas and dance-halls and cafes . . . greyhound racing and dirt tracts'. A slightly abridged Jubilee Edition, with eighty period photographs, was published in 1984. Beryl Bainbridge's *English journey, or the road to Milton Keynes* (London: Duckworth/BBC, 1984) is a diary kept whilst filming a TV documentary following Priestley's coach journey fifty years later.

51 **Journeys in England.**
   Edited by Jack Simmons.   Newton Abbot, England: David & Charles, 1969. 2nd ed. 288p.

Most of the passages in this anthology compiled from recorded accounts of journeys made in England are selected for their literary quality. Over half belong to the period 1760-1860 when travel ceased to be the exclusive prerogative of the wealthy and leisured classes. Although stated to be not intended as a disguised treatise on the history of travel in England, a twenty-page introduction provides a valuable historical summary.

52 **The itinerary of John Leland in or about the years 1535-1543.**
   Edited by Lucy Toulmin Smith.   London: Centaur, 1964. 5 vols.

John Leland (c. 1506-52) was appointed King's Antiquary in 1533, the only person ever to hold this office, and was commissioned by Henry VIII to search the country's libraries for surviving ancient chronicles which recorded Britain's history. For the next eight years he toured England and as his biographical and historiographical studies progressed he began to link them to the material remains of the past and eventually conceived the notion of a grand topographical work to be called *De antiquitate Britannica*. Although this never materialised, in 1545 Leland presented to Henry a plan of his proposed work, 'The laboriouse journey and serche of Johan Leylande for Englandes Antiquities geven of hym as a Newe Yeares Gyfte to King Henry the viii in the xxvii Yeare of his Raynge' in which he described his itineraries through England and the condition of castles, market towns and cities, their principal buildings and churches, recording the extent of common arable and enclosed land, meadows, woods and forests, the details of parishes and hamlets, the number and position of river bridges etc. Early printed editions of Leland's *Itineraries* appeared in 1549 and 1710; this edition was first published between 1906 and 1910. John Chandler's *Leland's itinerary* (Stroud, England: Alan Sutton, 1992. 448p.) adapts the original text into modern English and has rearranged it by counties. Leland's descriptions are complemented by county maps showing his routes and many of the places he mentions.

53 **Mr. Rowlandson's England.**
   Robert Southey, edited by John Steel.   Woodbridge, England: Antique Collector's Club, 1985. 201p.

This is not, as might first appear, a modern reprint of an early nineteenth-century work. The text originally appeared as part of *Letters from England*, ostensibly written by a visiting Spanish nobleman, but in reality penned by Robert Southey, poet laureate, and author of the life of Nelson. The 'Letters' mirror life in England in the early 1800s when inflation, unemployment, and foreign wars threatened national stability. Their bite and relevance are sharpened in this edition by Thomas Rowlandson's celebrated cartoons of the period.

14

54 **Notes on England.**
Hippolyte Taine.   London: Thames & Hudson, 1957. 296p.
The French philosopher, historian and man of letters, Hippolyte Taine published *Notes sur l'Angleterre* in 1872 after two visits to England in 1858 and 1871. In the only previous translation into English, serialized in the *Daily News* in the 1870s, a number of passages concerning the vulgarity of English design and English sexual life were suppressed. These are now restored. Taine's comments on the English social and political scene were sharply observed but he was impressed by what he saw as an apparent determination not to allow society to be regulated along religious lines.

55 **The English guide book c.1780-1870: an illustrated history.**
John Vaughan.   Newton Abbot, England: David & Charles, 1974.
167p. bibliog.
Guide books in the eighteenth and nineteenth centuries usually provided short descriptive inventories of places, institutions, and monuments. Based on the author's own guide book collection, this illustrated study examines their content and purpose, and explores some of their idiosyncrasies, before the arrival of more formal guides towards the end of the nineteenth century.

56 **Victorian travellers guide to 19th century England & Wales: containing charts of roads, railways, interesting localities, views of scenery and a comprehensive list of hotels.**
London: Bracken, 1985. 544p. 19 maps and charts.
A facsimile edition of *Black's guide to England and Wales* (London: A & C Black, 1864), this is a comprehensive illustrated guide to the outstanding landmarks and treasures along England and Wales' main roads and railway routes in the Victorian period.

57 **Thomas Platter's travels in England 1599.**
Translated from the German and introduced by Clare Williams.
London: Jonathan Cape, 1937. 245p. bibliog.
Thomas Platter, a newly qualified Doctor of Medicine at the University of Montpellier, maintained what today would be called a travel diary after landing at Dover in 1599. His leisurely tour took him to Canterbury, Rochester, Gravesend, London, Kingston, Hampton Court, Oxford, Greenwich, and Richmond, before returning to the Continent. He proves himself to be an observant tourist, noting and commenting on what he discovers around him, thus providing a valuable glimpse of contemporary English life. The translation of his diary comprises only eighty-seven pages of this edition, the rest is taken up with a background description of Elizabethan England.

Geography and Geology

Geography

58 **Contemporary Britain: a geographical perspective.**
A. G. Champion, A. R. Townsend.   London: Edward Arnold, 1990.
310p. 34 maps. bibliog.

Key geographical trends, the transformation towards a post-industrial society,
population changes, prosperous sub-regions, new sources of employment, and further
directions and policy issues, are some of the main themes of this integrated study of the
impact of the 1980s, including the growth of tourism and financial services, on the
geography of Britain.

59 **The Domesday geography of England.**
Edited by H. C. Darby.   Cambridge: Cambridge University Press,
1954-1977. 7 vols.

The volumes included in this series are: vol. one, *Eastern England*. 1971. 3rd ed. 400p.
110 maps; vol. two, *Midland England*, by H. C. Darby, I. B. Terrett. 1954. 482p.
159p. maps; vol. three, *South-East England*, by H. C. Darby, Eila M. J. Campbell.
1962. 658p. 179 maps; vol. four, *Northern England*, by H. C. Darby, I. S. Maxwell.
1962. 540. 143 maps; vol. five, *South-West England*, by H. C. Darby, R. Welldon Finn.
1967. 496p. 95 maps; vol. six, *Domesday gazetteer*, by H. C. Darby, G. R. Versey.
1975. 544p. + 65p. maps; vol. seven, *Domesday England*, by H. C. Darby. 1977. 416p.
111 maps. bibliog. For the first time Darby and his co-editors attempt here to form a
general picture of the relative prosperity of different areas of England and of local
variations both in the face of the countryside and in its economic life at the time of the
Domesday Survey. Details of settlements and their distribution, population, land use,
fisheries, mills, churches, and rural and urban life, for each county are explored in each
regional volume. With twenty-one statistical and bibliographical appendices, the
seventh volume provides a measured summing up of late eleventh-century England.

60   **An historical geography of England before AD 1800.**
Edited by H. C. Darby.   Cambridge, England: Cambridge University
Press, 1936. 566p. 87 maps.
Contains fourteen studies which examine: prehistoric southern Britain; human
geography in Roman Britain; the Anglo-Saxon settlement; the economic geography of
England AD 1000-1250; fourteenth century England; medieval foreign trade; Leland's
and Camden's England; the draining of the Fens; and the growth of London 1600-
1800. This 1936 edition was kept continuously in print but eventually an entirely new
but similar volume, based on the enormous amount of work done in the intervening
period, was published in 1973 entitled, *A new historical geography of England*. (Edited
by H. C. Darby.   Cambridge, England: Cambridge University Press, 1973, 767p. 156
maps). The topics considered in both volumes include political boundaries, the
landscape, place-names, the population, trade and industry, agriculture, taxation,
employment, steam and water power, and communications. *A new historical geography
of England before 1600* (1976. 316p. 63 maps) and *A new historical geography of
England after 1600* (1976. 460p. 94 maps) are hewn unaltered from the 1973 volume.

61   **A social geography of England and Wales.**
Richard Dennis, Hugh Clout.   Oxford: Pergamon Press, 1980. 208p.
(Pergamon Oxford Geographies).
In this penetrating study of the changing social geography of England and Wales from
pre-industrial times to the present day, the overall theme is urbanization and its effects
in different periods on the relationship between town and country. Topics discussed at
length include the geography of housing, the problems of the inner-city areas, and the
role of rural communities within an essentially urban society.

62   **An historical geography of England and Wales.**
Edited by R. A. Dodgshon, R. A. Butlin.   London: Academic Press,
1990. 2nd ed. 589p. maps. bibliog.
All aspects of human geography, population changes, agriculture, the towns and
industry, transport and communications, the landscape, and overseas trade, are
examined in this comprehensive survey. By and large three periods are distinguished:
the Middle Ages up to 1500; 1500-1730; and 1730-1914; with a concluding chapter on
the inter-war years. Since its first publication in 1978 a broadening of themes has
occurred to take in new socio-cultural and political topics, resulting in a greater range
of methodologies, and research among a wider array of sources, all of which are
evident in this revised and updated edition.

63   **A history of modern British geography.**
T. W. Freeman.   London: Longman, 1980. 258p. maps. bibliog.
Published in the year which marked the 150th anniversary of the Royal Geographical
Society of London, this history traces the development of the study of geography in
British universities, discusses seminal works of geography, and relates the growth of
geography as an academic discipline to contemporary intellectual, social and economic
circumstances. Biographies of over sixty leading British geographers are also included.

64 **British pioneers in geography.**
Edmund W. Gilbert. Newton Abbot, England: David & Charles, 1972. 2,271p. 7 maps.

Not a comprehensive account of British geographical thought, this collection of essays, derived from the author's lectures, is a personal selection with a heavy leaning to geographical studies at Oxford. 'Richard Hakluyt and his Oxford predecessors'; 'Victorian pioneers in medical geography'; 'British regional novelists and geography'; and 'Victorian methods of teaching geography', are some of the essays included.

65 **London a new metropolitan geography.**
Edited by Keith Hoggart, David Green. London: Edward Arnold, 1991. 255p. maps. bibliog.

Recent changes affecting London's future are the theme of this collection of thirteen essays which concentrate on the economic, political, and social issues of the nation's capital city. Chapters on rethinking London's government, and on London's uncertain future, highlight current problems which could seriously threaten its own and the nation's prosperity.

66 **The UK space: resources, environment and the future.**
Edited by J. W. House. London: Weidenfeld & Nicolson, 1973. 371p. maps. bibliogs.

Five significant themes are distinguished in this survey and interpretation of developments in Britain's spatial requirements and resources: the geographic regions economic planning problems; their population and employment prospects; the environment and land use; the industrial structure and the need for power; and the transport infrastructure.

67 **The changing geography of the United Kingdom.**
Edited by R. C. Johnston, V. Gardiner. London: Routledge, 1991. 2nd ed. 515p.

The first edition of this collection of papers was first published in 1982 as part of the celebrations marking the fiftieth anniversary of the Institute of British Geographers. Its purpose was to summarize what geographers in the UK had learned about its changing geography since the 1930s. Further changes have substantially altered the spatial variation in unemployment and relative prosperity, in the pattern of land use, and the relationship between society and the physical environment. This latest edition, almost entirely compiled by the original contributors, amounts to a totally new study.

68 **Great Britain geographical essays.**
Edited by J. B. Mitchell. Cambridge, England: Cambridge University Press, 1962. 612p. maps.

Introduced by general essays on relief, climate, vegetation and soils, and population, this volume covers the geography of Britain which has been divided into seventeen regions, including the Fenland, London, rural Yorkshire, and industrial Lancashire.

69 **Postcodes: the new geography.**
Jonathan Raper, David Rhind, John Shepherd.   Harlow, England:
Longman, 1992. 322p. bibliog.

Although postcodes derived from a need to automate the postal system their use now reaches much wider into many areas of British economic and commercial life. Since postcodes became available in computer form they have undoubtedly emerged as vital means of locating people and activities and analysing spatial patterns of consumer information. This outstanding book provides a background to their current use, and to the potential of postcode referenced information, in marketing, planning, retailing, transport, insurance, and health services. How to handle postcoded data and an account of the data held by government departments and agencies are included among the numerous appendices.

70 **The Ice Age in Britain.**
B. W. Sparks, R. G. West.   London: Methuen, 1972. 302p. 12 maps.
bibliog.

The general geography of the Ice Age and its causes; glacial landforms in Britain; the stratigraphy of British Ice Age deposits; Ice Age botany and zoology; dating Ice Age events; and the physical geography of the last interglacial period in Britain; are among some of the topics treated in this non-specialist account.

71 **British geography 1918-1945.**
Edited by Robert W. Steel.   Cambridge, England: Cambridge
University Press, 1987. 189p.

Edited by a former President of the Institute of British Geographers, this assessment of British geography between the wars is firmly based on the memories of some of those active in the discipline at the time. Geography's evolution from a distinctly fragile place in British universities to a respectable academic position, and the lively controversies it engendered, are the principal themes.

72 **The British Isles a systematic geography.**
Edited by J. Wreford Watson, J. B. Sissons.   London: Nelson, 1964.
452p. maps. bibliog.

Published to mark the 20th International Geographical Congress in 1964 the twenty-three essays assembled here constitute an inventory of the contemporary state of British geography. Contributed by leading geographers, they cover the individuality of Britain, the mapping of the British Isles, climate, hydrology, relief and structure, tertiary landscape evolution, the glacial period, the evolution of the climatic environment, prehistoric geography, historical geography from the Anglo-Saxon period to the Industrial Revolution, problems of land use, agriculture and fisheries, mineral resources and power, industry, transport, population, rural settlement, the towns, cultural geography, and the British Isles in the world context.

Catalogue of cartographic materials in the British Library 1975-1988.
See item no. 2351.

Maps and atlases

73 AA road atlas of the British Isles 1992.
Basingstoke, England: Automobile Association, 1991. 384p.

On a scale of three miles to the inch this atlas includes a colour feature, 'Tourist's British Isles', journey and route-planning information, street-indexed plans of almost seventy towns and cities, and eleven pages of London street mapping. The AA's bestselling road atlas is *Big road atlas Britain* (1993 ed. 244p.), also on a three miles to the inch scale, which includes London street maps, thirteen town plans, and locates over 350 roadside restaurants. A number of small-size glovebox atlases are also published including *AA Glovebox atlas Britain* and *AA Glovebox town plans of Britain*

74 The atlas of Britain and Northern Ireland.
Compiled by D. P. Bickmore, M. A. Shaw.   Oxford: Clarendon, 1963. 222p.

Described by L. Dudley Stamp as 'a landmark in the history of British cartography, with originality and freshness of approach as the most striking feature', this atlas contains physical geography, agriculture, fishery, industry, demography, housing, administrative, trade, and communication maps on various scales. The twenty-two page gazetteer has some 15,000 entries.

75 British cartography 1987-91: an overview.
The Cartographic Journal, vol. 28, no. 1 (June 1991), p. 3-107.

Apart from regular features like book reviews, recent literature, etc., virtually the whole of this issue is given over to twenty-seven authoritative articles dealing with governmental mapping, commercial cartography, academic cartography, and other activity in the period under review. *The Cartographic Journal* is published twice-yearly by The British Cartographic Society.

76 Britain from space: an atlas of Landsat images.
R. K. Bullard, R. W. Dixon-Gough.   London: Taylor & Francis, 1985. 128p. 39 maps.

The Landsat images in this atlas are generated from the Landsat mosaic produced by the National Remote Sensing Centre at Farnborough. One group systematically extends over the British mainland, another more specialized group illustrates natural and man-made features, whilst a third shows the different techniques employed and their various applications. Each image is accompanied by an interpretative map, drawn to a common specification, and a descriptive text which includes explanations of the evidence of soil types, underlying geological trends, and vegetation cover other than woodlands.

77 The early years of the Ordnance Survey.
Sir Charles Close.   Newton Abbot, England: David & Charles, 1969. 164p. bibliog.

First printed as a series of articles in the *Royal Engineers Journal*, and first published in book form by the Institution of Royal Engineers in 1926, this history by the Director of the Ordnance Survey 1911-1922 ranges from its eighteenth-century origins to the development of the English and Irish surveys of 1846. This edition contains an introduction by J. B. Harley who reviews Close's interpretation of the early years in the light of subsequent research.

78   **Ordnance Survey maps: a descriptive manual.**
     J. B. Harley.   Southampton, England: Ordnance Survey, 1975. 200p.
     maps. bibliog.

This authoritative manual describes the whole range of OS maps current at the time of writing. There are specific chapters on the national survey, the projection of OS maps and the national reference system, and on the OS's archaeological and historical maps. 'As much background is provided as seemed necessary to allow map users to understand the basic nature of the surveying, compilation, and production processes' (Preface).

79   **County atlases of the British Isles 1704-1742: a bibliography.**
     Donald Hodson.   Welwyn, England: Tewin, 1984. 200p.

A notable feature of this incomplete series which also includes *County atlases of the British Isles 1743-1763: a bibliography,* Donald Hodson (Welwyn, England: 1989. 193p.), is the meticulously detailed publication history of atlas production in the seventeenth and eighteenth centuries. A wide range of source material is used to disentangle the complexities of map engraving, book production, and retail outlets employed. In general these works will take the place of Thomas Chubb's *The printed maps in the atlases of Great Britain and Ireland: a bibliography* (London, Homeland Association, 1927. 479p.) which retains its reference value nevertheless.

80   **The tithe surveys of England and Wales.**
     Roger J. P. Kain, Hugh C. Prince.   Cambridge, England: Cambridge
     University Press, 1985. 327p. 12 maps. bibliog. (Cambridge Studies in
     Historical Geography).

The rural landscape of mid-nineteenth century England and Wales is depicted in minute detail in the large scale plans and schedules drawn for the Tithe Commission in connection with the Tithe Commutation Act of 1836. Information on field boundaries, rights of way, with schedules on the names of owners and occupiers, field names, and land use, is all available for over 11,000 parishes. This history discusses the nature of tithe payments, the 1836 Act, and the use made of the tithe maps and schedules in the study of early field systems, tracing land use, and in the understanding of farming practices.

81 **Historic towns: maps and plans of towns and cities in the British Isles with historical commentaries, from earliest times to 1600.**
Edited by M. D. Lobel. Vol. 1. *Banbury . . . Hereford, Nottingham, Reading, Salisbury.* London: Lovell-Johns/Cook, Hammond & Kell, 1969; vol. 2. *Bristol, Cambridge, Coventry, Norwich.* London: Scolar Press, 1975; vol. 3, *The City of London from prehistoric times.* Oxford: Oxford University Press, 1989.

Published for the Historic Towns Trust this series of large format atlases presents meticulously detailed colour maps, a textual commentary setting the towns in their historical context, and a gazetteer providing indispensable source material for known streets and buildings in the medieval period.

82 **Bartholomew gazetteer of places in Britain.**
Compiled by Oliver Mason. Edinburgh: Bartholomew, 1986. 2nd ed. 270p. 120p. maps.

Some 40,000 entries for inhabited places and physical features are contained in this gazetteer which was first published as *Bartholomew gazetteer of Britain* in 1977. Each entry provides a location reference to the 120-page map section and the distance to the nearest town of any size is noted in miles and in kilometres. An introductory section includes a brief etymology of place-names, population, statistics, and climatic information.

83 **The county maps of William Camden's Britannia 1695.**
Robert Morden. Newton Abbot, England: David & Charles, 1972. 50 maps.

With a new introduction by J. B. Harley this is a facsimile edition of a work originally published in 1695. There are separate maps for each of the English counties and for Roman and Saxon Britain. The maps' characteristics are studied in the context of the contemporary London map trade and there is a brief investigation of Morden's principal sources.

84 **The county maps of old England.**
Thomas Moule. London: Studio Editions, 1991. 126 maps.

Thomas Moule first published his highly individual series of county maps as *England's topographer or Moule's English counties delineated in the 19th century* in the 1830s. This handsome edition contains fifty-six specially coloured maps accompanied by the original text printed in *James Barclay's complete and universal dictionary* first published between 1842 and 1852.

85 **Ordnance Survey county street atlases.**
Southampton, England: Ordnance Survey; London: George Philip, 1988- .

Atlases so far published in this series, some in revised editions, include *Berkshire, Buckinghamshire, East Essex, North Hampshire, South Hampshire, Hertfordshire, East Kent, West Kent, Oxfordshire, Surrey, East Sussex, West Sussex,* and *Warwickshire.* They depict roads, streets and lanes, parks, woods, farms, bridleways and footpaths,

Post Offices, schools and libraries, museums, government offices, hospitals, fire stations, ferry ports and harbours.

86   Ordnance Survey gazetteer of Great Britain.
London: Macmillan, 1992. 3rd ed. 808p.

First published in 1987 this gazetteer lists 250,000 named features from the Ordnance Survey Landranger map series. The data provided includes county, national grid references, latitude and longitude, and an indication of what the name represents.

87   Ordnance Survey landranger maps.
Southampton, England: Ordnance Survey.

A total of 204 Landranger maps cover the United Kingdom, each one mapping an area of 675 square miles on a scale of one and a quarter inches to the mile. All maps show camping and caravan sites, picnic areas, viewpoints, and other tourist information. They are available either flat or folded.

88   Ordnance Survey maps, atlases and guides catalogue 1992.
Southampton, England: Ordnance Survey, 1992. 32p. annual.

Enjoying a world-wide reputation for meticulous accuracy, authority, and painstaking detail, the Ordnance Survey is Britain's national mapping agency. This illustrated catalogue provides details of all OS publications in print, motoring atlases, street atlases, leisure maps, and historical maps and guides.

89   Ordnance Survey motoring atlas of Great Britain 1992.
Southampton, England: Ordnance Survey, 1992. 144p.

On a scale of one inch to three miles for the whole of mainland Britain this motoring atlas which is revised annually also contains forty-five town plans, including central London, route planning pages, a distance chart, and travel information for the motorist. All the latest road changes are incorporated. A spiral bound edition allows the pages to lie absolutely flat for easy use.

90   Ordnance Survey national atlas of Great Britain.
Southampton, England: Ordnance Survey and Country Life, 1986. 256p. maps.

Seven thematic essays on Britain: land and countryside; people and history; energy and resources; communications; economy and industry; politics; power and the state; and leisure and heritage; statistical charts and diagrams; and four mile to the inch OS maps, are included in this national atlas. Noteworthy features include its detailed topography and its locations of places of interest.

91   Ordnance Survey road atlas of Great Britain.
Southampton, England: Ordnance Survey, 1992. 200p. 137 maps.

Revised periodically this road atlas is on a scale of one inch to four miles and is suitable for both business and holiday touring use. Complementary features include town centre maps, a separate London section, the M25 and routes into London, route planning maps. national and forest parks, long distance paths, and symbols indicating various types of tourist attractions.

92   **Ordnance Survey routemaster maps.**
     Southampton, England: Ordnance Survey.

Available either flat or folded these nine regularly revised one inch to four miles maps cover the United Kingdom and are ideal for motor touring use. Motorways, trunk roads, primary and secondary routes are all prominently depicted whilst relief detail is indicated by colour shading. Distances between major towns is tabulated. Titles include *Central Scotland and Northumberland, Northern England, East Midlands and Yorkshire, Wales and West Midlands, South West England & South Wales* and *South East England*.

93   **Ordnance Survey superscale atlas of Great Britain.**
     Southampton, England: Ordnance Survey.

The largest scale motoring atlas of Britain available, one inch to two and a quarter miles, this atlas recommends itself for in-car navigation use. Additional features include route planning maps, town plans, and a central London street plan.

94   **Ordnance Survey: map makers to Britain since 1791.**
     Tim Owen, Elaine Pilbeam.   Southampton, England: Ordnance
     Survey; London: HMSO, 1992. 196p. maps. bibliog.

Describing its origins and early map series, and the individuals who imprinted their personalities on its development, this fully illustrated history, which is published to mark the Ordnance Survey's 200th anniversary, charts its progress to its present pre-eminence in land surveying and map making.

95   **Mapping in the UK: mapping and spatial data for the 1990s.**
     C. R. Perkins, R. B. Parry.   London: Bowker Saur, 1993. 300p.

Detailed subject covering of both conventional hard copy products and digital data sets is provided in this authoritative guide to the current mapping of the UK.

96   **RAC motoring atlas Britain 1993.**
     Abingdon, England: RAC, 1992. 272p.

This popular large format atlas contains sixty-six pages of maps at 1:250,000 (one inch to four miles), a colour-coded route planning system, forty-nine town plans and urban approach maps, and assorted tourist information. A spiral bound edition is made available for car use. The Royal Automobile Club has also published a series of sheet maps on a scale of 1:200,000 (one inch to three miles) also with tourist information (e.g. golf courses, steam railways, and motorsport venues). Titles are: *South East, The South, South West, East Anglia, Midlands, Lancashire and Peak District, East Midlands and Lincolnshire*. A national map *England & Wales* contains the latest road information on a scale of around one inch to eight miles.

97   **Reader's Digest driver's atlas of the British Isles.**
     London: Reader's Digest, 1988. 368p.

The most distinctive feature of this popular motoring atlas, which includes 141 pages of three inch to the mile road maps, 128 town plans, and ten pages of London plans, is undoubtedly the map fold-overs linking maps on one page to the next. The gazetteer includes 27,000 place names.

98   **Marine cartography in Britain: a history of the sea charts to 1855.**
     A. H. Robinson.   Leicester, England: Leicester University Press, 1962.
     222p. bibliog.

This authoritative study includes biographical notes on the renowned surveyors and
chartmakers of the sixteenth century and a fifty page historical list of charts and
hydrographic surveys.

99   **A history of the Ordnance Survey.**
     Edited by W. A. Seymour.   Folkestone, England: Dawson, 1980. 394p.
     13 maps.

With contributions from a team of leading map scholars and historians, this
authoritative and comprehensive history is a handsome tribute to what is a model
national cartographic survey for many countries of the world. Among the themes
discussed are the OS's origins, the birth of the topographical surveys, the national grid,
OS's relations with government, its personalities and staff, and technical developments
in map production.

100   **County atlases of the British Isles 1579-1859: a bibliography.**
      R. A. Skelton.   Folkestone, England: Dawson, 1978. 272p.

Originally printed in parts between 1964 and 1970 and first published in book form by
Carta Press, this volume contains facsimiles of 124 county atlases issued from Tudor
times onwards. Each is briefly annotated with a short bibliographical description.
Appendices include a select list of maps of parts of the British Isles to be found in
general atlases before 1650, and a sketch of the London map trade before 1700,
together with a biographical list of London map publishers.

101   **The counties of Britain: a Tudor atlas.**
      John Speed.   London: Michael Joseph in association with the British
      Library, 1988. 288p. 69 maps. bibliog.

Originally published in 1616 as *The theatre of the Empire of Great Britaine presenting
an exact geography of the Kingdomes of England, Scotland, Ireland and the iles
adioyning: with the shires, hundreds, cities and shire-townes, within the Kingdome of
England, divided and described*, this facsimile edition was reproduced from a rare
contemporary colour version held in the British Library. It includes facsimiles of the
original title page and sixty-seven Tudor maps together with contemporary paintings,
illustrations and engravings. Nigel Nicolson contributes a concise biography of John
Speed whilst Alasdair Hawkyard describes the topographical features of each map and
explains the prevailing social conditions of each of the counties depicted.

102   **A directory of UK map collections.**
      Compiled by I. Watt.   London: McCarta for the British Cartographic
      Society, 1985. 2nd ed. 248p.

This guide to about 400 map collections includes those of the copyright libraries (in
England the British Library; Bodleian Library, Oxford; and Cambridge University
Library). The number and scope of their holdings, atlases, and their publications, are
all indicated.

Geology and geomorphology

103 **Field geology in the British Isles: a guide to regional excursions.**
J. G. C. Anderson. Oxford: Pergamon, 1983. 324p. maps.
Descriptions of 194 geological itineraries grouped according to the type of terrain are included in this field guide.

104 **The geological history of the British Isles.**
George M. Bennison, Alan E. Wright. London: Edward Arnold, 1969. 406p. 20 maps. bibliog.
This undergraduate textbook sketches the outline of the main geological events of the last 3,000 million years. The chronological stratographical framework is interpreted as a succession of events which changed the geography of the British Isles rather than as successions of strata.

105 **British fossils.**
London: HMSO for The National History Museum, 3 vols., 1975-83.
Acknowledged as the classic work of reference these authoritative volumes (vol. 1. *British Caenozoic fossils*, 1975. 5th ed. 136p. vol. 2. *British Mesozoic fossils*, 1983. 6th ed. 212p. vol. 3. *British Palaeozoic fossils*. 1975. 4th ed. 206p.) provide information on which types of fossils may be discovered in Britain. At the same time they are excellent guides to the identification of the species found. 'Amateur and professional palaeontologists alike will continue to find that these volumes are as important to their studies as their hand lens and geological hammer' (HMSO information sheet).

106 **British Geological Survey.**
London: HMSO, 1986. 47p. (Sectional List, no. 45).
This is a complete list of British Geological Survey publications in print including summaries of progress and annual reports, Bulletins of the Geological Survey of Great Britain, and one-inch and 1:50,000 sheet map memoirs.

107 **British Geological Survey maps.**
Southampton, England: Ordnance Survey.
The Geological Survey of Great Britain, which subsequently became a component of the Institute of Geological Sciences, now renamed the British Geological Survey, began making a geological map of Great Britain in the nineteenth century. The medium scale 1:63,360 (one inch to one mile) maps are now being replaced by metric equivalent 1:50,000 maps which may either be photographic enlargements of the previous maps, recompilations incorporating more recent resurvey work, or completely new compilations. Over 250 sheets cover England: twenty or so areas have not yet been mapped. They are generally accompanied by explanatory *Street Memoirs*, some of which cover one or more sheets, and whose titles usually read *Geology of the country around [place-name]*. For some areas warranting greater detail, usually for locations considered to be of outstanding interest, maps have been published on a scale of 1:25,000. Some of these are provided with *Explanatory Booklets* issued through HMSO. Full details are incorporated in British Geological Survey's *Catalogue of printed maps 1992 and associated literature*. Recent developments in BGS map

Geography and Geology. Geology and geomorphology

production are traced in K. Becken's 'Cartographic development in the British Geological Survey'. *The Cartographic Journal*, vol. 28, no. 1 (June 1991), p. 10-12.

108 **British landscapes through maps.**
Sheffield, England: The Geographical Association, 1960- . maps. bibliog.

'Great Britain exhibits a diversity of landscape types which is unsurpassed . . . In the one inch sheets of the Ordnance Survey, moreover, this country possesses a topographical map which is unexcelled in its clear and accurate representation of the surface features of our land. The aim of the present series of booklets is to interpret, through maps, the development of the principal types of landscape'. Volumes of interest are *The English Lake District*. F. J. Monkhouse. 1972. 2nd ed. 24p. *The Yorkshire Dales*. Cuchlaine A. M. King. 1960. 24p. *The Chilterns*. J. T. Coppock. 1962. 28p. *Merseyside*. R. Kay Gresswell, Richard Lawton. 1964. 36p. *The Scarborough District*. Cuchlaine A. M. King. 1965. 31p. *The Doncaster area*. B. E. Coates, G. M. Lewis. 1966. 44p. *Cornwall*. W. G. V. Balchin. 1967. 39p. *East Kent*. Aline M. Coleman. 1967. 30p. *Oxford and Newbury area*. P. D. Wood. 1968. 32p. *Dartmoor*. D. Brunsden. 1968. 55p. *The Norwich area*. Patrick Bailey. 1971. 30p.

109 **British regional geology series.**
London: HMSO for Natural Environment Research Council, 1948-1982. 11 vols.

Each book in this series contains an explanatory text, sketch maps, sections, and photographs. The titles are as follows: B. M. Taylor: *Northern England* (4th ed. 1971); W. Edwards, F. M. Trotter: *The Pennines and adjacent areas* (3rd ed. 1954); P. Kent: *Eastern England from the Tees to the Wash* (2nd ed. 1980); B. Hains, A. Horton: *Central England* (3rd ed. 1969); J. R. Earp, B. A. Hains: *The Welsh Borderland* (3rd ed. 1971); C. P. Chatwin: *East Anglia and adjoining areas* (4th ed. 1961); R. L. Sherlock: *London and Thames Valley* (3rd ed. 1960); R. W. Gallois: *The Wealden district* (4th ed. 1965); R. V. Melville, E. C. Freshney: *The Hampshire Basin and adjoining areas* (4th ed. 1982); G. A. Kellaway, F. B. A. Welsh: *Bristol and Gloucester district* (2nd ed. 1948); and E. A. Edmonds (et al.): *South-West England* (4th ed. 1975). All titles are kept in print.

110 **The geomorphology of the British Isles.**
Edited by Eric H. Brown, Keith Clayton. London: Methuen, 1976- . *Northern England*. Cuchlaine A. M. King. 1976. 213p. maps. bibliog. *Eastern and Central England*. Allan Straw, Keith M. Clayton. 1979. 247p. maps. bibliog. *Southeast and Southern England*. David K. C. Jones. 1981. 332p. maps. bibliog. *Wales and Southwest England*. Eric H. Brown, D. Q. Bowen, R. S. Waters. (not yet published).

Intended both for students and for those with a general interest in the evolution of the complex landforms of the diverse regions of the British Isles, these indispensable guides not only investigate their geological background, physiography, glaciation, and other features, but also enquire into the history of British geomorphological studies.

111 **The English medieval landscape.**
Edited by Leonard Cantor. London: Croom Helm, 1982. 225p. maps.

A group of historical geographers identify and describe major developments of the landscape during the period 1066-1485 in this authoritative study. They examine the medieval field system, forests and parks, marshland and waste, castles, fortified houses, monastic settlements, villages and towns, and roads and tracks.

112 **Catalogue of printed maps, 1992 and associated literature.**
Nottingham, England: British Geological Survey, 1992. 24p. 6 maps.

Full details of all British Geological Survey publications are listed in this annotated catalogue: regional geology guides; offshore regional reports; small, medium, and large scale Geological Survey maps and their accompanying sheet memoirs and explanatory booklets; and geophysical, geochemical, hydrogeological, engineering, and mineral assessment and reconnaissance maps.

113 **The history of British geology: a bibliographical study.**
John Challinor. Newton Abbot, England: David & Charles, 1971. 224p.

Challinor's purpose here is to outline the history of British geology by reviewing the written records of the progress of geological knowledge. First he lists the primary literature (reports of original research, summaries, and expositions of principles) in a chronological sequence and then, in a series of short bibliographical essays, groups these works in eighty-six major categories. Secondary and associated literature is included as an appendix.

114 **A bibliography of British geomorphology.**
Edited by Keith M. Clayton. London: George Philip, 1964. 211p.

For the purposes of this bibliography archaeology, pedology, geology, and ecology, are all included in a broad interpretation of what morphology embraces. The bibliography, which is divided into eleven thematic sections, includes entries for relevant books and articles published between 1945 and 1962 at which point *Geomorphology abstracts* began publication.

115 **The Penguin guide to the landscape of England and Wales.**
Paul Coones, John Patten. London: Penguin, 1986. 348p.

Six main topics feature in this guide: the natural landscape (relief and geology); prehistoric and Roman; medieval; pre-industrial landscapes; the Industrial Revolution; and the Victorian landscape. About a score of sites illustrate each category.

116 **Britain before man.**
F. W. Dunning (et al.). London: HMSO for the Institute of Geological Sciences, 1978. 36p. map.

This colourful booklet illustrates the geological eras of Britain starting with the earth's crust under the British Isles and proceeding from Pre-Cambrian times to the Ice Age and the period of early man. The names of the various geological periods, which can be a little daunting to the layman, are here explained and illustrated in clear fashion. A geological map of Britain and Ireland completes a very worthwhile publication.

117 **Stanford's geological atlas of Great Britain.**
T. Eastwood. London: Edward Stanford, 1964. 4th ed. 288p.
29 maps. bibliog.

Based largely on Horace B. Woodward's *Stanford's geological atlas of Great Britain and Ireland with plates of characteristic fossils preceded by descriptions of the geological structure of Great Britain and Ireland and their counties . . . and of the features observable along the principal lines of railway* (Stanford, 1914. 3rd ed. 214p.), still a useful reference work in its own right, this entirely new edition comprises authoritative textual commentaries on twenty-nine area maps derived from those of the ten mile Geological Survey. Although not intended as a geological textbook there are two introductory chapters on stratigraphy, and on the economic products associated with various rock formations.

118 **Discovering landscape in England and Wales.**
Andrew Goudie, Rita Gardner. London: Allen & Unwin, 1985. 177p.
maps. bibliog.

Written for the general reader in non-technical language, this is a guide to sixty-five of the more outstanding topographical features of the natural landscape, including Malham and the Pennines, Mam Tor, Dovedale, the Norfolk Broads, the Seven Sisters and Beachy Head, Cheddar Gorge, and Chesil Bank.

119 **Directory of quarries and pits.**
Edited by Bernard Hill. Nottingham, England: Quarry Managers
Journal, 1988. 22nd ed. various paginations.

Arranged by county this guide provides details of nearly 1,900 sites operated by almost 800 companies. Information is also given of plant, equipment, materials, and service companies, plant supply companies, and various quarrying industry organizations, research institutions, and professional bodies.

120 **English landscapes.**
W. G. Hoskins. London: BBC, 1977. 120p. map. bibliog.

Encompassing geology, topography, climate, and the history of landownership, this book, first published as a paperback in 1973, consists of ten illustrated essays interpreting different aspects of the English landscape.

121 **The making of the English landscape.**
W. G. Hoskins. London: Hodder & Stoughton, 1977. rev. ed. 326p.
17 maps and plans. bibliog.

A pioneer work when first published in 1955 this book may be said to have instigated the study of the evolution of the English landscape. It examines in turn the landscape before and after the English settlement; the colonization of medieval England; the Black Death, Tudor to Georgian England; parliamentary enclosures; the Industrial Revolution; roads, canals and railways; and the landscape of towns. Two of the author's premises are that previous estimates of population in prehistoric and Romano-British times were too low and that everything in the landscape is older than we think. This work spawned a number of regional works edited by Hoskins and Roy Millward in The Making Of The English Landscape series, e.g. H. P. R. Finburg's *The Gloucestershire landscape*, Arthur Raistrick's *West Riding of Yorkshire*, and many others. A new edition with an introduction and commentary by Christopher Taylor and photographs by Andrew Burton (1988. 256p.) points out some of the lines along which scholarship has taken landscape history since the 1950s.

122 **British rivers.**
Edited by J. Lewin. London: Allen & Unwin, 1981. 216p. maps. bibliog.

Describing and interpreting the physical nature of British rivers, this study includes chapters on river systems and regimes, contemporary erosion and sedimentation, mountain streams, channel forms and changes, water quality, and river management. Where possible nationwide information is presented in map form.

123 **The geologist's directory: guide to geological services, equipment and sources of geological information in the British Isles.**
Edited by E. McInairnie. London: Institution of Geologists, 1988. 4th ed. 219p.

Opening with information on the Institute of Geologists, this directory continues with sections on geology in government, education, and industry. Other sections include geological consultants, specialist services, a buyers guide, geological information sources, and a guide to companies overseas. This edition marks the tenth anniversary of the Institution.

124 **Mineral Reconnaissance Programme Reports.**
Nottingham, England: British Geological Survey. 1972- .

The Mineral Reconnaissance Programme was established in 1972 to carry out baseline mineral exploration to encourage and sustain private mineral enterprise. The information obtained is released in a series of reports prepared for the Department of Trade and Industry. To date over 120 have been published. No. 14 *The Mineral Reconnaissance Programme* (1990) contains summaries of all the previous 113 Reports in the series. New titles are advertised in *Mining Journal*.

125 **The National Trust rivers of Britain.**
Richard Muir, Nina Muir. Exeter, England: Webb & Bower, 1986. 225p.

All aspects of rivers, the geological events that formed them, their history and ecology, their bridges, fords and ferries, their fish, and their management, are covered in this immensely informative and readable volume.

126 **The stones of Britain.**
Richard Muir. London: Michael Joseph, 1986. 288p. 2 maps. bibliog.

Part geological textbook explaining the different processes by which rocks and stones were formed and the distinctive landscapes they produced, part archaeological guide to how prehistoric communities made use of stone, and part architectural treatise on the use of stone in church and secular buildings through the centuries, this book encourages the visitor and tourist to understand the use of stone in the British architectural heritage.

127 **National stone directory: dimension stone sources and services for Britain and Ireland.**
Maidenhead, England: Stone Industries, 1990. 8th ed. 160p.
Information on UK quarries in current production giving details of their owners, geology, the colour and weight of the stone quarried, its availability, suitability, its recent use, and lists of quarry operators, wholesalers, equipment and tools manufacturers, are the principal contents of this directory which was first published in 1968. Standards, education and training opportunities, trade organizations, conservation groups, and public bodies, are also featured.

128 **The landscape of Britain: from the beginnings to 1914.**
Michael Reed. London: Routledge, 1990. 387p. 5 maps. bibliog.
'The theme of the landscape historian is the evolution of that external physical world in which men and women have carried on the everyday business of their lives from the remotest period of prehistory down to the present' (Introduction). This study looks at the main factors in the evolution of Britain's landscape and man's use of the environment over hundreds of years, not only for the basic needs of food and shelter, but also for his intellectual needs.

129 **The Shell book of the British coast.**
Adrian Robinson, Roy Millward. Newton Abbot, England: David & Charles, 1983. 560p. 96 maps. bibliog.
After introductory chapters on various major themes, e.g. coastal life and habitats, land reclaimed from the sea, the climate for holidays and retirement, the main narrative of this profusely illustrated guide consists of an anti-clockwise progression round the coast from northwest England to the Scottish western isles. Conservation of the coastline, its accessibility, and its geological and climatic features, are among the predominant topics discussed.

130 **The coastline of England and Wales.**
J. A. Steers. Cambridge, England: Cambridge University Press, 1964. 2nd ed. 761p.
First published in 1946, this standard academic treatise is a detailed physiographical survey of each stretch of coastline working anti-clockwise from the Solway Firth round to the northeast coast. Because of its technical nature it is not suitable for casual readers and interested non-specialists should opt for the author's *The coast of England and Wales in pictures* (1960. 2nd ed.) which includes a general introduction and detailed notes.

131 **Natural landscapes of Britain from the air.**
Edited by Nicholas Stephens. Cambridge, England: Cambridge University Press, 1990. 288p.
Oblique and vertical aerial photographs have long been recognized by physical geographers as providing a valuable means of recording surface features and landscape patterns. In this beautifully produced volume a team of geomorphologists employ such photographs to examine the fossil effects of glacial erosion, the deposits left by glaciers and meltwater streams, the ground patterns caused by periglacial freezing, landscape

changes caused by rivers and variations in sea-level, and the effects of modern leisure activities and tourism.

132 **Down to earth: one hundred and fifty years of the British Geological Survey.**
H. E. Wilson. Edinburgh: Scottish Academic Press, 1985. 190p. bibliog.

This review of the British Geological Survey's origins, development, and expansion updates John Flett's *The first hundred years of the Geological Survey of Great Britain* (London: HMSO, 1937). By no means an 'official' history, the story is lightened by numerous anecdotes about some of the 'characters' who either helped or hindered its progress.

133 **The English landscape past, present, and future.**
Edited by S. R. J. Woodell. Oxford: Oxford University Press, 1985. 240p. maps. bibliogs.

Delivered as the Wolfson College Lectures in 1983, these papers by distinguished historians and scientists cover various aspects of the shaping of the natural environment in England. The titles are as follows: David K. C. Jones, 'Shaping the land: the geomorphological background'; B. W. Cunliffe, 'Man and landscape in Britain 6000 BC – AD 400'; Oliver Rackham, 'Ancient woodland and hedges in England'; M. W. Beresford, 'Mapping the medieval landscape: forty years in the field'; Joan Thirsk, 'The agricultural landscape'; Hubert H. Lamb, 'Climate and landscape in the British Isles'; F. M. L. Thompson, 'Towns, industry, and the Victorian landscape'; M. E. D. Poore, 'Agriculture, forestry, and the future landscape'.

Climate

134 **Sunny intervals and showers.**
David Benedictus. London: Weidenfeld & Nicolson, 1991. 208p.

In the wake of the hurricane of October 1987, and the severe storms of January 1990, this study examines meteorological statistics and examines the skills of the weather forecasters, comparing the performances and reputations of the high-tech professionals with the amateurs who rely on more traditional forms of the elusive art of weather forecasting. Little evidence of cataclysmic change emerges.

135 **Climate change: rising sea level and the British coast.**
L. A. Boorman, J. D. Goss-Custard, S. McGrorty. London: HMSO for Institute of Terrestrial Ecology, 1989. 24p.

According to some predictions global warming in the next century could lead to a rise in sea levels around Britain's coast which would possibly threaten flora and fauna in many areas. This timely report considers the biological implications and the impact on sea defence and coast protection.

Geography and Geology. Climate

136   British weather disasters.
Ingrid Holford.   Newton Abbot, England: David & Charles, 1976.
127p. 3 maps. bibliog.

A general picture of weather disasters in Britain caused by fresh and salt water floods, storms at sea, gale force winds, fog on motorways, blizzards, and, not least, by human neglect.

137   Meteorological Office.
London: HMSO, 1984. rev. ed. 10p. (Sectional List, no. 37).

Official handbooks, tables, charts, and reports, relating to meteorological data, climatological normals and averages, marine meteorology and sea-surface currents and ice, and weather over the oceans and coastal regions, are listed in this catalogue.

138   The potential effects of climate change in the United Kingdom.
London: HMSO for the Department of the Environment, 1991. 124p. bibliog.

The United Kingdom Climate Change Review Group was set up to consider the potential impact of climate change, and to establish what further research is needed. Their first report looks at the possible effects of future changes in climate and sea levels on various socio-economic factors notably on flora and fauna, the landscape, the coastal regions, the water industry, energy, mineral extraction, and recreation and tourism.

139   The weather of Britain.
Robin Stirling.   London: Faber, 1982. 270p. 87 maps. bibliog.

The weather and seas around Britain, high and low pressure systems, rainfalls and deluges, thunder and hail storms, tornados, drought, frost, snowfall, sunshine, and sensational months and seasons, underline the unpredictability of English weather in this historical survey.

140   British weather in maps.
James A. Taylor, R. A. Yates.   London: Macmillan, 1967. 315p. maps. bibliog.

Principally a guide to the analysis and interpretation of the primary source documents of the British climate, the daily weather reports, this study explains the significance and relevance of the atmosphere, air masses, fronts, and anticyclones. It includes a guide to the symbols used on weather maps, a map of the more important meteorological stations of the British Isles, the upper air stations, and the location of ocean weather ships.

141   Climatological maps of Great Britain.
E. J. White, R. I. Smith.   Cambridge, England: Institute of Terrestrial Ecology, 1982. 37p. bibliog.

The Institute of Terrestrial Ecology, whose task it is to study the factors detailing the structure, composition, and processes of land and freshwater systems, and of individual plants and animal species, was founded in 1973. It is one of fourteen sister institutes of the Natural Environment Research Council. This colour-coded series of maps show the mean air temperature, rainfall, visibility, sunshine hours, windspeed, and total snow depth of the British Isles.

142   **The great British obsession.**
Francis Wilson.   Norwich, England: Jarrold, 1990. 144p.

It is said that other countries have a climate; in Britain we just have the weather. This book, written by a former research scientist at the Meteorological Office, describes British weather in its global context, the effect it has on our minds and bodies, and its place in British history and the arts. Other topics covered include the history of meteorology, the factual basis of many traditional weather saws and beliefs, freak weather conditions such as the great floods of 1953 and the October 1987 hurricane, and professional methods of weather forecasting.

Flora and Fauna

General

143 **AA book of the British countryside.**
London: Drive Publications for the Automobile Association, 1973.
534p. maps.

A generously illustrated encyclopedic guide to the natural heritage and man-made landscape of the British Isles, with eighteen special wildlife features on the plants and animals to be found in different habitats (e.g. Beechwoods, bramble, canals, limestone country), this comprehensive work also includes forty-eight double-page essays on such varied topics as 'Animal behaviour', 'Colour and camouflage in Animals', and 'Painters of the countryside'. Instructive and informative notes on the County Code, country law, useful organizations, collective names for groups of animals, and a glossary of natural history terms, add to the value of a superbly produced volume.

144 **The naturalist in Britain: a social history.**
David Elliston Allen.   London: Allen Lane, 1976. 292p. bibliog.

In this context naturalists encompass all those who have contributed to our developing knowledge of the wild life and scenery of the British Isles: botanists; entomologists; geologists; ornithologists; and field club members, etc. This definitive social history of their professional societies, and their activities, seems destined to remain the standard work for many years to come.

145 **British Naturalists' Association guide to coast and shore.**
Brian Barnes, foreword by David Bellamy.   Marlborough, England:
Crowood Press, 1986. 128p. bibliog.

The British Naturalists' Association has provided opportunities for both beginners and more advanced students to share expert knowledge of wildlife since 1905. In this compact, highly readable guide the emphasis is on land and marine plants, invertebrates, amphibians, reptiles, mammals, butterflies, birds and fishes found on rock or sandy shores, shingle, mudflats, sand dunes, and estuaries. Ecological and conservation aspects are not overlooked and sites of key interest are spotlighted.

146 Macmillan guide to Britain's nature reserves.

Linda Bennet. London: Macmillan, 1989. 653p. 3rd ed. 58 maps.

This standard guide lists 2,500 major sites alphabetically by county. To qualify for inclusion the site must be accessible to the public either under common law rights or by virtue of membership of an appropriate club or society. Sites where rare or endangered species might be threatened by a mass invasion, or whose owners allow only limited access, are deliberately omitted. Without doubt the most comprehensive of all the nature reserve guides, its thumbnail sketches and site descriptions are enhanced with numerous location maps, and, not least, by almost 200 superb colour photographs.

147 Britain's wildlife, plants and flowers.

London: Reader's Digest, 1987. 420p.

More than 1,500 species of wild flowers, trees and shrubs, fungi, ferns and mosses, birds, butterflies and moths, mammals, amphibians and reptiles, fresh and salt water fish, are described and illustrated in colour in this single-volume work which owes a great deal to the separate volumes published in the Reader's Digest Nature Lover series. Background information for each species includes size, geographical distribution, and 'activity' times.

148 The Shell natural history of Britain.

Edited by Maurice Burton. London: Michael Joseph in association with Rainbird Reference Books, 1970. 481p.

Comprehensive coverage of plants, invertebrates, the seashore, fishes, amphibians and reptiles, birds and mammals, with sixty-four colour plates and 320 black-and-white illustrations, make this an excellent and instructive and plain language guide.

149 The complete guide to British wildlife.

Richard Fitter, Alastair Fitter, with illustrations by Norman Arlott.
London, Glasgow: Collins, 1981. 287p. bibliog.

Over 1,500 species are described and illustrated in this guidebook: trees and climbers; wildflowers; waterwoods; sedges, grasses and rushes; fungi; mammals; animal tracks; birds; snakes, fishes, butterflies, moths and other insects; the wildlife of the sea-shore; and farms, crops and livestock.

150 The Penguin dictionary of British natural history.

Richard Fitter, assisted by Maisie Fitter. London: A & C Black, 1968. 348p.

Designed for use by field naturalists, country lovers, and students in the field, the bulk of the 4,000 entries consists of the names of plants and animals, although natural history is interpreted in its broadest sense as including all living things and natural phenomena of the earth and its atmosphere. The names of internal organs are generally excluded but many words relating to external organs find a place. The scope of the entries, the notes on habitat, the classification of living entries, the drawings in the text, and the index of species, make it indispensable for both amateur and professional naturalists.

151 **British natural history books 1495-1900: a handlist.**
R. B. Freeman. Folkestone, England: Dawson, 1980. 437p.
Principally an alphabetical list by author of over 4,200 general natural history books dealing solely with British flora and fauna, this bibliography is completed with a title list in date order 1485-1800 and a thirty-five page subject index.

152 **British Naturalists' Association guide to wildlife in towns.**
Ron Freethy. Marlborough, England: Crowood, 1986. 128p. bibliog.
Illustrated with 100 photographs, many in colour, this guide describes the rich variety of plants, insects, birds, and mammals that flourish in urban settings, and also in rivers and canals, gravel pits, waterhouses, wall crevices, on wasteground and open spaces, and in churches and churchyards. Pollution and lead poisoning, and the behaviour of urbanized species, such as foxes and kestrels, are also considered.

153 **Pan/Ordnance Survey nature atlas of Great Britain, Ireland and the Channel Islands.**
Edited by Noel Jackson, Brian Eversham. London: Pan Books; Southampton, England: Ordnance Survey, 1989. 280p.
Produced with the co-operation of the Nature Conservancy Council, the Royal Society for Nature Conservation, the National Trust, and the Royal Society for the Protection of Birds, this authoritative and comprehensive natural history atlas covers nearly 2,000 easily accessible sites and constitutes an indispensable guide to British plants and wildlife. Regional gazetteers (South-West, South-East, Middle England, East Anglia and Northern England) provide detailed descriptions of what is to be found contributed by local naturalists together with practical information such as access and the best times to visit. Sites are plotted either on OS Routemaster maps (1:250,000) or else on Landranger maps (1:50,000) if of outstanding interest. A star rating system is employed to indicate sites which should on no account be missed.

154 **Nature watcher's directory.**
David Marsden. London: Hamlyn, 1985. 224p. map. bibliog.
With introductory information and advice on suitable clothing and equipment, bird and mammal watching, habitats, nature photography, and sound recording, the main part of this book consists of a regionally-arranged guide to over 200 sites where both flora and fauna may be seen to its full advantage.

155 **A nature conservation review: the selection of biological sites of national importance to nature conservation in Britain.**
Edited by D. Ratcliffe. Cambridge, England: Cambridge University Press, 2 vols., 1977. bibliog.
Volume one of this pioneering study outlines the ecological background to the selection of significant sites and describes the various types of ecosystem considered. Volume two contains a gazetteer of 735 locations with information on their size, geology, topography, soil, land-use, and plant and animal species.

156 **Nature in trust: the history of nature conservation in Britain.**
John Sheail. Glasgow, London: Blackie, 1976. 270p. 12 maps.
bibliog.

Drawing upon much previously unpublished archival material this history traces the development of the nature conservation movement in Britain from the nineteenth century, assessing the contributions of individual naturalists, the societies and pressure groups they formed, and the selection and management of the nature reserves they established.

157 **The natural history of Britain's coasts.**
Eric Soothill, Michael J. Thomas. London: Blandford Press, 1987.
256p. bibliog.

Birds, plants, snails, and seaweeds, inhabiting cliffs, rocky islands, sand dunes, and estuaries, are all featured in this reference work and field guide designed for birdwatchers, ramblers, naturalists, and holiday visitors. Ecological and conservational aspects are not forgotten and sites of key interest are spotlighted. Much factual information is crammed into the numerous appendices: seabird nesting sites; wildfowl and waders wintering sites; a flora checklist; a seaweed chart; and an introduction to sea-shore fossils.

158 **The biogeography of the British Isles: an introduction.**
Peter Vincent. London: Routledge, 1990. 315p. 52 maps. bibliog.

Biogeography is defined here as the study and interpretation of plant and animal distributions in geographic space. This pioneering work traces British biogeography over the last 200 years, and examines native ecosystems, habitats, and niches, in the context of animal and plant distribution. It also provides a definitive account of the development of biogeographical mapping and recording systems, and describes contemporary rural and urban distribution against the background of disruptive human activities.

159 **AA wildlife in Britain: a guide to natural habitats, safari parks, and zoos.**
Edited by Kenneth Williamson, Geoffrey Schomberg. Basingstoke,
England: Automobile Association, 1976.

In each of ten regional surveys there is a general essay contributed by a naturalist conversant with the area, which includes an assessment of the effect of the climate, geology, topography, and land use on wild life; a guide to natural habitats and a county gazetteer of important reserves and sanctuaries; a similar gazetteer of foreign animal collections assembled in safari parks, zoos, dolphinaria, and the like; and a regional map locating where animals can be seen either in the wild or in captivity. Throughout the emphasis is placed on conservation issues especially on preserving and breeding animals facing extinction.

Fauna

160 **A field guide to the reptiles and amphibians of Britain and Europe.**
E. N. Arnold, John A. Burton. London: Collins, 1978. 272p. 126
maps. bibliog.
The habitats, life-cycles, and distribution of European salamanders and newts, frogs
and toads, tortoises, terrapins and sea turtles, lizards, and snakes, are recorded and
described in this excellent field guide.

161 **Wildfowl in Great Britain: a survey of the winter distribution of the**
Anatidae and their conservation in England, Scotland and Wales.
Edited by G. L. Atkinson-Willes. London: HMSO, 1963. 368p.
61 maps. bibliog. (Monographs of The Nature Conservancy).
Prepared by the Wildfowl Trust, this survey of the distribution and habitats of wild
duck, geese, and swans, is arranged on a regional basis with maps showing the most
important concentrations. The wider migration of birds is discussed and there is an
explanation of the catching techniques used by ornithologists in the ringing of birds.
Reproductions of fifteen oil paintings by Peter Scott illustrate the text.

162 **The birds of the British Isles.**
David Armitage Bannerman. Edinburgh: Oliver & Boyd, 1953-1963.
12 vols.
After listing the species and distinguishing the different races, this mammoth
encyclopedic guide to British birds, which encompasses visitors as well as residents,
describes each bird in detail and gives an account of its distribution and migration and
a complete life history. Whenever possible its behaviour and habitat are described
from personal experience. Illustrated with 385 colour plates of George E. Lodge's
celebrated paintings, this massive work can be enjoyed by the interested general reader
and professional ornithologist alike.

163 **A complete guide to British butterflies: their entire life histories**
described and illustrated in colour from photographs taken in their
natural surroundings.
Margaret Brooks, Charles Knight. London: Cape, 1982. 159p.
After an introductory section outlining the biology of butterflies – their anatomy, life
cycle variations, enemies and diseases, and protective devices, and their recognition,
identification, nomenclature and classification – the main body of this very attractive
book is taken up with a photographic record of the eggs, caterpillars, chrysalises, and
adult male and female butterflies of every individual British species in its natural
surroundings. The accompanying text describes each stage in detail with information
on the butterflies' distribution, habitat, food plant, and anatomy. The result of sixteen
years' painstaking research, this is an indispensable work of reference and field guide,
not only for the amateur naturalist, but also for the professional entomologist.

164   **Tracks & signs of the birds of Britain and Europe: an identification guide.**
Roy Brown (et al.).   London: Christopher Helm, 1987. 232p. bibliog.

Tracks and trails, nests and roosts, feeding and behavioural signs, pellets and droppings, feathers, and skulls, are all considered in this comprehensive study. A list of European study and protection organizations is also included.

165   **Kingfisher guide to the mammals of Britain and Europe.**
John A. Burton.   London: Kingfisher, 1991. 192p. 160 maps. bibliog.

The key physical features, behaviour and distribution patterns, of 160 species of terrestrial and aquatic mammals are described in this superbly illustrated guide. Fact panels aid identification and provide supplementary information on each species' life cycle and conservation status, whilst outline maps illustrate their distribution.

166   **A field guide to caterpillars of butterflies and moths in Britain and Europe.**
David J. Carter.   London: Collins, 1986. 296p. bibliog.

Over 500 caterpillars and moths likely to be spotted in gardens, parks, and the countryside are described, family by family, in this splendidly illustrated field guide. Full details of their appearance, range and habitat, foodplants, and the times of the year when they are most likely to be seen are provided, and there is a colour plate section in which caterpillars are grouped by their foodplants, a novel and ingenious aid to identification.

167   **RSPB reserves visiting.**
Edited by Anthony Chapman.   London: Royal Society for the Protection of Birds, 1987. 240p.

The Royal Society for the Protection of Birds manages 120 nature reserves most of which are open to the public. This visitors' guide provides details of their location and facilities and of the birds and other wildlife that may be sighted. A bird checklist offers the opportunity to record when and where species are spotted.

168   **Collins guide to the insects of Britain and Western Europe.**
Michael Chinery.   London: Collins, 1986. 320p.

Covering all orders and major families of insects to be found west of a line drawn from Finland to the northern shores of the Adriatic, this illustrated guide stresses important identification points, aspects of insect behaviour, their food and habitats, and their general European distribution. An introduction outlines insect anatomy, life cycles, and their collection and preservation.

169   **The handbook of British mammals.**
Edited by Gordon B. Corbet, Stephen Harris.   Oxford: Blackwell for the Mammal Society, 1991. 3rd ed. 588p. maps. bibliog.

Twice extensively revised since its first publication in 1964, this comprehensive and admirably documented handbook is destined to remain the standard authoritative work on British mammals. Providing a full description and account of all current and extinct species, it includes details of their classification and nomenclature, recognition, distribution and habitats, breeding, food, predators and mortality, parasites and diseases, and their relations with man. There can be few doubts as to the importance of this impressive volume for all amateur naturalists and professional zoologists.

170   The seabirds of Britain and Ireland.
Stanley Cramp, W. R. P. Bourne, David Saunders.   London: Collins, 1976. 3rd ed. 287p. 32 maps. bibliog.

Emerging from a major survey, *Operation Seafarer*, conducted during 1969 and 1970, in which over 1,000 professional and amateur ornithologists combined to map and count all seabird colonies, this is a comprehensive and illustrated account of seabirds and their breeding places. An introductory section looks at their life history, their biology, and the dangers that threaten them. The main section comprises a detailed account of all twenty-four species frequenting the British Isles, with notes on their identification, their global distribution, and their prospects in British waters. Distribution maps record the location and size of all breeding colonies.

171   Lost beasts of Britain.
Anthony Dent.   London: Harrup, 1974. 138p.

Described as 'a hunt through British history on the track of certain splendid beasts which . . . have mysteriously disappeared', this book answers the questions how, when and why they vanished. In the main body of the text Dent assembles his evidence from contemporary hunting descriptions, from poetry, the bestiaries of medieval scholars, the plays of Shakespeare, and from old ballads, to account for the passing of wild boars, bears, wolves, and wild cats, etc.

172   Centipedes of the British Isles.
E. H. Eason.   London: Warne, 1964. 294p. bibliog.

All centipede species found in the British Isles, including those doubtfully recorded, are fully described and illustrated in this comprehensive guide. Eason emphasizes their structural characteristics which can be seen without too much dissection rather than their special morphological or physiological detail. Notes on their structure and life history, and an explanation of the principles governing their classification and distribution, are also included.

173   The scientific names of the Lepidoptera: their history and meaning.
A. Maitland Emmet.   Colchester, England: Harley, 1991. 288p.

A systematic list of over 300,000 scientific names of all British Lepidoptera forms the main section of this specialist work. It contains notes on their first use, on the person who named them, and a translation of the Latin term, supplemented by a directory of people commemorated in the names of butterflies, moths, and other winged insects. A brief introduction outlines the history of their scientific nomenclature for the non-specialist.

174 **Field guide to the animals of Britain.**
London: Reader's Digest, 1984. 319p. (Reader's Digest Nature Lover's Library).

Two introductory chapters on understanding and identifying animals precede the main section of this field guide which is taken up with recognition profiles of Britain's wild animals and farm animals most likely to be spotted. Special features illustrate animals associated with different habitats. There are also sections on fieldcraft, i.e. recognizing animal tracks and signs, watching and studying animals, and on Britain's 'lost beasts', wolves, brown bears, etc.

175 **Field guide to the butterflies and other insects of Britain.**
London: Reader's Digest, 1984. 352p. (Reader's Digest Nature Lover's Library).

The main section of this field guide contains over 500 recognition profiles of butterflies, other insects, spiders, and soil animals, with special features illustrating different species and their breeding grounds. Other material includes a section on butterfly watching as a hobby.

176 **Field guide to the water life of Britain.**
London: Reader's Digest, 1984. 335p. (Reader's Digest Nature Lover's Library).

Following two introductory chapters on understanding and identifying water life, the main section of this compact guide provides recognition profiles of the principal groups of marine and freshwater animals and plants commonly to be found in Britain together with a wide selection of the less common species. Other features describe and illustrate the wildlife associated with each main type of coastal or inland habitat.

177 **Reptiles and amphibians in Britain.**
Deryk Frazer. London: Collins, 1983. 256p. 16 maps. bibliog. (The New Naturalist).

Six species of amphibians are native to Britain, two of which are in danger of becoming extinct. This study, which replaces Malcolm Smith's *British amphibians and reptiles*, begins with a chapter on their anatomy, physiology, and evolution, and continues with separate chapters on frogs and toads, newts, lizards, snakes, and Chelonians, providing an overall picture of reptile and amphibian ecology in Britain.

178 **The complete birdwatcher's guide.**
John Gooders. London: Kingfisher, 1988. 360p. 200 maps.

This encyclopedic guide is divided into three major sections. 'All about birds and birdwatching' deals with birds' lifecycles, their structure and flight, and their feeding and sense organs. The second section comprehensively identifies 255 species seen regularly in the British Isles, whilst the third is a site directory of almost 200 birdwatching sites including transport and access information. A checklist of birds corresponds to the British Ornithologists Union's *Checklist of the birds of Great Britain and Ireland* (London: Witherby, 1952. 106p.).

179 **A field guide to the nests, eggs and nestlings of British and European birds.**
Colin Harrison. London: Collins, 1975. 432p.

Assuming that readers will have ready access to the identification of birds and to information on their distribution and general habitats, this work concentrates on their nests, breeding seasons, eggs, incubation, nestlings, and the nestling time period. There is a stern warning that the random unofficial collecting of eggs by amateurs is no longer scientifically justified.

180 **Atlas of butterflies in Britain and ireland.**
John Heath, Ernest Pollard, Jeremy Thomas. Harmondsworth, England: Viking in association with the natural Environment Research council and the Nature Conservancy Council, 1984. 158p. 62 maps. bibliog.

Commissioned by the Nature Conservancy Council, and produced by the Institute of Terrestrial Ecology, this atlas describes and maps the distribution of all resident species of butterfly in the British Isles together with all but the rarest immigrants. Using data from the National Butterfly Monitoring Scheme it explains each species' status and assesses changes in breeding patterns caused by ecological and other factors. Due to intensive farming methods many habitats suitable for butterflies have been altered out of recognition and a consequent decline in most species is recorded.

181 **The moths and butterflies of Great Britain and Ireland.**
John Heath, A. Maitland Emmet. Colchester, England: Harley, 11 vols., 1976- .

Already the volumes which have appeared in this series have been widely acclaimed as the most accurate, comprehensive, and up-to-date volumes available. When completed the series promises to be the definitive work in its field.

182 **A field guide to the butterflies of Britain and Europe.**
Lionel G. Higgins, Norman D. Riley. London: Collins, 1980. 4th ed. 384p. 384 maps.

First published in 1970, this completely revised edition describes and illustrates every species and every important sub-species to be found west of the Russian frontier. Details of their appearance, flight months, habitat, foodplants, altitude and range, distribution, and rarity, are recorded.

183 **British fresh-water fishes.**
W. Houghton, illustrated by A. F. Lydon. Exeter, England: Webb & Bower, 1981. 256p.

This splendidly produced facsimile reprint edition of a two-volume work first published in 1879 includes extensive descriptions of sixty-five species of fish of which forty-one are accompanied by full-page colour plates of an extremely high artistic standard. The scholarly text is not above family anecdotes, hints for fishermen, or cookery notes, and its delightful old-fashioned prose style is redolent of a bygone age.

184   **British names of birds.**
      Christine E. Jackson.   London: Witherby, 1968. 125p.

Based on H. Kirke Swann's *A dictionary of English and folk names of British birds, with their history, meaning and first usage* (Witherby, 1912), but omitting his Gaelic and Welsh names, this collection of 4,840 names given to British birds includes all birds for which there is a local or folk name, or an alternative common name. In addition there are lists of falconers' terms for birds of prey, wildfowlers' names, bird fanciers' terms, and swan keeper's specialist terminology. Bird names in literature, particularly poetry, collective nouns, and terms applied to more than one species, are also comprehensively recorded.

185   **The good birdwatchers guide.**
      Peter Jennings.   Llandrindod Wells, Wales: Ficedula, 1991. 482p.

This guide to more than 2,500 birdwatching sites is arranged alphabetically by county. It lists the site, its Ordnance Survey Landranger map number, its approximate location, the types of birds most likely to be spotted there, and nearby refreshment and accommodation facilities. A birds and weather feature for 1990 is a day by day record of sightings of rare or unusual birds. Other material includes a list of county bird record officers, regional representatives of the British Trust for Ornithology, a species checklist of 585 different birds of the British Isles, and advice on birdwatching clothing, binocular purchases, and reference books.

186   **A field guide to the land snails of Britain and North-west Europe.**
      M. P. Kerney, R. A. D. Cameron.   London: Collins, 1979. 288p.
      414 maps. bibliog.

Nearly 300 species of snails and slugs are systematically described and illustrated in this guide. An introduction gives a general account of their structure, reproductive habits and food.

187   **The naturalized animals of the British Isles.**
      Christopher Lever.   London: Hutchinson, 1977. 600p. bibliog.

This work describes how, when, where, and by whom twenty-two alien mammals, sixteen bird species, seven amphibians and reptiles, and fourteen fish, now living in the wild in Britain, were first introduced to these shores. All were either deliberately or unwittingly introduced by man and have now become self-supporting and self-perpetuating. Their effect on native flora and fauna, and on the environment, is also considered.

188   **A complete guide to British dragonflies.**
      Andrew McGeeney.   London: Cape, 1986. 133p. bibliog.

Forty-one species of dragonflies still surviving in Britain are fully described and illustrated in this comprehensive handbook. Their larvae, behaviour patterns, habitats, and distribution, are all recorded.

189 **Collins handguide to the fishes of Britain and Northern Europe.**
Peter Miller. London: Collins, 1980. 96p.
Individual descriptions of the characteristic features, habitats, diet, and breeding
habits, of 166 species of marine and freshwater fish, are included in this full-colour
guide.

190 **Collins guide to the sea fishes of Britain and North-Western Europe.**
Bent J. Muus, Preben Dahlstrom. London: Collins, 1974. 244p.
This richly illustrated handbook, first published in Denmark, deals with the structure,
habitat, distribution, and economic importance of the North Eastern Atlantic fisheries.
Its main section consists of a description and colour illustration of each species.

191 **The complete freshwater fishes of the British Isles.**
Jonathan Newdick. London: A & C Black, 1979. 127p.
All fish species, including hybrids, to be found in British waters are described and
illustrated in colour in this compendious and popular work. The brief, clear, but
authoritative text includes notes on each species' habitat, spawning, size, diet,
identification and a small distribution inset map. There is also a glossary and two
indexes of common and scientific names.

192 **A guide to zoos and specialist collections.**
John Nichol. London: Christopher Helm, 1989. 156p. map.
Over 200 zoos, bird parks, acquaria, falconry centres, butterfly farms, insect houses,
etc., open to the public are described in this guide. Full information is provided on
their locations, facilities, and services.

193 **Wildfowl of Britain and Europe.**
Malcolm Ogilvie. Oxford: Oxford University Press, 1982. 84p. map.
Thirty colour plates taken from volume one of OUP's seventeen-volume work,
*Handbook of the birds of Europe, the Middle East, and North Africa: the birds of the
western palearctic*, illustrate this study of British ducks, swans, and geese. In addition
to a detailed description of male and female birds, their plumage, song, and
distribution also receive attention.

194 **Field guide to British deer.**
Edited by F. J. Taylor Page. Oxford: Blackwell for The British Deer
Society, 1971. 2nd ed. 83p. bibliog.
There are five common species of deer in Britain with two other species limited to
specific areas. This guide, which was first published in 1957, offers basic information on
their habitats, signs and tracks, voice and identification, their behaviour in herds, their
seasonal changes of coat, their gait and age, and where best to watch them. A glossary
of venery, stalking, and forestry terms is included.

Flora and Fauna. Fauna

195   **Grasshoppers, crickets, and cockroaches of the British Isles.**
David R. Ragge.   London: Warne, 1965. 299p. 25 maps. bibliog.
(Wayside and Woodland Series).

Stick insects, cockroaches, grasshoppers, groundhoppers, wingless camel-crickets, bush crickets, and casual introductions and migrants, are all featured in this guide. Information on their distribution and history, a check list of species, and a glossary, add to its comprehensive usefulness.

196   **The spiders of Great Britain and Ireland.**
M. J. Roberts.   Colchester, England: Harley, 1985. 3 vols.

Comprising three volumes, (vol. 1. *Atypidae – Therdiosomatidae*. vol. 2. *Linyphiidae*. vol. 3. *Colour plates*), this authoritative textbook for the identification of over 300 species of British spiders covers their morphology, behaviour, nomenclature and classification. Volume three has 307 colour plates and there is a general introduction to arachnology in volume one.

197   **The Atlas of British bird life.**
Bob Scott.   Twickenham, England: Country Life Books, 1987. 208p.
298 maps. bibliogs.

A handsome addition to any ornithologist's bookshelf, this comprehensive and up-to-date atlas is divided into two parts. An illustrated checklist of British birds comprises almost 300 full colour distribution maps for each regularly occurring British bird, showing its relative abundance throughout Britain during the course of the year. The second part is a county-by-county guide to the best birdwatching country describing the landscape and its birdwatching potential, followed by descriptions of outstanding sites, including many Royal Society for the Protection of Birds reserves, all located by specially prepared county maps and Ordnance Survey grid references.

198   **The atlas of breeding birds in Britain and Ireland.**
Compiled by J. T. R. Sharrock.   Berkhamsted, England: Poyser,
1976. 477p. maps.

Fieldwork for this atlas was undertaken by 15,000 volunteers for the Biological Records Centre of the National Environment Research Council, the British Council for Ornithology, and the Irish Wild Birds Conservancy. It consists of location and distribution maps with facing texts and references.

199   **Woodland birds.**
Eric Simms.   London: Collins, 1971. 391p. 5 maps. bibliog. (The New
Naturalist).

Part one of this study examines the history of trees and their bird population since Pliocene times and the role of birds in modern forestry. Part two is a species by species account of British woodland birds, giving details of their distribution, status, and habitats.

200   **The Shell guide to Britain's threatened wildlife.**
       Nigel Sitwell.   London: Collins, 1984. 208p. bibliog.
The Wildlife and Countryside Act 1987 schedules some sixty-one plants, twenty
mammals, twelve reptiles, one fish, and nineteen invertebrates as needing protection.
In addition ornithologists have drawn up a list of fifty-nine of the most threatened
birds, making a total of 172 species in danger. A descriptive account is provided for
each of these species which includes a full-colour photograph and details of its habitat
and distribution.

201   **The butterflies of the British Isles: with accurately coloured figures of
       every species and many varieties. Also drawings of egg, caterpillar,
       chrysalis, and food plant and includes the new generic names.**
       Richard South.   London: Warne, 1962. rev. ed. 212p.
First published in 1906, this standard handbook for serious Lepidopterists serves as a
detailed descriptive guide to every indigenous species. It also contains the *Revised list
of the British butterflies according to the Report of the Committee of the Royal
Entomological Society of London on generic nomenclature* issued in 1934.

202   **The moths of the British Isles.**
       Richard South.   London: Warne, 1948. 2 vols. (Wayside and
       Woodland Series).
Revised by H. M. Edelstein this two-volume guide, which was first published in
1907-08, describes and illustrates all native species of moths, except for micro-moths,
arranged in family order.

203   **Land and water bugs of the British Isles.**
       T. R. E. Southwood, Dennis Leston.   London: Warne, 1959. 436p.
       bibliog. (Wayside and Woodland Series).
A descriptive natural history of the life cycles of 509 species of British flat, bark,
shield, ground, lace, bed and capid bugs, and pondskaters, this book also contains
useful notes for bug collectors.

204   **Dictionary of English and folk-names of British birds with their history,
       meaning and first usage; and their folk-lore legends etc., relating to the
       more familiar species.**
       H. K. Swann.   London: E. P. Publishing, 1977. 266p. bibliog.
First published by Witherby in 1913 this dictionary contains roughly 5,000 bird names.
Provincial, local, and dialect names in use in former times are discussed and explained.

205   **Birds of prey of Britain and Europe.**
       Ian Wallace.   Oxford: Oxford University Press, 1983. 88p. maps.
       bibliog.
Fifty species of diurnal birds of prey are identified in colour in this attractive study. An
introduction covers their classification, evolution, habitat, distribution, movements,
food, social pattern and behaviour, breeding, plumage, and their relationship with
man.

206 **The fishes of the British Isles and North West Europe.**
Alwyne Wheeler.   London: Macmillan, 1969. 613p. maps. bibliog.
Full descriptive accounts of all common species of British marine and freshwater fish
are provided in this definitive work which is arranged in three main sections: the
Marsipobranchii (i.e. lampreys and hagfish); Selachii (sharks, rays, and rabbit fishes);
and Osteichthyes (bony species).

207 **The handbook of British birds.**
H. R. Witherby, F. C. R. Jourdain, Norman F. Ticehurst, Bernard W.
Tucker.   London: Witherby, 1938-1941. 5 vols. maps.
According to Bannerman's *The birds of the British Isles* (q.v.) this comprehensive
handbook 'contains a wealth of information which can be found nowhere else'.
Constantly reprinted it is a descendant of *A handlist of British birds* first published in
1912. For each bird it gives its habitat, field characteristics and general habits, its voice,
display and posturing, breeding, food, distribution and migration, and its distribution
abroad. 'We have sought to make it as complete as possible as a book of reference on
British birds, and to arrange it in such a systematic and uniform way that it can be
consulted on any point about any species with ease' (Preface). Few ornithologists
would care to argue that it has not succeeded.

Flora

208 **Trees and shrubs hardy in the British Isles.**
W. J. Bean.   London: John Murray, 4 vols, 1970. 8th ed. 3410p.
William Jackson Bean (1863-1947) was born the son of a Yorkshire nurseryman. After
a long career in arboriculture he eventually became Curator of the Royal Botanical
Gardens at Kew. This standard work, first published in two volumes in 1914, is
intensely personal in tone and presentation. In addition to expert botanical
descriptions, and details of the history, distribution, characteristics, and cultivation of
trees and shrubs, it embodies Bean's personal experiences and references to individual
trees. The *Supplement* (D. L. Clarke.   London: John Murray, 1988. 616p. bibliog.)
updates the work in the light of modern advances in the taxonomy of temperate woody
plants and the introduction to gardens of new species and cultivars. There are also
sections on the pests and diseases of trees and shrubs.

209 **A new illustrated British flora.**
Roger W. Butcher.   London: Leonard Hill, 1961. 2 vols.
This mammoth encyclopedic work (a total of over 2,000 pages) identifies the name,
distribution pattern, and flowering period for all British native and well-established
non-indigenous plants.

210 **Flora of the British Isles.**
A. R. Clapham, T. G. Tutin, D. M. Moore. Cambridge, England:
Cambridge University Press, 1987. 3rd ed. 688p. bibliog.

It is a common misapprehension that a comparatively small British plant population
has long been fully described. This is not so, for modern field research has established
the existence of many distinct species and varieties not previously recognized. This
latest edition of the standard flora, first published in 1952, retains its main purpose of
ensuring the correct identification of indigenous and well-established alien plants,
providing information on their habitat, ecology, geographical distribution, and
agricultural significance. It also includes a historical survey of previous British flora
since the publication of John Ray's *Catalogus plantarum Angliae et insularum
adjacentium* in 1670. Of equal interest is the supplementary volume entitled *Flora of
the British Isles: illustrations.* Drawings by S. I. Roles. Cambridge, England:
Cambridge University Press, 1957-65. 4 vols. Clapham, Tutin and E. G. Warburg's
Excursion flora of the British Isles (1981. 3rd ed. 499p.) is a tall pocket-size concise
flora for students and amateur botanists and provides a convenient scientific
description of all plants commonly found in the British Isles.

211 **The Oxford book of trees.**
A. A. Clapham, illustration by B. E. Nicholson. Oxford: Oxford
University Press, 1975. 216p. bibliog.

Native British woodland trees, trees found in wet places, hedges, and introduced
conifers and flowering trees, are all covered in this beautifully illustrated field guide.
Some account is given of their ecology and distribution whilst a short glossary defines
the technical terms used.

212 **Poisonous plants in Britain and their effects on animals and man.**
Marion R. Cooper, Anthony W. Johnson. London: HMSO for
Ministry of Agriculture, Fisheries and Food, 1984. 305p. bibliog.

Thirty fungi and over 250 poisonous plants are identified in this government guide.

213 **Dictionary of British and Irish botanists and horticulturists, including
plant collectors and botanical artists.**
R. Desmond. London: Taylor & Francis, 1977. 3rd ed. 747p.

Descended from J. Britten and G. E. S. Boulger's *A biographical index of British and
Irish botanists*, published in 1893, this admirably comprehensive dictionary provides
authoritative information on 10,000 or so distinguished botanists. Desmond's
meticulous and painstaking research provides details of their birth and death dates,
education and qualifications, honours and awards, career details, publications, the
location of their plant collections, and plants commemorating their names.

214 **Introduction to British lichens.**
Ursula K. Duncan, assisted by P. W. James. Arbroath, Scotland:
Buncle, 1970. 292p. bibliog.

Strictly for students or readers with specialist knowledge, this guide to the
identification of British lichen is estimated to include sixty-five per cent of all native
species. The selection here is based on the relative frequency of species and on those of
special interest. A fourteen-page glossary and a forty-four page bibliography, which

lists some of the earliest items ever published, emphasize the specialist nature of this authoritative work.

215 A colour guide to rare wild flowers.
John Fisher.   London: Constable, 1991. 364p. maps. bibliog.

This guide briefly describes and illustrates in colour 150 species of rare wild flowers, fifty-one of which are protected under the 1981 Wildlife and Countryside Act.

216 Collins guide to the grasses, sedges, rushes, and ferns of Britain and Northern Europe.
Richard Fitter, Alistair Fitter.   London: Collins, 1984. 256p.
500 maps. bibliog.

Twenty-six different species of grasses, etc., including some well-established aliens, are distinguished in this colourfully illustrated distribution guide. Common English and scientific name indexes allow no confusion in identification.

217 British ferns.
Ron Freethy.   Marlborough, England: Crowood, 1987. 128p. bibliog.

Larded with anecdotes of fern enthusiasts of the past, from sixteenth century apothecaries to Victorian collectors, this beautifully illustrated book provides a comprehensive guide to all British ferns. Opening with a brief study of their evolution, and of the factors which contributed to their distribution patterns, this work continues with an up-to-date classification of all waterside, seaside, woodlands, and walls and hedgerows species.

218 Glossary of the British flora.
H. Gilbert-Carter.   Cambridge, England: Cambridge University Press, 1964. 3rd ed. 96p. bibliog.

First published in 1950, this glossary gives the meaning, pronunciation, and derivation of the generic, trivial, and varietal names of British plants.

219 A dictionary of English plant names (and some products of plants).
Geoffrey Grigson.   London: Allen Lane, 1974. 239p.

This descriptive and illustrated glossary provides the common English and scientific names of all species of English plant life from trees to seaweeds. Other information includes the date when each species was introduced into England, an approximate date for the first use of the plant name, the person who invented or first recorded it, and an historical or etymological explanation.

220 The Englishman's flora.
Geoffrey Grigson.   London: Phoenix House, 1955. 478p. bibliog.

Concerned with both the common and the rarer plants which are closely connected with man, 'this book is a mythology, a folk-lore, and a repository of magical ideas; it lists the superstition and the folk-knowledge of the countryside; it provides most of what is to be found in the old herbals . . . it touches upon the literary and artistic symbolism of plant life; and it provides . . . a long list of regional and vernacular plant names'. For all that, it is scientifically arranged, and provides much information on the origins and names of both indigenous and alien plants and trees.

221   **British trees: a guide for everyman.**
Miles Hadfield.   London: J. M. Dent, 1957. 468p. bibliog.
Illustrated by full page drawings of twigs and buds, foliage, fruit and flowers, this guide to over a hundred different species and varieties encompasses not only trees native to the British Isles but also those introduced either for ornament or for more utilitarian purposes.

222   **Royal Botanic Gardens Kew: gardens for science and pleasure.**
Edited by F. Nigel Hepper.   London: HMSO, 1982. 195p. bibliog.
The primary purpose of the Royal Botanic Gardens at Kew, and of Wakehurst Place, its Sussex annexe, is to serve as scientific collections and to maintain its long tradition of excellence in botanical and horticultural research. This lavishly illustrated guide to the collections, and to Kew's scientific work, comprises chapters contributed by senior members of staff, writing in laymens' terms of their own special fields of expertise. Among the topics discussed are Kew's involvement in worldwide botanical expeditions, its role in the classification and identification of plants, and the conservation of endangered species. James Bartholomew's *The magic of Kew* (London: Herbert Press in association with The Royal Botanic Gardens, 1988. 127p.) is an album of 100 photographs taken before the great storm of October 1987 which caused so much devastation.

223   **Grasses: a guide to their structure, identification, uses and distribution in the British Isles.**
C. E. Hubbard.   Harmondsworth, England: Penguin, 1984. 476p. bibliog.
Over 200 individual grasses are described and illustrated on facing pages in this authoritative standard work.

224   **Atlas of ferns of the British Isles.**
Edited by A. C. Jermy, H. R. Arnold, Lynne Farrell, F. H. Perring. London: The Botanical Society of the British Isles and The British Pteridological Society, 1978. 101p. 95 maps.
This atlas illustrates the spatial distribution of all British ferns, horsetails, and clubmosses. A short commentary accompanies each map.

225   **The illustrated field guide to ferns and allied plants of the British Isles.**
Clive Jermy, Josephine Camus.   London: HMSO for The Natural History Museum, 1991. 208p.
Notes on habitat requirements, distribution, conservation status, lists of hybrids to be found in each genus, and salient diagnostic points illustrated with line drawings, are included in this identification guide to British ferns, horsetails, and clubmosses.

226 **Mushrooms and toadstools: a field guide.**
G. Kibby. Oxford: Oxford University Press, 1979. 256p. bibliog.

A guide to mushroom and toadstool species, over 400 full colour illustrations of the larger fungi of Britain and continental Europe, and an invaluable glossary, are the principal features of this admirable field guide.

227 **The complete book of British berries.**
David C. Lang. London: Threshold, 1987. 223p. bibliog.

Every edible and poisonous plant bearing either a berry or a fleshy fruit is described and illustrated in colour in this comprehensive guide. Each plant's fruit, leaf, flower, ecology, and distribution is carefully detailed and there is also information on the symptoms of plant poisoning and recommendations for treatment.

228 **The concise British flora in colour.**
W. Keble Martin. London: Ebury Press and Michael Joseph, 1974. 3rd ed. 254p.

Sixty years of meticulous research snatched from the duties of a parish priest went into the making of this elegant reference work which was first published in 1965. The splendid draughtsmanship of its 1,486 illustrations (nearly 1400 in colour) contributed in small way to its success as it rushed into the bestsellers list. It is now a widely acclaimed 'classic'. *The new concise British flora* (1982. 247p.) adds details of eighteen species which may be native and of eighty introduced species. Keble Martin's autobiography, *Over the hills* (1968. 173p.) is worthwhile background reading.

229 **Hedgerows: their history and culture.**
Richard Muir, Nina Muir. London: Michael Joseph, 1987. 250p. bibliog.

A continuous history of hedges in the British countryside, from prehistoric, ancient, Roman, and medieval times to the parliamentary enclosures of the eighteenth and nineteenth centuries; regional variations in hedges; the future of hedges, and the dreadful consequences for the countryside if they continue to be destroyed, are the principal themes of this beautifully and lavishly illustrated account.

230 **Atlas of the British flora.**
Franklyn H. Perring, S. M. Walters. Wakefield, England: E. P. Publishing, 1976. 2nd ed. 432p. 1,623 maps.

Originally published by Nelson in 1962 for the Botanical Society of the British Isles, this atlas includes an introduction outlining the history of the mapping of plant distribution, the methods used, and their interpretation. This edition is accompanied by a *Critical supplement* (159p.) which gives distribution maps of 500 flowering plants and ferns with an explanatory text.

231 **Wild flowers of Britain.**
Roger Phillips. London: Ward Lock, 1977. 192p.

Arranged in order of flowering through the year this handbook illustrates over 1,000 British wild flowers in colour. The accompanying text provides information on each flower's common English, botanical and family name, its status (i.e. biennial, perennial, shrub or tree), its incidence, height, flowering period, habitat, and distribution.

232 **Hedges.**
E. Pollard, M. D. Hooper, N. W. Moore. London: Collins, 1974.
256p. 10 maps. bibliog. (The New Naturalist).

All aspects of hedges in Britain are covered in this authoritative study: their purpose and history; dating methods; their bird, mammal, reptile, and invertebrate life; their part in the countryside environment; and their cost and value to farmers.

233 **Field guide to the wildflowers of Britain.**
J. R. Press, D. A. Sutton, B. A. Tebbs. London: Reader's Digest, 1981. 447p.

Published in Reader's Digest's celebrated Nature Lovers Library this is a comprehensive identification guide to more than 550 of the most commonly encountered species of wild flowers, including grasses and sedges, in every type of habitat. Each species occupies a single page with a descriptive and informative text, a colour photograph of the plant growing in the ground, and five or more specially commissioned paintings displaying every prominent feature in close-up. Notes on how to identify flowers, the history of Britain's flowers, search and legal notes, some places to see rare plants, and a glossary, complete a handsome home reference and browsing volume.

234 **British plant communities.**
Edited by J. S. Rodwell. Cambridge, England: Cambridge University Press, 1991- . 5 vols.

Described and mapped in these five volumes (vol. 1. *Woodlands and scrub*. 1991. 395p. maps. bibliog. vol. 2. *Mires and heath*. vol. 3. *Grasslands and montane vegetation*. vol. 4. *Acquatic communities, swamps and tall herb fens*. vol. 5. *Maritime and weed communities*.) are over 250 plant communities. Their synonomy, species, physiognomy, habitat, sub-communities, distribution affinities, and floristic tables, are all presented in detail. This major project is the culmination of fifteen years work on a survey and analysis of British vegetation.

235 **Seaweeds of the British Isles.**
London: HMSO for The Natural History Museum, 1977- .

Not yet completed this set of volumes (*Rhodophyta. Pt. 1. Introduction, Nemaliales, Gigartinales*. Peter S. Dixon, Linda M. Irvine. 1977. 258p. *Rhodophyta, Pt. 2A. Cryptonemiales (sensu stricto), Palmariales, Rhodomeniales*. Linda M. Ervine. 1983. 120p. *Chlorophyta*. Elsie M. Burrows. 1991. 256p. *Fucophycae (Phaeophyceae) Pt. 1*. Robert L. Fletcher. 1987. 360p. *Tribophyceae (Xanthophyceae)*. Tyge Christensen. 1987. 38p.) will undoubtedly become the modern standard reference work in its field. It covers all the British and almost all the North Atlantic seaweeds.

236 **New flora of the British Isles**.
Clive A. Stace. Cambridge, England: Cambridge University Press, 1992. 1,264p. map. bibliog.

Now regarded as the standard British flora this scientific and rigorously compiled work is designed for professional use by taxonomists, plant geographers, ecologists, conservationists, and informed amateur botanists. It includes native and naturalized plants and recurrent casual plants and employs the sequence and nomenclature recommended in the Botanical Society of the British Isles standard checklist of British vascular plants issued in 1991.

237 **Field guide to the trees of Britain and Europe.**
David Sutton. London: Kingfisher, 1990. 192p. bibliog.

Concise descriptions of over 400 native and introduced trees are included in this compact guide, giving details of their physical features and their economic or ornamental uses.

238 **The Royal Botanic Gardens Kew: past and present.**
W. B. Turrill. London: Herbert Jenkins, 1959. 256p. bibliog.

Today Kew is renowned world wide for its scientific research and authority, and for its facilities for plant identification. This authoritative account, written by a former Keeper of the Herbarium and Library, tells its story from its beginnings in the sixteenth-century to the bicentenary of its foundation as a botanical garden by the Dowager Princess of Wales, Princess Augusta, in 1759.

239 **British mosses and liverworts: an introductory work, with full descriptions and figures of over 200 species, and keys for the identification of all except the very rare species.**
E. Vernon Watson. Cambridge, England: Cambridge University Press, 1981. 3rd ed. 519p.

Introductory or not, this study is intended for amateur and professional botanists and is not really general reader material although it claims to give the beginner an idea of the range of species most likely to be encountered in different parts of the country.

240 **A history of Britain's trees.**
Gerald Wilkinson. London: Hutchinson, 1987. 176p. map. bibliog.

Ranging from fossilized remains to twentieth-century trees and shrubs, this superbly illustrated work traces the history of all tree species from the time of their introduction to Britain.

Tourism and Travel Guides

Tourist industry

241 **Britain's leisure industry.**
London: Jordan, 1992. 58 + 69p.
An industrial commentary on the current trends and characteristics of the national leisure industry, including its general patterns, and a sectorial analysis of common leisure activities, is balanced in this report by summarized financial and other data on ninety-four leisure companies.

242 **The British Travel Association 1929-1969.**
London: British Tourist Authority, [n.d.]. 65p.
The principal objectives of the Travel Association of Great Britain and Ireland on its formation in 1929 were 'to increase the number of visitors from overseas' and 'to stimulate the demand for British goods and services'. This booklet includes a short history of Britain's national tourist organization, its advertising and overseas promotion, and the changing patterns in tourism. R. O. Baker's 'Fifty years young', *British Travel News*, no. 66, (summer 1979), p. 21-28, celebrates the first fifty years of the 'Come to Britain' movement from which the British Tourist Authority is ultimately derived.

243 **Law for the travel industry.**
John Downes, Patricia Paton.   Kingston upon Thames, England: Croner, 1991. 220p.
This practical approach to the law relating to business organizations, the tour operator and travel agent relationship, the holiday contract, consumer protection legislation, the settlement of disputes, employment law, and the carriage of passengers and their luggage, is intended primarily for students on tourism and travel courses and for those starting a career in the travel industry.

244 **The UK tourism and leisure market: travel trends and spending patterns.**
Kevin O'Brien.   London: Economist Intelligence Unit, 1990. 293p. bibliog.

This report 'analyses and assesses the levels and patterns of leisure taking and expenditure; examines the major trends and developments affecting the various sectors that comprise the leisure industry; discusses current practices with regard to leisure and tourism marketing, retailing and distribution channels; and examines the outlook for leisure and tourism in the 1990s' (Introduction).

245 **The Englishman's England: taste, travel and the rise of tourism.**
Ian Ousby.   Cambridge, England: Cambridge University Press, 1990. 244p. bibliog.

Omitting all purpose-built attractions such as spas or seaside resorts, this study of how the tourist map of England was created features literary shrines; country houses; ancient monuments and medieval ruins; and the natural landscape, which first attracted visitors in the eighteenth century when cultivated fashion encouraged outings to places like Chatsworth, Fountains Abbey, and the Lake District. A spirit of practical enquiry was in the air, which, with improvements in transport, laid the foundations of the English touring industry.

246 **Tourism in the UK.**
Hampton, England: Key Note, 1991. 7th ed. 43p.

This market sectorial overview contains an examination of the industry's structure, a consumer profile including the top ten UK tourist attractions, a survey of hotels, airlines and ferry operators, an estimate of market size and trends, and a survey of recent developments and future prospects.

247 **Tourism: Monthly News Views and Analysis of England's Travel and Leisure Industries.**
London: AMS Marketing for English Tourist Board, 1988- . monthly.

The October 1992 issue carries articles on the work and role of the parliamentary all-party tourism group; the implications of the European Community Holiday directive; the recession in the hotel industry; and on the positive role played by the tourist industry in the national economy. 'In the Travel Trade Market Place' is a regular feature giving notes and news on accommodation, travel agencies, business travel, and conferences, etc.

248 **Tourist Information Centres in Britain 1992/93.**
London: English Tourist Board, 1992. 39p. annual.

This is annual guide (or directory) to the 800 or so all-year-round and seasonal Tourist Information Centres, located up and down the British Isles, and to their services. Also included are the addresses of the regional tourist boards and of the British Tourist Authority and its overseas offices. Sadly the fifteen maps which enhanced the 1991/92 edition have disappeared.

249 **The UK Tourist: Statistics.**
London: English Tourist Board (and Scottish, Northern Ireland, and
Wales Tourist Boards). 1990- . annual.

Based on information drawn from *United Kingdom tourist survey* which was
commissioned jointly by the four national tourist boards, these statistics provide
detailed information of the annual volume and value of tourism undertaken by the
UK's resident population.

Guides

250 **AA book of British villages: a guide to 700 of the most interesting and
attractive villages in Britain.**
London: Drive Publications for The Automobile Association, 1980.
447p. 26 maps. bibliog.

A pictorial and descriptive gazetteer of Britain's most picturesque villages each
described by a local author who relates its history, local crafts, regional customs, types
of houses, and indicates its places of interest. Numerous essays on topics such as
'Discovering village history', 'How villages got their names', 'Lost villages', etc. place
this local information within a national context. There is also a county-by-county list of
villages where traditional craft workshops can be visited.

251 **AA budget guide Britain.**
Basingstoke, England: Automobile Association, 1993. 256p.

Regional tours which can be followed by car, 'bus, or train are included in this guide
which offers money-saving hints, information on local specialities and customs,
bargains of all types, inexpensive accommodation and places to eat out. What to avoid
is also indicated.

252 **AA country walks in Britain.**
Basingstoke, England: Automobile Association, 1991. 256p. maps.

Beautifully illustrated and packed with information on wildlife and habitats, this
ringbound looseleaf guidebook, which has a clear plastic wallet for individual leaf use
en route, describes 100 walks through some of Britain's finest wild areas and reserves.

253 **AA illustrated guide to Britain's coast.**
London: Drive Publications for The Automobile Association, 1984.
383p. maps.

A mile-by-mile guide and descriptive gazetteer starting at the Severn estuary, near
Bristol, and continuing anti-clockwise round the entire coastline of mainland Britain
and the principal offshore islands. Each section of approximately thirty-five miles
contains detailed information on what to see and do including safe swimming beaches,
powerboating, beachcombing, birdwatching and nature reserves, and inland sightsee-
ing alternatives on wet days. Part two: 'Exploring the living world of our seashore'

describes and illustrates the plants and animals of sandy shores, shingle beaches, and estuaries.

254   **AA illustrated guide to country towns and villages of Britain.**
London: Drive Publications for The Automobile Association, 1985.
445p. 36 maps.

This volume contains over 500 county towns and villages chosen for their outstanding beauty and places of interest. Each town and village is described and located and there are also overview essays on 'The country pub'; 'Crafts that live on'; 'Fairs, feasts and games'; 'The great house'; 'The old mill'; and 'The living past'.

255   **AA places to visit in Britain: a county-by-county guide to more than 2,400 castles, stately homes, gardens, theme parks, museums and other places of interest throughout England, Wales and Scotland.**
London: Drive Publications for The Automobile Association, 1988.
431p. 64 maps.

This is a magnificently illustrated guide and gazetteer 'that will enable you to pile the family into the car and say "Let's go to . . . for the day", in the confidence that everyone will find the outing worth while'. Special single and double-page features (e.g. Grasmere, Morwhellam Quay, Kew Gardens etc.) highlight showpiece sites.

256   **AA Touring Britain and Ireland.**
Basingstoke, England: Automobile Association, 1991. 288p. maps.

Forty-seven circular scenic tours are included in this superbly illustrated four mile to the inch touring atlas. Easy-to-follow directions, photographs, and descriptions of over 1,500 places of interest, are closely integrated in a series of double-page spreads.

257   **AA 250 tours of Britain: maps and easy-to-follow route instructions for day and weekend drives through England, Wales and Scotland, with descriptions of the natural wonders and man-made attractions to be seen on the way.**
London: Drive Publication for The Automobile Association, 1986.
415p. 8 maps.

A lavishly colour-illustrated guide showing tried and tested recommended itineraries, mostly on minor roads, to places of special interest, arranged on a regional basis (West Country, The South-East, Central Shires, Eastern England, North Country). Each itinerary includes a descriptive gazetteer and a detailed route map. Sources of touring and motoring information, national and country parks, and historic places, enhance an attractive guide for the experienced non-driving map reader.

258   **AA/OS leisure guides.**
Basingstoke, England; Southampton, England: Automobile
Association and Ordnance Survey, 1985- . 120p. maps.

In these guides historical and topographical sections precede descriptive gazetteers supported by an OS atlas. Other features include a monthly calendar of events, scenic walks and drives, and other things to do. Titles: *Cornwall*; *Cotswolds*; *Devon and Exmoor*; *East Anglia*; *Forest of Dean and Wye Valley*; *Isle of Wight*; *Lake District*;

New Forest; *North Yorkshire Moors*; *Northumbria*; *Peak District*; *South Downs*; *Wessex*; and *Yorkshire Dales*.

259 **AA/OS village walks in Britain.**
Basingstoke, England; Southampton, England: Automobile
Association and Ordnance Survey, 1991. 264p. maps.
This generously illustrated guidebook describes sixteen easy walks and points of interest along the way. A ringbound looseleaf format and a plastic wallet allows sheets for individual walks to be carried *en route*. Each walk, centred on one of Britain's most picturesque villages, has a detailed itinerary and information on terrain, local history, parking, opening times, and a large-scale Ordnance Survey local map.

260 **AA/OS walks and tours in Britain.**
Basingstoke, England: Automobile Association and Ordnance Survey, 1990. 319p. maps.
Fifty motor tours and 194 associated walks are planned in this lavishly illustrated guide. Relevant extracts from OS Pathfinder and Landranger maps, each on a separate sheet in a ringbinder, allow required sheets to be placed in a transparent protective wallet for use on the ground.

261 **Historic houses, castles and gardens open to the public 1992.**
Edited by Sheila Alcock. East Grinstead, England: British Leisure Publications, 269p. 12 maps.
Over 1,300 historic properties, ranging from cottages to castles, are located in this annual publication which was first issued in 1954. Opening hours, admission charges, and a brief historical introduction are given for each property. A supplementary list gives information on properties open only by appointment.

262 **Holy places of the British Isles: a guide to the legendary and sacred sites.**
William Anderson. London: Ebury Press, 1983. 176p. bibliog.
Intended for the thoughtful tourist and pilgrim, aware of the historical background, this profusely illustrated guide moves forward from Neolithic and Bronze Age sites to the Gothic cathedrals of the high Middle Ages, and ends with a gazetteer.

263 **The Ordnance Survey guide to great British ruins.**
Brian Bailey. London: Cassell, 1991. 224p. maps. bibliog.
Ruined castles, abbeys and priories, churches, halls and farmhouses, prehistoric and deserted villages, all feature in this lavishly illustrated gazetteer to over 600 sites in England, Wales and Scotland. Each entry provides historical information on the ruin, location details, who owns it, and public access. All sites are indicated on coloured Ordnance Survey maps.

264 **Monumental follies: an exposition on the eccentric edifices of Britain.**
Stuart Barton. Worthing, England: Lyle, 1972. 270p. 50 maps.
Arranged alphabetically by historic counties this book is a descriptive and illustrated guide to a wide cross section of buildings classed as follies: buildings erected, sometimes in bizarre shape, purely at the whim of a rich landowner able to indulge his

sentiment for a deceased wife, friend, or even pet, or else a sham tower or castle either to admire the view or to improve it. In fact, often no more than a foolish monument to greatness or a great monument to foolishness.

265 **The Shell book of the islands of Britain.**
David Booth, David Perrott. Leicester, England: Guideway/Windward, 1981. 192p. 80 maps.

A definitive guide to all the major island groups and to a number of rocks and rock formations round the coast of Britain which are included in this work for their historical and wildlife interest. Other aspects covered are legends, people, crafts and industries, vegetation, tourism facilities, and transport. Norman Newton's *Shell guide to the islands of Britain* (Newton Abbot, England: David & Charles, 1992. 208p.) is divided into two parts: part one examines the development and survival of the island way of life; whilst part two presents a close-up look at the various individual islands.

266 **Before you to to Great Britain: a resource directory and planning guide.**
James W. Brown, Shirley N. Brown. Camden, Connecticut: Shoe String Press, 1986. 201p. map.

An annotated list of the information resources for planning a visit rather than an actual travel guide, each chapter in this unusual but extremely valuable directory begins with a brief discussion of the topic in hand and proceeds through the various resources available, books and pamphlets, maps, audio-visual resources, and the relevant organizations and associations, where more detailed information can be obtained. Among the areas covered are travelling to Britain, national and regional travel guides, transport information, food and drink, sports, and specialist activities such as brass-rubbing and collecting antiques.

267 **Cityscapes: a tour round the great British cities.**
Anthony Burton. London: Deutsch, 1990. 218p. 18 maps.

Illustrated by some superb photographs, many in colour, sixteen English, two Scottish, and two Welsh cities are featured in this tour. Not the usual tourist attractions, these cities had formed themselves into the Great British Cities Marketing Group to promote themselves, 'claiming special qualities and character'.

268 **English market towns.**
Russell Chamberlain. London: English Tourist Board/Weidenfeld & Nicolson. 153p. map. bibliog. (ETB's Discover England Series).

Fifty historic towns are inspected in this handsome volume: their unique atmosphere, distinctive architecture, their local customs and traditions, and their places of interest, are all prominently on display. Brief details of twenty-five other towns, all of which could have legitimately featured in the main text, are included in a gazetteer.

269 **Churches in retirement: a gazetteer.**
London: HMSO for Redundant Churches Fund, 1990. 150p.

Since 1969 the Redundant Churches Fund has saved over 250 Saxon, Norman, and Gothic churches, from decay and ruin. This illustrated gazetteer provides a description of each church singling out their particular treasures.

270 **Discover England.**
London: English Tourist Board in conjunction with Weidenfeld &
Nicolson.
Prehistoric England (Richard Cavendish); *Roman England* (John Burke); *English
castles* (Richard Humble); *Villages of England* (Brian Bailey); *Great English houses*
(Russell Chamberlain); *English rivers and canals* (Paul Atterbury); and *English
cathedrals* (Patrick Cormack) are the first titles in this illustrated series on England's
history and heritage. Authoritative, inexpensive, lavishly illustrated both in colour and
black-and-white, with maps, plans and diagrams, these attractive books are ideal
companions for overseas visitors with little time to spare.

271 **A visitor's guide to underground Britain: caves, caverns, mines,
grottoes, tunnels.**
Richard Fells. Exeter, England: Webb & Bower, 1991. 144p.
Comprehensive details of seventy-five locations throughout Britain, including those
open to the public, together with precise instructions, and map references, are to be
found in this illustrated guide.

272 **Great medieval castles of Britain.**
James Forde-Johnston. London: Guild Publications, 1979. 208p.
3 maps. bibliog.
Built as military strongholds to prevent a conquered people from armed rebellion, the
great medieval castles of England and Wales remain an enduring feature of the
contemporary landscape, either in ruins, heavily restored, or pretty much as they were
first constructed. This generously illustrated volume is both a history of 300 years of
castle building and a guide to some 200 castles that can be seen today.

273 **The Guinness guide to superlative Britain.**
Enfield, England: Guinness, 1993.
Published in association with the four tourist boards of England, Scotland, Wales and
Northern Ireland, this magnificent new title which incorporates an authoritative text
with full-colour maps and illustrations undoubtedly ranks as one of the most attractive
and definitive guides to Britain currently on the market. It will prove irresistible to
English-reading overseas visitors.

274 **The Shell book of English villages.**
Edited by John Hadfield. London: Peerage, 1985. 384p. 15 maps.
Eight general chapters on such topics as the parish church, the village school, the
village shop, the village pub, etc. introduce over 1,000 villages selected for their
outstanding beauty and historical interest in this generously illustrated descriptive
guide book.

275 **Stanford's River Thames: a companion and boating guide.**
Graham Hayward. London: Stanford, 1988. 191p. 5 maps. bibliog.
This indispensable navigation guide and history of the Thames as a river for cruising
takes the form of an upriver travelogue from Teddington Lock, between Kingston and
Staines, to Inglesham Bridge, a mile above Lechlade in Gloucestershire, cross-
referenced mile-by-mile to *Stanford's River Thames map*, parts of which are

incorporated in the text. Details of 215 mooring sites and of twenty abandoned locks are also included.

276 **The Which? guide to harbours and marinas.**
Gill Heather, Basil Heather.   London: Consumers' Association and Hodder & Stoughton, 1991. 393p. 120 maps.

This guide to 180 ports of call for English Channel cruising holidays, extending from the Scillies to East Anglia, and the neighbouring continental coasts from southern Holland to the Channel Islands and Brittany, gives details of arrival procedures, mooring charges, the nearest telephone or launderette, boatyards and sailmakers, and fuel and water suppliers. Things to do or see ashore are also indicated.

277 **The encyclopaedia of Oxford.**
Edited by Christopher Hibbert, Edward Hibbert.   London: Macmillan, 1988. 562p. 3 maps. bibliog.

Indisputably the most comprehensive single-volume reference source for whatever aspect of England's premier university city, this encyclopedia contains over 1,000 entries on 'town and gown'. Its personages, places, university institutions and buildings, are featured along with more frivolous information on such topics as the estimated number of bicycles in use in Oxford or the burning question as to whether Sherlock Holmes was an undergraduate at Christ Church or St. Johns.

278 **The Cambridge guide to the historic places of Britain and Ireland.**
Kenneth Hudson, Ann Nicholls.   Cambridge, England: Cambridge University Press, 1989. 8 maps.

A supremely practical handbook for the tourist, this descriptive illustrated gazetteer to the amenities and attractions of over 1,500 monuments and buildings, including all the major National Trust and English Heritage sites, encompasses industrial monuments, battlefields, gardens, shops, theatres, literary shrines, and, of course grand stately homes and imposing cathedrals.

279 **Dark Age Britain: what to see and where.**
Robert Jackson.   Cambridge, England: Patrick Stephens, 1984. 208p. 6 maps.

Part narrative history, part visitor's guide, this well-illustrated book is perfect for a winter's night fireside planning of summer excursions to the material remains of an imperfectly understood period in British history. It reveals that the Dark Ages were not totally encased in Stygian gloom.

280 **Journeys into medieval England.**
Michael Jenner.   London: Michael Joseph, 1991. 256p. bibliog.

Superbly and sumptuously illustrated in colour, this travel book explores significant sites and remains throughout medieval England. It would make an ideal, not too expensive present (£18.00) for the committed motor-tourist with historical inclinations.

281   **Kid's Britain.**
Betty Jerman.   London: Piccolo, 1992. 2nd ed. 352p. 15 maps.
Arranged by official Tourist Board areas, this handbook describes suitable places for
family outings, and discusses the opportunities available at children's day and
residential camps.

282   **English Heritage Series.**
Edited by Stephen Johnson.   London: Batsford, 1989- .
A major popular series jointly conceived by Batsford, an experienced archaeological
publishing firm, and English Heritage, in which leading archaeologists interpret the
historic monuments of Britain, these bright and attractive books include over 100
maps, plans, reconstructions and photographs, and gazetteers of key places to visit.
Individual sites, e.g. *Hadrian's Wall, Stonehenge, Wharram Percy*, are re-examined in
the light of current knowledge, and placed in the context of the surrounding
contemporary landscape, whilst other titles e.g. *Prehistoric settlements, Roman towns,
Shrines and sacrifices, Viking Age Britain*, are more general in scope.

283   **Local heroines: a women's history gazetteer of England, Scotland and
Wales.**
Jane Leggett.   London: Pandora, 1988. 382p. 5 maps. bibliog.
A reaction to guidebooks featuring too many men and very few women, seen as yet
another example of women being virtually excluded from history, this county by
county gazetteer describes places associated with individual women and feminist
achievements. Some of the women are well known, many more deserve greater
recognition. Birthplaces, homes, schools, places of work, graves, and memorials, are
all included.

284   **'Holiday Which?' town and country walks guide.**
Edited by Tim Locke.   London: Consumers' Association, 1991. 656p.
maps.
Over 180 unusual and spectacular circular walks are described in this guide. For each
route there are detailed instructions, a list of points of interest, and a specially drawn
map by the editor. All walks follow recognized rights of way or an established path.

285   **The 'Holiday Which?' guide to the Lake District.**
Edited by Tim Locke.   London: Consumers' Association and Hodder
& Stoughton, 1989. 280p. maps.
The Lake District is one of England's most visited regions. This touring guide, divided
into four areas, includes recommended tourist routes. Clear maps pick out the major
places of interest.

286   **The traveller's key to sacred England: a guide to the legends, lore and
landscape of England's sacred places.**
John Mitchell.   London: Harrap Columbus, 1989. 323p. bibliog.
An historical overview, 'The making of the sacred landscape', introduces this
regionally arranged descriptive guide to abbeys and cathedrals, chapels and parish
churches, shrines and hermitages, holy wells, stone circles, and megalithic sanctuaries.

Tourism and Travel Guides. Guides

287 **English Heritage.**
Lord Montague of Beaulieu. London: Macdonald Queen Anne Press, 1987. 280p.

The Historic Buildings and Monuments Commission for England (popularly known as English Heritage) was formed in 1984 to care for England's rich legacy of historic buildings and ancient monuments. This superbly illustrated descriptive guide to over 350 sites of outstanding national and historical interest open to the public gives full details of their history, the buildings involved, and of what can still be seen. Lord Montague was the first Chairman of English Heritage. To accompany this guide *English Heritage map: a route planner to over 350 places to visit* (1989) is a single sheet map on the scale of one inch to twenty miles.

288 **National trail guides.**
Southampton, England: Ordnance Survey and Aurum Press. maps.

Published in association with the Countryside Commission these guides are intended for serious hikers, people on day excursions, cyclists, and horseriders. Local information, including refreshment and transport facilities, is amply provided. Titles include: *Offa's Dyke*; *Cleveland Way*; *The Ridgeway*; *Pennine Way*; *South West Coast Path*; *South Downs Way*; *North Downs Way*; *Wolds Way*; *Peddars Way & Norfolk Coast Path*.

289 **The National Trust atlas.**
National Trust and National Trust for Scotland. London: George Philip/National Trust, 1987. 3rd ed. 224p. maps.

Arranged in ten regional sections, each with separate features on coast and countryside; houses, gardens and parks; castles and abbeys; and archaeological and industrial sites, this atlas is a selective guide to the principal National Trust properties open to the public. Clearly reproduced maps, colour photographs, a glossary, and a list of architects and craftsmen, identifying the properties they worked on, make this an outstanding guidebook and gazetteer.

290 **Nicholson Ordnance Survey Guides to the Waterways.**
Edinburgh: Bartholomew, 1985. 2nd ed.

Produced on a scale of two-and-a-half inches to the mile these practical guides provide a wealth of navigational and leisure information and are illustrated throughout with two-colour Ordnance Survey maps. The titles are as follows: *South* (208p.) covering over thirty waterways mainly in the West Midlands region; *Central* (176p.), Staffordshire, Cheshire, Trent and Mersey Canal; *North* (176p.) i.e. Lancashire, Derbyshire, Leeds and Liverpool Canal; *Broads and Fens* (160p.) a guide to the holiday waterways of East Anglia; and *River Thames* (176p.) encompassing more than 140 miles downriver from Wiltshire to Greenwich, with special notes on navigating the tidal stretches. *Nicholson The Ordnance Survey inland waterways map of Great Britain* (scale seven miles to the inch) is a comprehensive folding route map for cruising Britain's inland waterways.

291 **New Shell guides.**
Edited by John Julius Norwich.   London: Michael Joseph, 1987- .
maps. bibliog.

Planned to cover the whole of Britain by the mid-1990s, in regional rather than county volumes as in earlier series, each of these volumes includes a number of introductory essays and a full descriptive gazetteer. Titles published to date are: *Cornwall and the Isles of Scilly*; *Oxfordshire and Berkshire*; *Northeast England*; *East Anglia*; *Sussex*; and *Gloucester, Hereford and Worcester*.

292 **Ordnance Survey Landranger guidebooks.**
Southampton, England: Ordnance Survey.

Published jointly with Jarrold this series of pocket guides is designed to help visitors enjoy some of the visually attractive areas covered by the OS Landranger maps. Each contains a comprehensive gazetteer to the towns, villages, and places of interest in the region illustrated with colour photographs, and extracts from OS maps. The series is particularly suitable for walking, cycling, or a motoring tour. Titles include: *The Cotswolds*; *Dorset*; *Lake District*; *London and beyond*; *North Devon, Exmoor and the Quantocks*; *The Peak District*; *Shakespeare country and the North Cotswolds*; *South Devon and Dartmoor*; *The Yorkshire Dales and York*; and *York and the Moors*.

293 **Ordnance Survey pathfinder series.**
Southampton, England: Ordnance Survey.

Each of these compact walking guides, published jointly by the Ordnance Survey and Jarrold, contains twenty-eight routes graded in order of difficulty thereby catering for leisurely family saunters or serious determined day-long hikes for no-nonsense ramblers. The walks are illustrated with colour photographs and extracts from OS maps and avoid private property. Titles include: *Cornwall walks*; *Cotswolds*; *Dartmoor*; *Dorset*; *Exmoor & Quantocks*; *Heart of England*; *Lake District*; *Norfolk and Suffolk*; *Northumbria*; *North York Moors*; *Peak District*; *Wye Valley & Forest of Dean*; and *Yorkshire Dales walks*.

294 **Ordnance Survey touring atlas of Great Britain.**
Southampton, England; Twickenham, England: Ordnance Survey and Hamlyn. 272p.

The features of this outstanding touring atlas include one inch to three miles mapping of mainland Britain, plans of provincial cities, the principal ferry ports and airports, a gazetteer of places of interest, and a full index of place names.

295 **Ordnance Survey touring maps and guides.**
Southampton, England: Ordnance Survey.

These maps cover popular tourist and holiday destinations. Many now have illustrated guides to the area in question with car tours and a gazetteer on the reverse to the map. Titles in the series are: *Dartmoor*; *North York moors*; *Lake District*; *Peak District*; *Exmoor*; *Yorkshire Dales*; *Cotswolds*; *Devon & Cornwall*; *Northumbria*; and *Wessex*.

296 **Traveller's guide to Celtic Britain.**
A. Ross, Michael Cyprien. London: Routledge, 1985. 128p. maps. bibliog.

The first in a series published by Routledge which covers various phases in early English history. The other titles are *Traveller's guide to Norman Britain* (T. Rowley, M. Cyprien. 1986); *Traveller's guide to early medieval Britain* (A. Goodman, M. Cyprien. 1986); *Traveller's guide to Roman Britain* (P. Ottaway, M. Cyprien. 1987). Each of these informative guides includes special essays on topics appropriate to the period, for example 'Magna Carta and the beginnings of Parliament' in the second volume, and a gazetteer of significant sites.

297 **Blue guide England.**
Ian Ousby. London: A & C Black, 1989. 10th ed. 822p. 4 maps.

This is the first revision for many years of an important title which traces its ancestry back to *Blue guide London and its environs* first published in 1918. Eighty-seven routes for motorists are outlined which completely avoid the motorways. Descriptive historical, art and architectural, and landscape information, are prominently featured whilst introductory material includes a five-page chronology of English history and a summary table of English sovereigns. This classic guide can be compared to the famous *Baedecker* guides.

298 **The Ordnance Survey guide to smuggler's Britain.**
Richard Platt. London: Cassell, 1991. 222p. 26 maps. bibliog.

Over 250 individual smuggling sites, fishing villages, seaside towns, beaches, caves, pubs, etc., where contraband was landed, are featured in this beautifully produced guide which traces the growth of smuggling from its modest beginnings in the thirteenth century to its peak in the late eighteenth and early nineteenth centuries.

299 **The traveller's guide to medieval England.**
Colin Platt. London: Secker & Warburg, 1985. 249p. 8 maps.

Eight regional weekend or short break historical tours are included in this gazetteer guide.

300 **Reader's Digest touring guide to Britain.**
London: Reader's Digest, 1992. 320p. 110 maps.

What distinguishes this particular touring guide in comparison with similar volumes is the double-page spread format made up of text and photographs on the left hand page and an accompanying map on the right. Touring maps in full colour, the majority on a scale of four inches to the mile, and over 4,000 text entries oozing practical information on places to go, thing to see, and things to do, all superbly produced to a very high standard, make this a unique combination of atlas and gazetteer guide-book.

301 **Ancient stone crosses of England.**
Alfred Rimmer. London: Garnstone Press, 1973. 159p.

First published in 1875 this delightful work, illustrated by seventy-five woodcuts, describes the extant market crosses, memorials, boundary crosses, and other monuments, that survived the Puritan revolution of the seventeenth century.

302 **The good beach guide: a guide to over 180 of Britain's best beaches.**
Anne Scott. London: Ebury Press, 1991. 192p. 7 maps.
Short essays on marine pollution, marine and coastal life, the seashore code, sea
sports, and coastal walks, precede the main text of this invaluable guide. Divided into
seven regional sections, there are entries for 450 beaches giving details of water
quality, litter, bathing safety, access and parking, seaside activities, walks and wildlife,
and wet weather alternatives. When compiling this guide, which was first published in
1988, the author was Pollution Control Officer at the Marine Conservation Society.

303 **Wildest Britain: a visitor's guide to the national parks.**
Roland Smith. Poole, England: Blandford, 1983. 224p. maps. bibliog.
All of England's national parks, Exmoor, the Peak District, Yorkshire Dales, North
Yorkshire Moors, the Lake District, and Northumberland, are included in this
attractive, illustrated guide. For each there is information on how to get there, where
to stay, places open to the public, maps, and lists of further readings.

304 **Town tours in Britain: a walker's guide.**
London: Reader's Digest, 1990. 448p. maps.
Two hundred walks through major towns and cities are described in this ringbound
looseleaf guide. Each individual town walk which includes a three-dimensional map
indicating points of interest can be detached for convenient *en route* use.

305 **Visitor's Guide Series.**
Ashbourne, England: Moorland. c. 250p. maps.
These eminently practical county and regional pocket guides give full information on
all places of interest in major tourist areas. Titles in the series are: *Chilterns*; *Cornwall*;
Cotswolds; *Devon*; *Hampshire and the Isle of Wight*; *Lake District*; *Kent*; *Peak District*;
Severn and Avon; *Sussex*; *East Anglia*; and *Yorkshire Dales and Northern Pennines*.

306 **Pictorial guides to the Lakeland Fells.**
A. Wainwright. London: Michael Joseph, 1955- . 7 vols.
Written with intense personal feeling, illustrated with Wainwright's own drawings,
adorned with snippets of wit and poetry, these guides which were originally published
in Lakeland at the author's expense have become 'classics' of their *genre* and
indispensable as fell walkers' companions. Their topographical features are cross-
refernced and indexed in Joan Newsome's *A companion to Wainwright's pictorial
guides to the Lakeland Fells* (London: Michael Joseph, 1992. 144p.).

307 **National Maritime Museum guide to maritime Britain.**
Keith Wheatley. Exeter, England: Webb & Bower, 1990. 206p.
2 maps.
Heritage docks, ship preservation, underwater archaeology, museums, maritime
research, the coastline, and leisure, are some of the topics which feature in this
definitive guide to Britain's maritime history.

308 **The 'Which?' guide to the West Country.**
London: Consumers' Association and Hodder & Stoughton, 1991.
337p.

Covering Cornwall, Devon, Somerset, and the Scilly Isles, each regional section gives a selection of recommended accommodation, access information to places of interest, and a two-tier system highlighting first and second division attractions. A separate chapter describes the best walking routes.

309 **White Horse 'by car' guides.**
Norwich, England: Jarrold.

Admirably designed for car use these compact booklets provide double-page spreads closely integrating strip route maps, mileage interval and driver instruction information, and notes and illustration of places of interest on the way. Titles include *Bath & Mendips*; *Chilterns*; *Mid-Cornwall*; *North Cornwall*; *Southeast Cornwall*; *Cotswolds*; *Dartmoor*; *North Devon*; *South Devon*; *Dorset coast*; *Exmoor country*; *Isle of Wight*; *East Kent*; *West Kent*; *Lakeland*; *New Forest*; *North Norfolk*; *Oxford Country*; *Shakespeare Country*; *Stour Valley* (*John Constable's countryside*); *East Sussex*; *West Sussex*; *Yorkshire Dales*; and *North Yorkshire Moors*.

310 **The American guide to Britain.**
Edited by Esmond Wright.   Topsfield, Massachusetts: Salem House, 1987. 294p. 15 maps.

Historical essays and a detailed gazetteer of over 1,500 towns and places to visit, including many with American associations, are the main features of this lavishly produced guide which was published in the United Kingdom as *AA the visitor's guide to Britain* (Exeter: Webb & Bower, 1987).

Tourists' London

311 **AA glovebox atlas London.**
Basingstoke, England: Automobile Association, 1991. 96p. maps.

Features of this compact atlas include over 6,500 street names, six inches to one mile maps, a M25 orbital London motorway map, and a gazetteer of places to visit.

312 **AA road map London.**
Basingstoke, England: Automobile Association, 1992.

On a scale of seven miles to one inch, this fold-out map of central London indicates one-way road systems, car parks, rail and Underground stations, AA centres, the principal places of interest, an indexed theatreland map, and maps of outer London approach roads.

313 AA the complete book of London.

Basingstoke, England: Automobile Association, 1992. 192p. maps.

Dividing London into thirty-one areas, each focusing on a main attraction together with a map showing other places of interest, all within walking distance, this intriguing guidebook also includes special features revealing lesser known places. The Thames is mapped and there are informative notes on markets and shops, hotels and restaurants.

314 A-Z London street atlas.

Sevenoaks, England: Geographers' A-Z Map, 1990. 2nd ed. 293p.

On a scale of approximately three miles to the inch 134 pages of clear and distinct four-colour street maps cover the whole of Greater London whilst a further twelve page on an enlarged scale of four and a half miles to the inch are allocated to Central London. Two other maps locate West End cinemas and theatres. An 140-page street index completes a remarkably inexpensive (£2.95) no-nonsense atlas. The less said about the map of the Underground system on the back cover the better (the use of a large magnifying glass is recommended). Similar street atlases are published for other English towns and cities.

315 London illustrated 1604-1951: a survey and index of topographical books and their plates.

B. Adams.   London: Library Association, 1983. 586p. + 24p. plates. bibliog.

The main section of this catalogue describes 238 books and sets of prints containing over 8,000 plates illustrating London. Each entry includes notes on the volume's publishing history and illustrations, a transcription of the title page, and a checklist of its London plates.

316 Nicholson London illustrated atlas.

Edited by Dominic Beddow.   London: Nicholson, 1992. 80p. 60 maps.

Maps of the internationally known shopping areas of London, street maps of Central London, a brief directory and location map of theatres and cinemas, information on travel, theatre booking, the emergency services, and an index of shops, sights, and places to eat, all feature in this extremely attractive atlas which is custom designed for overseas visitors.

317 London's historic railway stations.

John Betjeman.   London: John Murray, 1972. 126p.

The architectural features and background histories of London's mainline termini are revealed in this affectionate pictorial study which is further enlivened by the author's reminiscences of steam and electric railway journeys.

318 A guide to London churches.

Mervyn Blatch.   London: Constable, 1978. 434p. 13 maps. bibliog.

Limited to Inner London and to pre-nineteenth century churches, with a few later exceptions because of their special architectural, historical or social interest, this work is a compact and well-illustrated guide to 149 churches and seven surviving towers of churches blitzed during the Second World War. For each church there are descriptive notes on its dedication, history, interior and exterior fabric, furnishings, monuments, and associations.

319 **London statues: a guide to London's outdoor statues and sculpture.**
Arthur Byron. London: Constable, 1981. 433p. 16 maps. bibliog.

Covering an extensive area from Chiswick to West Ham, Finchley to Dulwich, this illustrated guidebook describes open air statues, obelisks and columns, and memorials of all descriptions. A final chapter is devoted to the most prolific sculptors, It succeeds Lord Edward Gleichen's *London open air statuary* published in 1928.

320 **The City of London its architectural heritage: the book of the City of London's heritage walks.**
David Crawford. Cambridge, England: Woodhead Faulkner in association with Commercial Union Assurance and Commercial Union Properties, 1976. 143p. 2 maps. bibliog.

This is a guide to two permanently signposted heritage walks introduced in 1975, European Architectural Heritage Year. Fifty buildings, from the Roman temple of Mithras to the Barbican housing development of the 1960s, are described and illustrated in terms of their architecture, site, and history.

321 **The parks and woodlands of London.**
Andrew Crowe. London: Fourth Estate, 1987. 367p. 30 maps. bibliog.

Greater London has sixty-seven square miles of public open land within its boundaries, almost eleven per cent of the city's total area. This refreshing guidebook is restricted to 100 of the most interesting larger parks with an additional annotated reference section on a further 200 smaller parks. The larger parks' history is traced at length and there are full descriptions of their buildings and monuments, gardens, lakes and ponds, trees and other plants, their wildlife and nature trails. A map of Greater London shows where each park is situated and travel directions and an indication of the facilities available are given for all 300 parks and woodlands included.

322 **The Blue Plaque guide to London.**
C. Dakers. London: Macmillan, 1981. 318p.

Over 600 celebrated London residents honoured by a Blue Plaque on the wall of their London home, or on whatever building now stands on that site, are listed alphabetically in this guide. Each entry gives the address, the legend inscribed on the plaque, and a brief descriptive essay. L. M. Palis' *The Blue Plaques of London* (Wellingborough, England: Equation, 1989. 212p.) is a selective guide.

323 **The Shell guide to the history of London.**
William Ronald Dalzell. London: Michael Joseph, 1981. 496p. maps. bibliog.

Historical maps, and notes on the origins of some famous street names are among the features of this generously illustrated chronological history of London.

324   **The map of London: from 1746 to the present day.**
Andrew Davies.   London: Batsford, 1987. 106p. 48 maps. bibliog.
In 1746 John Roque completed a six-and-a-half feet by thirteen feet map of London
and its neighbouring villages on a scale of twenty-six inches to the mile, with street
names, prominent buildings, and other landmarks clearly visible. After a short account
of Roque's career, and a comparative study of eighteenth-century London, this book
consists of Roque's map, divided into twenty-four sections, each section placed
alongside an equivalent section from a modern A-Z map, and accompanied by a
detailed commentary.

325   **Place-names of Greater London.**
John Field.   London: Batsford, 1980. 184p. map. bibliog.
Greater London in its present form came into existence in 1964. The main part of this
first comprehensive study of the place-names of the whole region consists of a
dictionary giving derivations of the district names, including places formerly in Essex,
Hertfordshire, Middlesex, and Surrey, and of London's street names.

326   **The markets of London.**
Alec Forshaw, Theo Bergstrom.   London: Penguin, 1989. 176p. maps.
bibliog.
By origins London is a market town, a Roman trading post set up at the lowest point
where the Thames was crossable. This illustrated guide traces the growth of London's
markets throughout its long history and describes individually the existing retail and
wholesale markets of inner London.

327   **Greater London street atlas.**
London: Nicholson, 1991. 7th ed. maps. 416p.
First published by Geographia in 1977, this atlas now contains 123 colour maps of
75,000 streets, covering 1,575 square miles in and around London on a scale of three
point one seven inches to the mile, with enlarged maps of Central London at five point
five inches to the mile. There is an information section providing details of
Underground and British Rail stations, theatreland, and places of interest.

328   **The Times London history atlas.**
Edited by Hugh Grout.   London: Times Books, 1991. 190p. maps.
bibliog.
Compiled by a team of twenty archaeologists, historians, and geographers this
magnificent colour atlas traces the growth of London from the Roman period to the
present day. A concise, lucid narrative text accompanies and elucidates the atlas'
specially drawn maps which incorporate the latest research into London's urban
history. An eight page thematic chronology charts London's history, politics and
society; its commerce, industry and infrastructure; building and architecture;
institutions and popular culture; and science and the arts. There is also an etymology
of London's rivers, districts (or villages), and of the street-names in the old city.

329 **The gourmet's guide to London.**
Elaine Hallgarten, Linda Collister. London: Ebury, 1992. 208p.

Recording over 450 places to buy, eat, or to learn how to prepare the best food in London, this guide covers all types of establishment from cheesemongers, fishmongers, and even fish and chip shops, to ethnic eating places and stores, tea and coffee merchants, restaurants, and street markets. Practical information on the location of the establishments entered in the guide is not lacking: opening times and credit card facilities are also noted.

330 **London.**
Elain Harwood, Andrew Saint. London: HMSO for English Heritage, 1991. 280p. (Exploring England's Heritage).

Some 200 buildings, ranging from Gothic churches and Tudor palaces, to an Edwardian pie shop and a 1950's 'bus garage, are described in this illustrated gazetteer of representative architecture in London.

331 **Catalogue of the oil paintings in the London Museum with an introduction on painters and the London scene from the fifteenth century.**
John Hayes. London: HMSO, 1970. 267p.

The collection of pictures, prints, and drawings assembled by the London Museum from its foundation in 1913 constitutes a valuable survey of the city's history since the early seventeenth century, recording its architecture, its ever changing panorama, and the lives and pleasures of its citizens. This illustrated catalogue is divided into three sections, topographical and. social scenes, portraits and theatrical pictures, and the reserve collection. Every oil painting is reproduced (the most significant are given a full page) and is accompanied by a detailed commentary on its content.

332 **Printed maps of London circa 1553-1850.**
James Howgego. Folkestone, England: Dawson, 1978. 2nd ed. 295p. maps. bibliog.

First published in 1964 this authoritative catalogue, regarded as the standard definitive work on its subject, lists 422 maps in chronological order of publication, with information concerning later editions, derivatives, and facsimiles.

333 **London's underground.**
H. F. Howson. London: Ian Allan, 1986. 2nd ed. 160p. maps.

In terms of mileage served by its trains the London underground system is the world's biggest. First published in 1951, this updated survey includes new chapters on the Victoria line, the Heathrow extensions, the Jubilee line, and the Docklands Light Railway. There is a chronology of the principal events of the Underground's history and also a list of routes giving the numbers of stations served and route miles.

334 **London termini.**

Alan A. Jackson. Newton Abbot, England: David & Charles, 1985.
2nd ed. 397p. map. bibliog.

Following an opening chapter explaining why they are situated where they are, each of London's mainline termini is looked at in detail. The history of Euston, Kings Cross, St. Pancras, Liverpool Street, Fenchurch Street, London Bridge, Cannon Street, Blackfriars and Holborn Viaduct, Waterloo, Charing Cross, Victoria, Paddington, and Marylebone, is accompanied by details of their sites and approaches, their architecture, the hotels that stand on them, their signalling, and accidents that have occurred. Since the first publication of this book in 1969 two stations have been completely rebuilt whilst others have endured the usual piecemeal improvements.

335 **No. 10 Downing Street: the story of a house.**

Christopher Jones. London: BBC, 1985. 192p. bibliog.

Standing on the foundations of a brewhouse once the property of the Abbey of Abingdon, the date when the present house was built is not exactly known but it was certainly occupied in the year 1677. It was granted by the Crown to Sir Robert Walpole in 1733 but he accepted it only on condition that it was entailed to the Office of the First Lord of the Treasury, an office that the Prime Minister of the day traditionally holds. This profusely illustrated book tells the story of the house from its earliest origins to the present day, describing not only the changes that have been made, but also the people who have lived there.

336 **A guide to the architecture of London.**

Edward Jones, Christopher Woodward. London: Weidenfeld & Nicolson, 1992. new ed. 448p. 18 maps.

First published in 1983 this practical guide to the best of London's architecture of all periods and styles by two practising architects contains over 950 entries and sixteen streetfinder maps to pinpoint the location of every building entered. This edition takes account of the changes in Dockland and in the City.

337 **London on £1,000 a day (before tea).**

Ferne Kadish, Shelley Clark. Basingstoke, England: Automobile Association, 1991. 432p.

What the well-heeled traveller needs to know: the best hotels, the most luxurious restaurants, where to hire a limousine or helicopter, the finest designer clothes or sports equipment, the sharpest jewellery, all presented with tongue-in-cheek expertise.

338 **A survey of London by John Stow reprinted from the text of 1603.**

Edited Charles Lethbridge Kingsford. Oxford: Clarendon, 1908.
2 vols. bibliog.

John Stow, one of the best known of the Elizabethan antiquarians, first published his *A survey of London. Conteyning the originall antiquity, increase, modern estate, and description of that city*, in 1598. It is based on walks round the London wards, on research into city and church records, crucially supplemented by oral historical research with individuals conversant with the ancient customs of London. Topics which claimed Stow's full attention include London's antiquity, its city walls, its ancient rivers, the town ditch, gates and bridges, its schools, hospitals, notes on the Stow family, a glossary, and a bibliography. *Stow's survey of London* (London: Dent, 1965. 533p. map. bibliog.) has a contemporary map of London and a full topographical index.

339   **Sherlock Holmes' London.**
   Tsukasa Kobayashi, Akane Higashiyama, Masaharu Vemura.   San
   Francisco: Chronicle, 1984. 128p. map. bibliog.
This photographic record follows the footsteps of Sherlock Holmes and Dr. Watson as they pitted their wits against jewel thieves, murderers, and master criminals in and around London. Sepia photographs of the period, and full contemporary colour illustrations, give the full flavour of late-Victorian London.

340   **The book of London.**
   Edited by Michael Leapman.   London: Weidenfeld & Nicolson, 1989.
   320p. 28 maps. bibliog.
Every aspect of London past and present is represented in this single-volume reference work which will appeal to London's residents and visitors alike. London's history and growth, the Thames, the City of London, Central London, the great houses and Georgian terraces, Victorian London, the suburbs, the medieval guilds, the Port of London, the markets, the Courts, theatres and concert halls, parks and gardens, fairs, museums and galleries, inns and pubs, pageantry and ceremonies, are all captured in print and illustration.

341   **A London docklands guide: a gazetteer to points of historical and**
   architectural interest in St. Katherine's, Wapping, Shadwell, Ratcliffe,
   Limehouse, Poplar, Blackwall, Isle of Dogs, Silvertown, North
   Woolwich, Beckton, Bermondsey and Rotherhithe.
   Peter Marcan.   High Wycombe, England: Marcan, 1986. 58p. maps.
   bibliog.
Short histories of each locality and imaginative accounts of their surviving landmarks are presented in this guide covering the London Boroughs of Southwark, Tower Hamlets, and Newham.

342   **London: Louise Nicholson's definitive guide.**
   London: Bodley Head, 1990. rev. ed. 382p. 14 maps. bibliog.
Of the making of London guidebooks there is truly no end. However, this guide has to be regarded as one of the finest available both for London residents and for visitors. It offers chapters on arriving and surviving (information sources, communications, getting around, health services, embassies, etc.); hotels; instant London (coach, in-depth, academic and thematic tours); London on wheels (by bus, train, underground and by bike to outstanding places of interest away from central London); rain (staying dry and having fun); London entertains; food and drink; shopping; and on fitness and fresh air. Add a month by month directory of events, a chronology, and a three-page bibliography, and it is easy to understand why it won the London Tourist Board's 'Best London Guide' award.

343   **Ordnance Survey London Central map.**
Southampton, England: Ordnance Survey.
This map covers the central area of London from Earls Court in the west to Spitalfields in the east, and from Regent's Park south to Lambeth. Features include one-way traffic routes, the river 'bus route, places of interest and entertainment, an inset map of the M25 and routes into London, and tourist information. Folded within hard covers, the inside cover text gives a short history of the Ordnance Survey in regard to its first home in the Tower of London.

344   **Crossing London's river: the bridges, ferries and tunnels crossing the Thames tideway in London.**
John Pudney.   London: Dent, 1972. 176p. map. bibliog.
The tidal reaches of the River Thames extend sixty-nine miles from the Nore to Teddington Lock. This historical survey effectively begins with the building of Old London Bridge in the twelfth century, and ends with the construction of the first Dartford Tunnel which was completed in 1963. Along the way it tells the story of the London watermen, the road and rail bridges of the nineteenth and twentieth centuries, the Tower Bridge, and the Woolwich Ferry, illustrating the diverse needs of those who wanted to navigate the river, and of those who simply wanted to cross it.

345   **Blue Guide museums and galleries of London.**
Malcolm Rogers.   London: A & C Black, 1991. 3rd ed. 360p. 6 maps.
No capital city in the world can boast of so many fine museums, art galleries, palaces, or even country houses, as London. This valuable guide provides a detailed description of over 160 museum and art collections in London, their buildings, furnishings, and outstanding exhibits and pieces.

346   **The art and architecture of London: an illustrated guide.**
Ann Saunders.   Oxford: Phaidon, 1984. 480p.
Extending over the City of London, the City of Westminster, and the London Boroughs north and south of the Thames, this exhaustive guide, over ten years in the making, introduces London's notable places, buildings and monuments, not forgetting the suburbs where little known village centres, medieval churches, and fine houses still stand.

347   **London's colourful pageantry: a month-by-month guide.**
Rachel Stewart.   Andover, England: Pitkin, 1989. 28p. map.
Royal and State ceremonies, military parades, recently established carnivals and festivals, history of the City of London's traditions, sporting occasions, etc. are included in this magnificently produced colour souvenir guide. A monthly calendar of events occupies the centre pages.

348   **Georgian London.**
John Summerson.   London: Barrie & Jenkins, 1988. 328p. bibliog.
Now furnished with twenty-three colour plates, and 160 other illustrations, this standard work, first published in 1945, consists of a series of essays on London's architectural history during the Georgian period. An epilogue, new to this edition, illustrates how Georgian London is still part of the capital's heritage. An appendix

contains a list of the churches, public buildings, and the more significant streets and houses surviving from the Georgian period in the City of London and in the London Boroughs.

349 Time Out Guides to London.
London: Time Out. 1986-89.

London for visitors (164p.), *Shopping in London* (228p.), *Eating out in London* (200p.), *Sport, health & fitness in London* (164p.), and *London student guide* (164p.), are all cheap (i.e. under £5.00), concise, colourful, informative guides, particularly suitable for overseas visitors.

350 London under London: a subterranean guide.
Richard Trench, Ellis Hillman. London: John Murray, 1985. 233p.

Buried and forgotten rivers, eighty-two miles of tube tunnels, crypts and cellars, hundreds of thousands of miles of cables and pipes, twelve miles of government tunnels, are all hidden beneath London's pavements and its uneven bed of gravel, clay, sand, and chalk. This definitive work plots and charts the tunnellers and borers who have burrowed under the city from Roman times to the present day. For the curious with itchy feet there is a gazetteer of exploration opportunities.

351 Oscar Wilde's London.
Wolf von Eckardt, Sander L. Gilman, J. Edward Chamberlin.
London: Michael O'Mara Books, 1988. 285p. bibliog.

Announced as 'a vivid portrait of the city that Oscar Wilde made and that made Oscar Wilde', in reality this plentifully illustrated book encapsulates *fin de siècle* London, from the autumn of 1879 when Wilde, just down from Oxford, rented rooms at 13 Salisbury Street, to the spring of 1897 when he left England for ever after his release from Pentonville Prison. It was at once a period of glorious imperial ceremonial and of industrial squalor, of trim garden suburbs and city-centre slums, of 'society' splendour and an awakening proletariat. All of these aspects are captured in this well-documented and readable American-inspired work.

352 London river: the Thames story.
Gavin Weightman. London: Collins & Brown, 1990. 160p. maps.

Accompanying a major London Weekend Television series, this illustrated volume takes the reader on a historical trip along the length of the River Thames, examining not only the tidal waters of its lower reaches but also the freshwater river above Teddington locks. Its bridges and ferries, its famous lighterman, its renowned frost fairs and regattas, its importance to national trade, the dangers of seasonal floods, the demise of the docks, and modern developments along its banks, are all featured. Michael St. John Parker's *London's royal river: a guide to the River Thames* (Andover, England: Pitkin, 1989. 28p.) is a superbly coloured souvenir guide to the celebrated buildings on both banks downstream from Royal Windsor and Eton to the Thames Barrier at Woolwich.

353   **The London encyclopedia.**
Ben Weinreb, Christopher Hibbert.   London: Macmillan, 1983.
1,029p.

Comprehensive in its scope, this enormous single-volume encyclopedia contains approximately 500 entries recording the important institutions, streets and buildings, people and events, in the history of Greater London.

354   **Where to stay in London 1992.**
London: London Tourist Board & Convention Bureau, 1991. 96p.

The official London Tourist Board guide to all types of accommodation.

355   **Guide to literary London.**
George G. Williams.   London: Batsford, 1973. 406p. 38 maps.

Thirty-eight guided tours arranged around a major author are presented here, each with its own map, and none taking any longer than an hour's steady walking. Not only where authors lived and died are featured but also where they met each other, attended church, or occasionally where they were thrown into gaol. The sites of historic theatres, bookshops and celebrated clubs and coffee houses are also indicated.

Prehistory and Archaeology

356 The handbook of British archaeology.

Lesley Adkins, Roy Adkins.   London: Macmillan, 1983. 319p. bibliog.

This is a paperback version of *A thesaurus of British archaeology* published by David & Charles in 1982. It offers clear definitions and explanations of the various technical terms used by archaeologists in a series of chronological chapters ranging from the Palaeolithic (Old Stone Age) period to Saxon times. A specialist chapter on archaeological techniques identifies and discusses terms used in locating and surveying sites, excavation, experimental archaeology, analysing artefacts, and dating whilst a miscellaneous chapter looks at terms employed in defining British archaeological periods, burials and hoards, agriculture, textiles, and prehistoric industries.

357 Arthur's Britain: history and archaeology AD 367-634.

Leslie Alcock.   Harmondsworth, England: Allen Lane, 1971. 415p. 11 maps. bibliog.

Exploiting both written and archaeological sources, this authoritative study sifts history from myth to conclude that King Arthur was a genuine historical figure of the late fifth and early sixth centuries. The author was Director of the Cadbury Castle excavations.

358 Ancient monuments and historic buildings.

London: HMSO, 1982. rev. ed. 20p. (Sectional List no. 27).

Guidebooks and souvenir guides to properties formerly under the care of the Department of the Environment are listed in this catalogue which is unfortunately no longer in print. Responsibility for these buildings have been transferred to English Heritage.

359 **Archaeological bibliography for Great Britain and Ireland.**
London: Council for British Archaeology, 1950-80. (biennially 1950-51 and 1952-53, then annually).
Arranged in two sections, a topographical section under county, period and subject headings, followed by a bibliography in author order, this publication which was discontinued in 1980 for financial reasons replaced the CBA's *Archaeological bulletin for the British Isles* (1940-49).

360 **An archaeology of the early Anglo-Saxon kingdoms.**
C. J. Arnold. London: Routledge, 1988. 224p. maps. bibliog.
Examining the evolving social and political structure of Anglo-Saxon England in the years 500-700 AD, with emphasis on the surviving archaeological evidence, this definitive study includes a history of early Anglo-Saxon archaeology and an extremely useful fifteen-page bibliography.

361 **Monumenta Britannica.**
John Aubrey, edited by John Fowles. Sherborne, England: Dorset, 1982. 2 vols. 9 maps.
John Aubrey (1626-1697) was granted letters patent by Charles II in 1671 commissioning him to conduct antiquarian surveys all over Britain. He devoted much time in collecting material for a detailed account of British field monuments from the prehistoric to the medieval period. *Monumenta Britannica: a miscellanie of British antiquities*, remained in manuscript form until printed in this limited edition of 595 copies. Here Aubrey's manuscript, perhaps the most important document in British archaeology, is reproduced in facsimile with a facing modern English printed text. Volume one covers temples, stone circles, camps, castles, and other military architecture. Volume two continues with barrows, sepulchres, ditches and highways, Roman pavements, coins, embanking and drainage, and also includes an editorial essay, 'John Aubrey and the Monumenta Britannica', Aubrey's family tree, and a memoir of Aubrey published in 1845. Michael Hunter's *John Aubrey and the realm of learning* (London: Duckworth, 1975) is a study of his writings.

362 **A prehistoric bibliography.**
Wilfred Bonser. Oxford: Blackwell, 1976. 425p.
Men and methods in archaeology; field archaeology; specific sites; material finds; and culture are the headings for the five main divisions under which 9,000 entries for books and journal articles are entered in this mammoth and monumental bibliography. They are subdivided into a general section and by zones corresponding to the group structure of the Council for British Archaeology.

363 **A guide to ancient sites in Britain.**
Janet Bord, Colin Bord. London: Latimer, 1978. 183p. maps. bibliog.
This regionally arranged descriptive and illustrated gazetteer of important prehistoric sites provides a key map for the region, basic archaeological information, location and access details, and information on whatever folklore, supernatural happenings, and unusual theories are associated with the site.

364 **Peoples of Roman Britain Series.**
Edited by Keith Branigan. Gloucester, England: Alan Sutton. 8 vols.

Originally published by Duckworth, and now relaunched, this series presents a comprehensive picture of the archaeology of Roman Britain. Each volume covers a single *civitas*, its settlement pattern and resources, and its reaction to an alien imposed civilization. Titles are as follows: *The Brigantes* (B. Hartley and L. Fitts); *The Catuvellauni* (Keith Branigan); *The Cantiaci* (Alex Detsicas); *The Cornovii* (Graham Webster); *The Carvetti* (Nicholas Higham and Barri Jones); *The Trinovantes* (Rosalind Dunnet); *The Iceni* (Helen Clarke and Peter Wade-Martins); and *The Parisi* (H. Ramm). The authors are all professional archaeologists experienced in research and fieldwork in the regions concerned.

365 **British Archaeological Abstracts.**
London: Council for British Archaeology, 1967- . biannual.

When first published this was intended to be a selective guide but since the annual *Archaeological bibliography for Great Britain and Ireland* folded in 1980 a more comprehensive coverage has been attempted. Some 1900 abstracts, arranged by period, extending from the Palaeolithic and Mesolithic Ages to post-medieval and industrial archaeology, allow scholars and researchers to keep abreast with the vast amount of literature now published.

366 **Recent archaeological excavations in Britain: selected excavations 1939-1955 with a chapter on recent air-reconnaissance.**
Edited by R. L. S. Bruce-Mitford. London: Routledge & Kegan Paul, 1956. 310p. 13 maps. bibliog.

Presented here are twelve reports, each one a personal account by the Director of excavations at particularly celebrated sites, mostly in northern, eastern, and southeastern England, including Star Carr, a mesolithic site in Yorkshire; the Lullingstone Roman villa; excavations in the City of London; the Sutton Hoo burial ship; and the deserted medieval villages at Wharram Percy. The editor was formerly Keeper of British and medieval Antiquities in the British Museum.

367 **Roman England.**
John Burke. London: English Touring Board/Weidenfeld & Nicolson, 1983. 152p. 2 maps.

This is a pictorial history of Roman England as recorded by its surviving monuments, artefacts, and antiquities. Fragments of walls, stretches of Roman roads, excavated villas and mosaic pavements, coins, lighthouses, tile works, shrines and temples, are all captured and reconstructed. Each regional chapter ends with a list of places to visit.

368 **The stone circles of the British Isles.**
Aubrey Burl. New Haven, Connecticut; London: Yale University Press, 1976. 410p. map. bibliog.

Over 900 stone circles, mostly situated in remote and isolated areas, dating from the middle Neolithic period to the Late Bronze Age (2,500-1,000 BC), attract thousands of visitors every year. Are they temple ruins or perhaps astronomical observatories? This scholarly but readable treatise presents the latest theories on their purpose and includes a thirty-five page county gazetteer of sites.

369 **The 'small towns' of Roman Britain.**
Barry Burnham, John Wacher.   London: Batsford, 1990. 388p. map.
bibliog.
The origins, physical development, and the most prominent buildings of fifty-four minor towns, potential cities, religious and industrial centres, and fortified and undefended settlements, are examined in this comprehensive survey. Each site is accompanied by a plan and an account of the most recent discoveries there.

370 **A guide to the archaeological sites of the British Isles.**
Courtlandt Canby.   New York, Oxford: Facts On File, 1988. 358p.
maps.
Information on more than 750 sites (monuments, churches, castles, etc.), ranging in time from the Palaeolithic period to the twelfth century, is arranged alphabetically by site in this illustrated guide. Although it is intended as a sourcebook for the amateur and professional archaeologist, it is a far from negligible guidebook for the interested visitor.

371 **Underneath English towns: interpreting urban archaeology.**
Martin Carver.   London: Batsford, 1987. 160p. 2 maps. bibliog.
Covering the period c. 40-1540 this study relates the achievements of urban archaeology over the last twenty-five years. Although intended 'for everyone who has worked as a volunteer on a dig; for visitors who look over the fence; for developers who are waiting for their site back; for contractors commissioned to build on it; for engineers, civil or otherwise; for local government and central government officers who have to justify the whole business, and for the press who want to a good story' (*Preface*), it also makes fascinating reading for the interested but unskilled amateur archaeologist.

372 **Neolithic Britain: new stone age sites of England, Scotland and Wales.**
Rodney Castleden.   London: Routledge, 1992. 432p. bibliog.
Although the Neolithic people of Britain erected some magnificent monumental architecture all too often only fragments remain. This descriptive gazetteer lists 1,100 domestic, ceremonial, and burial sites, belonging to the period 4700-2000 BC, some of which have only recently been excavated.

373 **Stonehenge complete.**
Christopher Chippingdale.   London: Thames & Hudson, 1983. 296p.
2 maps. bibliog.
Within the covers of this one book can be found a history and archaeology of Stonehenge since its re-discovery in AD 1130, an historical account of the English perception of the concept and purpose of Stonehenge, its builders, its astronomic significance, its place in art and literature, the threats to its continuing existence, and its preservation.

374 **The archaeology of medieval England.**
Helen Clarke.   London: British Museum, 1984. 224p. 7 maps. bibliog.

A rounded picture of English life in the period from 1066 to 1500 clearly emerges from this study of the archaeological evidence brought to light over the last forty years. Much has been derived from 'rescue' archaeology, that is *ad hoc* emergency excavations in response to imminent development programmes threatening to destroy valuable sites before they could be properly investigated or methodically interpreted. The archaeological significance of the countryside, parish churches, monasteries, castles, crafts and industries, and towns and trade, is evaluated and the author argues a convincing case for a more systematic approach to English medieval archaeology.

375 **Archaeological sites of Britain.**
Peter Clayton.   London: Batsford, 1985. 2nd ed. 239p. bibliog.

Over 250 of the most notable monuments are described in detail, with an Ordnance Survey map reference, in this illustrated gazetteer arranged in broad geographical divisions. Other sites are grouped and mentioned in passing. A glossary and an extended list of some museums to visit complete a very useful guide.

376 **A companion to Roman Britain .**
Edited by Peter Clayton.   Oxford: Phaidon, 1980. 208p. 6 maps. bibliog.

Six essays covering the major aspects of Roman Britain from the Conquest in AD 43 to the final withdrawal in the fifth century are followed by a gazetteer of the most important sites.

377 **The ending of Roman Britain.**
A. S. Esmonde Cleary.   London: Batsford, 1989. 242p. 5 maps. bibliog.

Based firmly on recent archaeological evidence rather than the dubious documentation which survives, this book explores events between the years AD 300 when Britain formed an established part of the Roman Empire and AD 500 by which time civilization had collapsed. It opens up a chronological gap, disturbing the orthodox view of continuity between the departure of the legions and the arrival of Anglo-Saxon marauders.

378 **The archaeology of Roman Britain.**
R. G. Collingwood, Ian Richmond.   London: Methuen, 1969. rev. ed. 348p. + 26p. plates. (Methuen's Handbooks of Archaeology).

First published in 1930, this standard work provides a systematic guide to the field monuments and the portable antiquities of Roman Britain. In turn magisterial chapters on roads, camps, forts and fortresses, signal stations, frontier lines, towns, villas, tombs and temples, native settlements, inscriptions, coins and pottery, brooches and weapons and other tools, enlighten the beginner and intrigue the armchair archaeologist.

379   **Post-medieval archaeology in Britain.**
David Crossley.   Leicester, England: Leicester University Press, 1990.
328p. bibliog.
Based on current research in this latest area of archaeological study, this overview
encompasses towns, the rural landscape, church archaeology, fortifications, shipwrecks,
the sources of power before the invention of the steam engine, metals, mining and
quarrying, glass, ceramics, and other industries.

380   **Iron Age communities in Britain: an account of England, Scotland and
Wales from the seventh century BC until the Roman Conquest.**
Barry Cunliffe.   London: Routledge, 1991. 3rd ed. 685p. maps.
bibliog.
Substantially revised since its first publication in 1974 this well-documented
monumental survey is the acknowledged standard work on the period. Introduced by
an essay on the development of Iron Age studies, it assesses and incorporates the latest
research on the distribution and pattern of Iron Age communities. A fifteen-page list
of the principal sites still visible adds to its reference value.

381   **Ancient Britain.**
James Dyer.   London: Batsford, 1990. 176p. bibliog.
Intended for the interested general reader, this copiously illustrated work presents a
readable account of current knowledge regarding prehistoric settlement, agriculture,
trade, industry, and ritual in Britain from the Upper Palaeolithic Age (c.450,000 BC) to
the Roman arrival in force in AD 43.

382   **The Current Archaeology down to earth guide to British archaeology.**
Supplement to *Current Archaeology*, vol. 11, no. 2 (Nov. 1990),
p. i-xxxiii.
Directory information on national and regional archaeological bodies and special
interest groups and on the various British Schools of Archaeology overseas is
contained in this special supplement produced in conjunction with *Down To Earth*, the
Channel Four television programme.

383   **Prehistoric Britain.**
Timothy Darvill.   London: Batsford, 1987. 223p. 10 maps. bibliog.
Special attention is given to six themes in this review of the development of human
societies in Britain from earliest times to the Roman Conquest: subsistence;
technology; ritual; trade; society; and population. The updating of knowledge brought
about by new technologies such as radiocarbon dating, and the analysis of the evidence
available, are also considered.

384   **The Penguin guide to prehistoric England and Wales.**
James Dyer.   London: Allen Lane, 1981. 384p. 6 maps. bibliog.
The main body of this comprehensive guide is a county-by-county descriptive gazetteer
of almost 1,000 scheduled ancient monuments regarded by the author as most
satisfying both for their intrinsic interest and for their natural surroundings. Excavation
discoveries, local legends, nearby archaeological museums, and topographical detail,

are all noted. Each entry is also provided with a bibliographical reference to a more complete source of information.

385 A guide to early Celtic remains in Britain.

Peter Berresford Ellis.   London: Constable, 1991. 272p. bibliog.

Containing careful descriptions of the physical features of hill-forts, cliff castles, hillside carvings, burial grounds, and permanent settlements dating from the eighth century BC to the arrival of the Romans in the first century AD, this regionally arranged illustrated guide includes all the most scenic and most significant sites.

386 Exploring England's Heritage.

London: HMSO for English Heritage, 1991- . irregular.

A series of illustrated gazetteer guides to the principal archaeological, architectural, and historical sites in England (*Devon and Cornwall*. Andrew Saunders. 1991. 117p. *London*. Elaine Harwood, Andrew Saint. 1991. 267p. *Cumbria to Northumberland*. John Weaver. 1992. 150p. *Dorset to Gloucestershire*. Martin Robertson. 1992. 144p.). Depending on the region industrial sites, landscapes, country houses, and parks and gardens are also featured.

387 A guide to the prehistoric and Roman monuments in England and Wales.

Jacquetta Hawkes.   London: Chatto & Windus, 1973. 2nd ed. 319p.

Arranged in regional sections, this guide which was first published in 1951 'attempts to reveal the monuments always in their proper setting of the countryside'. Over 600 sites described in the guide are listed in the twenty-four page gazetteer.

388 The Shell guide to British archaeology.

Jacquetta Hawkes, Paul Bahn.   London: Michael Joseph, 1986. 320p. 5 maps. bibliog.

This is a detailed and beautifully illustrated guide to over 600 of the most important archaeological monuments of Britain. Arranged on a regional basis, sub-divided alphabetically by county, each site is dated and described with map references and directions. The present whereabouts of significant artefacts found on site is indicated and there is a list of the more important museums.

389 Hill-forts of Britain.

A. H. A. Hogg.   London: Hart-Davis, Macgibbon, 1975. 304p. 6 maps. bibliog.

Arranged in two parts, this authoritative and well-illustrated study first deals with the various elements of hill-fort structures (they are defined as 'enclosures with ramparts built by prehistoric man to protect his settlements or stock') with appropriate background material to set them in their true historical and social context. The second section is a descriptive gazetteer of a representative selection of sites throughout Britain.

390   **Past imperfect: the story of Rescue Archaeology.**
      Barri Jones. London: Heinemann, 1984. 164p. bibliog.
Rescue Archaeology, the name given to the urgently imperative surveys and
excavations of sites about to be or in the process of being destroyed, dominated British
archaeology in the 1970s when the large scale destruction of archaeological sites was
threatened on an unprecedented scale by motorway construction programmes and city-
centre redevelopments. Written by the former Secretary of RESCUE, a trust for
British archaeology established in 1971, this is an account of the encounter between
archaeology and the contrasting worlds of big business property developers,
government finance and legislation, and local authority politics, and also of its
achievements in York, Gloucester, Lincoln, Peterborough, and in many other places
besides.

391   **A guide to medieval sites in Britain.**
      Nigel Kerr, Mary Kerr. London: Grafton, 1988. 270p. 8 maps.
This splendidly illustrated gazetteer of all types of buildings and monuments belonging
to the period between 1200 and 1485 consists of 160 entries incorporating historical and
architectural descriptions, plans, and map directions, of over 200 sites grouped in eight
regions. As a starting point for a tour of medieval Britain it could hardly be bettered.

392   **A guide to Dark Age remains in Britain.**
      Lloyd Laing, Jennifer Laing. London: Constable, 1979. 318p.
      11 maps. bibliog.
The Dark Ages stretched from the early fifth century when the Romans departed to
the mid-eleventh when the Normans invaded. Contrary to popular belief it was not
entirely a period of barbaric chaos but one in which a rich culture flourished as is
witnessed by its exquisite jewellery and illuminated manuscripts. This compact guide
arranged in nine regional chapters is designed to direct the non-specialist reader to
Anglo-Saxon remains both *in situ* and in museum collections.

393   **Archaeology in Britain since 1945: new directions.**
      Edited by Ian Longworth, John Cherry. London: British Museum,
      1986. 248p. 5 maps. bibliog.
Forty years progress in four areas of British archaeology is recorded in this well-
documented and generously illustrated survey. Prehistoric, Roman, Anglo-Saxon, and
medieval studies have all made considerable advances as a result of the application of
modern techniques such as radiocarbon dating, aerial photography, and large-scale
urban excavation. The period since the War has also been notable for a greater public
awareness of archaeology and a more responsible professional attitude to publication.

394   **Atlas of prehistoric Britain.**
      John Manley. Oxford: Phaidon, 1989. 160p. 14 maps. bibliog.
An up-to-date, informative, and eminently readable account of the development of
Britain's prehistoric societies from about 500,000 BC to the Roman conquest. Emphatic
use is made of specially drawn maps, site plans, reconstruction drawings, and some
striking colour photographs, to record the major prehistoric monuments.

395 **Introduction to British prehistory from the arrival of Homo Sapiens to the Claudian invasion.**
J. V. S. Megaw, D. D. A. Simpson. Leicester, England: Leicester University Press, 1979. 560p. maps. bibliog.

This well-documented series of papers deals authoritatively with the environmental background to British prehistory, pre-agricultural and agricultural communities, and the later Neolithic, Bronze, and Iron Ages. A forty-page bibliography is an invaluable guide to further research.

396 **Ordnance Survey historical maps and guides.**
Southampton, England: Ordnance Survey.

These maps show the position of buildings and monuments of the time overlaid in colour against a modern city plan. Those still surviving are highlighted to assist in their location. Each map includes an informative text and is illustrated with colour photographs. On a scale 1:2500 (25 inches to 1 mile), titles available include: *Roman & Anglian York*; *Viking & medieval York*; *Roman and medieval Bath*; *Georgian Bath*; *Roman and medieval Canterbury*, and *Roman London*. On a scale of 1:625,000 (1 inch to 10 miles) *Ancient Britain* and *Roman Britain* are now completely revised to allow historical information to be viewed in the context of the modern landscape. *Hadrian's Wall* (1¼ inches to 1 mile) is arranged in a series of strips each covering a section of the Wall.

397 **The Druids.**
Stuart Piggott. London: Thames & Hudson, 1968. 236p. 4 maps. bibliog. (Ancient Peoples and Places).

Thoroughly investigating what little documentary evidence survives, Piggott dispels the widespread popular misconceptions of the role and function of this Celtic priestly caste which would have them sharpening their sacrificial knives at Stonehenge at the height of the full moon.

398 **The Roman villa in Britain.**
Edited by A. L. F. Rivet. London: Routledge & Kegan Paul, 1969. 2990. 12 maps. bibliog.

'Roman villas are so well-established in Romano-British archaeology as to require, paradoxically, some explanation' (Sir Ian Richmond). These six essays on the Celtic background; the plans of Roman villas in England; the mosaic pavements; furniture and interior decoration; social and economic aspects; and on the future of Villa Studies, attempt to provide such an explanation.

399 **The archaeology of the English church: the study of historic churches and churchyards.**
Warwick Rodwell. London: Batsford, 1981. 192p. bibliog.

Church archaeology is a relatively recent academic study as opposed to church history and architecture. This pioneering work outlines its aims, methods, and achievements, in an attempt to demonstrate how much history remains to be uncovered in medieval churches. Among the topics discussed are church surveys; recording the fabric; churchyard archaeology; bones, burials, and monuments; and synthesis and publication. An appendix lists institutions relevant to church archaeology.

400   **English Heritage book of church archaeology.**
Warwick Rodwell.   London: Batsford/English Heritage, 1989. rev. ed.
208p. bibliog.

This account of the archaeology of churches and churchyards acts as an introduction to
the history, aims, methods and achievements of modern church archaeology. It
incorporates the results of much fresh information which has become available in
recent years due largely to new techniques in excavation and the recording of evidence.
With over 100 plans, reconstructions and photographs this is a complete guide for
anyone embarking on systematic visits to old churches.

401   **Royal Commission On The Ancient And Historical Monuments of
England. Inventories.**
London: HMSO, 1910- . 40 vols.

Set up to make an inventory of the ancient and historical monuments and constructions
connected with or illustrative of the contemporary culture, civilization, and living
conditions of ordinary people, the Royal Commission has published at intervals a
number of large format county volumes, each dealing with building materials,
earthworks, ecclesiastical buildings, etc., and each furnished with plans, maps, a
glossary, and detailed indexes. Much work needs to be done before these inventories
are anywhere near completed.

402   **The riches of British archaeology.**
A. Selkirk.   Cambridge University Press, 1988. 208p. maps.

Arranged in five chronological periods stretching from earlier prehistory to Saxon and
medieval Britain, this archaeological survey contains illustrated double-page spreads
devoted to each of fifty sites excavated in Britain since the 1960s. A list of museums
with significant collections is also included.

403   **England's undiscovered heritage: a guide to 100 unusual sites and
monuments.**
Debra Shipley, Mary Peplow.   London: Weidenfeld & Nicolson, 1988.
160p. 24 maps.

One hundred sites, follies, gardens, Roman remains, ancient earthworks, town houses,
towers, medieval churches, etc., selected from 400 properties in the care of English
Heritage, are featured in this profusely illustrated guidebook. The sites are arranged in
alphabetical order and each entry includes a description, an exact location, and
directions for getting there.

404   **Roads and tracks of Britain.**
Christopher Taylor.   London: Dent, 1979. 210p. 10 maps.

What happens to roads over long periods of time, how prehistoric tracks evolved into
Roman roads, Anglo-Saxon lanes, medieval highways, and modern trunk roads; their
dating; and the effect they had on the towns, villages, and countryside along their
routes, are the main themes of this study by a field archaeologist and former
Investigator for the Royal Commission on Historical Monuments (England). A select
list of some of the better known ancient trackways is included in a fifteen-page
gazetteer.

405 **A guide to prehistoric England.**
Nicholas Thomas. London: Batsford, 1976. 2nd ed. 270p. maps. bibliog.

Intended 'for people who love the countryside, who are interested in the past and may wish to plan their excursions around visits to prehistoric sites of various types', this work is a county arranged guide to sites to be used with an Ordnance Survey one-inch map. Each entry includes a physical description of the site together with notes on any discoveries made. A glossary of archaeological terms is also included.

406 **The archaeology of Anglo-Saxon England.**
Edited by D. M. Wilson. London: Methuen, 1976.

Agricultural and rural settlement, towns, ecclesiastical architecture, monastic sites, craft and industry, pottery and coins, animal resources, and the Scandinavian incursions, are the principal themes in this substantial and indispensable work which also includes a fifty-page gazetteer of accessible Anglo-Saxon sites. An earlier work of Wilson's, *The Anglo-Saxons* (London: Thames & Hudson, 1960. 231p. map. bibliog.), also looks at Anglo-Saxon archaeology and Christian antiquities besides considering the weapons and warfare of the period and Anglo-Saxon art.

407 **A guide to the Roman remains in Britain.**
R. J. A. Wilson. London: Constable, 1988. 3rd ed. 453p. 11 maps. bibliog.

First published in 1978, this is a thoroughly revised regional pocket-size guide to over 350 Roman excavations and earthworks grouped according to their nature and not necessarily by their proximity, accompanied by site and town plans. There is also a list of some museums displaying Romano-British material.

408 **Roman forts: an illustrated introduction to the garrison posts of Roman Britain.**
Roger Wilson. London: Bergstrom & Boyle, 1980. 96p. map. bibliog.

Over 240 Roman forts and fortresses are now known to exist in Britain although relatively few of these have been systematically excavated. Illustrated with fifty-nine reconstruction drawings, plans and diagrams, this compact guide first describes the layout of a typical fort and then traces the development of building techniques and construction methods.

History

General and reference

409 **Bibliography of British history.**
Oxford: Clarendon Press, 1928-1978. 6 vols. (vol. 1. *A Bibliography of English history to 1485*. Edgar B. Graves. 1975. 1,103p.; vol. 2. *Tudor period 1485-1603*. Conyers Read. 1959. 2nd ed. 624p.; vol. 3. *Stuart period 1603-1714*. Godfrey Davies, 1928. Mary Freer Keeler. 1970. 2nd ed. 734p.; vol. 4. *The eighteenth century 1714-1789*. Stanley Pargellis, D. J. Medley. London: Harvester Press, 1971. 642p.; vol. 5. *1789-1851*. L. M. Brown and I. R. Christie. 1977. 759p.; vol. 6. *1851-1914*. H. J. Hanham, 1978. 1,606p.).

Issued under the direction of the American Historical Association and the Royal Historical Society of Great Britain, this immense project traces its origins to a paper read by H. R. Tedder at the 1885 Plymouth meeting of The Library Association. The RHS involvement began in 1896 but it was not until 1909 that serious discussions were put in hand. Although each volume is complete in itself, they are all designed to a similar pattern and arrangement. Scholarly in nature they are more concerned with source material than with secondary authorities and each volume includes a selective survey of the material, brief descriptive and critical comments on many entries, and short introductory paragraphs indicating the more significant books to the main subdivisions. *Stuart period 1603-1714* has fifteen sections covering general reference works, political, constitutional, legal, ecclesiastical, military, naval, economic, social, cultural, and local history. The whole work stands as a monument to American and British historical scholarship.

410 **British historical and political facts series.**
London: Macmillan, 1977-1986. 6 vols. (vol. 1. *English historical facts 1485-1603.* K. Powell, Chris Cook. 1977. 228p. vol. 2. *English historical facts 1603-1688.* Chris Cook, J. Wroughton. 1980. 231p. bibliog. vol. 3. *British historical facts 1688-1760.* Chris Cook, John Stevenson. 1988. 252p. vol. 4. *British historical facts 1760-1830.* Chris Cook, John Stevenson. 1980. 208p. vol. 5. *British historical facts 1830-1900.* Chris Cook, B. Keith. 1975. 279p. vol. 6. *British political facts 1900-1945.* David Butler, Gareth Butler. 1986. 536p. bibliog.).

Each section in these compendious sourcebooks of facts, figures, and dates, is devoted to a specific subject area appropriate to the period in question. For example *1603-1688* has eleven sections: the monarchy; selected holders of major public offices; glossary of central government; biographies; Parliament; local government; the church; the armed forces; overseas trade and the colonies; education and learning; and population and the towns.

411 **British national archives.**
London: HMSO, 1984. rev. ed. 86p. (Sectional List no. 24).

Before the Public Record Office was established in 1938 official historical publications were the responsibility of the Record Commission (1800) and the State Paper Commission (1825). When the Public Record Office Act was passed the Master of the Rolls was empowered to print calendars, catalogues and indexes of the records in his possession. This sectional list includes all PRO publications, the reprints of the *Rerum Brittanicarum medii Aevi Scriptorum* (the Rolls series), publications issued by The Record Commissioners, and the House of Lords Record Office publications.

412 **Harrap's book of British dates: a comprehensive chronological dictionary of British dates from prehistoric times to the present day.**
Rodney Castleden. London: Harrap, 1991. 446p.

Year by year entries, with factual commentary to provide the necessary background information, give the dates for major political, dynastic, religious, and scientific events which have shaped and influenced British traditions and culture from about 8000 BC to the 1980s.

413 **Handbook of dates for students of English history.**
C. R. Cheney. London: Royal Historical Society, 1981. 2nd ed. 164p. bibliog.

Strictly limited to the dating of records which students of English history, both novices and experts, will commonly encounter, this compact and convenient guide includes sections on the different reckonings of time such as the Julian and Gregorian calendars, the rulers of England, Saints' days and festivals used in dating, a legal chronology, and the English calendar for the year 1752 when the new style calendar was adopted.

414   **The Oxford history of England.**
      Edited by Sir George Clark.   Oxford: Clarendon Press, 1934-1991.
      16 vols. (vol. 1A. *Roman Britain*. Peter Salway, 1981. 824p. bibliog.
      10 maps. [This volume replaced R. G. Collingwood and J. N. L.
      Myers' *Roman Britain and the English settlements*. 2nd ed. 1937];
      vol. 1B. *The English settlements*. J. N. L. Myers. 1986. 248p. bibliog.
      4 maps; vol. 2. *Anglo-Saxon England*. Sir Frank Stenton. 1971. 3rd ed.
      765p. bibliog. map; vol. 3. *From Domesday Book to Magna Carta
      1087-1216*. A. L. Poole. 1955. 2nd ed. 541p. bibliog.; vol. 4.
      The thirteenth century 1216-1307. Maurice Powicke. 1962. 2nd ed. 829p.
      bibliog. 4 maps; vol. 5. *The fourteenth century 1307-1399*. May
      McKisack. 1959. 598p. bibliog. 6 maps; vol. 6. *The fifteenth century
      1399-1485*. E. F. Jacob, 1961. 775p. bibliog. 6 maps; vol. 7. *The earlier
      Tudors 1485-1558*. J. D. Mackie. 1964. 699p. bibliog. 7 maps; vol. 8.
      The reign of Elizabeth. J. B. Black. 1959. 2nd ed. 539p. bibliog.
      6 maps; vol. 9. *The early Stuarts 1603-1660*. Godfrey Davies. 1959.
      2nd ed. 458p.; vol. 10. *The later Stuarts 1660-1714*. Sir George Clark.
      1956. 2nd ed. 479p. bibliog. 9 maps; vol. 11. *The Whig supremacy
      1714-1760*. Basil Williams. 1962. 2nd ed. 504p., bibliog. 10 maps;
      vol. 12. *The reign of George III 1760-1815*. J. Steven Watson. 1960.
      637p. bibliog. 4 maps; vol. 13. *The age of reform 1815-1870*.
      Sir Llewellyn Woodward. 1962. 2nd ed. 681p. bibliog. 6 maps; vol. 14.
      England 1870-1914. R. C. K. Ensor. 1964. 634p. bibliog. 7 maps;
      vol. 15. *English history 1914-1945*. A. J. P. Taylor. 1965. 709p. bibliog.
      8 maps; vol. 16. *Consolidated index*. R. Raper. 1991. 622p.).

Two characteristics distinguish this standard authoritative history compared with
previous histories: a special attention to geography, and a much greater emphasis on
social and economic affairs which receive equal treatment to constitutional and
political history. All volumes include a chapter surveying the contemporary state of
society and all end with an impressive bibliography. Although it is explicitly stated that
these bibliographical essays are not claimed to be exhaustive, it is clear that if printed
together in a separate volume they would constitute a far from neglible general
bibliography of English history. Publication of a *New Oxford history of England*, which
presumably will eventually supersede the original volumes, has begun with P.
Langford's *A polite and commercial people: England 1727-1783* (1989. 803p. bibliog.).

415 **Conference on British Studies bibliographical handbooks.**
Cambridge, England: Cambridge University Press, 1968-87. 8 vols.
(vol. 1. *Anglo-Norman England 1066-1154*. Michael Altschul. 1969;
vol. 2. *The High Middle Ages in England 1154-1377*. Bertie Wilkinson.
1978. 130p.; vol. 3. *Late-medieval England 1377-1485*. Delloyd G.
Guth. 1976. 143p.; vol. 4. *Tudor England 1485-1603*. Mortimer Levine.
1968. 115p.; vol. 5. *Restoration England 1660-1689*. William L. Sachse.
1971. 115p.; vol. 6. *Late Georgian and Regency England 1760-1837*.
Robert A. Smith. 1984. 114p.; vol. 7. *Victorian England 1837-1901*.
Josef L. Althoz. 1970. 100p.; vol. 8. *Modern England 1901-1984*.
Alfred Freeman Havighurst. 1987. 2nd ed. 109p.).
The Conference on British Studies was founded in 1951. It is now recognized as the official organization in the United States and Canada for scholars working in the field of British history and culture and as such is acknowledged by the American Historical Society to which it is affiliated. This series of bibliographical handbooks covers all aspects of British history except literature, and is specifically intended for research scholars, emphasis being given to the most scholarly publications. Each handbook contains over 2,000 annotated items classified under broad subject headings. For example *Modern England* has 2,670 entries divided into sixteen sections: bibliographies; catalogues, guides and handbooks; general surveys; constitutional history; political; foreign relations; social history; economic; labour; urban; agricultural; science and technology; military and naval; religious; fine arts; and intellectual history.

416 **Longman atlas of modern British history: a visual guide to British society and politics 1700-1970.**
Chris Cook, John Stevenson.   London: Longman, 1978. 208p. bibliog.
maps.
Contains thirty-eight separate subject sections, each with an introductory text, a selection of black and white maps, and statistical data, which help chart the course of modern British economic, social and political history.

417 **The Longman handbook of modern British history 1714-1987.**
Chris Cook, John Stevenson.   London: Longman, 1988. 2nd ed. 418p.
bibliog.
First published in 1983, this compendious handbook provides the essential facts and figures on the major aspects of modern British history from the death of Queen Anne to the beginning of Margaret Thatcher's third administration. Politics, social and economic conditions, foreign affairs and defence, all fall within its scope. This updated edition contains material on the women's movement and feminism, the Social Democratic Party and the Alliance, the Falklands War and the 1984/5 miners strike.

418   **A regional history of England series.**
Edited by Barry Cunliffe, David Hey.   Harlow, England: Longman,
1986- . 20 vols.

Dividing England into ten regions, this systematic history covers each region with two
linked but independent volumes; the first dealing with the region's prehistory and early
history up to AD 1000 which relies heavily on recent archaeological discoveries and
research, and the second volume recording changes and developments since that date.

419   **English historical documents.**
Edited by David C. Douglas.   London: Eyre Methuen; New York,
Oxford Press, 1953- . 14 vols. (vol. 1. *c.500-1042*. Edited by Dorothy
Whitelocke. 1979. 2nd ed. 952p. 3 maps. bibliog.; vol. 2. *1042-1189*.
Edited by David C. Douglas, George W. Greenaway. 1981. 2nd ed.
1083p. 4 maps. bibliog.; vol. 3. *1189-1327*. Edited by Harry Rothwell.
1975. 1032p. 7 maps. bibliog.; vol. 4. *1327-1485*. Edited by A.M.
Myers. 1969. 1235p. bibliog.; vol. 5. *1485-1558*. Edited by C.H.
Williams. 1967. 1082p. bibliog.; vol. 6. *1558-1603*. In preparation; vol.
7(1). *1603-1640*. In preparation; vol. 7(2). *1640-1660*. In preparation;
vol. 8. *1660-1714*. Edited by Andrew Browning. 1953. 966p. 21 maps.
bibliog.; vol. 9. *American colonial documents to 1776*. Edited by Merrill
Jensen. 1955. 888p. 3 maps. bibliog.; vol. 10. *1714-1783*. Edited by
D. B. Horn, Mary Ransome. 1957. 972p. 4 maps. bibliog.; vol. 11.
1783-1832. Edited by A. Aspinall, E. Anthony Smith. 1959. 992p.
4 maps. bibliog.; vol. 12(1) *1833-1874*. Edited by G. M. Young, W. D.
Handcock. 1956. 1017p. bibliog.; vol. 12(2) *1874-1914*. Edited by
W. D. Handcock. 1977. 725p. bibliog.).

The stated purpose of these massive volumes is 'to present to the general reader the
fundamental sources of English history which are today more often quoted than read
and more often sought than found'. Just how far the general reader would get in these
strictly academic collections of source documents is hard to determine but, as a
concession to the real world we live in, they are all printed in English translation
whenever the original text was in Anglo-Saxon, Norse, Latin, or Norman-French.
Each volume begins with a general introduction and a critical bibliography to assist
further research and a detailed contents list clearly indicates the classified extracts
which are arranged chronologically.

420   **Factbook of British history.**
Leicester, England: Galley Press, 1984. 237p.

This annotated and illustrated book of facts is divided into ten chronological sections.
A final reference section lists British rulers and prime ministers and brief biographical
information on some famous Britons.

421 **Historical atlas of Britain.**
Edited by Malcolm Falkus, John Gillingham. London: Kingfisher, 1987. rev. ed. 223p. bibliog.

A comprehensive chronological and thematic survey of British history from earliest times, reflecting contemporary historical thought, in which ninety distinct topics are separately presented with maps, diagrams, illustrations and an authoritative closely integrated text.

422 **British archives: a guide to archive resources in the United Kingdom.**
Janet Foster, Julia Sheppard. London: Macmillan, 1989. 2nd ed. 834p. bibliog.

Published originally in 1982 this invaluable guide for both experienced researchers and novices provides directory information, hours of opening, the historical background, the acquisition policy and major collections, and the funding aids and publications, of almost 1,050 British archive and record offices.

423 **Handbook of British chronology.**
Edited by E. B. Fryde (et al.). London: Royal Historical Society, 1986. 3rd ed. 605p. bibliog.

First published in 1941, with a second edition twenty years later, this standard reference work lists with dates the rulers of England, Wales and Scotland from the Saxon period onwards together with Officers of State (medieval post holders to present day ministries), the bishops and archbishops of England, Wales, Scotland, and Ireland; Dukes, Marquesses and Earls; English and British parliaments and related assemblies to 1832; and provincial and national councils of the Church in England c.600 to 1536. Background information is provided and the work opens with a bibliographical guide to the list of English office holders.

424 **Signposts to the past: place-names and the history of England.**
Margaret Gelling. Chichester, England: Phillimore, 1988. 2nd ed. 281p. 21 maps. bibliog.

The main aim of this work, first published in 1978, is 'to discuss the bearing of place-name evidence in English history, and to suggest maps in which archaeologists and historians may draw on this copious store of material' (Introduction). To this end there are chapters on the place-names of Roman Britain, Latin words in English place-names, the Celtic revival, the chronology of place-names, and Scandinavian and French names, with others on archaeology, and on boundaries and meeting places. The new material in this second edition consists of a series of chapter addenda, printed consecutively, outlining the advances in scholarship and interpretation since first publication.

425 **British history atlas.**
Martin Gilbert. London: Weidenfeld & Nicolson, 1968. 118p. 118 maps.

Black-and-white outline maps chart the economic, social, political, military, and territorial history of the British Isles and British interests overseas. They range from the Celts in Britain by the year 50 BC to the Western Pacific since 1945.

426 **The Cambridge historical encyclopedia of Great Britain and Ireland.**
Edited by Christopher Haigh. Cambridge, England: Cambridge
University Press, 1985. 3,920p. maps. bibliog.
Although it has attracted some criticism for attempting to cram too much information
into a one-volume work, this encyclopedia succeeds in integrating sixty specialist
interpretative essays, centred round dramatic historical events, and arranged in seven
chronological sections, extending from Roman Britain to Britain and Europe in the
1980s, with shorter descriptive entries, and 800 very brief biographies of historical
figures.

427 **History in print.**
London: HMSO, 1990. rev. ed. 28p. (Sectional List, no. 60).
Details of in print publications on historical subjects available from Her Majesty's
Stationery Office, formerly included in a number of sectional lists now discontinued
(no. 24 *British National Archives*, no. 27. *Ancient Monuments*, no. 50. *Miscellaneous*,
no. 59. *Royal Commissions*, and no. 60. *Histories of the First and Second World Wars*)
are incorporated in this revised list.

428 **The British Isles: a history of four nations.**
Hugh Kearney. Cambridge, England: Cambridge University Press,
1989. 236p. 6 maps. bibliog.
The writing of nation-based narrative history is firmly embedded in the nineteenth
century but, as Kearney illustrates, however much historians endeavour to keep within
a national framework they are led inexorably to wider dimensions. 'The viewpoint
adopted in this book is that the histories of what are normally regarded as four distinct
"nations" appear more intelligible if they are seen first within a general British Isles
context and secondly if they are seen in terms of "culture" and "sub-cultures".'.

429 **A dictionary of British history.**
J. P. Kenyon. London: Secker & Warburg, 1987. 415p. 12 maps.
With over 3000 entries for specific events, places, personalities, historical concepts and
movements, encompassing the domestic, political, social, and cultural history of the
British Isles, and its overseas possessions, from the Roman invasions to 1970, this is an
indispensable guide for general readers and students of history seeking authoritative
definitions of unfamiliar terms.

430 **A guide to English historical records.**
Alan Macfarlane. Cambridge, England: Cambridge University Press,
1983. 134p. bibliog.
In describing the nature of historical records created by the State and the Church
during the period 1200-1800, this work considers the administrative and judicial
processes which led to the documents being written, their survival and numbers, the
location and form of the various types of material, and the hidden errors and omission
– and deliberate deceptions – which sometimes plague them. This is not a book for the
aimless reader but it is of immense use both to amateur local historians and
genealogists and students of English archives.

431 **The illustrated dictionary of British history.**
Edited by Arthur Marwick. London: Thames & Hudson, 1980. 320p.
This A to Z companion to the main themes and personalities of British history encompasses political, social, diplomatic, religious, economic, and administrative history. Entries range from brief factual statements, or surveys of major events, and assessments of historical figures, to twenty interpretative essays on broader topics such as prehistoric Britain, feudalism, The Civil War, the women's movement, and the Welfare State.

432 **History of Britain series.**
Edited by W. N. Medlicott. London: Longman, 1959-1980. 9 vols.
(vol. 1. *The Anglo Saxon age c.400-1042*. D. J. V. Fisher. 1976. 384p.;
vol. 2. *The feudal kingdom of England 1042-1216*. F. Barlow. 1988.
4th ed. 496p.; vol. 3. *The later Middle Ages in England 1216-1485*.
B. Wilkinson. 1977. 434p.; vol. 4. *The Tudor Age 1485-1603*. J. A.
Williamson. 1979. 492p.; vol. 5. *The Stuart Age: a history of England
1603-1714*. Barry Coward. 1980. 512p.; vol. 6. *Eighteenth century
England 1714-1784*. Dorothy Marshall. 1975. 2nd ed. 572p.; vol. 7. *The
age of improvement 1783-1867*. Asa Briggs. 1959. 574p.; vol. 8. *England
1868-1914. The age of urban democracy*. Donald Read. 1979. 544p.;
vol. 9. *Contemporary England 1814-1964*. With epilogue 1964-1974.
W. N. Medlicott. 1976. 636p.).
Written by eminent academic historians, these narrative histories are ideal introductions to the dominant political, constitutional, social and economic, religious, cultural, foreign, and military themes of these periods for both students and general readers.

433 **A guide to the historical and archaeological publications of societies in England 1901-1933.**
E. L. C. Mullins. London: Athlone Press, 1968. 850p.
Compiled for the Institute of Historical Research this guide contains 6,560 entries for books and periodical articles issued by more than 400 local and national learned societies to their members. It neatly complements *Writings on British history 1901-1933* (W. Dawson. 1970. 2 vols.) which excludes society publications.

434 **Publications of the Royal Commission on Historical Manuscripts.**
London; HMSO, 1985. rev. ed. 28p. (Sectional List no. 17).
Included among the items listed in this official catalogue are the Reports and Calendars series, the reports on various collections, the Guide to Sources of British history series, and the Prime Ministers' Papers series consisting of descriptive catalogues of the papers of nineteenth-century Prime Ministers and Secretaries of State.

435   **Record repositories in Great Britain: a geographical directory.**
London: HMSO for Royal Commission on Historical Manuscripts,
1991. 9th ed. 46p.
First published in 1964 this directory lists 240 repositories which systematically collect,
preserve, and make available for public use, written records other than those of their
own administration. They include national and local record offices and national,
government, college, university, and public libraries, all arranged by region and then
alphabetically by town. Access, facilities such as cameras, microfilming, or repair
services, and published guides, are indicated.

436   **The Rolls Series: rerum Britannicarum medii aevi scriptores** *or*
chronicles and memorials of Great Britain and Ireland during the
Middle Ages.
London: Longmans Green, 1858-1911. 253 vols.
A proposal for the publication of primary source materials for the history of Great
Britain from the Roman invasions to the reign of Henry VIII was presented to the
Treasury by the Master of the Rolls, 26 January 1857. It was suggested that these
materials should be selected by competent editors who should introduce each volume
by adding an account of the manuscripts, their age and peculiarities, and a résumé of
the life and times of the author. Parliamentary approval was granted and the first
eleven volumes were published in 1858. *Descriptive catalogue of materials relating to
the history of Great Britain and Ireland to the end of the reign of Henry VII* (Edited by
Thomas Duffy Hardy, 3 vols in 4, 1862-1871) is a monumental work of scholarship,
recording and describing the sources of early British history both printed and in
manuscript, in which the material is arranged chronologically under the year in which
the latest event is recorded and not under the period when the author flourished. The
full story of this invaluable series may be followed in M. D. Knowles' Presidential
address. *Transactions of the Royal Historical Society.* 5th series, vol. 11, (1961),
p. 137-59.

437   **Royal Historical Society Annual Bibliography of British and Irish**
History.
Oxford: Oxford University Press, 1976- . annual.
This comprehensive and authoritative survey of books and articles published during
each calendar year is arranged in fourteen sub-divided form and chronological sections
beginning with archives, bibliographies and works of reference; general works; and
Roman Britain; and proceeding by historical period to Britain since 1914. The *1990*
volume (1991. 275p.) lists 1,221 books and 2,948 articles and also includes a history of
the bibliography by Professor G. R. Elton, its erstwhile editor. The great value of this
bibliography is that it is available before the end of the following year.

438   **Steinberg's dictionary of British history.**
Edited by S. H. Steinberg, I. H. Evans.   London: Edward Arnold,
1970. 2nd ed. 421p.
First published as *A new dictionary of British history* in 1963, itself a replacement for
J. A. Brendon's *A dictionary of British history* (1937), this co-operative work includes
entries for political, constitutional, diplomatic, administrative, legal, ecclesiastical and
economic events, people, and occasions. Literature, the arts, music, science, and

biographical material is excluded. The dictionary covers countries connected to Britain until such time as that connection lapsed.

439 **Who's who in British history series.**
Edited by G. R. Treasure. London: Shepheard-Walwyn, 1986- .
8 vols. (vol. 1. *Who's who in Roman Britain and Anglo-Saxon England.*
Richard Fletcher. 1989. 245p.; vol. 2. *Who's who in Early Medieval England.* Christopher Tyerman. 1992. 400p.; vol. 3. *Who's who in Late Medieval England.* M. Hicks. 1991. 400p.; vol. 4. *Who's who in Tudor England.* C. R. N. Routh. 1990. 476p.; vol. 5. *Who's who in Stuart Britain.* Peter Hill. 1986. 2nd ed. 466p.; vol. 6. *Who's who in Early Hanoverian Britain.* G. R. Treasure. 1991. 480p.; vol. 7. *Who's who in Late Hanoverian Britain.* G. R. Treasure. 1991. 480p.; vol. 8. *Who's who in Victorian Britain* not yet published).

'Each volume paints a portrait of an age. The persons selected are not confined to those who made their mark on church or state, but extended to a wider cross-section of society, including artists. explorers, scientists, entrepreneurs and eccentrics. The series differs from the conventional *Who's Who* in two major respects: entries are arranged in a broadly chronological rather than alphabetical sequence to facilitate reading about contemporaries; and secondly each essay conveys more than the bare facts of the subject's life; it places him in the context of his age and evokes what was distinctive and interesting in his personality and achievement' (Publisher's announcement). This series replaces the 'Who's who in history' series published by Basil Blackwell.

440 **Writings on British history: a bibliography of books and articles on the history of Great Britain from about 400 AD . . .**
London: Institute of Historical Research. 1934- . irregular.

Originally compiled for the Royal Historical Society these volumes were planned in an exhaustive record of the annual output of writings on British history in all languages. Publication began with the 1934 volume (1936) and since then the project has been carried forward to 1974 and back to 1901. Each volume is arranged in two parts: general works containing the auxiliary sciences, bibliography, historiography, British history in general, and English local history; and period histories in six chronological sections for pre-Conquest, medieval, Tudor, Stuart, and the eighteenth and nineteenth centuries. Later volumes add a section for the twentieth century. Volumes are as follows: *1901-1933*, contained five volumes in seven (*The auxiliary sciences and general works*; *The Middle Ages*; *The Tudor and Stuart periods*; *The eighteenth century*; *1815-1914*); 1934-1939 was covered in annual editions; *1940-1945* was complete in two volumes; and 1946-1974 was documented in volumes covering two or three years e.g. *1973-74* (published in 1986). The Institute of Historical Research assumed responsibility for publication in 1965.

Roman Britain

441   **A Romano-British bibliography (55 BC–AD 449).**
Wilfred Bonser.   Oxford: Blackwell, 1964. 442p.
This bibliography portrays in complete outline the pattern of the history of Britain and of its civilization during the 500 years before the arrival of the Anglo Saxon invaders. There are two main sections: thematic coverage (history, defence, geography, archaeology, numismatics etc.); and a regional record for local history, excavations, and finds. In all nearly 9,400 entries are recorded. An index is available in a separate volume (95p.).

442   **Britannia: a history of Roman Britain.**
Sheppard Frere.   London: Routledge & Kegan Paul, 1987. 3rd ed.
423p. + 32p. plates. 15 maps. bibliog.
When first published in 1967 this book was immediately perceived to be an outstanding study of the Roman period in Britain. A review of the pre-Roman Iron Age peoples introduces chapters on all aspects of the life and administration of the province. No attempt is made to discuss the archaeology of Roman Britain as such although this extensively revised third edition gives full weight to the evidence recovered from the most recent archaeological discoveries.

443   **An atlas of Roman Britain.**
Barri Jones, David Mattingley.   Oxford: Blackwell, 1990. 341p.
272 maps. bibliog.
Newly drawn maps chart the stages of the Roman invasion, conquest, and garrisoning, in this attractive atlas which outlines Britain's position on the periphery of the Roman World. Its rural and urban life, its religion and culture, and the economic development of its provinces, are all generously mapped. The accompanying text is based on the latest archaeological and historical research.

444   **The Saxon shore: a handbook.**
V. A. Maxfield.   Exeter, England: University of Exeter, 1989. 178p.
Based on the most recent research this handbook presents an up-to-date survey of the Saxon shore, its geographical setting, and the Roman fleets and forts guarding it. A fifty-page gazetteer of sites and a fourteen-page bibliography are distinctive features in this guide to a little explored area of study.

445   **Research on Roman Britain 1960-89.**
Edited by Malcolm Todd.   London: Society for the Promotion of
Roman Studies, 1989. 271p. maps. bibliog.
This collection of sixteen bibliographical essays begins with the later Iron Age in southern Britain, examines the northern frontiers, and the early cities, etc., and concludes with a prospect of Roman Britain.

446   **The towns of Roman Britain.**
      John Wacher.   London: Batsford, 1974. 460p. 6 maps. bibliog.
This magisterial account considers the circumstances surrounding the establishment of
the major administrative centres of Roman Britain, their political affiliations, and the
courses of their development and decline. A companion volume, Barry Burnham and
John Wacher's *The 'small towns' of Roman Britain* (Batsford, 1980. 388p. maps.
bibliog.) deals individually with fifty-four of the best-known sites grouped 'according to
the similarity of their morphological features and their identifiable functions'. Each site
is accompanied by a plan showing the most recent discoveries.

Anglo-Saxons

447   **An introduction to Anglo-Saxon England.**
      Peter Hunter Blair.   Cambridge, England: Cambridge University
      Press, 1970. 382p. 9 maps. bibliog.
In this well-received scholarly overview a summary of political and military events is
followed by separate studies of the Anglo-Saxon Church, government, economy, and
literary heritage.

448   **An Anglo-Saxon and Celtic bibliography (450-1087).**
      Wilfred Bonser.   Oxford: Blackwell, 1957. 574p.
Arranged under twelve broad subject headings, this comprehensive uncritical,
unannotated bibliography of textbooks, monographs, general works, and articles from
learned journals, relating to the period from the Anglo-Saxon invasions to the
compilation of Domesday Book, contains almost 12,000 items noting author and title,
an indication of its scope, and a citation similar to that of a journal article. A separate
Indices volume supplies author, subject, and topographical indexes.

449   **An atlas of Anglo-Saxon England.**
      David Hill.   Oxford: Blackwell, 1981. 180p. maps. bibliog.
Nearly 250 maps cover the political, economic and physical geography of Anglo-Saxon
England within the context of Viking Scandinavia, Iceland and Western Europe,
together with expert commentaries. Noteworthy features include: a long series of maps
documenting Viking invasions; a section covering royal itineraries; chronologies
of kings, princes, and bishops; and a chart of the location of mints and of coins struck
in the period between 871 and 1066.

450   **A history of the Anglo-Saxons.**
      R. H. Hodgkin.   Oxford: Oxford University Press, 1952. 3rd ed.
      2 vols. 34 maps.
Extremely well-documented, with generous illustrations, this general history of the
Anglo-Saxons begins with their tribal origins in Germany and ends with the death of
King Alfred. It encompasses political events, religion and literature, the conversion to
Christianity and the progress of the English Church, the Viking raids and Danish wars,
and the restoration of order and learning. First published in 1935 this third edition

includes an essay by R. L. S. Bruce-Mitford on the Sutton Hoo ship burial. There are also genealogical tables of the Mercian, Kentish, West Saxon, Northumbrian, and East Anglian kings.

451 **Anglo-Saxon settlements.**
Edited by Delia Hooke. Oxford: Blackwell, 1988. 317p.
Fourteen essays by historians, archaeologists, and geographers relate to such topics as settlement chronology, the developing outline of the medieval landscape, the establishment of a network of parishes and counties which lasted virtually unchanged for almost 900 years, place-names evolution, husbandry, and other economic factors.

452 **Anglo-Saxon England.**
Edited by Michael Lapidge. Cambridge, England: Cambridge University Press, 1972- . annual.
Thirteen specialist papers on 'some of the exciting new paths of enquiry which are currently being explored in many different fields of Anglo-Saxon studies – archaeology, legal history, palaeography, Old English syntax and poetic style, Latin classic learning with its many reflexes on Old English literature, and others' are contained in volume twenty of this annual publication (1991. 303p). Also included is a fifty-page bibliography of all books, articles, and signed reviews published in any branch of Anglo-Saxon studies in 1990.

453 **The age of Arthur: a history of the British Isles from 350 to 650.**
John Morris. Chichester, England, 1977. 3 vols. rev. ed. (vol. 1. *Roman Britain and the empire of Arthur*; vol. 2. *The successor states*; vol. 3. *Church, society and the economy*).
First published in 1973, this influential historical assessment of the period between the departure of Rome and the establishment of English, Scottish, and Welsh kingdoms, is complemented by nine volumes of Arthurian Period Sources: *Introduction, notes and index*; *Annals and charters; Ecclesiatics*; *People, places and Saxon archaeology*; *Texts and genealogies*; *John Morris papers 1957-1968* (seven papers dealing with studies on the courses of English Christianity and the chronology of the period); *Gildas*; *Nennius*; and *St. Patrick*. Together these sources provide the documented material upon which knowledge of sub-Roman Britain depends.

454 **The Anglo-Saxon Chronicle: a revised translation.**
Edited by Dorothy Whitelocke. London: Eyre & Spottiswoode, 1961. 240p. bibliog.
The *Anglo-Saxon Chronicle* was first compiled in the reign of King Alfred, possibly at the instigation of the King himself. The most important source for the political history of the period, it survives in the form of seven manuscripts and two fragments. From the tenth century onwards – it continues to 1140 – the manuscripts begin to show discrepancies. This edition is a composite transcription with a modern translation and includes a chronology, a note on its composition and circulation, and genealogies of the chief dynasties and noble houses recorded in the text. Other editions of interest include the version edited by G. N. Garmonsway in Dent's Everyman Library and that edited by Anne Savage (Heinemann, 1982. 288p) which conflates the four major manuscripts with notes on their background and provenance.

Medieval England

455 The minority of Henry III.
D. A. Carpenter. London: Methuen, 1990. 472p. 7 maps. bibliog.
At the time of Henry III's coronation in October 1216 England was on the verge of anarchy. The collapse of the King's authority after John's conflict with the barons boded ill, but the gradual application of the principles of *Magna Carta*, especially that the Great Council (or Parliament) should control the choice of the King's ministers, enabled stable government to continue. This detailed study of a crucial period in English history fully explores the significant constitutional changes being effected.

456 Anglo-Norman England 1066-1166.
Marjorie Chibnall. Oxford: Blackwell, 1986. 240p. 9 maps. bibliog.
This study points to the Reformation movements in the Western Church, the increasing literacy of government, the steady growth in population, and the changing patterns of trade, to account for the interaction between English and Norman institutions and traditions in the years following the Norman Conquest.

457 The reign of Stephen 1135-54: anarchy in England.
H. A. Cronne. London: Weidenfeld & Nicolson, 1970. 313p.
Contending that the traditional perception of Stephen's reign as no more than a period of violence, confusion, and breakdown of government, to be a gross over-simplification, Cronne provides studies on the Royal Household, on the revenues and the coinage, and on law and the administration of justice, to prove that the elaborate machinery of government bequeathed by Henry I to his successor, survived under Stephen, and became the basis for later reforms.

458 William the Conqueror: the Norman impact upon England.
David C. Douglas. London: Eyre & Spottiswoode, 1964. 476p.
2 maps. bibliog.
This extended study investigates how a single province of Gaul was able to conquer an ancient kingdom and effectively alter the political grouping of northwestern Europe with lasting consequences for both England and France.

459 England 1200-1640.
G. R. Elton. Cambridge, England: Sources Of History in association with Cambridge University Press, 1976. 225p.
First published by Hodder & Stoughton in 1969 this bibliographical essay examines the range of materials and sources available for the period. These include narrative histories, official state, church, and legal records, etc., and a chapter on the production and collection of books in medieval England.

460 **The Plantagenet encyclopedia: an alphabetical guide to 400 years of English history.**
Edited by Elizabeth Hallam.   London: Weidenfeld & Nicolson, 1990.
224p. 3 maps. bibliog.

Superbly illustrated, and set unobtrusively within a wider European context, over 1,200 entries provide easily accessible factual information on all aspects of England's history during the period 1100-1485.

461 **The handwriting of English documents.**
L. C. Hector.   Dorking, England: Kohler & Coombes, 1980. 136p.
bibliog.

Furnished with fifty-five document facsimiles and transcripts, this erudite guide to the physical problems of medieval manuscript records encountered by scholars and researchers deals comprehensively with writing surfaces, with Medieval Latin and Anglo-Norman French, with the conventional use of contractions and abbreviations, and with the different styles of handwriting employed.

462 **England in the later Middle Ages: a political history.**
M. H. Keen.   London: Methuen, 1973. 581p. 2 maps. bibliog.

Covering the turbulent period 1290-1485, which witnessed *inter alia* the deposition of Edward II, the usurpation of the throne by Henry IV, the Black Death of 1352, the Peasants Revolt thirty years later, the widespread religious dissent of the Lollards, and the Wars of the Roses, the constant theme of this definitive study is the heavy burden placed on the state by the incessant civil and foreign wars.

463 **Medieval England 1066-1485.**
Edmund King.   Oxford: Phaidon, 1988. 272p. bibliog.

Eighteen 'picture essays' (Domesday Book, University of Oxford, Rochester Castle, Order of the Garter, Robin Hood, etc.) are a feature of this expert overview of all aspects of the political, social, cultural and constitutional changes in England from the Norman invasions to the end of the dynastic wars of the fifteenth century.

464 **The Great Revolt of 1381.**
Charles Oman, introduction and notes by E. B. Fryde.   Oxford:
Clarendon, 1969. rev. ed. 219p. map. bibliog.

Although first published as long ago as 1906 this work still provides the best analysis and the most comprehensive narrative of the events of 1381 when a stringent poll tax excited the first major rebellion by the English labouring classes. The introduction to this edition contains a select bibliography of publications relating to all aspects of the rebellion published since this study first appeared.

465 **The reign of Edward III: crown and political society in England 1327-1377.**
W. M. Ormrod. New Haven, Connecticut: Yale University Press, 1990. 280p.

In contrast to the traditional view that the fourteenth century saw the centralizing policies of the thirteenth century monarchy collapse, Ormrod examines the history of Edward III's reign by focusing in turn on Edward's relations with each section of the active political classes, the ministers and magnates, the clergy, the gentry, and merchants, to rebut the charge that the power and prestige of the Crown declined.

466 **Medieval England.**
Edited by Austin Lane Poole. Oxford: Clarendon, 1958. 2 vols. 661p. bibliog.

The original plan of H. W. C. Davis' *Medieval England* published in 1924 is retained in this completely new and rewritten edition. All aspects of medieval society and its environment are described: the landscape; domestic architecture and town planning; towns and trade; the coinage; civil costume; arms and armour; heraldry; religious life and organization; ecclesiastical architecture; art; learning and education; books and libraries; science; and recreation.

467 **The Batsford companion to medieval England.**
Nigel Saul. London: Batsford, 1983. 283p.

Covering the period from the arrival of William the Conqueror in 1066 to the accession of Henry VII in 1485, this alphabetical compendium brings together short articles on all aspects of medieval society and its visible legacy today. Political, legal, constitutional, cultural, architectural, and ecclesiastical themes are all explored to inform the non-specialist reader.

468 **The first century of English feudalism 1066-1166.**
F. M. Stenton. Oxford: Clarendon, 1961. 2nd ed. 312p.

Based on the Ford Lectures delivered in the University of Oxford in 1929, this work which was first published in 1932 makes a study and assessment of Norman aristocratic society from the Conquest to the later years of the twelfth century. The Lord's household and court, thegns, knight's fees and services, including the castle-guard, are among the topics to receive special attention.

Tudors and Stuarts

469 **England under the Tudors.**
G. R. Elton. London: Routledge, 1991. 3rd ed. 525p. bibliog.

When this detailed narrative of the constitutional problems of Tudor government and politics was first published by Methuen in 1955 it occasioned a stir in academic circles because of its abrupt rejection of some long-held theories and interpretations of Tudor administration. 'Confronted with a choice between writing what I think to be true and repeating what I believe to be doubtful', Elton remarked, 'I could not but choose the former'. Elton is now Regius Professor Emeritus of Modern History in the University of Cambridge.

470 **The Cromwellian gazetteer: an illustrated guide to Britain in the Civil War and Commonwealth.**
Peter Gaunt. Stroud, England: Alan Sutton and The Cromwell Association, 1987. 241p. 8 maps.
County by county, this illustrated gazetteer explores the sites and buildings associated with the Parliamentary rebellion against the Crown 1642-60. The scenes of military conflict, including castles, battlefields, fortified houses and churches, sieges, and other locations significant in the lives of the leading Parliamentary politicians and soldiers, are all included. There is also a detailed chronology of the Cromwell family.

471 **England in the age of Caxton.**
Geoffrey Hindley. London: Granada, 1979. 266p. bibliog.
During William Caxton's lifetime (1422-91), England's economy moved rapidly from being an under-developed country to an industrial exporter. At the same time popular religious dissent entered a literary phase, the English landscape was permanently altered by enclosures, and the English people became aggressively patriotic after the military triumph of Agincourt. Drawn from contemporary sources this social history encompasses all these changes and events and ends with a chapter devoted to the most enduring event of the century, William Caxton's publication of the first English printed book in 1477.

472 **The Civil Wars of England.**
John Kenyon. London: Weidenfeld & Nicolson, 1988. 272p. 11 maps. bibliog.
'How did a small, poor, underpopulated nation, which had no regular army and no evident military tradition later than the fifteenth century, whose manufacturing industry was minuscule, whose parliaments prior to 1640 had insisted time and time again on the poverty of the taxpaying classes – how did this nation raise, equip, pay and sustain very substantial armies, reaching by 1644 a level of well over 30,000 men on each side, fight two civil wars with considerable skill and sophistication. . . .?' (Introduction). In answering this crucial question Kenyon's definitive study covers the military, financial, and political aspects of the English Civil Wars.

473 **Companion to the English Civil Wars.**
Peter Newman. New York, Oxford: Facts On File, 1990. 192p. 5 maps. bibliog.
In this valuable and indispensable historical dictionary over 1,000 entries, ranging between fifty and 200 words in length, define and describe the prominent participants, places and events, and the issues which divided the warring factions. Following the alphabetical section a ten-page list of dates ensures a tight chronological framework.

474 **The fall of the British monarchies 1637-1642.**
Conrad Russell. Oxford: Clarendon, 1991. 550p.

This history of the dramatic political events which led to the final collapse of the royal authority in England, Scotland, and Ireland in the early 1640s uncovers the full extent of Charles I's active participation in these events. Also treated at length are the wily plans of the Scots to further English divisions and the wide effect of the Irish rebellion on the royalist cause.

475 **Shakespeare's England: an account of the life and manners of his age.**
Oxford: Clarendon, 1962. 2 vols. bibliog.

This collection of essays presents a panorama of the lives, preoccupations, and leisure pursuits of the English people as the sixteenth century merged into the seventeenth. In two substantial volumes the different areas covered include religion, the court, the army and navy, voyages and exploration, land travel, education and scholarship, handwriting, commerce and coinage, agriculture and gardens, law, medicine, the sciences, folklore and superstition, the fine arts, heraldry, costume, the home, London, authors and their patrons, booksellers, printers and stationers, actors and acting, the playhouses, sports and pastimes, rogues and vagabonds, ballads and broadsides, and two overviews of the age of Elizabeth and Shakespeare's England. If ever there were a 'golden age' in English history, surely this was the time.

476 **The King's peace.**
C. V. Wedgwood. London: Collins, 1955, 1958. 2 vols. (vol. 1 1637-1641; vol. 2 1641-1647).

This universally-acclaimed narrative history of the Great Rebellion which cost Charles I his head and turned England into a republic fully examines its religious, political, and economic roots. Volume two assiduously follows the fluctuating fortunes of the royal and parliamentary armed forces as they fought to gain the upper hand.

Eighteenth and Nineteenth centuries

477 **British history 1815-1906.**
Norman McCord. Oxford: Oxford University Press, 1991. 544p. bibliog. (Short Oxford History of the Modern World).

This comprehensive political, social, and economic history provides an authoritative and readable account of the period when Britain was transformed from a predominantly rural society to the world's first industrial nation whilst simultaneously building one of the world's greatest empires. Divided into four chronological periods: 1815-1830; 1830-1850; 1850-1880; and 1880-1906, separate chapters in each section discuss the political background, administrative development, and contemporary social and economic issues. Among the major themes that dominated the entire period were the massive increase in population and the consequent widening scope of state activity in all areas of social and economic life.

478 **Victorian Britain: an encyclopedia.**
Edited by Sally Mitchell. New York: Garland, 1988; London:
St. James' Press. 1991. 986p. bibliog.

This massive work includes more than 400 authoritative, signed, cross-referenced
entries, covering individuals, institutions, topics, groups, and artefacts in Great Britain
during the period 1837-1901, each ending with brief bibliographies, and an eleven-page
chronology of events. Its intended purpose 'to serve as an overview and point of entry
into the complex interdisciplinary field of Victorian studies' (Preface) is underlined by
a lengthy annotated bibliography of research materials.

479 **Georgian England: a survey of social life, trades, industries and art from
1700 to 1820.**
A. E. Richardson. London: Batsford, 1931. 202p.

This panoramic survey reconstructs eighteenth-century England: its social scene; the
navy, army, and the church; trade and industry; sports and pastimes; architecture;
building crafts; internal decoration; its decorative arts; painting; sculpture; theatre;
music; and literature.

480 **Johnson's England: an account of the life and manners of the age.**
Edited by A. S. Turberville. Oxford: Clarendon, 1933. 2 vols.
bibliog.

A series of twenty-six descriptive essays depicts eighteenth-century English life in these
two imposing volumes. All aspects of English society and environment are portrayed:
the church; the army and navy; exploration and discovery; travel and communications;
London; town life in the provinces; industry and trade; agriculture and rural life;
poverty, crime and philanthropy; manners and domestic pastimes; sport; costume;
artistic taste; painting and engraving; sculpture, architecture and the garden; house
interiors; drama and the theatre; music; schools and universities; science, mathematics
and astronomy; medicine; law; authors and booksellers; and newspapers.

481 **Early Victorian England 1830-1865.**
Edited by G. M. Young. Oxford: Oxford University Press, 1934.
2 vols.

Work and wages, homes and habits, town life and London, life in the new towns,
country life and sports, the army and navy, the mercantile marine, the press, art and
architecture, music, the drama, holidays and travel, charity, expansion and emigration,
are the subjects treated in this full-scale portrayal of nineteenth-century English life.

Modern England

482   **The people's war: Britain 1939-45.**
Angus Calder.   London: Cape, 1969. 656p. bibliog.

'In 1940 and the years which followed, the people of Britain were protagonists in their own history in a fashion never known before . . . The war was fought with the willing brains and hearts of the most vigorous element in the community, the educated, the skilled, the bold, the active, the young, who worked more and more consciously towards a transformed post-war world' (Introduction). This history describes the effect of the War on all aspects of civilian life in Britain until the break-up of the wartime coalition government.

483   **British history 1945-1987 an annotated bibliography.**
Peter Catterall.   Oxford: Blackwell for the Institute of Contemporary British History, 1990. 843p.

Modelled to some extent on the Royal Historical Society's *Bibliography of British history series* (q.v.) (which it complements for the modern period) this massive work comprises 8,644 annotated entries arranged in fifteen main sections spreading over political and constitutional history, external relations, defence, the legal system, religion, social, economic and environmental history, education, and intellectual and cultural history. Many entries have long strings of further titles embodied so the true number of items included *in toto* is impossible to estimate but clearly it easily runs into five figures. Official publications, specialist articles from academic journals, bibliographies, and appropriate databases are all included. By delineating the existing literature of post-War British history, by its organization of the material, and by highlighting the principal themes and events, Catterall's work is without doubt a major contribution to the study of the period. It was justly awarded *Reference Reviews* Best Generalist Reference Work Prize for 1991.

484   **Contemporary Britain: an annual review.**
Edited by Peter Catterall.   Oxford: Blackwell, 1990- . annual.

Forty-one essays by different authors, analysing and interpreting legislation, reports and initiatives, and the year's events. The essays extend over politics, the media, law and order, external relations, the economy, social policy, society, the environment, religion, culture, and the regions. Peter Catterall is Executive Director of the Institute of Contemporary British History.

485   **Britain on the breadline: a social and political history of Britain between the wars.**
Keith Laybourn.   Gloucester, England: Alan Sutton, 1990. 222p. bibliog.

Unemployment stalked British politics in the 1920s and 1930s. Poverty and ill-health, social policy and housing, the whole economic, social and political impact of unemployment, are analysed in this study which encompasses the General Strike of 1926, the rise of the Labour Party and the decline of the Liberal Party, the appearance of British fascism on the streets of London, and the effect of the Spanish Civil War on public opinion.

486 **The people's peace: British history 1945-1989.**
Kenneth O. Morgan. Oxford: Oxford University Press, 1990. 558p.
bibliog.

Beginning with the 1945 Labour government which introduced social reform and reconstruction, and ending with the arrival of Thatcherism which deliberately sought to reverse Labour's achievements, this comprehensive study examines the transformation of post-War Britain. The fluctuations of the British economy from boom to bust, public disquiet at the ever increasing power of the state, the emergence of widespread personal prosperity measured against a stark social inequality, and coming to terms with the relinquishment of a colonial empire, and a complex relationship with Europe, are some of the dominant themes investigated.

487 **Great Britain since 1914.**
C. L. Mowat. Cambridge, England: Sources of History in association with Cambridge University Press, 1976. 224p.

Recent and contemporary history poses its own documentary problems. Vast quantities of material, including extensive official documentation, the recollections of participants in the events recorded, not including contemporary newspaper accounts, means that some form of bibliographical guidance is unavoidable. This series of essays examine standard and official reference works; cabinet papers; memoirs, diaries, and biographies; contemporary social surveys; audio-visual materials; and specialized categories of historical writing such as economic history, official history, and the history of science.

488 **Edwardian England 1901-1914.**
Edited by Simon Nowell-Smith. London: Oxford University Press, 1964. 619p.

Fifteen essays by separate hands on the Crown, politics, the economy, domestic life, science and thought, reading, art, architecture, the theatre, music, sport, the armed forces, and an Edwardian country childhood, revive Edward VII's England which disappeared and vanished in the maelstrom of the First World War.

489 **Macmillan dictionary of British and European history since 1914.**
Edited by John Stevenson. London: Macmillan, 1991. 437p. bibliog.

Alphabetically-arranged entries on the major events, individuals, political groupings, and issues, of British and European twentieth-century history are included in this compendium which is intended as a source of wide-ranging reference material for history students and teachers. Many of the cross-referenced entries end with recommendations for further reading.

Local history

490 **The book of British topography: a classified catalogue of the topographical works in the library of the British Museum relating to Great Britain and Ireland.**
John P. Anderson. Wakefield, England: E. P. Publishing, 1976. 472p.

First published in 1881, this catalogue contains nearly 14,000 titles relating to the general topography of the British Isles, to its constituent regions, and also to such specific topographical features as antiquities, lakes, railways, rivers and canals, schools, tours, views, and watering places. Although a catalogue of just one collection, the riches of the topographical collections of the British Museum Library virtually transform it into a general catalogue.

491 **A guide to British topographical collections.**
M. W. Barley. London: Council For British Archaeology, 1974. 159p.

Since the first edition of William Camden's *Britannia* in 1586 writers on antiquarian, topographical, or local history subjects have accepted that their printed works should be carefully illustrated. Consequently, Britain now possesses an enviable heritage of drawings of buildings and places. This guide briefly describes collections of topographical illustrations, drawings, prints, and photographs, to be found in public repositories and in a few private collections.

492 **The lost villages of England.**
Maurice Beresford. London: Lutterworth, 1954. 445p.

In this magisterial and well-documented work, now acknowledged as a classic in its chosen field, lost villages are defined as those 'where we have clear evidence of their existence as communities in the Middle Ages: but where we now have no more than (at most) a manor house and a farm and a church'. Archaeological and air reconnaissance evidence is used to describe such villages, and the occasions, motives and locale of their destruction are examined. Advice on how to conduct research and on the principal documentary sources follows. More than 1,000 sites are listed alphabetically by county and are located by a six-figure grid reference from one-inch or six-inch Ordnance Survey maps.

493 **Church and parish: an introduction for local historians.**
J. H. Bettey. London: Batsford, 1987. 174p. bibliog. (Batsford Local History Series).

For local historians the study of church sites and buildings provides valuable insights into the growth, and sometimes decline of local communities. This study serves two purposes: to describe the historic role of the Church in all aspects of community life; and to review the archaeological and architectural evidence, as well as the rich and diverse documentary resources, that may be exploited by the knowledgeable local historian.

494 **English place-names.**
Kenneth Cameron. London: Batsford, 1977. 3rd ed. 258p. bibliog.
2 maps.

The technique of place-name study; Celtic place-names and river names; the Anglo-Saxon kingdoms, shires, hundreds, and wapentakes; the Earliest English settlement names; Scandinavian place-names; the influence of French on English place-names; archaeology; placenames with pagan, mythological and Christian associations; the names of roads, rivers, marshland, hills and valleys, and woods, are all among the topics treated in this compact but comprehensive work.

495 **A companion to local history research.**
John Campbell-Kease. London: Black, 1989. 384p. maps.

First identifying the principal source materials available for the study of local history, indicating where they may conveniently be consulted, and setting local history into the national history context, this companion then proceeds to examine sixteen special topics including geological and geographical factors, archaeological evidence, place and field names, local organizations, heraldry, and chronology. A final section compiles the history of a fictitious locality by way of example. The author is honorary secretary of the Dorset Local History Group and chairman of the county Heraldry and Historical Genealogy Society.

496 **The Darwen County History Series.**
Chichester, England: Phillimore. 1976- . 34 vols.

Introduced by Lord Darwen in the early 1950s, this series was intended to provide concise and readable synopses of each county's history from prehistoric times to the present. It deals with the historic counties as they existed for a thousand years before they were superseded in many instances by the local Government reorganization of 1974. At the end of 1992 only Bedfordshire and Middlesex awaited inclusion in the series.

497 **The concise Oxford dictionary of English place-names.**
Eilert Ekwall. Oxford: Clarendon Press, 1960. 4th ed. 546p. bibliog.

It is now widely recognized that the study of place-names provides otherwise irretrievably lost information not only on the history and antiquities of town and countryside but also of the folklore, religious beliefs, and social conditions of the past. Among the topics encompassed in this standard and authoritative work are the historic and modern forms of over 10,000 place-names, counties, towns, parishes, villages, rivers, lakes, caves, hills, and coastal bays.

498 **Archives and local history.**
F. G. Emmison. Chichester, England: Phillimore, 1974. 2nd ed.
112p.

First published by Methuen in 1966, this basic guide describes the principal groups of local records to be found in county, diocesan, probate, manorial, borough, and national archives and record offices. An introductory chapter indicates relevant books and journals.

499 **English places: sources of information.**
London: British Library, 1979. 12p. (Humanities and Social Sciences
Public Services Reader Guide 6).

This short annotated guide to sources of information on English places in the
collections of Humanities and Social Sciences includes headed paragraphs on general
works and bibliographies, Victoria County History, directories, gazetteers and books
of travel, regional surveys, Domesday Book, buildings, place names, illustrations,
maps and atlases, newspapers and general periodicals, official publications, and
calendars and registers of archives.

500 **Place names of Great Britain and Ireland.**
John Field. Newton Abbot, England: David & Charles, 1980. 208p.
2 maps. bibliog.

Aimed at the general reader, this selective dictionary of 2,000 place-names explains
their derivations and probable meanings. It includes all the largest towns, the counties
and other administrative districts, and others chosen 'because the places are historically
important or otherwise interesting'. Entries give location, meaning, and brief
etymological and historical notes.

501 **The Batsford companion to local history.**
Stephen Friar. London: Batsford, 1991. 432p. maps.

Over 2,000 cross-referenced concise, descriptive and factual entries in dictionary order
are contained in this single-volume quick reference guide. They cover the local history
dimensions of archaeology, architecture, the landscape, history, heraldry, law, the
Church, education, place-names, and transport.

502 **Heraldry for the local historian and genealogist.**
Stephen Friar. Gloucester, England: Alan Sutton, 1992. 271p.
bibliog.

Many local historians are perplexed by heraldic language and conventions. This
delightfully produced work unlocks heraldry's complexities, its origins and significance,
the interpretation of its devices, the systems of marshalling and cadency (affiliation,
marriage and the identification of younger family members), and armory and blazonry,
are all described, explained and illustrated. A sixteen-page glossary adds a welcome
internal reference point.

503 **Latin for local history: an introduction.**
Eileen A. Gooder. London: Longman, 1978. 2nd ed. 173p.

As the study of local history has flourished on an unprecedented scale, so Latin as a
taught subject has drastically diminished as the number of grammar schools has
declined. Yet a knowledge of medieval Latin is almost indispensable in order to
decipher and interpret all types of historical records compiled before the sixteenth
century. This compact self-teaching manual, which originated from a course in Latin
for extramural students, has gained an enviable reputation since it was first published
in 1961. Now substantially revised it includes a formulary of different types of medieval
documents, a list of words likely to be encountered and, for the first time in this
edition, an introduction to Latin palaeography. Its value for those engaged in local
history with little or no Latin can hardly be exaggerated. J. Morris' *A Latin glossary*

for family and local historians (Birmingham, England: Federation of Family History Societies, 1989. 39p.) includes most of the more common Latin words and phrases which occur in parish registers, wills, and other records.

504 Local history and the library.
J. L. Hobbs, revised George A. Carter. London: Deutsch, 1973. 344p.

Public libraries traditionally regard the provision and maintenance of printed and manuscript material associated with their locality as one of their most important services and one which requires specialized knowledge and skills. First published in 1962, and extensively revised and rewritten here, this manual is of immense value to both local historians and librarians as it explores all aspects of local history, its records, and their care and exploitation.

505 Local history in England.
W. G. Hoskins. London: Longman, 1984. 3rd ed. 301p. 12 maps. bibliog.

When first published in 1959 this manual was hailed at the new standard work on the subject. A book of advice and guidance to all those studying local history and topography anywhere in England, and especially those intending to publish their own history of a particular locality, it covers the pre-nineteenth century community; parishes and manors; churches and chapels; the topography and social history of towns; buildings; health, disease and population; and writing and publishing.

506 A handbook of county bibliography: being a bibliography of bibliographies relating to the counties and towns of Great Britain and Ireland.
A. L. Humphreys. Folkestone, England: Dawson, 1974. 501p.

Some 6,000 bibliographies arranged alphabetically by county and sub-divided by individual towns and villages appear in this bibliography which was first published in 1917. It includes manuscript and periodical sources and is an essential reference point for all local history researchers.

507 Particular places: an introduction to English local history.
Christopher Lewis. London: British Library, 1989. 88p. bibliog.

Published to coincide with a major British Library exhibition commemorating the 200th volume in the *Victoria County History* series, this illustrated volume guides the novice local historian in researching the history of a house, school, family, or village. Christopher Lewis is a member of *VCH*'s editorial staff.

508 Local history.
Chris E. Makepeace. In: *Printed reference material and related sources of information*. Edited by Peter W. Lea, Alan Day. London: Library Association, 1990. 3rd ed., p. 230-65. bibliog.

This is both a guide to, and a critical and evaluative commentary on, the diverse range of source material existing for the study of local history. It covers books for beginners; national, private, local and parochial records; and the use of archival sources, newspapers and periodicals, parliamentary papers, directories, genealogical sources, census reports, place-name scholarship, biographical information, maps, photographs, ephemera, and tape-recordings. Six pages of references, citations and further readings lead the reader to further study.

509 **Greater London local history directory and bibliography: a borough by borough guide to local history organisations, their activities and publications, 1983-1987.**
Peter Marcan.   High Wycombe, England: Marcan, 1988. 83p.

Over 300 entries are listed alphabetically within each London Borough in eight categories: municipal collections and museums; historical and archaeological societies; community publishing projects and oral history groups; and amenity conservation societies, with separate sections on family, history societies, organizations spanning more than one Borough, and on record offices in adjacent counties. Based on information supplied by the various organizations involved, entries indicate contact addresses, interests and activities, and recent publications. This directory updates and supplements *London's local history* (2nd ed., 1985) (q.v.).

510 **London's local history an annotated catalogue of publications and resources issued by Greater London local authorities, local historical and archaeological societies, amenity societies and community publishing projects during the 1960's, 1970's and early 1980's, with listings of local history collections, museums, societies and notes on London wide historical societies and library collections.**
Edited by Peter Marcan.   High Wycombe, England: Marcan, 1985. 2nd ed. 58p.

First published in 1983 this guide to resources is supplemented by the editor's *Greater London local history directory and bibliography* (1988) (q.v.).

511 **A dictionary of English place-names.**
A. D. Mills.   Oxford: Oxford University Press, 1991. 388p. 2 maps. bibliog.

Over 12,000 entries describe the meaning and origin of all major English place names; their derivation, their Domesday and other early spellings, tracing their development from their earliest appearance to the present day. An introduction provides a chronology and discusses the various languages employed.

512 **British national archives and the local historian: a guide to official record publications.**
Ann Morton, Gordon Donaldson.   London: Historical Association, 1980. 52p.

This guide advises amateur local historians of the types of material held in the Public Record Office and what sort of information they each contain. Chancery, Exchequer and Judicial records, state papers, and Treasury, Privy Council, and parliamentary archives, are all considered.

513   **Phillimore catalogue 1992.**
Chichester, England: Phillimore, 1992. 40p. annual.
Phillimore's regionally-grouped catalogue provides a useful checklist of their town and county histories and their Domesday Book series. Long-established specialist publishers in local and family histories, Phillimore also distribute British Association for Local History publications.

514   **Exploring urban history: sources for local historians.**
Stephen Porter.   London: Batsford, 1990. 160p. bibliog.
A guide to where primary and secondary source materials can be located, how to interpret them, and how reliable they are, this manual considers their use in thematic sections dealing with the antiquarian and historical background, buildings, population and society, civic administration, the processes of government, and culture and leisure. The period covered stretches from the Tudors to the early twentieth century.

515   **The origin of English place-names.**
P. H. Reaney.   London: Routledge & Kegan Paul, 1960. 277p.
3 maps. bibliog.
Many English place-names are easy to explain but for others more than one interpretation is possible, indeed, some have successfully defied all attempts to interpret them. In an effort to dispel the rampant mythologies that bedevil popular and journalistic derivations, this book indicates to the general reader how a knowledge of philology and languages is essential for a correct historical interpretation. Successive chapters illustrate the ways in which the Celtic, Anglo-Saxon, Scandinavian, French and Latin languages have all left their mark on the English landscape.

516   **The local historian's encylopaedia.**
John Richardson.   New Barnet, England: Historical Publications,
1986. 263p. bibliog.
Divided into twenty sections this encyclopedic dictionary, which was first published in 1974, defines and explains the specialist terms encountered in local history research. The topics covered include land and agriculture; local communities; taxes and services; archives, documents and printed records; palaeography; museums, libraries and record offices; organizations and societies; genealogy; education; social welfare; law and order; utilities; roads and transport; religion; coins and tokens; the Militia; architecture and housing; archaeology; trades and occupations; and heraldry.

517   **Local history: a handbook for beginners.**
Philip Riden.   London: Batsford, 1983. 175p. bibliog.
A simple introduction to the study of local history for part-time amateurs with no previous experience of historical research, this useful work looks at the materials to be found in local libraries and record offices, investigates the importance of local maps, considers the evidence of buildings and the landscape, explores the resources of the Public Record Office and other national collections, and ends with practical hints on how to write and publish a local history.

518 **Record sources for local history.**
Philip Riden. London: Batsford, 1987. 253p. bibliog.

This detailed guide to archival sources available in England and Wales ranges from the eleventh century to the reform of local government in the 1970s. An introductory chapter concentrates on what is available either locally or centrally, where it is likely to be found, and on what aids to locating information exist. This is followed by a chronological survey of local and central government records from Domesday Book onwards.

519 **Dictionary of place-names in the British Isles.**
Adrian Room. London: Bloomsbury, 1988. 414p. bibliog.

The origins and derivations of over 4,000 familiar place-names are clearly explained in this dictionary which also includes an essay which discusses the role and lore of placenames, their sources, naming patterns, and a study of the word elements found in them. Room's *A concise dictionary of modern place-names in Great Britain and Ireland* (Oxford: Oxford University Press, 1983. 148p.) is a selective survey of over 1,000 post-1500 place names.

520 **Maps and plans for the local historian and collector: a guide to maps of the British Isles produced before 1914 valuable to local and other historians and mostly available to collectors.**
David Smith. London: Batsford, 1988. 240p. bibliog.

This detailed survey of cartographic sources available to local historians encompasses parliamentary deposited plans; estate, enclosure and title plans; regional and county, drainage, military and Ordnance Survey, and transport and communications maps; marine charts; parish; and urban plans; plans of London; and industrial and other thematic maps. In addition to a general bibliography there is a separate, three-page county bibliography of articles printed in county antiquarian and other learned society journals.

521 **A reader's guide to the place-names of the United Kingdom: a bibliography of publications (1920-89) on the place-names of Great and Northern Ireland, the Isle of Man, and the Channel Islands.**
Jeffrey Spittall, John Field. Stamford, England: Watkins, 1990. 341p.

This comprehensive bibliography, which includes all major works published between 1920 and 1989 and certain earlier titles, is arranged by county under area sub-divisions. It has an introduction on the history and development of place-name studies and ends with appendices on noteworthy publications (1850-1920), works on British place-names transferred abroad, and on Arthurian place-names.

522 **Sources for local history: studies in the use of historical evidence.**
W. B. Stephens. Cambridge, England: Cambridge University Press, 1981. 2nd ed. 342p. (Sources of History).

First published by Manchester University Press in 1973 this is an indispensable research tool both for beginners and experts. It takes the form of a detailed examination of the documentary sources for those areas of study which most frequently attract attention: population and social structure; local government and politics; poor relief and charities; prices and wages; industry and trade; agriculture; education; and religion.

523 **Manorial records.**
Dennis Stuart. Chichester, England: Phillimore, 1992. 160p.
For centuries the manor was the main unit of local government. Once the local historian has researched its history and development back beyond the mid-sixteenth century manorial records constitute his most reliable source of information. This manual is a comprehensive guide to their use, providing explanations of the nature of manorial court rolls, rentals and extents, accounts and custumals along with the Latin vocabulary used. A full glossary of all words normally found in manorial documents is of enormous help in their use.

524 **Survey of English place-names Series.**
English Place-Name Society. Cambridge, England: Cambridge University Press, 1924- .
The English Place-Name Society was formed in 1923 to carry out a survey of English place-names and to issue annual volumes publishing the results of these county by county surveys. Each volume contains a list of county names listed by hundred (a medieval local government administrative unit) with full notes on linguistic forms and derivations. Over sixty volumes have been published to date. Vol. one, part one, *Introduction to the survey of English place-names* (1924), and vol. one, part two, *Chief elements used in English place-names* are valuable sources of information.

525 **The parish chest: a study of the records of parochial administration in England.**
W. E. Tate. Chichester, England: Phillimore, 1983. 3rd ed. 369p. bibliog.
This almost indispensable guide to ecclesiatical and civil parish institutions and records was first published in 1946. Among local historians it enjoys an incomparable reputation for its wide coverage and detailed analyses. It includes a list of county and other major record offices.

526 **A bibliographical account of the principal works relating to English topography.**
W. Upcott. Wakefield, England: E. P. Publishing, 1978. 1,576p.
First published in 1818 in three volumes, this massive work describes and analyses some 1,500 general topographic works and county histories. Although its coverage is uneven in places it remains a well-respected reference resource.

527 **The Victoria history of the counties of England.**
London: Oxford University Press for the Institute of Historical Research, 1900- . maps. bibliog.
More usually known as the *Victoria County History*, this ambitious project was launched in 1899 to narrate the history of the English counties in a uniform and systematic way. At first it was thought that some 160 volumes would see the project completed within six years but it still remains unfinished although 180 substantial volumes, including a few index or bibliographic volumes, have now been published. Each county set consists of 'general' and 'topographical' volumes. The general volumes include those subjects considered suitable for county-wide treatment; prehistory, ecclesiastical and economic history, and a translation of the appropriate section from

the Domesday Book, whilst the topographical volumes describe individually each city, town or village within the county. Some county sets are complete in two or three volumes, others are still in progress, not a few are dormant, whilst Northumberland, Westmorland, and Yorkshire West Riding have still to be attempted. A *General introduction* (1970, 281p.) contains a history of the project, a list of the volumes published thus far, and the contents of all volumes together with author and title indexes. *Supplement to the General Introduction* (1989, 64p.) lists and indexes the fifty volumes published in the interim period. For the latest state of play it is necessary to consult Christopher Elrington's 'The Victoria County History', *The Local Historian*, vol. 22, no. 3, (Aug. 1992), p. 128-37 which sounds a warning about the project's future funding and estimates it will be at least another ninety years before the *VCH* is completed.

528 **Town records.**
John West. Chichester, England: Phillimore, 1983. maps. bibliog.
Combining a gazetteer of local sources of information, giving for each town the dates of its incorporation, present status, population, and the location of its archives, and a manual of municipal history and the types of records town administration has generated, this book is indispensable in its field. Among the records examined are medieval borough charters, gild and borough ordinances, town maps and plans, commercial directories, provincial newspapers, and the national censuses.

529 **Village records.**
John West. London: Macmillan, 1962. 208p. bibliog.
This collection of practical exercises for the amateur historian comprises studies on Saxon charters, Domesday Book, manorial court rolls, lay subsidy rolls, manorial extents, county maps, parish records, quarter sessions papers, inventories and wills, hearth tax returns, enclosure awards and maps, land tax and title records, and turnpike trust records. For village historians with little or no expertise who are embarking on projects this book will be a much needed eye-opener.

Domesday geography of England.
See item no. 59.

Historiography

530 **Recent historians of Great Britain: essays on the post-1945 generation.**
Edited by Walter L. Arnstein. Ames, Iowa: Iowa State University Press, 1990. 207p. bibliog.
It is the contention of this collection of essays that the late 1940s to the early 1970s constituted a golden age of British history. In this light eight historians assess the life, career, published works, and achievements of G. R. Elton, Joel Hurstfield, Christopher Hill, Lawrence Stone, J. H. Plumb, E. P. Thompson, Norman Gash, and F. S. L. Lyons.

531 **The First World War and British military history.**
Edited by Brian Bond. Oxford: Clarendon, 1991. 330p. bibliog.
The first systematic study of the historiography of the First World War, this collection
of eleven essays explores its themes and conclusions, many of them controversial,
which continue to excite interest not only in military strategy and tactics and the
political direction of the war, but also in the changing historical perspectives evident in
the diverse approaches of successive military historians.

532 **A liberal descent: Victorian historians and the English past.**
J. W. Burrow. Cambridge, England: Cambridge University Press,
1981. 308p.
The mid-nineteenth century witnessed a brilliant flowering of English narrative history.
This study concentrates on four major historians whose principal works focused on
crucial periods and themes in the building of England as a nation: E. A. Freeman's
History of the Norman Conquest (6 vols., 1867-79); J. A. Froude's *The history of
England from the fall of Wolsey to the defeat of the Spanish Armada* (12 vols., 1856-70);
T. B. Macaulay's *History of England from the accession of James II* (1848-55); and
William Stubbs' *The constitutional history of England in its origin and development*
(3 vols., 1874-78).

533 **Modern historians on British history 1485-1985: a critical bibliography
1945-1969.**
G. R. Elton. London: Methuen, 1970. 239p.
A personal commentary on the writings of his contemporaries, this bibliography was
compiled because publications in this area need to be re-examined in the light of the
material now available and the more precise methods of inquiry now adopted by
professional historians. It is arranged into thirteen chronological and thematic sections.

534 **Historical writing in England.**
Antonia Gransden. London: Routledge & Kegan Paul, 1974-82.
2 vols. (vol. 1. *c. 550 – c.1307*. 1974. 610p. vol. 2. *c.1307 to the early
sixteenth century*. 1982. 644p. bibliog.).
These two volumes form an extremely well-documented survey of early and late
medieval chronicles, annals, and local histories of prime importance in English
historiography. Both volumes have a chronological index of the principal literary
sources for English history in the medieval period.

535 **The evolution of British historiography: from Bacon to Namier.**
Edited by J. R. Hale. London: Macmillan, 1967. 380p. bibliog.
This historiographical overview opens with a lengthy critical analysis which examines
British historical writing as it developed from the end of the sixteenth century onwards
and provides a look back at the methods and purposes of the medieval historians. Its
main contents take the form of a representative sample of extracts from the published
works of twenty-one British historians which illustrate their individual contribution to
the historian's craft.

536 **The British Marxist historians: an introductory analysis.**
Harvey J. Kaye.   Cambridge, England: Polity Press in association with
Basil Blackwell, Oxford. 1984. 316p. bibliog.

Maurice Dobb and the debate on the transition to capitalism; Rodney Hilton on
feudalism and the English peasantry; Christopher Hill on the English Revolution; Eric
Hobsbaum on workers, peasants, and world history; and E. P. Thompson on the
making of the English working class, are the historians and themes explored in this
study.

537 **The history men: the historical profession in England since the
Renaissance.**
John Kenyon.   London: Weidenfeld & Nicolson, 1983. 322p.

Based partly on a series of articles for the *Observer Magazine* on great historians, this
study places individual historians in their contemporary class, political, religious
contexts, and also notes the professional animosities they indulged in. The
development of the study history in the universities, and the results of historical
research over the last hundred years in such fruitful areas of study as the Tudor
revolution in government, the absolutism of the Stuarts, and the work of R. H.
Tawney in social history, are also explored in depth.

538 **Humanism and history: origins of modern English historiography.**
Joseph M. Levine.   Ithaca, New York: Cornell University Press, 1987.
297p. bibliog.

How the new learning influenced the course of English historical study is the principal
theme of this masterly study. Among the major topics treated at length are Caxton's
histories; the attempt to disentangle fact from fiction at the close of the Middle Ages;
and the tracing of the transformation of amateur antiquarian studies into embryonic
scientific archaeology during the period from 1500 to 1800.

539 **Dark Age Britain: some sources of history.**
Henry Marsh.   Newton Abbot, England: David & Charles, 1970.

This study examines the most important British and English historians to shed light on
the history of Britain from the first English incursions to the reign of Alfred the Great.
These include Gildas, Nennius, the *Anglo-Saxon chronicle*, Bede, and Geoffrey of
Monmouth. There is also a useful note on the history of the texts and their
translations.

540 **English historical literature in the fourteenth century.**
John Taylor.   Oxford: Clarendon, 1987. 349p. bibliog.

Designed as a guide to the principal historical literature sources of fourteenth century
England, the last period of significant monastic chronicle writing, this study examines
the background and identity of the chronicle writers, the problems they encountered,
and the audience for whom they wrote. Because of their importance to English
historiography of the period several French chronicles also come under scrutiny.

Monarchy

541 **The Royal Encyclopedia.**
Edited by Ronald Allison, Sarah Riddell.   London: Macmillan, 1991.
632p. bibliog.
With unprecedented access to Buckingham Palace files, notably those built up over
forty years in the Press Office, and with much of the text written by members of the
Royal Household, this alphabetically-arranged encyclopedia enjoys quasi-official
status. Its 10,000 entries provide a comprehensive record and portrait of the present
Royal Family as well as articles on the constitution, the Commonwealth, the
responsibilities and duties of the Sovereign, royal pageantry and ceremonial, the royal
palaces and parks, and royal protocol, etc. The main emphasis is on the twentieth
century although, where necessary, all topics are placed in a full historical context.
Included among the twenty-three appendices are the Queen's antecedents, the burial
places of all English sovereigns, the Princes of Wales and Princess Royals, the foreign
orders and decorations held by the present Royal Family, their appointments in the
armed Forces, and the Royal gala film performances. This work is truly described as
'the complete guide to every royal subject . . . for every royal subject'.

542 **The crown jewels.**
Edited by Claude Blair.   London: HMSO, 1993. 2 vols.
Unquestionably the most scholarly historical account of the Crown Jewels ever to be
published, this splendidly produced two volume boxed set contains a general history of
coronations and coronation ritual, a history of English coronations before and after the
Commonwealth period, and an illustrated catalogue of the treasures in the Jewel
House at the Tower of London; the regalia, swords, plate, and the Coronation robes.
Tessa Rose's *The crown jewels of England* (HMSO. 1992. 128p.), a shorter guide for
the general reader, is based on this main work although it was published first.

543 **Royal faces: from William the Conqueror to the present day.**
Dana Bentley-Cranch. London: HMSO, 1990. 2nd ed. 67p.

Prepared from coins, effigies and death masks, illuminated manuscripts, painted panels, portraits and miniatures, stained glass windows, and photographs, this handsome National Portrait Gallery publication includes a general historical introduction and a short history of each reign.

544 **Royal Britain.**
Edited by Michael Butler. Basingstoke, England: Automobile Association, 1976. 216p.

Produced in co-operation with the British Tourist Authority, and with introductory information of the Queen's silver jubilee, the Royal Family, the grand occasions, the pomp and majesty, royal visits overseas etc., the main section of this descriptive and illustrated guide is devoted to tours throughout the realm based on places closely associated with the monarchy since the beginnings of recorded history.

545 **The Oxford illustrated history of the British monarchy.**
John Cannon, Ralph Griffiths. Oxford: Oxford University Press, 1988. 727p. 7 maps. bibliog.

Undoubtedly one of the most authoritative and comprehensive historical accounts of the Monarchy ever published for the general reader, this is both a study of the merging political and constitutional role of the Crown from the Dark Ages of the fifth century onwards, and a biographical commentary on individual kings and queens. There is no evidence of the cloying sentimentality which sometimes afflicts books on 'the Royals', although the widespread respect and affection the monarchy commands today is acknowledged and explained. There are genealogies of all the royal lines from Egbert, King of Wessex, who reigned from 802 to 839, and a list of English kings from Alfred the Great.

546 **Royal mistresses.**
Charles Carlton. London: Routledge, 1991. 208p.

For centuries members of Britain's royal houses have notoriously engaged in irregular liaisons with persons of the same or opposite sex. Sometimes merely providing unseemly tittle-tattle, at others possessing significant practical and constitutional implications, these liaisons have occasionally endangered the monarchy itself. This study is serious in purpose and it avoids unrewarding prurience.

547 **Kings and Queens of England and Great Britain.**
Eric R. Delderfield, Antony J. Lambert. Newton Abbot, England: David & Charles, 1990. 192p. bibliog.

The lineage and character of all reigning monarchs from the early Saxons to Queen Elizabeth II, and the principal events of their reigns, provide a royal background to English history. With the help of outline genealogical tables, the successive royal dynasties and the present line of succession are clearly indicated, and there is also an informative section on past and present royal residences.

548 The jewels of Queen Elizabeth II her personal collection.
Leslie Field. London: Thames & Hudson, 1992. 129p.
Published to coincide with a major Victoria and Albert exhibition, 'Sovereignty: a celebration of 40 years', this authoritative volume traces the 400 years' history of the British monarchy's family jewels. Bracelets and brooches, earrings, necklaces, tiaras, whether in diamonds, pearls, emeralds, rubies, or sapphires, are all included.

549 The lives of the Kings & Queens of England.
Edited by Antonia Fraser, Heraldic consultant J. P. Brook-Little.
London: Weidenfeld & Nicholson, 1975. 360p.
More than 900 years of English history are covered in this generously-illustrated volume which contains brief biographies of all forty occupants of the English throne since 1066. Even today English political and constitutional history is marked by its division into individual reigns, a practice that may still be justified when considering how the personalities of the various monarchs exerted an indelible influence on events.

550 The Monarchy and the British people: 1760 to the present.
J. M. Golby, A. W. Purdue. London: Batsford, 1988. 144p.
Starting in 1760 with the accession of George III, largely due to the fact that it was during his reign that the political power of the Crown diminished, this engaging study explores how the social significance and influence of the Royal Family has increased. The styles of successive monarchs as they attempted to come to terms with the roles demanded of them by changes in society, ending with the conflict between maintaining a proper royal reticence and dignity, and the danger of the Royal Family being presented as 'showbiz', are brought sharply into focus.

551 A guide to Royal Britain.
Leicester, England: Magna Books, 1984. 256p. 8 maps.
This sumptuously-illustrated volume is all that the committed 'royal-watcher' could wish for. Basically, this work takes the form of an atlas which encompasses a descriptive gazetteer to over 750 places that claim a significant contemporary or historical royal association, it also traces the rise of the British monarchy from its Saxon beginnings, and describes at length the role of the 'Royal Firm' today. There are special features on such topics as Royal heraldry, the Orders of Chivalry, Royal homes, the origins of Royal titles etc., which give a better understanding of the pomp and ceremony that is now inseparable from the political, social, and constitutional role of the Crown.

552 Royal fortune: tax, money and the monarchy.
Philip Hall. London: Bloomsbury, 1991. 241p.
This scholarly account of the royal finances, which is guaranteed to anger both ardent monarchists and fervent republicans, begins with the glorious revolution of 1688. But the most controversial aspect is its uncovering of the secret deal between Crown and Government at some undisclosed date between 1937 and 1952 whereby taxation on the monarch's personal investment income ended. Public unease on this point is not confined to anti-royalists especially as the Queen is generally accepted as the wealthiest person in England. This book may well prove to be something of a landmark in the modern history of the Royal Family. Certainly, the Queen later advised the Prime Minister that in future her personal income should be taxed although this did not

entirely allay public disquiet because of the uncertainty surrounding what her personal income comprised.

553   The political influence of the British monarchy 1868-1952.
Frank Hardie.   London: Batsford, 1970. 224p. bibliog.

This serious study of the declining political influence of the reigning monarch, from Queen Victoria to George VI, underlines their surviving constitutional importance.

554   Buckingham Palace.
John Harris, Geoffrey de Bellaigue, Oliver Millar.   London: Nelson, 1968. 320p.

First built as a comparatively modest house for the first Duke of Buckingham in the seventeenth century, Buckingham Palace has become not only a royal residence but a world renowned repository of works of art and other treasures. This lavishly-illustrated volume contains three authoritative essays on the Palace's architecture, its works of art, and its paintings.

555   The English regalia: their history, custody and display.
Martin Holmes, H. D. W. Sitwell.   London: HMSO, 1972. 83p.

This authoritative study outlines the history of the Crown Jewels and Coronation regalia, traditionally housed in the Tower of London, from the lost regalia of Edward the Confessor, which was destroyed in the English Civil War, to the seventeenth-century crown and sceptre that replaced it, and the later crowns and pieces used in the 1937 and 1953 coronations.

556   The royal palaces.
Philip Howard.   London: Hamish Hamilton, 1970. 276p. bibliog.

For centuries many of the dramatic diplomatic, dynastic, political, religious, and military events in English history took place in or close to the King's palaces. This survey of the private and public life of the Tower of London, Windsor Castle, Whitehall, the Palace of Westminster, Buckingham Palace, Hampton Court, St. James' Palace, Greenwich, Brighton Pavilion, and others, not only relates the significant episodes of English history that occurred there, but also enquires into why these palaces were built, and for what purpose, as well as examining such questions as what they were like to live in for the Royal household.

557   The Independent London News Royal Issue.
London: ILN Group, 1842- . 7 issues a year.

In response to readers' requests for more royal news and greater coverage of royal events, the *ILN* has since 1986 produced a special royal issue every year. The 1992 issue (*Royal issue 1992*. 90p.) includes essays on how state sovereignty and rule by consent are successfully reconciled in Britain; on Kensington Palace; on royalty's long cherished interest in alternative medicine; on royal portrait painters; and on a fifth century Welsh warlord who could be the legendary King Arthur.

558 **Queens of Britain.**
Norah Lofts.   London: Hodder & Stoughton, 1977. 192p.
Short illustrated biographical histories of Queens regnant, and royal consorts, from
Boadicea onwards, focus on the political and dynastic problems they faced.

559 **The Oxford book of royal anecdotes.**
Edited by Elizabeth Longford.   Oxford: Oxford University Press,
1980. 546p. bibliog.
This guided tour through the tangled history of the British monarchy is made by means
of a collection of anecdotes which is based on unimpeachable source material and
welded together by magisterial editorial interpolations.

560 **The Royal House of Windsor.**
Elizabeth Longford.   London: Weidenfeld & Nicholson, 1990. new ed.
288p. bibliog.
Three years after the outbreak of the First World War intense anti-German feeling
persuaded George V to announce that the Royal Family would cease to be known as
the house of Saxe-Coburg-Gotha and would henceforth assume the name of Windsor.
First published in 1974, this updated history chronicles the eventful years of the
Windsor dynasty since 1917 and examines the changing role of the Monarchy as part of
the constitutional, political, and social fabric of the nation.

561 **Chronicle of the Royal Family.**
Edited by Derrik Mercer.   London: Chronicle Communications, 1981.
624p.
The fourth of the major *Chronicle* titles to be published in Britain, this generously-
illustrated encyclopedic work follows the distinctive *Chronicle* pattern of reporting
historical events as if they had just happened. An introductory section, 'From tribes to
Kingdoms', traces the monarchy's beginnings to the year 850 AD from which point the
main chronicle takes the story forward to the modern monarchy, using diaries, official
biographies, and other sources, to give the most detailed treatment of the triumphs and
tragedies surrounding the throne in the twentieth century. An appendix provides a
descriptive gazetteer of all past and present royal palaces and residences whilst an
accompanying wall-chart displays the main lines of succession of the royal houses of
England and Scotland.

562 **The Queen's pictures.**
Oliver Millar.   London: Weidenfeld & Nicolson and the British
Broadcasting Corporation, 1977. 240p.
Established by the Kings and Queens of England from the Tudors onwards, the royal
collection of about 5,000 paintings is the property of the Crown held in trust for the
nation by The Queen and administered under the supervision of the Lord
Chamberlain. Thoroughly researched, well documented, with fifty colour and 250
black-and-white illustrations, this authoritative work traces its history and growth
under successive monarchs. Published on the occasion of the Queen's Silver jubilee, it
presents an account of acquisitions made since 1953, especially the Queen's collection
of miniatures, incontestably the largest in the world.

563 **The Royal line of succession.**
Patrick W. Montague-Smith. London: Pitkin Pictorials, 1972. 24p.

First published in 1952 and frequently reprinted in new covers, this colourfully illustrated, highly informative, and inexpensive booklet includes an introductory essay on the continuity of kingship and contains thirteen annotated genealogical tables charting the descent of the English Kings and their relationship with the Kings of Scotland, the Sovereign Princes of Wales, and the Kings of Ireland, from the sixth century onwards. Montague-Smith was consulting editor of *Debrett's Peerage*.

564 **Armorial bearings of the sovereigns of England.**
W. J. Petchey. London: Bedford Square Press, 1977. 2nd ed. 32p. bibliog.

This booklet traces the development of royal heraldry as it relates to English history and provides a summary of the changes in the sovereign's shields of arms, crests, supporters, badges, and mottoes.

565 **Royal heritage: the story of Britain's royal builders and collectors.**
J. H. Plumb. London: British Broadcasting Corporation, 1977. 360p.

Published to accompany a BBC television series this attractively-produced work shows how the royal art collections and buildings reflect the tastes and interests of successive monarchs from medieval times onwards. Paintings, miniatures, and drawings in the royal art collection, French furniture of the eighteenth century, porcelain and glass, jewels, postage stamps, bronzes, and royal palaces and strongholds are all featured.

566 **The Royal Maundy.**
Brian Robinson. London: Kaye & Ward, 1977.

The Royal Maundy is an annual service held on Maundy Thursday, the day before Good Friday. Part of the ancient service, which has its roots in the beginnings of the Christian church, is the distribution of monetary gifts by the monarch or her representative. This Maundy money is now increasingly regarded as a very desirable collectors' item. Numismatists especially will appreciate this comprehensive survey which examines the origins of Maundy money, the present-day ceremony, and the coins' value as collectors' pieces. Some readers may care to obtain a copy of Peter A. Wright's colourful booklet, *The pictorial history of the Royal Maundy* published by Pitkin Pictorials.

567 **The Crown Jewels of England.**
Tessa Rose. London: HMSO for The Tower of London, 1992. 128p.

Based on *The history of the Crown Jewels: a catalogue of the treasures of Jewel House* edited by Claude Blair (q.v.), this short guide for the general reader focuses on regalia used in the Coronation ceremony. The main topics discussed are the making of Kings; the establishment of a Coronation regalia; the symbols of kingship; the devices of ritual; and Coronation Day. Colonel Sir Thomas Butler's *The Crown Jewels and Coronation Ceremony* (Andover, England: Pitkin, 1989. 24p) is a descriptive colour booklet of individual pieces used at the Coronation.

568   **Sovereign legacy: an historical guide to the British monarchy.**
William Seymour.   London: Sidgwick & Jackson, 1979. 331p.
The salient historical facts of each reign, and short character sketches of each monarch,
from the Anglo-Saxon kings to George VI, cover 1,500 years of royal history. Each
chapter ends with a gazetteer of royal castles, churches, palaces that have survived and
can still be seen or visited.

569   **Lives of the Queens of England from the Norman Conquest.**
Agnes Strickland.   Bath, England: Cedric Chivers, 1972. 8 vols.
Intended for general readers inclined to history and biography Strickland's *Lives* were
first published in twelve volumes, 1840 to 1848. Finding a ready niche between
pedantic works of scholarship and over-imaginative historical novels, well-researched,
and with considerable narrative skill, they met with instant success, and were reprinted
many times. These facsimile reprint volumes were published at the request of The
London and Home Counties Branch of The Library Association because of constant
public library demand.

570   **Britain's royal families: the complete genealogy.**
Alison Weir.   London: Bodley Head, 1989. 386p. bibliog.
Described as not so much a family tree, more a family forest, this gigantic royal
genealogy descends from King Egbert who reigned *circa* 800 to Queen Elizabeth II,
comprehending both the English and Scottish royal families. Essays on the various
royal houses, coats of arms, and short bibliographies on each reigning monarch are
also included in this ingenious work of genealogical research.

571   **Debrett's Kings and Queens of Britain.**
David Williamson.   Exeter, England: Webb & Bower, 1986. 240p.
bibliog.
This comprehensive and illustrated appraisal of the monarchs of England, from the
early Celtic and Saxon Kings, to the House of Windsor, within the context of their own
times, shows how their actions were influenced and affected by their heredity,
environment, and contemporary political scheming. Twenty-two genealogical tables,
starting with 'Descendants of Woden', and ending with 'The descent of the Royal
Family from Irish Kings', prevent any errors of identification.

Biography

572 **The biographical dictionary of British feminists: Vol. 1: 1800-1930:**
Vol. 2: A supplement 1900-1945.
Olive Banks.   Hemel Hempstead, England: Harvester Wheatsheaf,
1985-90. 2 vols.

General biographical dictionaries often disregard all but the most eminent of feminist
leaders and even those who are admitted may be misrepresented and scant attention
given to their feminist activities. These two volumes print biographical essays on those
women, and occasionally men, who devoted their time, effort, and money, and
sometimes their health and happiness, to promoting the progress of the feminist
movement.

573 **The Sunday Times book of the rich: Britain's 400 richest people.**
P. Beresford.   London: Weidenfeld & Nicolson, 1990. 336p.

These biographical and career profiles narrating how their subjects obtained their
money, how they live, and how they maintain their power, are divided up in four
categories according to just how rich they are reputed to be. They descend from
billionaires with estimated fortunes of over £1,000 million, through the super rich (£100
million) and the very rich (£50 million), to mere millionaires (£20 million).

574 **Modern English biography containing many thousand concise memoirs**
of persons who have died between the years 1851-1900 with an index of
the most interesting matter.
Frederic Boase.   London: Frank Cass, 1965. 6 vols.

First published in Truro by Netherton & Worth (1892-1921), and based on research in
local newspapers, parish registers, and transactions of learned societies, this celebrated
work includes some 30,000 short biographical sketches of persons 'who achieved any
public importance whatsoever' and who died between 1851 and 1900. In most instances
the biographies are accompanied by a note of the particular sources used, details of
portraits, theatre performances, publications, and other facts sometimes omitted in

larger works of reference. *Index to biographies of women in Boase's Modern English biography* (Edinburgh: Peter Bell, 1986, 30p.) identifies 1,130 'female' entries.

575 British biographical index.
London: K. G. Saur, 1990. 4 vols.

Including 170,000 names ranging from the little-known to the very famous this must be the largest and most comprehensive single listing of British biographical information ever compiled. Each entry provides basic biographical detail plus a list of citations from 324 English language biographical reference works originally published 1601-1929 covering every aspect of British biography. However, the *Dictionary of national biography* and *Who's who* are excluded. Besides standing as a reference work in its own right the *Index* also acts as an entry into the publisher's *British biographical archive*, which is available on 1400 × 1:24 negative microfiches.

576 The Europa biographical dictionary of British women: over 1,000 notable women from Britain's past.
Edited by A. Crawford (et al.).   London: Europa, 1983. 436p.

Biographical details and the publications of over 1,000 women 'whose place in history is recognized', and 'whose work has had some sort of public impact', from the age of Boadicea to the present day, are contained in this biographical dictionary compiled by a team of six editors and eighty other contributors. It includes many women, such as the 'feminist' writers of the seventeenth and eighteenth centuries, and the suffragettes of a later period, who attempted to expand women's involvement in public affairs.

577 A dictionary of Edwardian biography.
Edinburgh: Peter Bell, 1987- . 36 vols.

First published by the Brighton publishers, W. T. Pike, in thirty-three county volumes (1898-1912), this reprint series omits the topographical material which had been originally included. Each volume consists of some 500 detailed and illustrated biographical sketches of local figures classified under occupational and professional headings.

578 **The dictionary of national biography.**
Oxford: Oxford University Press, 1885- . *The dictionary of national biography from the earliest times to 1900*. Edited by Sir Leslie Stephen, Sir Sidney Lee. Originally published London: Smith, Elder, 63 vols., 1885-1900. *First supplement*, 3 vols., 1901. *The twentieth century DNB 1901-1911*. Edited Sir Sidney Lee. 1912. 2,088p. *DNB 1912-1921*. Edited by H. W. C. Davis, J. R. H. Weaver. 1927. 623p. *DNB 1922-1930*. Edited by J. R. H. Weaver. 1937. 962p. *DNB 1931-1940*. Edited by L. G. Wickham Legg. 1949. 968p. *DNB 1941-1950*. Edited by L. G. Wickham Legg. 1959. 1,0312p. *DNB 1951-1960*. Edited by E. T. Williams, Helen M. Palmer. 1971. 1,150p. *DNB 1961-1970*. Edited by E. T. Williams, C. S. Nicholls. 1981. 1,170p. *DNB 1971-1980*. Edited by Lord Blake, C. S. Nicholls. 1986. 1,010p. *DNB 1981-1985*. Edited by Lord Blake, C. S. Nicholls. 1990. 608p. *DNB Missing persons*. Edited by C. S. Nicholls. 1993. 800p.

This vast collective biography of the influential and the élite in all fields of human endeavour was founded in 1882 'to supply full, accurate, and concise biographies of all noteworthy inhabitants of the British Isles and the Colonies (exclusive of living persons) from the earliest historical period to the present time'. Contributors as eminent as their subjects now join forces with a team of *DNB* staff writers to record the lives and achievements of such persons and to list their sources (often quoting 'personal knowledge') in authoritative and substantial essays. A gaping hole in *DNB*'s coverage, namely the inability in the programme to rectify serious omissions once the decennial supplements were published, is filled with the publication of a missing persons volume which includes 1,086 such people from all periods and occupation. The *Concise dictionary of national biography* (3 vols., 1992) presents the 36,500 lives so far included in a single chronological sequence. *DNB*'s antecedents and its early publishing history are admirably chronicled in J. L. Kirby's 'The Dictionary of National Biography', *Library Association Record*, vol. 60, no. 6 (June 1958), p. 181-91.

579 **People of today.**
Edited by Patricia Ellis.   London: Debrett's Peerage, 1992. 5th ed. 2,324p.

First published in 1988 as *Debrett's distinguished people of today*, itself the successor to *Debrett's handbook*, this biographical dictionary includes over 41,000 sketches of the most influential people from the highest echelons of British society. Revised annually, the entries outline their subjects' career, education, family, recreations, and club memberships. Factual detail of the Royal Family, the Order of Succession, the Royal Household, and H. M. Officers of Arms, are included. Among the introductory essays in this edition are 'The single European market', 'The way forward for British industry', and 'The Queen's forty years'. A spin-off series of county volumes is planned: the first is *Debrett's people of Kent*.

580 **The National Portrait Gallery collection.**
Susan Forster, Robin Gibson, Malcolm Rogers, Jacob Simon.
London: National Portrait Gallery, 1988. 248p.
Coloured portraits of 250 British men and women, including paintings and drawings, photographs, and sculptures, which constitute some of the Gallery's most notable items, are reproduced here with brief notes on the sitter and the artist.

581 **Who's buried where in England.**
D. Greenwood. London: Constable, 1990. 2nd ed. 352p. map.
The burial places of over 500 eminent men and women from all walks of life; royalty and the aristocracy, politicians, lawyers, scholars, scientists, engineers and industrialists, explorers, sportsmen, criminals etc., are all listed in this gazetteer.

582 **A history of British surnames.**
Richard McKinley. London: Longman, 1990. 230p.
Devoting a chapter to each of the main categories of surname; locative, topographical, occupational, personal, and nickname, this authoritative volume provides comprehensive information on the history of hereditary surnames in Britain. Historical, geographical, social and genealogical factors are all taken into account. McKinley was Director of the Survey of English Surnames at Leicester University for over twenty years.

583 **British autobiographies: an annotated bibliography of British autobiographies published or written before 1951.**
Compiled by William Matthews. Berkeley, California; Los Angeles: University of California Press, 1955. 376p.
Over 6,000 very briefly annotated entries for the autobiographies of persons either born in the British Isles or naturalized British subjects are included in this bibliography.

584 **British diaries: an annotated bibliography of British diaries written between 1442 and 1942.**
Compiled by William Matthews. Cambridge, England: Cambridge University Press, 1950. 339p.
This chronologically-ordered descriptive list includes diaries by Englishmen, Scotsmen, Welshmen, and Irishmen born in the British Isles, Europe, and on the high seas, and also the diaries of Americans and other travellers in the British Isles that were published in the English language in England.

585 **A dictionary of English surnames.**
P. H. Reaney, revised by R. M. Wilson. London: Routledge, 1991. 3rd ed. 509p. bibliog.
Originally published as *A dictionary of British surnames* in 1976, this standard work includes 16,000 surnames of which 4,000 are new to this edition. The change of title 'reflects a concentration on surnames of specifically English rather than Celtic in origin which has been increasingly apparent in successive editions' (Preface). Most names can be traced back to medieval times, the one general exception being those associated

with the influx of Huguenot refugees at the end of the sixteenth century. A scholarly introduction divides English surnames into four categories by which they can be identified: local; patronymic; occupational surnames; and those derived from nicknames. Reaney's *The origin of English surnames* (London: Routledge & Kegan Paul, 1967. 415p.) gives a general account of their development including changes in spelling and pronunciation, and the gradual use of hereditary family names.

586 **Asian who's who international.**
Compiled by J. S. Sachar. Ilford, England: Asian Observer, 1990. 5th ed. 280p.

Short biographical sketches of over 1,000 prominent Asians living and working in Britain are included in this biographical dictionary first published in 1975. Directory information on organizations involved in race relations, the ethnic minority press, religious festivals, and places of worship, is also included.

587 **Who's who: an annual biographical dictionary.**
London: A & C Black, 1849- . annual.

Eminent living persons worldwide are selected for inclusion in this prototype biographical dictionary which, nevertheless, is predominantly concerned with people native to, or resident in, the British Isles. Eminence is decided either on grounds of personal achievement or on interest to the public at large. However curious omissions sometimes persist. It is compiled from editorial questionnaires sent to those selected for inclusion and completed by the biographees themselves. The 1992 edition contained some 28,000 entries. *Who was who* consists of a series of decennial companion volumes and contains biographies removed from *Who's who* because of death with, in some instances, additional information to bring them up to date. The latest volume is *Who was who 1981-1990* (1992, 845p.). *Who was who: a cumulated index* 1897-1990 (1991, 850p.) provides a convenient access route.

Dictionary of British and Irish botanists and horticulturalists.
See item no. 213.

Dictionary of British educationalists.
See item no. 765.

Ghosts' who who
See item no. 887.

Biographical dictionary of modern British radicals.
See item no. 966.

The Blackwell biographical dictionary of British political life in the twentieth century.
See item no. 1006

Who's who in industry.
See item no. 1260.

Great engineers
See item no. 1285.

Lives of the engineers.
See item no. 1321.

Dictionary of labour biography.
See item no. 1447.

Who's who in the environment England.
See item no. 1513.

British historical portraits.
See item no. 1654.

British Music Hall: an illustrated who's who.
See Item no. 1769.

Illustrated who's who in British films.
See item no. 1806.

Biographical dictionary of English architects.
See item no. 1836.

English medieval architects.
See item no. 1854.

Dictionary of literary biography.
See item no. 1983.

Who's who in British athletics.
See item no. 2094.

Biographical encyclopedia of British flat racing.
See item no. 2136.

Religion

588   The pilgrims' way: shrines and saints in Britain and Ireland.
   John Adair.   London: Thames & Hudson, 1978. 208p. bibliog.
   2 maps.
Written primarily as a companion for those following the footsteps of medieval
pilgrims, this guide first explains how the practice of pilgrimage came into being before
embarking on descriptions of the routes and the shrines that were the pilgrims'
destinations. Two hundred photographs record the holy places and the inns and
countryside along the way.

**589   The English connection: the Puritan roots of Seventh-day Adventist
belief.**
   B. W. Ball.   Cambridge, England: James Clarke, 1981. 252p. bibliog.
Beginning with a history of Puritanism in England this study stresses its reliance on
biblical exegesis and examines its influence on later religious movements, notably
Seventh-day Adventism.

590   The Baptist Union directory for 1991-92.
   Didcot, England: Baptist Union of Great Britain, 1991. 349p.
A county list of churches with numbers of church members and attendances, and an
alphabetical register of accredited ministers, comprise the main contents of this long-
established directory. Ancillary material includes the constitution of the Baptist Union,
a directory of its various organizations, and the proceedings of the Baptist Assembly.

591   Evangelism in modern Britain: a history from the 1730s to the 1980s.
   D. W. Bebbington.   London: Unwin Hyman, 1989. 364p. bibliog.
This major historical study of the Evangelical Movement in Britain, from its inception
in the time of John Wesley, to the charismatic renewal in the 1980s, discusses its
impact in the nineteenth century, accounts for its resurgence since the Second World
War, and contends that developments in its ideas and attitudes were influenced by

changes in British culture. Fundamentalism, a particular form of Evangelism shaped by specific circumstances, also receives attention. The author is a Baptist deacon and lay preacher.

592 The Church of England in crisis.
Trevor Beeson. London: Davis-Poynter, 1973. 194p.

Concentrating on the visible malaise of the Church of England since the Second World War, this hard-hitting book analyses the basic facts of Church membership, finance, its relations with the State, and other Churches, and its new approaches to worship and Church government. The way forward is seen to be in the better deployment of Church resources at a local level rather than in the constant preoccupation with a centrally-managed Church.

593 A history of atheism in Britain: from Hobbes to Russell.
David Berman. London: Croom Helm, 1988. 253p.

Probably no other doctrine in modern British history has generated so much contumely as atheism. This pioneering study reveals that although avowed atheism surfaced in Britain for the first time as late as the end of the eighteenth century, it had its covert adherents as early as the mid-seventeenth.

594 A theological introduction to the Thirty-Nine Articles of the Church of England.
E. J. Bicknell, revised by H. J. Carpenter. London: Longman, 1955. 3rd ed. 463p. bibliog.

Intended not only as an introduction to the Thirty-Nine Articles but also as an aid to the further study of the Christian doctrine, this third edition has been revised in the light of fresh theological studies and new doctrinal emphases. It has been the standard work on the subject since it was first published in 1919.

595 The Penguin book of hymns.
Edited by Ian Bradley. London: Viking, 1989. 476p. bibliog.

Ninety-three of the 150 hymns included in this anthology are English in origin. Each hymn is printed in its full and original text and is accompanied by a commentary which gives biographical details of its author, notes on the circumstances in which it was written, and of the various tunes to which it might be sung. Every branch of English hymnody is represented.

596 The beginnings of Quakerism.
William C. Braithwaite, revised by Henry J. Cadbury. Cambridge, England: Cambridge University Press, 1970. 2nd ed. 607p. 3 maps.

Compiled from original source materials this volume and its successor (*The second period of Quakerism.* William C. Braithwaite, revised by Henry J. Cadbury. Cambridge, England: Cambridge University Press, 1961. 2nd ed. 735p.) were first published by Macmillan in their Rowntree Series of Quaker Histories in 1912 and 1919 respectively. They cover the history of Quakerism in Britain from its beginnings during the seventeenth-century Puritan revolution to 1725, and provide a well-documented account of the early days when George Fox and his adherents turned their backs on tradition, dogma, and external authority, and offered instead an immediate relationship with God and with each other.

597 Policy and politics in British Methodism 1932-1982.
George Thompson Brake.   London: Edsall, 1984. 880p. bibliog.

In 1932 the Primitive Methodists, the United Methodists, and the Wesleyans, came together to form the Methodist Church. This very detailed study records the process of that union and the first fifty years of a church which, numerically, is the largest of the denominations known as the English Free Churches. It is a factual account, based on official documents, and it examines all aspects of the Church's organization and activities, its doctrine and enterprises, and its property.

598 Christian England: what the 1989 English church census reveals.
Peter Brierley.   London: MARC Europe, 1991. 254p. 51 maps.

On Sunday, 15th October 1989 tens of thousands of Christian churches across England co-operated in a census to measure as precisely as possible the number of people attending church that Sunday. It followed a similar exercise in 1979; attendance figures then were published in *Prospects for the eighties. vol. 1* (Swindon, England: Bible Society, 1980). This detailed and well-documented study provides a quantified survey of the age and sex of churchgoers; the growth and decline of attendances; how beliefs are practised; when churches were built and congregations formed; the level of giving to the Third World; and the implications for the future. 'The hard facts will not be comfortable for church leaders, but they are facts to be faced, and facts to *act on*, if the influence of this country's historic Christian faith is not to disappear'.

599 UK Christian handbook 1992/93.
Edited by Peter Brierley, David Longley.   London: MARC Europe and Evangelical Alliance; Swindon, England: Bible Society, 1991. 880p. 25 maps.

First published under this title in 1964, the latest edition of this handbook appears after a three year interval in which work resulting from the English church had been completed. It comprises a series of seven directory type chapters giving details of accommodation by type and county; bookshops, libraries and publishers; churches including non-Christian churches preaching in Britain, with maps of diocesan and district boundaries; Evangelical missions and agencies; overseas missionary activities; the media, including musical and theatrical performers, newspapers and periodicals, and radio and television programme producers; and various social and welfare groups and services.

600 A social history of the Nonconformist Ministry in England and Wales 1800-1930.
Kenneth D. Brown.   Oxford: Clarendon, 1988. 244p. bibliog.

Based on statistical samples of the careers of Baptist, Congregational, Wesleyan, Primitive and United Methodist ministers, mainly culled from published obituaries, this study presents a picture of the private and professional lives of the less celebrated members of the Nonconformist Ministry.

601 **The Buddhist directory: a directory of Buddhist groups and centres in the United Kingdom and Ireland and other related organizations.**
London: Buddhist Society, 1987. 4th ed. 75p.

This county-arranged guide to Buddhist societies and organizations gives their contact names and addresses, their aims, and their activities and publications. Other sections indicate libraries with important Buddhist collections and retailers of Buddhist literature.

602 **The Catholic directory of England and Wales: for the year of Our Lord 1992.**
Manchester: Gabriel Communications for the Bishop's Conference of England and Wales, 1992. 153rd ed. 670p. map.

A directory of churches arranged alphabetically by diocese, giving the name of their incumbents, and of any religious order based on the church, and a list of religious and secular priests and permanent deacons, form the two main sections of this directory. Other information provided includes a list of Catholic members of parliament, diocesan child care organizations, religious houses, and Catholic societies.

603 **The Church of England year book 1992: the official year book of the General Synod of the Church of England.**
London: Church House Publishing, 1992. 108th ed. 423p.

The first part of this yearbook is concerned with the General Synod, its dates of session, constitution, officers, structure and composition. The second is a survey of the whole Anglican communion, including church organizations, church newspapers, and a who's who of General Synod members.

604 **Bede's ecclesiastical history of the English people.**
Edited by Bertram Colgrave, R. A. B. Mynors. Oxford: Clarendon Press, 1969. 618p. bibliog. (Oxford Medieval Texts).

If it were not for Bede's *History*, completed in AD 721, little would be known, certainly not documented, of the early history of Christianity in England or of the Anglo-Saxon invasions. This definitive edition makes use for the first time of an eighth-century manuscript now in Leningrad. Also included are long historical and textual introductions and an index of extant manuscripts. Dent's Everyman Library publishes a more accessible text under the title of *Bede's ecclesiastical history of the English nation* with an introduction by David Knowles.

605 **Crockford's clerical directory 1991/92: a directory of the Church of England, the Church in Wales, the Scottish Episcopal Church, the Church of Ireland.**
London: Church House Publications for The Church Commissioners for England and The Central Board of Finance of The Church of England, 1991. 92nd ed. 1,092p. 3 maps.

Biographies of the Anglican clergy and an index of English benefices and churches are the principal contents of this famous directory which was first published in 1858. Service, prison and hospital chaplains are also included. The anonymous prefaces of successive editions provide lively surveys of events concerning and influencing the Church of England.

606 A history of Anglican liturgy.
G. J. Cuming. London: Macmillan, 1969. 450p. bibliog.

This scholarly work on the Book of Common Prayer incorporates material gleaned from the reformed Primers, the 1689 proposals, and John Wesley's *Abridgement*. It is arranged on a chronological basis and replaces F. Proctor and W. H. Frere's *A new history of the Book of Common Prayer* published in 1901. A selection of documents provides translations of several texts not previously available in English and there is also an extensive bibliography.

607 A history of the Methodist Church in Great Britain.
Edited by R. Davies, G. Rupp. London: Epworth, 1965-88. 4 vols.

Approved and commissioned by the Methodist Conference, this work is a detailed survey of the origins of the Methodist Church, its development and influence, in the light of recent ecumenical perspectives, and based on modern historical and theological research. The first three volumes comprise essays on individual topics by various experts in a chronological sequence: volume one provides an account of the early history of the Church within John Wesley's lifetime; volume two takes the story to the mid-nineteenth century; and volume three outlines developments to the Methodist Union of 1932 and after. Volume four is a collection of source documents ending with an 150-page bibliography.

608 The English Reformation.
A. G. Dickens. London: Batsford, 1989. 2nd ed. 461p. bibliog.

Immediately acknowledged as a classic work of impeccable scholarship when first published in 1964, this substantially revised edition is virtually a new work. The fresh material incorporated includes a whole new opening chapter which places Tudor England in a wider temporal and geographical context; new sections on Sir Thomas More, Thomas Cromwell, and Anne Boleyn; expanded accounts of the reigns of Edward VI and the Marian reaction; and another completely new chapter on the influence of anti-clericalism, the uneven spread of Elizabethan Protestantism, and the intriguing concept that essentially the English Reformation was a youth movement.

609 Christian England.
David L. Edwards. London: Collins, 1981-84. 3 vols. (vol. 1. *Its story to the Reformation*. 1981. 351p. bibliog. vol. 2. *From the Reformation to the eighteenth century*. 1982. 520p. vol. 3. *From the eighteenth century to the First World War*. 1984. 378p.).

Described by the author as 'the first ecumenical history of English Christianity', these three volumes examine the impact which the Christian religion has made on the lives and imagination of the English people. More attention is given to literature, art, prayer, and to the Church's setting in the social and political life of the nation, than to ecclesiastical administration or theological controversy.

610 Leaders of the Church of England 1828-1978.
David L. Edwards.   London: Hodder & Stoughton, 1978. 383p. bibliog.

An updated edition of the author's *Leaders of the Church of England 1828-1944* (1971), this compact volume introduces the leading personalities whose beliefs shaped the modern Church's dogma and development. For this edition there is a new chapter on the trends in the leadership of the Church since 1945.

611 Faith in the countryside: a report presented to the Archbishops of Canterbury and York.
Worthing, England: Churchman, 1990. 400p.

Following the dramatic – and controversial – report *Faith in the city*, the two metropolitan archbishops authorised a companion study into the country areas of England by the Commission on Rural Areas. Its terms of reference were 'to examine the effects of economic, environmental and social change on the rural community; to describe the changing nature of the Church in the countryside; to examine the theological factors which bear upon the mission and ministry of the Church in rural areas; and to make recommendations for consideration and action'. Looking for signs of growth and evidence of engagement, the Commission found a Church identified with its community and one seeking to respond to whatever challenges which came its way.

612 English medieval pilgrimage.
D. J. Hall.   London: Routledge & Kegan Paul, 1965. 233p.

Holywell, Glastonbury, Lindisfarne and Durham, Walsingham, Canterbury Cathedral, Westminster Abbey, Verulamium, and Bromholm, are the shrines examined in historical detail in this attempt to explain the English pilgrimages as an integral part of the fabric of medieval English society.

613 A history of English Christianity 1920-1985.
Adrian Hastings.   London: Collins, 1986. 720p. bibliog.

Designed as a sequel to Owen Chadwick's *The Victorian church* (London: A. & C. Black, 1970. 2 vols.) published in the Ecclesiastical history of England series, this monumental wide-ranging study explores the modern history of the English churches and their role in national life since the end of the First World War. The beginnings of ecumenical discussions, the Church's role in modern society, the General Strike of 1926, internal politics and ecclesiastical life, pacifism, Communism and Fascism, the Second World War, the second Vatican Council, theology and society, are some of the subjects examined in detail.

614 British hymn writers and composers: a checklist giving their dates and places of birth and death.
Edited by A. J. Hayden, R. F. Newton.   Guildford, England: Hymn Society of Great Britain and Ireland, 1977. 94p.

About 2,500 names 'of those who were born or died in a known year in the British Isles and who wrote or shared in the making of a hymn in English or a tune . . . included in a major British hymnbook published between January 1901 and December 1875' (Preface).

615   **The pagan religions of the ancient British Isles: their nature and legacy.**
Ronald Hutton.   Oxford: Blackwell, 1991. 397p. bibliog.

Covering the period from the Old Stone Age (c. 30,000 BC) to the coming of
Christianity in early Anglo-Saxon times, this survey of religious beliefs ranges over a
wide aspect of archaeological evidence, folklore, and literary texts. A full account is
given of the decline of paganism and much fascinating evidence is mustered for the
convincing hypothesis that the early peoples of ancient Britain were immensely more
creative than was previously supposed. The survival of pre-Christian beliefs and
imagery into the Middle Ages is comprehensively traced.

616   **East meets West – a background to some Asian faiths.**
Muhammed Iqbal.   London: Commission for Racial Equality, 1981.
3rd ed. 130p. bibliog.

First published as *East comes West* by the former Community Relations Commission,
this work contains sections on the Hindu, Islamic, and Sikh religions, with a further
chapter on the customs of the Asian sub-continent, and a list of political, religious and
cultural festivals.

617   **The monastic order in England: a history of its development from the
time of St. Dunstan to the Fourth Lateran Council, 940-1216.**
David Knowles.   Cambridge, England: Cambridge University Press,
1963. 2nd ed. 780p. bibliog.

This magisterial work, along with its sister volumes, *The religious orders in England:
Vol. 1: the old orders 1216-1314* (1948. 350p.); *Vol. 2: the end of the middle ages* (1955.
407p.); *Vol. 3: the Tudor age* (1959. 522p.), provides an incomparable narrative
chronicle of all aspects of English monasticism and monasteries from their revival in
the tenth century to their suppression in the sixteenth. Supported by numerous
statistical, chronological and factual appendices, and by extensive bibliographies, these
volumes will not easily be replaced as the standard definitive accounts. *Bare ruined
choirs: the dissolution of the English monasteries* (1976) is an abridged illustrated
edition of volume three.

618   **The Jewish year book 1992. 5752-5753.**
Edited by Stephen W. Massil.   London: Jewish Chronicle, 1992. 306p.

A directory of synagogues in London and elsewhere in the United Kingdom, and a
'who's who' of prominent Jewish men and women, form the two principal sections of
this yearbook. Other material includes a brief history of British Jewry, a note on UK
legislation concerning Jews, and, in this edition, an article commemorating the 150th
anniversary of the *Jewish Chronicle*.

619   **Moore's introduction to English canon law.**
E. Garth Moore, Timothy Briden.   London: Mowbray, 1985. 2nd ed.
181p.

Originally published by the Clarendon Press in 1967, this extensively revised and updated
edition deals with the basic principles on which the Canon Law is determined and outlines
the legal constitution and framework of the Church of England. Chapter-length coverage
of topics includes the parish; non-parochial units; doctrine; worship; baptism, confir-
mation, and holy communion; matrimony; church property; ceremonial, furnishings,
and decoration; ecclesiastical courts and legal proceedings; and dispensations.

620 **A history of the Church in England.**
John R. H. Moorman. London: Adam & Charles Black, 1967.
2nd ed. 460p. bibliog.
First published in 1953 this is the standard single-volume history of Christianity in the British Isles which covers the arrival of the earliest missionaries to Christianity in present times. For this edition the last chapter on the Church since 1914 has been brought up to date. The definitive work is *A history of the English church* edited by W. R. W. Stephens and W. Hunt (London: Macmillan, 1899-1910. 8 vols in 9) which has been reprinted many times.

621 **Anglicanism.**
Stephen Neill. London: Mowbrays, 1977. 421p. bibliog.
Originally published by Penguin in 1958, this well-received book endeavours to explain what the Anglican Communion is, how it arrived at this point, what it stands for, and its role in ecumenical development. In view of its status as an established church, and of its claims to be 'Catholic, Apostolic, Protestant, and Reformed', some explanation of the Church of England's position, and of its worldwide communion, this scholarly work is thrice welcome.

622 **The English Catholic Church in the nineteenth century.**
Edward Norman. Oxford: Clarendon Press, 1984. 399p. bibliog.
Directed at the educated general reader, this account analyses the character and ideas of the leading Catholic hierarchy, assesses their achievements, and examines the influence and effects of such issues as Emancipation and Irish immigration on the English Catholic Church and its place in nineteenth-century society.

623 **Roman Catholicism in England: from the Elizabethan Settlement to the Second Vatican Council.**
Edward Norman. Oxford: Oxford University Press, 1985. 138p.
bibliog.
This brief study throws light on how the minority Catholic population has asserted its faith since the English Reformation and how they have reconciled their allegiance to the Roman pontiff with their secular loyalty to the English State.

624 **English Biblical translation.**
A. C. Partridge. London: Deutsch, 1973. 246p. bibliog.
(The Language Library).
This investigation of *The Bible* in English translation examines in some detail the Bibles of Wyclif (c. late fourteenth century), Tyndale (1534), Coverdale (1535), the Geneva Bible (1560), the King James I Authorised Version (1611), and the modern Moffat, Knox, Phillips, Jerusalem, and New English Bibles. Intended more for linguists than theologians, it explains and clarifies the more complex passages, traces the origins of errors in translation, and expands on the problems of producing an academically accurate translation which will be understood and appreciated by churchgoers and worshippers. Similar ground is covered in Peter Levi's *The English Bible 1534-1859* (London: Constable, 1974. 222p. bibliog.).

Religion

625 Religious books in print: a reference catalogue 1992.
London: J. Whitaker, 1992. 700p.

An annual publication since 1974 this bibliography currently lists over 25,000 titles. It also includes a directory of over 1,400 publishers and distributors.

626 Our Christian heritage.
Warwick Rodwell, James Bentley. London: George Philip, 1984. 254p. bibliog.

Published to mark Christian Heritage Year 1984/5, the main purpose of this lavishly-illustrated volume exploring the Church's impact on British society and culture from the Roman period onwards, and its material remains, is to reawaken interest in its rich ecclesiastical heritage and to discuss how the Church can secure its future.

627 Religion in England 1688-1791.
Gordon Rupp. Oxford: Clarendon, 1986. 584p. bibliog. (Oxford History of the Christian Church).

The 1688 Revolution transformed the official relationship of Church and State. This erudite work examines life and worship in the established Church in the years following the Toleration Act, the survival of intolerance, and the growth of the dissenting churches, the quandary of Roman Catholics, the moralism, mysticism and rationalism of the eighteenth century, the Evangelical revival, and the role of the clergy and the laity in the Georgian Church.

628 The clerical profession.
Anthony Russell. London: SPCK, 1980. 358p. bibliog.

Three main themes are pursued in this carefully researched book: the clergyman's role and the professional ideal; the professionalization of this role in the late eighteenth and nineteenth century; and its status in contemporary society.

629 The Salvation Army yearbook 1992.
London: International Headquarters of the Salvation Army, 1992. 270p.

First published in 1906 this yearbook contains facts and figures, details of Salvation Army periodicals, Salvation Army reports worldwide, and a Salvation Army who's who.

630 The history of the Salvation Army: vol. 1: 1865-1878; vol. 2: 1878-1886; vol. 3: 1883-1953 Social reform and welfare work; vol. 4: 1886-1904; vol. 5: 1904-1914; vol. 6: 1914-1946; vol. 7: 1944-1977.
Robert Sandall, A. R. Wiggins, F. Coutts. London: Thomas Nelson/ Hodder & Stoughton, 1947-1988. 7 vols. bibliog.

This monumental official history tells the story of The Salvation Army from its beginnings as an obscure mission, The East London Christian Revival Association, founded in the mid-1860s, to its present international status and reputation.

631   **A history of the Free Churches.**
Paul Sangster.   London: Heinemann, 1983. 216p. bibliog.
For the purpose of this book the Free Churches are defined as English Protestant Churches not controlled by the State. They include the United Reformed Church, the Baptists, Methodists, the Society of Friends (the Quakers), and the Salvation Army. Beginning with Wyclif and the Lollards in the fourteenth century, this popular work describes how the Free Churches were formed, their development and progress, and how they differ from each other. Particular attention is given to those individuals who decided to break away from the established national Church, George Fox, John Bunyan, the Wesleys, Elizabeth Fry, and General Booth, and others.

632   **The British: their religious beliefs and practices 1800-1986.**
Edited by Terance Thomas.   London: Routledge, 1988. 247p.
(The Library of Religious Beliefs and Practices).
An important source book for the study of religion in Britain during a period of change in the country's religious map, this series of well-documented essays explores the intra-religious pluralism of the growth of Christian denominations in nineteenth-century Britain and the religious aspect of multi-ethnic immigration. A final chapter poses the question 'How religious are the British?'.

633   **The United Reformed Church year book 1991/92: containing the lists of churches and ministers.**
London: United Reformed Church in the United Kingdom, 1991. 247p.
map.
As indicated in its title, the two main sections of this yearbook comprise a list of churches, arranged by province and district, and an alphabetical roll of ministers. The information provided includes the location, date of formation, and number of Reformed churches, the names and brief career outlines of ministers, and statistics on church attendances. This yearbook was first published in 1973.

634   **Anglicanism in history and today.**
J. W. C. Wand.   London: Weidenfeld & Nicolson, 1961. 265p.
bibliog.
The aim of this comprehensive work is 'to catch the general spirit of Anglicanism and to show how it originated, how it has maintained itself in history and how it expresses itself today'. To this end the author traces its historical development from its origins in the fusion of Celtic and Roman traditions, analyses the historical groups and movements within the Anglican Church, and examines its contemporary societies and institutions.

635 **How the Church of England works.**
Paul A. Welsby. London: Cio Publishing, 1985. 85p.
Published for the General Synod of the Church of England, this handbook to the administrative structures of the Church explains all the legal and administrative facts that a church officer needs to know in running a modern parish and its place in the wider Church. The diocesan and cathedral's role; the functions of the deanery and of the diocesan synods; the work of the General Synod and its boards and councils; its finances; the relationship between Church and State; and the worldwide Anglican Communion, are among the topics considered. The author has used much material (suitably updated) from his earlier work of the same title published by the Society for the Propagation of Christian Knowledge in 1960.

636 **The good retreat guide.**
Stafford Whiteaker. London: Rider, 1991. 240p. 8 maps.
Explaining what a retreat is, and distinguishing between Christian, Buddhist, Hindu, and New Age centres, this guide describes more than 200 places offering peace and spiritual renewal in the United Kingdom, Ireland and France. Their denomination, opening dates, permitted length of stay, facilities, and charges, are all noted.

Holy places of the British Isles.
See item no. 262.

Traveller's key to sacred England.
See item no. 286.

Anglican church plate.
See item no. 1632.

Lindisfarne gospels.
See item no. 1678.

Collins guide to parish churches of England and Wales.
See item no. 1821.

Abbey explorers guide.
See item no. 1822.

Medieval monasteries of Great Britain.
See item no. 1830.

Cathedrals of England.
See item no. 1833.

Discovering English churches.
See item no. 1849.

English cathedrals: the forgotten centuries.
See item no. 1857.

Blue guide churches and chapels.
See item no. 1858.

Inside churches
See item no. 1860.

Abbeys and priorities in England and Wales.
See item no. 1864.

Catholic churches since 1623.
See item no. 1866.

English medieval monasteries.
See item no. 1871.

Guide to the abbeys of England and Wales.
See item no. 1874.

Guide to the cathedrals of Britain.
See item no. 1875.

Church furnishing and decoration in England and Wales.
See item no. 1881.

English parish church.
See item no. 1882.

Blue guide cathedrals and abbeys in Britain.
See item no. 1887.

Collins guide to cathedrals, abbeys and priories of England and Wales.
See item no. 1891.

Society

Social history

637 **The people of England: a short social and economic history.**
Maurice Ashley. London: Macmillan, 1982. 214p.

Beginning with the Celts this compact and well-annotated history outlines the dominant themes and developments in English social and economic life: wealth and poverty; health and disease; land, labour, and wages; war and peace; and social class and population.

638 **A social history of England 1851-1990.**
François Bedarida. London: Routledge, 1990. 2nd ed. 384p.

Three fundamental questions are raised in this work which traces the evolution of English society from the Great Exhibition to the arrival of the European market. Is there something distinctive about the English? What did the England of 1889 have in common with the England of 1989? In what ways has it changed? English attitudes, behaviour, and psychology are all taken into account.

639 **Social and economic history of England series.**
Edited by Asa Briggs. London: Longman, 1964- . 11 vols.

To be completed in eleven volumes this substantial series offers an authoritative survey of the significant social and economic developments from the Anglo-Saxon settlement to the present day. The volumes published so far are *Anglo-Saxon England and the Norman Conquest*. (Henry Loyn. 1991. 2nd ed. 432p. maps); *Medieval England: rural society and economic change 1086-1348*. (E. Miller. 1978. 320p. maps); *The age of plunder: the England of Henry VIII 1500-1547*. (W. G. Hoskins. 1976. 280p. maps); *The age of Elizabeth: England under the late Tudors 1547-1603*. (D. M. Palliser. 1992. 2nd ed. 544p.); *England's apprenticeship 1603-1763*. (Charles Wilson. 1985. 2nd ed. 456p. maps); *The vital century: England's developing economy 1714-1815*. (John Rule. 1992. 352p.); *Albion's people: English society 1714-1815*. (John Rule. 1992. 288p.); *The rise of industrial society in England 1815-1885*. (S. G. Checkland. 1964. 486p. maps).

640 **A social history of England.**
Asa Briggs. London: Weidenfeld & Nicolson, 1983. 320p. 6 maps.
Extending from prehistory to modern times, this history of English society explores all
avenues, political, economic, demographic, and cultural history, in fact 'nothing is
irrelevant to it'. Vastly different from G. M. Trevelyan's *English social history* in style
and content, it is equally absorbing reading. The text is complemented by over 200
illustrations chosen not simply for their decorative appeal but as an integral part of the
unfolding historical narrative.

641 **Social trends 1992.**
Edited by Tom Griffin. London: HMSO for Central Statistical Office,
1992. 255p. bibliog.
A wealth of coloured charts brings life to this compendium, published annually since
1970, providing accurate analyses and breakdowns of statistical information on
population, households and families, education, employment, income and wealth,
health and personal social services, law enforcement, and other social aspects. Lists of
the major surveys scanned, and of definitions of the terms used, are given in an
appendix. This edition includes an article on the use and misuse of crime statistics.

642 **The English: a social history 1066-1945.**
Christopher Hibbert. London: Grafton, 1987. 785p. bibliog.
Based on diaries, letters, memoirs, official reports, and contemporary literature, this
one-volume social history enlivens every aspect of the daily life of all classes of the
English people over 900 years.

643 **Reshaping rural England: a social history 1850-1925.**
Alun Howkins. London: Unwin Hyman, 1991. 272p.
Four main themes dominate this history of the decline of Britain's agriculture from its
high point in the 1850s to the grim aftermath of the First World War: the creation of a
stable social order disguising widespread poverty; the economic collapse of the cereal
market in the 1870s; the emergence of trade unions in the farming industry; and the
changes in agricultural production during the war.

644 **Public life and the propertied Englishman 1689-1798.**
Paul Langford. Oxford: Clarendon Press, 1991. 616p. bibliog.
Middle class energy and activity is the dominant theme in this major reassessment of
English society in the eighteenth century. Thoroughly wedded to the concept of
property ownership conferring duties, responsibilities, and privileges, the burgeoning
middle classes scaled the social and political heights, effectively thrusting aside the
pretensions of the aristocracy who displayed their customary aplomb and ability to
adapt to new circumstances.

645 **An atlas of British social and economic history since c.1700.**
Edited by Rex Pope. London: Routledge, 1989. 255p. 255 maps.
Demography, agriculture, transport and trade, labour movements, religion, health and
housing, and education, are among the topics featured in this historical atlas which
covers the period from the mid-eighteenth century to the present.

Society. Social structure

646   The Cambridge social history of Britain 1750-1950.
Edited by F. M. L. Thompson.   Cambridge, England: Cambridge
University Press, 1990. 3 vols. bibliog.

This work follows the established pattern of co-operative Cambridge histories in that
each volume consists of a number of independent but integrated chapters by different
contributors. The first volume (*Regions and communities*, 608p.) presents a series of
studies of the social history of the various regions of the British Isles; the second
(*People and their environment*, 392p.) explores the questions of social structure, social
mobility, and class relations; whilst the third (*Social agencies and institutions*, 496p.)
discusses the institutions which affected social conditions and influenced social policy.
Together they offer an authentic account of the shaping of modern British society over
a 200-year period of intense demographic and socio-economic change.

647   English social history: a survey of six centuries Chaucer to Queen Victoria.
G. M. Trevelyan.   London: Longman, 1944. 628p. 7 maps.

Not since Macaulay's *History of England* had a serious historical work achieved such
instant acclaim as this book, written by Macaulay's great-nephew, when it was
published in wartime England. Conceived as a companion study to his own *History of
England*, it is concerned with 'the circumstances which have most influence on the
happiness of mankind, the changes of manners and morals, the transition of
communities from poverty to health, from knowledge to ignorance, from ferocity to
humanity', and it undoubtedly caught the popular mood as the Second World War
drew to an end. An illustrated edition, with a perceptive introduction by Asa Briggs,
was published in 1978. David Cannadine's *G. M. Trevelyan: a life in history* (Harper
Collins, 1992. 288p) examines Trevelyan's works in detail and also notes their
contemporary reception.

Social structure

648   Britain since 1945: choice, conflict and change.
Guy Arnold.   London: Blandford, 1989. 249p. bibliog.

First comparing Britain's position at the end of the Second World War in 1945, when
she was indisputably one of the Big Three powers imposing the post- war settlement,
with her 1988 situation as an unwilling partner in the European Community, Arnold
continues with an appraisal of Britain's economy during the intervening period, her
creaking social structure, the influence of the mass media, and ends with a glance at
the prospects for Britain in the 1990s.

649   **The British aristocracy.**
Mark Bence-Jones, Hugh Montgomery-Massingberd.   London:
Constable, 1979. 259p. bibliog.

Although much of this work is historical in content, dealing with the origins and history
of some of the great noble families of the British Isles, the aristocratic character, and
the ownership of land, there is a final chapter on how the aristocracy is faring in an age
of egalitarianism and in a climate of punitive and crippling taxation.

650   **The working class in Britain 1850-1939.**
John Benson.   London: Longman, 1989. 219p. bibliog. (Themes in
British Social History).

More an attempt to prove two hypotheses than a straightforward narrative, this fully
documented study questions the long-held assumption that working people in Victorian
and Edwardian England were moulded into an homogenous and readily identifiable
working class, and examines to what degree improving economic and social conditions
encouraged them to accept a capitalist society.

651   **British social attitudes cumulative sourcebook: the first six surveys.**
Compiled by Lindsay Brook (et al.).   Aldershot, England: Gower,
1992. various pagination. bibliog.

Core funded by Sainsbury Family Charitable Trust, the annual *British social attitudes*
survey series is a well-researched guide to Britain's changing social values based on
lengthy interviews of some 3,000 individuals. This sourcebook collates 1983-89 data
relating to citizenship, the role of government, and the constitution; crime, law
enforcement, and civil liberties; party politics; defence and international relations;
Northern Ireland; economic issues, income inequality, taxes, and public spending; the
labour market and employment; business and industry; education; social welfare and
poverty; health services; diet and lifestyle; morality and ethics; family relationships;
race; social class; religion; housing; and countryside and environment.

652   **The decline and fall of the British aristocracy.**
David Cannadine.   New Haven, Connecticut: Yale University Press,
1990. 813p.

In the last half-century the political decline of the aristocracy, baronage, and landed
gentry has become obvious. This magisterial work traces their diminishing influence in
the counties, the church, at the Bar, in the civil service, the armed forces, and even in
the House of Lords and the diplomatic service.

653   **British social trends since 1900: a guide to the changing social structure
of Britain.**
Edited by A. H. Halsey.   London: Macmillan, 1988. 2nd ed. 650p.
bibliog.

A sequel to *British society since 1900* (1972) this second edition consists of fifteen
essays from a distinguished group of Oxford University social scientists on various
aspects of Britain's social structure. Statistics and social trends, population, the
economic environment, the labour force, social mobility, education, urbanization and
local government, housing, health and welfare, religion, and immigration, are all
covered. Each essay provides a guide to contemporary trends.

149

654 **The English gentry 1500-1700.**
Felicity Hill.   London: Macmillan, 1993. 320p.
Themes explored in this analysis of the gentry in the early modern period include lineage and ancestry, land and inheritance, wealth, political power, education, social hegemony, religion, and patronage.

655 **The social structure of modern Britain.**
E. A. Johns.   Oxford: Pergamon, 1979. 3rd ed. 284p. bibliog.
First published in 1965, and now completely rewritten, this introductory textbook is a general overview of some of the main characteristics that make up the fabric of modern British society. Demographic issues like population trends and their socio-economic aspects, fertility and mortality, and immigration, are followed by chapters on the family, social class, education, leisure, and social controls and the maintenance of order, all placed in a historical and comparative context.

656 **The deluge: British society and the First World War.**
Arthur Marwick.   London: Macmillan, 1991. 2nd ed. bibliog.
Describing life on the home front between 1914 and 1918, and analysing the dramatic social changes of the 1920s, this classic study of a society in transition now contains in this second edition a long introductory essay on 'War and social change in twentieth-century Britain'.

657 **Rural life in Victorian England.**
G. E. Mingay.   Gloucester, England: Alan Sutton, 1991. 220p.
Taking each strand of the rural community in turn, landowners, tenant farmers, land agents, tradesmen, and craftsmen, this study, which was first published in 1971, provides a clear insight of a society in transition. Industrial and commercial expansion, the demand for cheap food, the exploitation of natural resources, the advance of the railways, transformed rural England at a bewildering pace.

658 **A social history of the English countryside.**
G. E. Mingay.   London: Routledge, 1990. 246p.
Although dealing with all the major aspects of rural society from medieval times to the Second World War, the emphasis of this pleasantly illustrated volume is on the changes of the eighteenth and nineteenth centuries. By the end of this period 'it was very clear that a great transformation had occurred: the rural population, and the occupations which supported it, once the mainspring of both government and economy, had wound down to become a disregarded appendage of the industrial state'.

659 **The Victorian countryside.**
Edited by G. E. Mingay.   London: Routledge & Kegan Paul, 1981.
2 vols. bibliog.
Life in rural England during the Victorian period, which was largely based on the horse for power, haulage, and personal transport, changed rapidly with the advent of the internal combustion engine and cheap food imports. The forty-six essays which make up these two volumes cover the land, agriculture, county towns and country industries, landed society, and labouring life during the period in question.

660 **British civilization: an introduction.**
John Oakland. London: Routledge, 1991. 2nd ed. 272p.
Providing a comprehensive introduction to contemporary British society, the law, local and central government, education, and the media, this extensively revised edition of a work first published in 1989 analyses recent developments in Britain, stressing that British society is both complex and dynamic, constantly facing new problems and situations. Unemployment, social mobility, industrial decline, and technological growth, are among contemporary issues challenging society. Oakland argues that conservative institutions will need radical transformation if they are to cope with these pressures.

661 **The rise of professional society: England since 1880.**
Harold Perkin. London: Routledge, 1989. 604p.
More and more 'modern society in Britain . . . is made up of career hierarchies of specialized occupations, selected by merit and based on trained expertise . . . the professions – not all of them equal in status or rewards, or stretching as far as the top – reach much further down the social pyramid than even landlordship or even business capital did, and embrace occupations formerly thought beyond the reach of professional aspiration' (Chapter one). This study thoroughly explores the professionalization of English society and its consequent impact on traditional class structures.

662 **The making of the English working class.**
E. P. Thompson. London: Gollancz, 1980. 958p. bibliog.
'A group of studies, on related themes, rather than a consecutive narrative', this seminal work has attained a landmark status in the literature of social history since it was first published in 1963. Divided into three parts, the first considers the continuing popular traditions of the eighteenth century, the second investigates the experiences of various groups of workers during the Industrial Revolution, whilst the third examines working class radicalism from the Luddites to the end of the Napoleonic Wars. Finally, the developing class-consciousness of the English working class in the early decades of the nineteenth century is placed under sympathetic scrutiny.

663 **English landed society in the nineteenth century.**
F. M. L. Thompson. London: Routledge & Kegan Paul, 1963. 374p. bibliog.
The landed classes virtually dominated English social and political life until the Great War of 1914-18. Benefiting from extensive research in the private and estate papers of many landed families, this penetrating study closely examines their structure and institutions, their social position, and their political power.

664 **Families and citizenship: values in contemporary Britain.**
Noel Timms. Aldershot, England: Dartmouth, 1992. 116p. bibliog.
Examining codes of behaviour and the nature of social bonds in contemporary Britain, this study discusses family, political, social, moral and religious issues. It follows *Values and social change in Britain* (Macmillan, 1985, 272p.).

665   **Family studies – information needs and resources: the report of the Review Panel of Family Studies.**
Jeffrey Weeks.   London: British Library, 1986. 123p. bibliog.
(Library and Information Research Report, no. 43).

This report presents the results of an investigation into the generation, transfer, storage, retrieval, discrimination and use of information by national agencies associated with research and practice in family studies.

666   **The sociology of an English village: Gosforth.**
W. M. Williams.   London: Routledge & Kegan Paul, 1956. 246p.

Essentially a survey of the rural parish of Gosforth, on the western fringe of the Lakeland fells of Cumbria, this well-documented study looks at its economy, family and kinship relationships, social classes, social activity, its religious life, and its own sense of identity, in an attempt to capture the manner in which its life was bonded together in the mid-twentieth century.

667   **Family and kinship in East London.**
Michael Young, Peter Willmott.   London: Routledge & Kegan Paul, 1986. 2nd ed. 234p. bibliog.

Families living in slums and due for rehousing in Bethnal Green in the 1950s were allocated new homes either in high-rise blocks of flats within the Borough (if the Borough Council was responsible for the demolition of their old home), or a flat not necessarily in the Bethnal Green area, or in a house on an estate outside London (if their home was demolished by the London County Council). These arrangements virtually ignored the long-established network of family relationships that had previously sustained working class communities and, it is argued, contributed in no small measure to the urban violence of the 1980s. This classic study was first published in 1957 and is now reprinted with a new introduction. Its lessons were learned too late.

Social problems

668   **Aids and drug misuse: report by the Advisory Council on the Misuse of Drugs.**
Department of Health.   London: HMSO, 1988-89. Printed in two parts.

The first part of this report concentrates on the measures which can be taken to tackle the spread of the HIV virus through drug injection, whilst the second considers ways in which health and social welfare services will need to develop in order to provide care to drug misusers who fall ill.

669   **Child sexual abuse: the search for healing.**
Christopher Bagley, Kathleen King.   London: Tavistock/Routledge, 1990. 276p. bibliog.

Whereas until very recently the problem of child sexual abuse was a taboo subject, it now attracts widespread media, academic and professional attention. This practical guide looks at its causes, its most effectual treatment, and its prevention. It also summarizes the many research studies undertaken recently on the nature and prevalence of the problem. Above all the emphasis is on the healing measures needed for all those involved, the victims, the offenders, and other members of their families.

670 **Hangmen of England: a history of execution from Jack Ketch to Albert Pierrepoint.**
Brian Bailey.   London: W. H. Allen, 1989. 206p. bibliog.
Many of the early hangmen were recruited from the prison population and some were eventually hanged themselves. This collective portrait of the men chosen to act as the public executioner – there was never a shortage of volunteers – clearly illustrates the brutal and degrading principle of capital punishment and its unbridled barbarity in practice. Capital punishment in the United Kingdom came to an end in 1969.

671 **The roots of urban unrest.**
Edited by John Benyon, John Solomos.   Oxford: Pergamon Press, 1987. 207p. bibliog.
Emerging from a symposium held at the University of Warwick in 1986, jointly organized by the Continuing Education Unit of the Department of Adult Education at the University of Leicester and the Centre for Research in Ethnic Relations at Warwick, whose purpose was to examine the deep-rooted causes of the violence which erupted in Britain's cities in the early 1980s, this set of papers investigates racial discrimination and disadvantage, unemployment, social deprivation, policing practices, and civil disorder in its historical context.

672 **Credit, debt and poverty.**
Richard Berthoud.   London: HMSO for the Department of Social Security, 1989. 42p.
Over half of unemployed families with children are seriously in debt. This study, commissioned at the beginning of the Government's Social Fund initiative, provides exact information on how debt adversely affects families on low income, especially those forced to rely on social security benefits.

673 **The investigation of crime: a guide to police powers.**
Vaughan Bevan, Ken Lidstone.   London: Butterworth, 1991. 576p.
Police powers of stop and search; of entry, search and seizure; of arrest and detention; and of treatment and questioning of persons in police detention, are the general themes in this successor to the author's *Guide to the police and Criminal Evidence Act 1984* (London: Butterworth, 1985. 554p.). This new work particularly takes account of the Prosecution of Offences Act 1985, the Public Order Acts of 1987 and 1988, and the Home Office's review during 1989 of the Codes of Practice that accompanied the Criminal Evidence Act 1984. Ken Lidstone was formerly Inspector in the South Wales Constabulary; both he and Bevan are now Senior Lecturers in Law in the University of Sheffield.

674 **Lone-parent families in the UK.**
Jonathan Bradshaw, Jane Millar.   London: HMSO for Department of
Social Security, 1991. 108p.

Lone-parent families currently number over one million. This survey provides
information on the routes into and out of lone parenthood, and lone-parents' financial
circumstances, housing, employment, attitudes, and behaviour.

675 **Misuse of drugs.**
Patrick Bucknell, Hamid Ghodse.   London: Waterlow, 1991.
2nd ed. 664p.

Since its first publication in 1986 this comprehensive work has established itself as the
definitive study of the legal and social-medical dimensions of drug abuse in the United
Kingdom. It examines the development of international control, and the most recent
UK legislation, notably the 1986 Drug Trafficking Offences Act, the 1988 Vienna
Convention, and the 1990 Criminal Justice (International Co-operation) Act. There is
a detailed analysis of important cases heard over the previous five years. Medical
aspects covered include the nature of addiction, the prognosis for treatment, with new
material on the detection of the presence of drugs in body fluids, and a table listing
controlled drugs and their trade names.

676 **Criminal Statistics England and Wales.**
London: HMSO for the Home Office, 1925- . annual.

Notifiable offences recorded by the police; offences in which firearms were used or
stolen; homicides; the number of offenders found guilty or cautioned; court
proceedings and sentences; and the use of police bail, are some of the topics
enumerated and analysed in this annual publication. Crime is also analysed by police
region.

677 **A land fit for heroin? Drug policies, prevention and practice.**
Edited by Nicholas Dorn, Nigel South.   London: Macmillan, 1987.
187p. bibliog.

The increasing availability of heroin in the 1980s prompted greater political efforts to
control its trafficking and increased concern for the treatment of those ensnared into drug
taking. In the context of an apparent failure to control the flow of heroin into Britain, this
study assesses the extent to which the problem is caused by social deprivation and how far
families and communities can contrive an effective response to addiction. It also discusses
how social welfare and medical care can best be co-ordinated.

678 **Crime and society in England 1750-1900.**
Clive Emsley.   London: Longman, 1987. 257p. bibliog. (Themes in
British Social History).

Four key questions are addressed in this study: what did contemporaries understand as
crime?; what patterns of crime were detected and have been detected subsequently by
historians?; who committed crimes?; what remedies were attempted to prevent crime
and to handle offenders? In finding answers the author challenges some time-honoured
perceptions – namely that crimes were mainly perpetrated by a criminal class; the
belief that changes in the criminal justice system resulted from the efforts of
humanitarian reformers; that working-class misery explains changing crime patterns;
and that emerging capitalism was somehow to blame.

679   **The English police: a political and social history.**
       Clive Emsley.   Hassocks, England: Harvester, 1991. 253p. bibliog.
County, Borough, and the Metropolitan police forces are covered in this historical
survey which extends from the eighteenth century to the 1990s. Modern recruitment
and training policies and practices are reviewed and there is a disturbing report of
police manipulation of suspects and of evidence presented in court.

680   **Faith in the city: a call for action by Church and Nation. The Report of
       the Archbishop of Canterbury's Commission on Urban Priority Areas.**
       London: Church House Publishing, 1985. 398p.
The Commission was appointed in July 1983 'to examine the strengths, insights,
problems and needs of the Church's life and mission in Urban Priority Areas and, as a
result, to reflect on the challenge which God may be making to Church and Nation:
and to make recommendations to appropriate bodies'. Urban Priority Areas (UPAs)
were defined as including inner city districts and many large Corporation estates. The
report aroused immediate political controversy: 'Chapter after chapter . . . tells the
same story: that a growing number of people are excluded by poverty or powerlessness
from sharing in the common life of our nation. A substantial minority – perhaps as
many as one person in every four or five across the nation, and a much higher
proportion in the UPAs – are forced to live on the margins of poverty or below the
threshold of an acceptable standard of living'. An urgent response from both Church
and government was called for.

681   **Trends in crime and their interpretation: a study of recorded crime in
       England and Wales.**
       Simon Field.   London: HMSO, 1990. 90p. bibliog. (Home Office
       Research and Planning Unit Report).
Confirming that the fluctuating rates of both property and personal crime is linked
directly with the ups-and-downs of the national economy, this report of a study of the
trends in crime during the post-War period shows that property crime grows faster
during years when consumer spending lessens. Conversely, personal crime (i.e. sexual
offences and violence against the person) increases in line with consumption. In England
and Wales these trends have remained constant since the beginning of the century.

682   **The crowd in contemporary Britain.**
       Edited by George Gaskell, Robert Benewick.   London: SAGE, 1987.
       273p. bibliog.
Focusing on events of the early 1980s, the purpose of this study is to investigate the
underlying nature of crowd behaviour as exemplified in crowd disorders. The historical
context of violent disorder in twentieth-century Britain; street life, ethnicity and social
policy; the front line supervision of the police; flashpoints of public disorder; crowd
solidarity; and the media sources for the study of recent events, are all examined.

683   **Excluding the poor.**
       Edited by Peter Golding.   London: Child Poverty Action Group,
       1986. 83p. bibliog.
This brief work shows how a lack of money prevents a large number of people from
participating in an extensive range of activities which are taken for granted by their

more affluent fellow citizens. It questions the common assumption that the provision of food, shelter, and clothing are all that is needed to ameliorate poverty, and points out that modern changes in the location and distribution of services, and in new technologies, actually increase poverty and social deprivation.

684 **The English highwayman: a legend unmasked.**
Peter Haining.   London: Robert Hale, 1991. 187p. + 16 plates.
Chronicling the exploits of the seventeenth-century Gentlemen (and Ladies) of the Road who flourished for a short time by holding up travellers before swinging at the end of the hangman's rope, this popular work allows a glimpse of historical truth to emerge from myth and legend.

685 **Inner city regeneration.**
Robert K. Home.   London: Spon, 1982. 188p. 5 maps. bibliog.
Riots in Liverpool, Manchester and London in 1981 brought into sharp focus the problems of Britain's inner cities. This book covers all government policies and current practices in the inner city regeneration programme, and examines in detail four specific government initiatives.

686 **The long affray: the poaching wars 1760-1914.**
Harry Hopkins.   London: Secker & Warburg, 1985. 344p. bibliog.
Readers who imagine the term 'poaching wars' to verge on sensational hyperbole will change their minds after reading this record of the bloody conflicts between poacher and gamekeeper in the nineteenth century which frequently ended with men murdered, transported or executed, all for the sake of a rabbit or pheasant. The harsh realities of rural life and justice, the inequalities of social rank and landed power as opposed to the economic dependence of the rural labourer, are portrayed in grim detail.

687 **Housing and Construction Statistics.**
London: HMSO for Department of the Environment. 1969- .
quarterly.
Part one which is published quarterly in March, June, September and December, contains tables on housebuilding performance, housing finance, and building materials whilst part two, published in April, July, October, and January, is concerned with construction activity and employment, and local authority housing loans and sales. *Housing and construction statistics 1980-1990*, an annual publication, with a number of informative maps and charts, provides a broad perspective on housing construction developments over the past decade.

688 **Housing the homeless: the local authority role.**
London: HMSO for the Audit Commission, 1989. 61p.
This report investigates local authorities' services for homeless people and the impact of government policies on that provision.

689 Child abuse: understanding the problem.
Paul Johnson. Marlborough, England: Crowood Press, 1990. 271p. bibliog.

Written from the perspective of a local authority social worker professionally involved with child abuse cases, and using authentic case histories to illustrate its complex nature, this study underlines the difficulties of children, parents, and welfare workers, in coming to terms with the problem and tackling it. Constant vigilance is urged.

690 Britain's inner cities.
Paul Lawless. London: Paul Chapman, 1989. 2nd ed. 194p. 3 maps. bibliog.

What can be certain in the next decade is that the problems of Britain's inner cities will not vanish overnight. This comparatively brief but expert review sets successive governments' policies since 1977 in their historical context, assesses the subsequent major urban initiatives, and concludes with an evaluation of the contribution of local government and independent organizations.

691 Crime and criminal justice since 1945.
Terence Morris. Oxford: Blackwell, 1989. 198p. bibliog. (Making Contemporary Britain).

With the relentless and inexorable increase in crime over the last four decades, which shows little sign of abating, the issue of law and order has been firmly placed on the political agenda. This work charts the growth of crime, and analyses British society's response, looking closely at the progress of legal and penal reform, and at the different styles of policing adopted to get on top of the alarming situation confronting them.

692 Poverty: the facts.
Carey Oppenheim. London: Child Poverty Action Group, 1990. 147p. 2 maps.

A regular publication in recent years, this expanded version is published to mark CPAG's twenty-fifth anniversary and to renew its campaign against poverty. Asserting that there is still a substantial minority living on low incomes, excluded from an acceptable standard of living, and barred from sharing the country's progress, this timely booklet presents a damning indictment of government policy.

693 Voice of protest: a history of civil unrest in Great Britain.
Harold Priestley. London: Leslie Frewin, 1968. 320p. bibliog.

From the agrarian and religious revolts of the fourteenth and fifteenth centuries to the Campaign for Nuclear Disarmament and the anti-Vietnam War protests of the 'fifties and 'sixties, this book examines the causes of protest and their effect on social and political history.

694 Chief Constables: bobbies, bosses or bureaucrats?
Robert Reiner. Oxford: Clarendon Press, 1991. 400p.

Based on interviews with the majority of chief constables in England and Wales, this study reports at first hand their views on the selection and training of the police's senior officers, their duties and responsibilities, and on the future shape and pattern of policing.

695 **'Rogues and vagabonds': vagrant underworld in Britain 1815-1985.**
Lionel Rose. London: Routledge, 1988. 254p. bibliog.
Poor relief; the successive Vagrancy Acts; Victorian dens of infamy and thieves'
kitchens; child vagrancy; and the post- war transition from lodging houses to bed and
breakfast accommodation for the homeless, are among the topics investigated in this
wide-ranging study of the street poor over the last 200 years. An eight-page
'Trampoloquia', a glossary of tramp slang, is also included.

696 **Crime in early modern England 1550-1750.**
J .A. Sharpe. London: Longman, 1984. 230p. bibliog. (Themes in
British Social History).
In this pioneering work of scholarship and synthesis the author examines the use of
criminal statistics culled from court archives, the incidence and causes of crime in
village communities, the problem of social crime, and élite attitudes to crime, and
some popular stereotypes of the criminal classes. A final chapter relates changes in
crime and its treatment to the wider context of socio-economic developments.

697 **The homes and homelessness of post-war Britain.**
Frederick Shaw. Carnforth, England: Parthenon Press, 1985. 287p.
bibliog.
In an attempt to present a general overview of how housing needs have developed
since 1945, this study reviews the different types of housing in use today. These include
privately rented, owner-occupier homes, council housing, housing association homes,
high-rise developments, mobile homes, institutional accommodation for children, the
destitute, and the elderly, the decayed inner city areas, slums, and the housing of
ethnic minorities. Changes in the law in the post- war period are also explained.

698 **The police and the public in England and Wales: a British crime survey.**
Wesley G. Skogan. London: HMSO, 1990. 74p. bibliog. (A Home
Office Research and Planning Unit Report).
Based on the findings of a 1988 survey, this report firstly examines why people call upon
the police and reveals their levels of satisfaction with the response they receive, and then
considers the contacts initiated by the police and the sources of complaints about police
methods and attitudes. The public's readiness to come forward either as witnesses or as
victims also comes under scrutiny. Two factors cause most concern: whilst the public
generally have a great deal of confidence in the police, this has steadily been eroded in the
last ten years; and secondly, there is a widening gap between the public's expectations and
the capacity of the police to meet them. Moreover, peoples experiences of the police, and
their assessment of police services, are consistently related to age, race, and gender. Both
police and public can find little comfort in this official report.

699 **Bricks of shame: Britain's prisons.**
Vivien Stern. London: Penguin, 1989. 2nd ed. 276p. bibliog.
Imprisonment is one of the least known aspects of British life, there is scant awareness of
the vast complexities of the prison system. In this well-researched and much lauded
investigation into the place of prisons in the British criminal justice system three major
questions are addressed. Why does the United Kingdom use imprisonment so much more
than most Western European countries? Why is the prison system expanding when it is
clear that it does little good and conditions worsen year by year? And, why is the prison

system so difficult to change? Written before the disturbances at Strangeways burst onto the television screen, this study looks at the use of prison sentences by the courts, the types of people sent to prison, the purpose of imprisonment, the resources swallowed up in running an inefficient system, and possible improvements which could be made. The author is Director of NACRO (National Association for Care and Resettlement of Offenders) and this book won for him the Oddfellows Social Concern Book Award.

700 **Poverty in the United Kingdom: a survey of household resources and standards of living.**
Peter Townsend. London: Allen Lane, 1979. 1,216p. bibliog.
An enormous amount of detailed information about income and wealth and the use of the social services over a wide social spectrum from the very rich to the very poor is collected in this ambitious and comprehensive survey. It first demonstrates what deprivation in the home, in the environment, at work, and in the community, really entails and continues by showing how poverty is systematically imposed on many social minorities, the elderly, the unemployed and the poorly-paid, through fundamental inequalities in the social hierarchy and the nature of public institutions. It concludes that poverty can only be banished, or even reduced, by a national determination to reform the major institutions through which wealth is earned and distributed.

701 **The strong arm of the law: armed and public order policing.**
P. A. J. Waddington. Oxford: Clarendon Press, 1991. 368p.
Dr. Waddington, Director of Criminal Justice Studies in the University of Reading, undertook three years' research into London's Metropolitan Police during which time he was allowed unprecedented access to the world of armed and public order policing. Here he describes police policy, their tactics and weaponry, and examines the selection and training of armed police officers, the growth of a paramilitary culture and organization, the preferred methods of dispersing rioting crowds, and the causes of riots. It is a sombre report on the current dilemmas surrounding the need to maintain public order whilst retaining public support and consent.

702 **The growing divide: a social audit 1979-1987.**
Edited by Alan Walker, Carol Walker. London: Child Poverty Action Group, 1987. 162p.
Contains fifteen papers which discuss the concept that social divisions in Britain are sharper and more pronounced after the first two Thatcher administrations, which are seen to have deliberately supported 'comfortable Britain' at the expense of the poorest and most vulnerable sections of society. The massive growth in poverty and unemployment, and the impoverishment of women and the ethnic minorities, are quoted to support this theory.

703 **Poverty and the workhouse in Victorian Britain.**
Peter Wood. Gloucester, England: Alan Sutton, 1991. 208p.
The 1834 Poor Law and the workhouses it established may be regarded either as a ruthless measure of social control of the poor or as one of the foundations of the modern welfare state. This study explores its myths and realities in a chronological context extending to the renewed attempts in the 1880s and 1890s to provide more effective institutional relief. How the authorities distinguished between the deserving and undeserving poor, the part voluntary and State agencies played in poor relief, the initial problems of the new Poor Law, and the contemporary financial restraints, are some of the issues debated.

Social Services and Welfare

704 Health policy and the National Health Service.

Judy Allsop. London: Longman, 1984. 324p. bibliog. (Social Policy in Modern Britain).

This study outlines the principles and structure of the NHS as they were when it was established in 1946, examines policy issues regarding its control and funding, accounts for the controversies that plagued its operations, and argues that in removing the threat to survival of severe illnesses, it has obscured the social bases of ill-health, created new needs for extensive care and counselling, and raised expectations that cannot yet be fulfilled. A final section contains thirty-three crucial documents in the NHS's history from 1946 to 1981 and a list of relevant reports and statutes 1858-1983.

705 Almhouses.

Brian Bailey. London: Robert Hale, 1988. 208p. bibliog.

Usually founded by local worthies and benefactors, almshouses eased the final years of the aged and infirm long before the advent of the Welfare State. Even today some 3,000 people live in this type of accommodation. This social and architectural history extends from medieval hospitals to instances of Victorian benevolence.

706 Housing policy an introduction.

Paul N. Balchin. London: Routledge, 1989. 2nd ed. 312p. bibliog.

First published in 1985, this critical analysis of housing issues under the Thatcher administration examines the sharp decline in housebuilding, the decline of private property for rent, the privatization of council housing, the controversies surrounding owner occupation, the inequalities of housing finance, and the escalation of house prices. A review of housing policies since 1985 includes specific consideration of the 1986 Housing and Planning Act and the 1988 Housing Act.

707 **Directory of child rights and welfare.**
Compiled by Claire M. Brennan. London: Woodhead-Faulkner, 1990. 323p. bibliog.

A wealth of information sources and advice agencies on a wide range of children's rights and welfare issues are listed in this directory. Government departments, local authorities, education and training agencies, health and safety, legal rights, holidays, play, sport and leisure, along with children's books and libraries, all are prominently featured.

708 **The voluntary sector in British social services.**
Maria Brenton. London: Longman, 1985. 266p. bibliog. (Social Policy in Modern Britain).

A fundamental move away from state provision and financing of the social services has placed an increasing responsibility on family help and the voluntary agencies. This study maps the agencies' major developments, and asks whether their assumption of tasks previously undertaken by the state is logically feasible or realistically desirable.

709 **A social history of housing 1815-1985.**
John Burnett. London: Methuen, 1986. 2nd ed. 387p. bibliog.

Every aspect of housing provision: physical, social, economic, and political, is examined in this survey of developments in urban and rural housing conditions. Its main aim is to describe the types of living accommodation available to the people from 1815 onwards.

710 **Social services made simple.**
Tony Byrne, Colin F. Padfield. Oxford: Made Simple, 1990. 4th ed. 496p.

Designed for students of social policy and administration, this textbook also serves an introduction to the Welfare State for general readers. It deals at length with social security, the health service, the problems of the aged and the handicapped, children and young persons, education, housing unemployment, environmental planning, finance, the treatment of offenders, and the need for information, advice, and legal aid.

711 **CANS (Citizens Advice Notes).**
London: National Council for Voluntary Organisations, 1991. 2 vols. Cumulative edition.

Supplements continually update this digest of social legislation. The areas covered include the administration of justice, British nationality and migration, business and industry, consumer protection, education, employment, housing and the Rent Acts, public health, health and welfare services, and town and country planning.

712 **Charities by counties and regions 1991.**
Walton-on-Thames, England: Will To Charity, 1991. 240p.

Intended for potential donors this directory also provides general guidance on the charities that exist and what functions and services they offer.

713 Charities digest 1992.

London: Family Welfare Association, 1992. 98th ed. 371p.

The number of charities registered under the 1960 Charities Act now exceeds 171,000. First published in 1882 as *The annual charities register and digest*, the main section of this directory is an alphabetical listing of some 2,000 national and regional charities, giving details of their foundation date, their status, named officers, and their aims and objectives. Other sequences include adoption societies, almshouses, citizens advice bureaux, legal advice centres, local associations for deaf, disabled and blind people, community trusts, volunteer bureaux, and hospice services. There is also information on the Charity Commissioners, the Registry of Friendly Societies, and other official bodies.

714 Housing and social policy.

David Clapham, Peter Kemp, Susan J. Smith. London: Macmillan, 1990. 274p. bibliog. (Studies in Social Policy).

Two key relationships, that between housing and political and social policies, and that between the provision of housing and the provision of other welfare services such as the health service, the education system, and social security, form the pervasive background to this thoughtful work which attempts to address British society's major concerns in the 1980s. Housing disadvantages, homelessness, community care, and housing management, all figure prominently.

715 The complete fundraising handbook.

Sam Clarke. London: Directory of Social Change in association with the Institute of Charity Fundraising Managers, 1992. 256p. bibliog.

Sound advice on all major aspects of fundraising is offered in this authoritative handbook: how to set about raising money; the range of funds available; understanding the difference techniques likely to be successful; and case studies of successful campaigns.

716 Dictionary of social services: policy and practice.

Joan Clegg. London: Bedford Square Press/NCVO, 1980. 3rd ed. 148p. bibliog.

Contained in this dictionary, first published in 1971, are nearly 600 cross-referenced, concise and matter-of-fact definitions of words and phrases commonly used in health, welfare, child care, housing and town planning, national insurance, and supplementary benefits. There is also a list of official reports relevant to the social services.

717 The health scandal: your health in crisis.

Vernon Coleman. London: Sidgwick & Jackson, 1988. 245p.

In every aspect of medicine, whether it be private health care, the National Health Service, drug companies, general practitioners, hospitals, or local authorities, the author perceives wastage, ignorance and incompetence. He exposes fifteen 'scandals' cumulatively paving the way to a medical doomsday about thirty years hence when a heavily outnumbered healthy and working population will be struggling to support an increasing number of elderly and disabled people.

718 **Directory for disabled people: a handbook of information and opportunities for disabled and handicapped people.**
Compiled by Ann Darnborough, Derek Kinrade. London: Woodhead-Faulkner, 1991. 6th ed. 444p.
Published in association with the Royal Association for Disability and Rehabilitation, this directory is the foremost guide to the services, facilities, and opportunities open to disabled people, their carers, and the providers of related services. Starting with a section on statutory services, it encompasses financial benefits and allowances, aids and equipment, housing, education and training, employment, mobility, holidays, arts, sports and leisure, personal relationships, and legislation affecting disabled people. A final section lists and describes some 300 helpful organizations.

719 **Directory of hospitals 1992.**
Harlow, England: Longman, 1992. 594p.
Over 2,300 National Health Service and 230 independent hospitals are listed in this directory. Entries for NHS hospitals give the address and telecommunication details, its type, number of beds, and the names of its unit general manager, senior nursing officer, and other chief officers and consultants. Details of regional and district health authorities and boards, family health services authorities in England and Wales, and first and second wave NHS Trusts, are also included in this edition.

720 **Directory of services for elderly people 1992.**
Harlow, England: Longman, 1991. 2nd ed. 321p.
The result of a collaboration between the publisher and the Centre for Policy on Ageing, this directory of services for the elderly is divided into two main sections: public and statutory services provided by central and local government agencies; and services created by private agencies. Brief details of services provided are given, and there are guides to appropriate government reports and legislations.

721 **Directory of youth services and child care in the United Kingdom.**
Harlow, England: Longman, 1991. 2nd ed. 346p.
This directory provides a reliable listing of all resource agencies and organizations working in the field of youth. The probation service, groups working with young people from ethnic minorities, counselling and advice services, professional associations, the media, research and development bodies, etc., are also covered in detail.

722 **Handbook of counselling in Britain.**
Edited by Wendy Dryden, David Charles-Edwards, Ray Woolfe. London: Routledge, 1989. 454p.
Published in association with the British Association for Counselling, this collection of papers by different authors offers a comprehensive overview of counselling activities in Britain. Their nature and practice, work with people in all age groups and settings, and the various themes and issues encountered, are all described and discussed.

723 **Employment, health and safety.**
London: HMSO, 1990. rev. ed. 40p. (Sectional List no. 21).

Expanded from previous lists which included only publications dealing with general employment matters, this edition also contains lists of Health and Safety Commission and Health and Safety Executive reports, surveys, Acts and Regulations, codes of practice, and guidance notes etc.

724 **CPAG's housing benefit and community charge legislation.**
Lorna Findlay, Martin Ward. London: CPAG, 1991. 4th ed. 495p. bibliog.

The standard authority on housing and community charge benefits, this handbook assembles all the relevant statutory material and subjects it to a detailed analysis and interpretation. Although it unravels the bureaucratic complexities associated with the two types of benefit in clear and unambiguous terms it still needs to be treated with caution by the untutored user.

725 **Unemployment and training rights handbook: the Independent Unemployment Unit and Youthaid's guide to rights when you are unemployed or on a Government Training Scheme.**
Dan Finn, Lucy Ball. London: Unemployment Unit, 1991. 291p. bibliog.

The definitive guide for the unemployed and school leavers, this handbook explains what benefits those in and out of work are eligible for, who can sign on as unemployed, the concepts of 'available for work' and 'actively seeking work', the penalties for refusing suitable employment, youth training, enterprise allowance schemes, and job clubs.

726 **How to . . . know your rights: patients: a handbook for every Health Service user.**
John Frain. Plymouth, England: How To Books, 1991. 144p. bibliog.

Formulated to answer the questions of ordinary patients who may be confused by the recent National Health Services changes, this handbook offers expert guidance to patients' and relatives' rights in respect of visits to doctors, clinics and hospitals, to matters regarding confidentiality, abortion, AIDS, consent to treatment, the right to information and to inspect medical records, and complaints and compensation. A medical glossary and a list of useful addresses add to this work's undoubted value.

727 **The health care consumer guide.**
Robert Gann. London: Faber, 1991. 350p. bibliog.

Based on the author's experience as librarian of Help for Health, a pioneering consumer health information service in the Wessex region, this guide first focuses on self-care and deals with such matters as 'green' health, how to cope with illness, and sensible and judicious use of the pharmacy. The second section concentrates on medical, dentist, and optician's services. Other sections are concerned with hospital services, private treatment, and how to find out about health. A directory of self-help organizations completes this remarkably useful publication.

728   **Understanding mental health.**
Angelina Gibbs.   London: Consumers' Association and Hodder &
Stoughton, 1986. 246p.

A straightforward guide to all aspects of mental health care, this handbook delves into
the causes of mental illnesses, explains why they occur, and what can be done to
prevent and treat them. Other sections deal with emotional problems, how to seek
help, and obtain specialist advice, living with mentally ill relatives, the legal aspects of
admission into psychiatric hospitals, and patients rights regarding their treatment and
discharge.

729   **The health and safety directory 1990/91.**
Edited by Margaret R. Hastings.   Kingston upon Thames, England:
Croner, 1990. 4th ed. 1,168p. bibliog.

A comprehensive reference source providing the names and addresses of all
organizations involved with health and safety, this massive work is concerned with
regulatory authorities and national bodies, including the Health and Safety Commission, regional and local public services, international organizations, health and safety
in industry, professional bodies, and safety organizations.

730   **Health and social security.**
London: HMSO, 1988. rev. ed. 32p. (Sectional List no. 11).

This catalogue provides a full guide to recent publications issued by the Department of
Health and Social Security relating to *inter alia* AIDS, spongiform encephalopathy
(mad cow disease), and all state benefits, allowances, and pensions.

731   **Cold comfort: the scandal of private rest homes.**
Bernadette Holmes, Andrew Johnson.   London: Souvenir Press, 1988.
188p. bibliog.

Appalling conditions, an inadequate diet, cramped living and sleeping accommodation,
lack of mental stimulation, the careless administration of drugs, as well as, at times,
actual physical and mental cruelty, have been the fate of many elderly people ending
their days in private rest homes. This investigation examines the causes of the declining
standards in residential care and sets down guidelines for their urgent improvement.

732   **Health, happiness, and security: the creation of the National Health
Service.**
Frank Honigsbaum.   London: Routledge, 1989. 286p. bibliog.

Meticulously researched, this study traces the part played by the Civil Service in the
creation of Britain's National Health Service and reveals how it influenced ministerial
decisions. The crucial role of Lord Moran, President of the Royal College of
Physicians, is also examined. Overall the conclusion is that the NHS could well have
come into existence more peacefully and less controversially had the Civil Service
shown more flexibility.

733 **Help with NHS costs.**
London: Department of Health and Central Office of Information, 1992. 24p.

Revised periodically, this booklet contains information on how to get free National Health Services prescriptions, dental treatment, vouchers for sight tests and glasses, hospital travel costs, wigs, milk and vitamins.

734 **The origins of the National Health Service: the medical services of the new poor law, 1834-1871.**
Ruth G. Hodkinson. London: Wellcome Historical Medical Library, 1967. 714p. bibliog.

Undoubtedly a pioneer work, and one not likely to be superseded, this comprehensive study of the growth of the State medical services in the nineteenth century takes into account the prevailing social and economic conditions, the poverty and ill-health, and the inadequacy of the existing poor law medical provision. The roles of the institutional provision for the sick and insane, the voluntary hospitals, the public dispensaries, are all examined, as is the growing awareness that the work of such bodies needed to be put on a more professional basis and to be more closely co-ordinated and controlled.

735 **Hospital and health services yearbook . . . an annual record of the hospitals and health services of Great Britain and Northern Ireland incorporating** *Burdett's hospitals and charities* **founded 1899.**
London: Institute of Health Services Management, 1991. 5,026p. bibliog.

Directory information on all British hospitals is included in this mammoth, single volume yearbook which also contains Statutory Instruments and circulars relating to health services, Health Service literature, and a directory of hospital suppliers.

736 **Government grants: a guide for voluntary organizations.**
Compiled by Maggie Jones. London: NCVO, 1991. 6th ed. 105p.

An essential tool for voluntary groups seeking government financial assistance, this guide covers grants from central government departments, quangoes, and local authorities. It provides easily understood information on the grant schemes available, the kinds of projects which can be funded, and the criteria for grant aid. It also gives practical advice on how best to apply for a grant and it prints a code of practice for voluntary societies when dealing with government departments.

737 **Benefits: CHAR's guide to means-tested benefits for single people without a permanent home: 1992/93.**
Emma Knights. London: CHAR, 1992. 13th ed. 257p.

Published with the assistance of the London Housing Foundation this guide offers expert advice on housing benefit, the community charge, how to negotiate payments from the social fund, with special sections for those either with no accommodation or living in temporary accommodation. The special rules applying to sixteen- and seventeen-year-olds, students, and prisoners, are also fully explained.

738 **Laing's review of private health care . . . and directory of independent hospitals, residential and nursing homes and related services.**
W. Laing.   London: Laing & Buisson, 1990. 3rd ed. 1,220p. map.

Over 12,000 private and voluntary homes for the elderly, other independent hospitals, screening units, and homes and hospitals for the mentally ill, are listed in this comprehensive directory.

739 **The development of the welfare state 1939-1951: a guide to the documents in the Public Records Office.**
Andrew Land, Rodney Lowe, Noel Whiteside.   London: HMSO, 1992. 254p.

This handbook provides researchers with a good working guide to the wealth of information contained in government departmental records relating to social welfare, social conditions, and social change.

740 **The early history of English poor relief.**
E. M. Leonard.   London: Frank Cass, 1965. 397p.

'A fairly effectual system of relieving the destitute by public authority has had in England a continuous existence since the seventeenth century'. This study, primarily based on the municipal records of London and Norwich, and which was first published in 1900, traces the secular control of poor relief since Anglo-Saxon times. Three main themes emerge: the early growth of local poor relief administration; constant central government pressure on local bodies; and the close connection between poor relief and the maintenance of public order.

741 **Housing year book 1992.**
Edited by Kate Lodge.   Harlow, England: Longman, 1991. 467p. bibliog.

First published in 1973 this guide to local and central government institutions and people involved in housing issues and problems includes sections on new towns and development corporations, housing advisory bodies, housing associations, specialist housing, homelessness, professional bodies and trade associations, and a final section on sources of further information.

742 **The welfare state in Britain since 1943.**
Rodney Lowe.   London: Macmillan, 1992. 320p.

Theoretical perspectives on the nature of the welfare state are followed in this historical account of welfare policy in Britain since the days of the Beveridge Report by an assessment of the successes and failures of government policy in social and employment policy, income maintenance, education, housing, and personal social services. Two clear periods are distinguished: consensus between 1943 and 1975; and ideological conflict 1975-1990, when the whole concept of the welfare state began to be questioned.

743 **Housing policy and practice.**
Peter Malpass, Alan Murie. London: Macmillan, 1987. 2nd ed. 350p.
bibliog. (Public Policy and Politics).

The expansion of home ownership, largely due to the privatization of local authority
housing, was a distinctive feature of the 1980s. Adopting as their main themes the
relationship between central and local government, and the growing government
dependence on private institutions to implement political policies, the authors outline
the causes and effects of home ownership. Other new features in this updated version
of a work first published in 1982 include the development of housing policy in the
nineteenth century, a study of the period 1979-1986, and housing finance. Finally, the
question is asked: who benefits from existing housing policies?

744 **The NHS handbook.**
London: Macmillan for the National Association of Health Authorities
and Trusts, 1991. 7th ed. 267p.

All aspects of the National Health Service, its funding and management, its provision
of care, community care and support services, are reflected in this handbook whose
aim is 'to make NHS easily understood by those without prior knowledge of its
structure and to provide an up-to-date reference document for those already working
in the NHS and related fields'.

745 **The home front: housing the people 1840-1990.**
Patrick Nuttgens. London: BBC, 1989. 160p. bibliog.

Based on six forty-minute television documentaries, this illustrated work examines how
the social changes caused by the Industrial Revolution made mass housing essential.
The early council estates of the Northern textile manufacturing towns, the model
villages, the garden city movement, slum clearances, the growth of the suburb, and the
coming of the high-rise blocks, all come under discussion. The thorny questions of
owner occupation and protected housing are also given a good airing. The author is
convinced that the dire mistakes of the past can be rectified and that mass housing will
remain a basic need for substantial sections of the population.

746 **The growth and development of the community health service.**
Roger Ottewill, Ann Wall. Sunderland, England: Business Education
Publishers, 1990. 540p.

For NHS management purposes a number of disparate services are grouped under the
collective title of 'community health services'. These include chriopody, health visiting,
family planning clinics, school health, district nursing, community midwifery,
vaccination and immunization, health education, home nursing aids, speech therapy,
and the community dental service. This study analyses the management and operations
of CHSs and examines their role within the National Health Service.

747 **Our NHS.**
David Owen. London: Pan Books, 1988. 197p. bibliog.

At one time a neurological and psychiatric registrar, the author sympathetically
reviews here the creation, structure and evolution of the National Health Service. He
then assesses its current position and examines how it can survive ideological and

political differences to develop into a modern, efficient, properly funded, comprehensive health service for the nation.

748 **The Guardian book of the Welfare State.**
Edited by R. A. Pearson. Aldershot, England: Wildwood House, 1988. 267p.
Divided into chronological sections which examine the central theses of housing, education, health, and social security and welfare, thereby ensuring an obvious progression of events in each specific social service, this book consists of selected reports from the *Manchester Guardian*, 16 January 1945 to 23 August 1948, the formative period of the 'welfare state'.

749 **Rights guide to non-means-tested benefits.**
Richard Poynter, Clive Martin. London: Child Poverty Action Group, 1992. 15th ed. 284p. bibliog.
Revised annually, and updated to cover the social security changes applying in 1992-93, this handbook aims to explain the non-means-tested benefit system for claimants to Department of Social Security benefits. Among the topics treated are unemployment benefit; disability benefit, including the new disabled living allowance; statutory maternity pay and sick pay; invalid care allowance; retirement pensions; industrial injuries and diseases; widows benefit; and how to appeal against DHSS rulings.

750 **The counselling handbook: a complete guide to what to expect and how to get the counselling you need.**
Susan Quilliam, Ian Grove-Stephenson. Wellingborough, England: Thorsons, 1990. 240p. bibliog.
Information on how to get in touch with a counsellor, what to expect from a counselling session, what to do after counselling has come to an end, and a complete list of all the principal counselling organizations, are all contained in this comprehensive consumer's guide.

751 **National welfare benefits handbook.**
Marcus Revell, David Simmons, Lynn Webster. London: Child Poverty Action Group, 1992. 22nd ed. 406p.
Explanations of who can claim income support; who is eligible for the new disability working allowance; how to claim from the social fund; how to obtain community charge rebates; who can claim family credit; the changes to the severe disability premium; and what the current maintenance rules are, are all in this extremely useful handbook.

752 **Directory of charities 1990-1991.**
Edited by Kerry Robinson. Tonbridge, England: Charities Aid Foundation, 1990. 2nd ed. 292p.
Information on 14,000 charities, giving their Charity Commission reference number, their aims and objectives, activities and projects, and their publications, is included in this directory.

753 **Social security statistics 1992.**
London: HMSO for Department of Social Security, 1992. 19th ed.
379p. map.

Statistical tables showing trends over several years are arranged in two main sections: benefits, pensions and allowances; and national insurance, finance, and prices. A brief descriptive note of the main features of the relevant benefit, as they currently apply, is printed before each section. Detailed analyses are provided for the most recent year available. The edition is updated annually.

754 **Social Service Abstracts: monthly summaries of selected documents.**
London: HMSO for Department of Health and Social Security, 1972- .
monthly.

Over 2,000 abstracts are published each year in this monthly publication. They encompass social policy, the social services, social work, services for the elderly, the handicapped, children and young people, Department of Health and Social Security circulars, and bibliographies. The emphasis throughout is on literature originating in and relating to Britain.

755 **Social Services year book 1991/92.**
Harlow, England: Longman, 1991. 802p. bibliog.

Included in this invaluable directory are details of all local authority social services departments, health authorities, advice and counselling services, voluntary services, and elderly people's welfare organizations.

756 **Consumer rights handbook.**
Anne Stanesby. London: Pluto, 1986. 236p.

This simple practical guide first sets out consumers' legal rights when buying goods, services, or credit, and then deals with problems that arise when their rights are infringed and violated.

757 **Dictionary of social welfare.**
Noel Timms, Rita Timms. London: Routledge & Kegan Paul, 1982.
217p.

Entries in this practical guide indicate the meaning, or range of meanings, of the words and terms employed in welfare, welfare legislation, policy controversies, and in social welfare practice. Most of then end with references to sources where a more extended treatment or elaborations on their application may be found.

758 **The voluntary agencies directory 1991.**
London: Bedford Square Press, 1991. 12th ed. 224p.

First published in 1928 as *Voluntary services handbook and directory*, and then as *Voluntary Organizations: an NCVO directory*, this standard reference work lists nearly 2,000 organizations, ranging from small specialist self-help groups to long-established national charities, giving concise descriptions of their objectives and activities, with details of their charitable status, their scope for volunteer participation, local branches, and of their membership and staffing. A quick reference list of abbreviations and acronyms assists access to individual agencies.

759   Social work, social care and social planning: the personal social services
      since Seebohm.
      Adrian Webb, Gerald Wistow.   London: Longman, 1987. 306p.
      bibliog. (Social Policy in Modern Britain).
Six key issues are identified in this analytical overview of the social services: the
problems caused by the need to combine social work, social care, and social planning;
the respective roles of the State and the voluntary sectors; the impact of central
government on local social services departments; whether there is a real shortage of
resources or whether they are used inappropriately; and whether there are real cuts in
the resources available or in resource growth.

760   The health services since the war: vol. 1. Problems of health care: the
      National Health Service before 1957.
      Charles Webster.   London: HMSO, 1988. 479p. 2 maps.
Given full access to official documents and archives, the author charts the politics of
health care and the state of health service from the inter-war period up to the tenth
anniversary of the 1946 National Health Service Act. He draws a sharp contrast
between the high ideals of those who conceived the NHS and the artificially (and
unnecessarily) low standards adopted and accepted in practice.

761   Which benefit? Social Security: a guide to Social Security and NHS
      benefits.
      London: Social Security Benefits Agency and Central Office of
      Information, 1992. 71p.
Information on all social security benefits, National Health Service costs, and war
pensions, is contained in this tall pocket-size Government booklet. These range from
National Insurance benefits to those directed at people on low income, the
unemployed, parents and guardians, young people, the sick, injured and disabled,
those in residential and nursing care, retired persons, and widows, etc. Help for those
receiving specific NHS treatment and appliances is also outlined. *Which benefit?* is
revised at least annually and sometimes more frequently as circumstances dictate. A
separate eighteen-page booklet, *Social security benefit rates* is inserted into the book.

762   The working parents handbook: a practical guide to the alternatives in
      childcare.
      London: Working Mothers Association, 1991. new ed. 92p.
Descending from *The working mothers handbook* (1981), this guide investigates all
aspects of reconciling child care and a return to paid employment. Information is given
on the widest choice of options and their legal implications.

763   Mastering social welfare.
      Pat Young.   London: Macmillan, 1989. 2nd ed. 337p.
This revised edition of a work originally published in 1985 has been updated to include
recent legislation on social security, housing, and education. It considers all aspects of
social welfare: poverty, unemployment, housing and homelessness, living in cities,
education, children in trouble, mental illnesses and handicaps, old age and disability,
the health service, and the contribution of the voluntary sector.

Education

764 **Access to UK higher education: a guide for overseas students.**
London: HMSO for British Council, 1992. 160p.

Compiled from data supplied by further and higher education institutions, this guide gives detailed information on the education and training facilities available in the UK to overseas students. Access ranges from undergraduate bridging courses to PhD research degrees. There is also much useful information on the scholarships available, the provision of family accommodation, and details of welfare services, at each institution.

765 **Dictionary of British educationalists.**
Richard Aldrich, Peter Gordon.   London: Woburn Press, 1978. 272p. bibliog.

About 450 educationalists who played a major part in the advancement of education in the United Kingdom from 1800 onwards are included in this biographical dictionary. Amongst their number are the chairmen of influential committees and also politicians and administrators whose careers took them into the educational world.

766 **South Kensington to Robbins: an account of English technical and scientific education since 1851.**
Michael Argles.   London: Longmans, 1964. 178p. bibliog.

The Committee on Higher Education, appointed in 1961, was asked 'to review the pattern of full-time higher education in Great Britain and in the light of national needs and resources to advise Her Majesty's Government on what principles its long-term development should be based'. Its report, published in 1963, the Robbins Report, was the most comprehensive account of higher education ever attempted in Great Britain and was plainly a landmark in scientific and technical education especially. This book relates the progress of scientific, technical and technological education in Britain from the year of the Great Exhibition onwards and is particularly valuable for its account of the post-war events leading up to the Committee's appointment.

767   **National vocational qualifications and further education.**
Edited by Mike Bees, Madeleine Swords.   London: Kogan Page in
association with the National Council for Vocational Qualifications,
1990. 223p.

This series of papers contributed by experienced practitioners address issues relevant
to college managers, tutors, and employers. The accreditation of prior learning,
adaptation and reform in Further Education, qualifying the workforce, the demographic
timebomb, and Further Education in an enterprise culture are all included.

768   **The student book 1993: the applicant's guide to UK colleges,**
polytechnics and universities.
Edited by Klaus Boehm, Jenny Lees-Spalding.   London: Macmillan,
1992. 14th ed. 775p. 7 maps.

A directory/guide to 250 universities, polytechnics, and colleges, with details of their
courses, admission requirements and procedures, library services, sports facilities, and
names of some well-known *alumni*, forms the main section of this student
compendium. Other sections include basic information on applying, funding, and how
to survive the first year.

769   **British qualifications: a complete guide to educational, technical,**
professional and academic qualifications in Britain.
London: Kogan Page, 1991. 22nd ed. 769p.

First published in 1966, this guide ranges from secondary school examinations,
qualifications from further education institutions, usually technical or commercial in
nature, to awards made by universities and polytechnics. But its core is without doubt
the section on trade and professional qualifications in over 200 career fields and
professions. *A dictionary of British qualifications: abbreviations and qualifying bodies*
(1985. 121p.) is a condensed version listing postnominal letters, their full meaning, and
the name and address of the awarding body.

770   **Choosing a state school: how to find the best education for your child.**
Caroline Cox, Robert Balchin, John Marks.   London: Hutchinson,
1989. 168p.

This heavily-used guide gives information on how to choose a good school, whether
state or private, primary or secondary. It explains parents' rights to choose, to secure
information, and to appeal against adverse decisions, and includes a step-by-step
approach on what to look for when visiting a school and what questions to ask. It also
instructs on how to compare examination results, how to read a school prospectus, and
gives guidance on the assisted places scheme. There is a fifty-page guide to career
educational requirements.

771 **The directory of resources for the GCSE: a guide to printed, audio-visual and software resources suitable for subject courses leading to the General Certificate of Secondary Education.**
Cambridge, England: Hobsons, 1988. 288p.

Part one of this directory sets out information about the background to GCSE, origins, objectives, syllabuses, administration and assessment. Part two consists single subject sections listing the aims and syllabus of each course and providing selection of suitable print and non-print resources.

772 **Education and science.**
London: HMSO, 1988. rev. ed. 28p. (Sectional List, no. 2).

Official reports and other literature issued by the Department of Education a Science and the House of Commons Education, Science and Arts Committee are liste in this catalogue. Relevant Public General Acts and Statutory Instruments referring education are also listed.

773 **The education authorities directory and annual 1992.**
Redhill, England: School Government Publishing, 1992. 1,296p.

First published as long ago as 1909 this compendium lists government department public offices, the examining boards, local authorities, secondary and middle school teachers' centres, further education colleges and institutions, polytechnics, teache training institutes and colleges, universities, special schools, directors of social service education psychological services, career centres, public library authorities, ai education publishers and equipment suppliers.

774 **Education Statistics for the UK.**
London: HMSO for Department of Education and Science, 1967- . annual.

Basic statistics are assembled in this annual compilation to illustrate the size and natu of educational activity within the UK. They cover areas such as educational financ teaching staff, schools, curriculum, further and higher education, qualifications, ai destinations.

775 **Directory of technical and further education.**
Edited by Michaela Evans.   Harlow, England: Longman, 1992.
23rd ed. 415p.

In this annual publication a tabular guide to courses in thirty-six subject area introduces strictly directory type information to government and public offices, th regional educational framework, PCFC colleges, universities and university college correspondence colleges, examining bodies, employment and career services, and th CBI and TUC and other organizations. It was formerly known as *Year book technical education and training for industry*.

776   **A guide to educational terms.**
Peter Gordon, Denis Lawton.   London: Batsford, 1984. 220p. bibliog.
Concise, cross-referenced working definitions of key terms in education, relating
mainly to educational institutions and practices, form the central core of this useful
guide. Ancillary material includes an outline of the education system of England and
Wales, landmarks in the development of English education since 1800, and a
chronological list of Ministers of Education.

777   **Education in the Second World War: a study in policy and
administration.**
P. H. J. H. Gosden.   London: Methuen, 1976. 527p. bibliog.
Planning for a fundamental reconstruction of the educational system started in 1940
and came to fruition with the passing of the Education Act in 1944. This expert study
shows how its framework was established and recounts the impact of evacuation; aerial
bombardment; the shortage of staff, materials and accommodation; rising truancy and
delinquency; and the development of welfare services, school meals especially, during
the Second World War.

778   **The complete degree course offers 1993 for entry into higher education:
the complete guide on admission to all higher education courses.**
Brian Heap.   Richmond, England: Trotman, 1992. 23rd ed. 440p.
bibliog.
Revised annually this guide provides information on grade requirements, admission
procedures, departmental strengths, attitudes on gap years (between school and
college), on possible questions at interview, courses with a European element, and on
employment prospects. It is recommended to all schools and career officers by the
Department of Employment.

779   **Higher education in the United Kingdom 1992-93: a handbook for
students and their advisers.**
Harlow, England: Longman for The Association of Commonwealth
Universities, 1992. 25th ed. 312p. map.
The Association of Commonwealth Universities was founded in 1913 and provides
factual information about university study and scholarship opportunities. The main
section of this handbook is a directory of subjects of study which lists available courses
by levels of study at higher education institutions. Introductory sections range over the
entire UK higher education scene: the academic year; admission procedures and
requirements; tuition fees; and student life.

780   **The history of adult education.**
J. W. Hudson.   London: Woburn Press, 1969. 238p. (The Social
History of Education).
This is a facsimile reprint of Hudson's *The history of adult education in which is
compressed a full and complete history of the Mechanics' and Literary Institutions,
Athenaeum, philosophical, mental and Christian improvement societies, literary union,
schools of design etc. of Great Britain, Ireland, America* first published by Longmans in
1851. It remains a valuable source for the theory behind the concept of self-
improvement and how it progressed in practice.

781 **The Which? guide to sponsorship in higher education.**
Alan Jamieson. London: Consumers' Association and Hodder & Stoughton, 1991. 372p.

Detailed information on various forms of sponsorship available to students taking first degree and HND courses is contained in this decidedly useful descriptive guide. General information on sponsorship is followed in a second section by a directory of 200 companies and organizations which offer bursaries, industrial training placements, or other sponsorship schemes. A third section lists institutions and departments covering subjects that attract sponsored students.

782 **The changing secondary school.**
Edited by Roy Lowe. Lewes, England: Falmer Press, 1989. 233p.

Major issues confronting secondary schools today are here placed in the general context of the recent history of English education. The establishment of secondary education in the immediate post-war years, the attempts by local authorities and pressure groups to achieve comprehensive education in the 1950s and 1960s, and the curricular developments sponsored by the Schools Council, lead up to an account of the rise of the New Right as a political force, and the consequent educational proposals which culminated in the 1988 Education Reform Act.

783 **Education year book 1992.**
Edited by Deborah Lyttleton. Harlow, England: Longman, 1991. 52nd ed. 684p.

First published in 1939 as *Education committees year book*, this edition takes into account the 1988 Education Reform Act, the city technology colleges, and schools which have 'opted-out'. Government and public offices, local authorities, independent secondary schools and non-maintained specialist schools, community homes and schools, higher, further and vocational education, the examining bodies, employment and careers, teachers' and other educational organizations, youth services, educational publishing, computers in education, and educational suppliers, all fall within its remit.

784 **Education re-formed: a guide to the Education Reform Act.**
Stuart Maclure. London: Hodder & Stoughton, 1989. 2nd ed. 180p.

'The Education Reform Act 1988 was the most important and far-reaching piece of educational law-making for England and Wales since the Education Act of 1944' (Introduction). This concise guide explains its wide-ranging implications: the increased powers of central government; the powers of choice and responsibilities of parents; the centrally controlled national curriculum; the diminishing of local educational authority responsibilities; the creation of a new category of Department of Education and Science maintained schools; and the new financial changes in Further and Higher Education. The author was editor of *Times Education Supplement* from 1969 to 1989.

785 **Macmillan/Pickup national training directory.**
London: Macmillan, 1991. 2 vols. 3rd ed. variously paginated.

This massive work provides a one-stop source of information on 15,000 short courses and training opportunities for school-leavers, unemployed adults, and employees. Each entry gives information on the course provider, clients and client level expected, entry qualifications, study mode, course length, starting dates, costs, and location. The

Professional Industrial, and Commercial Updating (PICKUP) scheme was launched by the Department of Education and Science in 1982.

786 Schools now: a parent's guide.
Charles Martin. Tring, England: Lion, 1988. 251p. bibliog.

Following the 1988 Education Reform Act parents are expected to express their views and to assume a more direct responsibility for their children's education. This book offers advice on the advantages and disadvantages of opting out of local educational authority control as well as providing information on such topics as the new grading and assessment procedures and on the role envisaged for parent governors.

787 A guide to the national curriculum.
Bob Moon. Oxford: Oxford University Press, 1991. 114p.

Detailed accounts of the three core foundation subjects: English, mathematics, and science, along with a review of recent developments in information technology, are included in this guide to the significance and implications of the national curriculum. Its structure, the way it is being introduced in the 1990s, the political and academic debates surrounding it, and its impact in the classroom, are among the specific topics considered.

788 English schools in the Middle Ages.
Nicholas Orme. London: Methuen, 1973. 369p. 7 maps. bibliog.

This study of the rise of schools and the growth in literacy in the medieval period comprises a sketch of the literary interest of different social classes; a discussion of school life and the curricula followed; and an outline of the history of religious and secular schools from the twelfth century to Elizabeth I. There is also a thirty-page list of medieval schools 1066-1530.

789 The primary school directory 1992.
Redhill, England: School Government Publishing, 1992.

The main feature of this directory is a systematic listing of school addresses, the names of head teachers, and numbers enrolled on the school registers in order of London Boroughs, metropolitan counties, and non-metropolitan authorities.

790 A history of secondary education in England 1800-1870.
John Roach. London: Longman, 1986. 342p. map. bibliog.

Concentrating on children between the ages of eleven and eighteen attending grammar schools, private schools, or the great public schools, this extremely well-researched and fully-documented study examines the structure of schooling in the nineteenth century, the curricula, some notable headmasters, innovations in teaching methods, and Nonconformist and Roman Catholic schools. It ends with a consideration of the reforms following the Clarendon examinations, more efficient administrative structures, and the introduction of new schools for girls.

791 **Comprehensive schooling: the impossible dream?**
Beverley Shaw. Oxford: Blackwell, 1983. 176p. bibliog.

The origins of the concept of comprehensive education, how it became public policy, and the organization of comprehensive schools, are all covered in this critical review. The sad conclusion is that it was an ill-devised reform based largely on doctrinaire and short-term political aims.

792 **The school effect: a study of multi-racial comprehensives.**
David J. Smith, Sally Tomlinson. London: Policy Studies Institute, 1989. 325p. bibliog.

This study is the outcome of a DES-funded research project carried out 1981-88 by the Policy Studies Institute and the Department of Educational Research, University of Lancaster, which followed a group of 3,000 children attending twenty multi-racial comprehensive schools over a five year period, from the time of transfer to the sitting of public examinations at the age of sixteen. Using statistical methods and techniques perfected at Lancaster, the study suggests there is wide scope for improvement in secondary schooling. The academic level at which a child is expected to compete depends more on the policies adopted by the school than on the child's own abilities. It also challenges the notion that ethnic minority children underachieve in secondary schools.

793 **The education fact file: a handbook of education information in the UK.**
June Statham, Donald Mackinnon. London: Hodder & Stoughton, 1991. 2nd ed. 196p. 7 maps. bibliog.

Although primarily intended as a set book for the Open University second level course, *Exploring education issues*, this fact file, first published in 1989, is designed to stand independently for other education courses and to give an insight into recent and current developments, including the implications of the 1988 Education Reform Act. Four areas are explored: the social and demographic background, including summaries of official reports and legislation about education; the education system encompassing education institutions and administrative structures, a 'who's who' in education, examinations and qualifications, and education finance; the school curriculum, and inequalities in terms of social class, sex, and ethnic groups; and a guide to educational terminology.

794 **Adult education.**
Michael D. Stephens. London: Cassell, 1990. 132p. (Education Matters).

Adult education is now recognized as being of crucial importance to the social and economic development of the nation and it is becoming increasingly clear that, in an age of fast-moving technological change, it is no longer possible to acquire sufficient knowledge and skills at school to last a lifetime. This book describes the origins and structure of adult education, and provides a comprehensive guide to its key developments, the Training Agency, distance education, and adult education in colleges of further and higher education.

795 **DUKHE 1991/92: The directory of UK higher education: a complete guide to first degree, HNC/D, and DipHE courses.**
Edited by James Tomlinson, David Weigall, Katy Goldberg. London: Hobsons, 1991. 302p.

First in this CRAC publication is a general information section on UK higher education institutions and on student grants and loans. Next a section on application requirements and qualifications for different types of courses, followed by a directory of courses broken down into eleven subject areas. A directory of institutions and the courses they offer completes a very useful publication.

796 **Graduate studies 1992/92: the complete reference source for postgraduate studies in the UK.**
Edited by James Tomlinson, Brenda Radcliffe, Katy Goldberg.
Cambridge, England: Hobsons, 1991. 1,176p.

Both this guide and *The students' guide to graduate studies in the UK 1992. A concise personal guide to research and postgraduate study in the UK* (704p.) provide summaries of research courses and facilities and basic information about institutions in which post-graduate studies are available, and both are divided into the same four subject areas: humanities and social sciences; biological, health and agricultural sciences; physical sciences; and engineering and applied sciences.

797 **University entrance 1993: the official guide.**
London: Association of Commonwealth Universities, 1992. 6th ed.
501p.

First published in 1987 as the successor to the *Compendium of university entrance requirements*, this guide provides an individual outline of all UK universities, including entrance policies and practices, and factboxes presenting details of student numbers, library facilities, and likely costs. Course tables giving detailed information on entry patterns, suitable GCSE subjects and grades, and alternative qualifications, for all courses, grouped in nine subject categories, are also included in this immensely useful reference work.

798 **Education A-Z: A-Z of sources on all major educational topics.**
Compiled by Elizabeth Wallis. London: Advisory Centre for Education, 1991. 5th ed. 242p.

The Advisory Centre for Education is a national charity, independent of both local and central government, which campaigns for a more open and a more responsible education service. This reference guide lists and describes major educational topics and organizations with information on education terminology, official reports, reference books, types of school, levels of courses etc. from Access courses to Zoning. It was first published in 1974.

Education

799 **Histories of old schools: a revised list for England and Wales.**
P. J. Wallis.   Newcastle upon Tyne, England: Department of
Education, University of Newcastle upon Tyne, 1966. 98p.

This basic bibliography of the history of schools that existed before 1700 lists the best
and most recent accounts of the history of particular schools, arranged on a county
basis. It was first published in the November 1965 and the May and November 1986
issues of *British Journal of Educational Studies*.

800 **A common policy for education.**
Mary Warnock.   Oxford: Oxford University Press, 1988. 185p.
bibliog.

Strongly critical of the government's reforms in the national education system,
particularly those relating to the City Technology Colleges, the tests in primary and
secondary schools at the ages of seven, eleven, and fourteen, and the proposal to
remove research facilities from some universities, this study presents alternative
developments for a common policy for the education system as a whole, including a
radical rethink on teacher training methods and an overhaul of teachers' salary
structures.

801 **Which degree 1993: the complete guide to all full-time and sandwich first
degree courses.**
East Grinstead, England: Newpoint, 1992. 5 vols. 25th ed.

Precise details of 17,000 courses nationwide are contained in this exhaustive series of
volumes (*Arts, humanities, languages.* 688p.; *Engineering, technology, the environment.*
640p.; *Mathematics, medicine, sciences.* 592p.; *Business, education, social sciences.*
560p.; *Universities, polytechnics, colleges: the complete guide to all institutions offering
first degree courses.* 448p.) each of which is divided into three sections. 'Essential
reading' gives advice and information on where to study, how to obtain a grant,
choosing a course, when to apply, and also includes a checklist of abbreviations.
'Course descriptions' of every course in all subject areas follow, and there is an index
to all single subject degree courses. The *Universities* volume provides concise
descriptions of all the 211 higher education institutions offering first degree courses
with information on the towns and cities in which they are located.

802 **Your child and the national curriculum: a parent's guide to what is
taught in schools.**
London: Department for Education, 1992. 2nd ed. 13p.

This illustrated pamphlet explains the purpose of the national curriculum, what
subjects it covers, and how it fits into the pattern of primary and secondary education
in England and Wales.

Population and Demography

803 **Population statistics: a review of UK sources.**
Bernard Benjamin. Aldershot, England: Gower, 1989. 355p.
Members of many professions from biologists and geneticists to sociologists and
accountants frequently need to interpret and employ demographic statistics. This guide
ranges over the whole field of demography related to the United Kingdom population
– conception, death, marriage and divorce, health and sickness, population censuses
and surveys, migration, and population estimates and projections. The descriptions of
the sources covered include the mode of data collection, the method of construction
of standard indices, the possible sources of error and bias, and guidance in the choice
of information for particular purposes.

804 **Birth statistics: historical series of statistics from registrations of births
in England and Wales 1937-1983.**
London: HMSO for Office of Population Censuses and Surveys, 1987.
206p.
A national system of vital statistics registration was introduced in England and Wales
in 1837. Parental age, season of births, area of residence, multiple births, and social
class, are among the data included in this historical series.

805 **Birth statistics: review of the Registrar General on births and patterns of
family building in England and Wales.**
London: HMSO for Office of Population Censuses and Surveys.
Compiled annually, mainly from information collected at birth registration, these
statistics also include details on parents' ages, their birthplace and social class. In this
annual review summary tables give data for the preceding ten years.

806 **This crowded kingdom: an essay on population pressure in Great Britain.**
Edwin Brooks.   London: Charles Knight, 1973. 176p. bibliog.

It is hard to argue with the premise that the present population of Great Britain is too large, is continuing to grow, and should be reduced. This study discusses the historical and statistical background of the population explosion in Britain and considers the effects of overcrowding notably the spread of large conurbations and housing problems. Other aspects covered include immigration, death control resulting from modern medical advances, and birth control measures.

807 **Census 1991 Reports.**
London: HMSO for Office of Population Censuses and Surveys, 1992- . irreg.

A series of county reports incorporating preliminary results from the 1991 Census are being published from June 1992 onwards. They provide information on the demographic and economic characteristics of the population, housing, tenure and amenities, households and household composition, and economic and employment status. Among the first batch of reports are *Isle of Wight*, *Northumberland*, *Cornwall*, *Cumbria*, and *Lincolnshire*.

808 **Population, economy, and society in pre-industrial England.**
J. D. Chambers, edited by W. A. Armstrong.   London: Oxford University Press, 1972. 162p. bibliog.

Topics covered in this survey include the general course of population change, marriage and fertility, social mobility, birth and death rates, and economic influences on the population.

809 **The British population: patterns, trends, and processes.**
David Coleman, John Salt.   Oxford: Oxford University Press, 1992. 680p. bibliog.

This comprehensive work combines a historical perspective with a study of Britain's contemporary demographic structure. It considers the changing distribution of population, fertility trends, marriage and divorce, households and families, differentials in mortality, Britain at work, internal and international migration, the ethnic minority populations, and the political economy of demographic change.

810 **Counterurbanization in England and Wales.**
D. F. W. Cross.   Aldershot, England: Avebury, 1990.

Three leading factors are identified in the change in population distribution away from metropolitan areas in the period 1971-86: retirement migration; long-distance commuting to work; and employment decentralization.

811   **The introduction to English historical demography: from the sixteenth to
the nineteenth century.**
D. E. C. Eversley, Peter Laslett, E. A. Wrigley.   London:
Weidenfeld & Nicolson, 1966. 283p. bibliog.
Included in this collection of essays are studies on population history and local history,
the exploitation of Anglican parish registers, on family reconstitution, social structure
from early census returns and listings of inhabitants, all closely linked to a twenty-
seven page bibliography.

812   **Family expenditure survey.**
London: HMSO for Central Statistical Office, 1957- . annual.
Based on a representative sample of about 11,500 private households in the UK, this
annual survey provides reliable information on family income and expenditure and
illustrates developments in spending on such items as food, clothes, fuel, and leisure
for more than a quarter of a century.

813   **General Household Survey.**
London: HMSO for Office of Population Censuses and Surveys,
1971- . annual.
Facts and figures on a wide spectrum of household variables are provided in this annual
survey which is based on a sample of the general UK population resident in private
households. Complementing *Family Expenditure Survey* (q.v.), it helps to fill the gaps
in information about social change between the decennial censuses in the area of
health, housing, employment, and education.

814   **Guide to census reports: Great Britain 1801-1966.**
London: HMSO for Office of Population Census and Surveys, 1977.
7,279p.
This invaluable guide outlines the significant developments in the scope and
organization of successive censuses, the particular questions addressed, and the gradual
refinement of the methods employed. A final chapter advises on how best to use census
reports.

815   **Making sense of the census: the manuscript returns for England and
Wales 1801-1901.**
Edward Higgs.   London: HMSO for Public Record Office, 1989. 156p.
Invaluable information on individuals, families, and communities during a period of
startling social change is available through the manuscript returns of the nineteenth-
century censuses. This introductory guide provides social science researchers with a
quick entry into the censuses' vast corpus of material.

816   **Regional demographic development.**
Edited by John Hobcraft, Philip Rees.   London: Croom Helm, 1980.
287p. bibliog.
Originally presented at a joint conference between the British Society of Population
Studies and the Population Study Group of the Institute of British Geographers, at
Liverpool University in September 1977, these ten papers from demographers,

geographers, statisticians, and policy makers, cover population history and regional trends, fertility, migration, and population forecasting.

817 The changing population of Britain.
Edited by Heather Joshi.   Oxford: Blackwell, 1989. 230p. bibliog.

Assembled under the joint auspices of the Centre for Economic Policy Research and the British Society for Population Studies, this collection of ten essays investigates the origins and effects of contemporary demographic and social changes and trends, and considers their relevance to the social problems and issues confronting Britain in the 1990s. The topics accounted for include the diminishing necessity of marriage for sexual relationships, the increase in one parent families, the temporary halt in population ageing, the growth of the middle class and the decline of traditional working class employment, and the concentration of non-white ethnic groups in particular inner cities.

818 Population.
R. K. Kelsall.   London: Longman, 1975. 3rd ed. 2 maps. bibliog.
(The Social Structure of Modern Britain).

Fertility, mortality, migration and social class, variations in family size, life expectation, and forecasting the size, age, sex structure, and regional distribution of the population, are the principal topics investigated in this brief account of Britain's current and future population.

819 Mortality statistics: review of the Registrar General on deaths in England and Wales.
London: HMSO for the Office of Population Censuses and Surveys. annual.

Published annually, this series collates data on death and arranges them according to certain variables. No. 1 *Mortality statistics: general* (c. 50p.) contains data on death classified by sex and age and by other characteristics such as method of certification and place of death; no. 2 *Mortality statistics: cause.* (c. 100p.) presents information arranged according to cause; no. 3 *Mortality statistics: perinatal and infant: social and biological factors* (c. 85p.) details numbers and rates of stillbirths and infant deaths classified by various characteristics and collected at birth and death registration; no. 4 *Mortality statistics: accidents and violence* (c. 60p.) arranges data by sex and age, cause, type, and place of accident, and month of occurrence; no. 5 *Mortality statistics: area* (c. 30p.) classifies death by cause, sex and age for the standard administrative and health areas of England and Wales; no. 6 *Mortality statistics: serial tables . . . deaths in England and Wales, 1841-1985* (c. 44p.) provides data on death rates per 1,000 population within sex and age groups 1841-1985, and deaths from accidents and violence, 1901-1985. This is the second in a series of volumes which will be published at five-yearly intervals.

820 The Government Social Survey: a history.
Louis Moss.   London: HMSO for the Office of Population Censuses and Surveys, 1991. 268p.

The Government Social Survey has studied many aspects of social and economic activities since its formation in 1941. It has contributed valuable data for policy formulation and evaluation in the areas of housing, health services, crime, employment, changes in the cost of living, education, nutrition, and transport. This history illustrates how the Survey's work has developed over the past fifty years.

821 **1991 census: preliminary report for England and Wales.**
London: HMSO for Office of Population Censuses and Surveys, 1991. 55p.

The statistics presented in this preliminary report provide new evidence about the population in local areas. A commentary brings out general patterns and more salient features of this subject.

822 **People count: a history of the General Register Office.**
M. Nissel. London: HMSO, 1987. 157p.

Registration practices before the GRO was established in 1837, the subsequent civil registration system, the story of the GRO and the Censuses over 150 years, and a chronology of the main events, are covered in this illustrated volume published to mark the GRO's 150th anniversary.

823 **Office of Population Censuses and Surveys.**
London: HMSO, 1987. 18p. (Sectional List, no. 56).

Preliminary and county reports of the 1981 census, historical tables, key statistical publications, migration reports, the OPCS monitors designed for the quick release of information as soon as it becomes available, studies on medical and population subjects, and handbooks and survey reports, are among the titles listed in this official catalogue.

824 **People in Britain: a census atlas.**
London: HMSO, 1981. 132p. 63 maps.

Prepared in collaboration with the Office of Population Censuses and Surveys, this atlas presents an easy-to-grasp picture of population distribution in Britain derived from data collected in the 1971 census. Part one has thirty-five maps on population, birthplace, demographic and socio-economic characteristics, travel to work, and households and housing, whilst part two brings out regional and local patterns with the assistance of a further twenty-eight maps.

825 **Population projections 1987-2027: population projections by sex and age for United Kingdom, Great Britain and constituent countries from mid 1987.**
London: HMSO for Office of Population Censuses and Surveys, 1989. 44p. microfiches.

Containing a summary of projections based on the estimated population at the middle of 1987, this report provides information on the methods used in compiling them and on the assumptions on which these projections are based. Detailed figures on a set of microfiche complement those printed in the book. This type of data was first published for the period 1970 to 2010.

Population and Demography

826 **Population trends**.

London: HMSO for the Office of Population Censuses and Surveys, 1975- . quarterly.

This journal opens with articles which cover a variety of population and medical topics and then prints a series of regular tables on population, population change, vital statistics, live births, marriages, divorces, migrations, deaths and abortions, etc.

827 **A census user's handbook**.

Edited by David Rhind. London: Methuen, 1983. 393p. bibliog.

With the exception of 1941, the Census of Population in Great Britain has taken place every ten years since 1801. Each census gives rise to an enormous amount of printed material. In 1971, for example, the census produced nearly 500 separately bound items, comprising over 40,000 pages of tables. This book, consisting of eleven chapters by different authors, is 'a guide to what is in and what can be obtained from the census, to what is good practice in analysing such data and what is definitely unwise'.

828 **Population and society 1750-1840: contrasts in population growth**.

N. L. Tranter. London: Longman, 1985. 230p. bibliog. (Themes in British Social History).

Taking full advantage of recent scholarship, this study explores the population revolution of the late eighteenth and early nineteenth centuries, particularly the rise and fall in fertility, and the economic and social consequences of the period's demographic trends. Other topics considered include illegitimacy, migration and emigration, and the decline in mortality rates. The viability of the principal source materials and methods of analysis is also investigated.

829 **Population since the Industrial Revolution: the case of England and Wales**.

N. L. Tranter. London: Croom Helm, 1973. 206p. bibliog.

Prominent among the topics discussed in this study of population growth since the early eighteenth century are the sources and techniques of population data and statistics, and the relationship between demographic change and social and economic development.

830 **Women and men in Britain 1991**.

London: HMSO for Equal Opportunities Commission, 1991. 37p.

The Equal Opportunities Commission regularly prepare reviews of the current position of women and men in Britain. This issue focuses on earnings. Graphs and tables are presented in seventeen sections showing, for example, earning differentials, the distribution of hourly and weekly earnings, employment by industry and occupation, the numbers of women in managerial positions, maternity rights and employment protection, etc.

831 **The population of Britain in the nineteenth century.**
Robert Woods.   London: Macmillan, 1992. 96p. bibliog.

Examining migration, marriage patterns, fertility, and mortality, Woods interprets the
causes of demographic change in the wake of the Industrial Revolution. He also
provides a guide to the sources of population data available to historians and
demographers and a glossary of demographic terms.

832 **The population history of England 1541-1871: a reconstruction.**
E. A. Wrigley, R. S. Schofield.   Cambridge, England: Cambridge
University Press, 1981. 779p. 15 maps. bibliog.

Already acknowledged as a classic work in its field, this formidable study is intended
for an academic audience and is not suitable for general readers. The authors assemble
a mass of vital statistical material which they use to determine, by novel methods of
analysis and interpretation, population size, gross reproduction rates, life expectation
at birth, age structure, and net migration totals, over a period covering three centuries.
The translation of 'raw evidence' into an incontrovertible picture of population trends
during that period represents a landmark in English demographic history.

Ethnic and Religious Minorities

833 **Modern British Jewry.**
Geoffrey Alderman. Oxford: Clarendon, 1992. 397p.
This political, social, and intellectual history of Jews in Britain over the last 150 years examines their social structure and economic base in Victorian England, traces their struggle for social emancipation, explores the effect of large-scale Jewish immigration in the early years of the twentieth century, and charts the course of the Zionist movement in Britain. Alderman brings his scholarly work to a close with a look at the concerns of Jews and their self-image in contemporary Britain's pluralist society.

834 **The myth of return: Pakistanis in Britain.**
Muhammad Anwar. London: Heinemann, 1979. 278p. bibliog.
Focusing on the Pakistani immigrant community in Rochdale this work explodes 'the myth that they are in Britain to save, invest, and eventually return to their villages back home. In reality, most of them are here to stay because of economic reasons and their childrens' future' (Preface). Among the topics under close scrutiny are kinship networks, economic activity, ethnic group mobilization and political participation, religion as a binding force, and their structure of leadership.

835 **Race and politics: ethnic minorities and the British political system.**
Muhammed Anwar. London: Tavistock, 1986. 182p. bibliog.
Ethnic minorities now make up five per cent of Britain's population, concentrated for the most part in inner-city and industrial areas. In this work the author, Head of Research at the Commission for Racial Equality, looks at immigration and settlement patterns, and the development of race relations on the political scene, and argues that the positive involvement of the ethnic minorities in all aspects of British political life is the only sure method to end racial discrimination and disadvantage.

836 **Employment of graduates from ethnic minorities.**
John Brennan, Philip McGeevor. London: Commission for Racial
Equality, 1987. 88p.

This report of a project at Bulmershe College of Education, sponsored by the
Commission for Racial Equality, provides information on a sample of Council for
National Academic Awards graduates from ethnic minorities who obtained their
degrees in 1982. It shows the courses on which they enrolled, how the graduates
themselves regarded their experience of higher education, and how they fared in their
quest for employment. It confirms that black ethnic minority graduates find it far more
difficult to obtain jobs than their white counterparts.

837 **Britain's black population.**
The Runnymede Trust and The Radical Statistics Race Group.
London: Heinemann, 1980. 160p. map. bibliog.

In the context of the active response of black minorities to discrimination and
disadvantage, and of the changing political scene, this study looks at Government
legislation, employment, education, health and social services, and housing. It also
finds severe words to describe the inadequacies of official statistics.

838 **The Club: the Jews of modern Britain.**
Stephen Brook. London: Constable, 1989. 464p. bibliog.

Two distinct aspects of modern British Jewry are closely examined in this
comprehensive study. Firstly, its influence on contemporary British society notably in
politics, commerce, the legal and medical professions, and show-business. And,
secondly, its own surprising internal tensions especially in the differing religious beliefs
and customs of Orthodox, Reform and Liberal Jews. The role of women in modern
Jewish life, the attitude of British Jews towards Israel, and the current state of anti-
semitism in Britain, are also debated.

839 **The Huguenots in England: immigration and settlement c.1550-1700.**
Bernard Coltret. Cambridge, England: Cambridge University Press,
1992. 317p. 2 maps. bibliog.

Persecution of French Protestants, or Huguenots, was endemic in the sixteenth century
and culminated in the religious wars of the 1550s and 1560s and the St. Bartholomew's
Day massacre in 1572. A measure of political and religious freedom was granted by the
Edict of Nantes 1598 which lasted precariously until it was revoked in 1685.
Throughout this strife-torn period many Huguenots emigrated to England; this
masterly study examines their reception and subsequent settlement.

840 **Control of immigration statistics United Kingdom.**
London: HMSO for the Home Office. c. 85p.

Data on passenger admission and refusal, acceptance for settlement, and enforcement
procedures, including deportation, are presented in this annual set of figures. Details
of nationality and the category of immigrants are also provided.

841 **Subjects, citizens, aliens and others: nationality and immigration law.**
Ann Dunnet, Andrew Nicol. London: Weidenfeld & Nicolson, 1990.
318p. bibliog.

This critical and historical analysis of British nationality and immigration laws first
relates the events that have influenced their enactment up to the nineteenth century
before examining the crucial period between 1880 and 1919 when three Aliens Acts –
The Aliens Act (1905); *British Nationalities and Status of Aliens Act* (1914 and 1918) –
were put on the statute book. Finally, the major developments of the post-war period,
the 1971 Immigration Act, the British Nationality Acts of 1981-83, the abandonment of
unrestricted Commonwealth entry, and the effect of Britain joining the European
Community, are all closely scrutinized.

842 **Ethnic minorities.**
London: HMSO, 1991. 96p. (Aspects of Britain).

Although this briefing provides a useful introduction to the statistics, legislation, and
institutions relating to United Kingdom ethnic minorities, it has to be born in mind
that it reflects Government justification of its actions to promote racial harmony and
equality of opportunity. The reality may not be quite so problem-free.

843 **Loosen the shackles: first report of the Liverpool 8 inquiry into race
relations in Liverpool.**
Lord Gifford, Wally Brown, Ruth Bundey. London: Karia Press,
1989. 262p. 2 maps. bibliog.

The Liverpool 8 inquiry was set up by Liverpool City Council in October 1988 at the
request of local organizations 'to enquire into policies and community relations there
with particular reference to the policies and practices of Liverpool City Council; the
causes of any tensions existing between the police and the people of Liverpool 8 (i.e.
Toxteth); the existence of any discrimination against black people in the law
enforcement process; social conditions relating to the deprivation and racist treatment
of Liverpool 8 people; and such other public issues as may be deemed relevant'. The
inquiry found disturbing evidence of racism, discrimination, racist abuse by police
officers, and of uncontrolled drug trafficking. It concluded that black people's
experiences in Liverpool over a long period had been 'uniquely horrific'.

844 **There ain't no black in the Union Jack: the cultural politics of race and
nation.**
Paul Gilroy. London: Hutchinson, 1987. 271p. bibliog.

Investigating the relationship between race, class and nation in contemporary Britain,
this authoritative study emphasizes the daunting complexity of racial politics, and
argues that racial prejudice transcends political divisions.

845 **Racial violence and harassment.**
Paul Gordon. London: Runnymede Trust, 1990. 2nd ed. 51p. bibliog.

'Not only is the existence of racism routinely denied, but Britain has for long been a
country where immigration policies have consistently defined the presence of black
people as a problem whose entry and growth must be controlled' (p. 36). This study
includes a short history of racist attacks in twentieth-century Britain, and sections on
the nature and extent of racial violence, the police response, the responsibilities of

local authorities, the policies of the Far Right, and the contextual social and political environment.

846 **Them: voices from the immigrant community in contemporary Britain.**
Jonathon Green.   London: Secker & Warburg, 1990. 421p.
One hundred first generation immigrants were interviewed and recorded on tape during 1989. As Green admits, these formed an infinitesimal fraction of the total immigrant population, not even enough to give a decent sample, but they did afford a cross-section of the proportion of one race to another. Asked for their experience of Britain and immigrant life, their responses confirm that 'for all its much vaunted liberal democracy, Britain is as racist, as insular and as self-protective as any other nation' and that 'to be poor, and worse than that, black too, is to lay oneself open to the least enviable of contemporary fates'. In fact, 'the multicultural society, a phenomenon much beloved by forecasters of every background, is still a demographic rather than a social concept'.

847 **The gypsies: waggon-time and after.**
Denis Harvey.   London: Batsford, 1979. 144p. bibliog.
This pictorial record of the travelling life in Britain deals with gypsy life: their livelihood, crafts, traditions, caravans, and dress, etc. Many of the photographs were taken by the author during his time on the road.

848 **Black British, white British: a history of race relations in Britain.**
Dilip Hiro.   London: Grafton, 1991. 355p. bibliog.
As in many other countries race remains an emotive issue in British society. The basic thesis of this revised and expanded study, which was first published in 1971, is that racism is deeply rooted in all social classes in Britain and that full integration will take generations to achieve. Although the bedrock of its research was carried out in the 1960s, and it might be considered that since that date some progress had been made, this thesis is hard to refute. This edition includes new chapters on the history of immigration policy and of the Asian and Afro-Caribbean communities in Britain in the 1970s and 1980s. Four appendices give the General Election results and Race and Immigration Laws since 1945; the figures of immigration from the Colonies and New Commonwealth 1948-88; the estimated ethnic minority populations of Great Britain; and the correlation between ethnicity and educational performance.

849 **Recruiting a multiracial police force: a research study.**
Simon Holdaway.   London: HMSO, 1991. 210p. bibliog.
At the beginning of 1990 there were just 1,306 police officers in England and Wales from the ethnic minorities. Worried by the failure of police forces all over the country to attract more such officers, the Home Office instigated an eighteen-month research project to investigate why they were not forthcoming. This report's findings indicate that ethnic minority recruitment is an issue which impinges on a very broad range of police policies and practices not only between police and the communities they serve but also the question of race relations in the police force itself.

Ethnic and Religious Minorities

850 **Immigrants and minorities in British society.**
Edited by Colin Holmes.   London: Allen & Unwin, 1978. 208p.
bibliog.

Seven essays by different contributors present an historical overview of immigration into Britain, a study of the growth of distinct ethnic and racial minorities, and separate studies of German, Irish, Chinese and Jewish immigrants. A final chapter looks at racial tolerance and intolerance in London's East End over the last hundred years.

851 **John Bull's island: immigration and British society 1871-1971.**
Colin Holmes.   London: Macmillan, 1988. 448p. bibliog.

Three main themes are addressed in this wide-ranging and well-documented survey of immigration into Britain in the hundred years before the Immigration Act of 1971. Which immigrant and refugee groups came to Britain and why did they come? What were the major distinguishing features of their social and economic history? And, how were these newcomers received by British society? However, only first generation immigrants are considered in this study.

852 **A tolerant country? Immigrants, refugees and minorities in Britain.**
Colin Holmes.   London: Faber, 1991. 144p.

No multicultural society has yet achieved a convincing degree of social harmony. This study dispels two misleading assumptions that have bedevilled efforts to understand and explain racial tension in Britain. First, that Britain was spared large-scale immigration before the post-war influx of New Commonwealth citizens, and that the British people are uniquely tolerant of ethnic minorities. In fact the experiences of nineteenth-century Irish, Polish and Jewish immigrants closely paralleled those of the Asian and Afro-Caribbean immigrants who arrived in Britain in the post-war period.

853 **Colour in Britain.**
Edited by Richard Hooper.   London: British Broadcasting
Corporation, 1965. 239p. 3 maps.

Based on a BBC radio series, this book examines and describes the position of colonial immigrants in Britain. The emphasis is on what practical action can be taken by such people as teachers, local councillors, trade unionists, and social workers to help immigrants integrate more fully into British society.

854 **Racism in Britain.**
Brian D. Jacobs.   London: Christopher Helm, 1988. 188p. bibliog.

The urban unrest of the 1980s is the backcloth to this study of racial antagonism in Britain today. Also under scrutiny are the ways in which racial minorities have attempted to overcome discrimination. Finally there is a look to the future and speculation whether these minorities will abandon the existing structure of national politics in favour of building up their own local community-based organizations.

855 **Racism and equal opportunity policies in the 1980s.**
Edited by Richard Jenkins, Jack Solomos. Cambridge, England:
Cambridge University Press, 1990. 2nd ed. 268p.
Examining the problems of racism and equal opportunity in employment, and
government attitudes in contemporary Britain, this collection of essays covers major
areas of debate such as the law, policies towards unemployment, job training and the
labour market, the role of trade unions, and crucially, the gap between stated policies
and high-sounding pronouncements on equal opportunities and implementation at
ground level.

856 **The politics of immigration: race and race relations in post-war Britain.**
Zig Layton-Henry. Oxford: Blackwell, 1992. 256p. bibliog.
An account of the history and politics of post-war black immigration, this scholarly
work analyses the politicization of race relations and immigration issues. The topics
covered include the role of populist politicians such as Enoch Powell and Margaret
Thatcher in influencing public opinion, the part played by the National Front in
provoking racial violence, the inner city riots, black participation in the political
system, and the dilemmas suffered by the Labour Party.

857 **The politics of race in Britain.**
Zig Layton-Henry. London: Allen & Unwin, 1984. 191p. bibliog.
Race relations and immigration issues have been in the forefront of British politics
since the New Commonwealth migration to the United Kingdom began in earnest soon
after the Second World War. This useful book traces the political response to the social
problems which culminated in the organized racism of the 1960s and 1970s and the race
riots of the early 1980s.

858 **The Jews of Britain: a thousand years of history.**
Pamela Fletcher Jones. Moreton-in-Marsh, England: Windrush Press,
1990. 198p. bibliog.
Published on the 800th anniversary of the mass suicide in the Clifford Tower in York
of 150 Jews rather than surrender to the mob howling for their blood outside, this work
traces the history of Britain's Jewish community from Roman times onwards. It also
takes a look at the Jewish way of life within the Jewish community and the place of the
Jews in British social history.

859 **Gypsy-travellers in nineteenth-century society.**
David Mayall. Cambridge, England: Cambridge University Press,
1988. 261p. bibliog.
Three main themes emerge from this historical study: the role of gypsies as a mobile
labour force; their position on the fringes of an industrial society resisting its
assimilating influences; and the identification of a racial and cultural minority. Only
now does their isolation from the majority of the population in cultural and economic
terms show signs of disappearing.

860 **New to the UK: a guide to your life and rights.**
Genevieve Muinzer. London: Routledge & Kegan Paul, 1987. 215p.
bibliog.

Over three million expatriates of all nationalities live in Britain at any one time. This comprehensive and readable guide, written by an American resident in the United Kingdom, lets people know what to expect when they arrive and advises them how to cope with the problems they will encounter. The British legal system, immigration law, pets and quarantine, passport information, services provided by embassies, insurance, welfare benefits, voting rights, family law, eligibility for British nationality, public and private health care, and taxation, are some of the topics of immediate interest covered. A second section deals with the social and psychological aspects of living as an expatriate in contemporary British society.

861 **The Irish in Britain.**
Kevin O'Connor. London: Sidgwick & Jackson, 1972. 188p. bibliog.

Largely descended from refugees who fled from the nineteenth-century famines, the Irish form the largest of all Britain's immigrant groups. This chronological and thematic account charts their social problems and their influence on British business, religious and political life from the end of the eighteenth century.

862 **Economic history of the Jews in England.**
H. Pollins. London, Toronto: Associated University Press, 1982.
339p. bibliog.

Following a brief introductory chapter on the medieval Jewish community in England this well-researched account concentrates on the economic activities and influence of the Jews from the seventeenth century onwards.

863 **The making of the black working class in Britain.**
Ron Ramdin. Aldershot, England: Wildwood House, 1987. 626p.
bibliog.

This history traces the making of the black working class in twentieth-century Britain as it relates to the development of British capitalism and its control and exploitation of black labour. Topics discussed in detail include the contribution of nineteenth-century black radicals to British working class struggles, the development of a black radical ideology in the 1920s and 1930s, and black working class consciousness in the 1970s and 1980s.

864 **Race and racism in contemporary Britain.**
John Solomos. London: Macmillan, 1989. 209p. bibliog.

This book combines an historical overview of the political debate and legislation concerning race and racism in Britain since 1945 with an analysis of the consequent racialization of such social issues as law and order, crime, the inner cities, and urban unrest.

865   **White bolts, black locks: participation in the inner city.**
      David N. Thomas.   London: Allen & Unwin, 1986. 252p.
Primarily concerned with Afro-Caribbeans and Asians, this study explores various
aspects of participation in general community groups and the subsequent reaction of
white individuals, groups, and institutions. There are three central themes: the issues
of ethnic participation in neighbourhood activities, and the interaction of non-white
and white residents; the extent and quality of communication between black, Asian
and white professional groups; and the development of the neighbourhood as a
significant force in the social structure of contemporary Britain.

866   **Irish in Britain directory.**
      Edited by Geraldine Vesey.   London: Brent Irish Advisory Service,
      1989. 4th ed. 140p.
This definitive guide to life in Britain for Irish people provides a directory of events,
organizations, and Irish businesses. An information and advice section gives the
necessary information on moving to Britain, and securing accommodation and
employment. Immigrants' rights as a citizen, student, householder, and tenant, and
how to claim welfare benefits and pensions, are also outlined.

867   **The English gypsy caravan: its origins, builders, technology and
      conservation.**
      C. H. Ward-Jackson, Denis E. Harvey.   Newton Abbott, England:
      David & Charles, 1986. 2nd ed. 221p. bibliog.
For all Romany and travelling people their distinctive, functional, and handsome
caravan was their most valued possession. First published in 1972 this study defines the
caravans' essential characteristics, describes and distinguishes six main types, and looks
at their interior furnishings and exterior decorations. An appendix gives details of
where caravans may be found.

868   **British Jewry in the Eighties: a statistical and geographical guide.**
      Stanley Waterman, Barry Kosmin.   London: Board of Deputies of
      British Jews, 1986. 56p. 8 maps. bibliog.
Since its inception in 1965 the Statistical and Demographic Research Unit of the Board
of Deputies of British Jews has made strenuous efforts to collect statistical data and to
monitor demographic trends among the Jewish population of Great Britain. This
statistical sketch of the Anglo-Jewish scene includes data on age–sex ratios, marriages
and divorce, residential distribution, Jews in London and Manchester, synagogue
membership and attendance, Jewish school, occupations, and social class.

The school effect: a study of multi-racial comprehensives.
See item no. 792.

Other languages of England.
See item no. 1906.

Folklore, Customs and Traditions

869 **Guide to ancient Britain.**
Bill Anderton. London: Foulsham, 1991. 224p. 6 maps.

Photographs and brief descriptions of ancient sites, standing stones, stone circles, burial grounds, holy wells, temples, esoteric carvings and symbols, are included in this pocket-size practical guide to the ancient and mysterious places of Britain. Arranged in six regional sections, it also contains a chapter on dowsing at ancient sites.

870 **A guidebook to Arthurian Britain.**
Geoffrey Ashe. London: Longman, 1980. 234p. 4 maps. bibliog.
(Longman Travellers Series).

Mainly an illustrated descriptive gazetteer to locations in Britain associated with the Arthurian legend, this guide also includes an introduction to the legend, the historical growth, and geographical extent, a look at earlier works similar in content, and a key which enables the reader to link individual sites with particular characters or themes.

871 **King Arthur's Avalon: the story of Glastonbury.**
Geoffrey Ashe. London: Collins, 1957. 384p. bibliog.

Not easily classified, this book, along with its companion volume, *From Caesar to Arthur* (Geoffrey Ashe. London: Collins, 1960. 320p. map. bibliog.) is not straightforward mainstream histories although they both adopt a more or less chronological narrative format. The first relates the rise of Christianity in Britain and, more specifically, the place of Glastonbury in the early history of England. Joseph of Arimathea's arrival in Britain, the advent of Arthur, and the emergence of the Grail stories from the dim mists of Celtic mythology, are among the episodes subjected to a sympathetic scrutiny. The second concentrates on that indistinct and blurred period between the departure of the Roman legions and the secure establishment of the Saxon kingdoms. Whatever wisps of truth that lie behind the Arthurian legend are revealed and endorsed.

872   **The landscape of King Arthur.**
Geoffrey Ashe, photographs by Simon McBride.   Exeter, England:
1987. 191p. bibliog.
Described as a personal tour of England, Scotland and Wales, this beautifully-
illustrated book identifies the chief locations associated with the Arthurian legends
beginning at Glastonbury and extending to Cadbury, Tintagel, the Lake District,
Winchester, Stonehenge and other lesser-known places.

873   **Mythology of the British Isles.**
Geoffrey Ashe.   London: Methuen, 1990. 304p. bibliog.
Covering the period from prehistory to the end of the ninth century AD, this study
provides a commentary on the surviving myths, legends, and stories, investigates their
sources, and attempts to trace their underlying ideas in the light of historical and
archaeological research. Among the topics explored are the mystery of the
construction and purposes of the megaliths, notably Stonehenge, and of the ancient ley
lines, King Brutus, King Lud, Old King Cole, and of course the Arthurian legend.
Ashe contends that all these tales are interrelated.

874   **The Quest for Arthur's Britain.**
Edited by Geoffrey Ashe.   London: Pall Mall Press, 1968. 238p.
6 maps. bibliog.
Eleven essays by different authors examine the historical foundations of the Arthurian
legends and present the results of excavations at South Cadbury Castle, the reputed
site of Camelot. A final chapter surveys twentieth-century imaginative Arthurian
literature.

875   **Folklore and customs of rural England.**
Margaret Baker.   Newton Abbot, England: David & Charles, 1974.
208p. bibliog.
Once of considerable importance in all aspects of rural life, folklore and customs have
long since ceased to exert any real influence. This book describes the more significant
country lore associated with the home, farm, village, and church.

876   **Ancient mysteries of Britain.**
Janet Bord, Colin Bord.   London: Grafton, 1986. 288p. 4 maps.
bibliog.
Both this book and its sequel *Mysterious Britain*. (Janet Bord, Colin Bord. London:
Garnstone Press, 1972. 262p. maps. bibliog.) contain a mixture of archaeology and
folklore combined with remarkable atmospheric photography as they present
prehistoric homes, tombs and temples, earthworks, rock carvings, early Christian
crosses, caves, Roman ruins, early churches, hill figures, holy wells, the Arthurian
legends, dragons, mazes, customs and traditions, leys and earth energies, and some
twentieth century mysteries. A small selection of the best places to visit, with location
details, are included at the end of each chapter.

Folklore, Customs and Traditions

877   **Atlas of magical Britain.**
Janet Bord, Colin Bord.   London: Sidgwick & Jackson, 1990. 192p.
17 maps. bibliog.

Prehistoric camps dating from 4000 BC, Arthurian sites, reputed haunts of Robin
Hood, hills full of fairy gold, ley lines, and early Christian centres, are among the 600
sites described on a regional basis in this colourfully-illustrated atlas. A calendar of
traditional customs and festivals still celebrated today is provided for each of the
sixteen regions.

878   **Dictionary of British folk-tales in the English language.**
Katherine M. Briggs.   London: Routledge, 1970-71. 4 vols. bibliog.

Arranged in two volumes entitled *Folklore narratives* and two volumes titled *Folk
legends*, this meticulously-researched collection has achieved classic status. *Folk
narratives* are tales told for entertainment but are not considered factually true. Five
categories are distinguished here: fables and exempla (animal stories in the manner of
Aesop either pointing to a moral or satirizing human frailties); fairy tales (narratives
containing a supernatural element); jocular tales (a corpus of drolls, noodle stories,
and bawdy tales); nouvelles (stories with no vestige of the supernatural); and nursery
tales for small children. Many of the narratives are printed in full, some are slightly
shortened, and many others are summarized. *Folk legends* are far more common in
England than folklore narratives and a representative collection is ordered in these
volumes under various archetypal headings: black dogs, bogies, devils, dragons, fairies,
ghosts, giants, etc.

879   **Glastonbury Abbey: the Holy House at the head of the moors
adventurous.**
James P. Carley, photographs by Simon McBride.   Woodbridge,
England: Boydell, 1988. 189p.

Glastonbury has been recognized as one of the most magical places in England since
before the dawn of the Christian era. Joseph of Arithmathea, St. Patrick and King
Arthur have all been associated with the Great Abbey whose history is recounted in
this volume.

880   **English fox hunting: a history.**
Raymond Carr.   London: Weidenfeld & Nicolson, 1976. 273p. bibliog.

'By 1830 fox hunting was the common activity of the English countryside, the
relaxation of substantial tenant farmers and the Chancellor of the Exchequer alike. It
was a regular sport, protected by convention if not by law, in which large crowds of
horsemen could charge across other peoples' fields . . . from its origin in the
destruction of noxious vermin it had been transformed into a rural mystique'
(Introduction). This well-documented study, which begins with fox hunting replacing
deer hunting in the early sixteenth century, focuses mainly on the nature of the
relationship between the hunts and the owners of the lands they hunted over in the
heyday of hunting from the middle of the eighteenth century to the outbreak of the
Great War in 1914.

881 **The weights and measures of England.**
R. D. Connor.   London: HMSO for Science Museum, 1987. 422p.
bibliog.

Much of what has been written on the history of English weights and measures, in medieval chronicles, statutes and cartularies, is not generally accessible. This difinitive work takes its source material from legislative orders, charters and other historical documents, from surviving physical standards and inferences drawn from old buildings, and from measures in use abroad. In a series of chronological chapters it looks at such topics as the Saxon gyrd, rod and acre, early currency, and the onset of metrication, carrying the story to the Weights and Measures Act of 1985. Regulation and enforcement, a brief account of the development of the metric system, and tables of English pre-metric measures are incorporated in appendices and there is a twelve-page glossary of unit terms.

882 **The British folklorists: a history.**
Richard Mercer Dorson.   London: Routledge & Kegan Paul, 1968.
518p. bibliog.

The word 'folklore' was first coined by William John Thomas in 1846 although the history of folklore began in a much earlier period. This study traces the development of the concept of folklore beginning in the sixteenth century and shows how its influences spread into the disciplines of literature, archaeology, philosophy, phychical research, and legal and medieval antiquities in the nineteenth. Dorson also edited *Peasant customs and savage myths: selections from the British folklorists* (London: Routledge & Kegan Paul, 1968. 2 vols.) which present extracts from the pioneering writings of distinguished Victorian scholars.

883 **A dictionary of pub names.**
Leslie Dunkling, Gordon Wright.   London: Routledge & Kegan Paul,
1987. 303p.

Pub names, which can trace their origins to the need of medieval ale-houses, inns and taverns to identify themselves to a largely illiterate population, are keywords to many aspects of English social history: folklore, military triumphs, heroes and heroines, natural history, trades and industries, sport, transport history, and many others. This dictionary lists more than 10,000 names.

884 **British teapots and tea drinking.**
Robin Emmerson.   London: HMSO for Norwich Museums Service,
1992. 368p.

The national habit of tea drinking became a passion in Britain about 1700. This delightful book charts its rise and explains how and why a previously exotic luxury became a staple part of the British diet. A growing demand for teaware stimulated the porcelain manufacture in the North Staffordshire potteries. The 564 teapots described and illustrated here date from 1720 to 1820 and are currently in the Twining Teapot Gallery at Norwich Castle.

885 Folklore, myths and legends of Britain.

London: Reader's Digest, 1973. 552p. maps. bibliog.

Folklore is defined as 'the study of beliefs which were once firmly held, but which have long ago lost their adherents'. This encyclopedic historical account claims to be the most comprehensive single-volume collection of British stories, customs, and superstitions ever assembled. It is divided into three sections: the world of nature (seasons and festivals, water guardians, green magic etc.); the world of man (house and home, death and burial etc.); and the world of twilight (old gods, unquiet graves, fabulous beasts). A major gazetteer section offers a quick reference guide to the places featured in the main text.

886 The traditional games of England, Scotland and Ireland.

Alice Bertha Gomme. London: Thames & Hudson, 1984. 531p.

Originally published by David Nutt in two volumes in 1894 and 1898, this dictionary of some 800 children's games presents consolidated information on how they were played, giving variant methods from different parts of the country, with details of any accompanying singing rhymes and their tunes. By dint of an anthropological analysis and interpretation, a seventy-five page memoir on their study identifies no less than thirty-four categories of games.

887 Ghosts' who's who.

Jack Hallam. Newton Abbot, England: David & Charles, 1977. 157p. bibliog.

Brief biographical sketches of about 450 phantoms associated with named individuals, including the manner and circumstances of their death, are packed within this guide.

888 Origins of festivals and feasts.

Jean Harrowven. London: Kaye & Ward, 1980. 188p. bibliog.

This is an amiable descriptive history of the customs, superstitions, games, and recipes traditionally associated with St. Valentine's Day, Shrovetide, Mothering Sunday, Easter, All Fools' Day, May Day, Whitsuntide, Harvest, Hallowe'en, Guy Fawkes' Day, Christmas, and New Year's Day.

889 Robin Hood.

J. C. Holt. London: Thames & Hudson, 1982. 208p. 4 maps. bibliog.

Man or legend, there is no historical certainty, Robin Hood has attracted more scholarly interest than any figure in history or legend with the exception only of King Arthur. In the popular mind he remains forever outwitting the dastardly Sheriff of Nottingham in Sherwood Forest, robbing the rich, and giving to the poor. This work assesses the evidence for a historical Robin Hood and traces the origins and development of the medieval legends. 'What began as an oral tradition ended as a television script'.

890 Death, ritual and bereavement.

Edited by Ralph Houlbrooke. London: Routledge, 1989. 240p.

Collectively these essays focus on English death-beds, funerals, burials, and mourning customs, in the period from 1500 to the 1930s, with half of them concentrating on the fundamental changes occurring in Queen Victoria's long reign. The importance of a comforting religious belief which asserted an immortal life after death, thus denying and rejecting its finality, is strongly underlined.

891 **Earth mysteries.**
Michael Howard. London: Robert Hale, 1990. 224p. bibliog.

'Earth mysteries' is a term coined in the 1970s to describe the study of ley lines (the alignment of ancient sites), stone circles, standing stones, hill figures, and the existence of terrestrial zodiacs. This book is a guide to such mysteries in the British Isles 'which will open the reader's eyes to a new view of Britain's prehistoric monuments'.

892 **The mystery of King Arthur.**
Elizabeth Jenkins. London: Michael Joseph, 1975. 224p. map. bibliog.

Possibly the most comprehensive survey of the Arthurian legend suitable for the general reader, this attractively and imaginatively illustrated book merges archaeology, folklore, history and literature. Facts and legends, early chronicles, medieval chivalry, the work of Sir Thomas Malory, the significance of the legend in Tudor and Stuart times, including Edmund Spenser's *The faerie queene*, the pre-Raphaelites, and Tennyson's *Idylls of the king*, are all blended into a compulsive narrative.

893 **The customs and ceremonies of Britain: an encyclopaedia of living traditions.**
Charles Kightly. London: Thames & Hudson, 1986. 248p. map. bibliog.

Arranged alphabetically by the name of the custom or ceremony, this encyclopaedia describes and explains the origins of folklore calendar customs, royal ceremonies, the remnants of long-vanished farming customs, church festivals, the relics of deep rooted pagan beliefs, and sporting traditions. A regional gazetteer gives details of place, custom, and date.

894 **The perpetual almanack of folklore.**
Charles Kightly. London: Thames & Hudson, 1987.

In Elizabethan, Stuart, and early Georgian times a printed calendar, or almanack, giving the dates of Saints day's, other festivals, the waxing and waning of the moon, and the rotation of the heavenly bodies through the zodiac, was almost indispensable. Amongst its other functions were weather forecasting for different periods; fortune telling; gardening; agricultural and husbandry tips, and the provision of much other miscellaneous information. Based on original almanacks, farming and herbal handbooks, early cookery books, and ephemeral works such as chapbooks, broadsides, and newspapers, this present book endeavours to reproduce this type of publication for present day use. Day by day, through the year, it offers advice and instruction on a variety of topics, cookery recipes, herbal remedies for all kinds of ailments, and the usual diary-type information.

895 **The new Arthurian encyclopedia.**
Edited by Norris J. Lacy. New York: Garland, 1991. 577p. map.
bibliog.

First published in 1986 as *The Arthurian encyclopedia* this truly comprehensive and critical illustrated treatment of Arthurian subjects, writers, and artists has been fundamentally revised, vastly expanded, and updated to include the most recent Arthurian scholarship and research. It includes brief informative entries devoted to particular subjects and authors along with extended essays consisting either of major studies on the more significant authors and texts or of broader thematic surveys covering all periods from the earliest legends to modern works of fiction and film making. In addition to the general bibliography most entries end with a generous selection of bibliographical references and there is a six-page chronology extending over the landmarks in Arthurian literature, archaeology, literature, music, etc.

896 **The Punch and Judy show: history, tradition and meaning.**
Robert Leach. London: Batsford, 1985. 192p. bibliog.

This fully-illustrated history of England's national puppet show traces its origins back to medieval fairs and festivals and outlines its development as an entertainment in pleasure gardens, at race meetings, as street entertainment, and as a summer holiday beach show. Along the way it examines the dexterous work of the unseen animators, analyses Mr. Punch's character, and tries to explain the secret of Punch and Judy's appeal.

897 **The English way of death: the common funeral since 1450.**
Julian Litten. London: Robert Hale, 1991. 272p.

A curator at the Victoria and Albert Museum, the author presents an intriguing survey of all aspects of English funerals from post-medieval pomp to more mundane present-day practices. Embalming techniques, burial vaults and mausoleums, and the work of contemporary undertakers, are among the topics discussed.

898 **Flora Britannica.**
Edited by Richard Mabey. London: Common Ground, 1994-95.
[n.p.].

Co-ordinated by Common Ground, the arts and conservation group, this project is planned to produce a cultural flora which will show how plants are rooted in the traditions, folklore and customs of a locality, in place-names, and in the treatment of illnesses. A second aim is to encourage people to compile their own cultural floras locally. The use of plants to mark parish boundaries, to decorate homes at festival times, to ward off evil spirits, and in herbal medicine, are some of the practices which, it is hoped, will be reliably recorded.

899 **The English ceremonial book: a history of robes, insignia and ceremonies still in use in England.**
Roger Milton. Newton Abbot, England: David & Charles, 1972. 216p. bibliog.

This historical survey provides the background information necessary for understanding the significance of the pageantry and symbolism associated with present-day English ceremonies. The robes, regalia, and insignia of the Coronation, and of peers, judges, barristers, and the orders of chivalry, are all separately treated.

900 **The folklore of the British Isles.**
Edited by Venetia J. Newall. London: Batsford, 1973- . 10 vols.

Legends, customs, and beliefs which once flourished, and some of which still survive, including stories attached to physical landmarks in the countryside, tales of witchcraft, and beliefs and practices relating to sickness and health, birth, marriage, and death, are all explored in these authoritative county volumes. Volumes published are as follows: *Sussex.* (Jacqueline Simpson. 1973. 187p.); *The Cotswolds.* (Katherine M. Briggs. 1974. 208p.); *East Anglia.* (Enid Porter. 1974. 192p.); *Cornwall.* (Tony Deane, Tony Shaw. 1975. 217p.); *Hampshire and the Isle of Wight.* (Wendy Boase. 1976. 212p.); *The Lake District.* (Marjorie Rowling. 1976.); *Somerset.* (Kingsley Palmer. 1976. 186p.); *Warwickshire.* (Roy Palmer. 1976. 208p.); *Wiltshire.* (Ralph Whitlock. 1976); *Hertfordshire.* (Doris Jones-Baker. 1977. 240p.).

901 **Children's games in street and playground.**
Iona Opie, Peter Opie. Oxford: Clarendon Press, 1969. 371p. 8 maps.

Prepared with the assistance of 10,000 children all over Britain, this scholarly study is limited to games played by children, between six and twelve years old, when out of doors, and out of sight of parents or other supervisors. No party, scout or team game is included. It details how over 2,000 chasing, catching, seeking, hunting, racing, duelling, exerting, daring, guessing, acting and pretending street games are played, together with their accompanying rhymes and chants.

902 **The lore and language of schoolchildren.**
Iona Opie, Peter Opie. Oxford: Clarendon Press, 1959. 417p. 11 maps.

Based on oral information gleaned from 5,000 'fun-loving, father-fearing' children attending some seventy primary, secondary modern, and grammar schools distributed all over Britain, this analytical survey records their strange and primitive culture. Seasonal customs, initiation rights, superstitious practices and beliefs, rhymes and chants, catcalls and retorts, stock jokes, ruderies, riddles, slang, and nicknames, are all captured, interpreted, and explained.

903 **The singing game.**
Iona Opie, Peter Opie. Oxford: Oxford University Press, 1985. 521p. bibliog.

Drawn from nationwide surveys previously exploited in their two previous works, *The lore and language of schoolchildren* (1959) and *Children's games in street and playground* (1969), and from information received from a further 112 schools, this survey of singing and clapping games includes a separate chapter for each different type of game. Within these chapters there is a general historical description, an account of each individual game, and a list of bibliographical and other sources.

904 Events in Britain: a complete guide to annual events in Britain.
Bernard Schofield. Poole, England: Blandford Press, 1981. 256p.

Details of 1,000 festivals, 400 fairs, 200 galas, 300 old customs, 600 agricultural and horticultural shows, and 1,500 sporting events, are presented county by county, month by month, in this sumptuously-illustrated guide.

905 Myths of Britain.
Michael Senior. London: Orbis, 1979. 241p. map. bibliog.

Intended for the interested layman rather than the specialist scholar, this broad review of the traditional material of Britain is largely concerned with the Arthurian legend although it also touches upon earlier British mythology.

906 The National Trust guide to traditional customs of Britain.
Brian Shuel. Exeter, England: Webb & Bower, 1985. 209p. maps. bibliog.

This pictorial volume gives a first-hand account of over 150 traditional customs and ceremonies, some familiar, some less so, which are maintained in Britain throughout the year on certain specified days, from Andrew's Dole which takes place in Bideford, Devon, 1st January, to longsword dancing in South Yorkshire on Boxing Day. There is a consolidated calendar of such events.

907 British dragons.
Jacqueline Simpson. London: Batsford, 1980. 160p. bibliog.

Drawing upon a wide range of sources, including folk songs, church inscriptions, and specialized collections of folk tales, this study opens with a historical survey of dragons before discussing the characteristics of British dragons, their appearance, size and habitats, and the dragon slayers and their preferred methods of despatching the foul beasts. The connection between dragons and specific localities (over seventy towns and villages claim a dragon tale or song), their appearance on tombstones and other church monuments, their effigies used in medieval plays, pageants and processions, and their religious, mythological, and politico-historical significance, are also investigated at length. There is a gazetteer of places associated with dragons and a chronology of dates relevant to British dragon legends.

908 English fairs.
Ian Starsmore. London: Thames & Hudson, 1975. 128p. bibliog. (Studies in Industrial Archaeology).

English fairs enjoy a long tradition and seem set to survive long into the future. This book examines their origins and characteristics, their daily routine, the secret of their popular appearance, and fairground equipment. It also provides a monthly calendar of established fairs.

909   The Glastonbury legends: Joseph of Arimathea, the Holy Grail and King
Arthur.
R. F. Treharne.   London: Cresset Press, 1969. 142p. bibliog.
Guaranteed to capture the interest and attention of even the most sceptical reader, this
delightful book re-examines the historical validity of the three notable legends
traditionally associated with Glastonbury.

910   **A gazetteer of British ghosts.**
Peter Underwood.   London: Souvenir Press, 1971. 256p. bibliog.
(Frontiers of the Unknown).
Over 200 locations of the most famous hauntings are recorded in this gazetteer,
ranging from the purely legendary to factually-presented and scientifically-investigated
phenomena.

911   **Albion: a guide to legendary Britain.**
Jennifer Westwood.   London: Granada, 1985. 448p. 13 maps. bibliog.
Drawn from medieval chronicles, seventeenth-century antiquarians, and the folklore
collectors of the nineteenth century, local folktales, myths, legends, and traditions are
retold within the context of their associated sites and locations which are grouped in
thirteen regions. Maps show the distribution of sites.

912   **British weights and measures: a history from antiquity to the
seventeenth century.**
Ronald Edward Zupke.   Madison, Wisconsin: University of Wisconsin
Press, 1977. 248p. bibliog.
From the first contact with the Romans in the first century BC to modern times there
was developed in Britain a complex, comprehensive, and sophisticated system of
weights and measures. Through the centuries constant attempts were devised to
simplify refine, and standardize this system either by legislation, the construction of
physical standards, inspection, or by verification and enforcement procedures. This
well-researched study follows these attempts and considers their scientific, linguistic,
medical, philosophical, social, and economic significance from antiquity to the end of
the Tudor period. It evolved from the author's earlier work, *A dictionary of English
weights and measures from Anglo-Saxon times to the nineteenth century* (1968. 224p.
bibliog.) which gives an etymology of all weights and measures terms, their meanings,
and dated illustrative citations.

Dictionary of English and folk-names of British birds.
See item no. 204.

Englishman's flora.
See item no. 220.

Constitution and Law

913 **All England Law Reports.**

London: Butterworths, 1936- . weekly.

Decisions of the various English courts are reported expeditiously in this law series. When these decisions are deemed to be of general significance editorial notes are added. An annual index includes a table of cases and a table of statutes judicially considered. *All England law reports 1558-1935* (a selection in the same style) were published in thirty-six volumes between 1966 and 1968.

914 **Freedom of information: the law, the practice and the ideal.**

Patrick Birkinshaw.   London: Weidenfeld & Nicolson, 1988. 291p. (Law in Context).

The notorious 1911 Official Secrets Act, the arguments for and against a Freedom of Information Act, including the need for personal privacy, and some possible ways forward, all feature in this well-annotated study. It addresses simply and starkly whether citizens have a right to expect more information from Government than they currently receive in the United Kingdom.

915 **A short guide to the records of Parliament.**

Maurice F. Bond.   London: House of Lords Record Office, 1980. 3rd ed. 25p.

Over the past 500 years Parliament has systematically preserved not only the records of its own proceedings but also the many petitions and other documents presented to it. This handbook gives a brief history of the records, describes how the parliamentary archives have been formed, explains what types of material are available for use, and how they are organized in the House of Lords Record office.

916 **Erskine May's treatise on the law, privileges, proceedings and usage of Parliament.**
Edited by C. Boulton. London: Butterworths, 1989. 21st ed. 1,079p.
Arranged in three main divisions this hallowed authority is the benchmark for parliamentary business and procedure: part one considers the constitution, powers, and privileges of Parliament; part two examines proceedings for public business; and part three covers private business. This work is not intended for general readership but for constitutional and parliamentary specialists. First published in 1844 *Erskine May* is one of those rare works that are simply known by their author's name.

917 **The origins of the English legal profession.**
Paul Brand. Oxford: Blackwell, 1992. 356p.
The modern English legal profession has emerged over seven centuries of change and development. This well-researched study provides an in-depth analysis of the first formative stage when the English Common Law evolved during the second half of the twelfth century. Brand also presents a detailed picture of the distinct legal profession which was established during the reign of Edward I, estimating its size, and examining the functions professional lawyers performed for their clients. Legal training, the control of entry into the profession, the development and enforcement of a code of ethics, and the canon lawyers who served the English Church courts, are also scrutinized.

918 **The legal profession 1990.**
Edited by Michael Chambers. London: Chambers, 1990. 686p.
A directory of the 1,000 largest law firms in England and Wales, and of all barristers, the two main sections comprise a list of solicitors specializing in thirty-nine different areas and a similar list of barristers accepting cases in twenty-two areas. An appendix prints a list of law centres. Michael Chambers is a legal recruitment consultant.

919 **County Court districts (England and Wales) index of place names.**
London: HMSO for Lord Chancellor's Department, 1991. 13th ed.
212p.
Some 30,000 place names giving the corresponding county court for each area are included in this index.

920 **Dod's guide to the General Election 1992.**
Etchingham, England: Dod's Parliamentary Companion, 1992. 350p.
Included in this parliamentary guide is a review of the 1992 general election, the Queen's speech on the opening of Parliament, biographies and photographs of all 651 MPs, full constituency results, Government and Opposition spokesmen, a history of the House of Commons, and a list of its principal offices and officials.

921 **Dod's parliamentary companion.**
Hurst Green, England: Dod's Parliamentary Companion, 1992.
160th ed. 1,000p.
Now published annually, *Dod's* is the definitive guide to parliament and the government. It includes a section on the Royal Family and biographical sketches of all Peers of the Realm, of all Members of Parliament, and of United Kingdom Members

of the European Parliament. It also outlines the activities of Whitehall, government departments, and public offices.

922 **Lobbying: an insider's guide to the parliamentary process.**
Alf Dubs.   London: Pluto Press, 1988. 228p. bibliog.

Using practical examples derived from his own experiences as a Member of Parliament, the author explains the democratic purpose and implications of such parliamentary procedures as Question Time, Early Day Motions, Private Member's Bills, Adjournment Debates, and Select Committees, to show how pressure groups, trade unions, and ordinary people can influence political decisions.

923 **Electoral statistics: parliamentary and local government electors in constituencies and local government areas of England, Wales, Scotland, and Northern Ireland 1991.**
London: HMSO for Office of Population Censuses and Surveys, 1991. 28p.

This particular set of statistics presents the number of voters on the electoral register for each of the 651 parliamentary constituencies and for all local government authorities.

924 **Taking liberties: the criminal jury in the 1990s.**
Sean Enright, James Morton.   London: Weidenfeld & Nicolson, 1990. 184p. bibliog.

At one time regarded as a basic freedom to be cherished, the right to trial by jury in criminal trials is now increasingly under threat and it is becoming fashionable to query the ability of ordinary jurors to competently discharge their duties especially in complicated cases of financial fraud. In this study two practising lawyers examine the evolution of the jury system and investigate the delicate relationship between the certainty of the state and the unpredictability of individual juries. Among the subjects discussed are the introduction of majority verdicts, jury vetting, and the reforms needed if the jury system is to survive.

925 **System of justice: an introduction to the criminal justice system in England and Wales.**
Mike Fitzgerald, John Muncie.   Oxford: Blackwell, 1983. 216p. bibliog.

This study of the organization and workings of the structures and processes of the English criminal justice system is divided into three main sections. In turn the organization, personnel, powers, policies and practices of the police, the courts, and the prisons are critically assessed; all three end with a discussion of the major issues and controversies surrounding these institutions and their working practices.

926 **The Parliament of Great Britain: a bibliography.**
Richard U. Goehlert, Fenton S. Martin. Lexington, Kentucky:
Lexington Books, 1983. 209p.

Focusing primarily on the historical development and legislative processes of
Parliament, and not with national politics or government policies, this bibliography
includes scholarly research material published in the English language in the last
hundred years. It is divided into two sections: reference works of all descriptions; and
specific works on the origins and development of parliament, the House of Commons
and House of Lords, the organization of parliament, its reform, and its legislative
machinery.

927 **Parliament: functions, practice and procedures.**
J. A. G. Griffith, Michael Ryle, M. A. J. Wheeler-Booth. London:
Sweet & Maxwell, 1989. 538p. bibliog.

Written with all the cumulated authority of the Emeritus Professor of Public Law in
the University of London, the Clerk of Committees in the House of Commons, and the
Clerk Assistant of the House of Lords, this formidable work has to be regarded as the
last word on the organizations, activities, procedures and practices of Parliament. Part
one analyses the House of Commons' functions, power and membership; part two
describes the physical and procedural framework for parliamentary business; part three
discusses how government business is conducted, the opportunities for Opposition and
backbench initiatives, and the structure, functions and powers of the Select
Committees; whilst part four deals with the composition, procedure and role of the
House of Lords. A final chapter poses the question 'Is Parliament effective?'.

928 **Halsbury's laws of England.**
London: Butterworths, 1989. 56 vols. 4th ed. re-issued.
vol. 1. *Administrative law, Admiralty*; vol. 50. *Weights and measures*;
vols. 51-52. *European Community*; vol. 53. *Consolidated table of
statutes, statutory instruments, and tables of European Community
materials*; vol. 54. *Consolidated index of cases*; vols. 55-56. *Consolidated
index 1990*.

The foremost encyclopedia for all areas of English law, the main work consists of
separate treatises on individual subjects amply complemented by case and precedent
studies. This is updated by an annual *Cumulative supplement* which incorporates all
material from previous years' *Supplements* still relevant, and new material to the end
of October of the previous year. A monthly *Current service* keeps Halsbury right up to
the minute. In addition there is an *Annual abridgement*, a complete survey of English
case law, statute law, and subordinate legislation, and other noteworthy items from
government papers, reports of committees, and legal periodicals. *Halsbury's laws of
England: a users guide* (1983. 30p.) gives advice on how best to use the main work,
vols. one to fifty are arranged alphabetically by subject, vol. 1 *Administrative law,
Admirality . . .* vol. 23 *Income and taxation . . .* vol. 33 *National Health . . .* vol. 40
Road Traffic . . . vol. 50 *Weights and measures*.

929 **Halsbury's statutes of England and Wales.**
London: Butterworths, 1985- . 50 vols. 4th ed.

First published in 1930 to accompany *Halsbury's laws of England*, this ambitious project aims to print an up-to-date version of every Public General Act or Ecclesiastical Measure still effectively in force with detailed annotations added to each section and schedule. A *Cumulative supplement* was published in 1989 as was *Tables of statutes and general index*. The whole work is an invaluable tool for tracing legislation relating to a particular subject or area.

930　**The noble lie: the British constitution and the rule of law.**
　　　Ian Harden, Norman Lewis.　London: Hutchinson, 1986. 334p.
　　　bibliog.

The 'noble' lie of the title refers to the orthodox doctrine that British constitutional aspirations are realized through the institutions and processes of the nineteenth-century liberal state. This challenging and stimulating work asserts that far from living under a system of open and accountable democratic government, in practice the British people suffer under an extremely secretive and unaccountable system geared in favour of an uncontrolled executive working through informal and obscure networks. The authors end with suggestions for a revised concept of law which would close the current extraordinary gulf between theory and practice. This book could still become a work of genuine seminal significance.

931　**The British constitution and politics.**
　　　J. Harvey, L. Bather.　London: Macmillan, 1982. 579p. bibliog.

First published in 1963 for undergraduates and for students preparing for professional examinations, this comprehensive textbook remains an excellent analysis of the main institutions of British government and of the principles and programmes of the major political parties. For this edition new sections have been added on Select Committees and on elections for the European Parliament.

932　**The Criminal Law Library.**
　　　Edited by Lord Havers of Edmundsbury.　London: Waterlow, 1985-91.
　　　9 vols. (vol. 1. *Fraud.* Anthony J. Arlidge, Jacques Parry. 1988.
　　　416p.; vol. 2. *Misuse of drugs.* Patrick Bucknell, Hamid Ghodse. 1991.
　　　2nd ed. 664p.; vol. 3. *Forensic medicine.* Evan Stone, Hugh Johnson.
　　　1987. 224p.; vol. 4. *Criminal evidence.* John A. Andrews, Michael
　　　Hirst. 1987. 688p.; *Supplement.* 1989. 88p.; vol. 5. *Sentencing.* Judge
　　　Eric Stockdale, Judge K. Devlin. 1987. 336p.; vol. 6. *Customs and
　　　excise cases.* Gavin McFarlane. 1988. 344p.; vol. 7. *Offences against
　　　property.* Jacques Parry. 1989. 416p.; vol. 8. *Sexual offences.* Peter
　　　Rook, Robert Ward. 1990. 488p.; vol. 9. *Offences of violence.* Peter
　　　Carter, Ruth Harrison. 1991. 338p.).

Each volume in this authoritative reference series, intended for law practitioners, has been written by experienced counsel, judges, or academic lawyers. Supplements and new editions are published when necessary to keep the series up to date.

933　**Mozley and Whiteley's law dictionary.**
　　　E. R. Hardy Ivamy.　London: Butterworths, 1988. 10th ed. 511p.

'The primary object of this work is to give an exposition of legal terms and phrases of past and present use. But as the mere exposition . . . would often be barren and unsatisfactory we have in many cases, especially when dealing with legal terms of the present day, added an exposition of the law bearing upon the subject-matter of the entry' (Preface). For this edition terms used in the commercial world have been added and the section on shipping law expressions has been expanded.

934 **Introduction to English law.**
Philip S. James. London: Butterworths, 1989. 10th ed. 591p.
Generations of first year undergraduates have acquired their basic knowledge of English public and private law from this classic conspectus which was first published over forty years ago. Much of the historical information previously so clearly in evidence has been excised in this revised edition.

935 **Parliament.**
Sir Ivor Jennings. Cambridge, England: Cambridge University Press, 1961. 2nd ed. 574p.
Long regarded as 'the standard work on Parliament for the ordinary citizen', this comprehensive and meticulous study on how the British parliamentary system operates has now largely been replaced by J. A. G. Griffiths, Michael Ryle, and M. A. J. Wheeler-Booth's *Parliament: functions, practice and procedures* (q.v.) although it still retains its historical value.

936 **The dictionary of English law.**
W. A. Jowitt, C. Walsh, edited by J. Burke. London: Sweet & Maxwell, 1977. 2 vols. 2nd ed. (supplement 1985). bibliog.
First published in 1959 this massive work amounting to almost 2,000 pages contains substantial definitions and explanations of English legal terms plus references to relevant statutes, cases, and definitive text books.

937 **Judicial Statistics Annual Report England and Wales.**
London: HMSO for Lord Chancellor's Department. annual.
Containing statistics on the criminal and civil business of the courts of England and Wales for which the Lord Chancellor is responsible, this annual report also includes brief descriptions of their functions, constitutions, and jurisdictions.

938 **The constitutional history of modern Britain since 1485.**
David Lindsay Keir. London: A & C Black, 1969. 9th ed. 600p.
This chronologically-ordered overview of the development of the British constitution describes its structure and the working of its main organizations of government. Keir interprets their evolution in the context of political, religious, social, and economic influences and shows how government has been conducted by successive administrations sharing a common political tradition. The twin theme of this classic text, first published in 1938, is that continuity has been the dominant characteristic of British constitutional growth and that its institutions have been regulated by constant and unwavering legal and philosophical principles.

939 Legal advice and assistance.
Elaine Kempson. London: Policy Studies Institute, 1989. 106p.

Currently, the legal advice and assessment scheme operating in England costs £60 million a year. Commissioned by the Law Society, this study investigates the amount of social welfare and assistance undertaken by solicitors either in private practice or in advice centres, focusing on three localities; the London Borough of Newham, the Metropolitan Borough of Oldham, and Cornwall. It also examines some of the proposals for change, especially ways of providing legal assistance at less cost.

940 The English legal system.
A. K. R. Kiralfy. London: Sweet & Maxwell, 1990. 8th ed. 309p.

No prior knowledge of the law is assumed in this general historical introduction to the English legal system. It contains chapters on the divisions of English law; a history of substantive law; sources (precedent, legislation, inherent jurisdiction, and in this edition, custom and practice, commercial efficacy, public policy and public interest, and legitimate expectation); European Community law; an outline history of the courts; criminal procedure and appeals; civil proceedings in the High Court; civil appeals, and special courts.

941 The office of Speaker.
Philip Laundy. London: Cassell, 1964. 488p. bibliog.

The Speaker is elected to office by MPs from their own ranks and is the principal officer of the House of Commons. He (or she) is the guardian of its privileges and its spokesman in its relations with the House of Lords and the Crown as well as the impartial conductor of its proceedings, presiding over its debates and maintaining order and discipline. This comprehensive work examines in detail the nature and functions of the Office and its historical development.

942 Law.
London: HMSO, 1991. 62p.

Arranged by title within broad subject categories, this catalogue assembles a selection of government publications relating to councils, committees, courts, and legal aid; employment, the environment; European and world affairs; finance, business, and industry; health and social issues; immigration and nationality; police and crime; and tax.

943 The Law Society's directory of solicitors and barristers 1993.
London: Law Society, 1993. 1313p.

Produced from the Law Society's own records this authoritative guide to solicitors and barristers in England and Wales is divided into geographical regions arranged alphabetically by town with separate sections for Greater London and overseas. Each firm's entry shows all qualified and admitted solicitors as at 31 January 1993 and their status within the firm (partner, assistant or consultant). Employed solicitors with a current practising certificate working in commerce, industry, the Crown Prosecution Service, and central and local government are listed separately. Barristers' chambers are entered alphabetically and individual barristers are listed in order of seniority. Additional information on agency solicitors, process servers, and expert witnesses, is included. The Law Society also publishes seven English *Solicitors' regional directories* presenting individual practices by town, a survey of services offered by each firm, and useful information on Independent Advice Centres and Citizens Advice Bureaux.

944 **The eclipse of Parliament: appearance and reality in British politics since 1914.**
Bruce P. Lenman. London: Edward Arnold, 1992. 284p.

The central theme of this study by the Professor of Modern History in the University of St. Andrews is that by 1914 genuine parliamentary government in Britain had been ousted by a rampant executive power. The consolidation of that change, the progressive winding down of the capacity of the House of Commons to check the executive powers of government, the steady growth of a prime ministerial system, the politicization of senior civil servants, and the resulting changes in party politics, parliament, and cabinet government, are the political and constitutional reality that Lenman so effectively explores.

945 **A history of the House of Lords.**
Lord Longford, introduction by Elizabeth Longford. London: Collins, 1988. 224p. bibliog.

Lord Longford has sat in the House of Lords since 1945, was for three years its leader, and played a major role in the 1968 debate on its reform. This history of the second chamber, 'a strange amalgam of hereditary peers, former members of the Commons, bishops, law lords and experts of every conceivable variety', traces its evolution from its obscure beginnings in the eleventh century and from its more documented appearance in the English body politic in the thirteenth and fourteenth centuries.

946 **Parliament at work.**
Oonagh McDonald. London: Methuen, 1989. 277p. bibliog.

Drawing upon her own experiences in the House of Commons, the author sets out in detail the way Parliament works, including the legislative process, private and private members' Bills, European legislation, public spending and raising taxes, the Select Committees, and the reporting of parliamentary proceedings. She also casts a critical eye at the effectiveness of these proceedings today. Information on how to visit Parliament and how to lobby MPs is included.

947 **The layman's dictionary of English law.**
Gavin McFarlane. London: Waterlow, 1984. 319p.

Concise definitions of some 3,300 legal terms expressed in everyday language are contained in this dictionary. Of necessity a few Latin tags and maxims are included as is a wide selection of terms in commerce and government.

948 **A concise dictionary of law.**
Editor Elizabeth A. Martin. Oxford: Oxford University Press, 1990. 2nd ed. 448p.

Over 3,400 cross-referenced entries define and explain the major terms, concepts, processes, and organization of the law, in this revised and expanded dictionary which was first published in 1983. Reflecting recent legislation such as the Criminal Justice Act 1988, the Children Act 1989, and the Police and Criminal Evidence Act 1984, it also encompasses changes in the law relating to conveyancing, consumer protection, bankruptcy and liquidation procedures, public order offences, the rights of illegitimate children, divorce proceedings, data protection, and state benefits.

949 Shaw's directory of courts in the United Kingdom 1991/92.
Edited by Gordon Morris. Crayford, England: Shaw, 1991. 257p.

First published in 1973 this directory includes The High Court, Crown Courts, County Courts, and Magistrates Courts of Summary Jurisdiction, stating their hours of session. Details of the Crown Prosecution Service and of penal establishments are appended.

950 The British constitution now.
Ferdinand Mount. London: Heinemann, 1992. 289p.

It is the concept of the unfettered supremacy of Parliament, in effect of the House of Commons, that forms the central theme of this seminal constitutional study. Mount argues that devolved government, European institutions, a reformed second chamber, a written Bill of Rights, and a Supreme Court, could equally guarantee the traditional legal and political freedoms of the United Kingdom. Constitutional issues are likely to be in the forefront of British politics during the next two Parliaments; this book questions the *status quo* and suggests a number of ways forward.

951 Hazell's guide to the judiciary and the courts with the Holborn Law Society's bar list 1992.
Edited by C. G. A. Parker. Henley-on-Thames, England: R. Hazell, 1992. 456p.

Published annually since 1985, this guide includes directory type information on the House of Lords (Lords of Appeal, the Judicial Committee of the Privy Council, the Lord Chancellor's department), the Courts in England and Wales (Circuits, Crown Courts, County Courts, circuit Judges, Magistrates Courts, Recorders, Stipendary magistrates, etc.), list of the Bar by chambers, and UK police forces.

952 Parliamentary papers: British parliamentary publications and procedural records of Parliament in the Official Publications and Social Sciences Reading Room.
London: British Library, [n.d.] 16p. bibliog.

Parliamentary papers are a rich mine of current and historical information. These notes not only provide a guide to the vast resources of the British Library, they also serve to explain just what parliamentary publications encompass. The purpose and background of *Reports of Select Committees*, the general and special indexes, the *Journals* of the House of Commons and House of Lords, the *Debates* of both Houses, the daily business papers, and the *Statutes*, are explained in detail.

953 Ministers of the Crown.
D. A. Pickrill. London: Routledge & Kegan Paul, 1981. 135p. bibliog.

Prime Ministers, Lord Chancellors, Lord Privy Seals, Paymaster-Generals, and the holders of all other ministerial offices, are listed here from their earliest known dates.

954 **Public general acts and measures.**
London: HMSO for Statutory Publications Office, 1831- . annual.
All Acts and Measures legislation passed during the calendar year are reproduced in chronological order in this annual publication. Access is by alphabetical and chronological indexes.

955 **International legal books in print, 1990-1991: an annotated bibliography.**
Edited by Donald Raistrick (et al.). London: Butterworths, 1991. 971p.
Prepared by an Editorial Board headed by Donald Raistrick of the Lord Chancellor's Department, this bibliography of English-language legal materials published or distributed in the UK, Europe, and current or former Commonwealth countries, lists more than 20,000 items. Full details are also provided of the 1,500 publishers whose works are listed in the bibliography.

956 **Mackintosh's The government and politics of Britain.**
Peter G. Richards. London: Hutchinson, 1988. 7th ed. 266p. bibliog.
John R. Mackintosh's classic textbook, first published in Hutchinson's University Library in 1970, was regarded by its author as an extended interpretative essay explaining how the British system of government worked. This latest edition attempts to show how that system is responding to contemporary political pressures although the text continues to develop broad constitutional themes: Parliament's role, the power and responsibilities of the Prime Minister, the functions of Whitehall departments and the Civil Service, and the changing – some would say diminishing – role of local government authorities.

957 **How Parliament works.**
Paul Silk, Rhodri Walters. London: Longman, 1989. 2nd ed. 272p. bibliog.
Chapters on the parliamentary building; 'who's who' in Parliament; officers, officials and helpers; Parliament's powers in theory and practice; the day-by-day organization of business; legislation; financial control and accountability; the inquisitorial factor (parliamentary questions and MP's letters and petitions); debates; Select Committees; Parliament and the European Communities; and parliamentary reform, provide an accurate, comprehensive, and up-to-date guide to the activities of the House of Commons and House of Lords.

958 **Statutes in Force.**
London: HMSO for Statutory Publications Office, 1972- . irreg.
Statutes in Force provides a constantly updated text of the current law of the land in 108 looseleaf binders. Acts of Parliament etc. are classified in 125 groups to allow customers to purchase only the sections they need. The *Statutes* contain unrepealed Acts of Parliament of England, Scotland, and the United Kingdom; Church Assembly and General Synod measures; and selected Acts from the *Local* and *Personal* series. *Index to the statutes*, two volumes updated annually, is an alphabetical list of subject headings. Under each of these sub-headings is a chronological list of every statute, together with its chapter number, and a reference to its location in the *Statutes*.

Constitution and Law

Chronological tables of the statutes, also revised annually, lists all Public General Acts and Measures from 1235 to date. It shows how and when each section of an Act has been amended or how and when it was repealed.

959   **Table of Government Orders.**
London: HMSO. annual.

This publication lists in chronological order all general subordinate legislation, Statutory Rules and Orders, Statutory Instruments, showing which are still in force, which have been amended or revoked, and by what authority. There is an half-yearly supplement.

960   **The Times guide to the House of Commons April 1992.**
London: Times Books, 1992. map.

Full information on the new Cabinet, a detailed constituency by constituency breakdown of the 1992 General Election results, biographies of the candidates who fought the election, reports and statistical analyses of the election campaign, and the main parties' election manifestos, are all included in this authoritative guide.

961   **Vacher's biographical guide 1992.**
Berkhamsted, England: Vacher's, 1992. 540p.

Biographies of the members of the House of Commons and the House of Lords are the principal features of this annual guide. For MPs the entries include their profession, political allegiance, their majority, birthdate, education, previous occupation, political career, and their personal and political interests. Biographies of British Members of the European Parliament and senior civil servants (Grades 1-3) are also included.

962   **The Oxford companion to law.**
David M. Walker.   Oxford: Clarendon Press, 1980. 1,366p. bibliog.

This alphabetical compendium provides concise information on the principal legal institutions, courts, judges and jurists, systems of law, branches of law, legal ideas and concepts, important doctrines, and the principles of law. Mainly concerned with the United Kingdom legal system it nevertheless includes material on the systems of other English-speaking nations. There is a comprehensive list of the holders of the various legal and constitutional offices since 1660.

963   **A foundation in English law.**
Geoffrey Whitehead, Abdul Kadar.   Cheltenham, England: Stanley Thornes, 1992. 564p.

Intended for students on law courses or business studies courses which contain a law module, this textbook provides a clear and comprehensive outline of the development of English law, the courts system, arbitration, criminal law, the law of persons, contract law, the law of tort, the law of property, constitutional and administrative law, employment law, trespass, nuisance, negligence, and defamation.

964   **An encyclopaedia of Parliament.**
       Norman Wilding, Philip Laundy.   London: Cassell, 1972. 4th ed.
       931p.

Concise and authoritative information on Parliament's powers and privileges, its procedures and customs, is provided in this authoritative work. Parliamentary history is dealt with under the reign of each monarch from Elizabeth I to Queen Victoria. Its earlier history is considered separately. Biographical entries are included, but only for those individuals who were personally concerned with parliamentary growth and development. There are thirty-four appendices, mostly lists of ministers, but including the parliaments listed according to regnal year and to the date of the first sessions of each parliament.

Law relating to the travel industry.
See item no. 243.

Moore's introduction to English canon law.
See item no. 619.

Subjects, citizens, aliens and others: nationality and immigration law.
See item no. 841.

Guide to the Data Protection Act.
See item no. 1215.

Labour law in Great Britain and Ireland.
See item no. 1479.

Countryside law.
See item no. 1522.

Sport and the law.
See item no. 2061.

Fair game: law of country sports.
See item no. 2064.

Copyright.
See item no. 2186.

Politics and Government

965 **Pressure groups and government in Great Britain.**
Geoffrey Alderman.   London: Longman, 1984. 164p. bibliog.
In this study of the relationship between pressure groups and the governing process, Alderman expresses the view that they form an integral part of government and are essential to the democratic process to voice demands and opinions which would otherwise go unheeded. He admits there could be grounds for concern over some groups' untoward influence but considers ways whereby they could be subjected to greater public accountability.

966 **Biographical dictionary of modern British radicals.**
Joseph O. Baylen, Norbert J. Gossman.   Brighton, England:
Harvester Wheatsheaf, 1979-88. 4 vols. (vol. 1. *1770-1830*. 1975. 565p.;
vol. 2. *1830-1870*. 1984. 556p.; vol. 3. *1870-1914*. 2 vols. 1988. 888p.).
For the purpose of this work 'radicals' are interpreted here as 'those persons whose programmes and work involved something more than a moderate adjustment of policy or minor change in the operation of political, social and economic institutions'. More specifically, this work includes 'those who hoped to change in some fundamental way the old order in which Britain was dominated by the landed aristocracy and the established Church' and 'those who sought to alter the social and economic structure of society through positive State action, to achieve a more equitable distribution of wealth and social welfare legislation'. In general the work was planned to supplement and to correct the *Dictionary of national biography* (q.v.).

967 **The British system of government.**
Anthony H. Birch.   London: Unwin Hyman, 1990. 8th ed. 286p. map.
bibliog.
First published in 1967, this study examines the social basis and constitutional framework of British political institutions. The party system, the working of parliament and the process of government, the Civil Service, the party system, and the relationship between the government and the governed, including a chapter on the

218

fraying relations between the public and the police, all fall within its scope. For this edition an entirely new chapter on foreign policy has been added.

968 **Public policy in Britain.**
Martin Burch, Bruce Wood.   Oxford: Blackwell, 1990. 2nd ed. 251p. bibliog.

First published by Martin Robertson in 1983, this study approaches the practice of government from the resource angle, the acquisition of the necessary money, land, and labour, and their allocation to the various policy programmes. The implementation of these programmes and their effect on British society are also examined. In practical terms, it is the whole process of public expenditure, taxes, budgets, and their impact, that is on view here.

969 **British general elections since 1945.**
David Butler.   Oxford: Blackwell, 1989. 128p. (Making Contemporary Britain).

This scholarly analysis of each general election since the war examines how much press conferences, advertising, opinion polls, photo-opportunities, and other mass media of communications activities, have changed the conduct of the democratic process in Britain. Other aspects considered include voters' behaviour and the electoral system itself.

970 **British political facts 1900-1985.**
David Butler, Gareth Butler.   London: Macmillan, 1986. 6th ed. 536p. bibliog.

With chapters on Ministries, political parties, parliament, elections, political allusions, the Civil Service, Royal Commissions, committees of inquiry and tribunals, the administration of justice, social conditions, employment and trade unions, the economy, nationalization, Royalty, local government, the Commonwealth, international relations, Europe, the armed forces, the press, the broadcasting authorities, and religion, this handbook covers the who, what, and when of twentieth-century British history. Compact and reliable data is here available at the turn of a page which otherwise might take hours to locate.

971 **The Far Left in British politics.**
John Callaghan.   Oxford: Blackwell, 1987. 249p.

Chiefly concerned with the Leninist Left, when Trotskyist and Stalinist factions found themselves on the same side, this study of Far Left politics since the Second World War focuses particularly on the 1983 general election when the programme of the Labour Party under Michael Foot enjoyed widespread Far Left support. In the face of Labour's worst performance for fifty years a new coalition of the Left took shape: the Bennites within the Labour Party, various Trotskyist groups, Stalinists from the Communist Party, and militant trade unionists. The Left's activities in the 1984-85 miners strike, the Labour Party – Militant confrontation in Liverpool, and the controversy over Black sections within the Labour Party, are also discussed.

Politics and Government

972 **Socialism in Britain since 1884.**
John Callaghan. Oxford: Blackwell, 1990. 279p. bibliog.

Concentrating primarily on socialist institutions and organizations in Britain from the founding of the Fabian Society in 1884, this overview of socialist ideology, strategies and policies, traces the importance of Marxism, guild socialism, Communism, the Labour Party, and the various and disparate left wing factions of the present day. The influence of writers such as the Webbs, George Bernard Shaw, H. G. Wells, G. D. H. Cole, R. H. Tawney, Harold Laski, and Anthony Crosland, is also examined.

973 **The British experience 1945-75.**
Peter Calvocoressi. London: Bodley Head, 1978. 253p.

Describing and evaluating the changes in Britain during the immediate post-war years, this thoughtful study looks at the social and political plans and achievements of the first Labour government, the economic crises of the period, the pressures of poverty and housing, and the changing role of Britain in the post-war world.

974 **On the record: surveillance, computers and privacy – the inside story.**
Duncan Campbell, Steve Connor. London: Michael Joseph, 1986. 347p.

This chilling and disturbing book outlines the threat to personal privacy posed by the major computer databanks holding information on large numbers of British citizens. It examines the potential damage of improper use, the effect of inaccurate information, the awesome power of the advanced technology information systems of central government, the use of confidential health records, the 'local intelligence' computer systems available to the police, and the data held on Special Branch and Security Service computers. A final chapter exposes the inadequacies of the 1984 Data Protection Act.

975 **The Civil Service.**
London: HMSO, 1982. rev. ed. 12p. (Sectional List, no. 44).

Handbooks and reports on internal Civil Service matters such as personnel management, recruitment policies, security, and training, and similar material relating to the Diplomatic Service, on computers in Government, and on Civil Service management techniques, are among the official publications listed in this catalogue.

976 **Civil Service year book 1992.**
London: HMSO, 1992. 802p.

Listing the royal household, parliamentary offices, all ministries and departments, libraries, museums, and art galleries, research councils, other organizations like English Heritage and the Countryside Commission, along with salary tables, this official guide outlines their responsibilities, and their senior Civil Servants. Essentially it is a 'who's who' of the higher echelons of government administration.

977 **Britain in agony: the growth of political violence.**
Richard Clutterbuck. London: Faber, 1978. 335p. bibliog. map.

During the period 1971-77 political violence in Britain reached its highest point for sixty years. This important study analyses the causes and effects of such incidents as the Saltley Coke Depot, the Shrewsbury pickets, Red Lion Square, Grunwick, the

Right to Work March, and the renewed IRA bomb campaign in England. These events are set in the context of the Industrial Relations Act, the so-called Social Contract, and the sudden upsurge in inflation and unemployment.

978 **Sources in British political history 1900-1951.**
Chris Cook. London: Macmillan, 1975-85. 6 vols.
Financed by the Social Sciences Research Council, a major project has been in progress at the British Library of Political and Economic Science (London School of Economics) since 1970 to locate important political archives and to make them available to historians. Each entry in this set of volumes relates to individual archives and their surviving unpublished historical papers. The volumes are as follows: vol. 1. *A guide to the archives of selected organizations and societies.* 1976. 330p.; vol. 2. *A guide to the papers of selected public servants.* 1976. 297p.; vol. 3/4. *A guide to the private papers of Members of Parliament.* 1977. 281p. + 272p.; vol. 5. *A guide to the private papers of selected writers, intellectuals and publicists.* 1978. 221p.; vol. 6. *First consolidated supplement.* 1985. 271p.

979 **Contemporary British politics: an introduction.**
Bill Coxall, Lynton Robins. London: Macmillan, 1989. 571p. bibliog.
Based on the conviction that political institutions and political issues are inseparable, this comprehensive textbook opens with a discussion on the nature and social context of politics, and on key political concepts and major ideologies. This is followed by a study of the institutions of politics, parliament, and government and of the issues and controversies which currently preoccupy politicians and voters. A final section examines the main theories concerning the distribution of power in British society and analyses the impact of Thatcherism in the 1980s.

980 **British electoral facts 1832-1987.**
Compiled by F. W. S. Craig. Aldershot, England: Dartmouth, 1989. 5th ed. 210p.
First published in 1965 as *British parliamentary election statistics*, this is exclusively a reference source to electoral statistics and makes no claim to be a study of either voting behaviour or of regional voting patterns. The main tables show the total votes won by candidates of the major parties in successive elections. Other tables provide information on the referendum on UK membership of the EEC; ministers defeated in general elections; the total numbers of the electorate; the reasons for calling elections; changes in the electoral system; Royal Commissions appointed to enquire into alleged corruption in individual constituencies; and even on the weather on polling day.

981 **British general election manifestos, 1959-1987.**
F. W. S. Craig. Aldershot, England: Dartmouth, 1990. 3rd ed. 521p.
Previous editions of this work have appeared as *British general election manifestos 1900-1974*. It contains the full text of the manifestos issued by the major political parties and serves as a guide to what was at the forefront of the public's attention in successive elections.

982 **The British electorate 1963-1987: a compendium of data from the British Election Studies.**
Ivor Crewe, Neil Day, Anthony Fox.   Cambridge, England:
Cambridge University Press, 1991. 572p.

Based on statistical information collected by the British Election Study research teams at Oxford and Essex universities, this authoritative reference guide to British voters and British elections covers a wide range of topics including voting patterns, turnout figures, party membership, and attitudes towards issues like nationalization, capital punishment, abortion, and welfare benefits. Statistical tables present the same data for each election in the twenty-five year period, allowing users to look up information on a specific election, to compare any two elections, or to distinguish trends across the whole period.

983 **Introduction to British politics: analysing a capitalist democracy.**
John Dearlove, Peter Saunders.   Cambridge, England: Polity Press, 1991. 2nd ed. 565p. bibliog.

First published in 1984, and continuously reprinted, this extensively revised edition focuses on the structure of power and policy-making in an analytical context of change and continuity in British politics. In particular the changing relationship between social class and voting patterns, the impact of New Right ideas on the politics of Conservative government, and the implications of entry into Europe on the erosion of national sovereignty, are closely pursued. The conclusion is that 'for good or bad, British politics can no longer be contained within the increasingly anachronistic boundaries of the territorial nation state'.

984 **Politics in Britain from Callaghan to Thatcher**.
J. Denis Derbyshire, Ian Derbyshire.   Edinburgh: Chambers, 1990. 2nd ed. 296p. bibliog. (Spotlight on Politics Series).

Equipped with a glossary of political terms, a chronology of events 1974-90, chapter notes, and an extensive bibliography, this guide to key political, economic and social changes during the Callaghan and Thatcher administrations is introduced by a consideration of the British political system and of political events since 1945.

985 **The history of the Liberal Party 1895-1970.**
R. Douglas.   London: Sidgwick & Jackson, 1971. 330p. bibliog.

At the beginning of this historical period the leader of the Liberal Party was either Prime Minister or Leader of Her Majesty's Opposition; at the end he led no more than a handful of Liberal MPs sharing a taxi to the House. This well-documented historical account charts the Party's downfall in fine style and detail.

986 **The Civil Service today.**
Gavin Drewry, Tony Butcher.   Oxford: Blackwell, 1988. 259p. bibliog.

This critical survey of the Civil Service outlines its history, provides a political profile of the modern service, and examines the organizational, constitutional and political framework in which it operates. It focuses on the key issues which have come into prominence in the 1980s, the problems of excessive bureaucratic secrecy, the shortcomings of ministerial accountability, the politicization of the civil service, and the increasing dilemma of civil servants facing crises of confidence in ministerial decisions, and on how Whitehall is affected by government campaigns aimed at improving efficiency and effectiveness. Special attention is paid to various recent *causes célèbres*; the ban on trade unions at GCHQ, the Ponting affair, the Westland crisis, and the vain attempt to suppress Peter Wright's *Spycatcher*.

987 A chronology of post war British politics.
Geoffrey Foote.   London: Croom Helm, 1988. 280p.

All major political events (e.g. general elections, government changes, significant legislation), social and economic developments, Britain's decline as a major colonial power, and its relations with the United States and the European Community, are given brief factual entries in this month-by-month chronology covering the period 1945 to the 1987 general election.

988 Britain since 1945.
Edited by T. R. Gourvish.   London: Macmillan, 1991. 400p. bibliog.

Tracing the nexus between economic performance and socio-political change in post-war Britain this set of expert papers evaluates the Conservative and Labour Party's attitudes towards the welfare state, the trade unions, housing, defence, education, and the nationalized industries, and concludes with an assessment of pop music and the pervasive youth culture of the period.

989 The British political tradition.
W. H. Greenleaf.   London. Routledge, 1983- . 4 vols.

Volume one (*The rise of collectivism*. 1983. 336p.) of this major study of the character of British politics over the last 150 years establishes its central theme: the extension of the role of Government at all levels. Volume two (*The ideological heritage*. 1983. 579p.) reviews the development of Liberalism, Conservatism, and Socialism and the ways in which all three political creeds have responded to this collectivist philosophy of government. Volume three (*A much governed nation*. (two parts). 1987) investigates how British political institutions reacted to the changing circumstances. This is undoubtedly an outstanding work which draws together all the diverse strands of the modern British political experience. A fourth volume, *The world outside*, is in preparation.

990 Public administration in Britain today.
John Greenwood, David Wilson.   London: Unwin Hyman, 1989.
2nd ed. 362p. bibliog.

An expanded version of *Public administration in Britain*, first published in 1984, this searching analysis takes full account of the fundamental changes in public administration that have occurred since 1984. Among the topics discussed are departments and departmentalism, co-ordinating the central administration, the cabinet system, the central administration in action, the administration and political context of local government, central–local government relationships, regional administration, parliament and accountability, and public administration and redress.

Politics and Government

991 H.M. Treasury and allied departments.
London: HMSO, 1984. rev. ed. 10p. (Sectional List no. 32).

Listed in this catalogue are reports, reviews, histories, texts of communiqués, abstracts of accounts, financial statements and budget reports etc., emanating from the Prime Minister's Office, the Cabinet Office, the Central Statistical Office, the Royal Mint, and HM Treasury.

992 Governing Britain: a guidebook to political institutions.
A. H. Hanson, Malcolm Walles. Glasgow: Fontana Press, 1990. 5th ed. 385p. bibliog.

Although Britain is a highly-developed country both in political and administrative terms, with long-established political and constitutional institutions, their evolution has been slow and gradual. This substantially-revised guide examines how central government has responded to the ever accelerating patterns of social and political change resulting from the shift away from consensual to confrontational politics in the 1980s. The changes in local government, the realignment of the political centre, and the concept of privatization of public services and utilities, are among the specific topics discussed.

993 Bibliography of the Chartist Movement 1837-1976.
I. F. C. Harrison, Dorothy Thompson. Hassocks, England: Harvester, 1978. 214p.

The Chartist Movement of 1837-54 was the most prominent working class movement for social and political reform in Britain before the rise of the modern Labour movement in the 1880s. It left a rich legacy of manuscript sources, contemporary printed sources, as well as published and unpublished secondary material, all of which is assembled here after years of research to provide an unparalled guide to primary source material.

994 Whitehall.
Peter Hennessy. London: Secker & Warburg, 1989. 851p.

Part history, part analytical study, part blueprint for reform, this thoroughly-researched and documented work examines how the Civil Service evolved and how the administrative machine functions in relation to Parliament and to the public. It also assesses how far its vaunted new look has genuinely changed its traditional attitudes.

995 Home Office.
London: HMSO, 1987. rev. ed. 16p. (Sectional List no. 26).

This catalogue includes in-print publications issued by the Home Office relating to animals; betting, gaming, and lotteries; broadcasting; charities; children; civil defence; community relations; crime; drugs; elections; fire; firearms; immigration and nationality; the police; prisons, probation, and aftercare; and publications of the Research and Planning Unit.

996 **A nation dividing? The electoral map of Great Britain 1979-1987.**
R. C. Johnston, C. J. Pattie, J. G. Alsopp.   London: Longman, 1988.
379p. 2 maps. bibliog.

When the dust and smoke of the 1987 general election cleared it was apparent that economic self-interest had produced a clear north-south division in British politics. South of a line drawn from Plymouth to Hull the Conservatives were overwhelmingly predominant whilst Labour strength was rooted in the north. This political and statistical study asks how the Conservatives can regain their support in the north, whether they need to, can Labour recover in the south without endangering their northern support, and is an electoral pact between Labour and the Democrat parties the only feasible alternative to continued Conservative governments?

997 **Consensus politics from Attlee to Thatcher.**
Dennis Kavanagh, Peter Morris.   Oxford: Blackwell, 1989. (Making Contemporary Britain).

Until Margaret Thatcher declared that her administration would be based on conviction government, post-war politics in Britain had evolved into consensus in key areas of policy. This study chronicles the rise and fall of consensus politics in five such areas: the mixed economy; full employment; trade unions; welfare; and foreign policy.

998 **The future of Whitehall.**
Oonagh McDonald.   London: Weidenfeld & Nicolson, 1991. 224p.

Crucial questions tackled in this powerful study of how Britain is governed include: Have twelve years of managerial reform streamlined the Civil Service and made it more efficient? What will be the impact of the Single European Act on Whitehall? Is open government essential for efficiency? and should public spending depend on the whim of government and be at the control of the Treasury?

999 **Policy networks in British government.**
Edited by David Marsh, R. A. W. Rhodes.   Oxford: Clarendon, 1992. 312p.

The 'policy networks' of the title denote the obscure world of civil servants, committees, and professional and vested interest groups, surrounding government policy decisions. This collection of papers cover policy-making in the areas of agriculture, civil nuclear power, youth employment, smoking, heart disease, sea defences, information technology, and exchange rate policy. An editorial assessment focuses on such questions as why networks change, which interests dominate and benefit from the network, and the consequences of the present system for democracy and the public interest.

1000 **Power, competition and the state.**
Keith Middlemas.   London: Macmillan, 1986-1991. 3 vols. (vol. 1. *Britain in search of balance 1940-61*. 1986. 416p.; vol. 2. *Threats to the postwar settlement: Britain 1961-74*. 1990. 480p.; vol. 3. *The end of the postwar era: Britain since 1974*. 1991. 608p.).

In the immediate post-war years both capital and labour co-operated with Conservative and Labour governments to sustain full employment in a mixed economy under the aegis of the welfare state. This comfortable state of affairs began to disintegrate in the

Politics and Government

1970s under the combined onslaught of seemingly unstoppable inflation, growing industrial unrest, and runaway public expenditure. The Thatcher 'miracle' halted all three, at least for a time. This interpretation of events achieves a masterly synthesis of contemporary political and economic history.

1001 **Labour people: leaders and lieutenants Hardie to Kinnock.**
Kenneth O. Morgan. Oxford: Oxford University Press, 1987. 370p. bibliog.

The careers and political significance of twenty-eight Labour leaders, 'parliamentary politicians, trade unionists, machine apparatchiks, intellectuals, journalists, prophets, and others', are analysed and reassessed in this important contribution to the history and ideology of the twentieth-century Labour Party.

1002 **Public bodies 1990.**
London: HMSO for Cabinet Office. Office of the Minister for the Civil Service, 1990. 123p.

Brief details about public bodies, the nationalized industries, public corporations, etc., for which Ministers have a degree of accountability, including financial information, and the number of ministerial appointments, are presented in this annual publication.

1003 **British government and politics.**
R. M. Punnett. Aldershot, England: Dartmouth, 1987. 5th ed. 572p. bibliog.

First published by Heinemann Educational Books in 1969, this firmly-established textbook has now been thoroughly revised. The impact of the Thatcher administration on the Cabinet system and the Civil Service, the parliamentary reforms of the 1980s, the changing perceptions of local government, the issue of privatisation of nationalized industries, electoral reform and the possible consequences of a 'hung' Parliament, are among the topics examined in this latest edition. There is also a completely new chapter on the influence the European Community exerts on British politics and government.

1004 **Fascism in Britain.**
Philip Rees. Hassocks, England: Harvester, 1979. 243p.

This annotated bibliography of 930 items covers the history of British fascism from its beginnings in 1923 when Roth Lintorn-Orman founded the British Fascisti. Writings by and on Sir Oswald Mosley are given prominence because of his long association with the British Union of Fascists.

1005 **The Thatcher decade: how Britain changed during the 1980s.**
Peter Riddell. Oxford: Blackwell, 1989. 236p. bibliog.

Mrs. Margaret Thatcher first led the Conservative Party to victory in the general election of May 1979, and won the two subsequent elections, to usher in over a decade of Tory rule. Among the many facets of Thatcherism, the eponymous driving force towards a new social revolution, this study concentrates on its nature, its economic policy, the labour market, privatization and popular capitalism, the welfare state, the social divide in terms of the distribution of income, wealth, employment, and the social cohesion of Britain.

1006   **The Blackwell biographical dictionary of British political life in the twentieth century.**
Edited by Keith Robbins.   Oxford: Blackwell, 1990. 449p. bibliog.
Although the primary focus of this work is on politicians, especially those who held important office in government or party, these career summaries also include church leaders, civil servants, soldiers, scientists, newspaper owners and editors, writers, etc. who made their mark in British political life, in political ideology, and in the continuity of political institutions. A complete coverage of Members of Parliament, however, is not attempted.

1007   **Politics in England: change and persistence.**
Richard Rose.   London: Macmillan, 1989. 5th ed. 381p.
Besides exploring the interrelated powers and functions of the Crown, the Prime Minister, Cabinet, and Parliament, this long-established study of English politics and public policy examines the electoral process, the communication of government information, and the political parties and their programmes. This edition has been revised and updated in the light of the events of the 1980s.

1008   **Parliamentary profiles.**
Andrew Roth.   London: Parliamentary Profiles, 1988. 2nd ed. 4 vols.
Individual biographies of each member of the 1987-1992 House of Commons contain details of their constituency, their majority, and an indication of their political outlook, history, education, qualifications, and personal and political traits. Memberships of the government and opposition front benches, select committees, and all party groups are also recorded.

1009   **Royal Commissions 1937-1981.**
London: HMSO, 1981. rev. ed. 10p. (Sectional List, no. 59).
Every published Royal Commission report and research paper is included in this official catalogue. They deal with such topics as capital punishment, the constitution, the distribution of income and wealth, gambling, local government, the National Health Service, the penal system in England and Wales, the press, standards of conduct in public life, and trade unions and employers' associations.

1010   **Third Party politics since 1945: Liberals, Alliance and Social Democrats.**
John Stevenson.   Oxford: Blackwell, 1993.
In the last ten to fifteen years the vicissitudes experienced by the Third Party in British politics have generated enormous interest. The inability to convert a large minority vote into parliamentary seats has cast grave doubts on the fairness of the British electoral system. This historical account follows the fortunes of the Third Party in British politics from the Liberal Party's near extinction in 1950 up to and following the 1992 general election.

1011　**The Prime Ministers: from Robert Walpole to Margaret Thatcher.**
George Malcolm Thomson.　London: Secker & Warburg, 1980.
260p. bibliog.

A series of forty-nine biographical and political vignettes traces the developing office of the Prime Minister in the transition from monarchical to parliamentary and cabinet government.

1012　**Treasury and Civil Service.**
London: HMSO, 1991. rev. ed. 30p. (Sectional List, no. 32).

Replacing two former sectional lists, *H.M. Treasury and allied departments* (no. 32), and *Civil Service* (no. 44), the scope of this new list has been widened so that in addition to covering in print publications from or about the Treasury and Civil Service which are available from Her Majesty's Stationery Office, it now includes those relating to the administration of government, government departments, and to many public services. For example, many National Audit Office and Committee of Public Accounts reports are listed here.

1013　**The almanac of British politics.**
Robert Waller.　London: Routledge, 1991. 4th ed. 717p. maps.

Essentially a guide to the 651 constituencies which form the membership of the House of Commons, this almanac presents a seat-by-seat geographical description and political history, including its electoral complexion and a note of boundary changes since the last election, and socio-economic data from the 1981 Census. Other features include lists of constituencies with the highest proportion of Asian and student voters, a list of marginal seats, maps of constituency boundaries, and an index of MPs and their constituencies.

1014　**The atlas of British politics.**
Robert Waller.　London: Croom Helm, 1985. 205p. 148 maps.

Concentrating on the evidence of the 1981 Census and the 1983 General Election, this atlas presents the regional realities of political power in Britain today. Topics treated include occupation and class, housing tenure, educational qualifications, rate of car ownership, levels of unemployment, and the location of non-white voters. The distribution of the party vote across the country is visually identified. Short explanatory essays elucidate the nature and importance of the statistics on which the maps are based. This work is intended as a complementary volume to the author's *Almanac of British politics* (q.v.).

1015　**Who's who of British Members of Parliament: a biographical dictionary of the House of Commons.**
Edited by Michael Stenton.　Hassocks, England: Harvester, 1976-79.
3 vols. (vol. 1. *1832-1885*. 1977. 444p.; vol. 2. *1886-1918*. 1978. 401p.;
vol. 3. *1919-1945*. Edited by Michael Stenton, Stephen Lees. 1979.
413p.).

Based on the annual volumes of *Dod's parliamentary companion* (q.v.) this work provides details of MPs' clubs, their dates of birth and death, their parentage, marriage, education, their careers before entering Parliament, their political beliefs and party affiliations, their views on important and controversial issues, their full parliamentary career, and their reasons for leaving Parliament and their subsequent history.

1016 The governance of Britain.

Harold Wilson.   London: Weidenfeld & Nicolson; London: Michael Joseph, 1976. 219p.

Written with the authority of a former Leader of the Labour Party and Prime Minister, this book analyses how the system of government operates in late twentieth-century Britain. It concentrates on the office of Prime Minister, its evolution since the eighteenth century, and its functions and powers *vis-à-vis* the majority party, Parliament, and the Cabinet, and on the Prime Minister's responsibilities for the national security agencies.

1017 British public opinion: a guide to the history and methodology of political opinion polling.

Robert M. Worcester.   Oxford: Blackwell, 1991. 231p. bibliog. (Making Contemporary Britain).

Robert Worcester is the founder, chairman, and managing director of MORI, a poll conducting organization. In this authoritative study he provides an historical overview of political opinion polling in Britain since the founding of the Gallup Poll in 1937. He also gives a detailed analysis of polling methodology, the art of asking questions, the science of sampling, and the correlation and publishing of the figures. An appendix prints the code of professional ethics and practices of the World Association of Public Opinion Research of which the author was President 1982-84.

Local Government and Administration

1018 **Audit Commission performance review in local government: a handbook for auditors and local authorities.**
London: HMSO, 1986. bibliog.

Two types of pressure were responsible for the introduction of performance reviews in local government: pressure for it to be accountable for the services it provides, and pressure on public spending at a time of changing social and economic circumstances. This handbook is a pack of ten separately published booklets contained within a spring-binder: *Introduction*; *Education*; *Environmental services*; *Housing*; *Law and order*; *Leisure and libraries*; *Planning and transportation*; *Social services*; and *Advice guide*. Each booklet begins with a brief description of the service followed by a section on trends and a résumé of key management issues. Finally there is a performance review guide in the form of a checklist for service managers with an annotated series of performance measures.

1019 **A history of the British fire service.**
G. V. Blackstone. London: Routledge & Kegan Paul, 1957. 484p. bibliog.

Covering the period from the fifth-century Roman *vigiles* to the county and county borough fire brigades of the 1950s, this history gives space to such topics as the growth and development of firefighting methods and equipment, the great fire tragedies, and the exploits of the National Fire Service in the Second World War.

1020 **Local government in Britain,**
Tony Byrne. London: Penguin, 1990. 5th ed. 468p. bibliog.

Taking into account the Local Government Finance Act 1988, and the Local Government Housing Act 1989, this definitive survey of the history, structure and functions of local government, first published in 1981, remains essential reading both for the student of government or politics and the general reader. It explains in non-technical prose the recent impact of local party politics and pressure groups, how councils and their committees operate, and offers an objective approach to such controversial issues as ratecapping and the abolition of the Greater London Council.

1021 **England – local government areas and parliamentary constituency boundaries.**
Southampton, England: Ordnance Survey.
Showing counties and districts created by the 1972 Local Government Act and by civil parishes, each of this series of thirty-seven maps on a scale of 1:100,000 (1 inch to 1½ miles) has a grey base map overprinted with local government information in red, and parliamentary boundaries in green. Specimen titles are: *Avon*; *Greater Manchester with Merseyside and Cheshire*; *Kent*; and *Wiltshire*.

1022 **Government and municipal contractors 1992.**
Epsom, England: Sell's, 1991. 56th ed. 556p.
Circulated to government departments, nationalized industries, municipal authorities, and major private work contractors, this buyer's guide contains an indexed directory of products and services, an alphabetical list of 8,000 companies supplying goods and services to local authorities, and a list of trade and brand names.

1023 **Greater London – local government and parliamentary constituency boundaries.**
Southampton, England: Ordnance Survey.
On a scale of 1:63,360 (one inch to one mile) this map shows the boundaries of the London Boroughs and the County of the City of London printed in red on a grey base with parliamentary boundaries in green.

1024 **Access to information in local government.**
Tim Harrison.   London: Sweet & Maxwell, 1988. 107p.
The 1985 Local Government (Access to Information) Act was instrumental in forcing local authorities to re-examine their internal procedures, and assembled in one place all the more important rights of access of the public to the deliberations of its elected representatives. This concise and practical guide also encompasses the implications of the 1984 Data Protection Act as it affects local Councils and the 1987 Access to Personal Files Act.

1025 **Opening the town hall door: an introduction to local government.**
Jane Hutt.   London: Bedford Square Press, 1990. 2nd ed. 141p.
bibliog.
Published for the National Council for Voluntary Organisations this little handbook shows how local government works and explains what services are provided by local councils, how decisions are made, how to go about finding sources of funding, how to make a complaint about services, or how to lobby for changes in local authority policies. This new edition deals at length with legislation enacted since 1987.

1026 **Local government and politics in Britain.**
John Kingdom.   London: Philip Allan, 1991. 282p. 5 maps. bibliog.
(Contemporary Political Studies).

Following the financial crises of the 1970s, and the interventionist Conservative
governments of the 1980s, local government has ceased to be a comparatively non-
controversial branch of public administration and has emerged as a dominant theme in
the political arena. This major introductory textbook encompasses the origins and
evolution of local government, what it does, its administrative context, local elections,
local political parties and pressure groups, local government boundaries, finance, and
the respective roles of elected members and their officers.

1027 **The local government companion: no. 19: 1991-92.**
Chichester, England: Local Government Companion, 1991. 546p.

This pocket-size publication gives the population and area of all local authorities in
England along with their Community Charge before and after capping and abatement
and the names of their chief executives and directors of their main departments.

1028 **Waterlow's 1991/92 local and public authorities directory.**
Edited by E. A. O'Connor.   London: Waterlow, 1991. 224p.

In addition to local authorities, central government departments, and public and
statutory offices, this directory also provides details of building societies and bank
headquarter offices, land registries, district probate registries, county courts, police
headquarters, and the Crown Prosecution Service. A detailed index of 15,000 place-
names indicates their County and District Council location.

1029 **Parish and town councils in England: a survey.**
London: HMSO for Department of the Environment, 1992. 105p.

Comprehensive data gleaned from a survey carried out between January and March
1991, accompanied by an explanatory text, provide an up-to-date picture of local
councils, their current activities, income and expenditure, the conduct of their
business, and their relationship with the communities they represent.

1030 **The Councillor.**
John Prophet.   London: Shaw, 1987. 10th ed. 109p.

Information on the structure of local government, the relationship between central and
local government, the status and conduct of local councillors, council meetings
procedures, and the role of local authority officers, is contained in this guide which was
first published over forty years ago.

1031 **The Parish Councillor's guide: the law and practice of parish, town and
community councils in England and Wales.**
John Prophet.   London: Shaw, 1988. 15th ed. 245p. bibliog.

Designed to meet the queries of parish councils and their clerks, this pocket-size guide,
first published in 1922, takes the form of notes on relevant topics likely to crop up at
parish council meetings.

1032 **Municipal year book 1992 and public services directory.**
Edited by Brian J. Rushbridge. London: Municipal Journal, 1992.
1992. 2 vols. 95th ed.

Volume one of this directory, which was first issued in 1898, is concerned with the functions of local authorities across the British Isles and the officers responsible for them. Arranged by local councils' departments and services, e.g. architecture and buildings, cultural activities, health, markets and fairs, refuse and salvage, and water, the names of the various chief officers are listed in alphabetical order of the various county, metropolitan district, and district councils. Volume two is a complete directory of all these councils with information on their population, debts, highways, amenities, topography, council members, committee chairmen, offices, and details of council meetings. It also includes information relating to parliament, the cabinet, and the development corporations.

1033 **A history of local government.**
K. B. Smellie. London: Allen & Unwin, 1968. 4th ed. 176p. bibliog.
(The New Town and County Hall Series).

First published in 1946 and substantially revised on the eve of a radical reconstruction, this study of how modern local government in England has developed since the Industrial Revolution, and the growth of political democracy after the 1832 Reform Act, begins with an outline of local government before that date and ends with a separate chapter on London. In discussing the causes of the various changes English local government has experienced the author neatly captures the structural and financial problems that still plague politicians and administrators.

1034 **Public authorities directory 1992.**
Edited by Geoffrey Smith. London: LGC Communications, 1992.
18th ed. 468p.

This authoritative and comprehensive guide to public authorities encompasses local authority counties and districts, local authority associations, the Audit Commission, the Commission for the New Towns, development corporations, combined police forces, residuary bodies, and health, fire and civil defence, and passenger transport authorities. For local authorities the information provided includes population, area, and the names of chief officers and heads of departments.

1035 **The future of local government.**
Edited by John Stewart, Gerry Stoker. London: Macmillan, 1989.
259p. (Government Beyond the Centre).

A substantial programme of legislation fundamentally altering the nature of local government was introduced by the Conservative government after its return to power following the 1987 general election. This set of papers, dedicated to the Institute of Local Government Studies on its twenty-fifth anniversary, is divided into two sections. The first examines some of the key areas of change in the legislation enacted or contemplated by the government, whilst the second assesses their implications for the structure and administration of local government in the future.

Local Government and Administration

1036 The politics of local government.
Gerry Stoker.   London: Macmillan, 1991. 2nd ed. 303p. bibliog.
(Public Policy and Politics).

Substantial new sections on local political parties, the internal politics of local authorities, the battles over local spending, the poll tax, the developments in privatizing local services, and the role of government and quasi-government agencies responsible for elements of local public service provision, update this wideranging analysis of the recent changes imposed on local government. The legacy left to local government in the immediate post-Thatcher era, and the likely directions local government will take in the 1990s, are also discussed. The author is Professor of Government in the University of Strathclyde.

1037 Guide to the local administrative units of England.
Edited by Frederic A. Youngs.   London: Royal Historical Society, 1980-91. 2 vols.

Divided by a line drawn from the Severn estuary to the Wash, the administrative history and boundaries of the ancient, civil and ecclesiastical parishes, other local government units, parliamentary constituencies, and dioceses of twenty-one historical counties and the City of London are encompassed in the southern volume (*Southern England*. 830p.) and a further eighteen counties in the northern volume (*Northern England*. 919p.) . It is the parish which is traditionally at the core of English local government. Here, the date of creation and abolition of each parish, the names of the other parishes from which is was formed, and the alteration of boundaries for any purpose, are all concisely chronicled. Heavy use is made of abbreviations and new readers are strongly advised to consult the preliminary pages which explain the guide's scope, organization, and format, before embarking upon its use.

Foreign Relations

1038   **British foreign policy 1918-1945: a guide to research and research materials.**
Edited by S. Aster.   Wilmington, Delaware: Scholarly Resources, 1984. 324p. bibliog.
A general introduction providing the historical background, chapters on the Foreign Office, and on research libraries and archives, and a bibliography of over 1600 items some of which refer to French and German language publications, are the main features of this important research guide.

1039   **British foreign policy in the twentieth century.**
C. J. Bartlett.   London: Macmillan, 1989. 144p. bibliog. (British History in Perspective).
Chronicling Britain's decline as a world power, this survey of Britain's foreign policy extends from the Fashoda Incident of 1898 to the Thatcher Government's relations with the European Community in the 1980s. During this period Britain witnessed the rise of other powers with the consequent diminution of her ability to influence world events with the same authority she claimed in the previous century.

1040   **The special relationship: a political history of Anglo-American relations since 1945.**
C. J. Bartlett.   Harlow, England: Longman, 1992. 224p.
Since the Second World War it has suited both the United Kingdom and the United States to avow that a special relationship exists between the two democracies. At times the close affinity between US Presidents and UK Prime Ministers has boosted the concept: Roosevelt and Churchill, Kennedy and Macmillan, Reagan and Thatcher. In this study Bartlett reconstructs the changing official perception of the relationship, explains how the two governments have grasped it when expedient, and demonstrates that although the relationship undoubtedly existed from time to time it was never constant nor permanent. A more popular study on the same theme is David Dimbleby

and David Reynold's *An ocean apart: the relationship between Britain and America in the twentieth century* (London: BBC/Hodder & Stoughton, 1988. 408p. bibliog.) which was developed from a BBC television series.

1041 **A handlist of British diplomatic representatives 1509-1688.**
Gary M. Bell. London: Royal Historical Society, 1990. 306p.
(RHS Guides and Handbooks, no. 16).

The dates of each embassy to European conferences and congresses, to the Holy Roman Emperor and Imperial Diets, to Denmark, France, the German States, Hanse Towns, the Italian States, Low Countries, North Africa, Persia and the Indian sub-continent, Poland, Russia, Scotland, Sweden, Turkey, and Venice, are all included in this handlist. The diplomatic rank of each envoy, the circumstances and purposes of their embassies, and a list of documentary instructions and diplomatic correspondence sources, are also listed.

1042 **A system of ambition? British foreign policy 1660-1793.**
Jeremy Black. Harlow, England: Longman, 1991. 296p.

It was during the eighteenth century that the roots of Britain's great power status were firmly entrenched. This study first examines the making of foreign policy and then proceeds to a detailed narrative interpretation of the policy in action.

1043 **Britain in Europe: the European Community and your future.**
Foreword by John Major. London: HMSO for Foreign &
Commonwealth Office, 1992. 24p.

The British Government's information booklet about how the Community works, the advantages of a single Market, and the changes that would be effected if the Treaty of Maastricht were to be ratified. Opponents would no doubt express other views.

1044 **'Pax Britannica'? British foreign policy 1789-1914.**
Muriel E. Chamberlain. London: Longman, 1988. 224p. 7 maps.
bibliog. (Studies in Modern History).

Two conflicting views of Britain's position in the world are discussed in this study of Britain's international role in her days of imperial splendour: that of men like Canning, Palmerston and Disraeli who acted as if Britain were the dominant world power, as opposed to Castlereagh, Wellington, Lord Aberdeen, and Gladstone, who considered Britain to be just one of four or five European powers. The influence of the press and of public opinion on British foreign policy is also calculated.

1045 **British security policy: the Thatcher years and the end of the Cold War.**
Edited by Stuart John Croft. London: Unwin Hyman, 1991. 256p.

This collection of essays examines the conduct of Britain's defence and foreign policy since 1979 and explores a number of alternative roles for Britain in the 1990s.

1046 **Inside the Foreign Office.**
John Dickie.   London: Chapmans, 1992. 338p. bibliog.
For thirty years John Dickie was diplomatic correspondent of the *Daily Mail*. This
penetrating investigation of how the Foreign office has handled the United Kingdom's
affairs abroad is based not only on his own experiences and insight but also on 150
interviews with politicians, ambassadors, and senior civil servants. He takes a close
look at conference and crisis diplomacy and diplomatic incidents, how the Foreign
Office is administered, the relations between the Prime Minister and the Foreign
Office, and at the wide influence and power wielded by the Principal Private Secretary.

1047 **The Diplomatic Service list 1992.**
London: HMSO for Foreign and Commonwealth Office, 1992.
27th ed. 339p.
Her Majesty's Diplomatic Service provides for the Foreign and Commonwealth Office
in London and for British Diplomatic and Consular posts abroad. This directory is
arranged in four sections: Home departments; British representatives overseas (by
country); chronological lists of Secretary of State, Ministers of State, Permanent Under
Secretaries, Ambassadors and High Commissioners since 1972; and biographical notes
of senior personnel including their current appointments.

1048 **Documents on British policy overseas.**
London: HMSO for the Foreign and Commonwealth Office, 1984- .
(*Series 1*. vol. 1. *The conference at Potsdam July-August 1945*. Edited
Rohan Butler, M. E. Pelly. 1984. 1,388p.; vol. 2. *Conferences and
conversations 1945: London, Washington and Moscow*. Roger Bullen,
M. E. Pelly. 1985. 951p.; vol. 3. *Britain and America: The negotiation
of the United States loan 3rd August-7th December 1945*. 1986. 453p.;
vol. 4. *Britain and America: Atomic energy, bases and food, December
1945-July 1946*. 1987. 417p.; vol. 5. *Germany and Western Europe
11 August-31 December 1945*. M. E. Pelly, H. J. Yasamee. 1990.
549p.; vol. 6. *Eastern Europe August 1945-April 1946*. M. E. Pelly,
H. J. Yasamee, K. A. Hamilton, 1991. 337p. *Series 2*. vol. 1. *The
Schuman Plan, the Council of Europe and Western European
integration May 1950-December 1952*. Roger Bullen, M. E. Pelly,
1986. 1,023p.; vol. 2. *The London Conferences: Anglo-American
relations and Cold War strategy, January-June 1950*. Roger Bullen,
M. E. Pelly, 1987. 406p.; vol. 3. *German rearmament September-
December 1950*. 1989. 421p.; vol. 4. *Korea, June 1950-April 1951*.
H. J. Yasamee, Ann Lane. 1991. 513p.).
The decision to publish these volumes, which follow the lines of *Documents on British
foreign policy 1919-1939*, was announced in the House of Commons in 1973. 'Her
Majesty's Government have decided to extend into the post-war period the practice
adopted for 1919-1939 of publishing documents on British foreign policy. The new
collection . . . will initially comprise two series to cover foreign policy in the periods
1945-1950 and 1950-1955 respectively'.

1049 **Chamberlain and appeasement: British policy and the coming of the Second World War.**
R. A. C. Parker. London: Macmillan, 1993. 256p. (The Making of the Twentieth Century).

Chamberlain's policy of appeasement of Nazi Germany, culminating in the Munich agreement of 1938, has aroused much political acrimony and controversy. Based on original archival research, this study examines the economic, diplomatic, and military factors which influenced Britain's foreign policy, especially with regard to the Axis powers, in the 1930s.

1050 **An index of British treaties 1101-1968.**
Clive Parry, Charity Hopkins. London: HMSO, 1970. 3 vols. 386p. + 1406p.

Compiled and annotated under the auspices of the International Law Fund, and the British Institute of International and Comparative Law, and prepared with the encouragement of the Foreign Office, this magisterial work forms a complete consolidated index to the Treaty Series published annually by the Foreign Office since 1892. It also includes the International Treaty series of the League of Nations and of the United Nations in addition to other British official and semi-official sources. The first volume contains the subject index to multilateral treaties and bilateral treaties by country whilst volumes two and three form a chronological index.

1051 **Offshore: Britain and the European idea.**
Giles Radice. London: I. B. Tauris, 1992. 192p.

Britain's role in Europe is a subject of intense political controversy. Radice, a staunch advocate of the European idea, examines the historical background to Britain's insular attitudes, and the suspicion that is never far below the surface in Britain that foreigners are not to be trusted. He argues that Britain's future success and prosperity depend very much on an active participation in Europe.

1052 **Britannia overruled: British policy and world power in the 20th century.**
David Reynolds. London: Longman, 1991. 392p. maps. bibliog.

Accounting for Britain's transition from an imperial global power to an off-shore island tentatively coming to terms with its role and status within the European community, this survey of Britain's overseas policy since the 1890s gives particular attention to antagonism and rivalry with both France and Germany, two World Wars, the special relationship with the United States, the Cold War, and colonial affairs.

1053 **Britain and the world: a study of power and influence.**
Jack Simmons. London: Studio Vista, 1965. 286p. bibliog. (A Visual History of Modern Britain).

This study of the impact made by Britain on Europe and the wider world concentrates on politics (but not overridingly so), technology, religion, the spread of English as the world's *lingua franca*, and on the development of European architecture.

1054 **Century of diplomatic Blue Books 1814-1914.**
Edited by H. Temperley, L. M. Penson.   London: Cass, 1966. 600p.
Originally published by Cambridge University Press in 1938 this work lists all
Parliamentary papers published 1814-1914 with a direct bearing on British foreign
policy. It is continued by R. Vogel's *A breviate of British diplomatic Blue Books 1919-
1939* (Leicester University Press, 1963. 474p.).

1055 **Treaty Series.**
London: HMSO for Foreign & Commonwealth Office, 1992- .
annual.
This government series lists those treaties to which the United Kingdom has become a
party to and which have come into force. The actual treaties are published in full as
parliamentary command papers.

1056 **The foreign policy process in Britain.**
William Wallace.   London: Royal Institute of International Affairs,
1975. 320p. bibliog.
First describing the policy making process in Whitehall, in particular the problems of
ministerial control and the domestic pressures against which ministers and civil servants
operate, this study continues by contrasting the pattern of relations with the United
States and Western Europe and that of foreign policy towards the rest of the world.
Wallace also includes case studies of policy making in both crisis and non-crisis
situations and conditions.

1057 **The Cambridge history of British foreign policy 1873-1919.**
Edited by A. W. Ward, G. P. Gooch.   Cambridge, England:
Cambridge University Press, 1922-23. 3 vols.
A co-operative history modelled on the *Cambridge modern history*, and based on
official documents, these volumes record the history of British foreign policy from an
admitted national point of view which openly seeks to vindicate the policies adopted
against their detractors. Each chapter is contributed by a British scholar and is
subdivided into sections on particular episodes. The work ends with a substantial
administrative history of the Foreign Office.

1058 **Britain and the world 1815-1986: a dictionary of international relations.**
David Weigall.   London: Batsford, 1987. 240p. + 12p. maps. bibliog.
Biographical entries, definitions of specialized diplomatic terms and concepts, major
entries on each war in which Britain has been involved, with shorter entries for key
battles, entries on underlying factors shaping events (e.g. economic developments,
strategic innovations, shifts in public opinion), and information on treaties and
diplomatic conflicts, are among the alphabetically arranged, cross-referenced entries
(from 100 to 3,000 words) which comprise this immensely valuable reference dictionary
on Britain's international relations.

1059   **Great Britain: foreign policy and the span of empire 1689-1971:**
       a documentary history.
       Edited by Joel H. Wiener.   New York: Chelsea House in association
       with McGraw Hill, 1972. 4 vols.

Documents from many diverse sources – treaties, judicial reports, memoirs, newspaper
accounts, contemporary tracts etc. – are edited, with commentaries, in these three
volumes. The broad perspectives of British foreign policy, Ireland, overseas
development, and the creation of the Commonwealth, are the principal themes.

Armed Forces and Defence

The Army

1060   A history of the British cavalry 1816-1919.
Marquess of Anglesey.   London: Leo Cooper, 1973- . 5 vols.
These well-researched volumes chronicle the origins, function, development, and employment, of the British Army's mounted division from the Napoleonic wars to the end of the First World War. Besides recording in detail the actions and campaigns in which the cavalry played a conspicuous part, they are equally concerned with peacetime soldiering.

1061   The Army list 1990.
London: HMSO, 1990. 2 vols.
Part one of this work lists Regular Army and Territorial Army officers by Army commands and establishments; part two includes officers on the retired list. The Army list was first published in 1814.

1062   A companion to the British Army 1660-1983.
David Ascoli.   London: Harrap, 1983. 319p. bibliog.
Orders of precedence at five crucial dates in the history of the British Army; the shifting pattern in the designation of its regiments and corps; their lineage, battle honours, and cap badges; and a chronology of the Army's political and military control, are all outlined in this authoritative reference work.

1063   All the Queen's men: the Household Cavalry and the Brigade of Guards.
Russell Braddon.   London: Hamish Hamilton, 1977. 288p.
Soldiers of the Life Guards, the Blues and Royals, and the Grenadier Coldstream, Scots, Irish and Welsh Guards, which together form the Household Division, are renowned for their discipline, the *élan* of their ceremonial drill, and for their

241

formidable prowess in battle. This account of their traditions and military history includes the history of their world famous regimental bands. Each regiment's history, battle honours, colours, and ceremonial duties are also outlined in a Pitkin London Guide, *The Guards* (Andover, England: Pitkin Pictorials, 1990. rev. ed. 28p.).

1064 **The handbook of British regiments.**
Christopher Chant. London: Routledge, 1988. 313p.

Provides an insight into the history and lineage of the approximately eighty-five regiments and corps that have survived a series of amalgamations and disbandments and which form the present-day Army. Arranged in order of precedence, each regiment or corps has a separate entry giving factual details, in a standardized layout, including current title, battle honours, uniform, history, affiliated and amalgamated regiments, nicknames, mottoes, and marches.

1065 **The records and badges of every regiment and corps in the British Army.**
H. M. Chichester, G. Burges-Short. London: Greenhill, 1986.
2nd ed. 984p.

First published by Gale & Polden in 1900 this is a reliable and informed account of all British regiments and corps, and their predecessors, up to the end of the nineteenth century. It incorporates information on regimental and corps badges, unit histories, and regimental colours and standards.

1066 **British Army uniforms and insignia of World War Two.**
Brian L. Davis. London: Arms & Armour Press, 1983. 276p. bibliog.

All badges of rank, uniform and insignia, and equipment, worn by the Army and Home Guard during the Second World War, are on view in this illustrated compendium.

1067 **Regimental badges.**
T. T. Edwards. London: Charles Knight, 1974. 6th ed. 361p.

Cap badges of all British Army regiments and corps, including the Territorial Army, Officers Training Corps, and also a number of discontinued badges, are recorded and illustrated in this comprehensive reference work.

1068 **Handbook on the British Army 1943.**
Edited by Chris Ellis, Peter Chamberlain. London: Arms & Armour Press, 1976. 234p.

This edition is basically a reprint of that originally issued by the United States Army in 1943 'to give an overall picture of the British Army, its equipment, uniforms, organization and tactics to the American soldier'. It remains a valuable and compact guide to the British Army in the middle of the Second World War.

1069   **Weapons and equipment of the Victorian soldier.**
Donald Featherstone.   Poole, England: Blandford, 1978. 130p.
bibliog.

During the Victorian period the British soldier fought at least 400 separate battles in more than sixty campaigns. From the Battle of Waterloo to the Crimean War he was given little new in either weaponry or equipment and, even after the reforms of Sydney Herbert, modernization was painfully slow. This is the story of the weapons employed – muskets and rifles, bayonets, swords, pistols and revolvers, the lance, machine guns, artillery, mountain guns, rockets – and of the equipment with which the infantryman marched, fought and died.

1070   **Modern British armoured fighting vehicles.**
Terry Gander.   Wellingborough, England: Patrick Stephens, 1986. 136p.

All types of armoured vehicles, including tanks and personnel carriers, ambulances, and signals and specialized engineering equipment, are covered in this concise guide. Photographs and constant scale drawings aid identification.

1071   **Regiments and corps of the British Army.**
Ian S. Hallows.   London: Arms & Armour Press, 1991. 320p.
bibliog.

The regimental system, widely recognized as the backbone of the British army, has survived the 1991 defence reorganization although a number of famous regiments seem destined to disappear. This authoritative book takes each regiment and corps in order of precedence and gives a brief outline of its history (formation, motto, regimental headquarters, recruitment area), its emblazoned and accredited battle honours, memorials, dress, marches, mascots, alliances with regiments overseas, journal, association, museum, record office, regimental histories, and its predecessor regiments. Other ancillary information provided includes a chronological chart of the raising of the regiments and corps and the Army's wars and campaigns; lists of the county regiments 1751-1958; regimental amalgamations and anniversaries; royal connections; and regiments and corps abbreviations.

1072   **History of the Great War: based on official documents by direction of the Historical Section of The Committee of Imperial Defence.**
London: HMSO, 1922-87.

This monumental, multi-volumed history, dealing mainly with the Western Front, but also covering military campaigns elsewhere, is uneven in quality and reliability but overall satisfactorily recounts the costly landbattles of the First World War in great detail. Assessments of its use and value, and of some of its faults, may be found in Robin Higham's *Official histories* (Kansas City, Kansas: Kansas University Press, 1970. 644p. bibliog.).

1073   **Head-dress badges of the British Army.**
Arthur L. Kipling, Hugh L. King.   London: Frederick Muller, 1972, 1979.

Over 3,000 badges are illustrated in this exhaustive work which extends from the eighteenth century onwards. The second volume *Head-dress badges of the British*

Army: vol. 2. From the end of the Great War to the present day, includes the Gurkha regiments of the British Army and the special units raised in the Second World War. Incidental to its main purpose, the work also provides a valuable and detailed guide to the successive amalgamations suffered by regular and reserve regiments of infantry, cavalry, and artillery, over the last 150 years.

1074 **The battle honours of the British and Indian armies 1695-1914.**
   N. B. Leslie.   London: Leo Cooper, 1970. 145p.
Battle honours won by British and Indian regiments and corps all over the world are recorded in this invaluable reference work.

1075 **Encyclopaedia of the modern Territorial Army.**
   Bob Peedle.   Wellingborough, England: Patrick Stephens, 1990.
   232p. 10 maps.
A detailed analysis of the TA's functional arms; the yeomanry, artillery, engineers, signal units, infantry, airborne units, and other corps and services, explaining their role, structure, weapons, and deployment, form the bulk of this admirably conceived and executed encyclopaedia. Regimental histories and regular army affiliations are also given in detail.

1076 **The Saturday night soldiers: the stirring story of the Territorial Army.**
   A. V. Sellwood.   London: White Lion, 1974. 214p. bibliog.
When first published in 1966 this history of the TA from its inception in 1908, notably its heroic part in two World Wars, was seen as a commemorative and valedictory volume in view of the ruthless root and branch reorganization it was then facing. Happily the TA soldiered on and this edition incorporates a chapter on the post-1966 structure of Britain's part-time volunteer defence force, which is directly descended from the militia and yeomanry units of the nineteenth century and earlier.

1077 **Kitchener's army: the raising of the New Armies, 1914-16.**
   Peter Simkins.   Manchester, England: Manchester University Press,
   1988. 359p. bibliog. (War, Armed Forces and Society).
Over five million men either volunteered or were conscripted in Britain's New Armies mustered in the Great War. This authoritative study describes how these millions of men were raised, reviews the political, economic and social effects of the sustained recruiting campaign of 1914-15, follows the experiences of officers and men once they joined, how they were fed, housed, equipped, and trained, before leaving for the front in Flanders and elsewhere.

1078 **British small arms of World War 2: the complete reference guide to weapons, makers' codes and 1936-1946 contracts.**
   Ian D. Skennerton.   Margate, Queensland, Australia: Skennerton,
   1988. 110p.
Arranged in numerical and alphabetical sequences this checklist of rifles, shotguns, pistols and revolvers, sub-machine guns and machine guns, anti-tank rifles and projectors, mortars and bomb throwers, etc., used by the armed forces in the Second World War, is an essential guide for the researcher and collector.

1079   **Gentlemen in khaki: the British Army 1890-1990.**
John Strawson.   London: Secker & Warburg, 1989. 292p. 7 maps.
bibliog.
This brief chronological account of the Army's colonial campaigns, its operations in all
theatres of two World Wars, and other conflicts, is placed firmly within the context of
geo-political and military strategy.

1080   **Women in khaki: the story of the British woman soldier.**
Roy Terry.   London: Columbus, 1988. 258p. bibliog.
In the post-war period Womens Royal Army Corps personnel have served in the
Middle East, Saigon, Singapore, Cyprus, Northern Ireland, and the Falklands. This
history, which celebrates the WAAC's golden jubilee, ranges from the earlier years of
this century, when prejudice hindered women from serving in the armed forces, to
present-day controversies such as combat training and career opportunities alongside
the regular Army.

1081   **Stand down: the orders of battle for the units of the Home Guard of the
United Kingdom, November 1944.**
Compiled by L. B. Whittaker.   Newport, Wales: Westlake, 1990.
153p.
The Local Defence Volunteers, soon to be renamed the Home Guard, were formed in
1940 when it seemed possible that the *Wehrmacht* would seek to invade and conquer
the British Isles. By 1944 the Home Guard had been transformed into a respectable
and far from negligible fighting force – as this order of battle demonstrates.

Royal Navy and Royal Marines

1082   **Encyclopaedia of the modern Royal Navy: including the Fleet Air Arm
and Royal Marines.**
Edited by P. Beaver.   Wellingborough, England: Patrick Stephens,
1987. 3rd ed. 329p. maps.
Separate essays in this guide to the modern (i.e. post-1945) Royal Navy concentrate on
its organization, warships, the Fleet Air Arm, Royal Marines, the auxiliary services,
equipment and weapons, and on its uniform and insignia.

1083   **The price of Admiralty: an indictment of the Royal Navy 1805-1966.**
Stanley Bonnett.   London: Robert Hale, 1968. 272p. bibliog.
This social history of lower-deck conditions in the Royal Navy, from the year of
Trafalgar, to the absorption of the Admiralty into the Ministry of Defence, in no way
accords with the views of other naval historians. Its premise is that the British public
were blinded by the Royal Navy's lustrous reputation to the appalling incompetence,
stupidity and sadism which the lower-deck experienced at the hands of the Admiralty.

1084 British vessels lost at sea 1914-18 and 1939-45.
Cambridge, England: Patrick Stephens, 1988. 304p.

This is a reprint of *Navy losses and merchant shipping losses* and *Ships of the Royal Navy: statement of losses during the Second World War and British merchant vessels lost or damaged by enemy action during the Second World War* published by HMSO in 1919 and 1947 respectively. The class, name, tonnage, date of completion and date of loss, how it was lost, and where, is given for each ship sunk.

1085 The future British surface fleet: options for medium-sized navies.
D. K. Brown.   London: Conway Maritime, 1991. 192p.

Outlining the political and historical background and setting the scene for the Royal Navy's likely future fleet requirements, this study by a distinguished naval architect considers the whole concept of warship design. Present circumstances which include the seemingly inexorable decline of the British shipbuilding industry and a noticeable dearth of experienced ship designers, due partly to a less than convincing career structure, lead to a strong advocacy of the setting up of a permanent warship design team.

1086 Badges and battle honours of HM Ships.
K. V. Burns.   Liskeard, England: Maritime Books, 1986. 208p.

Descriptions and colour illustrations of ships' badges, their mottoes and battle honours, with historical notes on previous ships of the same name, of all Royal Navy warships either in commission or being built at the time of writing, are provided in this attractive and scholarly study.

1087 Historic architecture of the Royal Navy: an introduction.
Jonathan Coad.   London: Gollancz, 1983. 160p.

Concentrating on the period 1700-1900, in particular on the era of sail, this survey draws attention to the creation and maintenance of the royal dockyards, victualling and ordnance depots, and the naval hospitals, that sustained the Royal Navy's supremacy at sea. Chatham, Sheerness, Portsmouth, Devonport, and Harwich are all featured.

1088 Ships of the Royal Navy: the complete record of all fighting ships of the Royal Navy from the fifteenth century to the present.
J. J. Colledge, foreword by David Brown.   London: Greenhill Books, 1987. 388p.

More than 14,000 entries provide details of the tonnage, dimensions, main armament, builders, yards, launch date, disposal, and name changes of Royal Navy warships. This is an indispensable reference work for both researchers and warship enthusiasts.

1089 Battleships and battlecruisers of the Royal Navy since 1861.
B. R. Coward.   London: Ian Allan, 1986. 120p. bibliog.

Details of displacement, length, beam, draught, armour, armament, engines, fuel, speed and ship's complement, together with design and historical notes, are given for every Royal Navy battleship and battlecruiser commissioned 1861-1960 in this encyclopedic work.

1090   **The WRNS: a history of the Women's Royal Naval Service.**
M. H. Fletcher. London: Batsford, 1989. 160p.
Presents a factual and illustrated record of the 'Wrens' through two World Wars to the present day.

1091   **The British sailor: a social history of the lower deck.**
Peter Kemp. London: J. M. Dent, 1970. 241p.
The gradual evolution of a social conscience in the Royal Navy through the leadership of enlightened senior officers, troubled by the execrable conditions in which the common sailor lived, worked, and frequently died, and their consequent improvement, is the thesis of this history from the sailing of the Spanish Armada to the outbreak of the First World War.

1092   **The British seaman 1200-1860: a social survey.**
Christopher Lloyd. London: Collins, 1968. 319p.
Mariners and seamen, not senior officers or great naval battles, are the focus of this account of those who sailed the seas from medieval times to the mid-nineteenth century when the establishment of continuous service and of a naval reserve fundamentally changed conditions in both the Royal and Merchant navies. How many seamen were called for, how they were recruited, and how they were fed, housed, and paid, are some of the issues explored.

1093   **British warship names.**
T. D. Manning, C. F. Walker. London: Putnam, 1959. 498p.
The names of the Royal Navy's fighting ships are anchored in its history. This comprehensive dictionary records the name of every warship of importance, explains its derivation, and notes what type of ship, the date of its completion, and of its ultimate fate, i.e. sunk, sold, broken up, or wrecked, and, not least, its battle honours.

1094   **Royal Navy aircraft carriers 1945-1990.**
Leo Marriott. London: Ian Allan, 1985. 144p. bibliog.
The full story of the Royal Navy's post-war carrier fleet including the passing of the big carriers, which transformed the form and purpose of British sea-power, is recorded here in full detail.

1095   **The Navy list 1992.**
London: HMSO, 1992. 361p.
First published in 1814, *The Navy list* includes an alphabetical list of serving officers in the Royal Navy, Royal Marines, Queen Alexandra's Naval Nursing Service, the Womens Royal Naval Service, giving their rank, seniority, and where they were serving. Other lists include a seniority list of officers on the active list; key RN personnel (attachés and advisers); a complete list of ships and units of the fleet and establishment; and a list of reserve and cadet force officers. Of further interest is: *The Navy list of retired officers together with the emergency list 1991* (London: HMSO, 1992. 144p.).

1096 **British battleships 'Warrior' 1860 to 'Vanguard' 1950: a history of design, construction and armament.**
Oscar Parkes. London: Seeley Service, 1966. rev. ed. 701p.

Derived from official returns, Admiralty ships' covers, and progress books, and illustrated with over 400 photographs, many of them never before published, this encyclopaedic work outlines the history of battleships in action, their influence on international affairs in war and in peace, and their structural design. The history of individual ships, their armament and purpose, the personalities of Sea Lords and politicians, critical examinations of ships' behaviour in battle, and in heavy weather, are also examined at length.

1097 **The ships that saved an army: a comprehensive record of the 1300 'little ships' of Dunkirk.**
Russell Plummer. Wellingborough, England: Patrick Stephens, 1990. 240p. bibliog.

A descriptive and illustrated record commemorates all ships known to have been involved in Operation Dynamo, the evacuation of the British Expeditionary Forces, 26 May to 3 June 1940, when more than 330,000 troops were lifted from the Dunkirk beaches.

1098 **History of the Royal Navy in the 20th century.**
Edited by Anthony Preston. Twickenham, England: Hamlyn, 1987. 224p. 10 maps.

The Edwardian Navy, naval uniforms, the Admiralty and the shipyards, warship design, the two World Wars, and the Falklands campaign, all feature in this popular narrative history.

1099 **The war at sea: Royal and Dominion Navy actions in World War 2.**
G. Smith. London: Ian Allan, 1989. 192p. maps. bibliog.

The main aim of this comprehensive work is 'to answer the question of what Royal Navy warships were lost, when, where, and in what circumstances'. The background events and major warship losses are shown month by month in the four main maritime theatres of war: the Atlantic, European waters, the Mediterranean, and the Indian and Pacific Oceans.

1100 **The Royal Marines: a pictorial history 1664-1987.**
Peter C. Smith, Derek Oakley. Tunbridge Wells, England: Spellmount, 1988. 256p. bibliog.

Over 350 early prints and painting, photographs, old recruiting posters, and cartoons illustrate this outline history of the Royal Marines, including the RM Artillery (1804-1923), the RM Light Infantry (1855-1923), and the Royal Navy School of Music (1903-1951). Details of its customs and traditions (Queen's and Regimental Colours, its motto, slow and quick marches, municipal freedoms), memorable dates in its fighting history, and its Victoria Cross awards, are provided in a series of appendices.

1101 **British naval aircraft since 1912.**
Owen Thetford.   London: Putnam Aeronautical, 1991, 6th ed. 512p.
This standard reference history of Royal Navy aviation which was first published in
1958 is a companion volume along identical lines to the author's *Royal Air Force
aircraft since 1918*. Over 100 main aircraft types are arranged alphabetically by aircraft
manufacturing company, and then chronologically by type. The information for each
aircraft encompasses a photograph, its history and service development, and technical
data. An appendix lists 160 other aircraft and airships which saw service with the Royal
Flying Corps (Naval Wing), Royal Naval Air Service, and the Fleet Air Arm. Details
are given of all the aircraft now held in the Fleet Air Arm Museum at Yeovilton.

1102 **A companion to the Royal Navy.**
David A. Thomas.   London: Harrap, 1988. 443p. 15 maps.
This encyclopedic work encompasses all aspects of Royal Navy history since the 1660s:
the office and political control of the Admiralty; ships' names and badges; fleet actions,
battles and campaigns; and battle honours. A twenty-five page chronology provides a
convenient reference point.

1103 **A dictionary of British ships and seamen.**
Grant Uden, Richard Cooper.   Harmondsworth, England: Allen
Lane & Kestrel Books, 1980. 591p. 7 maps.
This companionable guide encompasses individual seamen, ships, battles, trading
enterprises, uniforms, winds and weather, lighthouses, and seas and oceans. Line
drawings, eight coloured plates, contemporary prints, portraits, maps, and paintings,
illustrate the text.

1104 **The decline of British seapower.**
Desmond Wettern.   London: Jane's, 1982. 452p. bibliog.
Contending that economic problems, bureaucratic delays, and successive political
leaders' failure to understand the importance of seapower to the United Kingdom,
have inexorably led to a constant shortage of men, money, and ships. Wettern argues
for a larger and more efficient Navy to play its traditional role as the principal defender
of an island nation depending almost entirely on seaborne trade for its survival. A
forty-page appendix shows the strength of the Fleet 1947-81, a stark reminder of its
decline in numbers and power since the Second World War.

Royal Air Force

1105 **The Air Force list 1992.**
London: HMSO, 1992. 498p. biennial.
Provides details of serving officers who are listed by Command, branch, or
administrative unit, together with the date of posting. Also of interest is *The Royal Air
Force retired list 1992* (London: HMSO, 1992. 387p. biennial) in which officers who
have retired from their permanent commissions are listed in a single alphabetical
sequence.

1106 **History of the RAF.**
Chaz Bowyer. Twickenham, England: Hamlyn, 1985. rev. ed. 224p.
bibliog.
This pictorial history of British military aviation history not only tells of the wars and campaigns in which the Royal Air Force participated but also takes into account the technical qualities of British warplanes.

1107 **The aeroplanes of the Royal Flying Corps military wing.**
J. M. Bruce. London: Putnam, 1992. 642p.
Immediately recognized as the definitive work of its type when first published in 1982, this historical record encompasses every type of aircraft delivered to the RFC from the 1912 military trials to the formation of the Royal Air Force in 1918.

1108 **The Royal Air Force and two World Wars.**
Maurice Dean. London: Cassell, 1979. 10 maps. bibliog.
The formation of the Royal Flying Corps as part of the Army, its trial of strength in the First World War, the RAF's struggle with its rival Services in the post-war years, the rearmament programme in the 1930s, and the campaigns of the Second World War, are all covered in this authoritative history. The author was Private Secretary to the Chief of the Air Staff secretariat. He was Permanent Under Secretary at the Air Ministry 1955-1964.

1109 **Per Ardua Ad Astra: seventy years of the RFC and the RAF.**
Michael Donne, Cynthia Fowler. London: Frederick Muller, 1982.
191p. bibliog.
The Royal Flying Corps was constituted by Royal Warrant, on 13 April 1912, and combined with the Royal Naval Air Service to form the Royal Air Force on 1 April 1918. Material for this anniversary pictorial history was mostly drawn from official archives in the RAF's Historical Branch and at the Royal Aircraft Establishment at Farnborough.

1110 **Women in air force blue: the story of women in the Royal Air Force from 1918 to the present day.**
Beryl E. Escott. Wellingborough, England: Patrick Stephens, 1989.
312p. bibliog.
Based on the author's twenty-five years' service in the Women's Royal Air Force, and drawn from the remiscences of hundreds of former WRAFs, this study comprehensively recounts the history of a branch of the armed forces which played a vital role in the Second World War, not least in the Battle of Britain.

1111 **RAF Fighter Command 1936-1968.**
Norman Franks. Yeovil, England: Patrick Stephens, 1992. 253p.
bibliog.
Tracing the history and technical development of its aircraft, from silver biplanes to the supersonic vertical take off and landing warplanes of the modern era, this illustrated history of Fighter Command runs from its formation just three years before the outbreak of the Second World War to its merging into RAF Strike Command in 1968.

More concerned with conveying an impression of what it was like to be a fighter pilot than with the RAF's bureaucracy and political background, Franks naturally places heavy emphasis on the exploits of outstanding Second World War pilots, and on the prominent personalities of the Battle of Britain.

1112 **Encyclopaedia of the modern Royal Air Force.**
Terry Gander. Wellingborough, England: Patrick Stephens, 1987. 2nd ed. 256p. map.

All aspects of the RAF since 1945 are covered in this pictorial encyclopaedia. The organization and status of Strike Command, Support Command, RAF Germany, Air Cadets, WRAF, Royal Auxiliary Air Force, and the Royal Air Force Regiment are clearly outlined. The RAF's aircrafts and weapons, uniforms and insignia, are also described.

1113 **The modern Royal Air Force: a guide to Britain's air power.**
Terry Gander. Wellingborough, England: Patrick Stephens, 1988. 128p.

In addition to providing concise details of all aircraft in service, this guide also describes the role of RAF Strike Command, Support Command, RAF Germany, and the RAF Regiment. Aircrew training is not overlooked.

1114 **British service helicopters: a pictorial history.**
Richard E. Gardner, Reginald Longstaff. London: Robert Hale, 1985. 227p. bibliog.

A chronicle of helicopter operations, and a comprehensive record of all rotary-winged aircraft in service, from Second World War operations to the Falklands campaign, are the principal contents of this military history.

1115 **The Spitfire log: a 50th anniversary tribute to the world's most famous fighter plane.**
Compiled by Peter Haining. London: Souvenir Press, 1985. 144p.

This tribute by men who flew or admired the Spitfire includes a list of the twenty squadrons which took part in the Battle of Britain in the summer of 1940, an outline chronology of the Battle, and the whereabouts of seventy-two surviving Spitfires that are now on public view.

1116 **The British fighter since 1912: sixty-seven years of design and development.**
Peter Lewis. London: Putnam, 1979. 4th ed. 416p.

This is not an operational history but an authoritative technical account of the development of some 350 diverse types of British fighter aircraft by the designers, constructors, and test pilots concerned. Although 300 photographs and 104 three-view drawings enhance the text, this book is suitable more for the expert than the general reader.

1117 **Bombs gone: the development and use of British air-dropped weapons from 1912 to the present day.**
John A. MacBean, Arthur S. Hogben.   Wellingborough, England: Patrick Stephens, 1990. 320p.

The weapons employed (bombs, mines, and torpedoes), the development and technical capabilities of bomber aircraft, their operational performance, the bomber crews and their commanders, and the progress in target finding and marking techniques, are all recorded in this authoritative and comprehensive study.

1118 **Battle over Britain: a history of the German air assaults on Great Britain 1917-18 and July-December 1940, and of the development of Britain's air defences between the World Wars.**
F. K. Mason.   Bourne End, England: Aston, 1990. 539p. maps. bibliog.

This monumental study is divided into two parts. The first contains an account of the German raids over Britain in the First World War, and of the history of the Royal Air Force and the *Luftwaffe* in the inter-war years, whilst the second provides a detailed narrative of the Battle of Britain with accurate day-by-day tables of RAF and *Luftwaffe* losses. A long list of appendices includes details of the crews, the aircraft engaged, the *Luftwaffe* order of battle, British aircraft production and availability, awards of the Victoria Cross and the George Cross, Royal Navy losses in home waters July-October 1940, the bombing of British towns and cities, ground defences, and Air/Sea rescue services.

1119 **High commanders of the Royal Air Force.**
Henry Probert.   London: HMSO for Ministry of Defence, 1991. 162p.

Biographies of twenty-two senior RAF commanders, including nineteen past Chiefs of the Air Staff, are featured in this authoritative study. Their cumulative careers span the RAF's entire history.

1120 **Above the trenches: a complete record of the fighter aces and units of the British Empire Air Forces 1915-1920.**
C. Shores.   London: Grub Street, 1990. 397p. maps.

Over 800 biographical sketches, giving previous military service, and post-war careers, are contained in this extensively-researched record. A full list of the aircraft they shot down, including the date, time, location, and sources of information, is also indicated.

1121 **Aircraft of the Royal Air Force since 1918.**
Owen Thetford.   London: Putnam, 1988. 8th ed. 685p.

The main sections of this encyclopedic work contain full descriptions, technical specifications, operational histories, photographs and line drawings, of almost 300 types of aircraft designed and constructed for the RAF. Types not described or illustrated in the main text such as training or transport aircraft, and civil aircraft impressed during the Second World War, gliders, missiles, and a list of operational RAF squadrons, their bases and equipment, as at 1 April 1988, are included as appendices. This edition was published to mark the RAF's seventieth anniversary.

1122 **Men of the Battle of Britain: a who was who of the pilots and aircrew . . . who flew with Royal Air Force Fighter Command July 10 to October 31, 1940.**
K. G. Wynn.   Norwich, England: Gliddon, 1989. 470p. bibliog.
Short service biographies of 2,927 pilots and aircrew who were awarded the Battle of Britain clasp to the 1939-1945 Star, having flown at least one authorized operational sortie in the Battle of Britain, are included in this meticulously-researched 'who was who' volume.

Defence

1123 **British Defence Directory.**
London: Brasseys (UK), 1982- . quarterly.
Presents a computerized, regularly updated directory of senior military and civil personnel in the Ministry of Defence, Royal Navy, Army, Royal Air Force, NATO, and in service diplomatic posts. Part one contains an MoD hierarchical chart of designated permanent posts.

1124 **British defence since 1945.**
Michael Dockrill.   Oxford: Blackwell, 1988. 171p. bibliog. (Making Contemporary Britain).
At the end of the Second World War Britain faced enormous economic and financial problems exacerbated by a heavy military presence in Africa, Asia, and the Middle East. This study examines how British defence policy has balanced the need to maintain Britain's status as an independent nuclear power with its diminishing role in world politics, and concentrates on how that policy was applied in the Korean War, the Suez crisis, and the Falklands War.

1125 **A guide to the sources of British military history.**
Edited by Robin Higham.   London: Routledge, 1971. 630p.
Sponsored by the Conference on British Studies, Higham's *Guide* consists of twenty-five sub-divided bibliographical essays, and reviews of original source material in libraries and archives, on all aspects of British military history. *British military history: a supplement to Robin Higham's guide* (Edited by Gerald Jordan. New York: Garland, 1988. 586p.) picks up where the *Guide* left off and continues in the same pattern.

1126 **The Chiefs: the story of the United Kingdom Chiefs of Staff.**
General Sir William Jackson, Field Marshall the Lord Bramall.
London: Brasseys, 1992. 730p.
The integration of the Armed Forces into a civilian government administration has caused significant problems in many advanced democracies. Since 1906, when the Committee of Imperial Defence was founded, the UK government has been able to take expert advice on military matters from a properly constituted central organization. This work by two distinguished soldiers outlines the traditional responsibilities of the

Chiefs of Staff, and the effectiveness of the system, in the context of the personalities and issues involved.

1127 **Strongholds of the realm: defences in Britain from prehistory to the twentieth century.**
Charles Kightly, photographs by Peter Chèze-Brown. London: Thames & Hudson, 1979. 208p. bibliog.

The British Isles are geographically vulnerable to foreign invasion. This generously-illustrated work traces how successive generations and peoples attempted to defend their island home, and explains why fortifications were constructed where they were. Prehistoric hill-forts, Hadrian's Wall, the Saxon shore, Norman castles, coastal forts, and the Fylingdales early warning station, all take their place.

1128 **British nuclear weapons: for and against.**
Jeff McMahan. London: Junction Books, 1981. 165p.

In terms readily intelligible to the general reader, this assessment by an academic philosopher of the case on each side of the controversy about British nuclear disarmament examines the policy alternatives and discusses whether it was to Britain's advantage to retain its nuclear weapons. Published at a time when the danger of a third World War had by no means vanished, the conclusion was that Britain should unilaterally abandon these weapons.

1129 **Ministry of Defence; Navy Department, Army Department, Air Force Department.**
London: HMSO, 1986. rev. ed. 12p. (Sectional List, no. 67).

This catalogue of in-print publications includes Command Papers on British armed forces overseas, military histories, accounts of travel and discovery expeditions mounted by the services, manuals, and Queen's Regulations, etc.

1130 **The Nassau connection: the organisation and management of the British POLARIS project.**
Peter Nailor. London: HMSO, 1988. 133p. bibliog.

The Nassau Agreement 1962 between President John F. Kennedy and Harold Macmillan provided for the purchase of a submarine-launched ballistic missile system to replace the ageing V bombers as the sharp edge of Britain's nuclear deterrent. This is a study of how the Royal Navy organized the construction and deployment of its POLARIS submarines.

1131 **The best years of their lives: the National Service experience 1945-63.**
Trevor Royle. London: Michael Joseph, 1986. 288p. bibliog.

Three times this century, in 1916, 1939 and 1947, Parliament has agreed to compulsory military service. Based on the memories of those 'called-up', this is the story of over two million conscripts who served in the Armed Forces at a time when the Cold War was it its coldest, and when a general retreat from empire needed to be supervised with dignity and accord.

1132   **Britain's special forces.**
William Seymour, foreword by David Stirling.   London: Sidgwick &
Jackson, 1985. 334p. 14 maps. bibliog.

Perhaps because of its diminished resources Britain has in recent years made more use
of small *élite* forces, trained and equipped for special operations, than any other major
military power. The secrecy that continues to surround such operations had made an
authoritative history no easy task but, drawing upon a wide variety of documentary
sources and eye-witness accounts, this comprehensive study examines all Commando,
SAS, and Special Boat Squadron missions since the Lofoten Islands raid in 1942.

1133   **The Ordnance Survey complete guide to the battlefields of Britain.**
David Smurthwaite.   Exeter, England: Webb & Bower, 1984. 224p.
bibliog.

Over 100 major battles and engagements fought on British soil, starting with the
Roman invasion of 55 BC, and ending with the Battle of Britain, are explained in their
historical context. Detailed plans of the battles, based on modern archaeological and
documentary research, are superimposed on extracts from Ordnance Survey map
sheets.

1134   **A guide to military museums.**
T. Wise.   Doncaster, England: Athena, 1988. 6th ed. 80p.

Over 200 museums are listed in this guide which gives general descriptive information
and details of admission, etc. An index of regiments and their museums is also
included.

For gallantry

1135   **British gallantry awards: the standard reference work on awards for
gallantry or distinguished service 1855-1979.**
P. E. Abbot, J. M. A. Tamplin, edited by J. B. Hayward.   London:
Nimrod Dix, 1981. 316p. bibliog.

Forty-four gallantry awards and decorations are described in this work which was first
published by Guinness Superlatives in 1971. Their origins, citations, and numbers
awarded, are all noted.

1136   **The Victoria Cross roll of honour.**
James W. Bancroft.   Manchester, England: Aim High, 1989. 123p.
bibliog.

The Victoria Cross is the highest award for bravery available to members of the armed
forces of the Crown. Here its recipients are listed by their service, regiment, or corps,
in order of its seniority.

1137 **British battles and medals: a description of every campaign medal and bar awarded since the Armada, with the historical reasons for their awards, and the names of all the ships, regiments and squadrons of the Royal Air Force whose personnel are entitled to them.**
L. L. Gordon, edited by E. C. Joslin. London: Spink, 1988. 6th ed. 299p. bibliog.

First published in 1947 this standard work comprises sections on campaign medals from 1588 to 1982 in chronological order; Polar medals; United Nations medals; Army regiments of the line and corps as they stood in 1987 (now sadly further diminished); the precedence of corps and infantry regiments; and cavalry and infantry regiments, with useful indexes on medals and bars.

Guide to the castles of England and Wales.
See item no. 1848.

English castles.
See item no. 1857.

National Trust Book of British castles.
See item no. 1861.

Castles of England.
See item no. 1864.

Economy

1138 **Economic planning 1945-51: a guide to documents in the Public Record Office.**
B. W. E. Alford, Rodney Lowe, Neil Rollings.   London: HMSO for Public Record Office, 1992. 1,184p.

Arranged so that users can follow a particular planning decision, or locate related material among the vast range of government records housed in the PRO, this handbook gives a broad overview of the political and administrative context to economic planning by the post-war Labour Government.

1139 **Bank of England.**
London: Bank of England Economics Department, 1960- . quarterly.

An invaluable guide to the current state of the British economy, this quarterly publication includes articles, financial reviews and assessments, and extensive statistical analyses. Some of the material published here is not available elsewhere.

1140 **The medieval English economy 1150-1500.**
J. L. Bolton.   London: Dent, 1980. 400p. bibliog.

Topics treated in this review of medieval English economic history include the different patterns of settlement and society after the Norman Conquest; farming in the twelfth century; population contraction and expansion in economic change; the changes in an agrarian society; the growth of the towns; and the struggle of English and foreign interests to control overseas trade. No startling conclusions emerge, simply that the English economy in the Middle Ages remained primarily agricultural and under-developed, both in modern terms and in comparison with contemporary continental Europe.

Economy

1141 British historical statistics.
B. R. Mitchell.   Cambridge, England: Cambridge University Press, 1988. 886p.

The successor to *Abstract of British historical statistics* (1962), and its supplementary volume *Second abstract of British historical statistics* (1971), this work is mainly devoted to economic history although a wide selection of social statistics is also included. Topics covered at chapter length comprehend population and vital statistics, the labour force, agriculture, fuel and energy, metals, textiles, building, external trade, transport and communications, public finance, consumption, prices, and various miscellaneous statistics. Each chapter begins with an introduction for the non-specialist on the source, coverage, and major problems of the particular series of statistics involved.

1142 Years of recovery: British economic policy 1945-51.
Alex Cairncross.   London: Methuen, 1985. 527p. bibliog.

Concerned more with economic management and policy than economic theory, this study of the transition from a war to peace-time economy under the Labour governments 1945-51 gives a full account of the successive crises which confronted it, the coal and dollar crises of 1947, the 1949 devaluation, and rearmament in 1951. The underlying economic trends of a country uneasily poised between disaster and recovery are also examined.

1143 The inter-war British economy: a statistical abstract.
F. Capie. M. Collins.   Manchester, England: Manchester University Press, 1983. 118p.

British production, prices and retail sales, level of business activity, labour, overseas trade and shipping, money and banking, interest rates, and capital, are recorded statistically in this abstract.

1144 Bibliography of British economic and social history.
Compiled by W. H. Chaloner, R. C. Richardson.   Manchester, England: Manchester University Press, 1984. 208p.

First published in 1976 as *British economic and social history: a bibliography*, this revised version contains nearly 5,800 entries for books and periodical articles (as opposed to 4,200) divided into three chronological periods: 1066-1300; 1300-1500; and 1500-1700. Within each period these are arranged under numerous subject headings e.g. population; agriculture and rural society; prices, public finance, banking and financial dealings; classes and social groups; poor relief; charity and poor law.

1145 The pre-industrial economy in England 1500-1750.
L. A. Clarkson.   London: Batsford, 1971. 268p. bibliog.

Organized around a few basic economic concepts, notably that the pre-industrial period is best understood as a market economy hampered by low productivity and poorly-developed economic institutions and transport facilities, this compact study examines the structure of the English economy, agriculture and industry, commerce and communications, government policy, and wealth and poverty.

Economy

1146 The British economy since 1945.
Edited by W. F. R. Crafts, N. W. C. Woodward. Oxford: Oxford
University Press, 1992. 512p.

This undergraduate textbook includes chapters on the budget and fiscal policy, monetary policy, trade and the balance of payments, inflation, unemployment, economic growth, regional problems and policies, industrial organization and competition policy, nationalized industries, trade unions and industrial relations, and social welfare.

1147 The counties and regions of the UK: economic, industrial and social trends in local authority areas.
University of Warwick Business Information Service. Aldershot,
England: Gower, 1988. 201p. bibliog.

The UK as a whole has experienced the effects of both recession and economic boom in recent years. By presenting the key statistics in a county-by-county format on population trends, unemployment, earnings, housing completion, industrial floorspace, rateable value and local authority expenditure, the results of this economic instability can be measured in all UK regions. Commentaries on the statistics provide information on local authority initiatives to support the local economy, and on special developments in the new towns, enterprise zones, freeports, and science parks. Based on information from central government statistics, local authorities, development agencies, professional bodies, and private research organizations, this outline was first published in 1983.

1148 Understanding the UK economy.
Edited by Peter Curwen. London: Macmillan, 1992. 2nd ed. 489p.

Surveying the whole gamut of the British economy, maintaining a balance between analysis and description, and noting the growing importance of European integration, this textbook is particularly concerned to investigate how the UK functions – its history and politics, its macro-economy, financial system, its national spending, taxing, and borrowing, its employment and unemployment figures, and its social and economic inequality.

1149 British economic growth 1688-1959: trends and structure.
Phyllis Deane, W. A. Cole. Cambridge, England: Cambridge
University Press, 1967. 2nd ed. 350p. bibliog.

First published in 1962, this statistical and narrative study sets out the main long-term quantitative features of Britain's economy over 300 years, including the eighteenth-century origins of economic growth, industrialization and population change in the early 1800s, the changing structure of national product, and the trends in capital formation.

1150 Economic Trends.
London: HMSO for Central Statistical Office, 1953- . monthly.

Published monthly, this compilation brings together all the main economic indicators liberally sprinkled with charts and diagrams. It contains three regular sections. The first presents the most up-to-date statistical information available during the month; another shows movements of the key economic indicators over the previous five years;

whilst the third charts the movements of composite indexes over twenty years against a reference chronology of business cycles. Quarterly articles on the national accounts appear in January, April, July and October and on the balance of payments in March, June, September and December. *Economic trends annual supplement* gives long runs, up to forty years in some instances, of the key economic indicators, providing invaluable source material for economic historians.

1151   **Britain in decline.**

Andrew Gamble.   London: Macmillan, 1990. 3rd ed. 288p.

Britain's long decline as a great power, no longer obscured by military victories in two twentieth-century World Wars, has been accompanied by a severe decline in its economic fortunes. Gamble's widely acclaimed study of Britain's rise and fall discusses the main reasons which have been advanced to account for the decline and, in this third edition, assesses the claim of the Thatcher government to have reversed it.

1152   **Decade of discontent: the changing British economy since 1973.**

Nick Gardner.   Oxford: Blackwell, 1987. 236p.

The ten years following 1973 witnessed the fall of both a Labour and Conservative government through industrial action, the highest rate of inflation ever experienced in Britain, rising unemployment on a scale reminiscent of the 1930s, and the overthrow of previously unchallenged economic wisdom. This study examines the prevalent economic theories, policies, and events of the period extending from the first oil crisis to the end of the first Thatcher administration.

1153   **The economic history of England.**

E. Lipson.   London: A. & C. Black, 1956. 1959. 2 vols.

First published in 1915 and 1931 respectively, these two volumes (*The Middle Ages* [696p.] and *The Age of Mercantilism* [503p.]) were for many years acknowledged as the pioneering standard economic history of England from the medieval period to the eve of the Industrial Revolution. The first volume examines the manorial system, the open field agricultural system, the agrarian revolution, the growth of towns, fairs and markets, the guilds, the woollen industry, foreign trade, and public finance, whilst the second looks at trade, the Mercantile system, the control of industry, and relief of the poor. In general, Lipson concluded, the Industrial Revolution constituted no sudden break with the past; Mercantilist England evolved many capitalist features associated with modern England; and that the relaxation of the traditional restraints on free enterprise was due more to the growing influence exerted by the capitalist classes than to the theoretical considerations of Adam Smith.

1154   **The economic system in the UK.**

Edited by Derek Morris.   Oxford: Oxford University Press, 1985. 3rd ed. 940p.

Undoubtedly the most complete and comprehensive outline of the UK economy available to the general reader, this collection of twenty essays on the constraints within which the economy operates, and the policy and performance issues most important to its future, is arranged in seven sections: an introduction to the historical background; economic behaviour; macro-economic policy; the international context; the UK's long-term economic growth; industrial policy issues; and some conclusions on the topics considered.

1155   **OECD economic surveys: United Kingdom.**

Paris: Organisation for Economic Co-operation and Development, 1991. 131p.

Based on the Secretariat's study prepared for the annual review of the United Kingdom conducted by the Economic Development Review Committee, 24 June 1991, this survey observes that the UK economy entered a sharp recession in the summer of 1990 as consumers and businesses reacted to the Government's earlier tightening of monetary policy to check excess demands. The study reflects that the UK has proved inflation prone since the late 1960s and that a markedly better output and employment outlook would require a prompt and fundamental change in wage and price behaviour, compatible with the discipline imposed by the need to maintain sterling's competitive position in the ERM.

1156   **The development of the British economy 1914-1980.**

Sidney Pollard.   London: Arnold, 1983. 3rd ed. 440p. bibliog.

This standard economic history of Britain in the twentieth century incorporates three major changes in this edition: the earlier chapters are shortened and largely rewritten; the chapters dealing with the period 1914-1950 are revised in the light of recent research; and the post-Second World War period is split into separate thematic chapters on production and income, trade and finance, and government economic policy.

1157   **Who's who in British economics: a directory of economists in higher education, business and government.**

Edited by Paul Sturgess, Clair Sturgess.   Aldershot, England: Edward Elgar, 1990. 627p.

Based on questionnaires, this directory gives basic information only on British economists: their positions, qualifications, previous posts, offices held, area of expertise, and publications. It encompasses all practitioners whatever their employment might be.

Business (Commerce, Finance, Banking)

1158   **Longman dictionary of business English.**
       J. H. Adam.   Harlow: Longman, 1989. 2nd ed. 564p.

This defines words and phrases frequently used in modern business, commerce, and industry.

1159   **Advertisers annual 1993.**
       East Grinstead, England: Reed Information Services, 1992. 3 vols.
       67th ed.

If public relations and advertising oil the wheels of British business, industry, and commerce, this directory pumps the oil. Nearly 3,500 advertisers are now listed in these two volumes, *Agencies and advertisers: a complete guide to advertising agencies, PR, consultants and sales promotion throughout the UK, with coverage of national advertisers and their brand names*; and *UK media: a comprehensive guide to national and regional newspapers, consumer and business periodicals plus TV, radio and other media*.

1160   **The markets and fairs of England and Wales: a buyer's and browser's guide.**
       Roy Anderson.   London: Bell & Hyman, 1985. 175p. map. bibliog.

Based on information supplied by local authorities, the National Market Traders Association, the Showmens Guild, the Women's Institute, and the Department of the Environment, this gazetteer of some 150 markets and fairs provides information on their venues, the day(s) in the week when they are open, and their general nature.

1161 **Awards for business excellence.**
Compiled by The London Business School Information Service.
London: Lincoln Hannah MediaScan, 1990. 45p.

This register brings together the major UK awards for individual and company excellence in business in the areas of exports, the environment, design, management, the arts, and journalism. Information provided includes the name of the awarding body, the nature of the award, its value if there is a monetary prize, eligibility for the award, previous winners, and entry procedures.

1162 **Inside the Treasury.**
Joel Barnett. London: Deutsch, 1982. 200p.

Although a personal narrative, this account of Joel Barnett's appointment as Chief Secretary to the Treasury in the 1974-79 Labour government provides an authoritative summary of how the modern Treasury works. Among the events recorded are the continuous pressure on the pound sterling in 1976 and the consequent International Monetary Fund crisis faced by the Chancellor of the Exchequer.

1163 **Government funding for United Kingdom business: a complete guide to sources, grants and application procedures.**
Mishka Bienkowski, Rhona Walker, Kevin Allen, Lorraine Macdonald. London: Kogan Page, 1991. 7th ed. 685p.

Based on information from the on-line AIMS database, a continually updated information service on financial assistance schemes, this guide provides information on grants from government and other public sector sources for business investment and development, employment and training, and research and innovation.

1164 **BRAD advertiser and agency list 1992.**
Barnet, England: British Rate & Data, 1992. 700p.

There are nearly 2,100 entries in this directory of advertising agencies, creative and design consultants, direct marketing companies, outdoor and poster agencies, public relations companies, and sales promotion firms. Information includes when each company was established, the number of employees, annual billing totals, special services, and notable clients.

1165 **Britain's most successful companies.**
Bristol, England: Jordan, 1990. variously paginated.

Identifying the top performers by following their financial track record, this directory is arranged in three main sections. In the first 520 companies are listed in ranking order; the second is an alphabetical list of companies; whilst the third consists of summary tables of the companies' sales growth, profit growth, growth in profit per employee, the average return on net tangible assets, and the latest registered turnover. To qualify for inclusion companies must be publicly quoted, listed on the USM, or be privately owned.

Business (Commerce, Finance, Banking)

1166 **Britain's top foreign-owned companies.**
Bristol, England: Jordans, 1990. 7th ed. 397p.
Information on 2,500 companies selected from the publisher's database is available in this directory. A financial overview of each company is followed by comparative tables ranking the top companies by key performance measures, and financial profiles ranking companies in order of sales turnovers.

1167 **Britain's top privately-owned companies 1991.**
Bristol, England: Jordans, 1991. 5 vols. 10th ed.
A privately-owned company is defined here as a company controlled by individuals whose equity and capital are not listed on the Stock Exchange. These five volumes are incontestably the most up-to-date source of financial information on the leading privately-owned businesses in the United Kingdom, listing 10,000 companies in order of sales turnover, and ranking the top 2,000 companies in the order of their net tangible assets. Details include company name and address, the nature of its business, and the names of the chief executives.

1168 **Business information: a brief guide to the reference resources of the British Library.**
London: British Library Science Reference and Information Service, 1987. 32p.
This booklet is intended to help enquirers use the business stock of the Library and to call their attention to the Library's services. It is invaluable for indicating what type of material exists and the range available. Trade directories, market research reports, and business and trade journals, are all included.

1169 **The Observer how the new Stock Exchange works.**
Colin Chapman. London: Hutchinson, 1986. 182p.
The 'Big Bang' of 1985 was ostensibly no more than the abolition of a fixed commission on the buying and selling of shares on the London Stockmarket, and the removal of a number of traditional barriers between the principal operators, banks and merchant banks, brokers and jobbers, discount houses, and other financial institutions. Written in its immediate aftermath, this work provides a straightforward account of the Stock Exchange's transactions, examining the way stocks and shares are bought and sold and the power of the large institutions. It also cautiously assesses how average investors are likely to fare under the new system.

1170 **The City directory 1990: a guide to financial and professional services allied to the City of London.**
London: Director, 1990. 9th ed. 287p.
Published in association with the Institute of Directors this comprehensive guide is a structured and fully indexed list of companies and other institutions which comprise the City of London. The full range includes banks, money markets, the stock market, funds (i.e. investment and unit trust companies), insurance companies, building societies, financial services, commodity and bullion markets, shipbrokers and airbrokers, property, advertising and public relations, and the financial press.

1171 **The Bank of England: a history.**

Sir John Clapham. Cambridge, England: Cambridge University Press, 1970. 2 vols.

In tracing the growth of familiar bank practices like the use of bills, discounts, and cheques, and the progress of the Bank in relation to contemporary political and economic events, this authoritative history (*vol. 1. 1694-1797*. 305p.; *vol. 2. 1797-1914 with an epilogue: the Bank as it is.* 460p.) extends up to the Second World War. R. S. Sayer's *The Bank of England 1891-1944* (Cambridge, England: Cambridge University Press, 1976. 3 vols.) is also a valuable study of the Bank's role in monetary and economic history. John Giuseppi's *The Bank of England: a history from its foundation in 1694* (London: Evans, 1966. 224p. bibliog.) is intended more for the general reader.

1172 **The Daily Telegraph law for the small business.**

Patricia Clayton. London: Kogan Page, 1991. 7th ed. 347p. bibliog.

Separate chapters on establishing a business, capital and profits, premises, taxation and insurance, employment law, cash and credit, intellectual property (i.e. patents, copyright and trademarks), collecting debts, litigation, bankruptcy and liquidation, and takeovers and mergers, are printed in this reference guide. Recent changes in the law, including the 1989 Companies Act, and European Community directives, are incorporated in this edition.

1173 **Compendium of marketing information sources.**

London: Euromonitor, 1989. 258p.

Updating and expanding the *A-Z of United Kingdom marketing information sources*, published in 1984, this compendium serves as a one-stop guide to library services, abstracts and indexes, online databases and databanks, official and non-official sources of information, and market research agencies. Each section is preceded by an overview appraisal of the type of information covered, providing a useful *précis* of the advantages of that particular type of source.

1174 **The conference blue book: the technical guide to conference venues.**

Tonbridge, England: Benn, 1992. 608p. 5 maps.

Descriptive notes on the location and environs of conference venues, on their accommodation and special features, are followed in this directory and its companion volume, *The conference green book: the specialist guide to conference venues* (Tonbridge, England: Benn, 1992. 217p. 5 maps) by detailed information on their designated reading rooms, including the technical facilities and equipment available.

1175 **The marketing handbook 92/93.**

Edited by Claire Crossfield. East Grinstead, England, 1992. 3rd ed. 426p.

Provides directory information on market and market research consultants, graphic design companies, direct marketing agencies, sales promotion companies, and various marketing services.

Business (Commerce, Finance, Banking)

1176 **Directory of directors 1992: vol. 1 Key data on the 58,000 directors who control Britain's major companies: vol. 2 Financial data and information on 16,000 major British companies.**

East Grinstead, England: Reed Information Services, 1992. 2 vols.

Volume one of this long-established directory which was first published in 1880 is an alphabetical listing of company directors and the companies with which they are associated. Compiled from data supplied by company secretaries, volume two provides company information including a brief business description, whether it is a parent, subsidiary, or holding company, and information on the company's accounts, profit, turnover, assets and liabilities, and shareholders' funds.

1177 **Financial Statistics.**

London: HMSO for Central Statistical Office, 1962- . monthly.

Prepared in collaboration with the statistics divisions of government departments, and with the Bank of England, this monthly publication brings together key UK financial and monetary statistics. These include financial accounts and balance sheets of central government income and expenditure, as well as that of banks and building societies; money supply; institutional investment; company finance and liquidity; security prices; and exchange and interest rates. *Financial Statistics Explanatory Handbook*, published bi-annually, is a companion volume containing notes and definitions which are considered essential for a full understanding of the tables to be found in *Financial Statistics* and the relationships between them.

1178 **Stock Exchange official yearbook 1991-1992.**

Edited by Gavin Harrap Fryer. London: Macmillan, 1992. 117th ed. 1,134p.

Undoubtedly the most authoritative and comprehensive reference source for information about companies and their securities traded on London's markets, this edition incorporates the regulatory framework and revised features of the major trading and settlement systems. Divided into eight sections – the London Stock Exchange; the UK securities market; trading, settlement and transfer; taxation; trustees; Commonwealth, provincial and foreign government securities; an alphabetical list of companies and public corporations; and a register of defunct companies – the essential information provided includes the name of the company, its status, head office, registered number, capital, accounts and dividends, and other financial data.

1179 **UK small business statistics and international comparisons.**

Pom Ganguly. London: Harper & Row, 1985. 174p. bibliog.

A rational view on how small small firms are, statistics culled from VAT registrations, a detailed account of the work of the Department of Trade and Industry, the role of small firms in creating jobs, and the life cycles of UK small firms, are the principal subjects under discussion in this survey. Most of the material was first printed in the now defunct DTI weekly magazine *British Business*.

1180   **A bibliography of British business histories.**
Francis Goodall.   Aldershot, England: Gower, 1987. 638p. bibliog.
The items recorded in this bibliography mainly relate to UK companies in the
nineteenth and twentieth centuries although large overseas firms also find a place if
they had a direct interest in the UK economy.

1181   **British banking 1960-85.**
John Grady, Martin Weale.   London: Macmillan, 1986. 232p.
bibliog.
Bridging the gap between abstract monetary theory and institutional reality, Grady and
Weale show how Britain's banking system came near to collapse as parallel markets
developed outside the accustomed framework, and how the Bank of England's efforts
to revive the traditional system contributed to a banking crisis.

1182   **Town and country auctions in Britain: the bargain hunter's handbook.**
Eric Green.   Basingstoke, England: Automobile Association, 1992.
2nd ed. 233p.
First published in 1991 this handbook lists more than 400 salerooms holding regular
auctions of interest to casual browsers, interested amateurs, and professional dealers.
Arranged alphabetically first by county, then by town or city, it describes the nature of
archetypal sales, and gives information on buyer's premium, the dates and times of
sales and viewings, refreshments, parking, and practical details of storage, transport
and shipping.

1183   **The Hambro Company Guide.**
London: Hemmington Scott. 1985- . quarterly.
Company profiles giving details of each company's activities, directors, ordinary
capital, banks, gearing, assets, turnover, profits, share earnings and dividend, debts,
cash accounts, and five-year performance graphs, are all to be found in this
authoritative guide.

1184   **The business information maze: an essential guide.**
Edited by Jo Haythornthwaite.   London: Aslib, 1990. 243p.
Based on a series of lectures in the Department of Library and Information Studies,
Loughborough University, this guide reviews the business information potential of
online records; newspapers; official publications; management, company, marketing
and banking information sources; and patents and standards. Fee paying resources,
either from existing library services, or from information brokers, are also investigated.

1185   **Financial institutions' directory.**
Edited by John Hemming-Clark.   Chislehurst, England: Searchline,
1992. 2nd ed. 85p.
Banks, building societies, investment consultants and financial advisers, accountants,
solicitors, employment agencies, personnel consultants, computer system suppliers,
etc., all feature in this one-stop directory.

Business (Commerce, Finance, Banking)

1186   **City within a state: a portrait of Britain's financial world.**

Anthony Hilton.   London: Tauris, 1987. 199p. bibliog.

Crucial questions surrounding recent developments in the centre of Britain's financial world are examined in this important study. Was the City's trumpeted integrity no more than honour among thieves? To what extent is the City an exclusive club? How far does the City influence the government's economic policy? What is its role in financing, or failing to finance, British industry? To what extent has government policy favoured the City at the expense of the wider British economy? And, how important really are the City's invisible earnings to the economy?

1187   **Hollis press and public relations annual 1992-92.**

Edited by Nesta Hollis.   London: Hollis, 1991. 23rd ed. 1,011p.

This directory provides a classified guide to commercial, industrial, consumer, professional, and corporate news contacts; official and public information services; public relations consultancies; reference and research addresses; and to other services for the communications industry and the media.

1188   **The Institute of Chartered Accountants in England and Wales directory of firms 1992.**

London: Macmillan, 1992. 713p.

Incorporated by royal charter in 1880 the ICA now has 95,000 members and is one of the most respected professional associations in the world. Arranged alphabetically by town or city, this directory gives detailed information on all firms of accountants in which at least one ICA member is currently practising.

1189   **Insurance directory and yearbook 1992: Post Magazine Green Book.**

London: Buckley, 1992. 4 vols. (vol. 1. *Insurance companies. Lloyd's syndicates. Unit Trusts.* 605p.; vol. 2. *Brokers and intermediaries.* 690p.; vol. 3. *Statistics.* 596p.; vol. 4. *London market.*).

Plain, unannotated, factual information, and statistical data on the various components of the insurance business is to be found in this long-established directory which is now in its 150th year of publication. The first volume includes insurance companies; allied, amalgamated and wound-up companies; recruitment consultancies; and career information. The tables in volume three are based on returns to the Department of Trade and cover the period 1986/90.

1190   **UK business finance directory 1990/91: the guide to sources of corporate finance in Britain.**

Edited by Pauline Isbell.   London: Graham & Trotman, 1990. 270p.

Formerly known as *Sunday Telegraph business finance directory*, this publication contains separate sections for accountants, banks and securities houses, business expansion funds, factory companies, finance houses, insurance companies, investment trusts, public sector institutions, stockbrokers, and venture and development capital companies.

1191   **Dictionary of business biography: a biographical dictionary of business leaders active in Britain in the period 1860-1980.**
Edited by David J. Jeremy.   London: Butterworths, 1984-86. 5 vols.

Compiled by the Business History Unit at the London School of Economics, and Imperial College, this dictionary contains almost 1,200 individual biographies extending over the whole spectrum of business from mining and manufacturing, through the public utilities, construction, and servicing industries, to the distribution trades. It excludes academics, civil servants, trade unionists, and all those still active in business, and concentrates on those who have made a real impact regardless of their actual position or title of appointment. The information provided on each entrant includes a complete career profile: notable successes and failures, major innovations, industrial management style and policies, and outside business or political interests. An index volume is planned.

1192   **Directory of exhibition spaces.**
Edited by Susan Jones.   Sunderland, England: Artic Producers, 1989. 2nd ed. 495p.

Arranged alphabetically by town this directory includes museums, libraries, and galleries in educational institutions, in artists' studios or homes, community galleries, private galleries, publicly-funded galleries, galleries in heritage and leisure centres, and specialist darkrooms. Each entry provides a thumbnail sketch description of its activities and policies, its space, the procedures for exhibiting, and access details.

1193   **Information and business: an introduction.**
David Kaye.   London: Library Association Publishing, 1991. 219p.

Concerned primarily with the United Kingdom, and firmly based on the belief that it is essential to understand business processes in order to deliver an effective business information service, this expert study investigates information needs and sources entirely within the context of the business world. The structure and growth of business; its legal status; company finance; company information; patents; standards and regulations; brands, trade marks, prices and trade literature; markets and marketing; and online business information, are some of the topics explored.

1194   **Kelly's business directory 1992.**
East Grinstead, England: Reed Information Service, 1991. 105th ed. 2,251p.

Information on more than 84,000 industrial, commercial, and professional organizations is incorporated in this long-established reference work. A classified section contains details of manufacturers, merchants, wholesalers and firms offering an industrial service under some 15,000 trade and professional headings. This is complemented by an alphabetical listing of companies stating the trade engaged in, their address, and telecommunication details.

Business (Commerce, Finance, Banking)

1195 **Kelly's business link 1992.**
East Grinstead, England: Reed Information Services, 1991. 6th ed. 961p.

Described as an essential one-step purchasing guide to 12,000 leading suppliers, this directory consists primarily of a classified list of manufacturers, merchants, wholesalers, and firms offering industrial services. A second sequence lists those organizations who manufacture or supply products and services to the oil and gas industry.

1196 **Key British enterprises 1992: Britain's top 50,000 companies.**
High Wycombe, England: Dun & Bradstreet, 1992. 6 vols. annual.

Covering the agricultural, mining, construction, transport and communications, financial and insurance, wholesale and retail, manufacturing, and business services industries, the first four volumes of this mammoth venture consist of an alphabetical sequence of the 50,000 largest actively trading companies in Britain. Selected from the publisher's database of 1,400,000 companies, the information provided for each company includes its headquarters address, local branches, UK and US Standard Industrial Classification codes, trade names, royal warrants, parent company, bankers, trade abroad, export indicator, market served, the company registration number, its authorized and issued capital, names of its directors, and the number of its employees. Volumes five and six are index volumes.

1197 **Key business ratios 1992: the guide to British business performance.**
High Wycombe, England: Dun & Bradstreet, 1992. 6th ed. 764p.

This guide provides an analysis of percentages and ratios calculated from the audited accounts of over 200,000 registered UK companies. Two key sets of information are adduced: business ratios and balance sheet profit and loss accounts.

1198 **Key data: UK social and business statistics 1992/93.**
London: HMSO for Central Statistical Office, 1992. maps.

Compact and inexpensive this annually-published selection of official UK statistics extracted from other CSO publications is illustrated with tables, maps and charts. It includes a condensed guide to government statistical sources.

1199 **The 1992 insurance buyer's guide to schemes, packages and unusual risks.**
Edited by Norman Lawrence.   Kingston-upon-Thames, England: Kluwer, 1992. 10th ed. 394p.

Based on information provided by insurers and intermediaries, this specialist guide to services is arranged alphabetically under the type of service offered. Ancilliary information includes details of company name changes, mergers, and takeovers.

1200 **Market research: a guide to British Library holdings.**
Compiled by Michael Lydon.   London: British Library Science Reference & Information Service, 1991. 7th ed. 194p.

Market research reports dealing with the UK market, industrial surveys, and country profiles all published since 1986, are included in this catalogue of British Library's collection of publicly-available reports. Arranged alphabetically under subject headings, it gives details of publisher, title, year of publication, British Library shelf location, a geographic indicator, and whether a loan copy if available from the British Library's Document Supply Centre. A twenty-five page directory of publishers is also included.

1201 **The Economist pocket guide to the new City.**
Vince McCullough.   Oxford: Blackwell and Economist, 1988. 121p.
This is an A to Z guide to the people, institutions, and structures of the City of London's commercial and financial activities published in the wake of the 1985 'Big Bang' which so radically transformed the City's customs and practices.

1202 **Macmillan's unquoted companies 1991: financial profiles of Britain's top 20,000 unquoted companies.**
London: Macmillan, 1991. 2 vols. 6th ed.
Researched by ICC Business Publications this annual directory, first published in 1985, provides financial and market profiles of Britain's top unquoted companies whose turnovers exceed £3 million *per annum*. Each entry includes financial data over a three year period with key information on the company's location, details of its trade, and of its parent company. League tables record average returns on capital invested and average profit margins.

1203 **Markets year book 1992.**
Oldham, England: World's Fair, 1992. 32nd ed. 240p.
A directory of markets arranged alphabetically by town, stating their nature, operators, number of units, days and times; separate sequences for wholesalers and market operators; and a day-by-day market index, are the main features of this yearbook.

1204 **1992 guide to grants for business.**
Compiled by Michael Martin.   Swindon, England: Associated Management Services, 1991. 119p. map.
The objectives, benefits, eligibility, funds available, costs, and contact names for all UK Government enterprise initiative, manufacturing, business growth training, and export initiative grants, for the job centre disablement advisory services, and for energy efficiency, regional, and loan guarantee schemes, are outlined in this informative guide. European Community grants and loans and local grants are also included.

1205 **The City of London: continuity and change, 1850-1990.**
Ranald C. Michie.   London: Macmillan, 1992. 238p. bibliog.
Based on work in recent years by economic, social, and political historians, the general consensus has been that the City of London's commercial and financial interests have not always been compatible with the national interest in terms of production and manufacturing industry. This history presents 'a long-term perspective . . . seeking to examine, explain and evaluate the combination of trends and circumstances that have made it what it is today' (Preface).

1206   **Trade associations and professional bodies of the United Kingdom.**
        Edited by Patricia Millard.   Detroit, Michigan; Andover, England:
        Gale Research, 1991. 10th ed. 432p.

First compiled in 1962, this edition contains the latest information on nearly 4,000
associations and professional bodies (including 500 new entries) arranged alphabetically. Following the main sequence is a listing of Chambers of Commerce, Industry and
Shipping by town or city and an inventory of overseas Chambers of Commerce which
retain offices in the United Kingdom. A subject index consisting of over 500 broad
subject classifications and a geographical index allow easy access and reference.

1207   **The monopolies and mergers yearbook.**
        Edited by Robert Miller.   Oxford: Blackwell, 1992. 727p.

All decisions of the Monopolies and Mergers Commission, presenting an accurate
picture of the regulatory and policy framework for mergers and acquisitions in the
United Kingdom, are collected here in a single easily accessible volume. Covering the
period March 1989 to December 1990 this first *Yearbook* contains case summaries and
conclusions, recommendations and Department of Trade and Industry responses, a full
description of the role and structure of the Commission, a listing of Statutes relating to
the Commission's work, and expert analysis of the development of merger policy.

1208   **Standard catalogue of British coins: coins of England and the United**
        Kingdom 1993.
        Edited by Stephen Mitchell, Brian Reeds.   London: Seaby, 1992.
        28th ed. 367p. map. bibliog.

A guide to the retail value of all coins of the realm from Celtic times to the reign of
Elizabeth II, and so primarily intended for coin collectors, this catalogue provides an
illustrated history of the English coinage. Introductory material includes a beginner's
guide to coin collecting and a numismatic glossary whilst appendices are devoted to
foreign language legends on English coins and mintmarks and other symbols.

1209   **The London insurance market directory 1991.**
        Edited by Valerie Morrison.   London: Evandale, 1991. 302p.

This annually-published directory identifies all companies active in the London market
grouped according to their function: insurance companies; Lloyds maritime; aviation
and motor syndicates; brokers; underwriting agents; contact offices; lawyers; loss
adjusters; consultants; and accountants.

1210   **Guide to company information in Great Britain.**
        Paul Norkett.   Harlow, England: Longman in association with ICC
        Information Group, 1986. 209p.

This straightforward and practical handbook advises how and where to find and
interpret information on UK companies. Worked examples illustrate the use of
company annual reports and business ratios. There is a specialist chapter on the
techniques involved in using financial databases.

1211   **The Japanization of British industry: new developments in the 1990s.**
Nick Oliver, Barry Wilkinson.   Oxford: Blackwell, 1992. 2nd ed.
304p.

Japanese investment in British industry continues to develop. This work describes and
analyses British companies following Japanese management styles and considers their
effects on works organization and employee relations. The response of the Trade
Unions to the situation is also studied.

1212   **The postcode atlas of Great Britain and Northern Ireland: postcode
area and district boundaries.**
Edinburgh: John Bartholomew in association with the Post Office,
1989. 168p. maps.

Postcodes offer a unique business planning opportunity in that they allow companies to
accurately relate sales figures to specified areas. On a scale of four miles to one inch
(Greater London – 1 mile to 1 inch) this atlas clearly depicts postcode boundaries
superimposed on detailed background maps.

1213   **Register of defunct companies.**
London: Macmillan under licence from the International Stock
Exchange, 1990. 550p.

This 1989-90 edition represents the first accumulation of this sort of data since 1979-80.
It contains notes on 25,000 companies removed from the *International stock exchange
official yearbook* since 1875. In most cases this followed either liquidation, dissolution,
or winding up proceedings.

1214   **Retail directory 1992.**
London: Newman, 1992. 46th ed. 1,325p. maps.

Established in 1939 this directory incorporates details of all significant companies
involved in retail activities in the United Kingdom. The first sequence is a listing of
retail companies, shops, stores, supermarkets, and out of town outlets. Surveys of the
important shopping areas in 450 towns follow and there is also information on cash and
carry warehouses, co-operative societies, and mail order firms.

1215   **A guide to the Data Protection Act: implementing the Act.**
Nigel Savage, Chris Edwards.   London: Financial Trading, 1985.
2nd ed. 286p.

All individuals and organizations using computers to process personal information are
obliged under the terms of the 1985 Data Protection Act to apply for registration. This
guide examines the Act's scope and purpose, explains its complexities, and offers
advice to businessmen on how to respond. It contains the complete text of the Act and
completed specimen registration forms.

1216 **Chatset directory of Lloyds of London 1992.**
Edited by Charles Sturge, John Rew, Oliver Carruthers. London:
Chatset, 1992. 3rd ed. 312p.

Comprehensive information on Lloyd's council, committee, and syndicate structure, is contained in this authoritative guide to one of the UK's most famous institutions. Directory information on Lloyd's underwriting agents and brokers, insurance companies and accountants, financial services, and loss adjusters, is also included.

1217 **Treasury Bulletin.**
London: HMSO for H.M. Treasury, 1990- . triannual.

Regarded as HM Treasury's flagship publication, this *Bulletin* provides information on a wide range of issues which reflect the Treasury's functions and responsibilities, e.g. central government borrowing, the Treasury's forecasting performance, improvements to economic statistics, Civil Service Pay, and the transfer of responsibility for financial services to the Treasury.

1218 **Macmillan directory of UK business information sources.**
James Tudor. London: Macmillan, 1992. 3rd ed. 435p.

Of interest primarily to the non-business researcher this 'one-stop' guide to business information covers both published and organizational resources grouped according to the *Nomenclature Générale des Activités Économique* (NACE) number and heading. This edition takes full account of the increasing commercialization of business statistical information and the Europeanization of business activity in the run-up period to the implementation of the Single Market.

1219 **Introduction to patents information.**
Edited by S. van Dulken. London: British Library, 1992. 2nd ed.
bibliog.

This practical step-by-step guide covers patent searching on a worldwide basis but with particular emphasis on the UK and the rest of Europe, Japan, and the USA.

1220 **Who owns whom 1992: United Kingdom and Republic of Ireland.**
High Wycombe, England: Dun & Bradstreet, 1992. 2 vols.

First published in 1958 this directory is the definitive work on company ownership, giving full details of subsidiaries and associates of over 7,000 parent companies registered in the United Kingdom. The entire range of business ownership from the smallest companies to the largest corporate groups is covered. A list of consortia groups showing member companies is also included.

1221 **Debrett's bibliography of business history.**
Edited by Stephanie Zarach. London: Macmillan in association with
Debrett's Business History Research Ltd., 1987. 278p. bibliog.

Over 2,000 book titles, all twentieth-century English language material, ranging from slim privately printed booklets to specially-commissioned bumper volumes, are listed in this bibliography.

Industry and Industrial Archaeology

1222 Allied Brewery Traders' Association 1991 directory.
Wolverhampton, England: ABTA, 1991. 158p.
A membership list, a directory of trade names, and lists of UK brewers, cider makers, and soft drink manufacturers and producers, are the principal contents of this annual publication.

1223 The engineer buyers guide 1991.
Compiled by Peter Bealing, Laura Tierney. London: Morgan Grampian, 1991. 94th ed. 738p.
Divided into general and machine tool sections, this buyers' guide is limited to products or services supplied in the normal course of business. Other features include directory type information on manufacturers and suppliers, UK agents of overseas organizations, and associations, institutions and societies connected with the engineering industry.

1224 BEMA engineering directory.
Bristol, England: Bristol & Western Engineering Manufacturers Association, 1991. 52nd ed. 392p.
This long-established directory provides a classified buyers' guide to member companies of the Association offering castings and patternmaking; sheetmetal work, fabricating and welding; metal finishing and heat treatment; machinery and finished products; electrical and electronic engineering; plastics, rubber and non-metallic products and services; and technical and business services.

1225 English medieval industries: craftsmen, techniques, products.
Edited by John Blair, Nigel Ramsay. London: Hambledon, 1991.
446p. bibliog.

Only industries that resulted in the production of consumer goods, and where substantial numbers of medieval artefacts survive, are dealt with in this collection of fifteen essays on English medieval industries. Replacing L. F. Salzman's *English industries in the Middle Ages* (1913) as the definitive work on the subject, this book goes into detail on the housing, clothing, tools, vessels and ornaments of the craftsmen engaged in these industries, and highlights their skills, practices, careers, and craft guilds.

1226 BMIF year book and classified buyers' guide 1991/92.
Farncombe, England: Charles Smith, 1991. 272p.

The British Marine Industries Federation, which has been established for over seventy years, now has some 1,200 members involved in all aspects of the industry, although its main interest is boatbuilding. It offers legal, commercial and technical services geared to promoting the growth of the industry's products. First published under this title in 1987, this directory provides information on the BMIF's own structure and on the European market, the BMIF's export service and training opportunities, the role of the Yacht Harbour Association, and the Coastguard Safety Scheme. There is also a classified buyers' guide, a list of trade names, and a complete BMIF membership list.

1227 Twenty centuries of British industry.
Hugh Bodey. Newton Abbot, England: David & Charles, 1975.
208p. 2 maps. bibliog.

Ranging from the mining of tin, lead, and gold in Roman times, and the development of the wool trade in the Middle Ages, to the throes of the Industrial Revolution, this survey of the growth of British industry is firmly set within the complexities of its social and economic background.

1228 The Institute of Materials Management members' reference book and buyers' guide 1992.
Edited by Beryl Bowley. Birmingham, England: Guardian
Communications, 1992. 202p. bibliog.

Materials management is defined here as 'the procedures which enable an organization to achieve the means of ensuring that the right materials are available at the right place, at the right time, and the right quantity and quality, and at the right cost' (President's Message). This publication provides directory information on the Institute, a list of selected information sources, associated publications, British Standards related to materials handling, and includes a classified buyers' guide.

1229 Brewery manual and who's who in British brewing and Scotch whisky distilling 1992.
Hampton, England: Hampton Publishing, 1992. 278p.

An A to Z directory of brewery and related companies provides details of their head offices, directors, and senior personnel, their share capital, balance sheets, dividends, reserve funds, and a brief commercial history. A 'who's who' in British brewing gives only sparse information, sometimes no more than name, address, and company position. Other features include the brand names of beer, brewing organizations and conventions, hop merchants, and maltsters.

1230 **The British clothing industry year book 1991/92.**
Solihull, England: Kemps, 1991. 14th ed. variously paginated.

Sponsored by The British Knitting and Clothing Export Council, this directory provides the name and telephone numbers of houses and firms manufacturing menswear, womenswear and childrenswear. Other lists include brand names, fashion accessories, fabric and textile companies, machinery and ancilliary equipment makers, buying officers, and a more detailed alphabetical list of suppliers.

1231 **British Gear Association buyers guide and members handbook.**
Birmingham, England: BGA, 1991. new ed. 60p.

Founded in 1986 from the rump of the old British Gear Manufacturers Association, the BGA's purpose is to promote the competitive position of the UK gear and power transmission industry. This guide sets out the comprehensive range of products available from BGA members: loose gears, gear boxes, couplings, clutches, chain and belt drives, etc.

1232 **The United Kingdom patent system: a brief history.**
Neil Davenport.   Havant, England: Kenneth Mason, 1979. 136p.
bibliog.

Tracing separately each main feature from its origin, this comprehensive and indispensable handbook outlines the development of the United Kingdom patent system from its beginnings in the sixteenth century to the Patents Act 1977. A thirty-four page bibliography divided into five main sections: statutes and rules; law reports and digests; official publications; books on patent law and practice; and books on inventions, their history and exploitation, is unequalled for its practical use and value.

1233 **Who's who in bulk handling 1992.**
Edited by Allan Davies.   Rickmansworth, England: Turret Group, 1992. 140p.

Topical articles on different aspects of storage, packaging, weighing, dust explosions, and mechanical and pneumatic conveying, accompany a 'who's who' arranged by firm in this guide to the bulk handling industry. Other features include a product guide, an annotated list of relevant British Standards, and a directory of the industry's associations and organizations.

1234 **The definitive guide to working offshore.**
Liverpool, England: MS Offshore, 1991. 148p.

This guide for those seeking employment offshore also acts as a directory which provides an authoritative insight into how the UK oil industry operates, the levels of investment it attracts, the major companies, the location of their rigs and wells, and the short- and long-term prospects of the industry.

1235 **Digest of United Kingdom energy statistics.**
London: HMSO for Department of Energy, 1991. 146p.
After a section on general energy statistics this annual digest provides detailed data on the production, consumption, costs and prices of coal, crude oil and petroleum, gas, and electricity. The first annex presents long term trends whilst the second (new to this edition) is a section on renewable sources of energy which summarizes the results of a Department of Energy survey.

1236 **Directory to the furnishing trade 1992.**
Tonbridge, England: Benn, 1992. 34th ed. 444p.
Basic name and address etc. information on UK manufacturers and their overseas agents, a buyers' guide to finished products, a list of trade marks and brand names, a list of retail furnishers, and information on trade associations and charities, technical education, and research and training organizations, are the principal contents of this guide and directory.

1237 **Design directory 1989.**
Edited by Suzie Duke. London: Design Council, 1989. 2 vols.
One of the Design Council's functions is to assist industry in the implementation of successful designs. Volume one of this directory lists design consultants in the areas of engineering and industrial design.

1238 **England and the aeroplane: an essay on a militant and technological nation.**
David Edgerton. London: Macmillan, 1991. 140p. bibliog. (Science, Technology and Medicine in Modern History).
In contrast to received wisdom Edgerton argues that the evidence of the aviation industry suggests that twentieth-century England should be regarded as a techno-logically- and industrially-motivated nation.

1239 **Engineering buyers' guide and directory 1992-93.**
Halifax, England: Northern Advertising Agency, 1992. 24th ed. 183p.
Published for the Engineering Industries Association, this publication includes outline directory information on the Association and a buyers' guide of the products and processes of member companies and firms.

1240 **Printers yearbook 1991/92: BPIF guide to the printing industry.**
Edited by Debbie Fallshaw. London: British Printing Industries Federation, 1991. 262p.
This guide outlines BPIF's services to its members, and provides information on the law as it affects printers, industrial relations, and education and training. There is also a section giving technical information, a buyer's guide, an index of retail prices, a 'what's what' of printers' charities and other associations, and a 'who's who' of prominent people in the industry.

1241 **Freight industry yearbook 1992.**
Edited by B. Farnorth. Birmingham, England: Guardian
Communications, 1992. 268p.
Basically this directory is a buyers' guide to manufacturers and suppliers to the freight
industry and of freight road haulers and shippers.

1242 **Consultant engineers: the 1992 graduate's guide to consulting
engineering careers in the UK and Europe.**
Edited by Simon Fullalove. Twickenham, England: Anchorage,
1991. 312p.
Providing undergraduates and postgraduate students with independent and objective
advice on beginning their careers as consultant engineers either in private practice, the
public sector, or with consultancy wings of major contractors, manufacturers, or the
public utilities, this guide carries informative features on the Institution of Civil
Engineers, Institution of Structural Engineers, Chartered Institution of Buildings
Services Engineers, Institution of Mechanical Engineers, Institute of Marine
Engineers, Institution of Electrical Engineers, Institution of Water and Environment
Management, and other relevant professional bodies.

1243 **The concrete yearbook 1992.**
Edited by Siobhan Graham. London: Telford, 1992. 2 vols. 688p.
The contents of this comprehensive yearbook include a general introduction to
concrete together with a guide to further information sources; a list of relevant British
Standards and codes of practice; a directory of the concrete industry's manufacturers
and suppliers; UK and overseas organizations and associations; and lists of contractors
offering specialist technical services, consulting engineers, and plant and equipment
firms.

1244 **Electricity before nationalization: a study of the development of the
electricity supply industry in Britain to 1948.**
L. Hannah. London: Macmillan, 1979. 479p. bibliog.
Commissioned but not controlled by the Electricity Council, this volume, along with
*Engineers, managers and politicians; the first fifteen years of nationalized electricity
supply in Britain* (L. Hannah. London: Macmillan, 1982. 336p. bibliog.) is based on
full access to the Council's archives and on interviews with senior personnel in the
electricity supply industry. Together they constitute a reliable and well-documented
history which concentrates more on national events than on local issues. *Electricity
supply in Great Britain: a chronology from the beginnings of the industry to 31
December 1976* (London: Electricity Council, 1977. 2nd ed. 99p. bibliog.) includes
descriptive annotations of all relevant government legislation.

1245 **A history of factory legislation.**
B. L. Hutchins, A. Harrison. London: Cass, 1966. 3rd ed. 298p.
bibliog.
First published in 1903, this history recounts how a national system of regulation began
with protection of a minute section of the working population, pauper apprentices in
the textile mills, and expanded into legislation covering every manual worker in every
manufacturing industry in the country. Particular aspects of the legislation discussed

include hours of labour, sanitation, age of commencing work, protection against accidents, mealtimes, holidays, wages, the introduction of the normal day, women's rights, and health and safety regulations.

1246 **Industrial performance analysis: a financial analysis of UK industry and commerce.**
Hampton, England: ICC Business Publications, 1992. 300p.
Relative industrial sector performances, measured by a series of business ratios, are ranked and compared with the UK industrial average in this analysis. From the information presented it is possible to assess which sectors show the most profit, have the fastest sales growth, the highest levels of liquidity and productivity, or have suffered the most from high interest rates.

1247 **Institute of Housing yearbook 1992.**
Coventry, England: Institute of Housing, 1992. 176p.
By the terms of its Royal Charter the Institute of Housing is required to promote the art and science of housing, its standards, ideals, education, and training. This yearbook surveys its activities in the previous twelve months and provides a directory of its members according to their employing authority category: local government; housing associations; development corporation; public authorities; building societies, etc.

1248 **The Institution of Structural Engineers directory of firms, 1992.**
London: Structural Engineers Trading Organisation, 1992. 298p.
Planned as an annual publication, this directory of consulting and contracting engineering firms, arranged alphabetically by town, gives information on their size, key personnel, the geographical area of their operations, the nature of their expertise, and the location of branch offices.

1249 **The British wool textile industry 1770-1914.**
D. T. Jenkins, K. G. Ponting. Aldershot, England: Scolar Press, 1987. 389p. bibliog. (Pasold Studies in Textile History).
First published by Heinemann Educational Books in 1982, this analysis of the progress and performance of the wool industry looks at its structure and locations, its transition to factory production, its use of raw materials and new technology, its competitiveness in the home and overseas markets, and its place in the national economy.

1250 **A history of GKN.**
Edgar Jones. London: Macmillan, 1987-90. 2 vols. (vol. 1.
Innovation and enterprise 1759-1918. 1987. 480p.; vol. 2. *The growth of a business 1918-1945*. 1990. 448p. maps.).
Guest, Keen and Nettlefolds occupies a prominent position in the history of the British light steel industry. Using company records, this business history reveals the company's progress, its expansion into and withdrawal from the coal and heavy steel industries, and assesses the contributions of both management and the workforce.

1251   **British multinationals: origins, management and performance.**
Edited by Geoffrey Jones.   Aldershot, England: Gower, 1986. 212p.
bibliog.

Covering a wide spectrum of British industry, this series of papers, whose authors are
all associated with the Business History Unit of the London School of Economics,
focuses on Dunlop, Vickers, Cadburys, Courtaulds, Glaxo, GKN, and Pilkington, to
examine the origins and growth of British-based multinational manufacturing
companies. Based on hitherto confidential company records and archives it finds that
many British firms were hesitant and reluctant to expand overseas but that the
impositions of tariffs, and other commercial pressures, forced them to do so.

1252   **ICI: the company that changed our lives.**
Carol Kennedy.   London: Hutchinson, 1986. 209p.

Formerly registered on 7 December 1926, Imperial Chemical Industries quickly
became successful in the competitive world of plastics, petrochemicals, and
pharmaceuticals. This diamond jubilee history highlights a dozen or so inventions and
discoveries emerging from ICI's laboratories which have visibly transformed people's
lives: products like perspex, polythene, the anti-malarial drug Paludrine, and the beta-
blocker heart drugs.

1253   **Atlas of industrializing Britain 1780-1914.**
Edited by John Langton, R. J. Morris.   London: Methuen, 1986.
246p. 372 maps. bibliog.

Published as the result of a longstanding initiative on the part of the Economic History
Society, and the Historical Geography Research Group of the Institute of British
Geographers, this atlas, complete with a substantial analytical text, maps the spatial
patterns and relationships of over thirty vital social and economic aspects of a period of
almost totally unrestrained industrial growth. Among these are the physical
environment, regional structure and change, wages, chemicals, brewing and distilling,
shipbuilding, engineering, banking and finance, and unionization.

1254   **Industrial change in the United Kingdom.**
Edited by William F. Lever.   Harlow, England: Longman Scientific
& Technical, 1987. 272p.

The role of labour and capital; the availability of space and buildings; general
economic progress; the place of small firms; multiplant and multinational companies;
public sector industries; and national, regional and urban policies, are the main themes
explored in this analysis by sixteen British industrial geographers.

1255   **Companion to the industrial revolution.**
Clifford Lines.   New York, Oxford: Facts on File, 1990. 262p.
4 maps.

Over 1,000 cross-referenced entries relating to the people, places, events, and
technological changes which transformed Britain into the world's first industrial nation
are contained in this handbook. The areas covered include scientific discovery, law and
order, entrepreneurship, transport, disease, child labour, industrial archaeology, social
class, population studies, religion, politics, education, and the introduction of the
penny post.

1256 **Lovegrove's guide to Britain's North Sea oil and gas.**
Martin Lovegrove. Cambridge, England: Energy Publications, 1991.
2nd ed. 242p.

The British search for energy in the North Sea commenced 26th December 1964 when a rig started drilling a hole into the earth's crust to the depth of 9,000 feet, some 150 miles east of Teeside. Since then the exploitation of Britain's off-shore oil and gas reserves has been the country's most important recent industrial success. This comprehensive review of the industry examines the evolution of the Government's policies with regard to licensing, taxation, prices, and the development and abandonment of wells; the growth of such activities as project evolution and evaluation, and exploration and appraisal. It also outlines the issues which will affect the pace of work in the North Sea in the future.

1257 **Working boats of Britain: their shape and purpose.**
Eric McKee. London: Conway, in association with the National Maritime Museum, 1983. 256p. bibliog.

Analysing the factors which have traditionally determined the shape of British boats and why boat designs vary so much, as well as describing the techniques employed in British boat building, this book also serves as a historical survey of British small craft.

1258 **Inventing the industrial revolution: the English patent system, 1660-1800.**
Christine MacLeod. Cambridge, England: Cambridge University Press, 1988. 302p. bibliog.

Patents for invention have been granted in England since the mid-sixteenth century. This study examines their development and their relationship with the technical changes of the early years of the Industrial Revolution, MacLeod also analyses the contemporary legal and political framework, explores the motives and subsequent fortunes of industrial patentees, and gauges the reliability of patent statistics as a measure of technical change.

1259 **Manufacturing into the late 1990s.**
London: HMSO for the Department of Trade and Industry, 1989. 134p.

This DTI Enterprise Initiative report identifies the challenges, threats, and opportunities likely to affect British manufacturing industry in the short-term future, and offers practical suggestions on how it should address the key issues. It examines economic and market factors, the influence of technology, demographic influences, and industry's response.

1260 **Who's who in industry 1991/92: the biographical guide to the UK industrial and commercial community.**
Edited by Juliet Margetts. London: Fulcrum, 1991. 964p.

Biographical and career details of the leading 10,000 decision-makers in British industry are contained in this new 'who's who' volume which is planned to be an annual publication. The top 1,600 industrial companies were allocated a number of entrants according to their annual turnover. Other entrants include civil servants, trade associations, government agencies, industrial and business media personnel, trade unionists, politicians, consultants, and business academics.

1261 **The history of the British coal industry.**
Edited by P. Mathias. Oxford: Oxford University Press, 1984-1987.
5 vols. maps.

Commissioned by the National Coal Board these detailed and well-documented volumes (vol. 1. *Before 1700*; vol. 2. *1700-1830 The industrial revolution*. M. W. Flinn, D. Stoker. 1984. 528p.; vol. 3. *1830-1913 Victorian preeminence*. R. Church. 1986.; vol. 4. *1912-1946 The political economy of decline*. B. Supple. 1987. 700p.; vol. 5. *1946-1982 The nationalized industry*. W. Ashworth. 1986. 732p.) constitute a magisterial record of the British coal industry, its coalfields, coal distribution, the principal markets, and the structure of the industry itself. J. U. Nef's *The rise of the British coal industry* (London: Routledge, 1932. 2 vols. bibliog.) covers the period 1550-1750 and raises the question of the rightful ownership of natural resources.

1262 **The plastic industry directory 1992.**
Compiled by Nicky Mepham. Croydon, England: EMAP Vision, 1992. 196p.

Company information on firms engaged in the plastic industry, including notes on their functions and activities, is followed in this directory by listings of those companies supplying materials and machinery, moulds and dies, etc. A list of trade names identifying UK manufacturers, and a nine-page glossary of technical and industrial terms, are also included.

1263 **Science Park directory.**
Edited by Charles Monck. Sutton Coldfield, England: UK Science
Park Association. 2nd ed. 30 maps.

Science Parks are property-based units which have formal and operational links with higher education institutions whose aim is to encourage the formation and growth of knowledge-based business and other organizations normally resident on site. This directory provides authoritative information on the history, objectives, progress, and tenant services of thirty established UK Science Parks. A location map and site plan is given for each park.

1264 **Archives of the British chemical industry 1750-1914: a handlist.**
Peter J. T. Morris, Colin A. Russell. Faringdon, England: British
Society for the History of Science, 1988. 273p. (BSHS Monographs).

This record of industrial chemical firms' archives is arranged alphabetically by the firms' names. Each entry provides a short outline history of the company, a bibliography of source material, and a comprehensive summary of its surviving archives.

1265 **The selling of British Telecom.**
Karin Newman. London: Holt, Rinehart & Winston, 1986. 176p.

At the time of its privatization in 1985, British Telecom, the principal supplier of telecommunication services in the United Kingdom, was valued at £7,800 million. This study comprehensively reviews the unprecedented planning that led up to its flotation.

Intensive market research, and public relations on a massive scale, were followed by wide TV and press advertising, and direct mail shots, to attract over two million investors. It was a frightening example of how sophisticated, modern mass-marketing techniques can be applied to the privatization of a nationalized industry.

1266 **Bridging the years: a short history of British civil engineering.**
C. M. Norrie. London: Arnold, 1956. 212p.

Covering the years 1760-1914 this survey describes some of the most notable bridges, tunnels, canals, dams, harbour and river works constructed in Britain. A list of founder members of the Federation of Civil Engineering Contractors is also included.

1267 **A history of the Institution of Mechanical Engineers 1847-1947.**
R. H. Parsons. London: Institution of Mechanical Engineers, 1947. 299p.

In recording the history of the Institution this solid centenary commemorative volume provides a good summary of mechanical engineering as a profession, its inventions, and their industrial applications.

1268 **Nuclear power: its development in the United Kingdom.**
R. F. Pocock. London: Institution of Nuclear Engineers in association with Unwin, 1977. 272p.

Based on government papers, reports, journal articles etc. this is an authoritative and reliable account of the development of nuclear power in Great Britain by an engineer who was for many years employed in the nuclear industry.

1269 **Printing trades directory 1992.**
Tonbridge, England: Benn, 1992. 32nd ed. 524p.

A geographically-arranged directory of printers, a buyers' guide to specialist printers, and an alphabetical directory of printing manufacturers and suppliers, form the three principal sections of this annual publication. It also includes a list of suppliers' brand names, UK agents and distributors, and a guide to who owns whom.

1270 **A history of the Institution of Electrical Engineers 1871-1971.**
W. J. Reader. London: Peter Peregrinus for Institution of Electrical Engineers, 1987. 327p. map. bibliog.

Illustrating the three main stages of the development of electrical engineering, namely telegraph, power, and electronics engineering, this official centennial history also contains a chronology, the text of the Institution's Royal Charter, and biographical notes on its Presidents and Secretaries 1939-1986.

1271 **The CIRIA UK construction information guide.**
Compiled by B. G. Richardson. London: Spon, 1989. 361p.

The Construction Industry Research and Information Association is an independent body which initiates and manages research and information projects on behalf of its members. This guide contains an alphabetical list of UK local authorities and a similar list of construction information sources.

1272   The brewing industry: a guide to historical records.
        Edited by Lesley Richmond, Alison Turton.   Manchester, England:
        Manchester University Press, 1990. 485p.

First in series to be sponsored by the Business Archives Council, this book provides a
detailed list of the surviving records of nearly 650 brewing firms. Each company entry
contains a brief history, a summary of its archives and their location, and a
bibliography of related publications. Two well-documented introductory essays, 'The
British brewing industry since 1750' and 'Brewing archives: their nature and use', are
also included.

1273   The shipbuilding industry: a guide to historical records.
        Edited by L. A. Ritchie.   Manchester, England: Manchester
        University Press in association with the Business Archives Council,
        1992. 206p.

Shipbuilding has played a significant part in British industrial and maritime history well
into the second half of the twentieth century when it faltered and went into terminal
decline. This guide provides brief histories of some 200 businesses and indicates the
location of their surviving records.

1274   Victorian engineering.
        L. T. C. Rolt.   London: Allen Lane, 1970. 300p. bibliog.

This wide-ranging overview explains how during the nineteenth century Britain became
the workshop of the world, leading the way in locomotive and shipbuilding, in
bridgebuilding, and in the development of gas and electricity for industrial and
domestic consumption.

1275   BPI year book 1991: a statistical description of the British record
        industry.
        Edited by Peter Scaping.   London: British Phonographic Industry
        Ltd., 1991. 12th ed. 104p.

Statistics of trade deliveries, sales by price categories of singles, albums, cassettes, and
compact discs, of imports and exports, are the principal contents of this annual
publication. Other features include specialist charts, the BRIT awards, an essay on
anti-piracy activities, and a list of BPI members.

1276   Source guide to industrial market data.
        Compiled by Julie Scott.   London: London Business School
        Information Service, 1992. 137p.

Market data which includes information on production, prices, imports and exports,
trade names, buyers' guides, standards, patents, etc. can be used to build up industrial
sector profiles. This guide is intended not only to lead into the actual sources but also
to indicate the type of sources available in the areas of building and construction,
ceramics and glass, chemicals and pharmaceuticals, electronic and electrical engineering, energy, mechanical engineering, metals, mining and minerals, paper, printing and
packaging, rubber and plastics, textiles and clothing, transport and distribution, and
wood and furniture.

Industry and Industrial Archaeology

1277 **Sell's products and services directory 1992/93.**
Tonbridge, England: Benn Business Information Services, 1992.
107th ed. 1,310p.

A classified list of manufacturers, wholesalers, distributors, and companies supplying products and services to commerce and industry, is supported in this massive directory by a list of brand and trade names and a company data section. Details of 6,500 companies were added in this new edition.

1278 **A guide to the British food manufacturing industry.**
P. R. Sheard.   Bristol, England: Nova Press, 1991. 3rd ed. 295p.

Industrial statistics (i.e. marketing data, the top 100 food companies, acquisitions and mergers, companies taken into receivership) and company information (a brief history, recent developments, a produce guide, interim results, subsidiary companies, divisional organization, and a five year financial record) are the principal contents of this guide. The publisher's aim is to issue a new edition every two years.

1279 **Croner's health and safety at work.**
Edited by Paul Smith.   New Malden, England: Croner, 1991. 500p.

Comprising sets of looseleaf thematic sections gathered together in a spring-binder to allow for the insertion of updated and revised sections, this manual's objective is to be the first point of reference to the Acts, regulations, and codes of practice in the United Kingdom for the control of health and safety at work. Its main concern remains the 1974 Health and Safety at Work Act and the regulatory framework based on the Health and Safety Commission set up by the Act. Other legislation still in force includes the 1961 Factories Act and the 1963 Offices, Shops and Railways Premises Act. The most detailed treatment is given to topics considered to be most important to subscribers.

1280 **Space and industry: 1992 directory of UK capabilities.**
London: British National Space Centre, 1992. 152p.

Formerly published as *Directory of UK space capabilities* (1987) this directory is a guide to the space-related expertise to be found in UK manufacturers, agencies, and research institutions, listing their spheres of interest, key personnel, and industrial space resources.

1281 **Did Britain make it? British design in context: 1946-86.**
Edited by Penny Sparke.   London: Design Council, 1986. 168p.
bibliog.

The optimistically titled *Britain can make it* exhibition, held at the Victoria and Albert Museum in 1946, projected a future in which design would play an important part in establishing Britain as a world manufacturing power. This book sets out to determine what became of that dream, chronicling the fortunes of the British textiles and electronics industries, charting the dramatic upsurge in the influence of the retailing sector, and describing the evolving role of the professional industrial designer.

1282   **Design and British industry.**
        Richard Stewart. London: John Murray, 1987. 256p. bibliog.

Structured round the Great Exhibition of 1851 and the Festival of Britain in 1951 this illustrated study traces the history of British industrial design from the eighteenth-century Society for the Encouragement of Arts, Manufactures and Sciences to the work of the Council of Industrial Design which was established in 1944. A final chapter discusses current developments in engineering, innovation, and education.

1283   **The watermills of Britain.**
        Leslie Syson. Newton Abbot, England: David & Charles, 1980. 208p. bibliog.

Part one of this illustrated history traces the development of water power in Britain; part two concentrates on its use in milling; and part three consists of regional tours visiting the best remaining watermills. Syson's earlier work *British watermills* (London: Batsford, 1965. 177p. bibliog.) is concerned more with the craft of water milling.

1284   **UK Kompass register: the authority on British industry: 1992/93.**
        East Grinstead, England: Reed Information Services, 1991-92. 5 vols. 30th ed.

Endorsed by the Confederation of British Industry, the Institute of Purchasing and Supply, and the Chartered Institute of Marketing, the UK edition of *Kompass* includes industrial companies trading nationally with at least ten employees. It is without doubt the most detailed, up-to-date, and reliable source of information on British industry. The five volumes are as follows: vol. 1 *Product and services* (2,703p.) contains details of 41,000 different products and services offered by British industrial companies divided into sixty-four main industrial groups; in vol. 2 *Company information* (2,085p.) a trade name section lists trades names and their owners – the main section comprises companies arranged geographically under counties; vol. 3 *Financial data* (1,791p.) provides an alphabetically-arranged list of every company listed in volumes one and two along with their registration number, logo, trading address, year of incorporation, financial record, group details, etc.; vol. 4 *Parents and subsidiaries* (1,556p.) lists all parent companies and their subsidiaries, including UK companies registered overseas enabling corporate structures to be unravelled; vol. 5 *Industrial trade names* (844p.) contains 100,000 different trade names and their registered owners and also overseas companies and their UK agents and distributors.

1285   **Great engineers: a survey of British engineers 1937-1987.**
        Edited by D. Walker, A. Papadakis. London: Academic Editions/St. Martins in association with the Royal College of Art, 1987. 288p. bibliog.

Leading engineers, historians and industrialists contribute twenty-two essays on the major engineering figures of the nineteenth and twentieth centuries in this sumptuously-illustrated work. A second section adds another sixty biographical sketches and there is also a list of great British inventions as well as an extensive bibliography.

Industry and Industrial Archaeology

1286   The factory movement 1830-1855.
        J. T. Ward.   London: Macmillan, 1962. 515p. bibliog.
Based largely on local sources in the industrial districts, this study of the agitation for
the restriction of industrial labour, and the regulation of working conditions, traces the
history of the factory movement from its insignificant beginnings in the Northern
textile areas in the early nineteenth century to the parliamentary struggle for national
legislation.

1287   Reshaping nationalised industry 1979-1987.
        Edited by Christine Whitebread.   Newbury, England: Policy
        Journals, 1989. 245p.
From 1979 onwards successive Conservative administrations transformed the nationalized industries. Those remaining within public ownership were subjected to rigorous
financial control and public scrutiny. Many industries were taken out of the public
sector but it was still considered necessary to retain some form of public control. This
book examines how successfully the Government improved management in the public
sector, notably in the Post Office and in British Rail, and how it regulated the
privatized industries, water, gas, buses, and British Telecom. The role of the
Monopolies and Merger Commission, and the industries' accountability to Parliament,
and to the consumer, also come under close attention.

1288   A history of the British gas industry.
        T. I. Williams.   Oxford: Oxford University Press, 1981. 304. maps.
        bibliog.
The beginnings of the industry, its development up to the First World War, moves
towards nationalization by the Labour government after the Second World War, the
modern industry, and natural gas, are the main themes of this authoritative history.

1289   Industrial research in the United Kingdom: a guide to organizations
        and programmes.
        Edited by Brenda Wren.   Harlow, England: Longman, 1989. 13th ed.
        584p.
Some 3,000 UK laboratories active in a wide range of technical subjects are included in
this authoritative guide, industrial firms, research associations, consultancy agencies,
universities and polytechnics, training and development agencies, and learned and
professional societies. The areas covered include aerospace technology, agricultural
and environment sciences, chemical sciences, electronics and computer science, the
pharmaceutical, biomedical and biological sciences, and engineering. Funding agencies
are also considered.

Industrial archaeology

1290 A guide to Britain's industrial past.
Brian Bailey. London: Whittet Books, 1985. 187p. 4 maps.

Reflecting the changes to the rural landscape and to the urban scene caused by the Industrial Revolution, this descriptive gazetteer also records the remains of industries whose origins go back to prehistoric times. Biographical sketches of the engineering 'giants' such as Brunel, Abraham Darby, and Josiah Wedgwood, are also included.

1291 Industrial archaeology in Britain.
R. A. Buchanan. London: Allen Lane, 1980. 2nd ed. 475p. 7 maps. bibliog.

Two centuries of industrialization have made the United Kingdom a rich and diverse area for industrial archaeology. This pioneering work first looks at the definitions, techniques and historical framework of industrial archaeology, examines the social and economic background of heavy industry, power, transport and public utilities, and concludes with a six-part regional survey of industrial monuments. In the process a coherent academic discipline is forged.

1292 The National Trust guide to our industrial past.
Anthony Burton. London: George Philip and the National Trust, 1983. 240p. maps. bibliog.

Intended for the general reader, this account of British industrial development from prehistory to the end of the nineteenth century is augmented with a gazetteer of sites and monuments open to the public.

1293 The BP book of industrial archaeology.
Neil Cossons. Newton Abbot, England: David & Charles, 1987. 384p. bibliog.

A descriptive survey of Britain's industrial archaeology, its nature, various forms of power, industries, public utilities, and transport, is followed in this illustrated guide by a gazetteer of sites and industrial museums. First published in 1975 it seems set fair to be acknowledged as one of the few definitive general works so far published in this particular field.

1294 Guide to industrial archaeology sites in Britain.
W. Minchinton. London: Granada, 1984. 192p. maps. bibliog.

Almost 100 major sites are described in regional and county sections in this easy to follow, informative, and well-documented guide.

Industry and Industrial Archaeology. Industrial archaeology

1295 **England.**
Barrie Trinder, Michael Stratton. In: *The Blackwell encyclopedia of industrial archaeology*. Edited by Barrie Trinder. Oxford: Blackwell, 1992, p. 236-40. map. bibliog.

Outlining England's manufacturing inheritance from the pre-industrial period, this article draws attention to the salient features of English industrial archaeology and history. Museums holding industrial artefacts, conservation legislation, and associations and societies concerned with the preservation of the industrial heritage, are also covered. The encyclopedia contains over ninety separate entries relating to important industrial sites such as Bluebell Railway, Bridgewater Canal, Ironbridge, Severn Tunnel, and Weald and Downland Museum. Barrie Trinder is Lecturer and Historical Adviser at the Institute of Industrial Archaeology, Ironbridge.

Trade

1296 A-Z of UK marketing data.
London: Euromonitor, 1990. 4th ed. 153p.
Intended as a broad guide to a wide range of consumer markets, this pocket handbook provides a wealth of facts and figures for all types of consumer goods on sale in the UK. As well as information on over 400 products presented in a series of statistical tables covering the basic marketing parameters of retail sales, domestic production, imports and exports, 1984-1988, socio-economic information on consumer spending, demographics, employment, price indexes, advertising, income and housing, and a statistical profile of tourism, is also given for the same five-year period. Finally, there is a summary of trade and business press sources employed in compilation. The previous edition of this work was published in 1985.

1297 British exports 92: vol. 1: Products and services: vol. 2: Company information.
East Grinstead, England: Kompass-Reed, 1991. 24th ed.
Formerly (up until this edition) known as *Kelly's United Kingdom exports*, this directory lists more than 10,000 major UK exporters producing more than 16,500 different products and services. Illustrations and technical data concerning specific products are to be found in the *Company information* volume.

1298 Anglo-American trade directory 1993.
Edited by Shakpari Dolatshahi. London: American Chamber of Commerce (UK), 1992. 855p.
Published annually since 1916, and containing nearly 20,000 entries relating to companies with transatlantic business interests, this comprehensive directory is arranged in three major sections. An alphabetical sequence by company gives name, address, telecommunication details, principal executives, subsidiaries, agents and representatives, and main business interests; a classified sequence lists companies under US Government Standard Industrial headings; and a third section lists the companies within each UK and US region.

Trade

1299 Energy, trade and industry.
London: HMSO, 1988. rev. ed. 36p. (Sectional List, no. 3).

Recent annual reports and accounts, reviews, surveys, rules and regulations, and other official publications relating to all aspects of Britain's energy, trade, and industry, are listed in this catalogue, including consumer credit and protection, exports and imports, international and regional development, information technology, standard weights and measures, and tariffs and international trade regulations.

1300 A licence to trade: the history of English chartered companies.
Sir Percival Griffiths.   London: Ernest Benn, 1974. 318p. bibliog.

Following the maritime discoveries in the sixteenth century English merchants were anxious to expand their trade abroad. Because of the capital required and the costs and risks involved it was soon apparent that overseas trade was beyond the means of individual merchants. The solution was to form limited companies and to seek a monopoly of trade within a specified area by means of a royal charter. Besides the trading and plantation companies of the sixteenth and seventeenth centuries, this history also examines the administrative companies which followed in the nineteenth.

1301 Institute of Export members handbook 1992.
London: Cornhill, 1992. 200p.

This handbook provides practical and updated information on finance marketing, transport and distribution, information technology, communications, ports and shipping, and reference services, for exporters.

1302 Kelly's export services 1992.
East Grinstead, England: Reed, 1991. 6th ed. 100p.

This directory lists those UK companies which provide services to other firms exporting finished products. Information on government services for British exporters is also included.

1303 The invisible economy: a profile of Britain's invisible exports.
David Liston, Nigel Reeves.   London: Pitman and The Institute of Export, 1988. 376p.

Invisible exports traditionally play a vital part in Britain's economy contributing a significant surplus to the country's balance of trade each year. This comprehensive survey of Britain's international service industries describes not only the financial and City sector but also areas such as transport, travel and tourism, and what is known as the trade in knowledge, consultancies in engineering, health care and education, telecommunications, music, and computer software. It also assesses the effectiveness of education at school and professional level for ensuring the continuing success of Britain's invisible export industry.

1304 **The directory of British importers: vol. 1: England and register of importing firms: vol. 2: Indexes.**
Edited by Sarah MacLeod. Berkhamsted, England: Trade Research, 1991. 7th ed.

Sponsored by the British Importers Federation this directory provides a comprehensive register of about 4,600 importing firms, import agents and merchants, and manufacturing importers, giving a description of their business, the names of leading executives, the products imported, associated firms abroad, and annual import turnovers.

1305 **The McGraw-Hill handbook of British finance and trade.**
Stan Mason. London: McGraw Hill, 1983. 467p.

Every conceivable facet of the basic information on money and finance for firms and companies is contained in this handbook: interest rates, the national economy, financial incentives and inducements, taxation, investment, management analysis and techniques, sources and methods of finance, banks, and commercial institutions.

1306 **Trade marks: an introductory guide and bibliography.**
David C. Newton. London: British Library, 1991. 2nd ed. 202p.

Replacing Brenda M. Rimmer's *A guide to the literature and directory of lists of trade marks* (1976), and based on British Library's Science, Reference and Information Services' incomparable collection of trade mark literature, this guide provides succinct and reliable information on what exactly a trade mark is, trade mark history, UK trade mark law, and on how to conduct a trade mark search. A directory section includes over 700 lists of trade names published worldwide.

1307 **Overseas trade statistics of the United Kingdom 1992.**
London: HMSO for Central Statistical Office, 1993. variously paginated.

Compiled from declarations made to HM Customs & Excise, this general survey of trade provides the total import and export figures on a monthly basis followed by area of commodity and by country analyses. First issued in 1848 this annual publication was previously issued under the title *Overseas trade accounts of the United Kingdom*.

1308 **Retail prices 1914-1990.**
London: HMSO for Central Statistical Office, 1991. 109p.

The Retail Prices Index is the principal source of prices information as it reflects consumer spending. This volume contains the longest possible time series for each of the indices currently compiled. It includes all types of household spending with the exception of savings, investments, charges for credit, betting, and cash gifts. There are introductory notes on the structure of the RPI in 1991, price indicators, prices collection, weighting, and keeping the index up-to-date.

1309 **The British Monopolies Commission.**
Charles K. Rowley. London: Allen & Unwin, 1966. 394p. bibliog.

Convinced that market dominance by private enterprise organizations is not necessarily in the public interest, and perhaps works against it, the post-war Labour Government established the Monopolies Commission in 1948. This study of its first twenty years

Trade

commences by looking at the attitudes and conditions of the pre-war period that were to shape legislation and then examines the Commission's structure and constitution, and its investigating procedures. It continues with a critical scrutiny of the economics of market dominance, of the statistical measures of economic performance, and of the reaction of successive governments to the Commission's reports and findings.

1310 **Sell's British exporters 1991/92.**

Epsom, England: Sell's 1991. 75th ed. 682p.

A classified list of over 4,500 products and services, a directory of exporting companies, and a list of trade and brand names, are the principal features of this long established directory. Introductory material includes information of the BBC's Export Liaison Unit, government services for exporters, the Small Firm Information Service, and the Association of British Chambers of Commerce.

1311 **United Kingdom balance of payments: the CSO pink book.**

London: HMSO for Central Statistical Office, 1991. 80p.

Containing information on visible trade, invisible and capital transactions, and sections on specific aspects of the balance of payments, this annual publication provides detailed data for the past eleven years and summary figures for earlier years. A glossary of terms and an index are included and users are referred to other relevant sources where appropriate.

Transport and Communications

General

1312   **British passenger transport into the 1990s.**
Geography (Journal of the Geographical Association), vol. 77, no. 1
(Jan. 1992), p. 63-93. 6 maps. bibliog.
Ten short essays review current developments and outline the issues which will shape
transport policies into the 1990s: 'Introduction: the policy context'; 'British Rail
passenger policies'; 'The Channel Tunnel rail link; five years of British bus
deregulation'; 'Roads in the 1990s: expansion or restraint'; 'British airports'; 'Light rail
transit development in Britain'; 'London's transport system'; 'Transport for the
disabled'; and 'Transport and the environment'. Maps of the British Rail network, of
the proposed motorway network, of the locations of the major UK airports, of Light
Railway developments, and of the proposed Central London British Rail and London
Underground routes, are also included.

1313   **Travel in England: from pilgrim and pack-horse to light car and plane.**
Thomas Burke.   London: Batsford, 1946. 154p.
Essentially, this is a social history of road and rail travel in England from the earliest
times, incorporating primitive tracks and pathways. Roman roads, turnpikes, the great
coaching inns of the eighteenth century, the railways, and the motor-car. Legionaries,
medieval pilgrims, celebrated travellers, railway enthusiasts, and a host of others, take
their place in this historical cavalcade.

1314   **Royal Mail: the Post Office since 1840.**
M. J. Daunton.   London: Athlone Press, 1985. 388p.
Commissioned by the Post Office Board this book replaces Howard Robinson's
Britain's Post Office: a history of development from the beginnings to the present day
(1953) as the definitive history. Tracing the Post Office's progress both as an institution
and as a business with a widening range of activities, it begins with Rowland Hill and
the introduction of the postage stamp in 1840 and ends with its demise as a government

department under a Postmaster General and the separation of postal services from telecommunications which are no longer the Post Office's responsibility.

1315 **Lighthouses: their architecture, history and archaeology.**
D. B. Hague, R. Christie. London: Gower, 1975. 307p. maps. bibliog.

Confined almost entirely to the United Kingdom this illustrated study features lighthouse history, British lighthouse administration, their general design and construction, lighthouse builders, rock towers, and illumination and fog signals.

1316 **Modern British bridges.**
Dorothy Henry, J. A. Jerome. London: C. R. Books, 1965. 188p. bibliog.

Nearly 100 bridges, large and small, constructed in the decade 1957-1967, are featured in this compact reference work. An historical background to bridge building and an explanation of construction techniques are included in a short introductory text.

1317 **Lighthouses of England and Wales including the Channel Islands and the Isle of Man.**
Derrick Jackson. Newton Abbot, England: David & Charles, 1975. 176p. 3 maps. bibliog.

Illustrated with line drawings, this book outlines the history of all major rock and landfall lighthouses under the guardianship of Trinity House and the Northern Lighthouse Board and answers the questions: who designed and constructed them and when; how does the light work; what is its power and range; and is it open to the public? Information on this last point may soon be out of date as many lighthouses are soon to be automated with no staff on site.

1318 **The ancient bridges.**
E. Jervoise. London: Architectural Press, 1930-36. 4 vols. (vol. 1. *The ancient bridges of the South of England.* 1930. 138p.; vol. 2. *The ancient bridges of the North of England.* 1931. 146p.; vol. 3. *The ancient bridges of mid and Eastern England.* 1932. 164p.; vol. 4. *The ancient bridges of Wales and Western England.* 1936. 180p.).

As yet unsurpassed, these four volumes were compiled on behalf of the Society for the Preservation of Ancient Buildings. They include brief descriptions, the dates of their construction, and many illustrations.

1319 **The story of passenger transport in Britain.**
J. Joyce. London: Ian Allan, 1967. 208p. bibliog.

By the end of the eighteenth century the carrier's wagon, the stage coach, and the mail coach, had built up an intricate public transport network before they were eclipsed by the railways of the nineteenth century. In turn the railways were augmented by the private motor-car and by long distance coaches. This concise and readable history is told primarily from the passenger's point of view, and is imaginatively illustrated from contemporary prints and writings.

1320   **The National Trust book of bridges.**
       J. M. Richards.   London: Cape, 1984. 214p. bibliog.
Commencing with the medieval period this historical and architectural account of
British bridges ends with a discussion of the new styles and techniques in bridge
building in the last hundred years. Each chapter closes with a list of bridges especially
worth visiting.

1321   **Lives of the engineers with an account of their principal works**
       comprising also a history of inland communication in Britain.
       Samuel Smiles.   Newton Abbot, England: David & Charles, 1968.
       3 vols.
Virtually a basic history of the development of civil engineering in the United Kingdom
this acknowledged 'classic' describes within a biographical framework the gradual
accumulation of techniques and methods that made the Industrial Revolution possible.
It ranges from the earthworks of ancient Britain to the lives of George and Robert
Stephenson. At the time of its original publication in 1862 there were grave doubts as
to this book's commercial viability!

1322   **Transport statistics Great Britain, 1992.**
       London: HMSO for Department of Transport, 1992. 248p.
Tables and charts of every conceivable description along with separate sections for
road, rail, domestic waterborne freight, shipping, and air transport, are contained in
this wide-ranging volume which is intended to stimulate informed discussion of all
aspects of transport policies and development. A calendar of events from 1981 to 1991
is also included.

Road

1323   **The old roads of England.**
       Sir William Addison.   London: Batsford, 1980. 167p. 15 maps.
       bibliog.
Ancient trackways; Roman roads; Anglo-Saxon and Scandinavian farm-ways and
market ways; medieval roads, bridges, and pilgrim ways; packhorse tracks, drove roads
and lost roads; turnpike roads; coach roads; coaching inns; and roads for tourists, are
all featured in this pleasantly-illustrated book. A final chapter makes a plea for
stronger measures to protect ancient trackways and rights of way both on amenity
grounds and as historical and archaelogical records.

1324   **British motorcycles of the 1940s and 1950s.**
       Roy Bacon.   London: Osprey, 1989. 240p.
A complete alphabetical guide to all the well-known and obscure British marques,
nearly eight in number, which sought to satisfy the craving for personal transport in the
immediate post-war period, giving background information, descriptions, and a
photographic record of the machines produced.

1325   **The AA: a history of the first 75 years of the Automobile Association 1905-1980.**

Hugh Barty-King.   Basingstoke, England: AA, 1980. 319p.

This illustrated narrative history traces the development of motoring from the early days of 'automobilism', as it was known, to the post-war era and includes a chronology of events in the AA's history as well as brief biographies of all AA committee members. Pictorial features encompass AA badges, signs, uniforms, telephone boxes, vehicles, and its armorial bearings.

1326   **The little red book 1991/92: road passenger transport directory for the British Isles and Western Europe.**

Edited by Gavin Booth.   London: Ian Allan, 1991. 215p.

This directory provides information on vehicle suppliers and dealers, and on UK commercial, municipal, and independent 'bus and coach operators.

1327   **A history of British motorways.**

George Charlesworth.   London: Thomas Telford, 1984. 284p.

11 maps. bibliog.

The *British Standard glossary of highway engineering terms* (London: British Standards Institute, 1967) defines a motorway as 'a limited access dual-carriageway road with grade separation, completely fenced in, normally with hard shoulders. It is for the exclusive use of prescribed classes of motor vehicles'. No such road existed in Britain before 1958. In addition to indicating the engineering and other technical issues of motorway construction, this book looks at previous motorway proposals, their design and planning, their usage, the building of the first motorways in the late 1950s, and the environmental and social issues involved.

1328   **Roads and their traffic 1750-1850.**

John Copeland.   Newton Abbot, England: David & Charles, 1968.

206p. bibliog.

Based on local records, and early newspapers, this history describes the roads as they were maintained by the statute labour of the parishes, the improvements carried out by the turnpike trusts, and the carrying of goods, passengers, and mail. The problems faced by the coaching companies, the dangers and discomforts experienced by passengers, and the fierce competition with the railways, are also discussed.

1329   **Packhorse, waggon and post: land carriage and communications under the Tudors and Stuarts.**

J. Crofts.   London: Routledge & Kegan Paul, 1967. 147p. (Studies in Social History).

Tracing the development of land communications and its influence on social life in the sixteenth and seventeenth centuries, this book examines the contemporary road system, the types of transport, the work and role of the packers and waggoners, the use of footposts, the establishment of swift hackney stages, the posting system, the Royal posts and their privileges, and the early stage coaches. The main social impact was, of course, the constant erosion of the distinction between the town and the countryside.

1330   **The complete catalogue of British cars.**
David Culshaw, Peter Horrobin.   London: Macmillan, 1974. 511p.
Included in this encyclopedic work are 3,700 models in series production for at least
two years from nearly 700 manufacturers. Descriptive text and over 1,000 photographs
are linked to technical details giving year of production, number of cylinders, bore and
stroke, capacity, compression ratio, brake horse power, coolant, carburation,
wheelbase and length, track, weight, suspension, top gear ratio, etc. A series of
appendices give additional material on other cars like three-wheelers, steam cars,
electric cars, and also on coachwork styles, the names and addresses of manufacturers,
and motoring clubs and organizations.

1331   **The history of British bus services.**
John Hibbs.   Newton Abbot, England: David & Charles, 1989,
2nd ed. 306p. 10 maps. bibliog.
Immediately acknowledged as the definitive work on the subject when first published
in 1968, this pioneering study of the British 'bus industry examines its beginnings and
progress up to the 1930 Road Traffic Act. Its principal topics are the great combines
of the inter-war years, the struggle to avoid coming under railway company control,
the development of express coach services, the municipal 'bus fleets, their crews and
machines, and their licensing and control.

1332   **British lorries 1900-1945.**
C. F. Klapper.   London: Ian Allan, 1973. 159p.
Almost fifty marques are described in this pictorial history of British commercial
vehicles.

1333   **London buses 1929-1939.**
Gavin Martin.   Shepperton, England: Ian Allan, 1990. 144p.
The formation of London Transport in 1932 marked a determined effort to replace
obsolete and non-standard 'buses and to modernize London's 'bus fleet. By 1939 only a
handful of the 'buses inherited from the former independent operators remained. This
unashamed dip into nostalgia for the 'bus enthusiast follows these stirring years in
London's public road transport history and looks closely at design and engineering
developments. The illustrations come from the photographic archive of the London
Transport Museum.

1334   **British motor cycles since 1950.**
Steve Wilson.   Wellingborough, England: Patrick Stephens, 1987.
208p.
OEC, Panther, Royal Enfield, Scott, Silk, Sun, Sunbeam, and Tandon motorcycles,
are arranged by marque in this detailed account. Each section includes a brief history
of the marque, information on the major categories of the factory's road-going output,
a table of production dates, a year-by-year survey of each range of machine, and
information on the marque's engine and frame numbers, colour schemes, publications
and manuals, spares shops, and owner clubs.

Water

1335 **Heroes all! The story of the RNLI.**
Alec Beilby. Yeovil, England: Patrick Stephens, 1992. 224p.

The National Institution for the Preservation of Life from Shipwreck was founded in 1824 and renamed as the Royal National Life-Boat Institution thirty years later. Manned largely by volunteer crews some 200 RNLI stations are located round the coast ready day and night to go to the rescue of stricken ships. This splendid book recounts some of their exploits.

1336 **A boater's guide to the waterways.**
Watford, England: British Waterways, 1990. 64p. map.

Concise information on all its canals, region by region, is contained in this regularly up-dated British Waterways publication. The addresses and telephone numbers of all lock keepers, basin attendants, bridge keepers, and waterway managers; the maximum craft dimensions for each waterway; where to obtain windlasses and lock keys; opening times; closures; stretches of water given to either flooding or water shortage, are all included. Special payments for some stretches, extra charges for off-river basins, and for adjoining rivers not managed by British Waterways, are also covered.

1337 **The canal builders.**
Anthony Burton. London: Eyre Methuen, 1972. 230p. 6 maps. bibliog.

Between the opening of the Bridgewater Canal in 1761 and the coming of the railways early in the nineteenth century tens of thousands of men were involved in canal construction. This work looks at the promoters and financiers behind the various projects, the engineers who translated these schemes into reality, and the workers who laboured as 'navvies'.

1338 **Bradshaw's canals and navigable rivers of England and Wales.**
Henry Rodolph de Salis. Newton Abbot, England: David & Charles, 1969. 480p.

First published as *A handbook of inland navigation for manufacturers, merchants, traders, and others* (London: Henry Blacklock, 1904), which was compiled after the author, a director of a canal haulage firm, had travelled 14,000 miles over the whole national waterways network, this work provides an invaluable survey of British canals and rivers. De Salis cast an expert eye at arrangements for changing level (locks, weirs, lifts), tunnels and bridges, acqueducts, tides, the principal types of vessels, and the main through routes. A ten-page glossary of canal terms enables the canal novice to keep up.

1339 **Royal river highway: a history of the passenger boats and services on the River Thames.**
Frank L. Dix. Newton Abbot, England: David & Charles, 1985. 320p. bibliog.

For centuries all classes of people were accustomed to use the Thames both for business and pleasure but by 1850 the river's commercial traffic was under threat by the railway network and the improving road system. Eventually the river boats were forced to rely on week-end and holiday excursion traffic. This innovative study also looks at the new technologies, from petrol and diesel engines to hovercraft and hydrofoils, and at recent attempts to revive and re-establish regular waterbus and watertaxi services.

1340 **Inland waterways of Great Britain.**
L. A. Edwards. St. Ives, England: Imray, Laurie, Nurie & Wilson, 1985. 6th ed. 474p. bibliog.

Based on *Bradshaw's canals and navigable rivers of England and Wales* (q.v.) this comprehensive up-to-date compendium of the inland waterways opens with notes on locks, navigation weirs, lifts, tunnels, acqueducts, bridges, and tides. The main part of the work (p. 39-404) consists of a gazetteer directory of all England and Wales inland waterways with concise information on their routes, distance, features and facilities, and suitable vessel dimensions, length, width, draught and headroom. A long series of appendices feature the hiring of canal and river craft, canoeable rivers, types of inland waterways craft, the public right of navigation, waterways museums, a glossary, and a bibliography.

1341 **The Great Canal.**
Roderick Grant. London: Gordon & Cremonesi, 1978. 156p. bibliog.

One of the great engineering feats of the Victorian age, the Manchester Ship Canal was opened on 1 January 1894, enabling ocean-going merchant ships to anchor thirty-six miles inland, dramatically reducing the costs of the cotton trade between the southern states of America and Britain. The project was threatened by floods, accidents, bankruptcy, and civil disorder. The whole story, from start to finish, including the political and financial manoeuvrings, is covered in this well-researched study.

1342 **The canals of the British Isles series.**
Charles Hadfield. Newton Abbot, England: David & Charles, 1950- . 13 vols. maps. (vol. 1. *British canals: an illustrated history.* 1984. 7th ed. 367p. bibliog.; vol. 2. *South and south-east England.* 1969; vol. 3. *South-west England.* 1985. 2nd ed. 206p.; vol. 5. *West Midlands.* 1985. 3rd ed.; vol. 6. *East Midlands (including part of London).* 1970. 2nd ed.; vol. 7. *Eastern England* by J. Boyes and R. Russell, 1977; vols. 8-9. *North-west England.* 2 vols. 1970; vols. 10-11. *Yorkshire and north-east England.* 2 vols. 1970.).

Although not all of these titles are necessarily in print at the same time, this series of constantly-revised, descriptive, well-illustrated histories is arranged in three chronological periods: pre-1790; 1790-1845; and post-1845. Similar book-length works on individual canals (e.g. Kenneth R. Clew's *Dorset and Somerset Canal* and P. A. L. Vine's *London's lost route to Basingstoke*) are included in the same publisher's series, 'Inland Waterway Histories', which give full details of their history, construction, use, route, and present-day state of preservation.

1343 **The Shell book of inland waterways.**
Hugh McKnight. Newton Abbot, England: David & Charles, 1981.
2nd ed. 493p. 11 maps. bibliog.

The first part of this guide to the British canal system is taken up with its history, water supply, locks and lifts, bridges and acqueducts, tunnels, building and design, public houses, towns and villages, operation and maintenance, boats and carriers, pleasure cruising, boatyards and marinas, and animal and plant life. Waterway museums and Associations and Boat Clubs are also featured. The second part is a descriptive gazetteer of all canals in England and Wales, Scotland, and Ireland. Lavishly illustrated, this is a comprehensive handbook and guide for the committed canal enthusiast, the towpath walker, and for all those intent on exploring the waterways of Britain.

1344 **The complete book of canal and river navigations.**
Edward W. Paget-Tomlinson. Wolverhampton, England: Waine Research, 1978. 361p. bibliog. 32 maps.

Events in waterway history; waterway engineering; canal and river craft and navigation; boatbuilding; carriers, carrying, and crews, are all featured in this encyclopedic work.

1345 **Navigable waterways.**
L. T. C. Rolt. Harmondsworth, England: Penguin, 1985. rev. ed. 239p. 9 maps. bibliog.

'The British inland waterway system, consisting partly of navigable rivers and partly of still canals, combines beauty with utility to an enormous degree' (Introduction). First published by Longman in 1969 this work by an eminent industrial archaeologist first gives a detailed account of the great age of canal building and then charts the decline of the waterways and their recent upsurge as tourist attractions. An eight-page gazetteer of objects of outstanding interest on the waterways network emphasizes that today's canals and rivers are holiday amenities rather than commercial highways.

1346 **Britain's lost waterways.**
Michael E. Ware. Ashbourne, England: Moorland Publishing, 1989. 2nd ed. 189p. (Historic Waterways Scenes).

Once the major highways of Britain for the carrying of heavy goods, the canals declined when confronted with competition from rail and road networks in the nineteenth and twentieth centuries. Many of the smaller navigations are now no more than ditches, or have disappeared beneath urban development. Some have been restored by enthusiasts. This pictorial volume presents these 'lost' (but not forgotten) canals by means of old photographs linked by an historical and descriptive commentary.

Rail

1347   Titled trains of Great Britain.

Cecil J. Allen, revised by B. K. Cooper.   London: Ian Allan, 1983.
6th ed. 192p.

First published in 1946, this exercise in nostalgia for the committed railway enthusiast describes 135 named trains and their services of which only thirty still survive.

1348   Encyclopaedia of British railway companies.

Christopher Awdry.   Wellingborough, England: Patrick Stephens,
1990. 288p. bibliog.

Railway development in the United Kingdom was a haphazard operation involving over 1,000 separate companies which in 1923 were grouped into the 'Big Four', i.e. Great Western Railway; London and North Eastern Railway; London, Midland and Scottish Railway; and Southern Railway. In turn these companies were amalgamated as British Railways in 1948. This encyclopaedia lists all British companies which opened at least part of their projected lines, and provides information on their routes, their promoters, the dates of their authorization, buildings, opening, amalgamation or closure. 'Family trees' show how each company found its way into the 'Big Four', either by acquisition, absorption or merger, or into the London Passenger Transport Board, or, in some cases contrived to retain its independence to the end.

1349   Rail atlas Great Britain and Ireland.

Compiled by S. K. Baker.   Yeovil, England: Oxford Publishing,
1990. 6th ed. 123p.

The entire current British Rail network is outlined in this comprehensive atlas: all operational railways including freight only lines, London Transport, Tyne and Wear Metro, and the numerous independent standard or narrow gauge preserved and tourist railways. Information on the extremely detailed maps includes major power signal boxes, carriage sidings, freightliner terminals, junction names, freight marshalling yards, and tunnels.

1350   Brunel's Britain.

Derrick Beckett.   Newton Abbot, England: David & Charles, 1980.
222p. map. bibliog.

Adopting a uniform pattern to relate the lives and achievements of three outstanding engineers who contributed to much in the 'railway era', 1830-59, this study along with *Stephenson's Britain* (Derrick Beckett. Newton Abbot, England: David & Charles, 1984. 239p. 3 maps. bibliog.) and *Telford's Britain* (Derrick Beckett. Newton Abbot, England: David & Charles, 1987. 192p. 4 maps. bibliog.) opens with a chronology of events, looks in detail at their major triumphs, and suggests localized tours of regions where their engineering works may still be seen.

1351 **Great British tramway networks.**
Wingate H. Bett, John C. Gillham.   London: Light Railway
Transport League, 1962. 4th ed. 200p. 20 maps.

No less than 922 tramways and electric light railways which were either constructed, authorized, or seriously contemplated, are recorded in this region-by-region survey of tramway networks, their operations, and their rolling stock. First published in 1940 this standard and definitive work also indicates when services started and whether steam or horse-powered trams preceded them.

1352 **Great railway stations of Britain: their architecture, growth and development.**
Gordon Biddle.   Newton Abbot, England: David & Charles, 1986. 240p. bibliog.

Surveying the growth and development of Britain's mainline stations over 150 years, this illustrated study looks at their changing social and functional roles. The reasons for their location, their impact on local communities, and their contribution to city centre development, are all investigated, together with their varying styles of architecture. A five-page chronology of fifty-four stations sketches their history and progress.

1353 **The railway heritage of Britain: 150 years of railway architecture and engineering.**
Gordon Biddle, O. S. Nock.   London: Michael Joseph, 1983. 270p. 3 maps.

In 1981 the Secretary of State for the Environment suggested that industries and organizations should make available their rich heritage of historic buildings in published form. This is British Rail's response. It is an illustrated guide to the outstanding landmarks and other significant features along the main and branch lines of the entire national railway network in the form of four historical and descriptive gazetteers arranged by BR regions. There is a four-page glossary of terms and the complete list of BR's listed buildings is included as an appendix.

1354 **Railway stations of Britain: a guide to 75 important centres.**
Geoffrey Body.   Wellingborough, England: Patrick Stephens, 1990.

Smaller stations of historical significance as well as major junctions or termini are featured in this all-region guide. A wealth of information covering the selected stations' history and development, their facilities, routes and services, is further enhanced by national and area maps and station lay-out plans.

1355 **Historic railway sites in Britain.**
Michael R. Bonavia.   London: Robert Hale, 1987. 208p. bibliog.

Covering the chief regions of Britain, each section contains a general introduction on the area's special railway interest, followed by descriptive architectural and historical notes covering a representative selection of stations, viaducts, and tunnels. Most of the 120 sites discussed are still in British Rail's possession although a few which have been disposed of are included because they still retain a considerable railway history significance. An appendix on the Railway Preservation Societies includes notes on the principal preserved railways.

1356 **Twilight of British Rail?**
Michael R. Bonavia.   Newton Abbot, England: David & Charles,
1985. 207p.
Major upheavals sustained over fifty years, amongst them the effects of the Second
World War, nationalization, modernization, the Beeching rationalization, the loss of
freight traffic, questionable management decisions, damaging and disruptive strikes,
are the main talking points of this critical assessment of British Rail at a crucial period
when its future structure was increasingly under close scrutiny. Two earlier books by
this author are also of considerable interest: *The four great railways*, which contains a
study of the 'Big Four', the London Midland & Scottish, London and North Eastern,
the Great Western, and Southern Railways, and *British Rail: its first 25 years* which
describes the immense problems caused by unwieldy administration, the persistence
with steam, and by the Beeching years of savage contraction and closures.

1357 **Railways restored 1991/92 edition.**
Edited by Alan C. Butcher.   London: Ian Allan, 1991. 128p.
This guide to major preserved steam railways, railway museums, and preservation
centres, provides railway enthusiasts with a brief history of each, and information on
their central and other stations, their locomotives, facilities and services, and their
location.

1358 **Passengers no more.**
Gerald Daniels, Les Dench.   London: Ian Allan, 1980. 3rd ed. 144p.
Sadly, the ravages of Dr. Beeching on British Railway's vast network of routes and
stations were but the final blow in the decline of passenger numbers. This book lists in
two alphabetical sequences, for standard and narrow gauge railways, the location of all
lines and stations no longer in use, their former ownership, the date of closure,
together with a map reference.

1359 **A biographical study of the Father of Railways George Stephenson: on
the occasion of the 150th anniversary of the opening of the world's first
public railway the Stockton and Darlington 1825-1975 including an
account of railway mania and a consideration of Stephensonia today.**
Hunter Davies.   London: Weidenfeld & Nicolson, 1975. 337p.
bibliog.
Not the least interesting feature of this biography, which eschews technical engineering
data, is the light thrown on George Hudson, the first railway magnate, and
responsible, so the author claims, for the railway fever which swept early Victorian
England. A postscript, the George Stephenson tour, conducts the reader round places
with strong Stephenson associations and to where official documents, minute books,
plans, etc. may be found.

1360 **British railway history: an outline from the accession of William IV to
the nationalization of the railways, 1877-1947.**
Hamilton Ellis.   London: Allen & Unwin, 1954-59. 2 vols.
Intended for the general public as well as railway enthusiasts, this popular history (vol.
1. *1830-1876*. 1954. 443p.; vol. 2. *1877-1947*. 1959. 416p.), which takes the story up to
nationalization in 1947, encompasses the history of the various railway companies, the

leading personalities in the industry, railway architecture, mechanical, track, and signal developments, and, of course, the locomotives.

1361 **The Midland Railway – a chronology – listing in geographical order the opening dates of the lines and additional running lines of the company (with the powers under which they were constructed) together with the dates of the opening, re-naming, and closing of stations and signalboxes.**
John Gough.   Mold, Wales: Railway & Canal Historical Society, 1989. 392p. bibliog.

With its headquarters in Derby, the Midland Railway in its heyday extended to Manchester, Carlisle, Lincoln, Peterborough, Shoeburyness, St. Pancras, Bath, Bristol and Swansea. Joint ownership of lines took it to Chester, Liverpool, Southwestern Scotland, Ferrybridge, the East Anglian coast, and Bournemouth. This comprehensive list, and the track diagrams which accompany it, expertly charts the Midland's physical progress and must surely be the definite work on the subject.

1362 **Channel Tunnel – Le Tunnel sous la Manche**
Edited by Lesley Grayson.   London: British Library, 1990. 126p.

This bibliography includes both English and French language printed material dealing with the tunnel's commercial and environmental impact. It covers its history, construction and operation, fixed link options, its regional impact, and its competition with air and surface transport.

1363 **Eurotunnel: an illustrated history of the Channel Tunnel scheme.**
Peter Haining.   Channel Tunnel Group Ltd., 1989. 144p. bibliog.

No less than thirty-five proposals for a Channel Tunnel were presented to the British Parliament from the beginning of the nineteenth century, all to no avail until a scheme was finally approved in the 1980s. French support remained solidly in favour of the project. This history relies on contemporary illustrations and extracts from the writings of leading engineers, eminent statesmen and public figures, either staunch advocates of the project, or die-hard opponents.

1364 **Investigation into the Clapham Junction railway accident.**
Anthony Hidden.   London: HMSO for the Department of Transport, 1989. 220p.

Presented to the Secretary of State for Transport, this report provides an unprecedented insight into British Rail working practices in the 1980s. Its recommendations not only address the reasons for the signal maintenance failures which caused the disaster, but safety on British Rail generally, and also the responses of the emergency services in rendering aid and assistance.

1365 **Investigation into the King's Cross Underground fire.**
London: HMSO for the Department of Transport, 1988. 247p.

A catastrophic fire swept through King's Cross Underground station just after the peak evening rush hour, Wednesday 18 November 1987, claiming thirty-one lives. This is the report presented to Parliament on its causes and circumstances.

1366 **A chronology of the construction of Britain's railways 1778-1855.**
Leslie James. London: Ian Allan, 1983. 120p. 11 maps. bibliog.
All Britain's railways are listed in a chronological sequence of the dates when they
were opened for traffic. Details are given of the date of incorporation by Parliament,
to whom powers were granted, the routes of the lines constructed, the opening dates
for each section, and of their further history.

1367 **The tunnel: the Channel and beyond.**
Edited by Bronwen Jones. Chichester, England: Ellis Horwood,
1987. 334p.
For almost 200 years a channel tunnel has been a dream to some, a nightmare to
others. This study covers all aspects of the tunnel constructed in the 1980s: the financial
wheeling and dealing behind the scenes, the political manoeuvrings, the excavation and
dispersal of thousands of tons of chalk, the dangers faced by the workforce, the
environmental problems, and the public fears of rabies crossing the Channel,
terrorism, and accidents.

1368 **Jowett's railway atlas of Great Britain and Ireland: from
pre-grouping to the present day.**
Alan Jowett. Wellingborough, England: Patrick Stephens, 1989.
352p. bibliog.
This all-embracing historical railway atlas, reproduced from manuscript and hand
drawn maps, was compiled from the series of folding railway maps of England and
Wales produced by the Railway Clearing House in the early years of this century. The
maps not only act as a geographical guide to all British railways past and present, but
also as an historical record of British railway development. They illustrate the current
status of all stations and lines open for traffic, tunnels, sidings, junctions, viaducts,
engine sheds etc. Gazetteers facing the maps list all these details separately. Without
question this is an essential reference work for all railway enthusiasts.

1369 **Britain's steam railways: a guide to preserved lines and museums.**
Adrian Knowles. Andover, England: Pitkin, 1982. 32p. map.
More than just an attractive souvenir colour guide, this descriptive gazetteer of nearly
fifty of Britain's most celebrated steam railways provides full information on location
and travel directions, opening hours, station buildings, and locomotives. There is an
explanatory glossary of specialist terms for the non-technically minded. Timetable
information to ninety surviving lines can be found in *Wilson's preserved steam railway
timetable* (Leeds, England: Railway Promotion and Resources) which also lists special
railway events through the year.

1370 **The railway workshops of Britain, 1823-1986.**
Edgar J. Larkin, John G. Larkin. London: Macmillan, 1988. 266p.
bibliog.
The main railway workshops singled out for detailed treatment in this authoritative
history are those which were in operation when the amalgamation of the railways into
the Big Four came into effect under the 1921 Railways Act. There are specialist
chapters on works organization and management, the railway workshops in two World
Wars, and their financial control.

1371 **History of the Great Western Railway.**
E. T. MacDermot, O. S. Nock. London: Ian Allan, 1964. 3 vols.
maps. bibliog.

The first two volumes of this classic history, covering the periods 1833-1863, and 1863-1921 respectively, were first published in 1927. Subsequent research, especially into the history of the smaller railway companies which were later absorbed into the Great Western, led to this revised edition by C. R. Clinker in this edition. The third volume extends from the reorganization of the railway companies in 1922 to the formation of British Railways in 1947. Supported by statistical data, maps, and diagrams, this authoritative work enfolds all aspects of GWR's history, line construction, stations, services, locomotives, signals, and operational organization.

1372 **Collecting railwayana.**
John Mander. Ashbourne, England: MPC, 1988. 192p. bibliog.

A systematic guide to every important class of collectable railwayana short of actual locomotives or carriages: stations and their contents; goods transportation documentation; locomotive, wagon and carriage relics; signalling equipment; railway lamps; railway trackside artefacts; railwaymen's uniforms; and documents and publicity material. Hints on how and where to collect these items, a glossary of companies and jointly owned stations, and a helpful bibliography, complete this valuable pioneering work.

1373 **A history of the Southern Railway.**
C. F. Dendy Marshall, revised R. W. Kidner. London: Ian Allan,
1968. 555p. map. bibliog.

Histories of the earliest railways in the south of England and of the London and Southwestern Railway, the London, Brighton and South Coast Railway, the South Eastern and Chatham Railway, and of the Southern Railway, are included in this thoroughly revised edition of a work originally published in two volumes in 1937. It forms a complete history of this railway group from the earliest days of Southern Railway's constituent companies to SR's own absorption into British Railways. Details of the dates of lines opened and closed, the dates when services were electrified, and when stations were renamed, are included as appendices.

1374 **The national railway collection.**
London, Glasgow: Collins, 1988. 206p.

Written by the curatorial staff of the National Railway Museum at York, this book celebrates the history of the railways and describes and illustrates the national collection of railway relics, fully assuaging the perennially rampant national nostalgia for steam railways. It covers all aspects of the vintage railway years: signalling, civil engineering, shipping, hotels and catering, tickets and guides, railway heraldry etc.

1375 **Great British trains: an evocation of a memorable age in travel.**
O. S. Nock. London: Pelham, 1985. 212p.

This is the story of the prestigious 'named' trains, the *Flying Scotsman*, the *Golden Arrow*, etc., the pride of Britain's railways in the age of steam, from Edwardian days to the beginning of the Second World War. The author was privileged to ride on the footplates of many of the locomotives described.

1376   **A bibliography of British railway history.**
Compiled by George Ottley.   London: HMSO, 1983. 2nd ed. 683p.
Nearly 13,000 annotated and fully indexed items, books, extracts from books, and
pamphlets, on all aspects of the history of rail transport in Britain are grouped under
broad headings such as special types of railway and locomotion; engineering;
management and operation; heraldry and livery; humour; and the railway in art.
Highly technical works on specialized subjects are not included. Also of interest is *A
bibliography of British railway history. Supplement: 7951-12956* (Compiled by George
Ottley. London: HMSO, 1988. 544p.).

1377   **The 'rail centres' series.**
Shepperton, England: Ian Allan. 1981- . 12 vols. (*Brighton.*
B. Cooper. 144p; *Carlisle.* P. Robinson. 144p; *Clapham Junction.*
J. Faulkner. 128p; *Derby.* B. Radford. 128p; *Doncaster.* S. Batty.
144p; *Leeds/Bradford.* S. Batty. 160p; *Newcastle.* K. Hoole. 128p;
Oxford. L. Waters. 128p; *Peterborough.* P. Waszak. 128p; *Reading.*
L. Waters. 128p; *Shrewsbury.* R. Morris. 128p; *Wolverhampton.*
P. Collins. 128p.).
This illustrated series focuses upon the growth and development of the important
English railway towns.

1378   **George and Robert Stephenson: the railway revolution.**
L. T. C. Rolt.   London: Longman, 1960. 356p. bibliog.
Completing a consciously planned trilogy of famous engineer biographies (the others
were lives of Isambard Kingdom Brunel and Thomas Telford), this study of father and
son places them both on an equal footing. The elder never faltered in his vision and
faith in the power of railway locomotives; the younger, whose engineering ability was
superior, translated this vision into reality.

1379   **Red for danger: a history of railway accidents and railway safety.**
L. T. C. Rolt.   Newton Abbot, England: David & Charles, 1976.
3rd ed. 296p. bibliog.
Based on the annual reports of the Railways Inspection Department, this standard
work, first published in 1955, covers all the major accidents on British railways. It
examines the painstakingly thorough investigations by the Inspecting Officers of
Railways to ascertain their precise causes and the measures adopted to prevent similar
accidents occurring. There is a chronological index of accidents between 1830 and 1967.

1380   **The Victorian railway.**
Jack Simmons.   London: Thames & Hudson, 1991. 416p. map.
bibliog.
In many ways the railways were archetypal Victorian creations; simultaneously
representing progress, ugliness, and the destruction of a pristine peaceful and beautiful
landscape. This splendidly produced study shows how the railways affected Victorian
thought and language, how they were pictured in contemporary art and literature, how
they transformed internal communications, and the social revolution they caused in the
arrangements of ordinary people travelling to work and on holiday.

Transport and Communications. Rail

1381   **The railway and its passengers: a social history.**
David Norman Smith.   Newton Abbot, England: David & Charles,
1988. 192p. bibliog.

From the opening of the first Liverpool and Manchester passenger railway in 1830 to
their nationalization in 1947, the railways were constructed and operated entirely by
private enterprise. Often the interests of the railway companies clashed with those of
the travelling public. This study takes account of the impact of the railways on
passenger travel and the growth of the mass travel market in their historical social and
economic context. The different types of passenger services – mainline, rural,
commuter, leisure – and the companies' attempts to drum up business through
advertising and publicity, are prominently featured.

1382   **A regional history of the railways of Great Britain.**
Edited by David St. John Thomas, J. Allan Patmore.   Newton
Abbot, England: David & Charles, 1960-1989. 15 vols.

This important series recounts the detailed railway history of the major regions set
against their social, economic, and geographical background. The relevant titles are as
follows: vol. one *The West Country* (D. St. J. Thomas); vol. two *Southern England*
(H. P. White); vol. three *Greater London* (H. P. White); vol. four *North East England*
(K. Hoole); vol. five *The Eastern Counties* (D. L. Gordon); vol. seven *The West
Midlands* (Rex Christiansen); vol. eight *South and West Yorkshire* (David Joy); vol.
nine *The East Midlands* (Robin Leleux); vol. ten *The North West* (G. O. Holt); vol.
thirteen *Thames and Severn* (Rex Christiansen); vol. fourteen *The Lake Counties*
(David Joy).

1383   **Forgotten railways.**
H. P. White.   Newton Abbot, England: David & Charles, 1986.
240p. 15 maps. bibliog.

Since 1930 almost two-thirds of Britain's former railway network has been closed. This
book looks in depth at the whole question of the 'forgotten' railways: what they were
like in their heyday, the closure process, how they were dismantled, and the various
transformations they have experienced. Mainline and cross-country, urban, and rural
branch lines were all affected especially by the infamous Beeching cuts. Although a
self-contained work, this book also acts as an overall introduction to the publisher's
'Forgotten Railways' series which highlights the histories of the closed lines in a
number of regional volumes: *North East England* (K. Hoole); *East Midlands*
(P. Howard Anderson); *Chilterns and Cotswolds* (R. Davies and M. D. Grant); *South
East England* (H. P. White); *East Anglia* (R. Joby); *North West England* (John
Marshall); and *West Midlands* (Rex Christiansen).

1384   **Breakthrough: tunnelling the Channel.**
Derek Wilson.   London: Century in association with Eurotunnel,
1991. 144p.

Published to celebrate the breakthrough of the service tunnel under the Channel, this
colourfully-illustrated book gives a summary of the issues and wider dimensions of the
whole Channel Tunnel project. Its history, the engineering task, the men and machines
involved, the terminals, the environmental aspects and problems, the tunnel's future,
and the meeting under the Channel, are all authoritatively outlined.

310

1385   **Minor railways of England and their locomotives 1900-1939.**
George Woodcock.   Norwich, England: Goose, 1970. 192p.
A reference history for the enthusiast of twenty-four railway companies 'owning less
than ten engines at any one time which operated passenger traffic with one or more of
these same engines between the years 1900 and 1939'.

1386   **The Great Northern Railway.**
John Wrottesley.   London: Batsford, 1979-81. 3 vols. (vol. 1. *Origins
and development*. 1979. 256p. 7 maps. bibliog.; vol. 2. *Expansion &
competition*. 1979. 201p. 3 maps.; vol. 3. *Twentieth century to
grouping*. 1981. 220p. 4 maps. bibliog.).
The construction of its lines, including the engineering features, the early passenger
services, the coal traffic, the consolidation of the railway companies, the progress of
railway bills through Parliament, and the eventual loss of financial confidence, are
treated at length in this formidable three-volume history. The author, a former
President of the Railway Club, was for many years Special Assistant to the British
Transport Commission's Chief Legal Adviser.

Air

1387   **Flight international directory 1991/92: part 1 – United Kingdom:
incorporating who's who in British aviation.**
Edited by Malcolm Ginsberg.   Potters Bar, England: Flight
International, 1991. 534p.
All aspects of the aeronautical industry are represented in this directory: civil and
military aviation, airports and heliports, air transport and air taxi services, aviation
organizations including aircraft museums, recreational flying and gliding clubs, a major
section on trade and industry, aviation licence requirements and training facilities, and
the aeronautical press. Lastly an 130-page 'who's who' in British aviation provides
biographical sketches of prominent figures connected with aviation in industry and
commerce, the government, and the Royal Air Force.

1388   **Pooley's flight guide United Kingdom and Ireland 1992.**
Edited by Robert Pooley, William Ryall.   Borehamwood, England:
Elstree Aerodrome, 1992. 528p. Distributed by Airlife Publishing of
Cheltenham, England.
The main section of this all-encompassing guide which was compiled with the
assistance of the Civil Aviation Authority is a detailed directory of all British civil
aerodrome, private airfields, and landing fields. For the main aerodromes there is a
chart and details of their services, runways, opening hours, landing fees, hangers,
restaurant facilities, visual reporting points, and entry and exit lanes.

1389 **Airline: the inside story of British Airways.**
Arthur Reed. London: BBC, 1990. 160p.

In 1988 British Airways was twelfth in the world airline league table for its number of passengers (26.4 million) and tenth for its number of aircraft (204). This history shows how this respectable position has been attained since the company's formation from the merger of British Overseas Airways Corporation and British European Airways and investigates how BA has met the challenge of international terrorism and the subsequent decline in passenger numbers which, along with the rising price of oil, posed financial problems to all the world's major airlines in the 1980s. The change from the public to the private sector, and the merger with British Caledonian, also figure prominently. Other topics discussed include pilot training, freight capacity, marketing, and the issues involved in the purchase of new aircraft.

1390 **Aviation archaeology: a collector's guide to aeronautical relics.**
Bruce Robertson. Cambridge, England: Patrick Stephens, 1983.
168p. 8 maps.

Sections on veteran and vintage aircraft; aviation archaeology; reading, writing and researching; aircraft photographs; books, personal records, medals, and cigarette cards; etc., emphasize the diversity of collectable items sought after by aviation 'buffs'.

1391 **British airports.**
Alan J. Wright. London: Ian Allan, 1991. 4th ed. 112p. map.

Forty-eight airports are described in this illustrated gazetteer. Information is given on each airport's history, location and access, terminal, spectator facilities, operators, travel movements, and runways, along with an airport plan.

London's historic railway stations.
See item no. 317.

London's Underground.
See item no. 333.

London termini.
See item no. 334.

Crossing London's river.
See item no. 344.

London buses.
See item no. 1333.

Motorways versus democracy.
See item no. 1550.

Agriculture, Forestry, Fishing

Agriculture

1392 **Agricultural Statistics for the United Kingdom.**
London: HMSO for Ministry of Agriculture, Fisheries and Food.
1900- .
Data on agricultural topics is broken down into four main sections in this annual publication: agriculture (including area of agricultural land and distribution of holdings by type of agricultural activity); horticulture; county statistics; and prices. Trends in production, employment, and land use can be analysed from this data.

1393 **Agriculture, fisheries, food and forestry.**
London: HMSO, 1988. 18p. (Sectional List, no. 1).
Official publications listed in this catalogue relate to livestock; farm crops and grass; farm management; horticulture; plant pests and diseases; general farm pests; farm safety; climate, drainage and water supply; food; fisheries; forestry; and the Royal Botanic Gardens at Kew.

1394 **Agriculture in the United Kingdom 1991.**
London: HMSO for Ministry of Agriculture, Fisheries and Food,
1992. 75p.
Fourth in a series which followed the White Paper, *Annual Review of Agriculture*, this publication sets out data on the economic condition of, and prospects for, UK agriculture. It contains a summary of the year under review and sections on the structure of the industry, policy developments, output prices and input costs, commodities, agricultural incomes, land prices and balance sheets, farm business data, and public expenditure on agriculture.

1395 **Old farm tools and machinery: an illustrated history.**
Percy W. Blandford.   Newton Abbot, England: David & Charles,
1976. 188p. bibliog.

All aspects of the farming year – ploughing, sowing, cultivating, harvesting – are
touched upon in this fascinating expert study. Those tools still surviving are now
treasured collectors' items.

1396 **English land and English landlords: an enquiry into the origins and
character of the English land system, with proposals for its reform.**
George G. Brodrick.   Newton Abbot, England: David & Charles,
1968. 514p.

This history of land tenure and agriculture in England from the earliest period to the
end of the nineteenth century was first published by Cassell in 1881 for the Cobden
Club. It examines the working of primogeniture, family settlements, the dependent
position of farmers and farm labourers, and the distribution of land. A table compiled
in 1877 shows the various types of landowners with their respective acreage in each of
the English counties.

1397 **Agriculture in England: a survey of farming 1870-1947.**
Jonathan Brown.   Manchester, England: Manchester University
Press, 1987. 160p. bibliog.

For much of the period under discussion English farmers faced hard times. After
concentrating their resources on feeding the growing industrial population in the mid-
nineteenth century their livelihood came under threat when the adoption of free trade
allowed cheap food to flood in from overseas. This book looks at their search for new
products, their adoption of new techniques and machinery, their finances, and their
relations with government during the First World War and the inter-war period.

1398 **Farm machinery 1750-1945.**
Jonathan Brown.   London: Batsford, 1989. 118p.

All manner of machines, each requiring new skills and a back-up maintenance system,
made their appearance on English farms as almost every aspect of physical labour on
the land and in the farmyard was converted to horse power in the modern period. This
study traces the development and use of machinery from Jethro Tull's inventions in the
early eighteenth century to the Ferguson machines of the 1930s.

1399 **Windmills of England.**
R. J. Brown.   London: Robert Hale, 1976. 256p. bibliog.

No less than 10,000 windmills once added their distinctive shapes to the English
countryside before the advent of steam, and later oil and electricity, hastened their
demise. This exhaustive work discusses their design, machinery and workings in some
technical detail, and then describes over ninety preserved mills and their history, each
with a full-page drawing, and gives notes on a further twenty-four outstanding mills.

1400 The agricultural revolution 1740-1880.
J. D. Chambers, G. E. Mingay.   London: Batsford, 1966. 232p. map.

The Agrarian Revolution is defined here as 'the vital change from earlier systems to the scientific mass-production of food for the workshop of the world'. This study demonstrates that initially output was increased without large-scale mechanization which came well into the nineteenth century when demand finally outstripped home production. At first the agricultural system was carefully built up but eventually came to full maturity with new systems of rotation, improved fertility, heavier stocking, and mixed grain and animal husbandry, which enabled farmers to meet the upsurge in demand. The social and economic effects of reorganization and expansion, the significance of the enclosures, price movements, agricultural rents and wages, and labour conditions, are also treated at length.

1401 An agricultural atlas of England and Wales.
J. T. Coppock.   London: Faber, 1976. 2nd ed. 267p. 234 maps. bibliog.

This second edition of an atlas which was first published in 1964 is based on data extracted from the 1970 agricultural census. Its choropleth maps, which indicate the required differences by the density of shading, and their accompanying text, cover the physical basis of farming, its man-made framework, tillage crops, grasslands, horticulture, and livestock. There is a preponderance of coverage in favour of crops because crop data are 'less ambiguous' than those relating to livestock.

1402 The National Trust book of the farm.
Gillian Darley.   London: National Trust, Weidenfeld & Nicolson, 1981. 256p. map. bibliog.

First surveying the factors that determined the location and plan of farmsteads, the traditional building materials used in farmhouses and outbuildings, and the development of the farming landscape, this pictorial volume continues with a tour of the English agricultural regions, describing their origins and their characteristic building features. A third section provides a summary of the problems that surround the maintenance and continuous use of buildings and land.

1403 Farming: sources for local historians.
Peter Edwards.   London: Batsford, 1991. 226p. bibliog.

A chronological survey of farming and the marketing of agricultural products from the Middle Ages to modern times occupies the first part of this comprehensive guide to historical sources such as medieval tenures, estate accounts, Royal Agricultural Society records, and official crop and stock returns. Part two focuses on three important aspects of farming: tenure, the workforce, and technological developments in tools, equipment, and farm buildings. An extensive bibliography encourages further study and research.

1404 **English farming past and present.**
Lord Ernle. London: Heinemann; Frank Cass, 1961. 6th ed. 559p.
bibliog.

Originally based on *The pioneers and progress of English farming* (Longmans, 1888) and first published under this title in 1912, this sixth edition gives the text of the fifth edition of 1935 enhanced by two substantial introductory essays: G. E. Fussell's 'English farming before 1815' and O. R. McGregor's 'English farming after 1815'. Widely acknowledged as the standard text, it takes the form of a consecutive history extending from a discussion on the manorial system of farming and the break-up of the manor in the fourteenth and fifteenth centuries to the technical progress in agriculture after the First World War. Its theme is the transformation of traditional rural society caused by advances in agricultural skills, new methods, the application of new resources, and the inventions of new farm implements. A seven-page list of agricultural writings published before 1700 is included.

1405 **Farm buildings and equipment directory 1992.**
Kenilworth, England: Farm and Rural Buildings Centre, National Agriculture Centre, 1992. 64p.

Manufacturers and suppliers are listed under classified product headings in this directory which also includes a trade names section.

1406 **English field names: a dictionary.**
John Field. Newton Abbot, England: David & Charles, 1972. 291p.
bibliog.

Field names are defined here as the name of all pieces of land forming part of the agrarian economy of a town or village. To agrarian historians they are strongly indicative of the local history, the layout of open fields, crops grown centuries ago, or changes in the use of land. This dictionary interprets and explains the names listed giving their locations, meanings, and derivations.

1407 **Farms in England prehistoric to present.**
Peter Fowler. London: HMSO for Royal Commission on Historical Monuments England, 1983. 84p. bibliog.

This pictorial record of farms, farm buildings, fields, and crops, discusses the evolution of English farming and describes in some detail farm processes and the buildings and landscape in which they took place. Almost a hundred black-and-white photographs illustrate both the ancient and modern landscape of rural England, early farm machinery, as well as some posed romantic late-Victorian views of farmers and farm labourers 'at work'.

1408 **The farmer's tools: the history of British farm implements, tools, and machinery AD 1500-1900.**
G. E. Fussell. London: Orbis, 1981. 246p. bibliog.

Tools for field drainage, preparing seed beds, sowing, harvesting, and threshing are included in this technological history which also deals with barns and other machinery. A chronological list of farm tools, 1523-1904, adds a factual and historical perspective.

1409 Two hundred years of British farm livestock.
Stephen J. G. Hall, Juliet Clutton-Brock.   London: HMSO for the
Natural History Museum, 1988. 208p.

Over 200 photographs and contemporary paintings by nineteenth-century and modern
artists are included in this beautifully-produced book which looks at the development
of more than fifty breeds of British cattle, sheep, pigs, goats and horses. It was
published under the aegis of the Rare Breeds Survival Trust for the 1989 Celebration
Year of British Food and Farming.

1410 A history of the English agricultural labourer.
W. Hasbach.   London: Frank Cass, 1966. 470p. bibliog.

Originally published in Germany in 1894 and revised and updated in an English
language edition published by P. S. King in 1908, this solid work traces the
development of a class of free labourers out of medieval serfdom and the
demoralization of the agricultural proletariat before the Poor Law Amendment Act of
1834 and other social reforms allowed a return to comparative prosperity at the turn of
the century. In this edition the rise of the agricultural labour unions and the small
holdings movement in the period 1894 to 1906 are also considered.

1411 A history of farm buildings in England and Wales.
Nigel Harvey.   Newton Abbot, England: David & Charles, 1984.
2nd ed. 279p. bibliog.

Acting as central storage depots for fodder, manure, and machinery, as processing
shops, as homes for both farmer and livestock, and as the centre of operational
control, farm buildings are among the most conspicuous features of the rural
landscape. This study examines their evolution from primitive post-Roman structures
to the mechanized industrial unit of today.

1412 The English farm wagon: origins and structures.
J. Geraint Jenkins.   Newton Abbot, England: David & Charles,
1981. 3rd ed. 248p.

Published in co-operation with the Institute of Agricultural History and Museum of
English Rural Life, University of Reading, this widely acclaimed and definitive work
examines the design evolution of the wagon; its construction, the wheelwright's craft,
the details of its undercarriage, shafts, locks, ladders, and decoration, and ends with an
eight-page catalogue of wagons to be found in museums.

**1413 Countryside conflicts: the politics of farming, forestry and
conservation.**
Philip Lowe (et al.).   Aldershot, England: Gower, 1986. 378p.
bibliog.

With the Ministry of Agriculture and the farming and landowning community on one
side, and the conservation and protection agencies on the other, a conflict has emerged
in recent years over the impact on the countryside of modern intensive farming
methods. This report shows how the conflict has arisen and presents four case studies
to highlight the differing perceptions of the two opposing lobbies.

Agriculture, Forestry, Fishing. Agriculture

1414   **The vanishing countryman.**
       Edited by G. E. Mingay.   London: Routledge, 1989. 144p.
In the last hundred years English rural life has changed beyond recognition. Farming
has been transformed into a large-scale and capital intensive industry, farmworkers and
agricultural labourers have drastically declined in numbers, but have remained in the
lowest wage bracket, unable to compete with affluent newcomers in village
accommodation. The consequent inequality in the social composition of English
villages today is thoroughly chronicled and analysed in these studies.

1415   **The countryside encyclopaedia.**
       Richard Muir.   London: Macmillan, 1988. 240p.
Incorporating the latest archaeological research and developments in local and
landscape history, this lavishly-illustrated volume contains authoritative essays which
concentrate on the origins and functions of man-made features of the landscape.

1416   **Country life: a social history of rural England.**
       Howard Newby.   London: Weidenfeld & Nicolson, 1987. 250p.
       bibliog.
Dismissing the widespread romantic myths regarding English rural life, this history
explores the causes and effects of the eighteenth and nineteenth century agrarian
revolution when rural England was transformed into the world's first fully capitalist
society. The economic consequences, the changes in the law, the effect of the
Napoleonic Wars, the Repeal of the Corn Laws, the first steps towards unionization,
the changing perception of country living in architecture, literature and painting, the
advent of the European Economic Community, all fall under a thoroughly realistic
scrutiny.

1417   **A history of agricultural science in Great Britain 1620-1954.**
       Sir E. John Russell.   London: Allen & Unwin, 1966. 493p.
Director of the world famous Rothamsted Experimental Station from 1912 to 1943,
Russell presents the ideas of the great pioneers in British agriculture, men like Francis
Bacon, Robert Boyle, Humphrey, and John Evelyn, and reviews the scientific work of
the Royal Agricultural Society of England, the Animal and Plant Institute at
Cambridge, the Fruit Research Stations, and the Dairy Research Institute. A foreword
by Sir Bernard Keen provides a valuable insight into Russell's work at Rothamsted.

1418   **The silent revolution.**
       Quentin Seddon.   London: BBC, 1989. 250p.
Published to coincide with Food and Farming Year, and to accompany a series of
television programmes, this revealing study examines the drastic changes in English
agriculture since 1945 and discusses contemporary farming issues such as genetic
engineering, battery breeding, chemical spraying, and the growth of organic farming.
Finally Seddon peers into the future and discerns an unstoppable biotechnological
revolution and high-tech wizardry tempered with good sense (i.e. fewer chemicals and
natural livestock production). Designer bugs to fight pests and wonder crops for
massive harvests are two of his more startling predictions.

1419   **The land of Britain: its use and misuse.**
       L. Dudley Stamp.   London: Longmans Green in conjunction with
       Geographical Publications, 1962. 3rd ed. 546p.

Professor Stamp was Director of the Land Utilization Survey of Great Britain from
1930 until 1947. First published in 1948 this report opens with a history of the Survey
and continues with separate chapters on land use between 1931 and 1938, during which
period the Survey's fieldwork was carried out; the history of land use in Britain; the
distribution of grass, arable land, and orchards; market gardens and glasshouses;
moorland and rough grazing; forest and woodlands; soils; types of farming; and
wartime changes in land use between 1939 and 1945. For this edition there is a new
chapter on the results of the Town and Country Planning Act up to 1960.

1420   **The landowners.**
       Douglas Sutherland.   London: Muller, 1988. 2nd ed. 133p.

Since this study was first published in 1968 the United Kingdom's entry into the
European Community, the massive influx of foreign wealth, and the arrival of new
landowning concerns, have fundamentally altered the pattern of land tenure in Britain.
Whereas the first edition constituted a comprehensive survey of land ownership since
the eighteenth century, concentrating on the ability of the great landowners to adapt to
changing circumstances, this later edition examines the nature and function of land
ownership as an investment.

1421   **The agrarian history of England and Wales.**
       Edited by Joan Thirsk.   Cambridge, England: Cambridge University
       Press, 1967- . 10 vols in 8. maps. bibliog. (vol. 1 (1). *Prehistory*.
       Edited by Stuart Piggott. 1981; vol. 1 (2). *AD 43-1042*. Edited by
       H. P. R. Finberg. 1972; vol. 2. *1042-1350*. Edited by H. E. Hallam.
       1988. 1086p.; vol. 3. *1348-1500*. Edited by Edward Miller. 1991. 982p.;
       vol. 4. *1500-1640*. Edited by Joan Thirsk. 1967. 919p.; vol. 5 (1). *1640-
       1750 Regional farming systems*. Edited by Joan Thirsk. 1984. 480p.;
       vol. 5 (2). *1640-1750 Agrarian change*. Edited by Joan Thirsk. 1985.
       952p.; vol. 6. *1750-1850*. Edited by G. E. Mingay. 1989. 1215p.; vol.
       7. *1850-1914*. Edited by E. J. T. Collins. Not yet published; vol. 8.
       1914-1939. Edited by E. H. Whetham. 1978).

Based on extensive research in local record offices and in the national archives, this
exhaustive history presents an authoritative assessment and analysis of agrarian
methods and techniques over three millennia. Changes in the rural landscape, the
pattern of land settlement, estate management, the diversification of agriculture,
tenurial relationships, farming practices, building developments, yield ratios, and
marketing, are among the many topics discussed. The long delay in the appearance of
some volumes since the series' inception has called into question the currency of some
of the information printed in at least one volume. P. J. Fowler's *The farming of
prehistoric Britain* (1983. 246p. bibliog.) is a revised version of volume one (one).

1422   **A history of British livestock husbandry to 1700.**
R. Trow-Smith.   London: Routledge & Kegan Paul, 1957. 286p.
bibliog.
This volume and its successor, *A history of British livestock husbandry 1700-1900.*
(R. Trow-Smith.   London: Routledge & Kegan Paul, 1959. 351p. bibliog.) are widely
acknowledged as the definitive work on the origins and evolution of British breeds of
farm animals and the techniques of animal husbandry in Britain.

1423   **English parliamentary enclosure: its historical geography and economic history.**
Michael Turner.   Folkestone, England: Dawson, 1980. 247p. 3 maps.
bibliog. (Studies in Historical Geography).
During the period 1750-1850 up to seven million acres, one fifth of the total acreage of
England, were enclosed by acts of Parliament. Based on data taken from W. E. Tate's
A Domesday of English enclosure acts (1978), which Turner edited, this study
appraises the economic effects of these enclosures on prices, interest rates, harvest
yields, and population change.

1424   **Farm buildings in England and Wales.**
John Woodford.   London: Routledge & Kegan Paul, 1983. 150p.
bibliog.
Sixty-eight different types of farm buildings, divided into four categories, buildings
designed for livestock, for crops, processing and equipment, for auxiliary purposes,
and as farmsteads, are described and illustrated in this historical survey.

Forestry

1425   **British woodland produce.**
J. R. Aaron, E. G. Richards.   London: Stobart Davies, 1990. 224p.
bibliog.
This comprehensive account of the properties and uses of trees commonly grown in
British woodlands includes chapters on sawlogs and their conversion to sawn timber,
fencing; posts and preservation; fuelwood, charcoal, and wood gas and fire resistance;
the properties of coniferous and broadleaf species; the chemistry and structure of wood
and their implications for pulp production; and organizations involved in wood
marketing. A list of key British Standards relevant to British grown wood is appended.

1426   **The Woodland Trust book of British woodlands.**
Michael Allaby.   Newton Abbot, England: David & Charles, 1986.
224p. bibliog.
British woodland, the last remnants of the expanse of ancient 'wildwood', is fast
disappearing and being replaced if at all by commercial conifer forests. This
comprehensive study describes its principal trees and wild life, its unique ecosystem of
self-sustaining trees and other plants, animals, insects, and soil organisms, and includes

a thirty-five page descriptive gazetteer of woods and forests belong to or managed by the Woodland Trust, the National Trust, and the Forestry Commission, which are mostly accessible to the public, and a glossary of forestry terms.

1427 **The Shell book of country crafts.**
James Arnold. London: John Baker, 1968. 358p. bibliog.
This handy guide encompasses woodland and coppice industries, chairmaking, farriery, wrought-ironwork, wheelwrighting, thatching, wood-carving, pottery, dry-stone walling, saddlery, and many other crafts. It 'makes no distinction between those which are thriving, those which are no longer practised, and those which have been revived'.

1428 **Farm woodland management.**
John Blyth, Julian Evans, William E. S. Mutch, Caroline Sidwell.
Ipswich, England: Farming Press, 1991. 2nd ed. 196p. bibliog.
A compendium for all farmers involved in woodland management, this authoritative study considers the types and value of woodland, woodland improvements, hedges and hedgerow trees, woodland harvest, the agencies involved in land use, and, in this edition, details of recent government incentive schemes and tax concessions for woodland planting. A twelve-page appendix provides notes on the more important tree species commonly found on farms and suitable for farm planting.

1429 **The effects of the great storm: report of the Technical Coordination Committee.**
London: HMSO for the Department of the Environment, 1988. 52p.
To the great embarrassment of the BBC Television weatherman who confidently predicted that there would be no hurricane, storm force winds of well over 100 miles per hour swept across the southeastern corner of England in the early hours of 16 October 1987, the greatest storm disaster experienced in England since 1703. Serious damage was done to woodlands, nature reserves, parks and gardens, commercial nurseries, and to urban trees. This report presents guidelines for the management of damaged woods, makes recommendations for a replanting policy, and calls for long-term government funding.

1430 **Forestry Commission.**
London: HMSO, 1981. rev. ed. 8p. (Sectional List, no. 31).
Annual reports, bulletins, work studies, tables, forest records in book and leaflet form relating to silviculture, forest pathology, arboriculture, forest entomology, wildlife conservation, timber harvesting, and recreation and landscape, are listed in this catalogue.

1431 **The forests of England.**
Peter J. Neville Havins. London: Robert Hale, 1976. 208p. bibliog.
This survey of England's woodland landscape ranges from prehistoric times to the present. After a long period of gradual disappearance of the vast tracts of forest which once covered the English lowlands, there are encouraging signs of partial recovery. Specific topics of interest include the medieval laws of the forest, 'Greenwood' outlaws, surviving forests, and forest wildlife.

1432 **Forestry practice.**
Edited by B. G. Hibberd. London: HMSO for the Department of
the Environment, 1991. 239p. bibliog. (Forestry Commission
Handbook no. 6).

Intended for forest and woodland owners and managers, and for forestry students, this
handbook encompasses all aspects of British forestry: seed, nursery practice, tree
improvement, diseases and disorders, insect pests, wildlife management, wind
influences, timber production, forest roads, and recreation. Its bibliography includes a
subject index to all Forestry Commission publications.

1433 **Urban forestry practice.**
Edited by B. G. Hibberd. London: HMSO for the Department of
the Environment, 1989. 150p. bibliog. (Forestry Commission
Handbook no. 5).

Offering practical advice and information on the establishment and subsequent
management of trees and woodlands in urban and urban fringe areas, this handbook
includes a short history of urban forestry in Britain, a glossary, and a section on the
main diseases and pests of urban trees.

1434 **The forester's companion.**
N. D. G. James. Oxford: Blackwell, 1982. 3rd ed. 381p.

Published in co-operation with the Royal Forestry Society of England, Wales and
Northern Ireland, this concise and compact compendium of information on all aspects
of British forestry opens with short notes on broadleaf and conifer trees grown for
timber production. There follow sections on nursery work, planting, timber measuring,
forestry protection, diseases and pests, felling, extraction and transport, valuation and
the sale of timber, gates and fencing, hedges, amenity organizations connected with
forestry, forest gardens and parks, education and training, books, periodicals and
libraries, machinery and equipment, and a calendar of forestry work.

1435 **Forestry in the English landscape: a study of the cultivation of trees and
their relationship to natural amenity and plantation design.**
Roger Miles. London: Faber, 1967. 303p. 3 maps. bibliog.

A professional forester and landscape architect involved for many years in rural
planning, Roger Miles expertly relates the decline and revival of English forestry since
the late seventeenth century, the progress of the leisure and amenity movement, and
the establishment of the National Parks. After this general review he concentrates on
the Exmoor National Park which pioneered large-scale afforestation and woodland
surveys in England.

1436 **Trees and woodland in the British landscape.**
Oliver Rackham. London: Dent, 1976. 204p. maps. bibliog.
(Archaeology in the Field).

This disturbing account of the trees in Britain's woods and forests includes a history of
woodland management and of the irresponsible destruction of a large part of Britain's
woodland heritage.

Fishing

1437 **The sea-fishing industry of England and Wales: a popular account of the sea fisheries and fishing ports of those countries.**
F. G. Aflalo. London: Edward Stanford, 1904. 386p. map.
Following an account of the historical development and present (i.e. early twentieth-cer ,ury) grandeur of the fishing industry, and chapters on fish production, distribution, legislation, and scientific investigation, a regional survey of English and Welsh fishing ports provides a nostalgic glimpse of the fishing industry's former glories. A sea-fishing map shows the limits of the sea fishery districts, the chief fishing ports, railway routes to Billingsgate, and all marine biology stations.

1438 **The sea fisheries of Great Britain and Ireland: a record of the development of the fishing industry and its world-wide ramifications.**
George Lowe Alward. Grimsby, England: Albert Gait, 1932. 474p. + 55p. 8 charts.
Chapters on the exploration and development of Britain's inshore and deep-sea fisheries, fishing methods, and tide and currents, precede informative accounts of the growth of fishing at twenty-two English ports in this wide-ranging illustrated history. It ends with a detailed account of the work of the Marine Biological Association Laboratory at Plymouth.

1439 **Fish 'n' ships: the rise and fall of Grimsby – the world's premier fishing port.**
John Goddard, Roger Spalding. Clapham via Lancaster, England: Dalesman Publishing, 1987. 107p. bibliog.
A hard-hitting foreword by Grimsby's Member of Parliament, Austin Mitchell, blames the disastrous decline of the fishing industry on greedy big owners, politicians, and government. Based on two documentaries prepared for Channel Four television this history and pictorial record investigates the growth of what was once the world's premier fishing port.

1440 **Fleetwood's fishing industry: the story of deep-sea fishing from Fleetwood 1940-1990.**
Peter Horsley, Alan Hirst. Beverley, England: Hutton, 1991. 155p. bibliog.
The decline of the English fishing industry was exemplified as never before by the dissolution of the Fleetwood Fishing Vessel Owners' Association in 1979. This history and pictorial record recalls the port's early smacks and prawners, the steam trawlers, and the vital hauls in the Second World War. It also includes an index of Fleetwood vessels of over fifty tons 1890-1990 with details of when each vessel was constructed, its tonnage, length and owners, and what fate befell it.

1441 **The British whaling trade.**
Gordon Jackson. London: A. & C. Black, 1978. 310p. bibliog.
This historical survey presents a complete account of the British whaling industry from the early seventeenth century. Every aspect receives detailed consideration: the hazardous conditions the whale fishers experienced in Arctic and Antarctic waters, the huge market for oil and whalebone in the early years, the later demand for soap and margarine, and the fortunes of the leading firms engaged in the industry.

1442 **Atlas of the seas round the British Isles.**
Edited by A. Lee, J. Ramster. Lowestoft, England: Ministry of Agriculture, Fisheries and Flood, Directorate of Fish Research, 1981. 102p.
Seventy-five large loose-leaf coloured charts, with an accompanying text, depict map water movements, seabed features, dissolved chemicals, plankton, fisheries, oil and gas deposits, ferry routes, telephone cables, dumping areas, and marine safety systems.

1443 **Olsen's fisherman's nautical almanack: containing tide tables and directory of British fishing vessels.**
Edited by S. T. Smith. Scarborough: E. T. W. Dennis, 1992. 116th ed. 701p.
Every possible maritime aspect of the UK fishing industry is covered in this compendious almanac: a directory of the British Nautical Institute and other trade associations; a list of ports where ships' compasses may be adjusted; an explanation of compass terms; the distance of sea horizons in nautical miles; the Beaufort Wind Scale; and tidal stream charts for the North Sea. The main sections comprise the tide tables around the British Isles; the location of shipping buoys; a maritime directory of British ports giving information on their approaches, tidal range, port and harbour lights, traffic signals, port control, and facilities; and a list of all British fishing vessels giving their port letters, fishing number, when and where they were built, length, gross and net tonnage, power and owner. A directory of the appropriate government departments, and information on legislation bearing on the fishing industry, and on radio telephony and maritime VHF services, are also captured in this wide-ranging and long-established publication.

1444 **The economics of white fish distribution in Britain.**
R. A. Taylor. London: Duckworth, 1960. 240p.
This report of a study undertaken at the request of the White Fish Authority opens with an analysis of white fish landings, prices, and the pattern of consumption. An extended description of the structure and organization of the fish trade, and an examination of distribution costs, follow.

Labour, Trade Unions, Unemployment

1445 **The miners' strike 1984-5: loss without limit.**
Martin Adeney, John Lloyd.   London: Routledge & Kegan Paul,
1986. 322p.
Industrial editors respectively of the BBC and the *Financial Times*, the two authors
were closely involved in the day-to-day reporting of the strike which proved so
momentous for the trade union movement, 'in which the stakes for the main parties
concerned became so high that the price each was willing to pay, the loss each was
willing to sustain, excelled anything seen in an industrial dispute in Britain since the
Second World War'. Based on interviews with all but the two leading antagonists, this
book is not simply a chronological account of the strike, but an effort to convey a full
understanding of its political and industrial consequences.

1446 **A bibliography of British industrial relations.**
G. S. Bain, G. B. Woolven.   Cambridge, England: Cambridge
University Press, 1979. 665p.
This work 'brings together all the secondary source material, except that of an
ephemeral or strictly propagandist nature, published in English between 1880-1970 on
British industrial relations'. Over 15,000 items are arranged in seven sections; general
bibliographies and guides; employees' industrial attitudes and behaviour; employee
organization; employers' organizations; labour-management relations; the labour force
and conditions of employment; and the state and its agencies. Annual articles in the
British Journal of Industrial Relations update this bibliography. Also of interest is *A
bibliography of British industrial relations 1971-1979* (G. S. Bain, J. D. Bennett.
Cambridge, England: Cambridge University Press, 1985. 258p.).

Labour, Trade Unions, Unemployment

1447 **Dictionary of labour biography.**
Joyce M. Bellamy, John Saville.   London: Macmillan, 1972-1987.
8 vols.

Proceeding as a series of separate, self-contained A-Z volumes, but with a steady chronological thrust, this work enters 'all those who at any time in their lives were part of what we understand in general terms as the labour movement in Britain, either as members of a particular organisation, or because of their ideological attitude and approach'. Volumes two onwards include a list of bibliographies; volume five onwards have special notes on a random sample of organizations, movements and events which have tended to be neglected by others. For example volume eight has short essays on The Guild of St. Matthew, the Church Socialist League, and the British Labour Delegation to Russia 1920. The work is planned on the same basis as the *Dictionary of national biography* but it surpasses that work in its bibliographical coverage.

1448 **Women workers and the trade union movement.**
Sarah Beston.   London: Davis-Poynter, 1980. 326p. bibliog.

The theme of this study is the struggle of women workers to win recognition not only from employers but also from trade unions. One main factor stood in their way: the antipathy and opposition of male trade unionists, in direct contradiction of their own self-interests, by creating a pool of cheap labour threatening their own wage structure, working conditions, and jobs. Their opposition was, of course, a direct contradiction of their unions' socialist principles.

1449 **British labour statistics: historical abstract 1886-1968.**
London: HMSO for Department of Employment, 1971. 436p.

In 1886 the House of Commons resolved that 'immediate steps should be taken to ensure in this Country the full and accurate collection and publication of Labour Statistics'. This selection covers wage rates, earnings and hours worked, retail prices, employment and unemployment, vacancies and placings, household and family expenditure, trade union membership, industrial accidents and disputes, shift working, labour costs, etc. Introductory notes explain the concepts involved and the methods used in compiling the statistical information presented.

1450 **The English labour movement 1700-1951.**
D. Brown.   Dublin: Gill & Macmillan, 1982. 322p. bibliog.

Early trade unionism, Chartism, the emergence of Labour as a political force, the first Labour governments and their fall, and the post-war landslide election of 1945, are some of the main topics which feature in this outline account of the development of working class organizations in England since the Industrial Revolution.

1451 **British trade union and labour history: a compendium.**
Edited by L. A. Clarkson.   London: Macmillan, 1990. 290p. bibliog.

Edited for the Economic History Society, this book brings together four pamphlets originally published in the Studies in Economic and Social History series: *British trade unions 1800-1875* (A. E. Musson); *British trade unions 1875-1933* (John Lovell); *The aristocracy of labour in the nineteenth century* (Robert Gray); and *Women's work 1840-1940* (Elizabeth Roberts).

1452 **Directory of Employers' Associations, Trade Unions, Joint Organizations etc.**
London: HMSO for Department of Employment, 1962- . semi-annual.
Comprehensive lists of UK organizations whose purposes include the negotiation of wages or of wages recommendation are the principal features of this directory. In addition to employers' associations and trade unions these include joint organizations, wage councils, and arbitration boards.

1453 **Women in trade unions.**
Barbara Drake. London: Virago, 1984. 244p.
Originally published for a joint committee of the Labour Research Department and the Fabian Womens Group in 1920, this classic study surveys a number of different industries and unions, analysing the particular problems confronting women attempting to form their own organizations. The main obstacles were lack of recognition by male trade unions, the disruption of women's working lives by domestic responsibilities, little or no job training, and the refusal to grant equal pay for equal work. This edition contains a new introduction by Noreen Branson which gives a biographical sketch of Barbara Drake, and the background to the setting up of the joint committee.

1454 **Under new management: the story of Britain's largest worker cooperative – its success and failures.**
Tony Eccles. London: Pan Books, 1981. 416p. bibliog.
The Kirby Manufacturing and Engineering worker co-operative was set up in January 1975 and collapsed into voluntary liquidation 27 March 1979. At one time the concept of workers' co-operatives seemed to present a rational solution to the acerbic industrial relations that plagued Britain. This study by 'a participant observer' examines KME's history and the attitudes of the trade unionists and shop stewards, the industrial managers, the politicians and civil servants, and the bankers, who controlled and shaped its destiny.

1455 **Employment and training: Manpower plc.**
London: Mercury Books in association with CBI Initiative 1992, 1990. 194p. bibliog.
The CBI Initiative 92 project provides Britain with a comprehensive private sector intelligence resource to compete successfully in the single European market. In order to adapt to new legal requirements and to develop flexible and skilled workforces able to hold their own against European competition, companies will be compelled to engage in training and retraining their human resources. This book looks at the European legal framework, the impact of EC level employment legislation, training strategies for the 1990s, the recruitment and retention of staff, community education and training programmes, and language abilities.

1456 **Employment Gazette.**
London: HMSO for Department, 1971- . monthly.
Labour market data with information on employment, unemployment, vacancies, industrial disputes, earnings, and retail prices, are the principal contents of this monthly gazette.

1457 **Trade Unions and politics in the 1980s: the 1984 Act and political funds.**

Derek Fatchett.   London: Croom Helm, 1987. 135p. bibliog.

The continuation of trade union political funds was made conditional on the membership's approval by secret ballot under the terms of the 1984 Trade Union Act. Members voted overwhelmingly to maintain the political levy in the 1985/86 ballots. This book analyses the history of trade union funding, the relationship of the trade union movement with the Conservative government, and the political implications of the ballot result.

1458 **British unemployment 1918-1939: a study in public policy.**

W. R. Garside.   Cambridge, England: Cambridge University Press, 1990. 414p. bibliog.

Highlighting the argument between traditional economists and more radical politicians, industrialists, and economists such as J. M. Keynes, Oswald Mosley, and David Lloyd George, this study looks in detail at the nature and scale of unemployment in Britain between the two World Wars. As a guide to government policies and their reaction to the persistent patterns of unemployment this authoritative work could hardly be bettered.

1459 **Employment in the 1990s.**

Robbie Gilbert.   London: Macmillan, 1989. 292p.

A measure of agreement is emerging that the best prospect for a marked improvement in the levels of British unemployment is a revived and resuscitated industrial production sector. But this thoughtful study argues that in the long term only by more people working less will there be fewer totally workless. Robbie Gilbert, who was a special adviser at the Department of Employment in the early 1980s, also explores the possible social consequences of large numbers experiencing prolonged, and even permanent, unemployment.

1460 **Banners bright: an illustrated history of the banners of the British trade union movement.**

J. Gorman.   London: Allen Lane, 1973. 184p.

To the committed trade unionist his union's banner, behind which he and his brothers have marched in joy and anger, carries an almost religious significance. This study examines their history, style, and subject matter.

1461 **Graduate opportunities 1992.**

East Grinstead, England: Newport, 1991. 21st ed. 977p.

Following general information and advice on how to set about finding a worthwhile initial career post, this compendium gives detailed profiles and essential facts on some 1,700 employers who are seeking graduate recruits. Another section attempts to match employers' requirements with potential recruits' skills and qualifications. There is also a guide to some 1,500 further study options for those proceeding to postgraduate courses.

1462 **Industrial relations.**
G. D. Green. London: Pitman, 1991. 3rd ed. 280p.
Updated to include the latest statistical, factual, and legal information on such matters as the Social Charter, technological change, union recruitment strategies, and flexible working, this textbook covers every conceivable aspect of contemporary British industrial relations.

1463 **The Warwick guide to British labour periodicals 1790-1970: a checklist.**
Compiled by R. Harrison. Brighton, England: Harvester Press, 1977. 685p.
'Labour periodicals' are defined here as those produced 'by an organised body . . . of wage-earners or collectively dependent employees . . . in the avowed interest of the working class' and those 'produced for wage-earners by members of other social classes who sought to improve them, instruct them, or entertain them'. This checklist enters 4,125 such periodicals arranged alphabetically by title, with details of the dates and places of publication, editors and publishers, an indication of content, price, and the holdings of 138 libraries and repositories.

1464 **Labour and socialism: a history of the British labour movement.**
J. Hinton. Brighton, England: Wheatsheaf, 1983. 212p. bibliog.
At times the tangled relationship of the Labour Party's middle-class leaders and the Party's supporters in the broader working-class Labour movement has led to tensions and disunity. This work unravels the changing relationships of the Labour Party, the trade unions, and other independent socialist groups and factions.

1465 **A history of British trade unions since 1889.**
Oxford: Clarendon, 1964- . 3 vols.
This authoritative, detailed, and scholarly work replaces Sidney and Beatrice Webb's *History of trade unionism*, published in 1894, as the classic history of the trade union movement in Britain. Volume one (*1889-1910*. Hugh Armstrong Clegg, Alan Fox, A. F. Thompson, 1964. 524p.) covers the period when collective bargaining in its modern form began to take shape, when the trade unions played an influential role in the creation of the Labour Party, and when legal and parliamentary struggles established the unions on a statutory basis that was to last for seventy years. Volume two (*1911-1933*. Hugh Armstrong Clegg. 1985. 619p. bibliog.) relates the cycle of growth and decline in trade union membership, the titanic industrial strife culminating in the 1926 General Strike, the establishment of nation-wide collective bargaining in the place of district agreements, conflict between trade unions and government, and the emergence of a new philosophy of trade unionism.

1466 **The rise and decline of the English working classes 1918-1990: a social history.**
Eric Hopkins. London: Weidenfeld & Nicolson, 1991. 295p. bibliog.
Surveying all aspects of the changing life and labour of the working classes since the end of the First World War, this study deals especially with working and living conditions, the standard of living, trade unionism, health, poverty, family life, education, and leisure activities. Their decline is measured in terms of the reduction of the industrial workforce, the widespread adoption of a middle-class lifestyle, and a move from old central urban areas to new suburbs.

Labour, Trade Unions, Unemployment

1467 **British labour history 1815-1914.**
E. H. Hunt. London: Weidenfeld & Nicolson, 1981. 428p. bibliog.
Both the character and condition of the labouring classes and their organized response to changing economic and social conditions are treated at length in this history. So much of the strife between employers and the labour force, and the structure of the Trade Unions, had their origins in this formative period.

1468 **Jobfile 92: the comprehensive careers handbook.**
London: Hodder & Stoughton, 1991. 832p.
Compiled from information held on the jobfile of the JIIG-CAL computer-assisted careers education and guidance system of Edinburgh University, this handbook carries details of 641 jobs and careers covering all occupational levels from unskilled, through craft and technician to the graduate professional. Data on the file includes a job description, the qualifications required, skills and personal qualities which would prove useful, additional notes on the job in question, and references to books and leaflets which provide further information.

1469 **Wages and employment policy 1936-1985.**
Russell Jones. London: Allen & Unwin, 1987. 175p. bibliog.
Against the background of John Maynard Keynes' *The general theory of unemployment, interest and money* (Keynes' *Collected writings*. London: Macmillan, 1973, vol. 7), Russell Jones explains how the principle of full unemployment, advocated by Keynes, and adopted by successive post-war British governments, was formally dropped in 1981 when it was admitted that governments could no longer ensure high levels of employment.

1470 **Employer's guide to disabilities.**
Edited by Melvyn Kettle, Bert Massie. Cambridge, England:
Woodhead-Faulkner, 1986. 2nd ed. 144p.
First published by the Royal Association for Disability and Rehabilitation in 1982, this guide reminds employers what disabled people can do rather than stressing what they cannot, challenges popular misconceptions, and distinguishes between disability and handicap. An opening chapter lists thirty disabilities, explaining the nature and handicap of each, the implications for employment, health and safety considerations, and the sources of further specific and more detailed information. Other chapters discuss the statutory services, disability legislation, good practices in the employment of disabled people, and career services.

1471 **Labour force survey 1990 and 1991: a survey conducted by OPCS and the Department of Economic Employment in Northern Ireland on behalf of the Employment Department and the European Community.**
London: HMSO for Office of Population Censuses and Surveys, 1992. 73p.
Between 1984 and 1991 Labour Force surveys of households living at private addresses were carried out quarterly with households at sampled addresses called upon five times during the year. Boost surveys were conducted during the March-May quarter at over 44,000 households.

1472 **The Daily Telegraph recruitment handbook.**
Edited by Patricia Leighton. London: Kogan Page, 1990. 3rd ed.
212p.

This handbook first explores the key issues confronting personnel managers and recruitment officers in the 1990s, namely skills shortages, the recruitment of ethnic minorities, the use of paraprofessional staff, new selection techniques, and employee vetting. The major section consists of a directory of recruitment agencies and consultants grouped according to their areas of expertise.

1473 **The permanent revolution? Conservative law and the trade unions.**
John McIlroy. Nottingham, England: Spokesman for the Society of Industrial Tutors, 1991. 253p. bibliog.

A complete guide to the trade union legislation of the Thatcher and Major administrations, 1980-1990, and its ancillary measures, which together have revolutionized industrial relations in Britain, this study not only analyses the legislation in detail but examines also its relationship to the wider policies of government objectives. It explains why the trade union legislation was set in motion and considers the response of the Labour Party, individual unions, and the Trades Union Council.

1474 **Historical directory of Trade Unions.**
Arthur Marsh, Victoria Ryan. Farnborough, England: Gower.
1980- . 4 vols.

With introductory passages for each industry, this directory gives for each trade union its foundation date, name changes if any, amalgamations, winding up, characteristics of membership, its leadership and policy, outstanding events in its history, and membership numbers. Finally, there is a note on the sources of information and where documentation may be located. Over 5,000 British trade unions are listed. The volumes are as follows: vol. one *Non-manual unions* (1980. 228p.); vol. two *Engineering, ship-building and minor metal trades, coal mining and iron and steel, agriculture, fishing, and chemicals* (1984. 379p.); vol. three *Building and allied trades, transport, woodworkers and allied trades, leather workers, enginemen, and tobacco workers* (1987. 525p.); vol. four *Textiles, publishing and printing, retail distribution, government and general unions, and miscellaneous industries* (not yet published).

1475 **Trade Union handbook: a guide and directory to the structure, membership, policy and personnel of the British trade unions.**
Arthur Marsh. Aldershot, England: Gower, 1991. 5th ed. 424p.

First published in 1979 this handbook is arranged in four sections: a descriptive analysis of the Trade Union movement, including a discussion on current trends and issues, trade union structure, finance, and legal status; trade union organizations, giving their aims and purposes and their membership; a directory of trade unions, the handbook's principal section; and the addresses of government and other industrial relations institutions. Now in its fifth edition this publication is regarded as the definitive source of information on British trade unions.

1476   **Trades Union Congress: the growth of a pressure group 1868-1976.**
Ross M. Martin.   Oxford: Clarendon, 1990. 394p. bibliog.
At the 100th Congress held in Blackpool in 1968 over 1,000 delegates represented nine
million trade unionists and there were official observers from twenty government
departments, twelve embassies, and fraternal delegates from thirty-eight countries
overseas. In contrast, the first Congress, held in Manchester's Mechanics Institute,
attracted just thirty-four delegates representing 100,000 trade unionists. This study
traces the political career of the TUC, noting its changing relationships with ministers,
Parliament, individual trade unions, and with the major political parties.

1477   **The British labour movement 1770-1920: a history.**
A. L. Morton, George Tate.   London: Lawrence & Wishart, 1956.
313p. bibliog.
Exploring the causes of the considerable social and economic changes that were
effected from the end of the eighteenth century, this work by two Marxist historians
narrates the long struggle of the common people of Britain to secure fair wages,
reasonable working hours and conditions, adequate social welfare provision, and
democratic political rights.

1478   **Women in the workforce: the effect of demographic changes in the**
1990s.
Ginny Nevill, Alice Pennicott, Joanna Williams, Ann Worrall.
London: Industrial Society, 1990. 127p. bibliog.
By the mid-1990s the number of sixteen to twenty-four year olds in the population is
projected to fall by twenty per cent. Consequently employers will be keenly competing
to recruit and retain good staff. This study examines the major issues women and
employers will face, and the part women will play in the national workforce. The
Industrial Society is an independent, self-financing advisory and training body whose
aim it is to develop peoples' full talents and potential to maximise their contribution to
the nation's economic welfare.

1479   **Labour law in Great Britain and Ireland 1979-1990: a bibliography.**
Paul O'Higgins.   London: Mansell, 1992. 320p.
Four thousand publications are entered in this bibliography which is arranged in four
sections: British and Irish labour law, comparative aspects, and international labour
standards.

1480   **Paying for training: a comprehensive guide to sources of finance for**
adult training.
Andover, England: Gale Research, 1992. 5th ed.
Compiled by the Planning Exchange of Glasgow and Manchester, this guide present
details of 103 sources of finance and assistance for adult training. The different
schemes are grouped into national training programmes, Training and Enterprise
Council initiatives, Industry Training Organizations, regional and local training
schemes, and unemployed and disadvantaged groups. Information on each scheme
includes its purpose and description, the type of assistance available, eligibility, and
application and enquiry procedures.

1481   **A history of British trade unionism.**
Henry Pelling.   London: Macmillan, 1987. 4th ed. 344p. bibliog.

The emergence of trade unions from local clubs and societies to the formation of a national organization to seek legal recognition from Parliament, the unions' consolidation in the period 1880-1900, and the problems of national integration in the first half of the twentieth century, are the essential themes of this concise but well ordered history. An underlying *leitmotif* is the continuing union difficulty stemming from an apparent inability to discard attitudes moulded in earlier conflicts. This fourth edition is updated by two new chapters on the Industrial Relations Act and the 'Social Contract' in the 1970s and the trade union movement on the defensive in the 1980s.

1482   **Women workers and the Industrial Revolution 1750-1850.**
Ivy Pinchbeck.   London: Cass, 1969. 342p. bibliog.

With source material culled from Blue Books (q.v.), contemporary literature, and early newspapers, this study, which was first published in 1930, demonstrates that women wage earners existed in large numbers in the pre-industrial economy and that in most respects the Industrial Revolution proved beneficial to women.

1483   **Job book 1992.**
Edited by Jean Postle.   London: Hobsons, 1992. 472p.

Published for CRAC (Careers Research and Advisory Centre), this compendium contains nine distinct sections: the first on job applications and interview techniques; employer profiles; a location guide to employers; professional bodies and their qualifications; an A-Z directory of employers; a section on further education and training; a jobseeker's index; an information section including a glossary of the jargon used in employment circles; and a special section on careers in health care. CRAC is a non-profit making centre based in Cambridge whose aim is to link effectively the worlds of education and employment.

1484   **Six centuries of work and wages: the history of English labour.**
James E. Throrold Rogers, preface by G. D. H. Cole.   London: Allen & Unwin, 1949. 591p.

First published in 1884, this sympathetic history of the struggles and tribulations of the English working classes attempts to show that pauperism and the degradation of the English labourer was the result of a series of Acts of Parliament deliberately designed to compel the labourer to work at the lowest level of wages possible. Even so Rogers remained convinced that the English workman was neither socialist or anarchist and had no desire to struggle against capitalism but simply to improve his position within the capitalist system.

1485   **Occupation and pay in Great Britain 1906-79.**
Guy Routh.   London: Macmillan, 1980. 2nd ed. 269p.

Occupational tables of the population censuses between 1911 and 1971 show distinct changes in distribution by occupational class. Change is slow but its cumulative effect is significant. In the same period pay structure has normally remained rigid although, at intervals, it has changed sharply in response to high rates of inflation. This study provides a guide to the complex relationships between changes in the occupational composition of the labour force and in their pay structures.

Labour, Trade Unions, Unemployment

1486 **British trade unions 1750-1850 the formative years.**
Edited by John Rule.   Harlow, England: Longman, 1988. 275p.
Eleven specially commissioned essays are included in this history, which covers
workers and machinery in the eighteenth century, the roots of trade union law before
1875, the revolutionary period of general unionism, 1829-34, and employers and trade
unions 1824-50, amongst other general topics. There is also a substantial introductory
overview of these pioneering years.

1487 **Labour's grass routes.**
Patrick Seyd, Paul Whiteley.   Oxford: Clarendon Press, 1992. 284p.
After its disastrous defeat in the 1983 general election the Labour Party embarked on a
strategy of modernization to win back the voters. Although there was no clear
indication of the views of party members on matters of policy and internal party
organization, a constant theme was the concept of one member, one vote in order to
democratize the party at the expense of the influence wielded by party activists and the
block votes of the trade unions at the annual party conference. This study examines the
Labour Party's membership and explores their views on the party and its role in
society.

1488 **The state of the unions.**
Barrie Sherman.   Chichester, England: John Wiley, 1986. 175p.
Outlining the problems currently facing British trade unions from new technology
systems, social changes, changing trade patterns, and from unemployment, secondary
employment, and self employment, this study presents a number of positive
suggestions for a new way forward. Instead of a return to the heady days of the 1960s
and 1970s, which so many trade unionists advocate, Sherman talks of fewer unions
without permanent members, a different role for the TUC, and a different relationship
with both government and employers.

1489 **The General Strike 1926.**
Edited by Jeffrey Skelley.   London: Lawrence & Wishart, 1976.
413p.
Seventeen essays appear in this volume which was published to mark the fiftieth
anniversary of the General Strike, assessing its continuing significance in British labour
history. The realities of the nine days of the strike are remembered in a series of
regional studies and personal memoirs backed up by an introductory essay on its
historical background. A seven-page chronology of events, from April 1925 to
December 1926, is also included.

1490 **The British labour movement to 1970: a bibliography.**
Edited by H. Smith.   London: Mansell, 1981. 268p. bibliog.
This bibliography contains some 3,838 entries for books, pamphlets, and periodical
articles, arranged in historical and thematic sections e.g. Socialism, history and theory;
Early radicalism; Labour Party and Labour governments; Trade Unionism; and Co-
operative Society histories.

1491   **Women in British trade unions 1874-1976.**
       Norbert C. Soldon.   Dublin: Gill & Macmillan, 1978. 236p. bibliog.

This is a history of the growth of women's trade union organization from the founding
in 1874 of the Women's Protection and Provident League, the first effective women's
pressure group to foster the awareness of trade unionism for women, to the Equal Pay
Act of 1976.

1492   **A history of British industrial relations.**
       Edited by Chris Wrigley.   Brighton, England: Harvester, 1982-87.
       2 vols.

Aspects of the British labour market, the rise of the mass labour movement, dissent
and strikes, trade unions and the law, the government and industrial relations, are the
principal areas of investigation in the first volume of this authoritative history which
covers the period 1875-1914. Volume two looks at the impact of state intervention on
industrial relations in the 1914-18 War, trade union development and rank-and-file
movements in the interwar period, the growth of white collar trade unionism, the
employers' associations and management strategy, and the importance of social
welfare. Both volumes include a number of case studies.

Statistics

1493 **Annual Abstract of Statistics 1992.**
Edited by Geoff Dennis. London: HMSO for Central Statistical
Office, 1992. 347p.

Described by *The Independent* newspaper as 'the Government's own annual version of
trivial pursuit . . . a source of infinite pleasure to pedants, businessmen and social
analysts' (a formidable combination if ever there were one!), this bulletin, annual since
1865, is the most-quoted source of UK statistics published. Its tables cover every aspect
of economic, social, and industrial life, area and climate, population and vital statistics,
social services, justice and crime, education, employment, finance and insurance,
defence, production, agriculture and fisheries, transport and communications, the
distributive trades, the balance of payments, national income and expenditure, and
personal income and wealth. The data provided usually cover a ten-year period and
complement the figures available in *Monthly digest of statistics*.

1494 **Government statistics: a brief guide to sources.**
London: HMSO for Central Statistical Office, 1992. 44p.

Prepared by the Government Statistical Service (the statistics division of all major
government departments plus the two big collecting agencies, the Central Statistical
Office, and the Office of Population Censuses and Surveys), this annotated list of
government publications containing statistics is arranged under ten headings: general
background and reference, general digests, the economy, defence, external trade,
transport, distribution services, society, environment, and overseas aid. Departmental
responsibilities and contact points are also listed.

1495 **Guide to official statistics.**
London: HMSO for Central Statistical Office, 1986. 5th ed. (revised
1990). 192p. bibliog.

Official and significant non-official statistical sources are included in this invaluable
reference handbook. The content of statistical publications is fully outlined and the
availability of unpublished data is indicated where relevant.

1496   **Reviews of United Kingdom statistical sources.**
Edited by W. F. Maunder (to 1987), M. C. Fleming (from 1985).
London: Heinemann (vols. 1-5); Pergamon Press (vols. 6-21);
Chapman & Hall (vols. 21-), 1974- . (vol. 1. *Personal social services.*
2. *Voluntary organizations in the personal social field.* 1974. 180p.; vol.
2. *Central government routine health statistics. 4. Social security
statistics.* 1974. 257p.; vol. 3. *Housing in Great Britain. Housing in
Northern Ireland.* 1974. 229p.; vol. 4. *Leisure and tourism.* 1975.
115p.; vol. 5. *General sources of statistics.* 1976. 61p.; vol. 6. *Wealth.
Personal incomes.* 1978. 142p.; vol. 7. *Road passenger transport. Road
goods transport.* 1978. 127p.; vol. 8. *Land use. 15. Town and country
planning.* 1978. 219p.; vol. 9. *Health surveys and related studies.* 1979.
356p.; vol. 10. *Ports and inland waterways; and civil aviation.* 1978.
302p.; vol. 11. *Coal; Gas; Electricity.* 1979. 297p.; vol. 12.
Construction and the related professions. 1980. 650p.; vol. 13. *Wages
and earnings.* 1980. 161p.; vol. 14. *Rail and sea transport.* 1981. 268p.;
vol. 15. *Crime.* 1981. 406p.; vol. 16. *Iron and steel.* 1984; vol. 17.
Weather and water. 1985; vol. 18. *Ports and telecommunications.* 1986.
82p.; vol. 20. *Religion. Recurrent Christian sources; Non-recurrent
Christian data; Judaism; Other religions.* 1987; vol. 21. *Financial data
of banks and other institutions; Life assurance and pension funds.* 1988;
vol. 23. *Agriculture.* 1988; vol. 24. *Local government.* 1988; vol. 25.
Family planning. 1988. 220p.).
Published for the Royal Statistical Society and Economic and Social Research
Council, these volumes give detailed guidance on what data are available and facilitate
access for academics, market research workers, politicians, civil servants, and local
government officials. They replace M. G. Kendall's *Sources and nature of the statistics
of the United Kingdom* (1952-1957. 2 vols.).

1497   **Monthly Digest of Statistics.**
London: HM Stationery Office for Central Statistical Office. 1946- .
monthly.
Basic information on twenty topics including population, employment, prices, wages,
social services, production and output, energy, engineering, construction, transport,
retailing, finance, and the weather, is provided in this monthly digest. Its information
covers at least the previous two years in monthly or quarterly tables and in annual
figures for longer periods. *Monthly Digest Annual Supplement* giving definitions and
explanatory notes for each section is included in the annual subscription. These
definitions also apply to corresponding items in the *Annual Abstract of Statistics* and
Regional Trends.

1498   **Sources of unofficial UK statistics.**
   Compiled by David Mort.   Aldershot, England: Gower, 1990.
   2nd ed. 413p.

Substantially updated since its first publication in 1985 this useful sourcebook provides
details of over 1,000 statistical sources published by trade associations, professional
bodies, consultants, employer federations and trade unions, public companies, and
academic institutions. Each entry includes subject content, the source of the statistics,
publisher's address and contact for further information, frequency, and availability.

1499   **Statistical News: Developments in British Official Statistics.**
   London: HMSO for Central Statistical Office, 1968- . quarterly.

Providing a comprehensive account of current developments, this quarterly journal
contains articles giving detailed treatment to selected topics and shorter notes of the
latest developments in other fields. Reference is also made to closely related work not
carried out by government organizations. A cumulative index providing a guide to
developments in all areas of official statistics is published each November.

1500   **Regional Trends.**
   London: HMSO for Central Statistical Office, 1965- . annual.

Titled *Regional Statistics* for the first seventeen of its annual issues, this compilation is
the most important source of official statistics about the regions of the United
Kingdom. Its data, which include descriptive regional profiles, maps, and graphs,
encompass all manner of social, demographic, and economic topics such as population,
housing, health, law enforcement, education, employment, and provide comprehensive
up-to-date information on how Britain's regions are developing and changing.

1501   **United Kingdom National Accounts: The CSO Blue Book.**
   London: HMSO for Central Statistical Office, 1941- . annual.

Titled *National Income and Expenditure* up to 1983, and popularly known as *The Blue
Book*, this annual publication examines all aspects of the UK economy. It covers
industry; capital and financial accounts for the private sector, companies, public
corporations, and central and local government; and the current wealth of the nation in
terms of investment and capital consumption. Statistical tables go back twenty-two
years. Containing details of the concepts, definitions, statistical sources, methods of
compilation, and reliability of the various statistical series which together comprise the
national accounts, *United Kingdom national accounts sources and methods* (1985. rev.
ed. 285p.) is a definitive guide for analysis and forecasting. Earlier editions of this title
were published in 1956 and 1968.

1502   **Keeping score: the first fifty years of the Central Statistical Office.**
   Reg Ward, Ted Doggett.   London: Central Office of Information and
   the Central Statistical Office, 1991. 177p.

Based on personal reminiscences as well as minutes of meetings and public records,
this is an informative guide not only to the work of the CSO since its inception in 1941
but also to the earlier collection of trade and economic statistics ranging back to the
mid-eighteenth century.

Statistics

A-Z of UK marketing data.
See item no. 1296.

Overseas trade statistics.
See item no. 1307.

Retail prices.
See item no. 1308.

United Kingdom balance of payments.
See item no. 1311.

Transport statistics.
See item no. 1322.

Agricultural statistics of the United Kingdom.
See item no. 1392.

Environment, Planning, Green Issues

1503 **Acidity in United Kingdom fresh waters: second report of the UK Acid Waters Review Group.**
London: HMSO for the Department of the Environment, 1989. 62p. maps.
Scientists now better understand the differences between naturally acid waters and those which have been chemically polluted. This report examines this process and the consequences of acidification on water plants and wildlife. It also reviews historical and future trends, including the management and recovery rates of polluted waters.

1504 **Acid rain and the environment.**
London: British Library, 1984-1992. 3 vols.
Acid rain constitutes one of today's most serious environmental problems needing constant and careful monitoring and evaluation. These three bibliographies; *1980-1984* by Peggy Farmer; *1984-1988* and *1988-1991* both by Lesley Grayson, record the literature over the last decade.

1505 **What you can do for conservation – at work and at home: the Shell Better Britain campaign guide.**
Michael Allaby. London: Bloomsbury, 1990. 216p.
Published in association with Shell whose twenty-year old Better Britain campaign has sponsored conservation groups all over Britain, this guide shifts the onus for environment improvements away from governments, international agencies, and multinational companies, and concentrates more on what individuals can do at work.

Environment, Planning, Green Issues

1506   **A people's charter? Forty years of the National Parks and Access to the Countryside Act 1949.**
Edited by John Blunden, Nigel Curry.   London: HMSO for
Countryside Commission, 1989. 299p. 7 maps. bibliog.

The National Parks and Access to the Countryside Act, the first comprehensive legislation dealing with the protection and enjoyment of the countryside, undoubtedly laid the foundation of many of the statutory recreation powers that exist today. This publication marks its fortieth anniversary and records and evaluates progress in conservation of the countryside since it was placed on the Statute Book. It relates how the various countryside groups came together to bring pressure on the Government, and reflects on the success of the policy of designating areas of outstanding beauty.

1507   **New green pages: a directory of natural products, services, resources and ideas.**
Compiled by John Button.   London: Macdonald Optima, 1990. 352p.
bibliog.

A detailed and practical guide to a 'green lifestyle', this work was originally published as *Green pages* in 1988. One third of this version is taken up with either new or radically revised material. Products and areas covered include wholefoods, the environment, the home, clothes, health, therapy and spirituality, work and leisure, and technology. A useful guide to other information sources is included.

1508   **The greenhouse effect and terrestrial ecosystems of the UK.**
Edited by M. G. R. Cannell, M. D. Hooper.   London: HMSO for
the Institute of Terrestrial Ecology, 1990. 56p.

This collection of scientific research papers weighs up the current evidence for a 'greenhouse' effect on UK soils, plants, animals, and ecosystems. Some areas for future research are suggested.

1509   **The evolution of British town planning: a history of town planning in the United Kingdom during the 20th century and of the Royal Town Planning Institute, 1914-74.**
Gordon E. Cherry.   Leighton Buzzard, England: Leonard Hill, 1974.
275p.

Three main aspects of town planning are discussed in this diamond jubilee volume: the legal framework since the first Town Planning Act of 1909; the development of town planning practice; and the growth of the town planning profession.

1510   **Cleaner technology in the UK.**
London: HMSO for Department of Trade and Industry, 1991. 132p.

Identifying the most significant pressing environmental problems faced by the chemical, agrochemical, metal manufacturing, food processing, and waste incinerating industries, this study also examines work already in hand to improve matters and areas of cleaner technology with the potential for further development.

1511 **Conservation sourcebook.**
London: HMSO for the Conservation Unit, Museums & Galleries
Commission, 1991. 122p.

Completely revised and updated, this sourcebook provides information on many
diverse national and regional organizations concerned with the conservation of
buildings and other objects in the UK. It ranges over the entire spectrum of heritage
activities: research organizations, preservation societies, collectors' associations, and
government quangos, giving details of their aims and background, their publications,
their technical advice services, and their grants and awards.

1512 **Countryside: the Newspaper of the Countryside Commission.**
Cheltenham, England: Countryside Commission. 1983- . bi-monthly.

The Countryside Commission, whose work it is to conserve and enhance the beauty of
the English countryside, is the official adviser to the Government on countryside
matters. This newspaper is published to provide information about the Commission's
work and to act as a forum for discussions on countryside issues. The September-
October 1992 issue carries a centre-page spread on the work of the Countryside
Stewardship scheme in restoring England's wetlands, regenerating the moors,
recreating the chalk downland, and opening up the coast to the public.

1513 **Who's who in the environment England.**
Edited by Sarah Cowell, revised by Rachel Adatia, Barbara Gibson.
London: the Environmental Council, 1992. 388p.

This directory of national and regional organizations working towards a solution of
environmental problems, compiled from returned questionnaires, provides information
on their aims and activities, their status, publications, special services, photograph
libraries, staff, membership, and local branches.

1514 **Environmental planning 1939-1969.**
J. B. Cullingworth. London: HMSO, 1975- .

This series is the first of the official histories of peacetime announced for publication in
the House of Commons in 1966. Each volume examines in detail the evolution of
government policy, the pressure involved, and the ensuing legislation. Volume titles
are as follows: vol. 1. *Reconstruction and land use planning 1939-1947.* 1975. 283p.;
vol. 2 *National Parks and recreation in the countryside.* 1976. 177p. vol. 3. *New towns
policy.* 1979. 629p.; vol. 4. *Land values, compensation and betterment.* 1980. 582p.

1515 **Town and country planning in Britain.**
J. B. Cullingworth. London: Unwin Hyman, 1988. 10th ed. 460p.
bibliog.

Originally published in 1964, and now substantially revised, this standard textbook on
environmental planning includes chapters on planning controls, the legislative
framework, planning for traffic, recreation and the countryside, new towns and urban
renewal, and regional planning. A comprehensive bibliography of source documents
lists Department of the Environment circulars and inner city research programme
reports, ministerial letters, pollution programmes and reports, and Government White
Papers.

1516 **The urban environment: a sourcebook for the 1990s.**
Edited by Gerald F. M. Dawe. Birmingham, England: Centre for
Urban Ecology, 1990. 636p.

The Centre for Urban Ecology, an independent non-governmental body, was set up by
the Birmingham Settlement 'to investigate ways of improving the quality of the urban
environment, and to encourage more enlightened thinking by decision-makers
concerned with urban environmental policy' (Preface). This is its first publication. It
comprises 1,768 abstracts of books and periodical articles relating to the urban ecosystem, wildlife habitats, animals, plants, monitoring and analysis procedures, and the
human dimension. Secondary author, plant and animal, towns and cities, and subject
indexes, allow for convenient access to the wealth of information provided.

1517 **Drinking water 1991: a report by the Chief Inspector Drinking Water
Inspectorate.**
London: HMSO for Department of the Environment and Welsh
Office, 1992. 272p.

The 1989 Water Act requires the thirty-nine water companies to supply water that is
wholesome at the time of supply; the Drinking Water Inspectorate is responsible for
monitoring their progress. Details of their technical audit, water quality incidents and
research, and improvement programmes, are recorded in this annual report.

1518 **The effects of acid deposition on buildings and building materials in the
United Kingdom.**
London: HMSO for the Department of the Environment, 1989. 106p.
maps.

This report by the United Kingdom Building Effects Review Group publishes the
results of its investigations into the differences in the sensitivities of all kinds of
building materials to air pollutants and into the marked changes in major air pollutant
emissions that have taken place in recent years. It also draws attention to the reviewing
and monitoring programmes currently in operation.

1519 **The effects of acid deposition on the terrestrial environment in the
United Kingdom: first report.**
United Kingdom Terrestrial Effects Review Group. London:
HMSO, 1988. 120p. bibliog.

The Terrestrial Effects Review Group was established to monitor the damage caused
by acid deposition and its related pollutants on crops, trees, and natural vegetation.
This report was produced at the request of the Department of the Environment.
'Major agricultural crops in the United Kingdom', it concluded, 'are unlikely to be
damaged directly by current rural concentrations of sulphur dioxide and nitrogen
oxides'. Nevertheless the report urged that research aimed at understanding the basic
mechanisms by which pollutants affect plants should be maintained.

1520 **Environment.**
London: HMSO, 1991. rev. ed. 68p. (Sectional List, no. 5).

Not only in print publications from the various divisions of the Department of the
Environment but also a large number of other official organizations are represented in
this sectional list.

1521 **Directory for the environment: organisations, campaigns and initiatives in the British Isles.**
Monica Frisch. London: Green Print, 1990. 3rd ed. 263p. bibliog.
Information on the aims and activities of more than 1,500 national, regional, and significant country or local organizations concerned with the natural or human environment are incorporated in this directory. Government departments and other statutory bodies, academic and research institutes, learned societies, trade and professional associations, charities, campaigning groups, and a number of commercial and industrial organizations, are all represented.

1522 **Countryside law.**
J. F. Garner, B. L. Jones. Crayford, England: Shaw, 1991. 2nd ed. 240p.
Garner and Jones outline how recent legislation, including the 1990 Environmental Protection Act, tackles the twin problems of accommodating the public demand for recreation in the countryside whilst at the same time protecting it from irreparable harm and damage.

1523 **Environmental auditing: a guide to best practice in the UK and Europe.**
Edited by Lesley Grayson. London: British Library Science Reference & Information Service, 1992. 66p.
Identifying crucial UK and European regulations, this guide examines current best practice in both private and public sector organizations and reviews codes of practice and standards. Coverage includes the pressure for environmental auditing; legislation and policy; and environmental auditing in industry and local government.

1524 **Green belt, green fields and the urban fringe: the pressure on land in the 1980s: a guide to sources.**
Edited by Lesley Grayson. London: British Library & London Research Centre, 1990. 112p.
This bibliography makes use of a wide range of material retrieved from the London Research Centre's databases, ACOMPLINE and URBALINE. It lists material on government policy, the threat to the environment, land use, commerce and industry, housing, recreation, and the institutional use of land. No attempt has been made to cover the large number of planning documents issued by local authorities.

1525 **Recycling new materials from community waste: a guide to sources.**
Edited by Lesley Grayson. London: British Library, 1991. 154p.
Increasingly, national and local government, industry, action groups, and the general public, are becoming aware of the necessity to sensibly exploit and dispose of both natural and man-made resources. This guide identifies key United Kingdom and European regulations and legislation, good practice in public and private sector organizations, and the costs and benefits of recycling.

1526 **Green rights and responsibilities: a citizen's guide to the environment.**
London: Department of the Environment, 1992. 32p. (Citizens' Charter).

This guide outlines who is responsible for pollution control, people's legal rights, what action can be taken, and where more detailed advice can be found, for the six crucial areas causing most concern. These include the local government responsibilities for litter, refuse collection, and noise pollution; green consumer affairs; air and water pollution; and the conservation of land and historic buildings and monuments.

1527 **Hazard data sheets.**
Poole, England: BDH, 1990. 1,143p.

Over 2,250 health and safety sheets for products produced by BDH to enable their customers to meet the requirement of the new Control of Substances Hazardous to Health regulations are bound together in this compilation. For each product there is information on its hazard class, physical data, fire and explosion hazard, health hazard, first aid, spillage disposal, and suitable protection measures.

1528 **The directory of appropriate technology.**
Rose Heawood, Charmian Lake.   London: Routledge, 1989. 317p.

Appropriate technology is defined as technology which responds to human needs and is not imposed arbitrarily by unrepresentative groups. Specifically it is technology which is environmentally sound, non-pollutant, does not disturb existing ecosystems, and spares the earth's finite natural resources. This directory lists organizations and relevant publications in the areas of land; food and agriculture; health; water and waste; buildings and structures; energy; goods; skills and services; work and employment; and transport.

1529 **Urban trees: a survey of street trees in England.**
S. J. Hodge.   London: HMSO for Forestry Commission, 1991. 32p.

In 1989 the Forestry Commission surveyed 3,600 trees in thirty towns and cities selected at random. This report provides information on vandal damage, tree growth and condition, planting locations, and soil types. It will contribute to the future planning and design of urban tree planting programmes.

1530 **Water pollution law (including 1989 supplement).**
W. Howarth.   Crayford, England: Shaw, 1989. 500p.

This study provides both an introduction to the background and policies of the water pollution regulations and a comprehensive guide to their widest ramifications.

1531 **London: world city moving into the 21st century: a research project.**
Richard Kennedy.   London: HMSO, 1991. 268p.

Published on behalf of the London Planning Advisory Committee to mark the major World City Symposium, held at the Guildhall, London, on 24 November 1991, this research study examines wealth creation, jobs and income, the quality of life, and the necessary enabling infrastructure, for London's urban development in the next century. It is seen as the foundation for a reassessment of London's strategic planning policies.

1532 **Environmental information: a guide to sources.**
Nigel Lees, Helen Woolston. London: British Library, 1992. bibliog.
Highlighting the unique resources of the British Library, this literature guide includes
details of all types of environmental information sources, journals, reports, books, and
databases, which cover legislation, business matters, recycling, waste management,
energy, and conservation.

1533 **The green index: a directory of environmental organisations in Britain
and Ireland.**
Edited by J. Edward Milner, Carol Filby, Marian Board. London:
Cassell, 1990. bibliog.
This directory includes some 5,200 entries for national, regional, and local
organizations involved in environmental issues: natural history societies, government
bodies and quangos, action groups campaigning on particular issues, botanical gardens
and arboreta, animal welfare organizations, common land preservation societies, and
specialist biological study groups.

1534 **Monitoring of radioactivity in the UK environment.**
London: HMSO for the Department of the Environment, 1988. 75p.
bibliog.
This report describes the environmental monitoring programmes to detect unaccept-
able levels of radioactivity which have been devised by nuclear site operators and
government bodies.

1535 **1992 pollution handbook.**
Edited by Loveday Murley. Brighton, England: National Society for
Clean Air and Environmental Protection, 1992. 383p. bibliog.
Since its first publication in 1985 this annual handbook has firmly established itself as
the essential guide to UK pollution law and practice. Updated to December 1991 this
edition provides full details of all relevant UK legislation, and EEC directives,
including the Environment Protection Act of 1990, its subsequent regulations and
implementation timetable, and the Water Acts of 1991. It provides a comprehensive
overview of air, noise, waste, and water pollution, with information on early
legislation, regulatory controls, and likely developments in the future.

1536 **An atlas of renewable energy sources in the UK and North America.**
Julian E. H. Mustoe. Chichester, England: Wiley, 1984. 202p.
16 maps. bibliog.
With its main focus on the UK, this atlas surveys the energy potential offered by solar,
wind, wave, tidal, geothermal, bio-fuel, and riverine sources of power.

1537 **The greening of cities.**
David Nicholson-Lord. London: Routledge & Kegan Paul, 1987.
270p. bibliog.
Environmentalism and ecology first emerged as a persuasive force for social reform in
the 1960s, providing the impetus for improvements in city architecture and planning.
This study examines the historical development of urbanism, nature, and wilderness

347

and how they have been expressed in landscaping, and discusses the range of current 'greening' practices and initiatives in Britain's cities.

1538   **Britain's nuclear waste: siting and safety.**
        Stan Openshaw, Steve Carver, John Fernie.   London: Belhaven, 1989. 207p. maps. bibliog.

Radio-active waste disposal is recognized as a long-term problem. This book reviews the government's policy, the disquiet expressed in Parliament, and discusses the work of the Nuclear Industry Radioactive Waste Executive (NIREX) which was set up in 1982 to solve the civilian radwaste problem in a speedy and efficient manner. How NIREX selects sites for dumping radwaste is given special attention.

1539   **Environmental hazards in the British Isles.**
        A. H. Perry.   London: Allen & Unwin, 1981. 191p. 28 maps. bibliog.

This comprehensive account of hazards and disasters encompasses meteorological, pollution, seismic, geomorphological, and biological dangers, and includes a threefold methodology of study and research into their incidence, causes and frequency, and social impact.

1540   **Pesticides: code of practice for the safe use of pesticides on farms and holdings.**
        London: HMSO for Health and Safety Commission and Ministry of Agriculture, Fisheries, Food, 1990. 75p. + leaflets in plastic wallet.

This booklet and its accompanying leaflets are published for the benefit of farmers, agricultural contractors, and commercial crop growers using pesticides. Essentially it is intended to encourage greater vigilance and control of their use.

1541   **P is for pollution: your guide to pollution and how to stop it.**
        Brian Price.   London: Green Print, 1991. 149p. bibliog.

Pollution is defined here as 'the introduction of something into the environment, by human activities, which causes harm'. This guide, which assumes no prior scientific knowledge, looks at the scientific processes which cause pollution, provides a directory of pollutants from acid rain to zinc, and ends with a section on legal controls, practical measures individuals can take, and on the pressure groups actively campaigning against pollution.

1542   **River quality in England and Wales: a report of the 1985 survey.**
        London: HMSO for the Department of the Environment and the Welsh Office, 1986. 42p. map.

In the 1985 survey of water quality in England and Wales water authorities classified waters as either good, bad, poor, or fair. According to the survey ninety per cent of river and canal length, and ninety-two per cent of estuarial length, is judged to be either of good or fair quality. Some doubts are expressed as to the consistency of methods between the various water authorities to determine these results.

1543 **Poisoned harvest: a consumer's guide to pesticide use and abuse.**

Christopher Robbins. London: Gollancz, 1991. 320p.

Although accepting that pesticides may be necessary, this guide claims that government and industry pay insufficient attention, to the point of neglect, to establishing the degree of risk to health from their use. Supermarkets display a far more cautious attitude to the presence of pesticides in the food chain. There is a detailed list of the main pesticides used in the United Kingdom, showing the foods and other products most likely to contain them. The force and effectiveness of recent legislation and regulations, notably the 1985 Food and Environment Protection Act, the 1990 Food Safety Act, the 1986 Control of Pesticides Regulations, and the 1988 The Pesticides (Maximum Residue Levels in Food) Regulations, is critically assessed.

1544 **The greening of British party politics.**

Mike Robinson. Manchester, England: Manchester University Press, 1992. 246p. (Issues in Environmental Politics).

Based on sixty interview with politicians of the three main parties, between 1986 and 1990, and on analyses of official and quasi-official party policy statements, green briefing documents, and so on, this study assesses the emergence and cost of environmental concern in Britain and the political response. The reasons for the marginalization of the UK Green Party, seen as falling between a UK pressure group and a fully fledged political party as seen in Europe, attract a particularly close scrutiny.

1545 **A new London.**

Richard Rogers, Mark Fisher. London: Penguin, 1992. 255p. bibliog.

People of all political persuasions would agree that London is at crisis point. Behind the façade of the main tourist attractions the city is dirty, overcrowded, its public transport effectively near to breakdown, and with its political infrastructure atrophied. This study, written in association with the Labour Party, by Richard Rogers, the head of an internationally renowned firm of architects, and Mark Fisher, Shadow Minister for the Arts and Media, presents their plan for London's rebirth, one that involves architecture, urban design, and the development of its under-used resources. Recommending that a democratically elected authority for London to concentrate on the city's strategic regeneration, they argue that London should learn to regard itself not simply as the capital of the United Kingdom but as a European city.

1546 **The dirty man of Europe: the great British pollution scandal.**

Chris Rose. London: Simon & Schuster, 1990. 360p. bibliog.

To justify his title Chris Rose points to various incontestable facts: that Britain is the European Community's biggest producer of carbon dioxide, the principal cause of acid rain; that it is the only nation pouring large volumes of sewage into the North Sea; that the British government has lagged behind in implementing measures for diminishing pollution control; and that it has consistently attempted to evade European nitrate regulations. He examines three areas in particular: water pollution in British seas, rivers, wells, and taps; air pollution mainly dealing with industrial exhalations; and urban, domestic, and toxic waste.

1547 **The solid waste and water environmental pocket book.**
Northampton, England: Taylor Marketing Services, 1992. 435p.

Up-to-date information on the personnel involved in relevant government departments, local government, consultancies, and trade organizations, is included in this pocket book which is planned to be an annual publication.

1548 **Britain's planning heritage.**
Edited by Ray Taylor, Margaret Cox, Ian Dickins. London: Croom Helm, 1975. 230p. 15 maps. bibliog.

Arranged in fifteen regions, each with a map and a gazetteer of sites, this historical guide to town and country planning in Britain provides examples ranging from prehistoric sites to new towns and modern shopping centres. A site index and a glossary define the characteristics of the principal Planning Acts referred to in the text.

1549 **Urban planning under Thatcherism: the challenge of the market.**
Andy Thornley. London: Routledge, 1991. 253p. bibliog.

Since 1979 the Thatcherite market-oriented economy has steadily gnawed away at the town planning system created by the post-war welfare state. By linking theory to practice this study assesses the dramatic changes in the planning system, analyses the modifications to the relevant legislation, and investigates the new initiatives which have introduced new procedures in order to bypass the customary checks and balances.

1550 **Motorways versus democracy: public enquiries into road proposals and their political significance.**
John Tyme. London: Macmillan, 1978. 166p.

This record of the author's involvement and participation in public inquiries, endeavouring with little success to halt the inexorable advance of the motorways, is based firmly on his conviction that the motorway building programme constituted the most costly mistake in the nation's transport history. Motorways obliterate living communities which lie in their path; destroy other, more efficient methods of transport; drain badly needed resources from housing, school and hospital programmes; and encourage the nation's dependency on the motor car. To add frustrating insult to grievous injury decisions are made by faceless technocrats, not by the democratic process.

1551 **Who's who in the water industry 1992.**
Rickmansworth, England: Turret, 1991. 284p. 11 maps.

The biographical content of this publication is confined to just twenty-five pages of biographical and career sketches of senior executives of the UK water industry. Basically it is a directory of the ten Water Service companies in England and Wales giving details of their areas, population, water and sewage treatment works, reservoirs, and board members. Information on the National Rivers Authority and government departments and other organizations associated with the water industry is also incorporated.

1552   **Britain and the beast.**
Edited by Clough Williams-Ellis.   London: Dent, 1937. 332p.

An early expression of disquiet at the steady erosion of the British countryside by arterial roads, their straggling suburbs, and decaying factories, this collection of twenty-six articles and essays was intended not only to awake the nation to the perils threatening rural England, but also to act as 'the sort of politico-aesthetic-economic treatise that can move government to action' (Editor's introduction).

1553   **National directory of recycling information.**
Compiled by Jonathan Wooding, Sue Reiss.   London: Waste Watch, 1991. 2nd ed. 114p.

The 1990 government White Paper, 'The common inheritance', indicated the need for renewed emphasis on recycling as a method of dealing with household waste. Under the terms of the Environment Protection Act of the same year all local authorities were required to have a Recycling Plan. This directory provides information on local authority and other organizations' recycling services and facilities.

1554   **Our backyard: how to challenge the threats to your health and environment.**
Edited by Martin Wright.   London: Hodder & Stoughton, 1991. 178p.

Published in conjunction with Channel Four's television series of the same name, this book breaks down the key issues in land development, roads and transport, the quality of food and water, waste and recycling, and major earthworks, and advises on what action private individuals can take when environmental threats emerge. Part two is a guide to campaigning – how to get the support of the media, politicians, and the law.

Science and Technology

1555 Public science – private view.
David W. Budworth. Bristol, England: Adam Hilger, 1981. 183p.

A critical review of British science policy from the mid-1950s onwards, this book is written from the point of view of a scientist who has witnessed at close quarters government policies and practices towards the administration of science and technology. Dr. Budworth demonstrates how unwise decisions have resulted in a waste of valuable scientific resources and he has much to say on the best use of scientific manpower.

1556 Who's who of British scientists 1980/81.
Edited by S. Boff. Dorking, England: Simon Book Directories, 1980. 3rd ed. 589p.

First published by Longman in 1971, this edition has entries for some 5,500 British scientists employed in universities, research associations, and industry.

1557 James Joule: a biography.
Donald S. L. Cardwell. Manchester, England: Manchester University Press, 1989. 333p.

James Prescott Joule (1818-1889) gave his name to the international unit of energy. This biographical and scientific study deals with the sources of his ideas and theories and provides an account of his discovery of the laws of electrical energy. The economic, social and technological implications of Joule's discoveries are not neglected.

1558   The organization of science in England.
        D. S. L. Cardwell.   London: Heinemann, 1972. rev. ed. 268p.
        bibliog.
This wide-ranging study, which was first published in 1957, sheds light on the social
origins of applied science in England and traces the factors at work in transforming the
study of science from an amateur leisure pursuit into a professional and co-operative
vocation. Within this context the development of English scientific institutions, science
education, and scientific research, all fall neatly into place.

1559   British scientists of the nineteenth century.
        J. G. Crowther.   London: Routledge & Kegan Paul, 1935. 332p.
        bibliog.
Every aspect of the lives and work of five famous British physical scientists (Humphry
Davy, Michael Faraday, James Prescott Joule, William Thomson, and James Clerk
Maxwell) is recorded in this biographical study. Crowther contends that it was the
growth of industry that caused the pre-eminence of physical scientists in the ranks of
nineteenth-century British science.

1560   British scientists of the twentieth century.
        J. G. Crowther.   London: Routledge & Kegan Paul, 1952. 320p.
        bibliog.
Joseph John Thomson, Ernest Rutherford, James Hopwood Jeans, Arthur Stanley
Eddington, Frederick Gowland Hopkins, and William Bateson, are the six British
scientists commemorated in this study which explores the relationship between their
discoveries and the contemporary social scene. The main facts of each scientist's life
and an outline of their chief discoveries, are followed by quotations from their
published works, to provide an overall assessment of British twentieth-century science.

1561   Scientists of the Industrial Revolution.
        J. G. Crowther.   London: Cresset, 1962. 365p. bibliog.
Joseph Black, the founder of quantitative chemical analysis; James Watt, the inventor
of the steam engine; Joseph Priestley, the father of modern chemistry, and discoverer
of oxygen; and Henry Cavendish, the discoverer of the constitution of water, are the
four scientists celebrated in this biographical study which emphasizes the links between
science and industry.

1562   Statesmen of science.
        J. G. Crowther.   London: Cresset, 1965. 391p. bibliog.
It is Crowther's hypothesis in this study of nine British scientists of the last two
centuries that the growing role of science in national and international life has raised
new problems for government both in the use of science for the benefit of the people
and in the organization of science itself. Men who address these problems are a new
kind of statesmen. Those singled out here are Henry Brougham, William Robert
Grove, Lyon Playfair, Prince Albert, the seventh Duke of Devonshire, Alexander
Strange, Richard Burdon Haldane, Henry Thomas Tizard, and Frederick Alexander
Lindemann. Their failure to create a scientific order, and to make full use of the
national scientific talent was due, it is argued, to the inhibiting effect of a capitalist
society.

1563 **Current Technology Index.**
London: Bowker-Saur, 1981- . bimonthly.

Formerly titled *British Technology Index* (1962-80) this publication indexes about 20,000 journal items a year in the fields of general technology, applied sciences, engineering, chemical technology, and manufacturing and technical services. Until 1990 it was published by the Library Association.

1564 **British inventions in the 20th century.**
Peter Fairley.   London: Hart-Davis, 1972. 239p.

Centring around the National Research Development Corporation, which was founded to encourage the financing, patenting, and safeguarding of British inventions, this study not only examines its role of liaising with industry, agriculture, and marine businesses, but also relates some of the triumphs of British inventive skill. A brief history of the patent system provides an effective historical background.

1565 **The Newton handbook.**
Derek Gjertsen.   London: Routledge & Kegan Paul, 1986. 665p.
bibliog.

Isaac Newton stood like a Colossus in seventeenth-century English science. Few scientists have equalled the influence he exerted on his contemporaries or on later scientists, and few have written so prolifically on such a diversity of subjects. This handbook reveals his interest in alchemy, church history, theology, chronology, and biblical prophecy, and contains entries for all Newton's published works, with full bibliographical details. There are two exhaustive modern biographies: Richard S. Westfall's *Never at rest: a biography of Isaac Newton* (Cambridge, England: Cambridge University Press, 1980. 908p. bibliog.) and A. Rupert Hall's *Isaac Newton: adventurer in thought* (Oxford: Blackwell, 1992. 448p.). Both are essential reading for a full understanding of Newton's complex genius.

1566 **UK science policy: a critical review of policies for publicly funded research.**
Edited by Maurice Goldsmith.   London: Longman, 1984. 275p.

Nine major fields of government activity are selected for attention in this first review by the Science Policy Foundation of research and development in agriculture; big science (i.e. astronomy and physics); biotechnology; defence; energy; health service; higher education and research training; social sciences; and transport. The central questions addressed include: what should be the policies for the development of basic research; how should they be developed and funded; and how should the state decide on priorities in allocating resources?

1567 **Scientists in Whitehall.**
Philip Gummett.   Manchester, England: Manchester University Press, 1980. 245p.

The Government's approach to science, the role of the scientific civil service, the problems associated with offering scientific advice in a political context, are among the issues debated in this overview of the relationship between science and the Government's administrative machine. There is also an analysis of how departmental research policies are formulated and implemented, and a close scrutiny of the Research Council system.

1568 **Weighed in the balance: a history of the Laboratory of the Government Chemist.**
P. W. Hammond, Harold Egan. London: HMSO for Laboratory of the Government Chemist, 1992. 240p.
Founded in 1842 the Laboratory is now one of the world's most modern analytical laboratories. This history of its work and development illustrates the growth in scientific support of health, environmental and revenue protection in Britain in the last 150 years.

1569 **Highlights of British science: based on the subjects of exhibits arranged for the Jubilee Exhibition at the Royal Society 20 to 25 June 1977.**
London: The Royal Society, 1978. 240p.
Outstanding British achievements in astronomy, weather forecasting, oceanography, agriculture, nuclear energy, electronics, electron microscopy, chemistry, the intra-cellular electrode, biology, and drug treatment for high blood pressure, during the previous twenty-five years, are recounted here by leading British scientists.

1570 **Greenwich time and the discovery of longitude.**
Derek Howse. Oxford: Oxford University Press, 1980. 254p. bibliog.
Charles II founded the Royal Observatory in his park at Greenwich in 1675 with the objective of discovering a method for establishing longitude at sea. Such was the observatory's pre-eminence that the meridian at Greenwich was chosen to mark zero degrees longitude in 1884 in preference to Paris, Washington, or the Great Pyramids in Egypt. This history recounts its progress and achievements.

1571 **The politics of British science.**
Martin Ince. Brighton, England: Wheatsheaf Books, 1986. 227p. bibliog.
New technology springing from scientific research is now essential for strong innovative industries to encourage and to bolster national economic prosperity. Serious questions are raised in this work as to the Government's efficient planning and co-ordination of basic research and its promotion of stronger links between academic laboratories and industry on a declining budget. A transformation is called for in the existing state-funded research system.

1572 **Humphry Davy: science and power.**
David Knight. Oxford: Blackwell, 1992. 248p.
Based on Davy's notebooks and scientific correspondence, this biography underlines his crucial importance in the progress of English science. Besides his pioneering work in the invention of the safety lamp, in the use of laughing gas. Davy was also instrumental in bringing science to public notice and attention in Regency Britain, notably by his lectures at the Royal Institution.

1573   **The Jodrell Bank telescopes.**
Bernard Lovell.   Oxford: Oxford University Press, 1985. 292p.
bibliog.

This authoritative account of the UK politico-scientific scene (1960-1980), describes the visionary schemes for constructing radio telescopes of unprecedented size, the events that led to their abandonment, and the response of the Jodrell Bank astronomers in modifying their existing telescopes. The author was Professor of Astronomy in the University of Manchester and Director of the Nuffield Radio Astronomy Laboratories from 1951 to 1981. Dudley Safari's *Bernard Lovell* (London: Robert Hale, 1984. 320p.) is an authorized biography. Lovell's *Astronomer by chance* (London: Macmillan, 1990. 380p.) tells his own story.

1574   **Out of the Zenith: Jodrell Bank 1957-1970.**
Bernard Lovell.   London: Oxford University Press, 1973. 255p.

This work deals with the main aspects of the scientific work carried out at Jodrell Bank in Cheshire from 1957 when the 250 foot aperture steerable radio telescope came into operation until 1970 when it was temporarily taken out of service for modification and improvement. An earlier work, *The story of Jodrell Bank* (1968), describes the construction of the telescope and the serious political and financial problems that had to be overcome.

1575   **The parliament of science: the British Association for the Advancement of Science 1831-1981.**
Edited by Roy MacLeod, Peter Collins.   Northwood, England: Science Reviews, 1981. 308p.

The British Association has played a major part in British science. Formed in 1831 its objectives are 'to give a stronger impulse and a more systematic direction to scientific inquiry . . . to obtain more general attention for the objects of science and the removal of any disadvantages of a public kind which impede its progress'. This collection of nine essays by different contributors examines the Association's role in scientific impulse and inquiry, its work abroad, and the public perception of science. Jack Morrell and Arnold Thackray's *Gentleman of science: early years of the British Association for Advancement of Science* (Oxford: Clarendon, 1981. 592p. bibliog.) is a brilliant exposition of the Association's progenitors. It used to be the case that for their annual meeting in various provincial cities a regional scientific survey would be published. For example *Durham County and City with Teeside* (1970. 522p.) included chapters on geology, geomorphology, soils, climate, hydrology and water use, civil engineering, biology, vegetation, freshwater biology, conservation, archaeology, history, economic development, rural settlement, place-names, agriculture, coalmining, shipbuilding, chemical industry, transport, population, modern settlement, social structure and social change, education, and a history of Durham. Since the Second World War similar volumes have been published on Birmingham, Southeastern England, Merseyside, Oxford, Bristol, Sheffield, York, Norwich, Manchester, Southampton, Cambridge, Nottingham, and Leicester.

1576   **History of British space science.**
Harrie Massey, M. O. Robins.   Cambridge, England: Cambridge
University Press, 1986. 514p.

Not a book to be approached casually or lightly, this formidable work narrates the
history of British space science after the Second World War. University departments of
physics, combined with government research establishment technology, and with major
British firms in the electronic and aerospace industries, combined to develop a totally
new branch of science. Among the topics discussed are the initiation of the Skylark
rocket programme, the Ariel programme, the European Space Research Organisation,
and significant scientific studies undertaken by British space scientists.

1577   **Science and technology in the industrial revolution.**
A. E. Musson, Eric Robinson.   Manchester, England: Manchester
University Press, 1969. 534p.

Mainly concerned with the development of the engineering and chemical industries in
the UK, this meticulously researched volume poses two important questions: what
were the connections between the scientific and industrial revolutions? How was
technical knowledge developed and disseminated? The conclusions are that the
Industrial Revolution was far from being a product of uneducated empiricism and was
in fact an intellectual movement arising from the inter-relationship of science and
technology in eighteenth-century England.

1578   **Science and technology in the United Kingdom.**
Edited by Sir Robin Nicholson, Catherine M. Cunningham, Philip
Gummell.   Harlow, England: Longman, 1991. 312p.

This authoritative overview of UK science and technology and its associated research
and development since the Second World War is in three parts. The first consists of an
outline of science and technology policy and organization from the late 1940s to the
present day within its social, political and economic context; the second deals with
those areas of technology predominantly state funded such as energy, defence,
agriculture, the environment, health, and space; whilst part three is concerned with
areas where private funding is evident, as in the chemical and pharmaceutical industry.
The guide ends with a directory of research establishments, giving full contact details,
and a brief summary of their activities.

1579   **Going critical.**
Walter C. Patterson.   London: Paladin, 1985. 184p.

'Going critical: reaching the point at which a chain reaction becomes self-sustaining;
starting up a nuclear reactor; asking embarrassing questions'. This unofficial history,
i.e. 'a history of certain key aspects of British nuclear power, told from outside the
British nuclear establishment', spotlights the ways in which successive governments
have poured taxpayers' money into ambitious nuclear projects which have prodigiously
outrun their budgets without success.

1580   **Edmond Halley: genius in eclipse.**
         Colin A. Ronan.   London: Macdonald, 1970. 251p. bibliog.

Although Edmond Halley (1656-1742) is best known today for the comet named after him, his contemporary reputation rested upon his all-round scientific work, notably his treatises on the trade winds and his invention of a marine diving helmet. This meticulously researched work reveals the full scope of Halley's scientific interests and achievements.

1581   **Science and Technology Policy.**
         London: British Library Science Reference and Information Service, 1988- . bi-monthly.

Each issue of this review of recent events addresses the questions of the day relating to science policy: how government and industry allocate resources to education and research in science and technology; the impact of those decisions on the size, structure, resources, and creativity of scientific and technical research; and how effectively British companies exploit new developments. A bibliography, abstracts, and a subject index help to locate specific scientific information.

1582   **English science, Bacon to Newton.**
         Edited by Brian Vickers.   Cambridge, England: Cambridge University Press, 1987. 244p. bibliog. (Cambridge English Prose Texts).

Two issues are highlighted in this study: the development of experimental method in scientific investigation from the purely empirical approach, and the seventeenth-century discussion concerning the proper nature of scientific language. The emphasis is on the 1660s, one of the most fruitful decades in the history of English science, when important papers were published by such distinguished scientists as Robert Boyle, Robert Hooke, Isaac Newton, Henry Power, Thomas Spratt, and John Wilkins, all of whom receive individual attention in this erudite volume.

1583   **British science and politics since 1945.**
         Tom Wilkie.   Oxford: Blackwell, 1991. 142p. (Making Contemporary Britain).

Although British science is extraordinary creative in ideas and experiments in the field of pure science, it seems unable to translate this creativity to practical advantage. Since the Second World War, when it seemed to be established that no modern state can survive without harnessing its full scientific potential, the Government has gradually retreated from its previously active role in sponsoring research. This history of British science and scientists in relation to Government policy charts its fall from the high promise of the immediate post-war years to its disillusion and decline in the Thatcher years of the 1980s.

1584 **Rutherford simple genius.**
David Wilson. London: Hodder & Stoughton, 1983. 639p. bibliog.
Ernest Rutherford (1871-1937) discovered the nature of radioactivity and was the first to identify alpha, beta, and gamma rays. The atom was first split in his Manchester University laboratory and in the 1930s he presided over the famous Cavendish Laboratory in Cambridge and its renowned School of Physics. This extremely well documented biography is a worthy memorial to one of Britain's most formidable scientists.

Visual and Decorative Arts

General

1585 **Guide to the antique shops of Britain 1991.**
Compiled by Carol Adams. Woodbridge, England: Antique
Collectors' Club, 1990. 19th ed. 1,107p. maps.

Arranged by county, with a map coded to locate shops in towns, cities, and villages,
this guide contains details of nearly 7,000 establishments. Opening hours, the nature of
the stock, showroom size, price range, the date the shop was established, and the
owner's affiliations to trade associations etc., are all included.

1586 **The art atlas of Great Britain and Ireland.**
Bruce Arnold. London: Viking, 1991. 489p. maps.

The main body of this 'atlas' which is published in association with the National Trust
(although it is by no means confined to Trust properties) is a regional survey of fine art
collections open to the public and an alphabetical by county gazetteer providing
practical access information and a short critical description of each collection.
Introductory material includes special assessments of the Ashmolean Museum in
Oxford and the British Museum and Victoria and Albert Museum in London.

1587 **The golden age of Anglo-Saxon art 966-1066.**
Edited by Janet Backhouse, D. H. Turner, Leslie Webster. London:
British Museum, 1984. 216p. bibliog.

Rooted in the reign of King Alfred, the religious and cultural revival in the tenth
century encouraged the production of sumptuously-illuminated manuscripts and other
works of art. Published in connection with the exhibition celebrating the millenium of
the death of St. Aethelwold, Bishop of Winchester, this book describes and illustrates
the exhibits – manuscripts, ivories, jewellery, and metalwork of the period – centring
round Aethelwold's splendidly illuminated *Benedictional* which is now one of the
British Library's most treasured possessions.

360

1588   **The Thames and Hudson encyclopaedia of British art.**
        Edited by David Bindman.   London: Thames & Hudson, 1985. 320p.
        bibliog.

Compiled by an impressive array of scholars, this specialist handbook and guide covers
the whole spectrum of British painting, sculpture, and printmaking, not forgetting
medieval goldsmith's work and embroidery from the Anglo-Saxon period to the
present day. Its entries provide information on the more important artists, schools,
techniques, institutions, patrons, and writers. There is also a world gazetteer of
museums and art galleries containing British art.

1589   **The Oxford history of English art.**
        Edited by T. S. R. Boase.   Oxford: Clarendon Press, 1949- . 11 vols.
        (vol. 1. *English art to 871 AD*. In preparation; vol. 2. *871-1100*.
        D. Talbot Rice. 1952. 280p.; vol. 3. *1100-1216*. T. S. R. Boase. 1953.
        331p.; vol. 4. *1216-1307*. Peter Brieger. 1957. 299p.; vol. 5. *1307-1461*.
        Joan Evans. 1949. 272p.; vol. 6. *1461-1553*. In preparation; vol. 7.
        1553-1647. Eric Mercer. 1962. 287p.; vol. 8. *1625-1714*. Margaret
        Whinney, Oliver Millar. 1957. 391p.; vol. 9. *1714-1800*. Joseph Burke.
        1976. 425p.; vol. 10. *1800-1870*. T. S. R. Boase. 1959. 352p.; vol. 11.
        1870-1940. Dennis Farr. 1978. 405p.).

Still incomplete, this history gives similar treatment to its subject as the *Oxford history
of England* (q.v.) gives to general English history. It describes the development of
English visual arts in recognized periods of English history which do not necessarily
always coincide with the beginning or close of artistic periods or movements. Volume
eleven is arranged in six parts: painting and sculpture 1870 to 1900 and 1900 to 1930;
architecture and the decorative arts 1870 to 1920; architecture and design 1920 to 1930;
the modern movement in England; and patronage and collecting 1870 to 1940. All
volumes include extensive bibliographies and ninety-six pages of plates (except
volumes nine and eleven which have 120 pages) chosen to illustrate the different
branches of art discussed and the main stylistic variations of the period in question.

1590   **The fine and decorative art collections of Britain and Ireland.**
        Jeannie Chapel, Charlotte Gere.   London: Weidenfeld & Nicolson,
        1985. 360p. 3 maps.

An essential reference work for museum professionals and art historians, this
monumental guide covers the whole field of fine and decorative arts, arms and armour,
costume and jewellery, furniture, metalwork, toys, textiles, paintings and drawings,
and prints. With the exception of those collections in the care of the National Trust,
and the Department of the Environment, it aims to include all the great works held by
public museums and art galleries in the British Isles. Besides information on access and
opening hours it also gives details of the origins and history of the collections.

1591 **Dictionary of British art.**
Woodbridge, England: Antique Collectors' Club, 1971- . 7 vols. (vol. 1. *The dictionary of sixteenth and seventeenth century British painters*. Ellis K. Waterhouse, 1988. 308p. bibliog.; vol. 2. *The dictionary of eighteenth century painters in oils and crayons*. Ellis K. Waterhouse, 1981. 442p. bibliog.; vol. 3. *The dictionary of romantic painters (1790-1840)*. Geoffrey Ashton. 1992; vol. 4. *The dictionary of British artists 1880-1940*. J. Johnson, A. Greutzner. 1986. 576p. bibliog.; vol. 5. *The dictionary of Victorian painters (1840-1900)*. Christopher Wood. 1978. 2nd ed. bibliog.; vol. 6. *Dictionary of British twentieth century painters and sculptors*. Frances Spalding. 1990. 700p.; vol. 7. *Dictionary of contemporary British artists*. Bernard Dolman. 1981. 553p.).

Although subsumed within a general series title, not all these volumes follow an exact or uniform pattern. For example, Johnson and Greutzner's work was compiled entirely from the catalogues of exhibitions held at forty-nine named galleries and heavily abbreviates the information contained in its 41,000 entries to help keep it within reasonable limits. Nevertheless they all give brief biographical and professional details of an incredibly large number of artists.

1592 **The arts funding guide.**
Anne-Marie Doulton.   London: Directory of Social Change, 1991. 2nd ed. 336p.

First published in 1989 this guide provides a directory of sources available to fund raisers, giving advice on planning fundraising strategies and approaching prospective donors and sponsors, and offering ideas for earning more money. It outlines the policies of the Arts Council of Great Britain, Regional Arts Boards, and other funding bodies such as the Crafts Council, the Museums and Galleries Commission, local authorities funding sources, grant awarding trusts, and industrial sponsors.

1593 **The Cambridge guide to the arts in Britain.**
Edited by Boris Ford.   Cambridge, England: Cambridge University Press, 1988. 9 vols. (vol. 1. *Prehistoric, Roman and Early Medieval*. 308p. bibliog.; vol. 2. *The Middle Ages*. 302p. bibliog.; vol. 3. *Renaissance and Reformation*. 356p. bibliog.; vol. 4. *The seventeenth century*. 356p. bibliog.; vol. 5. *The Augustan age*; vol. 6. *Romantics to early Victorians*. 338p. bibliog.; vol. 7. *The later Victorian age*. 363p. bibliog.; vol. 8. *The Edwardian age and the inter-war years*. 367p. bibliog.; vol. 9. *Since the Second World War*. 369p. bibliog.).

Designed for general readers who are familiar with the arts in Britain these volumes follow a uniform pattern. First a chapter on the cultural and social setting of the age, then a series of specialist chapters by different hands, and finally a bibliography for reference or further reading. The last volume, for example, contains chapters on music, ballet, the visual arts, New Towns, the crafts, literature and drama, the film, architecture, housing at Roehampton, and industrial design. Each volume reveals the changing emphases in the national culture in any one period. A paperback edition was published under the general title of *The Cambridge cultural history of Britain* in 1992.

1594 A dictionary of marks.
Edited by Margaret MacDonald-Taylor. London: Ebury, 1990.
319p. (The Antique Collector's Guides).
The provenance, period, and maker's name, of pieces of metalwork, ceramics, and even tapestry and furniture, can often be deduced from marks when all other sources have been exhausted. This dictionary lists all the essential marks for the student or collector.

1595 A dictionary of artists of the English school: painters, sculptors, architects, engravers and ornamentists: with notices of their lives and work.
Samuel Redgrave. Bath, England: Kingsmead, 1970. 498p.
The aim of this work which was first published in 1874 is 'to include the name of every artist whose works may give interest to his memory, whether to the lover of art, the art collector, or the antiquary'. Only those artists native to England are included. This is a facsimile reprint of the 1878 second edition.

1596 British art since 1900.
Frances Spalding. London: Thames & Hudson, 1986. 252p. bibliog.
Equal weight is given to Edwardian post-Impressionism, to the neo-romanticism of the 'thirties, and to the conceptualism and post-modernism schools, in this concise account of twentieth-century British painting and sculpture.

1597 The artists directory.
Heather Waddell, Richard Layzell. London: A. & C. Black, 1988.
3rd ed. 247p.
Information on art exhibitions, reviews, magazines, and bookshops; a regional directory of art galleries; a section on studios, workshops, grants, awards, scholarships, and prizes; and advice on art and the law, and buying and selling art, are the main features of this comprehensive directory.

1598 The Arts Council of Great Britain.
Eric W. White. London: Davis-Poynter, 1975. 326p.
The author of this study was Assistant-Secretary to the Council for the Encouragement of Music and Arts and to its successor, the Arts Council, for almost thirty years. He was also the Council's first Literature Director. Established in 1946 the Council was incorporated, in the words of its second charter of 1967, 'to develop and improve the knowledge, understanding and practice of the arts and to increase the accessibility of the arts to the public throughout Great Britain'. White scrutinizes the Council's relationships with the various Ministers responsible for the arts, the government departments concerned, and the national network of art organizations. He also takes a close personal view of its work in drama, music and ballet, music, the visual arts, and literature.

1599 **Who's who in art: biographies of leading men and women in the world of art today – artists, designers, craftsmen, critics, writers, teachers and curators, with an appendix of signatures.**
Havant, England: Art Trade Press, 1992. 25th ed. 598p.

Compiled from information personally provided by artists, from artists' clubs and societies, and from art publishers, this work contains some 3,000 (mainly British) artists and 500 signatures. There is also a fourteen-page annotated directory of art academies, groups, and societies.

1600 **Anglo-Saxon art: from the seventh century to the Norman Conquest.**
David M. Wilson. London: Thames & Hudson, 1984. 224p. bibliog.

This work by a former Director of the British Museum illustrates and discusses every important work of Anglo-Saxon art from the Sutton Hoo ship burial, and the magnificent illuminated manuscripts of the period, to the surviving sculptural crosses found in many churchyards. It succeeds Sir Thomas Kendrick's *Anglo-Saxon art to AD 900* (1938. 2 vols.) as the definitive survey.

Sculpture

1601 **The monument guide to England and Wales: a national portrait in bronze and stone.**
Jo Darke. London: Macdonald, 1991. 256p.

Divided into six regional sections, this is principally a detailed descriptive gazetteer of the nation's most significant monuments ranging from royalty and celebrated war leaders, to poets, and local dignitaries. Besides factual detail on location, sculptor, and casting, there is anecdotal material on the monument's commissioning and siting, and the public response to the finished article. Its present state of repair is also noted.

1602 **A dictionary of British sculptors: from the XIIIth century to the XXth century.**
Maurice Harold Grant. London: Rockliff, 1953. 317p.

In his introduction the author remarks that sculpture has never been a major prepossession of the British people and that there is little to record of British sculpture. Nevertheless he has amassed an impressive amount of information on the career details of sculptors although no authorities or sources are cited on the curious grounds 'that the writer hopes he has consulted them all'.

1603 **Dictionary of British sculptors 1660-1851.**
Rupert Gunnis. London: Abbey Library, 1968. rev. ed. 514p.

First published by Odhams in 1953 this dictionary provides biographical details of 1700 sculptors who flourished from Restoration times to the Great Exhibition of 1851. Each entry includes a list of known works either attested from actual signatures, or sufficiently documented from manuscript or printed sources. No attributions are hazarded on stylistic grounds.

1604 **Open air sculpture in Britain: a comprehensive guide.**
W. J. Strachan. London: Zwemmer in association with the Tate
Gallery, 1984. 279p. 10 maps. bibliog.
More than 552 pieces of original three-dimensional creations by 195 modern sculptors,
including reliefs, but excluding statues and memorials, are described, illustrated, and
located in this regional guide. A special chapter on the methods of producing sculpture
relates specifically to the most recent sculpture. A list of sculptors and their works
includes biographical notes.

Pottery and porcelain

1605 **The dictionary of Minton.**
Paul Atterbury, Maureen Batkin. Woodbridge, England: Antique
Collectors' Club, 1990. 370p. bibliog.
Extensively researched in the Minton archives, this encyclopedic work is surely
destined to become the standard definitive history of the company, its wares, and its
craftsmen. Two main sections present a dictionary of Minton ware and biographies of
the artists, designers, modellers, decorators, engravers, and gilders, either employed
by Minton, or associated with the company over its 190 years of production.

1606 **18th century English porcelain figures 1745-1795.**
Peter Bradshaw. Woodbridge, England: Antique Collectors' Club,
1981. 327p. bibliog.
Beginning with a survey of ceramic activities in China, at Meissen, Germany, and in
France, the main corpus of Bradshaw's scholarly study comprises a series of historical
summaries of English factories concerned with figure production, describing their paste
and glaze, their modelling characteristics, and their enamel colours. He also examines
the decline of porcelain figures and the practical aspects of reproductions, fakes,
restorations, and figure collecting.

1607 **A dictionary of British studio potters.**
Pat Carter. Aldershot, England: Scolar, 1990. 187p. bibliog.
Brief career details, including a list of exhibitions held, and an illustration of a notable
piece of work, are given in this dictionary of 170 outstanding twentieth-century British
studio potters. A list of galleries selling contemporary ceramics, and another of
museums with permanent collections of modern pottery, are included.

1608 **Royal Doulton 1815-1965: the rise and expansion of the Royal Doulton
Potteries**.
Desmond Eyles. London: Hutchinson, 1965. 208p.
In June 1815 John Doulton invested his life savings of £100 in a partnership in a small
back-yard pot-house in Lambeth. Published to mark the firm's 150th anniversary this
work traces the rise of the world famous Royal Doulton pottery from that humble
beginning. The evolution of salt-glaze stoneware, bone china, and *rouge flambé*, and

365

the Doulton contribution to the mid-nineteenth century Sanitary Reform Movement, are among the Company's high spots. Information on some 200 former artists and designers, and a complete list of Doulton monograms, trademarks and backstamps, and other guides to dating, appears as an appendix.

1609   **Royal Doulton figures produced at Burslem c.1890-1978.**
Desmond Eyles, Richard Dennis.   Stoke-on-Trent, England: Eyles & Dennis, 1978. 432p.

Resulting from a meticulous study of pattern books, old catalogues, price-lists, trade journals, supplemented by discussions with artists and designers, this collector's handbook contains full details of the figures produced at Burslem during the period under review. Their size and colour, the dates of production and withdrawal, their designers, and other relevant details, are all recorded and illustrated in colour.

1610   **British porcelain: an illustrated guide.**
Geoffrey A. Godden.   London: Barrie & Jenkins, 1974. 451p. bibliog.

This volume together with *British pottery: an illustrated guide* (Geoffrey A. Godden. London: Barrie & Jenkins, 1974. 452p. bibliog.) virtually constitute a visual history of British ceramics from the seventeenth century to the present day. Between them they contain 1200 illustrations specially chosen to cover some of the lesser-known factories. The porcelain guide presents a pictorial coverage of the main manufacturers alphabetically by factory, giving a short history of each firm, and details of the significant artists employed. The pottery volume is a chronological review of the different types of slipware, Delft, stoneware, salt-glazed ware, Whitdon and Sussex ware, etc., being more concerned with the main classes of pottery than with individual makes.

1611   **Encyclopaedia of British porcelain manufacturers.**
Geoffrey A. Godden.   London: Barrie & Jenkins, 1988. 855p. bibliog.

The whole range of British porcelain manufacturing firms from the 1760s, when commercial manufacture of 'china ware' was introduced, is included in this monumental encyclopedia. Shortlived small pot banks, well-known and long-established companies, modern studio potters, and even some manufacturers of the early period which have as yet no attributed pieces, all find a place. For each firm there is information on its working period, its relationship with earlier and later firms, an outline of its history, and an indication of the type of articles it produced. Introductory sections include an article on the basic types of porcelain, a general guide to makers' marks and pattern numbers, and a checklist of British porcelain manufacturers 1740-1840.

1612   **English china.**
Geoffrey A. Godden.   London: Barrie & Jenkins, 1985. 362p. bibliog.

Revised and edited from the author's other standard reference works, this encyclopedic work reviews the establishment and growth of the ceramic industry in England. A thirty-page illustrated glossary of the basic types of English china is included.

1613 **The handbook of British pottery and porcelain works.**
Geoffrey A. Godden. London: Barrie & Jenkins, 1972. rev. ed.
193p. bibliog.

'The object of a ceramic trade mark is to enable at least the retailer to know the name
of the manufacturer . . . In the case of larger firms the mark also has publicity value
and shows the buyers that the object was made by a long-established firm with a
reputation to uphold . . . To the collector the mark has greater importance, for not
only can he trace the manufacturer of any marked object, but he can also ascertain the
approximate date and manufacture' (Introduction). First published in 1968, and
frequently reprinted, this handbook lists manufacturers and factories in alphabetical
order with illustrations of their marks. A pictorial glossary, a checklist of initials, and
combinations of initials, used as marks by British manufacturers from about 1775, add
to the scholarly detail.

1614 **Victorian porcelain.**
Geoffrey A. Godden. London: Herbert Jenkins, 1961. 222p. bibliog.
(The Victorian Collector Series).

Intended for collectors of Victorian porcelain, this illustrated volume provides a
general survey of the main English porcelain factories. Lists of the principal artists
employed, many of them recruited from the Continent, are included. Factory marks,
so vital for dating and identification, are also printed. The author was allowed access to
factory archives.

1615 **Examples of early English pottery named, dated, and inscribed.**
John Eliot Hodgkin, Edith Hodgkin. East Ardsley, England: EP
Publishing, 1973. 187p.

This is a well-produced facsimile edition of a notable work first published in a limited
edition of 550 copies in 1891. It provides an almost complete list of all pieces of early
English pottery of significance, complete with details of when they were made, where,
by whom, or for what purpose. But it is not simply an exhaustive descriptive catalogue,
it is also a directory of early collectors, including the authors, who were responsible for
preserving so many items, and who virtually pioneered the study of ceramics in
England.

1616 **Old English porcelain: a handbook for collectors.**
W. B. Honey, revised by Franklin A. Barrett. London: Faber, 1977.
3rd ed. 440p. bibliog.

First published in 1928 this manual remains the definitive study of English porcelain
1745-1860. The technical and artistic characteristics which distinguish the work of
individual factories are illustrated by examples readily accessible in public collections.
An appendix contains all the well-established factory-marks and there is an extensive
bibliography.

1617 **A collector's history of English pottery.**
Griselda Lewis. Woodbridge, England: Antique Collectors' Club,
1987. 4th ed. 360p. bibliog.

Pottery-making is the oldest surviving craft practised by man. This pictorial history, first published in 1969 by Studio Vista, contains over 760 monochrome and colour illustrations, and describes English pottery from the fragmentary remains of primitive Stone Age ware onwards. In illustrating its trends and developments through the years Lewis pays particular attention to slipware, Delft ware, stoneware and earthenware, the work of Josiah Wedgwood, enamel coloured figures, stone china, a wide sample of popular nineteenth-century pottery, the modern artist potters, and twentieth-century factory made pottery up to 1985.

1618 **Understanding miniature British pottery and porcelain 1730 – present day.**
Maurice Milbourn, Evelyn Milbourn. Woodbridge, England:
Antique Collectors' Club, 1983. 183p.

A definitive work according to the publisher's dustjacket, a preliminary assessment assembled in the hope of forming the foundation for a further work according to the authors' preliminary note, this pioneering study which is based on the authors' own collection deals with pottery and porcelain mostly too large for a dolls house and too small for ordinary use. Providing guidance in dating, it also establishes the general characteristics of miniature ware, and defines its trends in terms of shape, style, and decoration.

1619 **Pewter of Great Britain.**
Christopher A. Peal. London: John Gifford, 1983. 247p. bibliog.

Important for both the novice and connoisseur, this enthusiastic handbook is a completely revised enlarged version of the author's *British pewter and Britannia metal* (1971). It offers expert advice on the acquisition and collecting of British pewter, and on its cleaning and repairing. It is particularly useful for its tips on new types of pewter previously unrecorded and for its warning on the snares of fakes and reproductions. Peal is a former President of the Pewter Society and his earlier works include *More pewter marks* (Norwich: Peal, 1976) which complements H.H. Cotterall's *Old pewter its makers and marks* (London: Batsford, 1929, reprinted 1963) and *Addenda to more pewter marks* (1977).

1620 **English pottery.**
Bernard Rackham, Herbert Read. East Ardsley, England: EP
Publishing, 1972. 143p. + 102p. plates. bibliog.

This is a facsimile edition of a renowned critical assessment of the history and aesthetics of English pottery, first published in 1924, which for the first time established the work of English potters in ceramic mainstream history. In contrast to earlier works which often took the view that English ceramic art steadily improved from the rougher wares of the seventeenth century, the authors take the opposite view that excellence has declined since factory methods and industrial standardization superseded hand thrown pottery.

1621 **Medieval English pottery.**
Bernard Rackham. London: Faber, 1972. 2nd ed. 39p. + 96p.
plates. bibliog.
This detailed study of medieval earthenware was a pioneering work when first
published in 1948. Whilst not drastically altering its general premise that medieval
English pottery can be admired for its nobility of form, this edition has been revised in
the light of the strides made in medieval archaeology which has contributed a great
deal to existing knowledge in the intervening period.

1622 **The dictionary of Wedgwood.**
Robin Reilly, George Savage. Woodbridge, England: Antique
Collectors' Club, 1980. 414p. bibliog.
Almost every facet of the Wedgwood pottery, its wares and manufacturing processes,
the subjects of the decorations employed, and the principal personnel, is covered in
this definitive history of the Wedgwood family firm which takes its story from the early
beginnings of the Industrial Revolution to today's large industrial complex. The largest
pottery and porcelain group in the Western world, it is one of the UK's most successful
exporters.

1623 **The illustrated guide to Worcester porcelain 1751-1793.**
Henry Sandon. London: Barrie & Jenkins, 1975. 2nd ed. 265p.
bibliog.
Worcester is the only porcelain factory founded in the mid-eighteenth century to have
continued an unbroken manufacture to the present day. Helped by access to the
original factory records, the author, Curator of the Dyson Perrins Museum and the
Worcester Royal Porcelain Co. Ltd., presents in this book and its companion volume
Royal Worcester porcelain: from 1862 to the present day. (Henry Sandon. London:
Barrie & Jenkins, 1975. 2nd ed. 265p. bibliog.) an unrivalled history, giving full details
of shapes, factory marks, painters' and trade marks, pattern names, etc.

Metalwork

1624 **History of old Sheffield plate: being an account of the origin, growth,
and decay of the industry and of antique silver and white or Britannia
metal trade . . .**
Frederick Bradbury. Sheffield, England: Northend, 1968. 535p.
First published in 1912 the object of this massive study is 'to extend a knowledge of the
now highly valued specimens of Old Sheffield plated wares; to trace the origin of the
process by which they are made, to give some particulars of the manufacturers and
their factories, the localities, the workmen and the methods employed; with other
details that may be of interest both to collectors and to those who deal in the products
of an old-time industry that has today fallen almost entirely into disuse'. It is still
unrivalled in its field.

1625 **Hallmarks on gold and silver plate: illustrated with revised tables of annual date letters employed in the Assay Offices of England, Scotland and Ireland.**
W. Chaffers, edited by C. A. Markham. London: Reeves, 1922. 10th ed. 395p. bibliog.

First published in 1865 this renowned catalogue includes historical data, tables of marks, notes on standards, and a chronological list of plate specimens. Chaffers' *Handbook to hallmarks on gold and silver plate Great Britain and Ireland* . . . (London: Reeves, 1975. 11th ed. 135p.) is a reduced version.

1626 **Catalogue of rubbings of brasses and incised slabs.**
Muriel Clayton. London: HMSO for Victoria & Albert Museum, 1929. 250p. + 72p. plates. bibliog.

The V & A Museum's *List of rubbings of brasses* was first published in 1915: this 1929 revised edition was reissued in its original form without alteration in 1968. It differs from other catalogues in that its arrangement is chronological rather than topographical. A place-name index allows for location access.

1627 **Old pewter its makers and marks in England, Scotland and Ireland: an account of the old pewterer and his craft.**
Howard Herschel Cotterell. London: Batsford, 1963 reprint. 432p. bibliog.

Illustrating all known marks and secondary marks of the old pewterers, with a series of plates showing the chief types of their wares, this scholarly study was instantly recognized as the definitive work on its subject when first published in 1929. Alphabetical lists of pewterers and their marks, and of marks which bear only the initials of their owners' names, are included. In short, all that was known of the maker, the locality, and the date, of any marked piece of British pewter is stored in this book which is now supplemented by Christopher A. Peal's *More pewter marks* and *Addenda to more pewter marks* (Norwich, Peal: 1976 and 1977).

1628 **Old English plate: ecclesiastical, decorative and domestic: its makers and marks.**
Wilfred Joseph Cripps. East Ardsley, England: EP Publishing, 1977. 519p. bibliog.

First published in 1878, this is a reprint of the 1901 Library Edition. So comprehensive is it that it played a decisive and indispensable part in establishing the systematic study of old plate, virtually non-existent when it first appeared, and its authority is still widely acknowledged today. Beginning with a survey of gold and silver, and their alloys, it continues with a history of the goldsmith's and silversmith's crafts and the complex legislation by which they were governed. Plate marks are the subject of exhaustive examination with over 2,600 illustrations. There are two appendices: a chronological list of the examples used as authority for London date-letters and maker's marks; and tables of the date-letters used by English, Scotch and Irish assay-halls.

1629 **Silver boxes.**

Eric Delieb. London: Herbert Jenkins, 1968. 120p.

Based on the author's premise that any receptacle which possesses a lid, whether it is attached or not, and which is intended to accommodate anything but food, may legitimately be classed as a box, this illustrated study concentrates on the development of the silver box in England from the sixteenth to the late nineteenth century. A strong emphasis is placed on technical developments and on silver box ornament.

1630 **British biscuit tins 1868-1939: an aspect of decorative packaging.**

M. J. Franklin. London: New Cavendish Books, 1979. 215p. bibliog.

'Although examples of decorated tin ware are known to exist before 1868, the advent of the British biscuit tin signalled a new era in decorated packaging' (Foreword). Some 40,000 different biscuit tins are known to have been manufactured in the period up to the beginning of the Second World War. This scholarly treatise, which is based on Franklin's own pioneering collection, includes essays on the methods of manufacture, the shapes of biscuit tins, their designers and artists, a list of biscuit making firms, and a descriptive catalogue of tins, giving their date, company, title manufacturer, size, and history.

1631 **Old silver spoons of England.**

Norman Gask. London: Spring Books, 1973. 192p.

First published in 1926 this is an expert survey of spoons from the early medieval period. A detailed look at the marks on old London spoons is complemented by an assessment of spoons made elsewhere in England. The book ends with some suggestions for their collection and preservation.

1632 **Anglican church plate.**

James Gilchrist. London: The Connoisseur and Michael Joseph, 1967. 120p. bibliog.

'The story of Anglican church plate depends as much on theology and sacramental devotion for its forms as on artistic taste' (Introduction). Both ingredients are traced in this monograph on the evolution of Anglican plate from the ninth-century Trewhiddle Chalice, the earliest extant piece, through the secular designs of the post-Reformation era, to the nineteenth-century Tractarian restoration of pre-Reformation shapes.

1633 **Silver in England.**

Philippa Glanville. London: Unwin Hyman, 1987. 366p. bibliog. (English Decorative Arts).

Four well-documented aspects of silver, that most recyclable of all metals, are presented here: its historical use in England from the medieval period; its craft and governing authorities; its design and ornament; and the development of silver collecting, which includes sections on antiquaries, collectors, and fakers. An extended bibliography adds to the value of this delightful book which is of the utmost value to collectors and students of English silverware.

1634 **The London goldsmiths 1200-1800: a record of the names and addresses of the craftsmen, their shop-signs and trade-cards.**
Compiled by Sir Ambrose Heal. Newton Abbot, England: David & Charles, 1972. 280p.

Compiled from the records of The Most Worshipful Company of Goldsmiths of London, and other contemporary sources, the main part of this invaluable reference work, first published in a limited edition in 1935, consists of an alphabetical list of nearly 7,000 goldsmiths, jewellers, bankers and pawnbrokers who plied their trade in the City of London over a 600-year period.

1635 **Three centuries of English domestic silver 1500-1820.**
Bernard Hughes, Therle Hughes. London: Lutterworth, 1952. 247p.

Each chapter in this carefully detailed work deals with a specific item of domestic silver. The course of its development is explained through each phase of its design, ornament, and manufacturing technique. Long overdue attention is given to production processes such as raising, casting, rolling, stamping, engraving, empressing and chaising, and bright-cutting. The hallmarks of London and the provinces also receive special notice in this practical guide to recognition and identification for the amateur silverware collector.

1636 **An illustrated dictionary of British steel engravers.**
Basil Hunnisett. Aldershot, England: Scolar, 1989. 180p. bibliog.

This is a much enlarged edition of Hunnisett's *Dictionary of British steel engravers* published in 1980. With 644 entries and over sixty pages of plates it recreates the impeccable artistry of the line engravers who played a major part in satisfying the huge demand for illustrated books which surfaced in the early years of the nineteenth century.

1637 **An anatomy of English wrought iron.**
John Seymour Lindsay. London: Alec Tiranti, 1964. 60p. 175 plates.

Essentially a book of detailed drawings with accompanying textual notes, this appreciation of the blacksmith's art and methods extends from the end of the tenth century to 1800.

1638 **Identifying antique British silver.**
T. R. Poole. London: Bloomsbury, 1988. 327p. bibliog.

The principal sections in this guide are an illustrated dictionary of artefacts and a descriptive list of makers' marks. Hallmarks, punch shapes, date letters, styles, and a chronology, are treated in an introductory section.

1639 **The National Trust book of English domestic silver 1500-1900.**
Timothy Schroder. Harmondsworth, England: Viking in association with The National Trust, 1988. 338p. bibliog.

With a biographical appendix of the most prominent silversmiths, detailed chapter notes, and a bibliography, a six-page glossary, an index of silversmiths and manufacturers, an index of collections, and countless illustrations, complementing an authoritative text, this work has strong claims to be regarded as a definitive study. Its approach is chronological but it takes full account of such factors as economic pressures and the availability of alternative materials. Many of the illustrations are of silverware owned by the National Trust and still to be found in the great houses for which it was originally commissioned.

Glass

1640 **Dictionary of British antique glass.**
Douglas Ash. London: Pelham, 1975. 210p. bibliog.
Ranging from the late sixteenth to the early nineteenth century, this compact guide provides a wealth of information on the history and stylistic evolution of all manner of glass objects from the simplest domestic vessels to the most outstanding masterpieces of design. The work of individual artists, manufacturing processes, technical terms, shapes and motifs, the influence of other applied arts, inscriptions, and developments in taste and fashion, are some of the themes encountered.

1641 **English glass: and the glass used in England,** *circa* **400-1940.**
R. J. Charleston. London: Allen & Unwin, 1984. 288p. bibliog.
(English Decorative Arts).
This general history of glass in England from Anglo-Saxon times to the twentieth century is far more than a review and description of historic pieces. More mundane topics like the use of glass for windows, lighting, and medical diagnosis, the main types of glass produced, and the social and technical features exerting an influence on design and production, are all discussed at length.

1642 **A guide to stained glass in Britain.**
P. Cowen. London: Brewer, 1982. 201p. bibliog.
The history and design of stained glass in Britain takes up the first part of this illustrated guide; the second is a county-by-county gazetteer of buildings where stained glass is on view.

1643 **Stained glass in England 1180-1540.**
London: HMSO for the Royal Commission on the Historical Monuments of England, 1987. 104p.
Not only the great cathedrals but also many parish churches possess colourful and intricate medieval stained glass windows. This illustrated work, which explains the basic techniques and development of stained glass in the high medieval period, is designed for the appreciation of both the experienced church visitor and for the tentative newcomer.

1644 The identification of English pressed glass 1842-1908.
Jenny Thompson. Kendal, England: Dixon Printing Co. for the author, 1990. 165p.

Pressed glass was mass produced in England during the second half of the nineteenth century in response to a middle class demand for cut or engraved domestic glassware. This comprehensive guide not only provides an analysis of the characteristic designs of individual firms but also includes original drawings from the Patent Office Design Register never before published.

Furniture

1645 Dictionary of English furniture makers 1660-1840.
Edited by Geoffrey Beard, Christopher Gilbert. Leeds, England: Furniture History Society in association with W. S. Maney, 1986. 1,046p. bibliog.

Compiled over seven years by 400 researchers this definitive reference work must be the starting point for all serious attempts at identifying furniture makers known previously only through faint inscriptions, faded labels, or fugitive records. Entries on the major furniture makers were specially commissioned from recognized scholars. The coverage is wide and includes picture frame, clock and barometer, box, and spinning wheel makers as well as furniture inlayers. Also of interest is *Index to the dictionary of English furniture makers 1660-1840* (compiled by Angela Evans, 1990. 166p.).

1646 English furniture styles from 1500 to 1830.
Ralph Fastnedge. London: Jenkins, 1962. 320p.

'To unite elegance and utility, and blend the useful with the agreeable, has ever been considered a difficult, but honourable task' (*Preface to George Hepplewhite's The Cabinet-Maker and Upholsterer's Guide* London: I. & J. Taylor, 1794. 3rd ed.). This comprehensive historical survey of the evolution of English furniture draws upon contemporary manuals, memoirs, diaries and letters to recreate the social conditions in which designers and makers operated. To add further authenticity there is a list of cabinet-makers and designers, a short list of cabinet-makers established in London in the year 1803, chronologies of the favoured periods of oak, walnut, and mahogany, a glossary, and 100 line drawings and sixty-four plates.

1647 English vernacular furniture 1750-1900.
Christopher Gilbert. New Haven, Connecticut: Yale University Press, 1991. 304p.

Over twenty types of vernacular furniture are distinguished in this lavishly-illustrated magisterial survey by the Director of Leeds City Art Gallery. Furniture made for schools, prisons and lunatic asylums, Quaker meeting-houses, army barracks, alehouses, shops, and railway premises, are all featured, demonstrating that common furniture holds as much interest as more fashionable collected pieces.

1648 **English furniture.**
John Gloag. London: A. & C. Black, 1973. 6th ed. 184p. + 40p.
plates. bibliog. (The Library of English Art).
Intended to describe and illustrate how the evolution and development of all types of
English furniture from the late fifteenth century has reflected changes in taste, design
and decoration, this manual for antique furniture collectors, first published in 1934, has
been updated to include a chapter on the post-war introduction of new materials and
their effect on design.

1649 **The Englishman's chair: origins, design, and social history of seat
furniture in England.**
John Gloag. London: Allen & Unwin, 1964. 485p. bibliog.
This expert history of English chairs begins in the fifteenth century, when a
recognizable native style began to emerge, and ends with the mid-twentieth century
genesis and development of the modern movement in design. It demonstrates the
varying importance of dignity, elegance, and comfort, in different periods depending
on whether social life was formalized, relaxed, casual, comfortable, or downright
careless.

1650 **The dictionary of English furniture from the Middle Ages to the late
Georgian period.**
P. A. MacQuoid, Ralph Edwards. Woodbridge, England: Antique
Collectors' Club, 1983-86. 3 vols. 2nd ed.
This exhaustive work was first published between 1924 and 1927. It includes signed
entries for craftsmen, designers, materials, technical terms, and furniture styles and
provides an unparalleled insight into the history of English domestic furniture.
Edwards' *The shorter dictionary of English furniture* (London: Hamlyn, 1964. 684p.) is
a much reduced version.

1651 **History of English furniture.**
P. A. MacQuoid. Woodbridge, England: Antique Collectors' Club,
1987. 2 vols.
Themes treated at length in this standard and definitive history include the influence of
foreign furniture makers, the social and political context in which a native English style
flourished, and contemporary architectural practices. MacQuoid first published this
book in 1904.

1652 **Adam and Hepplewhite and other neo-classical furniture.**
Clifford Musgrave. London: Faber, 1966. 223p. + 96p. plates.
bibliog.
The furniture of the Adams period continues to be admired for its eloquence and
refinement. This illustrated survey examines the development of Adams' style and its
evolution in the independent work of great craftsmen of the whole neo-classic period,
the Chippendales, John Cobb, John Linnell, Ince and Mayhew, Samuel Norman,
William France, Peter Langlois, and others, who contributed to its development.

1653   **Victorian furniture.**
R. W. Symonds, B. B. Whineray.   London: Country Life, 1962. 232p.

If the eighteenth century was the heyday of the English furniture craftsmen, the Victorian period marked the decline of individual craftsmanship, and the advent of factory produced furniture for the thousands of new houses that were being built. This lavishly-illustrated account studies the furniture of the whole Victorian age, its fluctuations in style and taste, and also the materials used by the leading furniture manufacturers.

Painting

1654   **British historical portraits: a selection from the National Portrait Gallery with biographical notes.**
Cambridge, England: Cambridge University Press for the National Portrait Gallery. 1957. 266p.

The National Portrait Gallery was founded in 1856, largely on the initiative of the fifth Earl Stanhope, to house the portraits of the most eminent persons in British history. This selection of 382 portraits, with accompanying biographical notes, is taken from the 4,000 or more now held.

1655   **British painting, modern painting and sculpture.**
London: Tate Gallery, 1984. 8th ed. 350p.

This catalogue lists all 12,817 paintings, drawings, prints, and sculptures held by the Tate Gallery at the end of December 1983.

1656   **Courtauld Institute Gallery.**
Dennis Farr.   London: Scala, 1990. 128p. (Museums of the World).

Now housed in Somerset House, the Courtauld Galleries were founded by Samuel Courtauld, the rayon manufacturer, in 1931. Their holdings include Italian Renaissance, Flemish and Dutch masterpieces, and the largest collection of Impressionist and post-Impressionist works in Britain. This fine volume which is arranged in chronological chapters provides a short introduction to each period followed by colour reproductions of the Gallery's most notable works.

1657   **British portrait miniatures: a history.**
Daphne Foskett.   London: Methuen, 1963. 199p. bibliog.

Confined to artists working in Britain, this history of portrait miniatures begins with the arrival of Hans Holbein in England in 1526. Illustrated with fourteen colour plates, and almost 200 black-and-white photographs, it discusses the artists, their techniques, signatures, and patrons.

1658 **English painting: a concise history.**
William Gaunt. London: Thames & Hudson, 1985. 288p. bibliog.
(World of Art).

For all its obvious susceptibility to foreign influences, English painting still retains its own individual character. First published in 1964 as *A concise history of English painting*, this guide covers such topics as medieval painting, landscape painting, rural life and sport, eighteenth-century portraiture, watercolours of the picturesque, William Blake and his followers, J. M. W. Turner, the Pre-Raphaelites, and twentieth-century painting.

1659 **The British Institution 1806-1867: a complete dictionary of contributors and their work from the foundation of the Institution.**
Algernon Graves. Bath, England: Kingsmead, 1969. 618p.

First published in 1875 this dictionary adopts the same pattern as Graves' *The Royal Academy of Arts: a complete dictionary of contributors and their work . . . 1769-1904* (1905-06) (q.v.). This is a facsimile reprint edition.

1660 **A dictionary of artists who have exhibited works in the principal London exhibitions from 1760-1893.**
Algernon Graves. Bath, England: Kingsmead, 1969. 314p.

First published in 1884, this is a facsimile reprint of the 1901 third edition of the dictionary. One-line entries for over 25,000 artists give the first and last years they exhibited paintings, the types of works most associated with them, and their memberships of professional societies. Over half of the artists included are not to be found in other reference works.

1661 **The Royal Academy of Arts: a complete dictionary of contributors and their works from its foundation in 1769 to 1904.**
Algernon Graves. Weston-super-Mare, England: Kingsmead, 1989. 4 vols.

This is a facsimile reprint edition of a work first published in 1905. Compiled with the sanction of the President and Council of the Royal Academy, it lists chronologically by artist the paintings hung in the summer exhibitions. It is supplemented by *Royal Academy exhibitors 1905-1970: a dictionary of artists and their work . . .* (Calne, England: Hilmarton Manor Press, 1986. 4 vols.) and a further volume covering 1971-1989 (1989). These are purely factual reference volumes and there is no commentary or analytical text.

1662 **The Society of Artists of Great Britain 1760-1791: the Free Society of Artists 1761-1783: a complete dictionary of contributors and their work from the foundation of the societies to 1791.**
Algernon Graves. Bath, England: Kingsmead, 1969. 354p.

A facsimile reprint of the original 1907 edition, this list of exhibitors extends back to 1760 when the first public exhibition of paintings was held in England. It complements Graves' *The Royal Academy of Arts: a complete dictionary of contributors and their work . . . 1769 to 1904* (1905-06) (q.v.) and follows the same pattern. Accounts of the two societies compiled from Edward Edwards' *Anecdotes of painters* and John Pye's *Patronage of British art* are also included.

1663 **The history of the Royal Academy 1768-1986.**
Sidney C. Hutchinson. London: Robert Royce, 1986. 2nd ed. 314p.
bibliog.

The Royal Academy 'is certainly the oldest established society in the British Commonwealth solely devoted to the fine arts and it appears to be unique in the world as a self-supporting, self-governing body of artists which, on its own premises, conducts art schools, holds open exhibitions of the work of living artists' (Introduction). Primarily based on the Academy's minute books, annual reports, and exhibition catalogues, this scholarly and authoritative review was first published in 1968 to mark the Academy's bicentenary. It covers in detail the Academy's origins, its homes, its problems and achievements, and its famous summer exhibitions.

1664 **British watercolours in the Victoria and Albert Museum: an illustrated summary catalogue of the National Collection.**
Compiled by L. Lambourn, J. Hamilton. London: Sotheby Parke Bernet in association with the Victoria and Albert Museum, 1980. 455p. bibliog.

This illustrated catalogue lists over 5,600 works by 1,600 different artists. Information is provided on the painter, size, and provenance of each item.

1665 **A world of their own: twentieth century British naïve painters.**
Jill Leman, Martin Leman. London: Pelham, 1985. 128p.

In 1984 the Royal Academy for the first time devoted a whole room to naïve painters in their Summer Exhibition, an indication of the growing interest in their work. Forty-four artists are featured in this chronological catalogue which provides biographical and career commentaries to accompany representative colour plates of their paintings.

1666 **Victorian narrative paintings.**
Raymond Lister. London: Museum Press, 1966. 159p. bibliog.

Narrative painting was a genre remarkably suited to the Victorian age. Usually presented in a highly moral tone, sometimes comic, but more often extremely pathetic, it offered a reassuring and sanitized vision of society, glossing over and obliterating its ugly and nasty reality. This scholarly work examines sixty well-known paintings.

1667 **The dictionary of British watercolour artists up to 1920.**
H. L. Mallalieu. Woodbridge, England: Antique Collectors' Club, 1976-90. 3 vols.

Over 6,000 watercolour artists who produced a significant body of work are listed in volume one (*The text*, 1986. 2nd ed. 390p.) along with details of their professional work and publications and the locations where their most important paintings may be seen. Volume two (*The plates*, 1979. 557p.) gives 800 black-and-white plates. A recreation of the Haldimand Collection, dispersed in the 1820s, and a study of a number of watercolours once attributed to Tom Girtin, are the principal contents of the third volume (*A wider perspective*, 1990 288p.).

1668   **The dictionary of British equestrian artists.**
Sally Mitchell.   Woodbridge, England: Antique Collectors' Club,
1985. 517p. bibliog.

Biographical sketches of 870 artists who flourished from the early seventeenth century
to the present day are included in this outstanding reference work. A thirty-page essay
on the development of British equestrian art, a chronology of the main equestrian
artists and events 1600-1980, and a pictorial chronology of dress, saddlery, and the
dressing of manes and tails, complement the sketches.

1669   **The National Gallery illustrated general catalogue.**
London: The National Gallery, 1986. 2nd ed. 744p. (Supplement,
1988. 16p.).

The National Gallery collection is widely regarded as one of the most balanced and
representative collections of Western European paintings, being particularly strong in
its Italian Renaissance and Dutch seventeenth-century paintings. This comprehensive
volume serves not only as an illustrated guide giving brief factual information on all its
2000 paintings and sculptures, but also as a handbook to the major European artists
from the Italian masters of the fourteenth century to the works of Matisse and Picasso.
Normally the whole of the National Gallery's collection is on view.

1670   **Dictionary of British portraiture.**
Edited by Richard Ormond, Malcolm Rogers.   London: Batsford in
association with the National Portrait Gallery, 1979-1981. 4 vols.
(vol. 1. *The Middle Ages to the early Georgians.* Andriana Davies.
1979. 157p.; vol. 2. *Later Georgians and early Victorians.* Elaine
Kilmurray. 1979. 231p.; vol. 3. *The Victorians.* Elaine Kilmurray.
1981. 230p.; vol. 4. *The twentieth century.* Andriana Davies. 1981.
176p.).

From information taken principally from a comprehensive archive held by the National
Portrait Gallery and from *Dictionary of National Biography* entries, these four volumes
list the portraits of some 5,000 figures in British history held in galleries and other
institutions open to the public. For each person listed there is information on their
profession or occupation, and their known portraits either as a painting or drawing or
on a manuscript, silhouette, sculpture, tapestry, stained-glass window, print,
caricature, or photograph, and where these likenesses can be inspected.

1671   **Early Victorian portraits.**
Richard Ormond.   London: HMSO for the National Portrait Gallery,
1973. 2 vols. 626p. + 1,046 plates.

Over 1,000 portraits of people active in the period 1830 to 1860, owned by the National
Portrait Gallery, are described in this massive work which consists of one volume of
text and another of black-and-white plates. In addition to full details of each portrait
(name of sitter, a concise biographical description, medium, name of artist, etc.),
Ormond provides a list of all known images of the sitters, thereby transforming a
catalogue raisonné into a vast index to the portraiture of every major figure of the
period.

1672 **Catalogue of British oil paintings 1820-1860.**

Ronald Parkinson. London: HMSO for Victoria and Albert Museum, 1990. 334p.

Representing roughly half of the V & A's collection of British oil paintings, this catalogue includes landscapes and seascapes, portraits and genre paintings, depictions of famous events, and characters in history and literature, by artists of the calibre of Turner, Millais, and Landseer. Entries are arranged alphabetically by artist; the annotations include a short biographical outline and details of the painting's commissioning and subsequent history.

1673 **Modern English painters: vol. 1. Sickert to Lowry; vol. 2. Nash to Bowden; vol. 3. Hennell to Hockney.**

John Rothenstein. London: Macdonald, 1984. rev. ed. 2 vols.

Widely acclaimed when first published in 1952 these biographical and critical studies of modern English artists, are arranged in chronological order of birth date 'to emphasize the individuality of their subjects by cutting them off from all fortuitous and ephemeral groupings'.

1674 **The Shell guide to the great paintings of England.**

Nigel Viney, edited by David Piper. London: André Deutsch, 1989. 318p. 11 maps.

This descriptive and illustrated guide and gazetteer pinpoints 350 public galleries and private houses where English paintings of some significance are on view. There is a biographical index to the 1,000 artists mentioned in the text.

1675 **Dictionary of British artists working 1900-1950.**

Grant M. Waters. Eastbourne, England: Eastbourne Fine Art, 1975. 2 vols. plates.

Over 5,500 biographies and career details of artists working in the period are included in the first volume of this detailed and comprehensive work. Some 1,100 supplementary biographies and almost 400 black-and-white plates appear in the second.

1676 **Handbook of modern British painting 1900-1980.**

Edited by Alan Windsor. Aldershot, England: Scolar Press, 1992. 400p.

This comprehensive but portable guide, which contains over 1,500 biographies of British artists, outlining their careers, and with a brief characterization of their work, is intended for on-the-spot consultation at art exhibitions. It also covers major collectors and dealers, and includes information on art terms, schools, techniques, genres, and movements.

1677   **National Portrait Gallery complete illustrated catalogue 1856-1979.**
Compiled by K. K. Yung, edited by Mary Pettman.   London:
National Portrait Gallery, 1981. 749p.
Comprising 5,500 entries this comprehensive checklist and illustrated record of every
painting, miniature, photograph and work of sculpture is the most extensive survey of
British portraiture ever attempted. Each entry provides the name, profession, and
dates of the sitter, the medium worked in, size, source and year of acquisition. A list of
paintings grouped in named collections, and an index of painters, engravers, and
photographs, are useful ancillary features.

Illustration

1678   **The Lindisfarne Gospels.**
Janet Backhouse.   Oxford: Phaidon in association with the British
Library, 1981. 96p. bibliog.
Named after the Northumbrian island monastery where it was produced in the seventh
century, the illuminated manuscript known as the *Lindisfarne Gospels* is now one of
the British Library's most cherished possessions. This study tells the story of the
monastery at Lindisfarne, of St. Cuthbert, in whose honour the Gospels were written,
and places the manuscript in its full historical context.

1679   **British print makers 1855-1955.**
Devizes, England: Garton, 1992. bibliog.
This dictionary of printmakers contains entries for 400 artists and includes full
descriptions of the development of wood engraving, etching, lithography, linocuts,
colour woodcuts, monotype, and poster-prints. Checklists of prints, artists, and
exhibitions are appended.

1680   **English prints for the collector.**
Stephen Calloway.   London: Lutterworth, 1980. 232p. bibliog.
With the development of printing and the introduction of new techniques prints
became immensely popular as decorative objects in the eighteenth and nineteenth
centuries. This authoritative illustrated survey covers the works of all major artists and
engravers and many lesser known printmakers, examining their styles, techniques, and
subjects. A final chapter on the care of prints looks at how to frame, mount, and store
them.

1681   **The Department of Prints and Drawings in the British Museum: user's
guide.**
Anthony Griffiths, Reginald Williams.   London: British Museum,
1987. 189p.
Access to the British Museum's Department of Prints and Drawings is not easy for the
inexperienced researcher. No single catalogue or index records the entire collection
which is divided into many different series and sub-collections organized in different

ways whose access and retrieval of information is varied and complex. This handbook is a reliable guide to the collections, its inventories and registers, and to the holdings of individual artists' works.

1682 **The dictionary of British book illustrators and caricaturists 1800-1914: with introductory chapters on the rise and progress of the art.**
Simon Houfe. Woodbridge, England: Antique Collectors' Club, 1981. rev. ed. 520p. bibliog.

Book illustration is defined here as 'any pictorial subject in topography, architecture, genre or literature which aids a text, however slender'. In this dictionary, which was first published in 1978, ten chronological overview essays precede alphabetical entries for 2,500 popular and significant book illustrators giving details of their careers, the books which they illustrated, and the periodicals to which they contributed, exhibitions held, and current museum collections of their work.

1683 **British prints: dictionary and price guide.**
Ian Mackenzie. Woodbridge, England: Antique Collectors' Club, 1987. 359p. bibliog.

Written by the Head of Sotheby's Print Department, and illustrated with forty-four colour plates, and 650 in black-and-white, this dictionary gives brief biographies of British printmakers, and of foreign printmakers, who either worked in Britain, or who reproduced paintings by British artists. It also encompasses plates made for books which are often sold as separate prints. An introductory essay discusses the principles of evaluation, condition and rarity, subject matter, identification, and the various processes used in print-making.

1684 **Dictionary of British book illustrators: the twentieth century.**
Brigid Peppin, Lucy Micklethwait. London: Murray, 1983. 336p. bibliog.

Career details of 800 book illustrators, primarily of poetry and fiction, whose work was first published in Britain 1900-75, are contained in this beautifully produced dictionary. Entries incorporate basic bibliographical information, a list of books and periodicals illustrated, and a list of references to further reading.

1685 **Guide to British topographical prints.**
Ronald Russell. Newton Abbot, England: David & Charles, 1979. 224p. bibliog.

Topographical prints of wild and remote districts of the British Isles, of picturesque scenery, of the early railways, and popular resorts, appealed to a wide public in the eighteenth and nineteenth centuries. This guide devotes separate chapters to each of the major print-making processes: early etching and line engraving on copper; aquatint and lithography; line engravings on steel; wood cutting and engraving; and etching.

1686   **English books with coloured plates 1790 to 1860: a bibliographical account of the most important books illustrated by English artists in colour aquatint and colour lithography.**
R. V. Tooley.   Folkestone, England: Dawsons, 1987. 2nd ed. 424p.

In the first half of the nineteenth century a flood of colourfully illustrated books on travel, antiquities, military exploits, sport, landscape, and inventions, catered for the cultural tastes of the fashionable wealthy and leisured classes of society. Publishers were able to employ well-known artists, engravers, and colourists for book illustration. This checklist, which was first published in 1935 as *Some English books with coloured plates*, now includes over 500 titles. Works on botany and ornithology are excluded.

Performing Arts

Music

1687 A book of British music festivals.

Richard Adams. London: Robert Royce. 1986. 224p. 2 maps.

'A music festival is a garden fete with string quartet' is one definition but not one which accurately describes the 200 festivals featured in this survey of the classical music festival scene of the mid-1980s. Intended as a practical guide for regular festival concertgoers, it encompasses all festivals in which music plays a major role, from modest village occasions to celebrated international events.

1688 The Blackwell history of music in Britain.

Oxford: Blackwell, 1981- . 6 vols.

Originally conceived in 1974 as *The Athlone history of music in Britain* this project was taken over by Blackwells in 1988. The first part of each volume deals with music and musicians in the society of the period whilst the second concentrates principally on the music itself. Contributions by leading music historians and musicologists are edited by recognized experts on the period concerned. Titles already published are *The eighteenth century* (Edited by H. Diack Johnstone, Roger Fiske. 1990. 534p. bibliog.) and *The Romantic Age 1800-1914* (Edited by Nicholas Temperley. 1981.). Titles in preparation are: *The Middle Ages*; *The sixteenth century*; *The seventeenth century*; and *The twentieth century*.

1689 Brass bands in the 20th century.

Edited by Violet Brand, Geoffrey Brand. Letchworth, England: Egon, 1979. 239p.

Every aspect of the brass band movement in Britain is covered in this authoritative work: its nineteenth century beginnings, instrumental developments, the National and Belle Vue championships, famous bands and their conductors, the contemporary repertoire, the National Youth Brass Band of Great Britain, and the Salvation Army bands and their music. There is a discursive historical discography and a list of the

384

results of the British Open Championships 1953-1978 and of the National Championships 1900-1978, giving the winning band, its conductor, and test piece. In his long career Geoffrey Brand has been professional conductor of the Black Dyke Mills band and adviser to the Brighouse and Raistrick band; he and his wife were joint editors of *British Bandsman*, 1967-1975.

1690 The folk-carol of England.
Douglas Brice. London: Herbert Jenkins, 1967. 174p. bibliog.

Concerned principally with folk-songs relating to the Christmas story, the early encounters of the Holy Family, and the life of Christ, this scholarly survey encompasses both medieval and modern carols.

1691 British Catalogue of Music.
London: British Library National Bibliographic Service, 1957- .
2 interim issues and an annual cumulation.

Based on material deposited at the British Library's Legal Deposit Office at Boston Spa, *BCoM* is a record of new music published in the UK and of foreign music available in the UK through a sole agent. The annual cumulation has composer, title, and subject indexes. A cumulation, *British catalogue of music 1957-85* (London: Bowker-Saur, 1987. 10 vols.) is arranged in a single classified sequence of some 60,000 items.

1692 British pop singles 1975-84: title index.
Hastings, England: John Humphries, 1985. 492p.

An essay by Bob Macdonald, '1975-84 the Single Revolution', introduces this index of over 51,000 seven and twelve inch records released or reissued in Great Britain in this formative decade. The entries provide the title, the artist(s) involved, the catalogue number, label, record company, distributor, format, and release and deletion dates.

1693 The music guide to Great Britain: England, Scotland, Wales, Ireland.
Elaine Brody, Claire Brook. London: Robert Hale, 1975. 240p.

Information on the birthplaces, homes, and monuments of famous British composers and musicians; the leading opera houses and concert halls; music publishers, instrument repairers, conservatories and music schools; and on music libraries, archives, and instrument collections, is all to be found in this comprehensive single-volume guide.

1694 Blues – the British connection.
Bob Brunning. Poole, England: Blandford, 1986. 256p.

A founder-member of the British band, Fleetwood Mac, Bob Brunning also played with most of the American touring bands in the 1970s and 1980s. His 'inside story' relates the fortunes of some twenty-five bands in that formative period. A later work, *Fleetwood Mac: behind the mask* (London: New English Library, 1990. 208p.), which includes a discography, recounts its chart-topping career over two decades as one of the most successful bands of all time.

1695 **British music yearbook 1992.**
Edited by Annabel Carter. London: Rhinegold, 1991. 18th ed. 734p.

Over 12,000 names are listed in this directory which is arranged in ten sections: official organizations, artists and agents, venues and promoters, jazz and light music, early music, recording and broadcasting, competitions and scholarships, education, marketing, and suppliers and services.

1696 **The Penguin book of rounds.**
Rosemary Cass-Beggs. Harmondsworth, England: Penguin, 1982. 128p. bibliog.

Rounds consist of three or more short sections which together produce a pleasing sound. This collection from the hundreds composed from the sixteenth to the nineteenth century to be sung in taverns and clubs is transcribed into modern spelling and musical notation. Songs relating to love and romance, to revelry and humour, to town and country life, and patriotic songs, are all included. A short essay on the round and its history sets them in context.

1697 **The end of the Beatles?**
H. Castleman, W. Padrazik. Ann Arbor, Michigan: Popular Culture, 1985. 581p.

This exhaustive discography updates two earlier volumes, *All together now: the first complete Beatles discography 1961-75* (Ann Arbor, Michigan: Pierian Press, 1975. 379p.), and *The Beatles again* (Ann Arbor, Michigan: Pierian Press, 1975. 280p.). Coverage extends to the end of 1983.

1698 **POMPI: Popular Music Periodicals Index.**
Chris Clark, Andy Linehan. London: British Library National Sound Archive, 1984- . annual.

In effect a contents catalogue of the periodical holdings of the National Sound Archive, this index provides subject access to the feature articles and interviews, but not record or performance reviews, printed in seventy (mainly British) popular music and jazz magazines and journals many of which are not indexed elsewhere. The two compilers are Curators for jazz and popular music respectively at the National Sound Archive. Clark's 'POMPI: Popular Music Periodicals Index', *Fontes Artis Musicae*, vol. 38, no. 1 (Jan.-March 1991), p. 32-37 outlines its background, describes its indexing policy (but not its indexing system), and lists the periodical titles currently indexed. Inaugural double issues for 1984-1986 and 1986-1988 preceded this journal's annual publication.

1699 **Medieval English songs.**
E. J. Dobson, F. L. Harrison. London: Faber, 1979. 331p.

Presenting the entire corpus of English text songs down to the beginning of the fifteenth century which have survived with their music – some thirty-three songs in all – this definitive work outlines the songs' historical contexts and discusses their literary and musical significance. Dobson is Professor of English Language at the University of Oxford whilst Harrison is Emeritus Professor of Ethnomusicology at the University of Amsterdam.

1700 **Cliff.**
Patrick Doncaster, Tony Jasper in co-operation with Cliff Richard.
London: Sidgwick & Jackson, 1981. 240p. bibliog.
Cliff Richard's career now spans five decades, an incredibly long time in the transient world of rock and pop music. This musical biography ends with a facts sections, giving his diary of events 1959-81; a detailed discography, including non-UK releases; films and videos; radio, stage and television appearances; and a list of books either on or by him.

1701 **A bellringer's guide to the church bells of Britain.**
Compiled by Ronald H. Dove. Aldershot, England: Viggers, 1976.
5th ed. 198p.
Lists of church towers hanging five or more bells, rings of bells by counties, British cathedral bells, notable bells, and of carillons of the British Isles, are all included in this comprehensive catalogue.

1702 **The music profession in Britain since the eighteenth century: a social history.**
Cyril Ehrlich. Oxford: Clarendon Press, 1985. 269p. bibliog.
Without question this wideranging book is the definitive study of the music profession in Britain. Securely set in its social and economic context, it relates musicians' struggle for survival, their education and training, their employment prospects at various times, and assesses the impact of two World Wars and the technological innovations hurtling along in their wake. The progress of the Musicians Union is also followed.

1703 **English madrigal verse 1588-1632.**
E. H. Fellows, revised by Frederick W. Sternfield, David Greer.
Oxford: Clarendon, 1967. 3rd ed. 798p.
First published in 1920 this work prints the poetic texts of most of the madrigal collections and song-books issued in England. Part one contains poems set as madrigals whilst part two those set as lute songs. In both instances the various collections are arranged alphabetically by composer or compiler.

1704 **Old English instruments of music: their history and character.**
Francis W. Galpin. London: Methuen, 1965. 4th ed. 254p. bibliog.
Originally published in the Antiquaries Books series in 1910, this learned study is confined to musical instruments in use in England prior to the end of the eighteenth century at which point the familiar instruments of the modern orchestra were beginning to emerge. Among the instruments discussed are the rote and harp, the gittern and citole, the mandore and lute, the dulcimer, the rebec and viol, the shawm and pipe, and the trumpet and sackbut.

1705 **The Guinness book of British hit singles.**
Paul Gambaccini, Tim Rice, Jonathan Rice.   Enfield, England:
Guinness, 1991. 8th ed. 406p.

First published in 1977, this discography now covers the period 14 November 1952 to 29 December 1990 and is arranged in two main parts. First, an alphabetical list of artists consisting of 4,021 chart facts, and chronological title lists, giving the date each disc first hit the charts, its label and catalogue number, its highest position in the charts, and the number of weeks it remained there. A second sequence of 15,048 titles, including different versions of the same song, and different songs of the same title, indicates the year of initial chart entry. Lastly, a 'Facts and feats' section gives details of chart record breakers, most weeks in the charts, most top ten hits, the longest intervals between chart hits, the top twenty acts of all times, Christmas hits, the oldest chart toppers, number one hits, and other vital information. The same team also compiled *The Guinness book of British hit albums* (5th ed. 416p.).

1706 **The Guinness book of top forty charts.**
Edited by Paul Gambaccini, Tim Rice, Jonathan Rice.   Enfield,
England: Guinness, 1992. 800p.

Every week's official singles chart is listed in this definitive record of pop music's development from the hit parade of the early 1950s to the top forty of the 1990s.

1707 **Music On Record 1: Brass bands.**
Edited by Peter Gammond, Raymond Horricks.   Cambridge,
England: Peter Stephens, 1980. 152p. bibliog.

Besides a discography of brass band music on long playing and extended play records this publication also includes an essay on the brass band repertoire and a thirty-five page 'who's who' in the brass band world.

1708 **A history of jazz in Britain.**
Jim Godbolt.   London: Quarter, 1984. 2 vols.

Based on research in the files of *Melody Maker*, and specialist jazz magazines such as *Swing Music* and *Hot News*, this two-volume study is the most detailed and comprehensive survey of jazz from the British perspective so far published. Volume one, *A history of jazz in Britain 1919-50*, examines the arrival of jazz music in Britain with the Original Dixieland Jazz Band tour in 1919, the big-band era, the influence of visiting American bands, the roots of British trad jazz, and the disastrous effects of the Musicians Union ban of overseas musicians. Volume two, *A history of jazz in Britain 1950-70*, covers a much smaller period. Both volumes pay particular attention to jazz journalism and both include selected discographies. Godbolt was at one time editor of *Jazz Illustrated*.

1709 **The early English carols.**
Edited by Richard Leighton Greene.   Oxford: Clarendon Press,
1977. 2nd ed. 689p. bibliog.

Collected in this volume are all those Middle and Early Modern English lyrics extant and accessible either in manuscript or printed sources earlier than 1550 to which the term 'carol' can properly be applied. An introductory text includes chapters on the carol as a *genre*, as a dance or popular song, its relationship with religion, and on its

Latin background. This scholarly work, first published in 1935, and here substantially revised, concludes with extensive notes and a forty-four page bibliography of original source material.

1710 **The British Bandsman centenary book: a social history of brass bands.**
Alf Hailstone. Baldock, England: Egon, 1987. 272p.

The British Bandsman: a monthly magazine for Bandmasters and Members of Military and Brass Bands was first published in September 1887. In this centenary history the author, a contributor to the magazine, has effectively chronicled the growth of the brass band movement, setting it in its wider social and economic context.

1711 **The brass band movement in the 19th and 20th centuries.**
Edited by Trevor Herbert. Milton Keynes, England: Open University Press, 1991. 224p. map.

By the end of the nineteenth century there were 40,000 brass bands in Britain playing to packed concert audiences. This study investigates their musical, social and historical background, their origins earlier in the century, their relationships with commercial, military and church organizations, their changing functions in working-class social life, and the attitude of the musical establishment towards them. The technical development of brass band instruments is also discussed.

1712 **300 years of English partsongs: glees, rounds, catches, partsongs 1600-1900.**
Edited by Paul Hillier. London: Faber, 1983. 87p.

The words and music of thirty pieces, both familiar and lesser known, including some bawdy songs, are arranged for male voices in this collection. There is an informative essay on the English partsong.

1713 **The British union catalogue of music periodicals.**
Compiled by Anthony Hodges, edited by Raymond McGill.
London: Library Association in association with the International Association of Music Libraries, Archives and Documentation Centres United Kingdom Branch, 1985. 145p.

Location details of music periodicals held in major UK libraries are provided in this union catalogue.

1714 **Music publishing in the British Isles: from the earliest times to the middle of the nineteenth century: a dictionary of engravers, printers, publishers and music sellers, with a historical introduction.**
Charles Humphries, William C. Smith. London: Cassell, 1954. 354p. bibliog.

Of the 2,200 names listed in this dictionary, only 400 were included in Frank Kidson's *British music publishers, printers and engravers* (London: W. E. Hill, 1900), which it updates and, to a large extent, replaces. Details are given of their business history, of particular works published, and of the important catalogues that they issued. Both on the professional staff of the British Museum's Department of Printed Books, the two compilers enjoyed unrivalled access to original source material which included long runs of early newspapers.

1715 **Bells in England.**
Tom Ingram.   Newton Abbot, England: David & Charles, 1987.
204p. bibliog.

Tracing the origins and history of a whole variety of bells, and demonstrating their influence and impact on everyday life through the centuries, this illustrated account investigates the rituals and traditions associated with medieval timekeeping, the art of change ringing, the archaeology of church towers and spires, the skill of casting bells, and the routine work in bell foundries.

1716 **Four faces of British music.**
Norman Hyde.   Worthing, England: Churchman, 1985. 248p.

Music at court, from Henry V to the royal wedding in 1981; music in the inn from seventeenth-century catch clubs to the working men's clubs of today; music in schools; and music in the concert halls, which includes the prominent London and provincial orchestras, constitute the four faces of British music alluded to in the title. Each is firmly embedded in this identification of the British musical heritage.

1717 **The top twenty: the official British record charts 1955-1990.**
Tony Jasper.   London: Batsford, 1991. 5th ed. 528p.

Produced in association with Music Week and Chart Information Network, this catalogue indexes every song title's entry into the top twenty charts. It is 'official' in the sense that its information derives from charts printed in *Record Mirror* used by the BBC for its Radio 1 programmes and for its television 'Top of the Pops' feature since 1968.

1718 **The Hallé tradition: a century of music.**
Michael Kennedy.   Manchester, England: Manchester University Press, 1960. 424p. bibliog.

Two main themes are explored in this official centenary history: the music the Hallé Orchestra has played, including new compositions, and the responses not only of the public, but also of its own players; and, secondly the Hallé tradition, the role of its principal conductors, its soloists, and its finances, radio and television performances, and its relationship with the city of Manchester. Kennedy's *The Hallé 1858-1983: a history of the orchestra* (1982. 152p. bibliog.) chronicles the Hallé's changing fortunes, its relationship with the city council, and the colourful characters among its players, administrators, critics, and supporters.

1719 **Folksongs of Britain and Ireland: a guidebook to the living tradition of folksinging in the British Isles and Ireland, containing 360 folksongs from field recordings sung in English, etc.**
Edited by Peter Kennedy.   London: Cassell, 1975. 824p. maps.
bibliog.

The words and music of songs of courtship, true and false love, seduction, uneasy wedlock, of various occupations, country life, and of the travelling people, are recorded here. Comprehensive and informative notes are added.

1720   **The BBC Symphony Orchestra: the first fifty years 1930-1980.**
Nicholas Kenyon.   London: British Broadcasting Corporation, 1981.
543p. bibliog.
Drawing upon unpublished BBC archive material, this historical study examines the
administrative and artistic policy decisions that have marked the Orchestra's progress,
tracing for the first time in print the full background to several important and
sometimes controversial episodes. A discography of the Orchestra's recordings, a
complete membership list of the Orchestra, and a list of first performances, provide
factual back-up.

1721   **Printed music in the British Museum: an account of the collections, the
catalogues, and their formation up to 1920.**
Alec Hyatt King.   London: Clive Bingley, 1979. 210p. bibliog.
Three closely interwoven themes are evident in this authoritative and erudite study:
the origins and growth of the collections and successive acquisition policies; the
planning and control of the catalogues; and the technical procedures adopted to
effectively organize and exploit the collections. Alec Hyatt King was Superintendent of
the British Museum Library's Music Room for forty years.

1722   **Music in London: a history and handbook.**
Norman Lebrecht.   London: Aurum, 1992. 183p.
Following an informative and entertaining historical outline of musical activities in
London, concentrating mainly on the last two centuries, a consumer guide to
everywhere music is played to the public in present-day London, the major concert
halls, smaller halls, parks etc., provides details on how to book seats, their price,
nearby eating places, and overnight accommodation. Shops selling printed and
recorded music are also listed in this reasonably-priced guide.

1723   **The Oxford book of English madrigals.**
Edited by Philip Ledger.   London: Oxford University Press, 1978.
402p.
Madrigals composed in the late sixteenth and early seventeenth centuries include some
of the finest music ever written in England. The words and music of sixty are included
in this anthology in which major composers are represented by several works and
lesser figures by their best known compositions.

1724   **Folk song in England.**
A. L. Lloyd.   London: Lawrence & Wishart, 1967. 433p. bibliog.
The relationship between the development of English folk songs and the evolution of
English society is the leading theme explored in this classic study. Subsidiary topics
include the structure of English folk melody, the decorative art of English singers, and
a comparison with the folk songs of other nations.

1725   **Travellers' songs from England and Scotland.**
Ewan MacColl, Peggy Seeger.   London: Routledge & Kegan Paul,
1977. 387p. bibliog.

Extensively researched in southern England and central and northeastern Scotland, the
words and music of some 130 travellers', tinkers', and gypsy songs, some in more than
one version, are included in this definitive collection, the first to be published since
Alice Gillington's *Songs of the open road* (1911). Traditional ballads, bawdy, tragic and
humorous songs and songs about love, work, and death, are all represented. Textual
notes expand on their folkloristic and historical interest.

1726   **A social history of English music.**
E. D. Mackerness.   London: Routledge & Kegan Paul, 1964. 307p.
bibliog.

Music holds a distinguished place in many spheres of public life – in religious services,
the drama, dancing, in national occasions and celebrations, and simply as entertainment. The main purpose of this work is to determine why certain kinds of music and
musical activities came into prominence at different periods, in the Middle Ages, in the
eighteenth century, and subsequently, with popular music infiltrating and capturing the
attention of all social classes.

1727   **The new Grove twentieth century English masters.**
Diana McVeagh, Anthony Payne, Hugh Ottaway, Imogen Holst,
Ian Kemp, Peter Evans.   London: Macmillan, 1986. 307p. bibliog.
(New Grove Composers Biography Series).

These seven biographical essays on Edward Elgar, Frederick Delius, Ralph Vaughan
Williams. Gustav Holst, William Walton, Michael Tippett, and Benjamin Britten, are
reprinted from the multi-volume *The new Grove dictionary of music and musicians*
edited by Stanley Sadie (London: Macmillan, 1980). Each essay includes musical
criticism, a detailed work list, and an extensive bibliography.

1728   **The Royal Society of Musicians of Great Britain: list of members
1738-1984.**
Compiled by Betty Matthews.   London: Royal Society of Musicians,
1985. 253p. bibliog.

Based on membership records held in the Society's archives, this list of members
indicates their individual professional accomplishments. Pippa Drummond's essay,
'The Royal Society of Music in the eighteenth century' (*Music and letters*, vol. 59,
no. 3, July 1978) is reprinted.

1729   **Music Week directory '91: the comprehensive guide to the UK music
industry and ancillary service companies.**
London: Music Week, 1990. 365p.

Areas covered in this annually-published directory include multiple market outlets, the
record companies; music publishers; videos; distributors; industrial, business and tour
and recording services.

1730   **The 1991/92 folk directory.**
London: English Folk Dance & Song Society, 1991. 160p.

Formed in 1932 from an amalgamation of the Folk Song Society (1898) and the English
Folk Dance Society (1911), the English Folk Dance and Song Society's key aims and
objectives are to preserve English folk songs and dances and to encourage their
practice in their traditional forms. It publishes dance instructions, song books, and the
journal *English Dance and Song*, and issues records. A county guide to societies
engaging in ritual dancing and folk singing forms the main section of this directory and
there is also a classified section listing performers and services.

1731   **A musical gazetteer of Great Britain and Ireland.**
Gerald Norris.   Newton Abbot, England: David & Charles, 1981.
352p. map.

Arranged regionally by county, this musical gazetteer indicates places associated with
over 3,000 conductors, singers, composers, and pianists. Considerable space is given to
contemporary musicians. The location of famous musical occasions is also indicated.

1732   **The Oxford history of English music: vol. 1: From the beginnings to
c. 1715.**
John Caldwell.   Oxford: Clarendon Press, 1991. 691p. bibliog.

The first of two volumes in this magisterial survey of the whole field of music by
English composers begins with the cultivation of church music after St. Augustine's
missionary visit to England in 597. An account of medieval music is followed by the
story of the growth of a distinctly English musical tradition from the early fifteenth
century to the achievements of the Tudor and Stuart period. The work of Dunstable,
Taverne, Byrd, and Purcell, is placed in the context of their contemporaries' music.

1733   **A ballad history of England: from 1588 to the present day.**
Roy Palmer.   London: Batsford, 1979. 192p. bibliog.

Over eighty ballads ranging from 'The Invincible Armada' (1588) to 'Hop picking'
(1931), 'The Blitz' (1940), and 'Great Train Robbers' (1963) show how ordinary people
have reacted to social change and national events over the last 400 years. Palmer
provides an historical commentary and well-selected quotations from contemporary
writers to set each ballad in its historical context.

1734   **Everyman's book of British ballads.**
Edited by Roy Palmer.   London: Dent, 1980. 256p. bibliog.

Traditional ballads, music-hall ballads, ballads of the supernatural, of death and
disaster, of deeds of daring, of crime and punishment, of true and false love, in fact
ballads of all types and of all periods, are included in this collection.

1735   **Everyman's book of English country songs.**
Edited by Roy Palmer.   London: Dent, 1979. 256p. bibliog.

An anecdotal account of the singers and the collectors of English country songs
introduces this collection of 147 such songs many of which are published here for the
first time. The songs are arranged thematically: songs of work and protest, songs
relating episodes of rural crime, songs of love and marriage, and songs celebrating
country sports, seasons, and ceremonies.

393

1736 **Folk songs collected by Ralph Vaughan Williams.**
Edited by Roy Palmer. London: Dent, 1983. 209p. bibliog.
In the early years of this century Ralph Vaughan Williams travelled extensively throughout England listening to and writing down the words and music of 800 folk songs. Many survive only because of his efforts. This collection publishes 121, seventy of them for the first time.

1737 **The Oxford book of sea songs.**
Edited by Roy Palmer. Oxford: Oxford University Press, 1986. 343p. bibliog.
Over 150 ballads and shanties, chiefly from England, and most with their tunes, are collected in this anthology. The editor adds technical detail and historical background in his introduction and commentaries.

1738 **Edwardian popular music.**
Ronald Pearsall. Newton Abbot, England: David & Charles, 1975. 207p. bibliog.
If musical comedy most characterizes English Edwardian music, the music hall, shop ballads, and outdoor music such as concert party performances, barrel organ music, German bands and military bands, were also typical of the period. This study embraces them all along with music pirates, musical evenings for middle-class families, the gramophone, and the coming of ragtime. An appendix prints extracts from Edwardian record catalogues.

1739 **Popular music of the twenties.**
Ronald Pearsall. Newton Abbot, England: David & Charles, 1976. 176p. bibliog.
In many respects a transitional period in popular music, the 1920s scene is captured here in its entirety: the changing face of musical variety, musical comedy and operetta, the translation of ragtime into jazz, Tin Pan Alley, the influence of the wireless, and many of the elements which foreshadow the pop scene of today.

1740 **Victorian popular music.**
Ronald Pearsall. Newton Abbot, England: David & Charles, 1973. 240p. bibliog.
The whole panorama of Victorian popular music is unrolled in this authoritative slice of social history: opera and ballet, music hall, drawing-room, songs, brass bands, street organs, massed choirs, and above all, the domestic piano recital.

1741 **The LSO at 70: a history of the orchestra.**
Maurice Pearton. London: Gollancz, 1974. 240p.
Adopting a 'social' approach, showing the Orchestra as its players viewed it in different periods of its development, rather than simply chronicling its memorable performances, this history reflects how audiences and fashions in music changed, and how the business and finance of concert-giving and concert-going has developed since the orchestra came into existence at the turn of the century; from the start it was self-governing and for many years it has toured overseas. Both of these aspects are visible

in J. B. Priestley's *Trumpets over the sea* (London: Heinemann, 1968. 160p.) sub-titled 'a rambling and egotistical account of the London Symphony Orchestra's engagement at Daytona Beach, Florida, in July-August 1967'.

1742 **Music in British libraries: a directory of resources.**
Edited by Barbara Penney. London: Library Association, 1981. 452p.

Arranged alphabetically by authority, institution, or library, this directory gives details of the music books and periodicals, manuscript and printed sheet music, and sound recordings, available from a wide range of libraries. Supplementary information includes the names of chief librarians and senior staff responsible for music and record libraries, access, charges, special collections, publications, and services.

1743 **Philharmonia Orchestra: a record of achievement 1945-1985.**
Stephen J. Pettit. London: Robert Hale, 1985. 285p.

Formed by Walter Legge in 1945, suspended in 1964, and reformed as the self-governing New Philharmonia Orchestra, its history is both chequered and dramatic. With access to the official archives Pettit carefully unravels why this desperate measure was necessary and charts its subsequent progress. A discography of the Orchestra's recordings available in April 1985 is arranged in conductor order.

1744 **The English musical renaissance.**
Peter J. Pirie. London: Gollancz, 1979. 270p. bibliog.

This strictly chronological account of English music in the twentieth century examines the way in which social and political factors have influenced music, and places English music in its contemporary world context. Pirie steers a clear path between those critics who pretend that every piece of English music is a great composition and those who automatically condemn it as wholly negligible.

1745 **A dictionary of old English music & musical instruments.**
Jeffrey Pulver. London: Kegan Paul, 1923. 247p.

Mainly confining its attention to late Tudor and early Stuart music, this descriptive dictionary covers the musical forms, instruments, and terms commonly in use during those periods.

1746 **British union catalogue of orchestral sets.**
Edited by Tony Reed. Boston Spa, England: British Library Document Supply Centre in cooperation with IAML (UK), 1989. 2nd ed. 380p. bibliog.

Produced to facilitate inter-library lending, this catalogue lists orchestral sets housed in sixty-six UK libraries giving details of their composers, titles, thematic catalogue key numbers, the duration of the work, its orchestration, and a number of library locations.

1747   **The English folksinger: 159 modern and traditional folksongs.**
Edited by Sam Richards, Tish Stubbs.   London: Collins, 1979. 224p.

The words and music of songs concerned with work and labour, of motion songs
(dancing, marching songs and sea shanties), songs in praise of drink and singing, songs
on love and marriage, bawdy songs, children's rhymes, and songs commemorating
historical events, many previously unpublished, are included in this collection. The
compilers are professional folksingers based in the West Country.

1748   **Tell me why: a Beatles commentary.**
Tim Riley.   London: Bodley Head, 1988. 423p.

'As a microcosm of the rock experience, nothing equals the Beatles' catalogue: it
illustrates the best of what came before and signals the array of styles that would soon
follow' (Introduction). This deeply researched commentary on the Beatles discography
examines the personal, political, and global influences on their work, taking each
album in turn, and breaking down their individual songs to perceive and analyse their
particular patterns.

1749   **Philharmonic.**
Thomas Russell, introduction by J. B. Priestley.   London:
Hutchinson, 1942. 180p.

Written by a former playing member, and later secretary and business manager of the
London Philharmonic Orchestra, this short book deals with many aspects of the
symphony orchestra, its evolution, its leaders and conductors, its finances, its audience,
and its programmers. Jerrold Northrop Moore's *Philharmonic jubilee* (London:
Hutchinson, 1982. 110p.) celebrates its fiftieth anniversary.

1750   **British dance bands 1912-1939.**
Compiled by Brian Rust, Edward S. Walker.   London: Storyville,
1973. 458p.

Based on dedicated research in the files of *Melody Maker*, *Rhythm*, *The Era*, *The
Dancing Times*, and *The Gramophone*, this publication provides a full discography of
all well-known bands in the spotlight either in hotels or nightclubs up to the outbreak
of the Second World War. Rust and S. Forbes' *British dance bands on record 1911-
1945* and *Supplement* (Harrow, England: General Gramophone Publications, 1989.
1,390p. and 72p. respectively) extends and corrects the original work.

1751   **English folk-song: some conclusions.**
Cecil J. Sharp.   London: Simpkin & Novello, 1907. 143p.

The accurate and scientific collection and preservation of English folk-songs owes
much to the distinguished author of this book. This preliminary work on the
evolutionary origin of the folk-song is based on his own collection of 1500 tunes mostly
gathered from four years fieldwork in Somerset. There is a list of seventeen books
containing English folk-songs which have been taken down directly from folksingers.

1752 **The English medieval minstrel.**
John Southworth. Woodbridge, England: Boydell Press, 1989. 191p.
bibliog.

Based on thorough scholarship and research, this account of minstrelsy in medieval England names 332 individual performers. Amongst them are fools, acrobats, actors, conjurors, puppeteers, and dice-throwers – singing alone was never enough in a minstrel's repertoire. A check-list of royal harpers and fools as recorded in the State Papers is appended.

1753 **The Penguin book of English madrigals for four voices.**
Edited by Denis Stevens. Harmondsworth, England: Penguin
Books, 1967. 158p.

In this collection each madrigal is prefaced by an edited version of the poem which notes features of special interest whilst the music is edited to help singers to achieve a richer balance and ensemble.

1754 **Brass bands.**
Arthur R. Taylor. London: Granada, 1979. 356p. bibliog.

This well-researched account of the brass band movement contains a history of brass bands in Britain from the beginning of the nineteenth century; thumb-nail sketches of current events and occasions; and a reference section which includes appendices covering the contest results of the British Open Championship at Belle Vue and of the top section of the National Championships in London, a month by month calendar of national, regional, and local contests, BBC radio coverage, the Salvation Army bands, and a valuable bibliographical essay.

1755 **The music of the English parish church.**
N. Temperley. Cambridge, England: Cambridge University Press,
1979. 2 vols. bibliog.

Outlining the changes in church music, and investigating why they occurred, this definitive work extends from pre-Reformation times to the twentieth century. Volume one ends with a massive fifty-page bibliography; volume two is mostly taken up with examples of notable examples of church music.

1756 **Directory of recorded sound resources in the United Kingdom.**
Edited by Lali Weerasinghe. London: British Library National
Sound Archive, 1989. 173p.

Listing 489 collections in libraries and museums, record and archives offices, learned societies, radio stations, and in business and industry, all arranged alphabetically by county, this directory covers jazz and pop, dance and theatrical music, and other recorded material, and provides information on the size and contents of each collection together with details of access.

1757 **The Penguin book of English folk songs.**
Edited by R. Vaughan Williams, A. L. Lloyd. Harmondsworth,
England: Penguin Books, 1959. 128p. bibliog.

Selected from the *Journal of the Folk Song Society* and its successor, the *Journal of the English Folk Dance and Song Society*, this slim volume presents the words and music of seventy English folk-songs in alphabetical order of title.

1758 **Tudor music.**
David Wulstan. London: Dent, 1985. 378p. bibliog.

All the main categories of Tudor music are discussed in the context of their historical and technical background in this analytical survey: street and minstrel music; court and household music; music for organs and virginals; church music, etc. The works of well-known composers like Tallis, Byrd, Gibbons, and Taverner, are explored but lesser-known composers are also by no means neglected. Wulstan, who is Professor of Music in the University of Wales at Aberystwyth, also deals with the interpretation of Tudor music for present-day performances, and the problems of pitch, notation, and editing.

1759 **Music's great days in the spas and watering places.**
Kenneth Young. London: Macmillan, 1968. 228p. bibliog.

Today live music concerts outside London and the main provincial cities is comparatively rare but during its halcyon years, between 1880 and 1950, there were few self-respecting resorts who could not boast of a professional spa, pier or municipal orchestra capable of playing the whole range of the concert repertoire, providing important stimuli and showcases for both composers and conductors. This is the story of the music, who played it, and what they played.

1760 **A history of British music,.**
Percy M. Young. London: Benn, 1967. 641p.

Ranging from the martial music of the Celts to music in post-war Britain, this comprehensive history firmly places music within its social, political, and historical contexts which so crucially affected its composition in every period. Neglected English composers are reassessed and, in one instance, reinstated; and the full value and significance of English provincial music life is generously reappraised.

Penguin book of hymns.
See item no. 595.

Theatre, opera, dance

1761 **English theatrical literature 1559-1900: a bibliography.**
James Fullarton Arnott, John William Robinson. London: Society
for Theatrical Research, 1970. 486p.

Incorporating Robert W. Lowe's *A bibliographical account of English theatre literature*,
published in 1888, long regarded as the standard reference work indispensable to any
student of theatrical literature, this bibliography includes over 4,500 entries arranged
under fourteen subject and form headings.

1762 **The story of Sadler's Wells 1683-1977.**
Dennis Arundell. Newton Abbot, England: David & Charles, 1978.
2nd ed. 353p.

Tracing Sadler's Wells' history from its seventeenth-century beginnings as a music-
house for summer visitors to its present-day standing as a national ballet and opera
centre, this study which was first published in 1965 recalls its past glories and
performances.

1763 **The Gilbert and Sullivan companion.**
Leslie Ayre. London: W. H. Allen, 1972. 485p.

The comic operas created by Gilbert and Sullivan in the last three decades of the
nineteenth century established new landmarks in English music and popular culture.
This alphabetically arranged companion contains biographical notes and anecdotes
about the composers, the actors who played leading roles at different periods, concise
accounts of each of the operas, and the full texts of the main songs and ensembles.

1764 **The Gilbert and Sullivan book.**
Leslie Baily. London: Spring Books, 1966. rev. ed. 475p.

Originally published by Cassell in 1952, this spacious work is largely based on the
correspondence and diaries of the two men whose personalities were not always
compatible but who fashioned a popular and peculiarly English form of popular
entertainment. Their Savoy Operas, *Trial by Jury*, *HMS Pinafore*, *The Pirates of
Penzance*, *Iolanthe*, *The Mikado*, and the rest, have justified Lytton Strachey's
observation that they would prove to be the most permanent legacy of the Victorian
Age. This bumper book, generously illustrated with contemporary playbills and
programmes, is one Gilbert and Sullivan buffs and enthusiasts cannot afford to be
without. The author included some updated material from this classic study in his
Gilbert and Sullivan and their world (London: Thames & Hudson, 1973. 128p.
bibliog.).

1765 **A companion to post-War British theatre.**
Philip Barnes. London: Croom Helm, 1986. 277p.

Playwrights and their plays, career details of prominent directors and actors, theatre
groups, the alternative theatre, 'schools' of dramatic practice and technique, stage
history, and theatrical terminology, all take their place in this single sequence
alphabetical guide to the contemporary British theatre.

Performing Arts. Theatre, opera, dance

1766   **The Royal Shakespeare Company: a history of ten decades.**
Sally Beauman.   Oxford: Oxford University Press, 1982. 388p.
The Shakespeare Memorial Theatre opened in Stratford-upon-Avon, 23 April 1879.
This centenary history records the consolidation of its acting companies into the Royal
Shakespeare Company, highlighting the ideals which inspired the efforts of individuals,
actors, directors, and administrators, and describes the celebrated productions of the
last thirty years. The Company's relations with the Arts Council and the National
Theatre also come under the spotlight.

1767   **The original British theatre directory 1992.**
Edited by Samantha Blair.   London: Richmond House, 1992.
20th ed. 587p.
London and provincial venues, the fringe theatre, municipal theatres, personal
managers, concert promoters, literary agents, appropriate publishers and booksellers,
ballet and opera, drama schools, suppliers and services, all feature in this directory,
sometimes described as 'the Bible of British theatre'.

1768   **The Royal Ballet: the first fifty years.**
A. Bland.   London: Threshold/Sotheby Parke Bernet, 1981. 320p.
This comprehensive history and record book covers both the Royal Opera House and
Sadler's Wells Theatre. A dancers' 'who's who', including the earliest traceable dates
of their first appearances, their choreographers and chronologies of their ballets, and
information on each company's repertoire, provide a complete record of all the Royal
Ballet's performances.

1769   **British music hall: an illustrated who's who from 1850 to the present
day.**
Roy Busby.   London: Elek, 1976. 191p.
Owing much to patient research through the files of *The Performer*, the official organ
of the Variety Artists Federation, this 'who's who' details the careers of some 500 of
the truly great British music hall and variety artistes. An attempt is made in these
biographical sketches to capture their reception by contemporary audiences. An
outline history of the popular music halls provides the essential background.

1770   **Other theatres: the development of alternative and experimental
theatre in Britain.**
Andrew Davies.   London: Macmillan, 1987. 249p. bibliog.
(Communications and Culture).
From the late nineteenth-century the theatres in London's West End have inevitably
dominated the whole theatre scene in Britain, especially in the types of play put on and
the methods of acting employed. This study on the important tradition of alternative
and experimental theatre over the last 200 years examines Yiddish drama, suffragette
theatre, the repertory movement, the little theatres between the wars, Joan
Littlewood's Theatre Workshop, and alternative and political theatre since the 1960s.
Davies also expertly covers the relationship of the alternative theatre with the
mainstream commercial theatre.

1771 **Foundations of English opera: a study of musical drama in England during the seventeenth century.**
Edward J. Dent. New York: Da Capo, 1965. 242p.

First published by Cambridge University Press in 1928, this book quickly attained standard work status in its field of English operatic activity in the seventeenth century and its relationship with Italian opera. Henry Purcell's music for *Dido and Aeneas*, *King Arthur*, and *The Faerie Queene*, and English opera's close links with Masque, are among the other topics discussed. The author's life and work, and his place in English musicology, is assessed in a new introduction to this edition.

1772 **The Royal Opera House in the twentieth century.**
Frances Donaldson. London: Weidenfeld & Nicolson, 1988. 238p.

This official history discusses the Royal Opera House's achievements in Covent Garden and abroad, examines the attitude of the English people towards opera, accounts for the crusade for opera to be sung in English, and follows Covent Garden's internal politics as they affect its central administration. Due attention is also paid to the larger-than-life personalities associated with its productions.

1773 **The guide to drama training in the UK.**
Sarah Duncan. London: Cheverell, 1990. 251p.

Based on personal visits to the institutions concerned, this guide contains detailed information on over 400 drama and performing arts courses in drama schools, colleges and universities, ranging from degree courses to summer schools, and from straight drama and musical theatre to mime and clowning skills.

1774 **The history of the National theatre.**
John Elsom, Nicholas Tomalin. London: Cape, 1978. 342p. bibliog.

Although the first proposal for a National Theatre was made by Effingham Wilson, a London publisher and bookseller, in 1848, it was not until 1976 that it at last moved into its new home on the South Bank. This history sketches the early days of the campaign for a National Theatre, but concentrates on the post-war period, when it struggled to life, surviving press criticism, political and economic vicissitudes, and high level personality clashes.

1775 **Funny way to be a hero.**
John Fisher. London: Frederick Muller, 1973. 336p. bibliog.

The giants of British music hall and variety stage and radio and television comedy are celebrated in this penetrating study of their own individual idioms, techniques, and popular appeal.

1776 **Ballet in England: a bibliography and survey c.1700-June 1966**.
F. S. Forrester. London: Library Association, 1968. 224p.

Arranged by date of publication 664 books and periodical articles are divided into form, chronological, and thematic sections, *viz.* publishing and bibliography, encyclopedias, directories and yearbooks, general works, history, ballet companies, choreographers, dancers, design and costume, music, film and television, fiction, and periodicals.

Performing Arts. Theatre, opera, dance

1777 **The British musical theatre: vol. 1. 1865-1914; vol. 2. 1915-1984.**
Kurt Ganzl.   London: Macmillan, 1986. 2 vols.
Recording in minute detail the history of the British light musical theatre from pre-Gilbert and Sullivan days to the musicals of Tim Rice and Andrew Lloyd Webber, these two massive volumes deal in chronological order with every original British musical performed in London's West End, and many provincial productions as well, totalling over 1,000 in all, providing critical analyses of their libretti, lyrics and music, extracts from contemporary reviews, a history of theatrical events, and biographical notes on many hundreds of writers, actors, and producers. Performance details including the theatre, the length of run, creative credits, casts and cast changes, and revivals and American productions, are given at the end of each chapter. In theatrical terminology this definitive work will run and run.

1778 **The Savoy operas.**
W. S. Gilbert.   London: Macmillan, 1926. 698p.
Constantly reprinted, this collection contains the complete texts of all the Gilbert and Sullivan Savoy Operas originally produced in the years 1875 to 1896.

1779 **Britain's Royal National Theatre: the first 25 years.**
Tim Goodwin.   London: National Theatre in association with Nick Hern Books, 1988. 108p.
This pictorial record contains an outline of the beginnings of the National Theatre, an annotated chronology of key events 1963 to 1988, a production scrapbook of National Theatre successes for those years, with commentaries and complete cast lists, an architectural study, and a management overview.

1780 **Directory of theatre resources: a guide to research collections and information services.**
Compiled by Diana Howard.   London: Library Association Information Services Group and the Society for Theatre Research, 1986. 2nd ed. 144p.
First published by The Arts Council of Great Britain in 1980 as *Directory of theatre research and information research in the United Kingdom*, this directory and guide not only provides information on private and public collections, and their locality and terms of access, but also on theatrical associations and societies.

1781 **Glyndebourne: a history of the festival opera founded in 1934 by Audrey and John Christie.**
Spike Hughes.   Newton Abbot, England: David & Charles, 1981. new ed. 288p.
First published in 1965 this history of a rural opera house established in John Christie's ancestral home contains a critical appraisal of every Glyndebourne season, complete cast lists of the operas performed, and a Glyndebourne discography.

1782 **The complete Gilbert and Sullivan opera guide.**
Alan Jefferson.   Exeter, England: Webb & Bower, 1984. 352p.
bibliog.
The libretti of all fourteen Savoy Operas, checked and passed by W. S. Gilbert shortly
before he died, are printed in this listener's and viewer's guide. It also includes notes
on their recordings and films.

1783 **British alternative theatre directory 1991-1992: the complete guide.**
Edited by David McGillivray.   Cardiff: Rebecca Books, 1991. 307p.
First published in 1979, this directory provides very clear details on all alternative
theatre companies, which include touring companies, community theatres, street
entertainers, cabaret artists and London fringe theatres. In addition, separate sections
cover childrens and young people's theatre, puppet companies, rehearsal rooms,
theatre and cabaret venues, theatre training, arts councils, national festivals, and
theatrical suppliers.

1784 **The lost theatres of London.**
Raymond Mander, Joe Mitchenson.   London: Hart-Davis, 1968.
576p. 2 maps.
This definitive study chronicles the famous central London theatres now vanished
either because of enemy action, 'development', or because of bankruptcy. Their
buildings, their bewildering changes of name, and their stage triumphs, are
exhaustively recorded. A trenchant review of previous works on the subject appears in
the preface.

1785 **The handbook of Gilbert and Sullivan.**
Compiled by Frank Leslie Moore.   London: Arthur Barker, 1962.
264p. bibliog.
Part one of this handbook contains synopses of all the Savoy Operas, including a
complete list of characters and their involved relationships, a description of the setting
of each scene, a complete list of arias, ensembles and choruses, and lengthy historical
notes on their writing and production. Part two provides biographical sketches of
William Gilbert, Arthur Sullivan, and Richard D'Oyly Carte, a list of members of the
Savoy Company, and a chronology of the Gilbert and Sullivan era.

1786 **Theatre at Stratford-upon-Avon: a catalogue-index to productions of
the Shakespeare Memorial/Royal Shakespeare Theatre 1879-1978:
vol. 1. Catalogue of productions: vol. 2. Indexes and calendar.**
Edited by Michael Mullin, Karen Morris Muriello.   London: Library
Association, 1980. 1,038p.
The Royal Shakespeare Theatre, and its predecessor, not only have presented
productions of all Shakespeare's plays in Stratford but also the works of other
dramatists in London and on international tours. Records of all those performances are
preserved in the substantial theatrical archive the Company maintains. Now, for the
first time, this archive is accessible to the public in this computer produced catalogue
which lists each production by play title and gives the date of its first performance, the
playwright and director, lighting designer, actors and actresses, and a list of review and
reviewers.

1787 **A history of English drama 1660-1900.**
Allardyce Nicoll.   Cambridge, England: Cambridge University Press,
1952-1959. 6 vols. (vol. 1. *Restoration drama 1660-1700.* 1952. 4th ed.
462p.; vol. 2. *Early eighteenth century drama.* 1952. 3rd ed. 467p.;
vol. 3. *Late eighteenth century drama 1750-1800.* 1952. 2nd ed. 423p.;
vol. 4. *Early nineteenth century drama 1800-1850.* 1955. 2nd ed. 668p.;
vol. 5. *Late nineteenth century drama 1850-1900.* 1959. 2nd ed. 901p.;
vol. 6. *A short-title alphabetical catalogue of plays produced or printed
in England from 1660 to 1900.* 1959. 565p.).
Published with the aim of tracing the fortunes of English dramatic literature from the
accession of Charles II to the end of Queen Victoria's reign, this monumental history,
which has experienced a number of revisions, is universally acknowledged as the most
authoritative and comprehensive standard work on its subject. Each of the first five
volumes begins with a study of the contemporary theatre, the audience, the theatre
buildings, interiors, equipment, the size and shape of the stage, and the actors,
managers and authors. Appendices provide factual information on the playhouses'
history, the history of the English stage, and handlists of plays. The final volume serves
as a guide to the earlier volumes.

1788 **The official British theatre directory seating plan guide.**
London: Richmond House, 1992. 92p.
Seating plans of forty-four London theatres, eleven major London concert venues, and
of fifteen provincial arenas and theatres, seventy plans in all, are included in this guide.
It is intended for use when booking seats for theatre and concert performances by
telephone.

1789 **The revels history of drama in English.**
Edited by L. Potter.   London: Methuen, 1975-83. 8 vols. (vol. 1.
Medieval drama. Edited by A. C. Cawley. 1983. 348p.; vol. 2. *1500-
1576.* Edited by N. Sanders. 1980. 290p.; vol. 3. *1576-1613.* Edited by
J. L. Barroll. 1975. 526p.; vol. 4. *1613-1640.* Edited by P. Edwards.
1981. 337p.; vol. 5. *1660-1750.* Edited by J. Loftis. 1976. 331p.; vol. 6.
1750-1880. Edited by M. R. Booth. 1975. 304p.; vol. 7. *1880 to the
present day.* Edited by H. Hunt. 1978. 298p.).
Each period of English drama is set in its social and literary context in this multi-
volume history which covers theatres and actors, playwrights and their plays, together
with detailed chronologies of plays and theatrical and historical events. The eighth
volume relates to American drama.

1790 **The rise of the English actress.**
Sandra L. Richards.   London: Macmillan, 1992. 352p. bibliog.
Tracing the actresses' rise to social and professional pre-eminence and respectability,
this pioneering study discusses the work of the foremost actresses at each period of the
English stage, including Sarah Siddons, Ellen Terry, Sybil Thorndike, Edith Evans,
and Peggy Ashcroft. Entry into the theatre, acting styles, famous roles, salaries, and
relations with theatrical managers, are some of the themes explored.

1791 **London theatre: from the Globe to the National.**
James Roose-Evans. Oxford: Phaidon, 1977. 160p. bibliog.

Four centuries of the London stage are celebrated in this history, from Burbage's Theatre in Shoreditch completed in 1576, to the opening of the National Theatre in 1976. All forms of drama and entertainment are considered, including street processions, puppet plays, pantomimes, music hall, and modern experimental plays.

1792 **The repertory movement: a history of regional theatre in Britain.**
George Rowell, Anthony Jackson. Cambridge, England: Cambridge University Press, 1984. 230p. bibliog.

Repertory is the name given to mainly provincial theatres which house a resident company of actors and which present each season a programme of plays to cater for all sections of the community. This account of the origins, development, and current state of the repertory theatre, includes consideration of the major landmarks in recent theatrical history, the effects of two world wars, the growth of alternative forms of entertainment like the cinema and television, and the introduction of State funding for the Arts. It concludes with detailed studies of six regional repertory theatres.

1793 **The Theatre Museum: Victoria and Albert Museum.**
Compiled by Alexander Schouvaloff. London: Scala Books, 1987. 144p.

The Theatre Museum, Covent Garden, one of the largest collections of theatre memorabilia in the world, was officially opened in September 1974. Two million items, costumes, programmes, photographs, etc. are represented in this scrapbook which also includes a short history of the collections. The frustrations along the way, and the ultimate triumph of the drive towards the Museum's foundation, are well told in Jean Scott Rogers' *Stage by stage: the making of the Theatre Museum* (HMSO for Victoria & Albert Museum, 1985. 88p.).

1794 **The history of the English puppet theatre.**
George Speaight. London: Robert Hale, 1990. 2nd ed. 366p.

With preliminary sections on English puppetry's Mediterranean and European antecedents, and on medieval English clowns, this detailed and lavishly illustrated account traces the history of the puppet theatre in England from the high medieval period onwards to the television age, taking in the story of Punchinello, the puppet theatre in eighteenth-century London, the evolution of Punch and Judy, and nineteenth-century marionettes. A list of puppet showmen in England, 1600-1914, attempts to include the name of every puppet-show proprietor who played in England before the First World War. Speaight's meticulous research is also displayed by a list of all puppet plays performed in England from 1500 onwards of which any record survives. First published by Harrap in 1955 this is now universally recognized as the definitive work on the English puppet theatre.

1795 **The annals of English drama 975-1700.**
Edited by Sylvia Stoler Wagonheim. London: Routledge, 1990.
3rd ed. 352p.

An analytical record of all plays, extant or lost, chronologically arranged, and indexed
by author, title, and dramatic company, this latest edition of a work first published in
1940 includes over 1,000 new entries, clarifications, corrections, and deletions. Each
entry provides information on author, title, date of first performance, type of play, the
circumstances of its first production, earliest text, and latest modern edition.

1796 **The London stage . . . a calendar of plays and players.**
J. P. Wearing. Metuchen, New Jersey: Scarecrow, 1976- .
6 vols in 14.

Provides day-by-day calendars of plays produced at the major West End theatres in
London. Accurate cast lists which note changes during the production's unbroken run,
production details, and locations of contemporary reviews, and comprehensive
indexes, provide exhaustive coverage. The 1940-49 volume lists 2,409 productions,
including operas and ballets, in chronological order. The years covered are as follows:
vol. one *1890-1899*; vol. two *1900-1909*; vol. three *1910-1919*; vol. four *1920-1929*;
vol. five *1930-1939*; vol. six *1940-1949*.

1797 **The history of English opera.**
Eric Walker White. London: Faber, 1983. 472p.

Tracing English opera from its origins in Elizabethan incidental music and in Jacobean
court masques to the post-war opera renaissance in London and the provinces, this
historical survey not only tells the story of the principal composers and librettists, but
examines also how opera productions have been financed and staged. The recent
history of Sadler's Wells and the Royal Opera House is well covered and the whole
work is leavened and lightened with anecdotal records of celebrated composers and
performers.

Cinema

1798 **Britain can take it: the British cinema in the Second World War.**
Anthony Aldgate, Jeffrey Richards. Oxford: Basil Blackwell, 1986.
256p.

Eleven key films of the period receive in-depth attention, including consideration of
their scripts, reviews, and box office returns, in this detailed overview of how the
British cinema sustained morale in the Second World War. Much light is thrown on the
delicate relationship between official government propagandists and the film-makers
and each film is firmly placed in its historical, social and political context.

1799 **A critical history of the British cinema.**
Roy Armes.   London: Secker & Warburg, 1978. 374p. bibliog.
Eighty years of British film history are chronicled in this detailed study. The author
stresses the unsung achievements of British film makers who, although struggling in a
tighter environment, were too often compared unfavourably with their Hollywood
counterparts.

1800 **Researcher's guide to British newsreels.**
Edited by James Ballantyne.   London: British Universities Film &
Video Council, 1983, 1988. 2 vols.
Illustrating the history and development of British newsreels and cinemagazines,
between 1910 and 1959, this guide contains abstracts of books, pamphlets, periodical
articles, and reports relating to their genesis, growth and eventual demise; a directory
of newsreel organizations; their staffing; and newsreel libraries and archives. Coverage
is updated to 1987 in a supplementary volume.

1801 **The beginnings of the cinema in England.**
John Barnes.   Newton Abbot, England; David & Charles, 1976.
240p.
Two inventions, the Kinetograph and the Kinetoscope, first demonstrated in England
in 1894, represent the first practical method of cinematography. Starting with the
Kinetoscope this book and its sequels *The rise of the cinema in Great Britain: vol. 2.
Jubilee year 1897* (John Barnes. London: Bishopgate, 1983. 272p.) and *Pioneers of the
British film: the rise of the photoplay* (John Barnes. London: Bishopgate, 1983. 256p.),
trace technical developments in the cinema to 1901 by which time the film had become
a major attraction in English music halls and the film producers had turned their
attention to simple photoplays. The third volume focuses primarily on the careers of
pioneer filmmakers in Bradford and Leeds.

1802 **Ealing studios.**
Charles Barr.   London: Cameron & Tayleur in association with
David & Charles, 1977. 198p.
A roll-call of notable British film successes in the twenty-one year period 1938-1959
would include many emanating from Ealing Studios. Outstanding Ealing comedies,
particularly those belonging to the middle of this period, would be particularly
prominent. This admirably illustrated critical history ends with details of all ninety-five
feature films produced by Sir Michael Balcon for Ealing.

1803 **British National Film and Video Catalogue.**
Edited by Maureen Brown.   London: British Film Institute, 1963- .
quarterly.
Published quarterly, with annual cumulations, this catalogue attempts to provide
details of all films and videos released for loan or sale in the United Kingdom,
including education and training films, independent productions, documentaries,
television programmes, and feature films, but not straight advertising films, or the bulk
of videos made available to the public in retail outlets. Entries are arranged according
to the Universal Decimal Classification scheme and give details of availability, a

content summary, and an indication of the prospective audience. Directory type information on producers and distributors is also printed. In compiling this catalogue the BFI relies on the goodwill and co-operation of the production companies, there is no statutory requirement to deposit copies of films and videos in a national library or archive.

1804   **The golden gong: fifty years of the Rank Organization, its films and its stars.**
Quentin Falk.   London: Columbus Books, 1987. 208p. bibliog.

'In those days your British film industry was, basically, the Rank Organization', Michael Caine remarks in his foreword. How accurate he was is obvious as this pictorial history unfolds, A J. Arthur Rank filmography brings this nostalgic volume to an end.

1805   **The British film catalogue 1895-1985: a reference guide.**
Dennis Gifford.   Newton Abbot, England: David & Charles, 1986. 2nd ed. bibliog.

Under the terms of the Cinematograph Films Act of 1927 British film production companies are required to register film titles and footage. This comprehensive catalogue of every British entertainment film produced for public release, contains details of length, type of censors' certificate, whether silent or sound, in black-and-white or colour, its screen ratio, production and distribution company, producer and director, screenplay and story source, cast and characters, plot summaries, and any awards it may have received. Information on films produced before 1927 has been gleaned from extensive research in trade papers, fan magazines, and film production catalogues, preserved in the British Film Institute archives.

1806   **The illustrated who's who in British films.**
Dennis Gifford.   London: Batsford, 1978. 334p. bibliog.

The career details of over 1,000 stars, character actors, and directors in British films are featured in this biographical reference work which covers the period 1895 to 1977. All film appearances are listed chronologically and there is a bibliography of film biographies. Film buffs will happily browse within its pages for hours.

1807   **British Film Institute film and television handbook 1992.**
Edited by David Leafe.   London: BFI, 1991. 332p.

Beginning with information on the BFI's own facilities and services, the Museum of the Moving Image, the National Film Theatre, and the National Film Archive, this annual review of the previous year's developments covers British film production, key events in film and video distribution, cinemagoing, and television and radio programmes. Lastly, there is a directory of suppliers and services including archives and libraries, bookshops, cable and satellite, festivals, film societies, production companies, film releases, and studios, etc.

1808 **The history of the British film.**
Rachel Low, Roger Manvell (vols. 1-2). London: Allen & Unwin,
1948-1985. 7 vols. bibliog. (vol. 1. *1896-1906*. 1948. 136p. vol. 2. *1906-
1914*. 1948. 309p. vol. 3. *1914-1918*. 332p. vol. 4. *1918-1929*. 1971.
544p. vol. 5. *Documentary and educational films of the 1930s*. 1979.
vol. 6. *Films of comment and persuasion of the 1930s*. 1979. vol. 7.
Film making in 1930s Britain. 1985. 452p.).
To mark the fiftieth anniversary in 1946 of the appearance of the cinema as a regular
form of entertainment in Britain, the British Film Institute established a Research
Committee to initiate and to support research into the history of the early years of the
British cinema both as an art form and as an industry. Because research into the
invention of the cinematograph was not included in the Committee's terms of
reference, technical developments are only referred to if they directly impinge on their
main theme. Although primarily intended for reference, these volumes are nevertheless immensely readable narrative histories. Strictly reference material is confined to
appendices or to other specialized sections like the lists of British films of the period
included in all but the first volume. Rachel Low was one of the original five members
of the Research Committee.

1809 **Researcher's guide to British film and television collections.**
Edited by Elizabeth Oliver. London: BUFVC, 1989. 3rd ed. 185p.
bibliog.
This directory of national archives; regional collections; television company holdings;
newsreel, production, and stock shot libraries; and specialized collections, contains
details of some 200 collections. The bibliography includes acts of Parliament and
Government reports and surveys relevant to the British film and television industries.

1810 **British film actors' credits 1895-1987.**
Scott Palmer. London: St. James Press, 1988. 917p.
Nearly 5,000 performers, virtually every British actor who made at least three films,
with complete filmographies, and a quarter of a million film titles, are listed in this
definitive work. The factual entries provide birth and death dates, a chronological list
of all films (including television films) in which the performer appeared, and brief
character descriptions. Separate lists of actors and actresses awarded titles, those who
appeared in 100 films, and those who won film awards, are also printed.

1811 **British sound films: the studio years 1928-1959.**
David Quinlan. London: Batsford, 1984. 407p. bibliog.
Recalling an era when British studios tried desperately hard to break into the
international market, hampered by the dubious quota system by which a percentage of
films exhibited in British cinemas had to be produced in Britain, Quinlan adopts a
decade-by-decade approach to his work. Over 3,000 British film releases are recorded
complete with lists of key technical staff, cast lists, plot summaries, and with brief
critical assessments.

1812   **Documentary diary: an informal history of the British documentary film 1928-1939.**

Paul Rotha.   London: Secker & Warburg, 1973. 305p. bibliog.

In the 1930s British documentary films enjoyed an unparalleled period of success and achieved a high reputation for their gritty portrayal of British society. This study by an acknowledged master of the medium relates the origins of the documentary film movement in Britain factually and critically and also tells of his own experiences as director and producer.

1813   **British official films in the Second World War: a descriptive catalogue.**

Frances Thorpe, Nicholas Pronay.   Oxford: Clio Press, 1980. 321p.

Sponsored by the Imperial War Museum, this catalogue provides a record of 1,887 films officially produced and distributed by British government agencies 1939-1946 which were intended both for internal consumption and to project Britain's image in neutral countries abroad.

1814   **Hollywood, England: the British film industry in the sixties.**

Alexander Walker.   London: Harrap, 1986. 493p.

The author, a former *Evening Standard* film critic, presents a chronological account of the British film industry in its contemporary social context which he claims is 'an attempt to illustrate the diversity of talents and motives, economic changes, historical accidents and occasional artistic achievements' of the industry 'during a brief, turbulent part of its existence'. Of additional interest is *National heroes: British cinema in the seventies and eighties*, also by Alexander Walker (London: Harrap, 1985) which 'places the emphasis on the people with power (producers, financiers, entrepreneurs, corporate bosses) and the ways they have asserted it through the films they have made or caused to be made'. Both books end with a substantial chronology.

1815   **British films 1971-1981.**

Edited by L. Wood.   London: British Film Institute, 1985. 154p.

This catalogue is divided into two main sections: commercial films from British producers released in the UK with information on their director and running time; and films in production in identified British studios, noting their director and production company. The British Film Institute has embarked on a retrospective project leading up to this volume: the first title to be published is Wood's *British films 1927-1939* (1986. 143p.).

Architecture

1816   **The literature of British domestic architecture 1715-1842.**
John Archer.   Cambridge, Massachusetts: MIT Press, 1985. 1,078p.
A work of immense scholarship based on an extensive search of major library
collections, this study traces the evolution of architectural ideas by examining
architects' own literary output. Entries are arranged in three sections: architecture and
the book trade (i.e., publication practices, chronological trends in publication activity,
etc); format and content; and theory and design. A full standard bibliographical
description of each book includes descriptions of all known editions, and a
commentary analysing the text and plates and focusing on the author's ideas and
approach to design issues.

1817   **Architects of Europe – United Kingdom edition.**
Melbourne: Images Publishing Group, 1990. 183p.
Described as a 'unique and current portrayal of the cream of UK architects and their
architecture', this magnificently-illustrated work is given over to profiles of contemporary British architects, landscape architects, and architectural artists. Full details of
their most recent projects are provided.

1818   **The National Trust book of the English house.**
Clive Aslet, Alan Powers.   Harmondsworth, England: Penguin in
association with the National Trust, 1986. 312p. bibliog.
Concerned primarily with middle-class, middle-sized houses in England, this National
Trust book traces their evolution from their medieval origins to their counterparts in
the New Towns of the late twentieth century. The authors perceive these houses as the
houses of rich merchants, successful businessmen, younger sons of the aristocracy,
farmers, churchmen, and clever lawyers. One wonders how many of these classes, or
their modern counterparts, are living in the New Towns today.

1819 **The Shell book of the home in Britain: decoration, design and construction of vernacular interiors 1500-1850.**
James Ayres. London: Faber, 1981. 253p. map. bibliog.

'The vernacular interior was not designed on paper in an office; it evolved on carpenter's bench and mason's 'banker' and was built *in situ*. In other words, vernacular building is arrived at either by individuals constructing shelter for themselves or by trained craftsmen . . . inspired and disciplined by local materials and climate' (Introduction). This historical survey covers such constructural features as walls, doors and doorways, windows, floors and ceilings, stairs, and paint and painting. A gazetteer provides details of museums containing relevant items.

1820 **Suburban style: the British home 1840-1960.**
Helena Barrett, John Phillips. London: Macdonald Orbis, 1987. 224p. bibliog.

It is estimated that more than half of Britain's population live in suburban areas. Both an appreciation of the design features of suburban houses, and a practical guide to restoration and renovation, this generously-illustrated work demonstrates with great clarity the architectural designs and furnishings adopted in suburbia from the High-Victorian period to the 'by-pass variegated' style of the 1960s. A comprehensive gazetteer lists nationwide stockists and suppliers of renovation materials.

1821 **Collins guide to parish churches of England and Wales including the Isle of Man.**
Edited by John Betjeman. London: Collins, 1980. 4th ed. 528p.

First published in 1958, this widely acclaimed guide and gazetteer to over 4,000 parish churches 'worth bicycling twelve miles against the wind to see' has been completely revised and rearranged within the boundaries of the 'new' counties. Introduced by Sir John Betjeman, who explains the inspirations, structure, and architectural features of parish churches from pre-Conquest times onwards, and with drawings by John Piper, this is an accumulation of a number of county guides by local experts. Map references are provided for each church. Those churches, all too many, that have been declared redundant or demolished since the first edition was published have been omitted.

1822 **The abbey explorer's guide: a guide to abbeys and other religious houses.**
Frank Bottomley. London: Kaye & Ward, 1981. 248p. bibliog.

The first section of this pocket-size handbook is an alphabetical illustrated glossary covering all major aspects of abbey buildings, their use, officials, customs, work, and prayer. The second is a gazetteer of the notable religious houses of England, Wales, and Scotland, giving brief details of their location, foundation, type, access, and remains. Unaccountably there are no maps.

1823 **English medieval architecture.**
Hugh Braun. London: Bracken, 1985. 2nd ed. 297p.

First published by Faber in 1951 this superbly illustrated book examines the work of medieval builders, the constructional problems they encountered, and the development or architectural design, before concentrating on specific types of ecclesiastical and secular buildings. The methods, techniques, and styles of stonemasons and other craftsmen are also clearly and authoritatively described.

1824 Tracing the history of houses.
Bill Breckon, Jeffrey Parker. Newbury, England: Countryside Books, 1991. 192p. bibliog.

Outlining the history and development of English houses from the departure of the Romans to the present day, this book charts the social, economic and political influences on their development. It also makes a detailed study of basic house components such as roofs, walls, doors and windows, floors and ceilings, chimneys, and staircases. Finally, the authors present a step-by-step guide on how to establish a house's date.

1825 Timber-framed buildings of England.
R. J. Brown. London: Robert Hale, 1986. 368p. bibliog.

England enjoys a magnificent heritage of timber buildings. This popular work looks at their structure and construction, their architectural features, and at timber-framed churches, homes, farms, and public and industrial buildings.

1826 Illustrated handbook of vernacular architecture.
R. W. Brunskill. London: Faber, 1987. 3rd ed. 256p. 12 maps. bibliog.

Increasing public and academic interest in vernacular architecture over the last forty years on the part of social and economic historians, topographers, medieval archaeologists, geographers, sociologists, and conservationists, stresses the need for a handbook to provide basic information on buildings such as manor houses, farms, cottages, barns, mills, stables, and inns and shops. First published in 1971 this book quickly achieved classic status for its authoritative text closely integrated with clear, accurate and explanatory drawings and diagrams. The enormous variety and profusion of old houses and farm buildings is evident from Brunskill's *Traditional buildings of Britain: an introduction to vernacular architecture* (London: Gollancz, 1981. 160p. bibliog) which discusses in general terms where outstanding examples may be found, when they were placed there and why, and what kinds of house plans were adopted by people of different social levels at different times.

1827 Timber building in Britain.
R. W. Brunskill. London: Gollancz in association with Peter Crawley, 1985. 239p. bibliog.

Primarily concerned with traditional mainstream carpentry, this well-documented work examines the construction of timber roofs and buildings. An illustrated glossary explains carpentry terms and a chronological survey of timber buildings inspects some outstanding examples of the carpenter's craft.

1828 English churchyard memorials.
Frederick Burgess. London: Lutterworth, 1963. 325p.

Only now perhaps is the primitive impulse to perpetuate the memory of the dead by erecting stone monuments losing its power. In the past the majority of tombs and monuments were restricted to men of substance, but by the seventeenth century more humble people were beginning to commemorate their dead in similar fashion. This book describes the origins and development of churchyards, analyses the different types of monument in each period, and examines the symbolism, ornament, and lettering of the memorials commonly to be found in English churchyards. A concluding section looks at the training of stonemasons and their methods of working.

1829   **The historic houses handbook.**
Neil Burton.   London: Macmillan, 1981. 639p. 8 maps.

Visiting historic houses and stately homes has become one of the most popular leisure pursuits of modern times. This guide to 550 houses regularly open to the public gives a brief historical and architectural account of each house, its treasures, collections, gardens, times of opening, and general facilities.

1830   **Medieval monasteries of Great Britain.**
Lionel Butler, Chris Given-Wilson.   London: Michael Joseph, 1979. 416p. maps. bibliog.

An introductory text (p. 13-129) tells the story of English monasticism from the earliest period, of the new orders of monks which revitalized the English Church after the Norman Conquest, and of the arrival of the Friars in the thirteenth century. An illustrated gazetteer describes the architecture and history of eighty of Britain's largest monastic houses. There is also a glossary of architectural terms and a list of monastic sites not mentioned in the text.

1831   **The best buildings in Britain: a catalogue of Grade 1 buildings and Grade A churches in England . . .**
Iain Clark, Clive Aslet, Louise Nicholson.   London: Save Britain's Heritage, 1980. 87p.

Before this list was produced official lists of buildings of special architectural interest were not published although they were available for inspection at local planning offices. Here the information given for Grade One buildings (i.e. those the Department of the Environment consider 'of exceptional interest') is their location, date, and type of ownership; for churches the town and date.

1832   **Church builders of the nineteenth century: a study of the Gothic Revival in England.**
Basil F. L. Clarke.   Newton Abbot, England: David & Charles, 1969. 296p.

According to the *British Citizen* English towns in the 1830s were places 'of ungodliness, profligacy, intemperance, improvidence, turbulence, filth, riot, sullenness, ferocity, desperation, disease: the unmitigated and intolerable penury which is seen at the heels of vice and low debauchery; the destruction of physical, mental, moral and spiritual health; the murder of soul and body; the atmosphere of pollution spreading and propagating itself without a check'. Clearly, in the social climate of the time, the established Church was expected to act to combat this appalling state of affairs and, as church building had not kept pace with the growing population, a vast programme was put in motion. This book, acknowledged as a pioneering study when first published in 1938, examines the reasons for church expansion, the architects involved, and the new and restored church buildings.

1833   **The cathedrals of England.**
Alec Clifton-Taylor.   London: Thames & Hudson, 1967. 288p. map.

Concentrating primarily on 'the outstanding excellences of English cathedrals' architecture and decoration', this is an indispensable handbook for all those intending to visit cathedrals who wish to become knowledgeable on their architectural features. Over 200 illustrations, historical summaries and ground plans of the twenty-six English medieval cathedrals, and a glossary of architectural and ecclesiological terms, are included.

1834   **English stone building.**
Alec Clifton-Taylor, A. S. Ireson.   London: Gollancz, 1983. 285p.

What varieties of stone have traditionally been available to English stonemasons? Where was the stone quarried? How was it worked? These and other questions are tackled in this delightful book by a well-known architectural historian and a former master mason. There are specific chapters on mortars and pointing, stone roofs, and substitutes used instead of stone at various times.

1835   **English cathedrals the forgotten centuries: restoration and change from 1530 to the present day.**
Gerald Cobb.   London: Thames & Hudson, 1980. 176p. bibliog.

The transformation in the fabric and furnishings of England's greater churches in the four hundred years after the Reformation was prodigious in scale. For a number of reasons, the need for structural repairs, an antiquarian zeal for 'correctness', or simply because of shifting fashions, choir-stalls, pulpits, altars, stalls, and statuaries, were all swept away whilst the introduction of large church organs led to further changes. This book selects ten English cathedrals as a representative sample and by means of documentary evidence and pictorial records demonstrates how their interiors were 'restored' almost beyond recognition.

1836   **A biographical dictionary of English architects 1660-1840.**
H. M. Colvin.   London: Murray, 1954. 821p.

Covering the whole period of English classical architecture, this biographical reference work includes over 1,000 professional architects and master builders. Brief career details are given together with buildings with which the architect or builder is chiefly associated. No building is listed which is not reliably documented. A revised edition, *A biographical dictionary of British architects 1600-1840*, including Scottish and Welsh architects, was published in 1978.

1837   **The history of the King's works.**
Edited by H. M. Colvin.   London: HMSO, 1963-82. 6 vols.

This authoritative series of volumes presents an exhaustive history of public buildings erected for government administration, defence, the royal household, and worship, in England and Wales from pre-Conquest times to the year of the Great Exhibition. Titles are as follows: vols. one and two *The Middle Ages* (1963. 1,139p.); vols. three and four *1485-1660* (1975-82. 469p.); vol. five *1660-1782* (1976. 535p.); vol. six *The period of reform and experiment 1782-1851* (1973. 744p.).

1838 **British building firsts.**

David Crawford.   Newton Abbot, England: David & Charles, 1990. 192p. bibliog.

This book is an alphabetical guide to the first, earliest known, or oldest surviving example of twenty-nine categories of public buildings ranging from Roman churches to multiscreen cinemas, from Bronze Age harbours to international airports. There are notes on the architects, engineers, and craftsmen involved in their construction, and a list of outstanding buildings and sites to visit.

1839 **How old is your house?**

Pamela Cunnington.   London: A. & C. Black, 1988. rev. ed. 253p. bibliog.

A comprehensive guide to the dating of houses from internal and external evidence, this book is as much concerned with changes in the way people have lived as in changes in architectural styles and fashions. Beginning with an explanation of documentary evidence, and where it may be found, it pays specific attention to the ways in which the status and function of a house may change from one generation to the next. Accommodation for travellers, and how to determine whether a period appearance is genuine or fake, are also closely examined.

1840 **English architecture: an illustrated glossary.**

James Stevens Curl.   Newton Abbot, England: David & Charles, 1986. 2nd ed. 192p. bibliog.

First published in 1977 this is the first really comprehensive glossary of English architectural terms to have appeared for many years. Including 300 photographs and drawings it is a delightful book in which to browse as well as being an excellent work of reference.

1841 **Directory of official architecture and planning 1992.**

Harlow, England: Longman, 1991. 31st ed. 381p.

This directory includes information on appropriate government departments, local authorities, development and planning bodies, public services and statutory authorities, parks and tourist boards, universities and ecclesiastical buildings, staff architects attached to commerce and industry, and professional and training bodies. Sources of professional information are also listed.

1842 **Victorian architecture.**

Roger Dixon, Stefan Muthesius.   London: Thames & Hudson, 1978. 288p. bibliog.

The surviving buildings of Victorian England are among the most varied and colourful in England's architectural heritage. Here domestic architecture, buildings designed for all types of entertainment, new materials and new building types, industry and commerce, civic architecture, churches, and the architecture of education, their visual appeal, historical style, and their designers' artistic development, all come under scrutiny. There is also a comprehensive listing of over 300 architects and their most renowned buildings.

1843   **The architecture of Wren.**
Kerry Downes.   London: Redhedge, 1988. 139p. + 96p. plates.
bibliog.

Sir Christopher Wren held the post of Surveyor of the King's Works for almost half a century. This work places his career in a biographical context and asserts his genius by examining his artistic principles, his working methods, and the influences that shaped and conditioned them.

1844   **The handbook of British architectural styles.**
David N. Durant.   London: Barrie & Jenkins, 1992. 208p.

For tourists and week-end outings enthusiasts with no specialized knowledge of architecture this portable guide has much to offer. By virtue of its chronological approach the emergence and development of successive architectural styles is clearly recognized and a correct historical sequence is easily distinguished.

1845   **A broken wave: the rebuilding of England 1940-1980.**
Lionel Esher.   London: Allen Lane, 1981. 326p.

The German blitz of 1940-41 provided an unlooked for opportunity to rebuild England's towns and cities. This book focuses on five case studies, London, Newcastle upon Tyne, Sheffield, Liverpool, and the New Town of Milton Keynes, to discover how English planners and architects met, or failed to meet, the challenge.

1846   **Seven Victorian architects.**
Edited by Jane Fawcett.   London: Thames & Hudson, 1976. 160p.

This volume, a joint enterprise of the publishers and the Victorian Society, presents essays on William Burn, Philip Charles Hardwick, Sydney Smirke, John Loughborough Pearson, George Frederick Bodley, Alfred Waterhouse, and Edwin Lutyens, whose work has generally been neglected by architectural historians.

1847   **The architecture of the Anglo-Saxons.**
Eric Fernie.   London: Batsford, 1983. 192p. bibliog.

Exploiting fresh information brought to light by archaeological research in the 1960s and 1970s, this book investigates Anglo-Saxon domestic and urban architecture in addition to ecclesiastical architecture which has usually preoccupied previous studies. It embraces not only buildings which survive above ground but also important structures uncovered by excavations and others known only from contemporary descriptions.

1848   **A guide to the castles of England and Wales.**
James Forde-Johnston.   London: Constable, 1981. 352p. 10 maps.
bibliog.

A brief survey of castle building during the years 1066-1485 introduces this pocket-size guidebook which is divided into ten regional sections for easy reference. More than 350 castles are listed, 115 of them are described in detail, each with a concise architectural and historical account, a ground plan, and photographs.

1849 **Discovering English churches: a beginner's guide to the story of the parish church from before the Conquest to the Gothic revival.**
Richard Foster.   London: BBC, 1981. 295p.

This lavishly-illustrated book accompanied the BBC television series of the same title first broadcast on BBC2, October to November 1979. It sets the parish within the wider context of national history and aims to encourage readers and viewers to embark on voyages of discovery in unfamiliar churches. The book ends with a list of 1,001 of some of England's most interesting churches, and a twenty-page illustrated glossary of architectural and ecclesiastical terms.

1850 **The English tradition in architecture.**
John Gloag.   London: A. & C. Black, 1963. 258p. 2 maps. bibliog.

Written for the non-specialist this well-illustrated survey of the history of architecture in England concentrates on the development of the characteristically English approach to the use of materials and to the adventurous and common-sense attitudes of English architects, builders, and craftsmen.

1851 **English architecture since the Regency: an interpretation.**
H. S. Goodhart-Rendel.   London: Constable, 1953. 304p.

This chronological survey, intended for a non-specialist audience, and redolent of the author's own reasoned philosophy of architecture, is now generally accepted as one of the most readable and entertaining guides to Victorian architecture ever written.

1852 **The National Trust guide: a complete introduction to the buildings, gardens, coast and country owned by the National Trust.**
Lydia Greeves, Michael Trinick.   London: National Trust, 1989. 4th ed. 402p. 16 maps.

Established in 1895 to protect places of historic interest or of natural beauty, the National Trust is now the third largest private landowner in England. This encyclopedic illustrated work, which was first published in 1973, is the only comprehensive guide to the National Trust's principal properties and the treasures they contain. Brief details of properties not described in the text and of buildings not open to the public are listed and annotated in an appendix.

1853 **British architectural books and writers 1556-1785.**
Eileen Harris.   Cambridge, England: Cambridge University Press, 1990. 571p.

In this bibliographical survey biographical essays present overviews of 220 architectural authors followed by full and detailed bibliographical descriptions of their books and successive editions. Substantial introductory essays look at books on the architectural orders, design and pattern books, carpenters' manuals, measuring and pricing books, archaeological works, books on bridges, publishing and bookselling, and architectural engravings.

1854 **English medieval architects: a biographical dictionary down to 1550 including master masons, carpenters, carvers, building contractors and others responsible for design.**
John Harvey, Arthur Oswald.   Boston, Massachusetts: Boston Book & Art Shop, 1954. 412p.

Sepulchral inscriptions, official enrolments relating to the Royal Works, licences to crenellate, accounts and contracts, churchwardens' fabric accounts, are among the unusual sources drawn on for this well-researched biographical dictionary of the architects, artists, and craftsmen, who designed the buildings of medieval England.

1855 **Sources for the history of houses.**
John H. Harvey.   London: British Records Association, 1974. 61p.

Concerned with the practical use of the sources, and not with their nature, this book is designed to help the ordinary occupier of a pre-1850 house to answer questions about its history: When was it built or altered? Who built it? What families owned it? Who have been the occupiers? With what events has it been connected? Documentary sources and architectural evidence are both examined.

1856 **The country house described: an index to the country houses of Great Britain and Ireland.**
M. Holmes.   Winchester, England: St. Paul's Bibliographies/Victoria & Albert Museum, 1986. 320p. bibliog.

Based on the contents of 135 general architectural works, county histories, guides, and sale catalogues, held at the National Art Library, Victoria & Albert Museum, there are entries for 4,000 houses in this meticulously researched publication.

1857 **English castles.**
Richard Humble.   London: English Tourist Board/Weidenfeld & Nicolson, 1984. 152p. bibliog.

The sites of seventy-five of England's finest castles which are easily accessible by car are described and illustrated in this handsome volume. An introductory section explains why individual castles were erected in particular locations, how they were planned, and what their functions were.

1858 **Blue guides: churches and chapels.**
S. C. Humphrey.   London: A. & C. Black, 1991. 2 vols.

Detailed descriptions of the most interesting churches in terms of their antiquity, historical associations, and architecture and fittings, are included in these two volumes (vol. one *Northern England*, 544p.; vol. two *Southern England*, 606p.), arranged alphabetically by traditional counties, which usually correspond to the Church of England's diocesan boundaries. Each volume includes an architectural and ecclesiological glossary, an informative introduction to church history, and brief accounts of the development of regional church building.

Architecture

1859 **English country houses open to the public**
Christopher Hussey, John Cornforth.   London: Country Life, 1964.
4th ed. 256p.
Brief accounts of the history, and the particular distinctive features of 409 country
houses are arranged chronologically in this pictorial volume which goes a long way to
justify the claim that English country houses are the supreme achievement of the visual
arts in England.

1860 **Inside churches.**
London: Capability Publishing in association with the National
Association of Decorative & Fine Arts Societies, 1989. 244p. bibliog.
Originating as a practical handbook for the Church Recorders of NADFAS, this
encyclopedic guide is now aimed at those visitors to churches who may be baffled by
what they see around them. Terms used in church architecture, costume, crosses,
decoration, and heraldry are defined; the materials used in church construction are
explored; and various objects such as clocks, memorials and monuments, and musical
instruments are described in detail. Every description or definition is accompanied by a
drawing, greatly facilitating recognition and identification of items likely to be
encountered inside churches.

1861 **The National Trust book of British castles.**
Paul Johnson.   London: National Trust, 1978. 288p. bibliog.
Beginning with Iron Age hill-forts, this sumptuously-illustrated work traces each stage
of development in the design, construction, and purpose of British castles.
Technological developments in the art of warfare, which eventually nullified the
castle's effectiveness as a military stronghold, and the conditions faced by their
inhabitants, are fully explained. Castle restoration, and the building of mock castles in
the eighteenth and nineteenth centuries, are also considered.

1862 **Industrial architecture in Britain 1750-1939.**
Edgar Jones.   London: Batsford, 1985. 239p. bibliog.
Two main lines of enquiry are followed in this general history of British industrial
architecture. One examines the process whereby factories and warehouses won
respectability as suitable subjects for architectural study and not treated as an inferior
class of building apart from the mainstream. Particular attention is paid to those
architects who made a conscious decision to specialize in industrial commissions. The
other investigates the way in which textile mills, engineering works, warehouses,
gasworks, chemical plants, and the rest, were influenced by changing architectural
fashions and practices. Some industrial structures actually generated original
architectural concepts, notably in the field of safety and environmental hazards.

1863 **British and Irish architectural history: a bibliography and guide to
sources of information.**
Ruth H. Kamen.   London: Architectural Press, 1981. 249p.
Compiled by the Head of the RIBA's Library Information Service, this bibliographical
guide contains 900 fully annotated entries divided into seven sections: a guide to
architectural literature; architects and buildings; published and unpublished sources,
periodicals, and periodical indexes; societies, institutions and organizations; sources of

architectural photographs; and a selective bibliography of British and Irish architectural history providing full citations and descriptive comments on the essential reference material and the most important works.

1864 **Abbeys and priories in England and Wales.**
Bryan Little. London: Batsford, 1979. 216p. bibliog.

Abbeys and priories which are still active are considered in this impressively-illustrated volume as well as the medieval foundations suppressed under Henry VIII. A general survey includes terms and meanings, the growth of monasteries, friars and hospitals, the Dissolution, and the modern scene. A regional gazetteer provides information on the history and the surviving architecture of those abbeys and priories most worthwhile visiting.

1865 **Architecture in Norman Britain.**
Bryan Little. London: Batsford, 1985. 191p. bibliog.

This thematic study of Norman buildings, encompassing military, ecclesiastical and domestic architecture sets them in the context of European Romanesque art and architecture. A wide range of evidence is adduced not only from buildings surviving intact, or partially in ruins, but also from ground plans of recently excavated sites.

1866 **Catholic churches since 1623: a study of Roman Catholic churches in England and Wales from penal times to the present decade.**
Bryan Little. London: Robert Hale, 1966. 256p. bibliog.

From the end of the eighteenth century onwards Roman Catholic churches became increasingly prominent in England's religious architecture. This expert study concentrates on their architectural history and design and on the architects employed. In a final chapter the circumstances surrounding the building and planning of Liverpool's Roman Catholic cathedral are given a thorough airing.

1867 **A history of the English house: from primitive times to the Victorian period.**
Nathaniel Lloyd. London: Architectural Press, 1931. 487p.

Still regarded as the standard work in its field this exhaustive study of the development of English domestic architecture is arranged in two parts. A chronological narrative is followed by 900 photographs illustrating architectural features such as plans and exteriors, wall treatments, entrances, windows, chimneys, ceilings, fireplaces, and staircases.

1868 **The Royal Institute of British Architects: a guide to its archive and history.**
Angela Mace. London: Mansell, 1986. 378p. bibliog.

Founded in 1834 the RIBA is today one of the world's foremost professional architects' association. This practical guide and companion to its archives is arranged on a thematic basis. Each section contains an introduction, a descriptive list, and a bibliography. A concise history of the RIBA and an essay, 'Using the RIBA archive: a historian's view', are also included. The Association publishes an annual *Directory of Members*, an alphabetical listing of over 28,000 architects and a *Directory of practices* (London: 1989, 410p.), a list of architectural firms listed by town or city.

Architecture

1869   New British architecture.
Robert Maxwell.   London: Thames & Hudson, 1972. 199p.

After a lengthy introduction which examines the British architectural tradition, and its post-war theory and practice, this expert study inspects fifty examples of recently completed private homes, university, city, cultural, and commercial buildings, sports centres, hospitals and schools, mostly dating from the 1960s, whose designs the author considers to have extended tradition and convention. A number of important architectural questions are raised: whose interest is more important, the client's, or the user's? To whom is the building designed to appeal? Can it be understood by the man in the street, or only by a knowledgeable few?

1870   English vernacular houses.
Eric Mercer.   London: HMSO for Royal Commission on Historical Monuments England, 1975. 246p. bibliog.

Covering all major aspects of vernacular architecture, from house plans and construction methods to the influence of architectural styles and trends exhibited in the houses of the more affluent classes in society, on smaller and humbler dwellings, this study of rural houses from medieval times to the nineteenth century emphasizes the rich variety of regional characteristics within the overall context. A ninety-page descriptive list of selected recorded monuments is arranged alphabetically by county.

1871   English medieval monasteries (1066-1540).
Roy Midmer.   London: Heinemann, 1979. 385p. 8 maps. bibliog.

This comprehensive work of reference opens with a survey of the contemplative, mendicant, and minor orders, and of the alien priories, Knights Templar, and the Knights Hospitallers, active in England during the medieval period. Background information on monastery finances, visitations, the Black Death, and the Dissolution, is also included. The main section is a complete A-Z gazetteer of monasteries giving historical, archaeological, and architectural notes and references to sources of more detailed information.

1872   Modern British architecture since 1945.
Edited by Peter Murray, Stephen Trombley.   London: Frederick Muller in conjunction with RIBA Magazines, 1984. 185p. bibliog. (RIBA Guides to Modern Architecture).

Edited by the editor and deputy editor of the Royal Institute of British Architect's *Journal*, this tall pocket-size handbook is an illustrated guide to 336 post-war buildings which notes their significance in the contemporary environment. The guide is divided into thirteen regions and gives directory and access information for those who may wish to visit particular buildings.

1873   The English terraced house.
Stefan Muthesius.   New Haven, Connecticut; London: Yale University Press, 1982. 278p. bibliog.

The ordinary house built rapidly, economically, and to a standardized design, provides the central focus of this book which charts the development of terraced houses from the fashionable residences of the later Georgian period to the strictly working class accommodation of late Victorian and Edwardian times. The method, management, and control of English speculative building is first discussed. More complex issues such as the variety of working class housing in the North, the way in which changes in domestic life influenced house plans, the effect of new styles and technological developments on the use of common building materials, the distinction between the size and type of house in the context of the social stratification of Victorian society, and the eventual demise of the terraced house as the most fashionable form of everyday living, are also treated at length. This book was awarded the Sir Banister Fletcher Prize of the Authors' Club for 1982 for the most deserving book in the field of architecture and the fine arts.

1874   **A guide to the abbeys of England and Wales.**
Anthony New.   London: Constable, 1985. 465p. 2 maps.
A step-by-step architectural and historical description of 243 abbey sites or buildings and their contents, together with an Ordnance Survey National Grid six figure reference, and details of care or ownership, are included in this convenient pocket-size guidebook. A quality audit of each building's architectural setting, its printed guide, and its accessibility, is presented in tabular form.

1875   **A guide to the cathedrals of Britain.**
Anthony New.   London: Constable, 1980. 462p. maps.
No less than 106 cathedrals and twenty-seven churches which were once cathedrals, of all denominations, are fully described in this extremely useful pocket size guide. In addition to architectural detail there is information on the craftsmen and designers who were engaged on the building and decoration of Britain's splendid cathedrals: embroiders and tapestry-makers; furniture makers; workers and artists in stained glass; metalworkers; organ builders; sculptors; and mosaic and ceramic artists.

1876   **The architecture of Southern England.**
John Julius Norwich, photographs by Jorge Lewinski, Mayotte Magnus.   London: Macmillan, 1985. 720p. 9 maps. bibliog.
Covering those counties lying to the south of a line drawn from the River Severn to the Wash, this is a 'personal anthology' of some 1,200 buildings primarily, although not exclusively, concerned with those 'in which the English architectural genius shows itself at its brilliant best: with churches and cathedrals on the one hand, and with country and manor houses on the other'. Each county section begins with an historical introduction and ends with a short list of further buildings for which the limitations of space allowed only a brief description. This is truly a highly readable and informative book to be cherished by all those who have a feeling for old buildings and who delight in visiting them.

1877   **Blue Guide Victorian architecture in Britain.**
Julian Orbach.   London: Black, 1987.
All types of Victorian buildings are described in this comprehensive county-by-county guide: banks, churches, civic buildings, clocktowers, hotels, mausoleums, memorial towers, mills and factories, offices, railway stations, stately homes, etc. An introduction outlines architectural development in the Victorian period and there is a ten-page glossary of architectural and cultural terms.

1878 **Buildings of England series.**
Nikolaus Pevsner. Harmondsworth, England: Penguin, 1951- .
48 vols.

Pevsner began his architectural survey of England in 1946. This mammoth descriptive inventory of English acclesiastical and secular buildings, comprising some 20,000 pages, and encompassing forty-eight county volumes, offers tourists, sightseers and architectural historians an authoritative and definitive guide to every worthwhile building in England, not only those of national and international standing, but lesser buildings such as old churches and garden follies, pubs and pumping stations etc. Each volume contained an introductory survey, a detailed descriptive gazetteer, a glossary of architectural terms, and various indexes. The first two titles published were *Cornwall* and *Nottinghamshire* in 1951. Since Pevsner embarked on his monumental task the townscapes have changed beyond recognition, many of the buildings he recorded have been demolished. Revised, updated editions have consequently been issued at frequent intervals. For example *North Devon* and *South Devon*, first published in 1952, were combined into a single revised *Devon* volume (1989. 2nd ed. 974p.). This includes ten introductory essays, a bibliography, and a list of architects 1660-1800. *The best buildings of England: an anthology* (Edited by Bridget Cherry, John Newton. Penguin, 1986. 232p. bibliog.) was published to coincide with the forming of the Pevsner Memorial Trust. This contains 101 of Pevsner's most illuminating accounts of individual buildings. Both editors have long been associated with the series; Cherry has been editor of the project since 1983 and has been responsible for the continuing revision programme. Pevsner's and P. Metcalfe's *The cathedrals of England* (1985. 2 vols.) includes descriptions of sixty-two medieval and modern cathedrals extracted from the county volumes of the Buildings of England series.

1879 **The styles of English architecture.**
Hubert Pragnell. London: Batsford, 1984. 176p. bibliog.

Copiously illustrated with the author's own drawings and plans, this concise visual guide describes the major developments in English architecture from the Anglo-Saxon period onwards. Some specific types of buildings, such as medieval churches, or nineteenth-century mills and factories, are given detailed treatment at the appropriate point in the chronological text.

1880 **The traditional buildings of England.**
Anthony Quiney. London: Thames & Hudson, 1990. 224p. bibliog.

Successive generations' building traditions, and the buildings that emerged, are the principal themes of this authoritative and magnificently illustrated study. The making of a native tradition of building, the materials to hand, timber framing, medieval houses, innovations, town buildings, agricultural and industrial buildings, and the Gothic revival, are all featured in this overall architectural assessment.

1881 **Church furnishing and decoration in England and Wales.**
Gerald Randall. London: Batsford, 1980. 240p. bibliog.

A wide coverage of Church furniture is evident in this illustrated historical introduction. Porches, fonts, pulpits and lecterns, chests and almsboxes, screens, altars and communion tables, piscinas, Easter sepulchres, memorials, and many other types, are examined and discussed.

1882 **The English parish church.**
Gerald Randall. London: Batsford, 1982. 192p. bibliog.
Some parish churches have been in continuous use for over a thousand years.
Beginning in the Saxon period, this evolutionary history draws upon historical and
theological background material, and present-day descriptive information, to present
the successive stages of church building from one generation to another.

1883 **The Shell book of cottages.**
Richard Reid. London: Michael Joseph, 1977. 12 maps.
'A pictorial celebration of thatched, oak-beamed, rough-plastered dwellings', this
guide introduces twelve regional descriptive and illustrated gazetteers of outstanding
country cottages by a number of thematic essays on their history, construction, and
place in rural life. The *Financial Times* was moved to describe it as 'probably the
definitive work to carry with you at all times'.

1884 **The National Trust book of English architecture.**
J. M. Richards. London: National Trust/Weidenfeld & Nicolson,
1981. 288p. bibliog.
This fully-illustrated survey of England's architectural heritage concentrates on
buildings that may still be entered as well as simply looked at. Whilst representative
buildings of all types, and of every period since Anglo-Saxon times, are covered, there
is especial emphasis on the nineteenth and twentieth centuries. The work of leading
architects, and the advances in building methods and materials, are examined in detail.

1885 **The ice-houses of Britain.**
Susan Roaf, Sylvia P. Beamon. London: Routledge, 1990. 576p.
By the end of the nineteenth century most large country houses enjoyed the benefit of
an ice-house. In the first half of this carefully researched illustrated book the
constructional problems of siting, access and drainage are fully discussed whilst an
historical account of ice-houses establishes their form and function from the earliest
times. Part two constitutes a gazetteer of 3,000 British ice-houses.

1886 **The architecture of Northern England.**
John Martin Robinson, photographs by Jorge Lewinski, Mayotte
Magnus. London: Macmillan, 1986. 380p. bibliog. 4 maps.
This is a companion volume to John Julius Norwich's *The architecture of Southern
England* (q.v.). Illustrated with over 230 photographs, it comprises 575 entries which
relate to old and new buildings, religious and secular, arranged alphabetically by
county, to be found in England north of the Cotswolds. Together, the two volumes
provide a comprehensive and exuberant guide to English architecture.

1887 **Blue Guide cathedrals and abbeys of England and Wales.**
Keith Spence. London: Ernest Benn, 1984. 327p. 3 maps. bibliog.
Bridging the gap between large scholarly tomes on medieval architecture and short
guides with limited space, this volume, like all others from the same stable, compresses
a wealth of information into its comparatively modest size. Divided into seven regional
sections, it includes a description of all Church of England and Roman Catholic
cathedrals, the Greek Orthodox cathedral in London, and of 200 abbeys and abbey

churches either standing or in ruins, together with ground plans and illustrations. Introductory information includes short essays on the layout of monasteries and the Rule of St. Benedict. A production miracle, it easily falls into the indispensable class.

1888 **The English house 1860-1914: the flowering of English domestic architecture.**
Gavin Stamp, Andre Goulancourt. London: Faber, 1986. 254p. bibliog.

Developing from an exhibition of photographs and drawings sponsored by the Building Centre Trust and Redland Ltd. in 1980, this book features descriptive portraits of some eighty or so houses arranged according to broad themes in roughly chronological order. English houses prior to this period are described and there are commentaries on late-Victorian country houses, Classical and neo-Georgian houses, town and suburban houses, and on the architectural and social concepts embodied in the garden suburbs.

1889 **Architects in Britain 1530-1830.**
John Summerson. London: Penguin, 1983. 7th ed. 624p. 6 maps. bibliog. (The Pelican History of Art).

First published in 1953, this descriptive and historical survey extends from the early Renaissance to the post-Waterloo Greek and Gothic revival. More emphasis is given in this edition to the technical changes of the period, especially at the close of the eighteenth century, when architecture first felt the impact of the Industrial Revolution. There is a new chapter on materials and methods in the Age of Improvement. As is the case in all volumes of the Pelican History of Art series, this survey is profusely illustrated with contemporary prints, plans, and drawings.

1890 **Anglo-Saxon architecture.**
H. M. Taylor, Joan Taylor. Cambridge, England: Cambridge University Press, 1965. 2 vols.

Forming a complete catalogue of the Anglo-Saxon fabric surviving in English churches, this immense work of scholarship is in three parts. The first is a short introduction reviewing pre-Conquest architectural features and the reasons for assigning them to the Anglo-Saxon period, whilst the second is a detailed description of individual churches arranged alphabetically by parish. Nearly 280 photographs complete this definitive and exhaustive inventory. A list of fifty-three churches which have been claimed as Anglo-Saxon, in whole or in part, but which are not regarded sufficiently definite to include in the text, are listed in an appendix.

1891 **Collins guide to cathedrals, abbeys and priories of England and Wales.**
Henry Thorold. London: Collins, 1986. 332p. 2 maps.

Arranged by diocese, each of the forty-eight English and Welsh cathedrals, and a multitude of abbeys and priories still regularly used for worship, are described and illustrated in detail. The historical and architectural features of each building are carefully explained and there is a glossary of historical and architectural terms. Although too big and heavy for field use, this is nevertheless an admirable work for planning visits.

1892   **A short dictionary of British architects.**
      Dora Ware.   London: Allen & Unwin, 1967. 312p. bibliog.
This dictionary records the life and works of 500 British architects from the Norman
period onwards, giving biographical and professional detail, including their publications, and a list of their principal and existing buildings.

1893   **English architecture: a concise history.**
      David Watkin.   London: Thames & Hudson, 1979. 216p. bibliog.
Chapters on Anglo-Saxon and Norman architecture, the early Gothic style; Decorated,
Court Style and Perpendicular; later Tudor and Jacobean country houses; Inigo Jones
to James Gibbs; the classical revival; Victorian architecture; and the twentieth century,
present a balanced and authoritative account of the major masterpieces of English
architecture. A glossary, a detailed bibliography, and 309 illustrations further enhance
the text.

1894   **The castles of England.**
      Frederick Wilkinson.   London: George Philip, 1973. 191p. 7 maps.
This A-Z gazetteer is limited to sites and buildings commonly designated as 'castles'.
All others, with the single exception of the Tower of London, are rigorously excluded.
The main section includes only those sites 'of which real evidence survives on the
ground' although there is a list of other sites excluded because they are 'both physically
unimpressive and historically obscure'. Major sites are provided with a short history, a
description of its original form, and conditions of access.

1895   **British architects 1840-1976: a guide to information sources.**
      Lawrence Wodehouse.   Detroit, Michigan: Gale Research, 1978.
      353p. (Art and Architecture Information Guide Series).
Part one of this guide consists of general reference works, books on the architecture of
towns, cities and counties, and books on various building types, whilst part two consists
of a selected annotated biographical dictionary of British architects 1840-1976.

1896   **The English medieval house.**
      Margaret Wood.   London: Phoenix, 1965. 448p. bibliog.
This definitive and scholarly work allocates specific chapters to the main architectural
features of medieval English houses: halls and chambers; vaulted cellars; oriels;
doorways, porches and gatehouses; timber houses; kitchens and fireplaces; roofs and
roof coverings; and many more.

A guide to London churches.
See item no. 318.

London statues.
See item no. 319.

The City of London its architectural heritage.
See item no. 320.

A guide to the architecture of London.
See item no. 336.

Architecture

A London docklands guide.
See item no. 341.

The art and architecture of London.
See item no. 346.

Georgian London.
See item no. 348.

Language

General

1897 **Annual Bibliography of English Language and Literature.**
London: Modern Humanities Research Association, 1920- . annual.
Volume sixty-three: *1988* (1992. 588p.) has 9,247 entries for books, pamphlets, and journal articles, arranged under form and chronological headings, e.g. *Festschriften*; bibliographies; language, literature and the computer; newspapers and other periodicals; English language (general studies, phonetics and phonology, grammar, vocabulary, lexicography, names, dialect, etc.); traditional culture, folklore and folklife; and English literature (by period).

1898 **The treasure of our tongue: the story of English from its obscure beginnings to its present eminence as the most widely spoken language.**
Lincoln Barnett. London: Secker & Warburg, 1966. 253p. bibliog.
Easy to learn, although difficult to use with precision, English became the *lingua franca* of the world in the years following the Second World War. This study which had its origins in a series of articles in *Life* magazine 1961-62, first discusses the origins of human language, traces the evolution of English to its Elizabethan flowering, and ends with a discussion of its future as an international language.

1899 **A history of the English language.**
Albert C. Baugh, Thomas Cable. London: Routledge & Kegan Paul, 1978. 3rd ed. 438p. 5 maps. bibliog.
Scholarly bibliographical essays to each chapter underline the academic nature of this standard work first published in England in 1951. It gives equal prominence to the early roots of the English language and to its later developments. The political, social, and intellectual influences affecting the language at different periods are also investigated.

1900 **The English language.**
Edited by W. F. Bolton, David Crystal. London: Sphere, 1987.
362p. bibliog.
Ten essays by different authors examine the phonology, morphology, syntax, vocabulary, style, history, and social context of the English language, in this comprehensive and authoritative study. The development of English into a world language is examined in a final chapter.

1901 **The English language.**
Robert Burchfield. Oxford: Oxford University Press, 1985. 194p.
map. bibliog.
This scholarly and well-documented introduction to the nature, origin, and development of the English language, seen as a successor to Logan Pearsall Smith's *The English language* (1912), pays special attention to the recording of the language in dictionaries and grammars, vocabulary, pronunciation and spelling, and to dispersed forms of English overseas. The author, chief editor of the *Oxford English dictionary*, concludes that 'English as it is spoken and written by native speakers looks like remaining a communicative force, however slightly or severely beyond the grasp of foreigners, and changed in whatever agreeable or disagreeable manner, for many centuries to come'.

1902 **The changing English language.**
Brian Foster. London: Macmillan, 1968. 263p.
This survey of contemporary English traces the changes affecting the language in the latter half of the century. The impact of American usage, foreign contributions, and the new society, are seen as important influences.

1903 **The Cambridge history of the English language.**
Edited by Richard M. Hogg. Cambridge, England: Cambridge
University Press, 1992- . 6 vols. (vol. 1. *The beginnings to 1066*.
Richard M. Hogg. 1992. 616p. maps. bibliog.; vol. 2. *1066-1476*.
N. F. Blake. 1992. 692p. 2 maps. bibliog.).
When complete this authoritative co-operative history will provide a full account of the English language extending from strict linguistics to more specialized topics like personal names and placenames. Earlier volumes are treated on a chronological basis whilst those dealing with later periods employ a geographical coverage. To date only vols. one and two in the series have been published, projected volume titles are as follows: vol. three *1476-1776* (Roger Lass); vol. four *1776-present day* (Suzanne Romaine); vol. five *English in Britain and overseas: origins and development* (Robert W. Burchfield); vol. six *English in North America: origins and development* (John Ayto).

1904 **The Oxford companion to the English language.**
Edited by Tom McArthur. Oxford: Oxford University Press, 1992.
960p.
Written by over ninety specialist contributors this Oxford companion includes articles ranging from the core aspects of the English language, its grammar, pronunciation, history, and usage, to wider topics like linguistics, accents and dialects, education,

literature, technology, and geography. There are entries for individuals, books, and institutions which have shaped the language, or of its study, and there is also broad coverage of English as a worldwide language. A chronology of the language from its origins to the present day is also featured.

1905 **The story of the English language.**
Mario Pei. London: Allen & Unwin, 1968. 430p. bibliog.
First published as *The story of English* in 1953 this historical guide now contains a section on American English. Other topics discussed include prehistory and Anglo-Saxon English, the enhancement and degradation of the language, teaching English, and spelling reform.

1906 **The other languages of England.**
Edited by Michael W. Stubbs. London: Routledge & Kegan Paul, 1985. 429p. bibliog.
Languages originating in South and East Asia and in Southern and Eastern Europe, considered to be important in everyday life in some areas of urban England, are the 'other' languages referred to. This study, compiled by members of The Linguistic Minorities Project based on the Institute of Education, University of London, provides information about language patterns of children and adults, about usage in different social contexts, and about the teaching of these languages. It seeks to destroy the concept of English monolinguism and argues that the minority languages constitute a valuable social and economic resource.

1907 **The archaeology of English.**
Martyn Wakelin. London: Batsford, 1988. 191p. 30 maps. bibliog.
Not strictly a history of the English language but more an examination of the physical evidence which forms the basis of any such history, *viz.* inscriptions, manuscripts, place-names, writings of all kinds, and descriptions of the state of the language at various stages, this study combines a chronological narrative with close analyses of selected passages from texts of all periods to the present day.

Old and Middle English

1908 **A dictionary of archaic and provincial words: obsolete phrases, proverbs, and ancient customs, from the XIV century.**
James Orchard Halliwell-Phillips. London: Routledge, 1924. 7th ed. 960p.
A twenty-seven page essay, 'The English provincial dialects', precedes this dictionary of the early English language. It contains some 50,000 words 'many of which have never appeared even in scattered glossaries'. The definitions are supported by illustrative quotations from the original authorities.

1909 **A grammar of Old English: vol. 1. Phonology.**
Richard M. Hogg. Oxford: Blackwell, 1992. 352p.
Taking full advantage of the *Dictionary of Old English* project in Toronto, which enabled a much wider range of data to be checked and assessed than previously, this reference grammar is based on the most recent developments in Old English studies and in linguistic theory. Vol. two, *Morphology*, is in preparation. When completed it will serve as an essential modern reference tool.

1910 **A guide to Old English.**
Bruce Mitchell, Fred C. Robinson. Oxford: Blackwell, 1992. 5th ed. 376p. bibliog.
Part one of this standard introduction to Old English language and literature covers orthography and pronunciation, inflexions, word formation, syntax, and an introduction to Anglo Saxon studies in language, literature, archaeology and history. Part two consists of selected passages from important Old English texts.

1911 **Middle English dictionary: containing words used by writers from the twelfth to the fifteenth century.**
F. H. Stratmann, revised by H. Bradley. London: Oxford University Press, 1963. 708p.
First published in 1891 this dictionary lists over 20,000 entry words giving their etymology, meanings, and illustrations of their usage.

Etymology

1912 **Bloomsbury dictionary of word origins.**
John Ayto. London: Bloomsbury, 1990. 583p.
The purpose of this dictionary, which includes some 8,000 cross-referenced entries, is 'to uncover the often surprising connections between elements of the English lexicon that have become obscured by centuries of language changes' (Introduction). It demonstrates how present-day English has developed from its Indo-European origins and how the different main influences on the language have intermingled.

1913 **The Oxford dictionary of English etymology.**
Edited by C. T. Onions, G. W. S. Friedrichsen, R. W. Burchfield. Oxford: Clarendon Press, 1966. 1,024p.
Widely regarded as the most reliable etymological dictionary of the English language ever published, this erudite work stands as the principal source of information on the origin, formation, and development of English words. Its 28,000 main entries give the earliest recorded date of each word, tracing it to its ultimate source 'so far as this is known or is reasonably to be presumed', and states whether it is of Old English or German descent or has been admitted from other languages. *The concise Oxford dictionary of English etymology*, which is based on the main work, provides a clear

guide to the origins and history and sense-development of modern English including both basic words of the language and a wide selection of the derivative forms.

1914 **Origins: a short etymological dictionary of modern English.**
Eric Partridge. London: Routledge & Kegan Paul, 1966. 4th ed. 972p.

Some 20,000 of the most common English words are defined by derivation in this standard compact lexicon first published in 1958. To assist the student of etymology there is a 150-page section comprising lists of prefixes, suffixes, and elements of words employed in specialist vocabularies of scholarship and learning.

1915 **Why do we say . . .? Words and sayings and where they come from.**
Nigel Rees. Poole, England: Blandford Press, 1987. 224p.

Some 500 well-known phrases and sayings are dissected in this pithy reference work whose purpose is 'to compare the many explanations on offer and to test them, even if in the end it serves to emphasize that in this field hard and fast conclusions are difficult to come by'.

1916 **Dictionary of changes in meaning.**
Adrian Room. London: Routledge & Kegan Paul, 1986. 292p. bibliog.

English is a dynamic language and it is by no means unusual or extraordinary for words to change their meanings, sometimes quite dramatically, over the centuries. This dictionary charts the progress of 1,300 such words.

Dialect

1917 **English dialects.**
G. L. Brook. London: André Deutsch, 1963. 232p. 7 maps. bibliog. (The Language Library).

This study of English dialects rests upon two premises: that the word 'dialect' refers to the everyday speech of a group of people smaller than the group who share a common language, and that the basis of sub-division of a language into dialects may be social, occupational, or geographical (thus 'standard English' is itself a dialect which, for strictly non-linguistic reasons, has acquired greater prestige than others). It covers Old English, Middle English, Modern English, English overseas, class and occupational dialects, dialect research, and dialect and literature.

1918   **A directory of English dialect resources: the English counties.**
Compiled by Viv Edwards.   Swindon, England: Economic & Social
Research Council, 1990. 83p.

Based on the Survey of British Dialect Grammar project at Birkbeck College, this
directory provides a bibliography of books, the sources for records and cassettes,
details of sound recording and local studies collections, and of various dialect centres
and societies, for each English county.

1919   **Survey of English dialects.**
H. Orton, E. Dieth.   Leeds, England: E. J. Arnold for the
University of Leeds, 1962-1971. 5 vols. (vol. 1. *Introduction*. 1962.
112p. map; vol. 2. *The six northern counties and the Isle of Man*.
3 parts, 1962-63; vol. 3. *The West Midland counties*. 3 parts, 1969-71;
vol. 4. *The East Midland counties and East Anglia*. 2 parts, 1969-70;
vol. 5. *The southern counties*. 3 parts, 1967-68).

Presented here in these volumes are the findings of a fieldwork survey carried out 1950-
61 of the dialect 'normally spoken by elderly speakers of sixty years of age or over
belonging to the same social class in rural communities'. Orton's *The linguistic atlas of
England* (London: Croom Helm, 1978. 450p.) is a cartographic representation of the
Survey and has 249 phonological maps, sixty-five lexical maps, and nine syntactical
maps. Orton and N. Wright's *Word geography of England* (London: Seminar Press,
1974. 302p.) has 251 distribution maps illustrating regional dialect words and phrases
also based on the *Survey*.

1920   **The dialects of England.**
Peter Trudgill.   Oxford: Blackwell, 1992. 176p. 34 maps. bibliog.

English dialects have emerged over 1,500 years of linguistic and cultural development.
Celebrating the rich diversity of English regional and social dialects, this study outlines
in non-technical language the differences of vocabulary, accent, grammar, and
literature, still to be found in late twentieth-century England. The trend towards
linguistic uniformity is uncompromisingly denounced.

1921   **Word maps: a dialect atlas of England.**
Clive Upton, Stewart Sanderman, John Widdowson.   London:
Croom Helm, 1987. 228p. 200 maps. bibliog.

Based on the material of the Survey of English dialects, collected from over 300
localities between 1948 and 1961, 200 maps are arranged by a title which consists of a
standard English word, or a group of words, depicting regional variations in vocabulary
and usage.

1922 **The English dialect dictionary: being the complete vocabulary of all dialect words still in use, or known to have been in use during the last two hundred years.**
Edited by Joseph Wright. London: Oxford University Press, 1970.
6 vols. bibliog.

Twenty-three years in the making, this massive learned reference work, comparable in authority and standing to the *Oxford English Dictionary*, was based on the publications of the English Dialect Society and on the contributions of innumerable local correspondents. Its definitions give exact geographical area, quotations, and reference source; pronunciation; and etymology. American and colonial words still in use in the United Kingdom, or which can be found in early printed dialect books and glossaries, are also included. Volume six contains a Supplement, a fifty-page bibliography, and a substantial Grammar which brings out the principal characteristic features of all the dialects covered.

Bad language

1923 **Dictionary of jargon.**
Jonathon Green. London: Routledge & Kegan Paul, 1987. 616p.
bibliog.

Jargon is defined by the *Oxford English Dictionary* as 'any mode of speech abounding in unfamiliar terms, or peculiar to a particular set of persons, as the language of scholars or philosophers, the terminology of a science or art, or the cant of a class, sect, trade, or profession'. Vastly expanded from the author's earlier work, *Newspeak: a dictionary of jargon* (1984), this later work contains some 21,000 jargon words, phrases, acronyms and abbreviations of specialist occupational slang ranging 'from marketing to medicine, from advertising to artificial intelligence, from skiing to sociology, and from technology to tiddlywinks'.

1924 **What a word! Being an account of the principles and progress of 'The Word War' conducted in 'Punch', to the great improvement and delight of the people, and the lasting benefit of the King's English, with many ingenious exercises and horrible examples.**
A. P. Herbert. London: Methuen, 1935. 286p.

Sir Alan Herbert, poet, humorist, law reformer, parliamentarian, and wit, was early in the ring against the monstrous regiment of 'piratical, ruffianly, masked, braggart, and ill-bred words' constantly invading the English language. Here he invites all lovers of good words 'to buckle on their dictionaries' in the fight to repel them.

1925 **The Faber dictionary of euphemisms.**
R. W. Holder. London: Faber, 1989. 408p. bibliog.

Five thousand words and phrases are defined and their usage illustrated by a printed quotation in this dictionary. It supersedes Holder's *A dictionary of American and British euphemisms* (Bath, England: Bath University Press, 1987).

Language. Bad language

1926   **The dictionary of diseased English.**
       Kenneth Hudson.   London: Macmillan, 1977. 267p. bibliog.
Clumsiness, carelessness, the desire to shock, a conscious and cynical combination of
iconoclasm and seeking after novelty, and a longing for grandeur, are diagnosed as
being the causes of diseased English, the villainies and absurdities perpetrated by
management experts, industrialists, social scientists, advertisers, and entertainment
impressarios upon an ailing English language. This selection identifies some of the
worst cases, makes an attempt to explain their meanings, and endeavours to shame
them out of existence. Also of interest is *The dictionary of even more diseased English*
(Kenneth Hudson. London: Macmillan, 1983. 159p.).

1927   **Swearing: a social history of foul language, oaths and profanity in
       English.**
       Geoffrey Hughes.   Oxford: Blackwell, 1991. 304p. bibliog.
Despite a long period of relative decorum in the eighteenth and nineteenth centuries
England has a long tradition of hard swearing. Whether it be Anglo Saxon invocations
of magical charms, medieval blasphemy, or the foul-mouthed sexual swearing of the
late twentieth century, widely disseminated by undiscriminating sections of the mass
media, it is all charted in this admirably detailed and wide-ranging study.

1928   **A dictionary of slang and unconventional English: colloquialisms and
       catch phrases, fossilised jokes and puns, general nicknames, vulgarisms
       and such Americanisms as have been naturalised.**
       Eric Partridge, edited by Paul Beale.   London: Routledge & Kegan
       Paul, 1984. 8th ed. 1,400p.
After publishing *The songs and slang of the British soldier 1914-1918* and an annotated
edition of Francis Grose's *The classical dictionary of the vulgar tongue* (1785), Partridge
was commissioned to prepare a dictionary of slang. When published in 1935 it met with
immediate success and was to become his most celebrated lexicographical work. A
further 7,500 entries are included in this latest edition which comprises material
Partridge accumulated after the 1967 edition went to press and other terms and phrases
that have subsequently gained currency. Beale's *A concise dictionary of slang and
unconventional English* (London: Routledge, 1991. 534p.) lists 1,500 new words. *The
Routledge dictionary of historical slang* (edited by Jacqueline Simpson. London:
Routledge, 1973. 1,006p.) consists of 50,000 entries drawn from Partridge's *Dictionary*
with the emphasis on expressions coined before 1914.

1929   **Slang today and yesterday: with a short historical sketch and
       vocabularies of English, American and Australian slang.**
       Eric Partridge.   London: Routledge & Kegan Paul, 1970. 4th ed.
       476p.
The etymology, origins and history of slang, a wide coverage of the slang employed in
various trades and professions, and rhyming slang, are all to be found in this
authoritative study.

436

1930   **A dictionary of invective: a treasury of curses, insults, put-downs, and other formerly unprintable terms from Anglo-Saxon times to the present.**
Hugh Rawson.   London: Robert Hale, 1991. 435p.

Tracing the origin, use and abuse of personal insults, political vilification, and Anglo-Saxon four-letter words (once normal parlance but which dropped out of polite use over the centuries), this guide illustrates the constant conflict and stress between social taboos and freedom of expression.

1931   **Bloomsbury dictionary of contemporary slang.**
Tony Thorne.   London: Bloomsbury, 1990. 583p.

This dictionary contains some 5,000 terms and 15,000 definitions likely to be encountered by anyone reading modern fiction and journalism, listening to popular music, or watching films and television. It presents an accurate record of the vocabulary that has enriched and debauched the English language worldwide since the 1950s.

Idioms

1932   **A book of English idioms.**
V. H. Collins.   London: Longman, 1958. 3rd ed. 258p.

Current idioms in frequent use, including colloquialisms, and a few slang phrases, have their meanings explained. Where possible, their origins are also given. A *Second* and *Third book of English idioms* are also available.

1933   **A dictionary of catch phrases; British and American from the sixteenth century to the present day.**
Eric Partridge, edited by Paul Beale.   London: Routledge & Kegan Paul, 1985. 2nd ed. 384p.

'A catch phrase is a phrase that has caught on, and pleases the populace'. Definitions, explanations of origins, and illustrative quotations are the bread and butter of this dictionary. In this considerably augmented second edition greetings, toasts, exclamations and exhortations, threats, invitations, jokes and puns, popularly accepted misquotations, modern proverbs, adages and maxims, are all added in significant numbers.

1934   **A dictionary of clichés: with an introductory essay.**
Eric Partridge.   London: Routledge, 1978. 5th ed. 261p.

More and more clichés are being inflicted on the English language, notably by politicians and 'media' personalities who now enjoy unrivalled access to our homes and schools through newspapers, magazines, radio and television. This chronicle of the origins and progress of hackneyed phrases, over-used idioms, and familiar quotations, all long past their sell-by-date, should be on the shelves of everyone in the public eye who intends to voice his opinion, or to advance her views.

Language. Synonyms

1935 **A concise dictionary of English idioms.**
B. A. Phythian. Sevenoaks, England: Headway Hodder &
Stoughton, 1986. 4th ed. 250p.

This useful dictionary is a practical guide, giving both definitions and illustrative quotations, to the most frequently used English idiomatic expressions 'which everyone uses, which usually evade the normal rules of grammar, and which often have implications quite unconnected with the normal meanings of the words themselves'.

1936 **Longman dictionary of English idioms.**
Edited by Della Summers. Harlow, England: Longman, 1979. 387p.
bibliog.

Based on a study of contemporary printed and audio-visual sources, and liberally furnished with examples and quotations, this dictionary is designed to help teachers and students of English to comprehend and become familiar with the complexities of English idiomatic usage. It lists and explains over 4,500 idioms and their derivatives.

Synonyms

1937 **Crabb's English synonyms arranged alphabetically with complete cross references throughout.**
George Crabb. London: Routledge, 1961 reprint of 1916 Centenary edition. 716p.

George Crabb first published his *English synonyms explained* in 1816, and it is a tribute to his scholarship that his name is itself regarded as synonymous with his title. He pioneered the practice of not only giving meanings of the generic or key words, but also writing at paragraph length on the shades of meaning of alternative words.

1938 **The new Nuttall dictionary of English synonyms and antonyms.**
Edited by Rosalind Fergusson. Harmondsworth, England: Viking, 1986. 442p.

Previously published as *The Nuttall dictionary of English synonyms and antonyms*, this is an entirely new, updated, and considerably enlarged edition of a work which collects together groups of words of similar meaning arranged under headwords, listed alphabetically. Each headword is followed by a selection of synonyms grouped according to the various senses of the word.

1939 **The new Collins thesaurus.**
London: Collins, 1984. 768p.

Unlike *Roget* this practical wordfinder is arranged in dictionary order so that the user may go straight to the word for which he needs an equivalent. Sixteen thousand headwords quarried from the core of the English language extend to over 270,000 synonyms, but no matter how many synonyms a word has they are all listed in one entry.

438

1940 **Reader's Digest reverse dictionary.**
London: Reader's Digest Association, 1989. 765p.

Part one of this ingenious work is a dictionary which endeavours to work from the definition of a word to the 'target' word required. This it does by employing three basic strategies: by the use of synonyms; by collocations, or familiar phrases; and by antonyms. Cue words lead direct to the target word or refer to a chart of terms on a particular subject, or to an illustration on which the target word is pinpointed. In some respects it equates to a scaled-down, alphabetically arranged Roget's *Thesaurus*. Part two is a lexicon of difficult words.

1941 **The synonyms finder.**
J. J. Rodale, revised by Laurence Urdang, Nancy La Roche.
Aylesbury, England: Rodale Press, 1987. 1,353p.

Containing more than 1,500,000 synonyms, grouped in related clusters, this completely revised work is undoubtedly the largest and most comprehensive dictionary of synonyms in print.

1942 **Roget's thesaurus of English words and phrases.**
Peter Mark Roget, updated by Betty Kirkpatrick. Harlow, England:
Longman, 1987. 7th ed. 1,254p.

Without doubt one of the most widely known of all English language reference works, and one for which countless aspiring writers have had good reason to be thankful, the first edition of *Roget* was first published in 1852. By an ingenious system of subdivided and cross-referenced paragraphs words and phrases are arranged not in dictionary order but classified according to their concepts and meanings within six main sections: abstract relations; space; matter; intellect; volition; and emotion, religion and morality. This edition boasts of 11,000 new terms (in a total of 250,000) and includes Roget's original introduction and a detailed plan of the classification. Roget has often been imitated but never surpassed. D. M. Emblem's *Peter Mark Roget: the word and the man* (Longman, 1970. 368p. bibliog.) is a well-researched biography.

1943 **Chambers 20th century thesaurus: a comprehensive word-finding dictionary.**
Edited by M. A. Seaton, G. W. Davidson, C. M. Schwarz,
J. Simpson. Edinburgh: Chambers, 1986. 750p.

Unlike Roget's *Thesaurus* this work is arranged alphabetically with 18,000 entries providing the key to over 350,000 synonyms and antonyms. A series of forty-one classified word lists (e.g. alphabets and writing systems, collective nouns, prosody, and units of measurement) and a twenty-three page list of words arranged by their endings, complete an invaluable *vade-mecum* for authors, journalists, and everyone who needs to extend their vocabulary.

1944 **The Oxford thesaurus: an A-Z dictionary of synonyms.**
Laurence Urdang. Oxford: Oxford University Press, 1991. 1,024p.

Containing some 275,000 synonyms, including unusual phrases, idioms, and dialectal expressions, this useful dictionary is suitable for house, school, and business use.

1945   **The rhyming dictionary of the English language: in which the whole language is arranged according to its terminations, with an index of allowable rhymes.**
John R. Walker, revised and enlarged by Lawrence H. Dawson, Supplement compiled by Michael Freeman.   London: Routledge, 1990. 683p.

First published in 1775, and substantially revised in 1924, this dictionary is grouped in strict alphabetical order by reverse spellings. There is a confident, but scarcely credible, statement that 'the arrangement is perfectly simple, and after two or three tries the reader will be able to find his way about this reverse-order dictionary as rapidly and conveniently as he can over those constructed on the usual principles'.

Usage

1946   **The Oxford writer's dictionary.**
Compiled by R. E. Allen.   Oxford: Oxford University Press, 1990. 448p.

This authoritative and up-to-date dictionary of writing style and usage for writers, journalists, editors and publishers, is a corrected version of *The Oxford dictionary for writers and editors* (1981) and is based on the Oxford University Press house style. It provides a straightforward guide to common spelling difficulties, the names of people and places, foreign words and phrases, abbreviations, and to some broader aspects of usage such as punctuation and capitalization.

1947   **Word perfect: a dictionary of current English usage.**
John O. E. Clark.   London: Harrap. 1987. 490p.

More than 4,500 alphabetically-arranged and cross-referenced entries are contained in this editorial guide to contemporary English writing style whose basic premise is that the chief object of the printed word is to communicate clearly and effectively. Common errors of spelling, meaning, grammar, and sentence construction, are all included as are the use of synonyms, homonyms, archaisms and clichés, and notes on prefixes and suffixes, irregular verbs, and technical editing and publishing terms.

1948   **A dictionary of modern English usage.**
H. W. Fowler, revised by Sir Ernest Gowers.   Oxford: Oxford University Press, 1968. 2nd ed. 725p.

First published in 1926, *Fowler's modern English usage*, to use its more accustomed form, is much more than a pedantic and prescriptive manual of usage. Some entries such as '-edly', 'elegant variations', 'mute', 'negative mishandling', 'than', and 'that', are short essays, encyclopedic in their nature and range. In many respects, not least in its clear thinking, and the proper use of precise words, it cannot be outdated, but such is the relentless march of the English language that some of its more refined rulings have been long disregarded and superseded. This present edition, prepared by Sir Ernest Gowers of *Plain words* fame, declines to make substantial alterations for fear of losing the authentic Fowler flavour, although a modicum of pruning and consolidation has brought it more up-to-date. It also contains a brief biographical sketch of the author.

1949 The King's English.
H. W. Fowler, F. G. Fowler.   Oxford: Clarendon Press, 1931.
3rd ed. 383p.

This renowned guide to good English makes no comment on those rules of grammar which are rarely, if ever, broken but concentrates instead on 'all blunders that observation shows to be common'. Vocabulary, syntax, airs and graces (e.g. humour, archaisms), and punctuation are the main topics discussed together with less significant chapters on euphony, quotations, grammar, meaning, style, and ambiguity. But it is not so much the coverage that excites admiration as the wealth of examples of incorrect usage assembled and used in evidence.

1950 The complete plain words.
Sir Ernest Gowers, revised Sidney Greenbaum, Janet Whitcut.
London: HMSO, 1986. 3rd ed. 285p. bibliog.

Sir Ernest Gowers, a distinguished civil servant, wrote *Plain words* (1954) at the request of the Treasury who were anxious to improve and simplify the convoluted English perpetrated by government departments. It was followed by *The ABC of plain words* (1951) and the two were combined under the present title in 1954. This new revision, published as part of HMSO's 1986 bicentenary celebration, retains the essential flavour and authority of the original although it has been updated to correspond to contemporary practice in vocabulary and style. Its main purpose remains to help government officials in their use of written English so that the recipients of official letters will be left in no doubt as to what they are intended to convey.

1951 Literary companion dictionary: words about words.
David Grambs.   London: Routledge & Kegan Paul, 1985.

Excluding poetry and classical drama terms, etymology, and discursive derivational lore, the entries in this literary dictionary come from journalism, linguistics, book reviewing, grammar and rhetoric, political speechwriting, editing, and publishing. There are also twenty 'special entries' judged to merit or to need particular scrutiny, among them newsroom headline jargon, mixed metaphors, scholarly (bibliographic) terms, and weasel words commonly used in advertising.

1952 Usage and abusage: a guide to good English.
Eric Partridge.   London: Hamish Hamilton, 1965. 6th ed. 392p.

Once described as 'Fowler admired, enlarged, quoted, disagreed with and brought up to date', this book, first published in 1942, was intended to be 'less Olympian and less austere' than its illustrious predecessor. Most serious writers would consider it an indispensable *vade-mecum*.

Grammar, spelling, punctuation

1953 **English grammar.**
B. A. Phythian. Sevenoaks, England: Hodder & Stoughton, 1980.
287p.

This is a revised version of Gordon Humphreys' *Teach yourself English grammar* first published in 1945. It devotes separate chapters to the principal parts of speech before dealing with punctuation and sentence construction. A series of exercises tests and reinforces the student's comprehension.

1954 **The Oxford guide to English usage.**
Compiled by E. S. C. Weiner. Oxford: Clarendon Press, 1983.

Intended as a practical guide to the formation and use of English words, this book concentrates on acknowledged areas of difficulty and controversy. It is divided into four sections: word formation, pronunciation, vocabulary, and grammar, with appendices on the principles of punctuation, clichés and modish and inflated diction, and English overseas.

1955 **Current English usage.**
Frederick Wood, revised by Roger Flavell, Linda Flavell. London:
Macmillan, 1990. 3rd ed. 329p.

First published in 1962, this edition provides a simple guide to contemporary standard written English. Less academic, and more up-to-date than Fowler's *A dictionary of modern English usage* and Eric Partridge's *Usage and abusage*, it covers idiom, style, spelling, punctuation, syntax, and modern usage generally.

1956 **An introduction to the pronunciation of English.**
A. C. Gimson. London: Edward Arnold, 1980. 3rd ed. 352p.
bibliog.

In the years since its first publication in 1962 this text has been generally acclaimed as the standard description of spoken British English. For this edition an appendix on teaching the pronunciation of English has been added.

1957 **Everyman's English pronouncing dictionary: containing over 59,000 words in international phonetic transcription.**
Daniel Jones, edited by A. C. Gimson. London: Dent, 1988.
14th ed. 576p. bibliog. (Everyman's Reference Library).

This fourteenth edition widens the questionable basis that the 'Received Pronunciation' of the English language is that used in ordinary conversation by typical Southern English people who have attended English public (i.e. private) schools, this dictionary indicates the approved pronunciation of 60,000 words by symbols used by the International Phonetics Association. The general public's measure of familiarity with these symbols can best be gauged by the inclusion of a twenty-two page 'Explanation' section.

1958 **You have a point there: a guide to punctuation and its allies.**
Eric Partridge. London: Routledge & Kegan Paul, 1953. 230p.
bibliog.
Structured on progressive lines so that the reader may accumulate knowledge in a
practical and systematic way, this comprehensive guide deals with the theory and
practice of recent and modern punctuation and such accessories, or 'allies', as capitals,
italics, quotation marks, hyphens, and paragraphs.

1959 **Word Spell: a spelling dictionary.**
Edited by Bud Wileman, Robin Wileman. London: Harrap, 1988.
371p.
Drawn from a range of spelling tests and lists of commonly misspelled words, this
dictionary presents a lexicon of correctly and incorrectly spelled words in one
sequence. Alongside each incorrect word is the correct spelling.

1960 **A history of modern colloquial English.**
Henry Cecil Wyld. Oxford: Basil Blackwell, 1936. 3rd ed. 433p.
bibliog.
First published in 1920, this book is primarily an account of the history of English
pronunciation from the early fifteenth century to the beginning of the nineteenth.
Evidence for the arguments and conclusions is drawn from three main sources: the
phonetic spellings found in surviving private letters and diaries; the statements of early
writers on pronunciation; and from rhymes and verses.

1961 **A handbook of English grammar.**
R. W. Zandvoort, J. A. Van Ek. London: Longman, 1978. 7th ed.
349p. bibliog.
Originally designed as a bilingual manual of English grammar for Dutch students, this
descriptive grammar was first published in 1945. It provides a comprehensive study of
the characteric features of modern English accidence and syntax.

Dictionaries

1962 **The Penguin rhyming dictionary.**
Rosalind Fergusson. Harmondsworth, England: Viking, 1985. 530p.
Based on phonetic rather than orthographic principles, this ingenious dictionary was
prepared by running words with their phonetic transcriptions through a computer
programmed to sort them into phonetic order. Words are arranged in numbered
groups according to the vocal sounds of their final syllables. Rhyming words are found
by consulting the alphabetical index.

1963 **Collins COBUILD English language dictionary**.
Edited by Gwyneth Fox, Rosamund Moon, Penny Stock. London:
Collins, 1987. 1,703p.

COBUILD is the Collins Birmingham University International Language Database and gives its name to this dictionary because it was developed in the English Department in the University as part of a language research project commissioned by Collins. Designed 'for people who want to use modern English', the dictionary was compiled with the use of advanced computer technology. By scanning a large representative group of English texts a corpus of words in current use was built up. Hence the claim that 'it offers more, and more accurate, information on the way modern English is used than any previous dictionary'. Its most noticeable feature is an extra column to the right of the definitions which gives students and teachers detailed grammatical information about how each sense of each word can be used. This avoids the use of conventional phonetic symbols. *Collins COBUILD essential English dictionary* (1989. 960p.) is intended for intermediate learners.

1964 **Neologisms: new words since 1960**.
Jonathon Green. London: Bloomsbury, 1991.

About 3,000 new words which have forced their way into English mainstream vocabulary, excluding jargon and slang, are recorded in this register. Science, especially computer science and information technology, bears a heavy responsibility but so too do feminism, environmentalism, and an upsurge of interest in a healthy diet.

1965 **Collins English dictionary**.
Edited by Patrick Hanks. London: Collins, 1991. 3rd ed. 1,771p.

Advertised as the first major new English dictionary in forty-five years when first published in 1979, this single volume dictionary contains some 170,000 entries. In size it slots in about midway between the *Shorter Oxford* and the *Concise Oxford*. Its strengths are its coverage of science and technology, commerce, and culture, and of worldwide contemporary English usage and it has attracted many supporters in the increasingly competitive world of English-language dictionary publishing.

1966 **A dictionary of the English language**.
Samuel Johnson. London: Longman, 1755. 2 vols.

Nine years in the making, Johnson's famous *Dictionary* was published in two large folio volumes each the size of a lectern *Bible*. Because of its original and elegantly composed definitions, and its copious literary quotations, it is generally acknowledged as the first standard English dictionary worthy of the name. It included a history of the English language, a grammar, and 40,000 words, and was unrivalled for almost a century. A *de luxe* facsimile edition was issued by the original publishers in 1990 which incorporated Johnson's 'The plan of a dictionary of the English language', and his proposals to write the *Dictionary* published in 1747. With the aid of recently discovered manuscripts Allen Reddick's *The making of Johnson's dictionary 1746-1753* (Cambridge, England: Cambridge University Press, 1990. 296p.) examines its conception, composition, writing, and revision, and analyses its political and theological aspects.

1967 **Longman dictionary of the English language.**
Harlow, England: Longman, 1991. 2nd ed.

Noted for its thorough and comprehensive coverage of contemporary English worldwide, and for its extensive advice on grammar and usage, this parent etymological Longman dictionary which was first published in 1984 contains 90,000 headwords and 225,000 definitions. An ingenious re-spelling system indicates preferred pronunciations. Its celebrated currency is maintained by public involvement in spotting new words and meanings through the Longman 'Wordwatch' scheme. *Longman concise English dictionary* (1985. 1,651p.) has 50,000 headwords, 10,000 definitions, and 100 illustrated pages of encyclopedic information.

1968 **Which dictionary? A consumer's guide to selected English-language dictionaries, thesauri and language guides.**
Brendan Loughridge. London: Library Association, 1990. 177p.

The number of English language dictionaries published continues to grow unabated as publishers take advantage of computer technology to compile enormous databases of words and citations which allow them to produce all types of dictionaries aimed at different user groups and to revise and update them more frequently than in the past. With the emphasis very much on native English, this practical guide expertly evaluates standard, concise, pocket, and school dictionaries, examining their intelligibility, structure and organization, definitions, and basic value for money.

1969 **Longman Guardian new words.**
Edited by Simon Mort. Harlow, England: Longman, 1986. 219p.

Scientific and technical terms, the terminology of politics and business, social issues, leisure, and examples of the trend usage of words, are included in this popular guide to new words and meanings in the English language. Extracted from the Longman dictionary database, these precise dictionary definitions embrace existing words that have taken on new meanings, new compound words, and completely new words, tracing the development of the language as it occurs. *The Longman register of new words* (1989-90. 2 vols.) charts the latest word usage in the fields of politics, medicine, finance, international relations, economics, computer science, and the pop music scene.

1970 **Caught in the web of words: James A. H. Murray and the *Oxford English Dictionary*.**
K. M. Elisabeth Murray. New Haven, Connecticut: Yale University Press, 1977. 386p.

James Murray was a schoolmaster at Mill Hill when he was invited to edit the *New English Dictionary*, later known as the *Oxford English Dictionary*. He built a scriptorium in his back garden and from there assembled the materials for the *Dictionary* which he grappled with for the next thirty-five years until his death in 1915. This biography by Murray's granddaughter is based on Murray's correspondence and other manuscript material held in the family. It throws fresh light on the *Dictionary's* origins and on those members of the Philological Society who breathed life into it.

Language. Dictionaries

1971 Longman new generation dictionary.
Edited by Paul Proctor. Harlow, England: Longman, 1981. 798p.

Designed for the eleven to sixteen age group, this dictionary contains some 40,000 entries (partly selected from an analysis of school textbooks) whose definitions are given using only a basic vocabulary of 2,000 words. In no way biased towards literary or scholarly words, idioms and colloquialisms are included.

1972 Longman dictionary of contemporary English.
Edited by M. Rundell. Harlow, England: Longman, 1987. 2nd ed. 1,428p.

Particularly suitable for overseas students learning English as a foreign language, this dictionary which was first published in 1978 contains about 56,000 words and phrases. Definitions use a carefully chosen basic 2,000 word vocabulary to assist users to grasp difficult concepts and words likely to be confused. Students mastering these 2,000 words, always simpler than the words they describe, should in theory be able to understand most of the English language. Both British and American pronunciations are indicated by means of the International Phonetic Alphabet.

1973 The Oxford English Dictionary.
Prepared by J. A. Simpson, E. S. C. Weiner. Oxford: Clarendon Press, 1989. 20 vols. 2nd ed. bibliog.

Without doubt the *OED* is the largest and most authoritative dictionary of the English language and it is generally recognized as the ultimate arbiter of the meaning and usage of English words and phrases. Incorporating the twelve-volume 1933 reprint of the original *New English dictionary on historical principles* (1884-1928. 10 vols.) and the four-volume *Supplement* (1972-1986), this second edition includes 5,000 new words and meanings and presents in a single sequence the entire vocabulary of the English language. It provides an unchallengeable historical record of the development and change of meaning of each word by virtue of nearly two-and-a-half million illustrative quotations selected from literary, technical and other sources. Volume one contains a twenty-six page history of the *OED* whilst the last volume includes a 138-page bibliography of those works which have most commonly quoted in the *Dictionary*. Donna Lee Berg's *A guide to the Oxford English Dictionary* (1992. 192p.) provides an authoritative insight into the compilation of this second edition. Part one analyses the components of a typical entry: its pronunciation, part of speech, its area of origin and use, variant forms of the word, the definition itself, and a supporting quotation. Part two covers *OED's* history, and the individuals who have influenced its terminology and methods. *The shorter Oxford English Dictionary* (1973. 2 vols. 3rd ed. 2,702p.) is an abridgement of the main work for those not requiring a full scholarly apparatus. It includes not only recent literary and colloquial words but also common scientific and technical words, and a considerable number of obsolete, archaic, and dialectal words.

1974   **BBC English dictionary: a dictionary for the world.**
       Edited by John Sinclair.   London: BBC English and Harper Collins,
       1992. 1,374p.

Compiled from a databank of seventy million words from the BBC's World Service's output, and a further ten million from National Public Radio in the United States, and collated on the University of Birmingham's COBUILD computer, this dictionary defines words according to the way they are most frequently used. Words or phrases must be used on the air ten times a year to qualify for inclusion. Many people will be gutted that trendy announcers and newscasters are putting the kibosh on the language especially as the BBC has traditionally been regarded as a stalwart guardian of standard English usage.

1975   **The Oxford dictionary of new words: a popular guide to words in the
       news.**
       Sara Tulloch.   Oxford: Oxford University Press, 1991. 320p.

In this popular guide 2,000 words and phrases that have recently entered the language in all areas of modern life, from technology and the environment, to youth culture, big business, health, and war, are defined in an easy style. Each of the 750 articles provides etymological details and illustrates usage from a wide range of international sources.

1976   **Isms: a dictionary of words ending in -ism -ology, and -phobia: with
       some similar terms arranged in subject order.**
       Compiled by Mary Walton, revised by Phyllis E. Charlesworth.
       Sheffield, England: Sheffield City Council, 1968. 2nd ed. 100p.

Devised initially by Sheffield City Library staff to answer readers' enquiries of the 'What do you call a man who studies/collects/hates/loves/ believes/kills such and such' type, this imaginative dictionary records those terms markedly different from the usual English word for the subject.

Literature

1977 **A checklist of women writers 1801-1900: fiction, verse, drama.**
R. C. Alston. London: British Library, 1990.
Based on a personal examination of British Library's incomparable collection of
nineteenth-century literature, this comprehensive catalogue lists all editions of women
writers of imaginative literature published in the British Isles or in British dependent
territories. Almost 15,000 fiction, 2,079 verse, and 298 drama titles are listed
alphabetically by author.

1978 **Annals of English literature 1475-1950: the principal publications of
each year together with an alphabetical index of authors with their
works.**
Oxford: Clarendon Press, 1961. 2nd ed. 380p.
Updated from the 1935 edition, and with a wider scope for Commonwealth and United
States writers, these annals present the main literary output year by year.

1979 **The concise dictionary of British literary biography.**
Edited by Matthew J. Bruccoli, Richard Layman. Detroit, Michigan:
Gale, 1992. 8 vols.
Recognizing the need for a more compact work than the *Dictionary of literary
biography* (q.v.) which has now reached over 100 volumes, the editors have extracted
172 relevant entries from the main work, updated them where necessary, and
reassembled them in an eight-volume chronological sequence: vol. 1. *The Middle Ages
and Renaissance to 1660*; vol. 2. *The Restoration and 18th century*; vol. 3. *The
Romantic period 1789-1832*; vol. 4. *Victorian writers 1832-1890*; vol. 5. *Late Victorian
and Edwardian writers 1890-1914*; vol. 6. *Modern writers 1914-1945*; vol. 7. *Writers
after World War II*; vol. 8. *Contemporary writers 1960 to the present*. Each article
begins with a chronological bibliography of the author's works, continues with a
biographical and critical essay indicating how their works were received by
contemporary readers, and ends with plot summaries and quotations.

1980 **The English and Scottish ballads.**
Edited by Francis James Child. New York: Folklore Press in
association with Pageant, 1957. 5 vols. in 3. bibliog.

Originally published in Boston between 1882 and 1898, these volumes are universally
regarded as the definitive reference source for the study of traditional English ballads.
All known versions of 305 ballads, 'the whole extant mass of material' are contained
within its pages. For each ballad there is a full account of its sources, prefatory
historical information, and a scholarly textual analysis. This edition includes a nine-
page biographical and literary sketch of Child by G. L. Kitredge who saw the work
through to completion after Child's death in 1896. Volume five includes a glossary and
an extensive bibliography.

1981 **The Everyman history of English literature.**
Peter Conrad. London: Dent, 1985. 740p.

Not so much an encyclopedic survey but more a personal interpretation with an
emphasis on the continuity of major literary forms and on the way in which leading
literary figures transform their traditions, this history examines the relations and links
between authors rather than their relation to the society and times in which they live.

1982 **Literary landscapes of the British Isles: a narrative atlas.**
David Daiches, John Flower. New York: Paddington, 1979. 287p.
17 maps. bibliog.

A series of essays illustrating how a sense of place has coloured literary imagination is
followed by an atlas and gazetteer section plotting the localities associated with 225 of
Britain's most celebrated writers.

1983 **Dictionary of literary biography.**
Detroit, Michigan: Gale, 1978- . In progress.

This American series pays a great deal of attention to British literature. Each volume
contains lengthy career biographies on the main authors of particular genres or
periods. Bibliographies of the authors' works and of biographical and critical studies
are also included. The relevant volumes are as follows: vol. ten *Modern British
dramatists 1940-1945* (2 parts); vol. thirteen *British dramatists since World War II* (2
parts); vol. fourteen *British novelists since 1960* (2 parts); vol. fifteen *British novelists
1930-1959* (2 parts); vol. eighteen *Victorian novelists after 1885*; vol. nineteen *British
poets 1880-1914*; vol. twenty *British poets 1914-1945*; vol. twenty-one *Victorian
novelists before 1885*; vol. twenty-seven *Poets of Great Britain and Ireland 1945-1960*;
vol. thirty-two *Victorian poets before 1850*; vol. thirty-four *British novelists 1890-1929:
Traditionalists*; vol. thirty-five *Victorian poets after 1850*; vol. thirty-six *British novelists
1890-1929: Modernists*; vol. thirty-nine *British novelists 1660-1800* (2 parts); vol. forty
Poets of Great Britain and Ireland since 1960 (2 parts); vol. fifty-five *Victorian prose
writers before 1867*; vol. fifty-seven *Victorian prose writers after 1867*; vol. fifty-eight
Jacobean and Caroline dramatists; vol. sixty-two *Elizabethan dramatists*; vol. seventy
British mystery writers 1860-1919; vol. seventy-seven *British mystery writers 1920-1939*;
vols. eighty, eighty-four and eighty-nine *Restoration and eighteenth-century dramatists*;
vol. eighty-seven *British mystery and thriller writers since 1940*; vols. ninety-three and
ninety-six *British romantic poets 1789-1832*; vol. ninety-five *Eighteenth-century British
poets*; vols. ninety-eight and one hundred *Modern British essayists*; vol. 101 *British
prose writers 1660-1800*.

1984 **The Oxford companion to English literature.**
Edited by Margaret Drabble. London: Oxford University Press, 1985. 5th ed. 1,155p.

This edition is a fundamental revision of Sir Paul Harvey's widely acclaimed *Companion* which was first issued in 1927. Seven thousand entries, mostly relating to English authors and their books, but also including literary societies, printers, publishers and booksellers of lasting importance, 'quickly, easily and clearly satisfy the immediate curiosity of the common reader and direct that reader to further sources of information'. Out go Harvey's 'allusions commonly met with', such as 'pieces of eight' and 'the Cinque Ports', to make way for contemporary writers born since 1939, and coverage of comic strips, detective stories, science fiction, and children's literature. Discussions of literary movements are retained and updated. Censorship and the law of the press and notes on the history of English copyright are included as appendices.

1985 **The Oxford literary guide to the British Isles.**
Edited by Dorothy Eagle, Hilary Carnell. Oxford: Clarendon Press, 1977. 447p. 13 maps. bibliog.

Even in the age of television pilgrimages to places with strong literary associations are still widely popular. This gazetteer describes towns and villages, schools, inns, houses and castles, lakes and rivers, and other topographical features where several hundred authors, from the Venerable Bede to J. R. R. Tolkien, have lived, worked and died, or in some way made famous. Travel directions and hours of opening are given whenever possible. Also of interest is *The Oxford illustrated literary guide to Great Britain and Ireland.* Edited by Dorothy Eagle, Meic Stephens, Hilary Carnell. (Oxford: Oxford University Press, 1992. 2nd ed. 272p. 13 maps. bibliog.).

1986 **The new Oxford book of seventeenth century verse.**
Edited by Alastair Fowler. Oxford: Oxford University Press, 1991. 831p.

Responding to the changes in critical taste since J. H. Grierson and G. Bullough's *The Oxford book of seventeenth century verse* was published in 1934, this new collection strikes a balance between Metaphysical and Jonsonian poetry, and remedies the previous neglect of popular verse.

1987 **The new Oxford book of English verse 1250-1950.**
Edited by Helen Gardner. Oxford: Clarendon, 1972. 974p.

Although sharing many poems with Quiller-Couch's *Oxford book of English verse*, this is not a revision of his renowned collection but a completely new anthology. Gardner regards it not simply a personal collection like Quiller-Couch's but as representative of 'the critical consensus of the age in which it is compiled'.

1988 **Longman companion to English literature.**
Christopher Gillie. London: Longman, 1978. 2nd ed. 885p. 2 maps.

Long essays on political history and institutions of England from 1066; society and the arts; religion, philosophy and mythology; narrative literature from the romance to the novel; drama in Britain; poetic form since 1350; and the history of English critical thought, comprise part one of this companion. The second consists of 2,750 alphabetically-arranged entries relating to major authors, significant works, literary forms and themes, important journals, and literary movements.

1989 **The Oxford book of late medieval verse and prose.**
Edited by Douglas Gray. Oxford: Clarendon, 1985. 586p.

Although the period in English literature from the death of Chaucer to the early years of Henry VIII's reign is relatively unexplored, it produced an extensive variety of rich and fascinating work. This anthology represents not only familiar authors like Malory, Skelton, and Sir Thomas More, and well-known types of literature such as songs and lyrics, ballads and romances, but also neglected texts either never before published or else in very obscure editions. Private letters, scenes from the medieval chronicles, and extracts from books on medicine and alchemy, and hunting and fishing, are also included, and there is a seventy-page glossary of words, forms or senses unfamiliar to modern readers.

1990 **A chronology of English literature.**
Martin Gray. Harlow, England: Longman, 1989. 276p.

Literary works that have achieved classic status or were influential in their time, or simply characteristic either of an individual author or of a historical period, are placed in the flow of historical events in this ingenious chronology. Three main literary periods are distinguished: Old English literature; and Middle English; both treated in parallel columns of literary and historical dates; and Literature 1500 to 1900 in which annual historical resumés are followed by short lists of the more important prose, dramatic, and poetic work published during the year. Winners of the Booker and Whitbread prizes for literature, the dates of English-language *Bibles* and of *Books of Common Prayer*, and the hundred books most frequently borrowed from public libraries July 1987 to June 1988, are listed as appendices.

1991 **Dictionary of anonymous and pseudonymous English literature.**
S. Halkett, J. Laing. Edinburgh: Oliver & Boyd, 1926-62. 9 vols.

About 70,000 entries arranged alphabetically by title, giving brief bibliographical details, and their author's actual name, are listed in this authoritative dictionary which was first published in four volumes between 1882 and 1888. Volume six is the first supplement, volume seven is an index volume, whilst volumes eight and nine contain new material 1900-50. A projected revised edition giving precise documentary evidence for the attributions of authorship has not progressed beyond volume one and appears to have lapsed: *A dictionary of anonymous and pseudonymous publications in the English language, vol. one: 1475-1640* (Edited by John Horden. London: Longman, 1980. 271p.).

1992 **A literary atlas & gazetteer of the British Isles.**
Michael Hardwick. Newton Abbot, England: David & Charles, 1973. 216p. 32 maps.

Nearly 4,500 localities associated in some way with authors representing all periods of English literature are listed in this useful gazetteer.

1993   **Now read on: a guide to contemporary popular fiction.**
Mandy Hicken, Ray Prytherch.   Aldershot, England: Gower, 1990.
328p.

Divided into nineteen writing *genres*, e.g. advent stories, thrillers, country life, perceptive women's works, etc., this guide is arranged alphabetically by author within each *genre*. Each author entry includes brief biographical information, an indication of the major characteristics of the author's works, and a dated list of novels published. At the end of each entry there are instructions on what to read next in the same vein. Revised editions are contemplated.

1994   **Later English broadside ballads.**
Edited by John Holloway, Joan Black.   London: Routledge & Kegan Paul, 1975-79. 2 vols. bibliog.

Based on the 75,000 printed songs and lyrics amassed by Sir Frederic Madden (1801-1873), Keeper of the British Museum Department of Manuscripts, now in Cambridge University Library, these volumes reveal the anarchic and often bawdy sub-culture of eighteenth and nineteenth century England. A brief commentary accompanies many of the texts.

1995   **Index to British literary bibliography.**
T. H. Howard-Hill.   Oxford: Clarendon, 1969-92. 7 vols. (vol. 1.
Bibliography of British literary bibliographies. 1987. 2nd ed. 886p.;
vol. 2. *Shakespearian bibliography and textual criticism.* 1971. 322p.;
vol. 3. *British bibliography to 1890*; vols. 4-5. *British bibliography and
textual criticism: a bibliography.* 1979; vol. 6. *British literary
bibliography and textual criticism 1890-1969: an index..* 1980; vol. 7.
British literary bibliography 1970-1979: a bibliography. 1992.
912p.).

This vast research enterprise, based at the University of South Carolina, is invaluable to all branches of English literary scholarship. For example, volume one, first published in 1969, now lists over 7,000 bibliographies published in the English language since 1890 on British writers active since the beginning of the Tudor period.

1996   **The new Oxford book of sixteenth century verse.**
Edited by Emrys Jones.   Oxford: Oxford University Press, 1991.
769p.

Covering possibly the greatest period in English poetry, this collection displays its riches in their full scope and diversity. Although including many of the acknowledged masterpieces, ample space is also given to satirical verses, epigrams, and political, social, and religious verse. A large number of long poems are printed intact. This new anthology complements rather than replaces Sir Edward Chambers' *Oxford book of sixteenth century verse* published in 1932.

1997 **The Oxford book of short poems.**
Edited by P. J. Kavanagh, James Michie. Oxford: Oxford University
Press, 1985. 307p.

Six hundred and fifty poems are included in this collection which attempts 'to bring
together the best that has been written, among poems below a certain length, from
medieval times to the present day'. A limit of thirteen lines is imposed, thus avoiding
sonnets which find their way into other anthologies, but allowing for the inclusion of
much unfamiliar work from poets better known for their longer poems.

1998 **The Oxford book of ballads.**
Edited by James Kinsley. Oxford: Clarendon, 1969. 711p.

Since Sir Arthur Quiller-Couch's *The Oxford book of ballads* was first published in
1910 'notions of what a ballad is, and of what is excellence in balladry, have grown
broader and more critical; editorial principles and standards have changed; and we
have learned again what generations of scholars had forgotten – that ballads are
narrative songs in which music and poetry are independent' (Preface). Most of the
ballads included in this collection are taken from the definitive Child *canon*. Nearly all
the texts are based on a single version as close as possible to its original oral tradition.

1999 **Reference guide to English literature.**
Edited by D. L. Kirkpatrick. London: St. James Press, 1991. 3 vols.
2nd ed. 2,143p. bibliog.

Derived from earlier encyclopedic works from the same publisher, this is a valuable
companion to the study of English literature from Britain and Ireland, Australia, New
Zealand, Canada, and English-speaking countries in Africa, Asia, and the Caribbean.
The first volume starts with a series of essays outlining a history of British and
Commonwealth Literature. The remainder of the first and the entire second volume
are given over to some 900 author entries, each with a biographical sketch, a list of
works, a short bibliography of critical studies, and an evaluative essay. Further essays
on the best-known works of English literature and historically important works, some
600 in all, are in the third volume.

2000 **British authors before 1800: a biographical dictionary.**
Edited by Stanley J. Kunitz, Howard Haycraft. New York: Wilson,
1952. 584p. bibliog.

A companion volume to that cited below, this dictionary contains 650 biographical
sketches, varying in length from 300 to 1,500 words. The authors' principal works are
listed along with the date of their original publication.

2001 **British authors of the nineteenth century.**
Edited by Stanley J. Kunitz, Howard Haycraft. New York: Wilson,
1936. 677p. bibliog.

One thousand biographical sketches, 100 to 2,500 words long, depending on the
author's stature, are presented in this volume. Preference for inclusion is given to
strictly 'literary' writers although an attempt is made to summarize the lives and
achievements of eminent figures in science, religion, philosophy, travel and
exploration, jurisprudence, political economy, sociology, and education, who published
works of lasting value.

2002 **Literary Britain: a reader's guide to writers and landmarks.**
Frank Morley. London: Hutchinson, 1980. 510p. 8 maps.

Beginning in London this discursive literary and historical guide explores the six major roads of old England, the Great North Road, the Dover Road, and so on, 'which were from the start the carriers of speech and writing', scanning *en route* their literary landmarks and landscapes. It is a pleasantly engaging book not lightly to be put down.

2003 **A dictionary of literature in the English language: from Chaucer to 1940.**
Edited by Robin Myers. Oxford: Pergamon Press, 1970. 968p. Index volume p. 969-1497.

This dictionary, along with *A dictionary of literature in the English language for 1940-1970: complete with alphabetical title-author index and a geographical-chronological index to authors* (Edited by Robin Myers. Oxford: Pergamon, 1978. 519p. bibliog.) provides outline biographical and bibliographical information on 4,800 authors writing in English over a 600-year period. Novelists, dramatists, essayists, poets, and other writers such as historians, scientists, economists, lawyers, and statesmen, who influenced their own times, are all included. A select list of literary prizes and awards, and their winners, 1940-1973, is to be found in the latter volume.

2004 **A reader's guide to the classic British mystery.**
Susan Oleksiw. London: Blandford, 1989; Boston: G. K. Hall, 1988. 582p. map.

Encompassing detective, police procedural, and suspense novels, this guide provides brief summaries (without revealing 'whodunit') of over 1,400 titles by 121 authors from the turn of the century to the present day. An author's books are grouped by series characters and listed chronologically by the time period of the story. Also presented are lists of creators and characters (and *vice versa*); occupations of series characters; period of stories; locations outside England; settings; the Metropolitan Police and local Forces; and 'One Hundred Classics of the *Genre*'.

2005 **The Oxford book of narrative verse.**
Edited by Iona Opie, Peter Opie. Oxford: Oxford University Press, 1983. 407p.

Ranging through time from Chaucer to W. H. Auden, most of the poems in this collection are printed in their entirety. They include such well known favourites as The Rime of the Ancient Mariner, The Pied Piper of Hamelin, and Sohrab and Rustem. Extracts from book length narratives are also included. Editorial notes trace the sources of the poets' inspiration and demonstrate how the material is transformed into the completed work.

2006 **Blue Guide literary Britain and Ireland.**
Ian Ousby. London: A. & C. Black, 1990. 2nd ed. 423p. 19 maps.

This illustrated guidebook explores the topographical associations of British authors and is divided into two parts. The first is given over to individual entries (sub-divided by region) for seven towering figures of English literature whose lives and works are indelibly associated with particular localities, Charles Dickens; Thomas Hardy; James Joyce; Wordsworth, Coleridge and Southey (the Lake poets); and William Shakespeare.

The second is limited to shorter entries for writers of lesser reputation or achievement 'who make less conspicuous or precise use of place in their work'. A list of properties open to the public and a useful map section enhance the practical value of this comprehensive work.

2007 The Cambridge guide to literature in English.
Ian Ousby. Cambridge, England: Cambridge University Press, 1988. 1,100p.

The successor to *The Cambridge guide to English literature* edited by Malcolm Stapleton (1983. 992p.), this is a reference guide to literature produced by all the English-speaking cultures. Over 4,000 entries arranged alphabetically cover authors, major works, literary *genres*, literary movements, important journals, literary clubs, etc.

2008 The golden treasury of the best songs and lyrical poems in the English language selected and arranged by Francis Turner Palgrave with a fifth book selected by John Press.
London: Oxford University Press, 1964. 5th ed. 615p.

First published in 1861 'this little collection differs, it is believed, from others in the attempt made to include in it all the best original lyrical pieces and songs in our language, by writers not living, and none besides the best'. Undoubtedly the most celebrated anthology of poetry in the English language it has never been out of print. This new edition includes poems written in the hundred years following its first publication.

2009 The English Association handbook of societies and collections.
Edited by Alicia C. Percival. London: Library Association for the English Association, 1977. 139p.

Founded in 1906, the English Association exists to further interest in all aspects of English studies. This handbook lists and describes national and local societies and associations concerned with the study of English language and literature. Major libraries with relevant collections are also listed.

2010 English humour.
J. B. Priestley. London: Heinemann, 1976. 208p.

A scholarly and highly entertaining, chronological *tour de force* of the landmarks of English humour as expressed in English literature from Chaucer to P. G. Wodehouse, with special chapters on 'Feminine humour', 'Clowns and the comic stage', and a forty-eight page gallery of 'English comic art'. Not to be confused with the same author's *English humour* (London: Longmans Green, 1929. 180p.).

2011 The Oxford book of English prose.
Edited by Sir Arthur Quiller-Couch. Oxford: Clarendon, 1925. 1,092p.

Constantly reprinted, this anthology was for many years regarded as the official choice of all that was best in English prose literature. Ranging from an extract of John Trevisa's translation of Rannulph Higden's *Polychronicon* in the fourteenth century, to a prose work of Rupert Brooke's published in 1914, it represents 'that subdued and hallowed emotion which . . . should possess any man's thoughts standing before the tomb of the Black prince in Canterbury Cathedral: a sense of wonderful history written silently in books and buildings'.

2012   **The Oxford book of English verse 1250-1918.**
       Edited by Sir Arthur Quiller-Couch.   Oxford: Clarendon, 1939.
       new ed. 1,166p.

Very much a personal collection, this first and most famous of all the Oxford anthologies was inspired by Palgrave's *Golden Treasury* (q.v.). Primarily a collection of lyrical verse which in places confidently excised a few superfluous stanzas if Quiller-Couch was of the opinion that the poem would be improved, it did not include any extracts from longer poetical works, thus removing some of the finest poetry in the English language. First published in 1900, with a further hundred pages added in this edition, this anthology earned a permanent place in English literature.

2013   **English poetry of the First World War: a bibliography.**
       Catherine W. Reilly.   London: George Prior, 1978. 402p.

This bibliography identifies no fewer than 2,225 poets, either civilians or serving in the armed forces, and lists some 3,000 separately printed works of poetry and 131 anthologies.

2014   **The Oxford illustrated history of English literature.**
       Edited by Pat Rogers.   Oxford: Oxford University Press, 1987. 528p.
       2 maps. bibliog.

According to the editor's foreword the aim of this history 'is to make the reading of poems, plays and novels more satisfying because (the reader is) better informed, and more profound because (the reader is) more comprehending'. To that end nine essays by different authors, each taking a distinct period, Old and Middle English to mid-twentieth century literature, excluding writings in English by non-English writers, present an entertaining narrative which takes into account not merely the literature itself but the ideas and outlooks that nurtured it.

2015   **Macmillan's handbook of Elizabethan and Stuart literature**.
       James E. Ruoff.   London: Macmillan, 1975. 468p. bibliog.

More than 500 entries relating to significant plays, poems, essays, and prose tracts, and broader topics such as literary genres, schools and movements, and to general subjects with a direct bearing on the literature of the period, like puritanism, astronomy, and the Inns of Court, are contained in this reference handbook. For individual writers the information includes basic biographical detail, a discussion of his artistic development, and an appraisal of his lasting successes and influence. For specific titles there is concise information on its composition and either a précis or a detailed synopsis. In both instances there are bibliographies of critical biographies or of major critical writings.

2016   **St. James Press Series.**
Chicago, London: St. James Press.

The volumes in this series follow an identical format: main entries in the form of critical essays contributed by a large team of invited experts on individual writers, supported by biographical notes, a complete checklist of published books, and at times comment by the writer under discussion. Not only English but also American and Commonwealth writers are to be found in these volumes. Works in the series are as follows: *Contemporary dramatists.* Edited by D. L. Kirkpatrick. 1988. 4th ed. 785p.; *Contemporary literary critics.* Edited by E. Borklund. 1982. 2nd ed. 600p.; *Contemporary novelists.* Edited by Lesley Henderson. 1991. 5th ed. 1,050p.; *Contemporary poets.* Edited by Tracy Chevalier. 1991. 5th ed. 1,179p.; *Twentieth-century children's writers.* Edited by Tracy Chevalier. 1989. 3rd ed. 1,288p.; *Twentieth-century crime and mystery writers.* Edited by Lesley Henderson. 1991. 3rd ed. 1,294p.; *Twentieth-century romance and history writers.* Edited by Lesley Henderson, 1990. 2nd ed. 856p.; *Twentieth-century science-fiction writers.* Edited by N. Watson, P. E. Schellinger. 1991. 3rd ed. 950p.

2017   **An encyclopedia of British women writers.**
Edited by Paul Schlueter, June Schlueter.   Chicago, London:
St. James Press, 1988. 516p. bibliog.

After a long period of neglect interest in women writers continues to grow. This encyclopedia contains informative and readable articles on 'a broad cross-section of women writers', some 400 in all, who were either British by birth or by adoption. However, number of well-known contemporary writers are inexplicably omitted. Consistent bibliographical coverage is achieved through chronological lists of the author's titles and other relevant biographical or critical works.

2018   **British writers.**
Edited by Ian Scott-Kilvert.   New York: Scribner's, 1985. 8 vols.
bibliog.

These chronologically-arranged volumes contain the text of 154 fifty-page booklets in the Writers and their Work series originally published by Longmans for the British Council. Ranging from the late fourteenth to the twentieth century, each booklet offered a 10-15,000 word critical appraisal of an individual author, or very occasionally a *genre*, a checklist of the author's publications and of studies and biographies of the author. Volume eight is an index volume. *Supplement 1* (1987. 465p.) adds twenty-three contemporary writers.

2019   **The Oxford book of medieval verse.**
Edited by Celia Sisam, Kenneth Sisam.   Oxford: Clarendon, 1970.
617p.

Covering the period from 1150, when post-Conquest English begins, to 1500, a date generally recognized as marking the end of the medieval period, this collection allows copious space to unfamiliar anonymous verses which take their place alongside extracts from the work of Chaucer, Gower, Langland, and others. A gesture is made to untutored readers by glossing difficult words at the foot of each page.

Literature

2020   **A concise chronology of English literature.**
P. J. Smallwood.   London: Croom Helm, 1985. 220p.

Emphasizing the increasing tendency to relate the teaching of English literature to its social and historical context, this chronology consists of parallel unannotated lists of literary and historical events on facing pages.

2021   **Prizewinning literature: UK literary award winners.**
Anne Strachan.   London: Library Association, 1989. 267p.

Based on information supplied by the administrators of the awards and prizes, this list of fifty-eight awards gives the purpose and value of each prize, the prizewinners in chronological order, with full bibliographical detail. For the Booker Prize shortlisted titles are also noticed.

2022   **The Oxford book of literary anecdotes.**
Edited by James Sutherland.   Oxford: Clarendon, 1975. 382p. bibliog.

For the purposes of this anthology an anecdote is considered to be 'the narrative of a detached incident, or of a single event, told as being in itself interesting or striking' (*Oxford English Dictionary* [q.v.]). Strictly speaking, a literary anecdote is one by or about a writer in his professional capacity as an author but in this collection of over 500 anecdotes, which ranges from Caedmon in the seventh century to Dylan Thomas in the twentieth, the worlds of the printer, the publisher, and the librarian, are all invoked.

2023   **Dictionary of British women writers.**
Edited by Janet Todd.   London: Routledge, 1989. 762p.

Over 400 British and Commonwealth women writers of all types find a place in this comprehensive guide, novelists, poets, dramatists, essayists, literary critics, biographers and historians, and children's writers, from the Middle Ages to the present. The entries, of about a page and a half each, give dates of birth and death, pseudonyms, a biographical sketch, a discussion of major works and key themes, a list of works, and a number of critical references.

2024   **The writer's handbook 1992.**
Edited by Barry Turner.   London: Macmillan, 1991. 5th ed. 698p.

First published in 1987, this guide for professional writers provides guidance on where to place material, the type of material commonly sought, how best to present work, and on fees and royalties. Professional associations and societies, writers' courses and workshops, press cuttings agencies, picture libraries, and proofreading, are all covered in detail.

2025   **The new Cambridge bibliography of English literature.**
Edited by George Watson, J. R. Willison.   Cambridge, England: Cambridge University Press. 1969-1977. 5 vols.

Replacing *The Cambridge bibliography of English literature* published in four volumes in 1940, and its *Supplement* (1957), this monumental work consists of four chronological volumes: *600-1600*, *1600-1800*, *1800-1900*, and *1900-1950*, with a fifth *Index* volume. It lists works by and works about literary authors either native to or wholly resident in the British Isles. The twentieth-century volume includes an introductory section encompassing general works, book production and distribution; poetry (general works and individual poets); novelists; dramatists; prose writers (literary scholars, essayists, humourists, historians, autobiographers, and writers on politics, economics, philosophy, theology, the natural sciences, and psychology). A final section list newspapers and periodicals. The Index volume, compiled by J. D. Pickles, includes anonymous works, and pseudonyms. The whole constitutes a work of great scholarship and reference value both as a source of learning and as a starting point for research.

2026 **The Oxford history of English literature.**
Edited by F. P. Wilson (et al.). Oxford: Clarendon Press, 1945- .
12 vols. (vol. 1. pt. 1. *English literature before the Norman Conquest.*
Not yet published; pt. 2. *Middle English literature.* J. W. Bennett,
1986. 496p.; vol. 2. pt. 1. *Chaucer and the fifteenth century.*
H. S. Bennett, 1947. 327p.; pt. 2. *English literature at the close of the
Middle Ages.* E. K. Chambers. 1945. 248p.; vol. 3. *English literature
in the sixteenth century (excluding drama).* C. S. Lewis. 1954. 696p.;
vol. 4. pt. 1. *The English drama 1485-1485.* F. P. Wilson. 1969. 244p.;
vol. 5. *English literature in the earlier seventeenth century 1600-1660.*
D. Bush. 1962. 2nd ed. 680p.; vol. 6. *English literature in the late
seventeenth century.* J. Sutherland. 1969. 569p.; vol. 7. *English
literature in the early eighteenth century 1700-1740.* Bonamy Dobrée.
1959. 701p.; vol. 8. *The mid-eighteenth century.* J. Butt. 1979. 671p.;
vol. 9. *English literature 1789-1815.* W. L. Renwick. 1963. 293p.;
vol. 10. *English literature 1815-1832.* Ian Jack. 1963. 643p.; vol. 11.
pt. 1. *English literature 1832-1890, excluding the novel.* P. Turner.
1989. 522p.; vol. 12. *Eight modern writers.* J. I. M. Stewart. 1963.
704p.).
This authoritative standard history interprets literature in its broadest sense to include biography, history, travel writing, religious writing etc. Each volume contains exhaustive bibliographies.

2027 **Writers and artists yearbook: a directory for writers, artists,
playwrights, writers for film, radio and television, photographers and
composers.**
London: A. & C. Black, 1992. 85th ed. 599p.
Part one of this long-established yearbook advises on where best to place all forms of literary material. Part two is concerned with general information on such matters as financial law and regulations, publishing practices, word processing and desktop publishing, picture research, literary prizes, and professional associations and societies.

2028 **Bloomsbury guide to English literature.**
Edited by Marion Wynne-Davies. London: Bloomsbury, 1989.
1,066p.
Twelve substantial essays on the most important literary issues, from medieval literature, to contemporary critical theory, and on the history and development of the

main genres – poetry, drama, and the novel – are followed by a huge reference section which complements the essays, and amasses factual information about the ideas, authors and texts already discussed, along with major works, literary forms, literary journals and movements, and explanations of the historical and cultural events influencing the literature of their times. There is also a chronology of literary dates and significant historical events.

2029 **The Year's Work in English Studies.**
Oxford: Blackwell, 1921- . annual.

Volume seventy-one, *1990* (1992. 1,000p.) contains critical notices of some 1,500 books. A series of bibliographical essays cover reference, literary history, and bibliography; literary theory; English language; Old English literature; thirteen chronological periods of English literature; and four essays on overseas literature written in English. Each essay ends with bibliographical notes.

Children's Literature and Reading

2030 **In the realms of gold: the story of the Carnegie Medal.**
Keith Barker.   London: Julia Macrae Books in association with the
Youth Libraries Group of the Library Association, 1986. 61p. bibliog.

Named after Andrew Carnegie, the Scottish-born American philanthropist, whose
enormous fortune was instrumental in establishing many of Britain's public libraries,
the Carnegie Medal was instituted in 1936 to be awarded annually 'for the best
children's book published during the year by a British author'. This informative
booklet looks at who selects the winners, what sort of books are honoured, and how
the award is publicized and promoted. It ends with a chronological history and a list of
the medal winners and commended books.

2031 **Information books for children.**
Edited by Keith Barker.   Aldershot, England: Ashgate, 1992. 245p.
bibliog.

Information book publishing accounts for forty per cent of the 5,000 children's titles
which currently appear every year. This selection guide contains about 470 reviews by
teachers and librarians who regularly review books for *The School Librarian*. All areas
of knowledge are covered but there is no attempt to find recommended titles in every
specific subject, the quality of the book is the sole criterion for inclusion. Each review
gives full publication and bibliographical details and an indication of the suitable age
range.

2032 **You're a brick Angela! A new look at girls' fiction from 1839 to 1975.**
Mary Cadogan, Patricia Craig.   London, Gollancz, 1976. 397p.
bibliog.

It was not until the end of the nineteenth century that a separate body of girls' fiction,
recognizing the particular nature and interests of young girls, came into being. Since
then girls have been depicted as passive, domesticated, brainless, and decorative, and
it is only in recent times that they have been allowed careers and adventures. This
situation is no more than another instance of literature reflecting the prevailing social

461

context. In this historical account the authors explore the whole gamut of girls' fiction, select important titles for close analysis, distinguish general themes and trends, reveal the contribution to social history, and indicate the lines along which it is likely to change.

2033 **The Oxford companion to children's literature.**
Humphrey Carpenter, Mari Prichard. Oxford: Oxford University Press, 1984. 587p.

Equal attention is paid to British, American, and Commonwealth publications in this encyclopedic work which contains 900 biographical entries for children's authors, illustrators, and publishers. A further 2,000 entries cover major works of fiction, notable characters in children's literature, and children's play and learning processes.

2034 **Secret gardens: a study of the golden age of children's literature.**
Humphrey Carpenter. London: Allen & Unwin, 1985. 235p. bibliog.

Rooted in the belief that the work of the great children's writers in the period 1860-1930 forms a coherent pattern of themes and ideas, this study tries to explain why so many children's classics should have appeared in England over that seventy year span. A close examination of the works of Charles Kingsley, Lewis Carroll, George MacDonald, Kenneth Grahame, Edith Nesbit, Beatrix Potter, J. M. Barrie, A. A. Milne, and others, will reveal, or so the author argues, that they were all, in one way or another rejecting and satirising contemporary adult English society and seeking to replace it with alternative worlds in which their own unconventional and unorthodox attitudes might flourish.

2035 **Twentieth-century children's writers.**
Edited by T. Chevalier. Chicago: St. James Press, 1989. 3rd ed. 1,288p. bibliog.

First published in 1978 this encyclopedia covers 800 English-language authors of fiction, poetry and drama. Each entry includes a biography, a definitive list of all separately published books, critical assessments by expert contributors, and, in some instances, comments by the authors themselves. An appendix surveys some important nineteenth-century writers.

2036 **The children's annual: a history and collector's guide.**
Alan Clark. London: Boxtree, 1988. 160p.

Children's annuals, nearly always appearing early in the Christmas season, have been published for over 150 years and have been seriously collected for almost as long. This richly-illustrated guide charts their long history from *The Boy's Own Paper* and *Ally Sloper's Christmas Holidays* to *Bubbles Annual*, *Schoolgirls' Own Annual*, *Rupert*, and *Batman*. It ends with a collector's price guide to nearly 100 titles.

2037 **The Nesbit tradition: the children's novel in England 1945-1970.**
Marcus Crouch. London: Ernest Benn, 1972. 239p.

A personal appreciation and criticism of post-war children's books, this authoritative work seeks 'the qualities which make the true novel: vivid, sustained and developed narrative, honestly observed and consistent characterization, a critical examination of society, and identifiable objectives, the whole presented in a style which is adapted to its purpose yet still expresses the personality of the writer'. There is also a list of children's books for adults.

2038 Treasure seekers and borrowers: Children's books in Britain 1900-1960.

Marcus Crouch. London: Library Association, 1962. 162p. bibliog.

This comprehensive chronological survey of children's books in the twentieth century was an attempt to relate changes in social behaviour to children's books of successive generations. In the event it 'proved difficult to find a close relationship between the children's books of the century and the changes taking place all around their authors and publishers'. Not only works of quality are examined, 'formula stories' with no originality or any other commendable feature are also taken into account. Winners of the Library Association's annual Carnegie and Kate Greenaway Medals are listed since their inception in 1936 and 1955 respectively.

2039 English children and their magazines 1751-1945.

Kirsten Drother. New Haven, Connecticut: Yale University Press, 1988. 272p. bibliog.

Drother's central argument in this pioneering full-length study is that children's magazines must be interpreted as 'emotional interventions in the everyday lives of their readers'. Her approach is strictly from a popular culture and reading perspective, not from a children's literature or children's book collectors' standpoint.

2040 British children's books in the twentieth century.

Frank Eyre. Longman, 1971. 208p. bibliog.

Primarily concerned with original work by British authors, the principal object of this revised and considerably expanded version of a work first published in 1952 as *Twentieth century children's books*, is to call attention to the outstanding children's books of the period. After an introductory section summarizing the historical development of children's literature there follows a critical examination of its main *genres*, school and adventure stories, historical and fantasy novels, and books for younger readers. It ends with a list of Carnegie, Kate Greenaway, and other award winners. The author was for many years in charge of the children's book department of Oxford University Press.

2041 The British comic catalogue 1874-1974.

Denis Gifford. London: Mansell, 1975. 210p.

The first comic paper to be published was *Funny Folks*, which made its appearance on the news stands 12th December 1874, whilst the first separate children's comic was *The Rainbow*, on sale continually from 14th February 1914 to 20th April 1956. The adult comic disappeared and did not re-emerge until the 1970s. Based on the author's own unrivalled collection, which includes some otherwise unknown titles, this centenary catalogue lists 1900 comics. Each entry provides information on the date of the first and last issues, the total number of issues published, the publisher and distributor, its original price and subsequent changes, amalgamation and incorporation into other comics, the names of strip characters and their original artists with the years of their first appearance, and editors' names.

Children's Literature and Reading

2042 Encyclopedia of comic characters.
Denis Gifford.   London: Longman, 1987. 256p.

The earliest recorded cartoon character who survived into a series is Ally Sloper who made his debut in a full-page strip, 'Some of the mysteries of loan and discount' which first appeared in *Judy*, a weekly humorous magazine, 14 August 1867. Over 1,200 comic strip heroes and heroines, each one illustrated with a typical picture from the author's own vast comic collection, are included in this encyclopedia. Arranged alphabetically by the name of the character, it provides information on the original creator or illustrator, the comic(s) in which the character appeared and dates, and the comic's publisher.

2043 Tellers of tales: an account of children's favourite authors from 1800 to 1968 with a chronological table of famous children's books to the present day and lists of titles by each author.
Roger Lancelyn Green.   London: Kaye & Ward, 1969. rev. ed. 320p. bibliog.

'I have tried to tell something about the authors who have been, or are likely to be, the favourites of most children and young people at some time or other, and to say something about their books and how they came to write them', the author remarks in his introduction. Lewis Carroll, George MacDonald, Charlotte Mary Young, Juliana Horatia Ewing, Mrs. Molesworth, Andrew Lang, Robert Louis Stevenson, Rider Haggard, Edith Nesbit, J. M. Barrie, Rudyard Kipling, Kenneth Grahame, Beatrix Potter, and Hugh Lofting, are the main authors discussed. How many of these, it might be asked, will survive into the next century?

2044 Dictionary of British children's fiction: books of recognized merit.
Althea K. Heilbig, Agnes Regan Perkins.   Westport, Connecticut: Greenwood, 1989. 2 vols. bibliog.

Based on 387 books published in the three hundred year period, from 1687 to 1985, and on finalists for literary awards, this dictionary includes over 1,600 entries relating to authors, titles, major characters, memorable settings, literary terminology, and plots of significant children's fiction.

2045 Children's fiction sourcebook: a survey of children's books for 6-13 year olds.
Margaret Hobson, Jennifer Madden, Ray Prytherch.   Aldershot, England: Ashgate, 1992. 285p.

Although North American, Australasian, and other Commonwealth writers are included, there is a distinct UK bias to this list of 140 of the 'best and most popular' authors of children's fiction. Entries, which are usually from twenty to seventy words in length, give guidance on the author's style and content, and indicate the age range of each book. Coverage is extended with sections on children's book series, prize winners, and television tie-ins.

2046 **The promise of happiness: value and meaning in children's fiction.**
Fred Inglis. Cambridge, England: Cambridge University Press, 1981.
333p. bibliog.

Written to answer the question: 'which books should our children read, and why?' this is an authoritative study of the best children's fiction of the past hundred years which strongly takes into account its social context. It concentrates on stories intended for the nine to thirteen age group and contrasts the delights to be gained from the recognized ancient and modern books of outstanding merit.

2047 **The men behind boys' fiction.**
W. O. G. Lofts, D. J. Adley. London: Howard Baker, 1970. 361p.

In addition to well over 2,000 biographies of authors and editors active in boys' fiction, including pseudonyms, and papers and publishers they contributed to, this nostalgic work also carries a trenchant introduction by Leslie Charteris, and three short essays on the D. C. Thomson papers, the Claude Hamilton schools, and the Sexton Blake roll of honour.

2048 **50 years of the Carnegie Medal.**
Derek Lomas. London: Library Association Youth Libraries Group and the Carnegie United Kingdom Trust, 1986. 60p.

This commemorative review by a former chairman of the Youth Libraries Group's selection committee offers an objective critical assessment of all the winners of the annual award in its first fifty years.

2049 **A nursery companion.**
Iona Opie, Peter Opie. Oxford: Oxford University Press, 1980.
128p.

There began to be published in London in the early nineteenth century a number of booklets containing nursery rhymes which, although obviously intended for children, could also be appreciated by adults. This illustrated collection reproduces some of these rhymes including the *Comic adventures of old Mother Hubbard*, *The history of the house Jack built*, *Cock Robin*, and *Peter Piper's practical principles of plain and perfect pronunciation*.

2050 **The Oxford book of children's verse.**
Edited by Iona Opie, Peter Opie. Oxford: Clarendon Press, 1973.
407p.

This notable anthology assembles the verse written for children, or written with children prominently in mind, which was either cherished in its own day, or which has successfully withstood the ravages of time, over the last 500 years. Arranged chronologically, it contains more than 300 poems and verses. A forty-page authors and verses section provides valuable background information.

2051 **Early children's books: collector's guide.**
Eric Quayle.   Newton Abbot, England: David & Charles, 1983.
256p. bibliog.

Eric Quayle's collection of early children's books is one of the finest in the world and includes many titles which are known only by the copy in his care. In this descriptive guide he not only discusses all types of childrens literature, from its beginnings in the late Tudor period, to the periodicals, annuals, and penny dreadfuls which proliferated in the early years of this century, but also sets out the ways by which first editions and other valuable items may be identified, describing some interesting individual titles to look out for. Many of the items discussed, he claims, can still be acquired at prices that enable beginners to search on equal terms with experienced and more affluent collectors.

2052 **The heirs of Tom Brown: the English school story.**
Isabel Quigly.   Oxford: Oxford University Press, 1982. 296p. bibliog.

The public school stories of Dean Farrar, Thomas Hughes, Talbot Baines Reed, F. W. Anstey, Rudyard Kipling, P. G. Wodehouse, Hugh Walpole, Angela Brazil, and Frank Richards, are all given particular attention in this literary, social, and cultural history. It is no mere nostalgic ramble through childhood reading; it investigates the whole social ethos in which the fictitious schools prospered. The real schools behind the school stories, headmasters of fact and fiction, the school story as an imperial training manual, and the school story at war, are some of the themes explored.

2053 **Children as readers: a study.**
John Spink.   London: Clive Bingley, 1989. 129p. bibliog.

A qualified librarian, the author brings together various aspects of literary theory, child psychology, and children's literature, to investigate how the perception of words and images can affect a child's developing personality. There are discussions of the parts played by works of acknowledged merit, and books of no great merit except for holding the young reader's attention or interest, and of the ways children's libraries can best cater for young readers. The successful promotion of reading, and the social distractions that threaten its future, are also treated at length.

2054 **Seen and not heard: a garland of fancies for Victorian children.**
Nigel Temple.   London: Hutchinson, 1970. 272p. bibliog.

Taken from the author's own collection of illustrated nineteenth-century juvenile books, this is an anthology of the improving tracts and pious horror stories administered to Victorian children for their own moral good.

2055 **Written for children: an outline of English-language children's literature.**
John Rowe Townsend.   Harmondsworth, England: Penguin, 1987.
3rd ed. 364p. bibliog.

When first published by Garnet Miller in 1965 this vigorous appraisal was limited to children's prose fiction written in England. This revised and expanded edition incorporates all works of imagination first published in the English language. It discusses the best books of the best writers, adhering firmly to the principle that 'a good children's book must not only be pleasing to children: it must be a good book in its own right'.

2056 Boys will be boys.
E. S. Turner. London: Michael Joseph, 1975. rev. ed. 280p.

Described by the author as a 'refresher course' when first published in 1948, this entertaining work is an unashamed wallow in nostalgia for the gripping yarns of derring-do of such immortals as Jack Harkaway, Buffalo Bill, Deadwood Dick, the Famous Five of Greyfriars School, and other renowned schoolboy heroes of yesteryear. Recognized as a classic study of the *genre*, it is a refreshing antidote to all the earnest studies of the books children's librarians and other self-appointed experts cherish, but which are often non-starters in the eyes of children themselves.

2057 Tales out of school.
Geoffrey Trease. London: Heinemann, 1948. 199p. bibliog.

Dealing with all the main types of writing for children, and based initially on his own childhood memories, this critical survey of books read by British children since the publication of John Newbery's *Little pretty pocket book* in 1744 discusses what is good and what is not in children's literature. It is an intensely personal book by a renowned children's writer and one which still commands and merits a close attention.

2058 The child and the book: a psychological and literary exploration.
Nicholas Tucker. Cambridge, England: Cambridge University Press, 1981. 259p. bibliog.

Ranging from nursery rhymes and fairy tales to comics and modern bestsellers this erudite work explores the relationship between children and fiction and asks why certain themes and approaches in children's literature are so popular with young readers. Among other topics examined are the issues raised by the possible censoring of children's books and why some children show more interest in reading than others.

2059 A history of children's book illustration.
J. I. Whalley, T. R. Chester. London: John Murray with the Victoria and Albert Museum, 1988. 268p. bibliog.

Based almost entirely on British children's books this authoritative historical survey covers chapbooks, comics, and instructive works.

Children's books in print.
See item no. 2352.

Sport and Recreation

General

2060 **Sport in Britain: a bibliography of historical publications 1800-1988.**
Richard William Cox.   Manchester, England: Manchester University Press, 1991. 285p.

Over 7,000 monographs, theses, periodical articles, and conference papers are registered in three main sections: nationwide histories of sport (including general surveys and histories of sixty-nine different sports), local studies by county, and biographical works. Richard Cox was the founder of the British Society of Sport History and the bibliography continues in the Society's *Bulletin*.

2061 **Sport and the law.**
Edward Grayson.   London: Butterworths, 1988. 376p.

Set in the context of football violence on and off the field, the taking of performance-enhancing drugs, and sponsorship rows, this study outlines the legal pitfalls that can cause confusion in many sporting activities. It emphasizes that the rules of play and the rule of law in society must work together.

2062 **Sport and the British: a modern history.**
Richard Holt.   Oxford: Oxford University Press, 1989. 416p.

Such differing themes as the persecution of early female cyclists in their 'rationals' (i.e. rational clothing, to wit 'bloomers') and the reason why Rugby Union football in England is a middle-class game as opposed to being a near religion to the people of Wales, are included in this well-researched study of the changes in organized sport since 1800. It goes a long way to explain why sport holds centre-stage in the lives of people of all social classes.

2063 **Sport in Britain: a social history.**
Edited by Tony Mason. Cambridge, England: Cambridge University Press, 1989. 363p.

Ten essays by different contributors examine the growth and organization of the major mass-participation sports in contemporary Britain: angling, athletics, boxing, cricket, football, golf, horse-racing, tennis, rowing, and rugby union. The topics treated include the social background of both players and spectators, gambling, media coverage, the impact of television, and professionalization.

2064 **Fair game: law of county sports and the protection of wild life.**
Charlie Parkes, John Thornley. London: Pelham, 1989. rev. ed. 268p. bibliog.

All aspects of the law regarding poaching and trespass, the possession and use of firearms, the rights to game, wildfowling, deerhunting, foxhunting, hare coursing, cockfighting, badger baiting, the control of predators, and cruelty to animals, are explained in this comprehensive guide. This edition is revised to include major changes in the firearms law made in the 1988 Firearms (Amendment) Act.

2065 **Official rules of sports and games 1992-93.**
Edited by Tony Pocock. London: Kingswood, 1992. 18th ed. 856p.

Compiled with the full co-operation of the various governing bodies, this compendium of the official rules of thirty-one competitive sports played in Britain and overseas was first published by Nicholas Kaye in 1949.

2066 **Pay up and play the game: professional sport in Britain 1875-1914.**
Wray Vamplew. Cambridge, England: Cambridge University Press, 1988. 394p. bibliog.

Concentrating on four major sports, association football in England and Scotland, county cricket, horse racing, and rugby league, this work outlines the progress of commercialization, the development of professional gate-money sport, concluding with an examination of the long association of commercial sport with gambling, players' misconduct, and spectator violence. Football hooliganism, for one, has a longer history than is generally assumed.

Angling

2067 **Angling Times good fishing guide: coarse fishing.**
London: Headline, 1992. 336p.

Drawn from information gleaned from commercial fisheries, recreational organizations, hotels and holiday operators, Tourist Information Centres, the National Rivers Authority, and the Forestry Commission, this illustrated guide, along with its equivalent on game fishing (*Angling Times good fishing guide: game fishing*. London: Headline, 1992. 336p.) provides information on fish stocks and typical weights, cost of tickets, bag limits, restrictions in terms of techniques and flies, facilities, and directions to more than 1,000 venues.

2068   **Angler's Mail encyclopedia of fishing.**
       Edited by Julian Brown.   London: Hamlyn, 1991. 192p.

A complete A-Z guide to fishing in the British Isles, this colourful encyclopedia covers all the fundamentals of coarse, sea and trout fishing, including tackle, bait, and techniques, and the most popular species of fish.

2069   **Angler's directory.**
       Brian Morland.   Twickenham, England: Hamlyn, 1985. 224p.
       12 maps.

Listing over 400 locations in Britain where good fishing may be found, this descriptive gazetteer is divided area by area into major river authorities. It is a ready reference to the rivers, streams, lakes, and reservoirs which can be fished free of charge or by a written permit. Each venue is described in detail with information of the licences required, by-laws, local conditions, techniques, baits, and the species likely to be caught. Additional information includes local and national records of fish weights, advice on legal matters, lists of angling publications, and useful addresses.

2070   **Where to fish 1992-1993.**
       Edited by D. A. Orton.   Beaminster, England: Thomas
       Harmsworth, 1992. 83rd ed. 515p.

Fishing in England takes up 220 pages in this worldwide guide to where to fish. After introductory paragraphs on the National River Authority, the close season, and licence dues, the main section is a gazetteer to English fishing stations, describing over 1,000 freshwater and sea angling stations first along the principal rivers, and then the tributaries, noting the fish likely to be hooked.

2071   **Collins new encyclopaedia of fishing in Britain and Ireland.**
       Michael Prichard.   London: Collins, 1990. 216p.

If only angling was as easy as this book would have us believe! With colour photographs, drawings, or paintings on every page, this compendium provides splendid support and background for anglers of all persuasions whether they favour winter pike, match fishing, rock fishing for conger, wrasse and dogfish, dry-fly fishing, salmon-runs, or stillwater fishing.

Association football

2072 **The Football League 1888-1988.**
Bryon Butler. London: Macdonald, 1987. 353p.
The Football League is reputedly the toughest football competition in the world. This popular history traces its development and considers the social significance of English football. Championship triumphs, relegation issues, yesterday's and today's prominent players, are all featured as are the annual League tables.

2073 **The Football Association yearbook 1991-1992.**
London: Pelham, 1991. 216p.
Complete records of the FA Challenge Cup, Challenge Trophy, and Challenge Vase winners, of England's international matches 1872-1991, England goalscorers 1946-91, England match reports 1990-91, and England teams 1946-91, are included in this yearbook.

2074 **Football spectator violence: report of an official working group.**
London: HMSO, 1984. 61p.
A joint Foreign Office/Home Office/Department of Transport ministerial working group was set up 'to consider further action by the Government and football authorities to deal with spectator violence at home and abroad' following serious outbreaks of hooliganism at two England football matches against Luxemburg and France in the winter of 1983/84. This report includes recommendations for action by the football authorities, the law enforcement authorities, and by central government.

2075 **England football fact book.**
Chris Freddi. Enfield, England: Guinness, 1991. 264p.
Published to coincide with the preliminary group matches leading to the European Championship in 1992, this book provides information on the matches, scorers, players, and opposition involved in England's performances over the last 100 years, with a complete 'who's who' of all those who have played for England at full international level.

2076 **The official Football League yearbook. 1992.**
Edited by Barry J. Hugman. Ickleford, England: Valiant Sporting Books, 1991.
A concise summary of how each of the ninety-three Barclays League clubs fared during the previous season, with full team line-ups, goalscorers, and attendances for all League matches; a club by club directory giving ground details, crowd capacities, location street maps; and a brief history (including major honours, individual record appearances, and goalscorers), are the main ingredients in this annual publication. Other regular features include coverage of the Rumbelows League Cup, the Zenith Data Systems Cup, the Leyland DAF Cup, and the new season's fixtures.

2077   **Rothman's Football League players records: the complete A-Z 1946-1981.**
Compiled by Barry J. Hugman.   Aylesbury, England: Rothmans, 1981. 500p.

The career record of every single player who appeared in a Football League match for the first thirty-five post-war seasons (some 16,000 in total) is outlined in this massive volume. At-a-glance information is given of every player's date and place of birth, his non-League and Football League clubs, seasons played, his total appearances and goals scored, and of his international career. In addition there are biographical sketches of four hundred of the most illustrious players.

2078   **The football grounds of Great Britain.**
Simon Inglis.   London: Willow Books, 1987. 2nd ed. 368p.

Many changes in English football grounds carried out as a result of the Popplewell enquiry after the Bradford fire disaster in 1985 are incorporated in this descriptive and illustrated guide which was first published in 1983 as *The football grounds of England and Wales*. There are introductory essays on the history, design, and the safety of grounds.

2079   **An English football internationalists who's who.**
Douglas Lamming.   Beverley, England: Hutton, 1990. 300p.

Biographical sketches of 1,003 players capped for England, 1872-1988, are contained in this 'who's who' volume: birth and death dates, career details, their total number of caps, and other honours. Lists of double football and cricket internationals, England schoolboys who earned senior caps, and the total appearance record of players with twenty or more caps, are also included.

2080   **Arsenal: a complete record 1886-1990.**
Fred Ollier.   Derby, England: Breedon, 1990. 2nd ed. 416p.

Undoubtedly the best-researched and most accurate record book ever published on perhaps the most famous of English football clubs, this work includes features on Arsenal's six home grounds and thirteen managers, and a 'who's who' of most first team players. A season-by-season playing record, including wartime matches, for all competitions played in, a list of Arsenal's home international players, and top goalscorers, augment this remarkably comprehensive volume. Similar 'complete record' titles on other FA Premier League and Football League clubs are also published. Also from the same publisher is Gordon Smailes' *Breedon book of Football League records* (1992. 257p.) which lists every League, League Cup, and FA Cup result to the end of the 1990-91 Season.

2081   **100 years of the FA Cup: the official centenary history.**
Tony Pawson.   London: Heinemann, 1972. 299p.

This is a pictorial record of the first hundred years of the Football Association Challenge Cup, the world's oldest football competition. Tony Pawson, also a capped Kent cricketer, played for the famous amateur club, Pegasus, and turned out for Charlton Athletic in the Football League.

2082　**Rothmans football yearbook 1992-93.**
　　Edited by Jack Rollin.　London: Headline, 1992. 23rd ed. 1,024p.
A six page-section is devoted to each of the ninety-three Football League clubs in this long-established annual publication. Coverage of English domestic football also includes a day-by-day record of the previous season, a summary of major non-League football, and fixtures for the new season. Jack Rollin is a soccer columnist on the *Sunday Telegraph.*

2083　**Soccer who's who.**
　　Jack Rollin.　Enfield, England: Guinness, 1992. 6th ed. 400p.
A complete statistical season-by-season record of all League appearances, and goals scored, for every player in the Football League in the 1991-92 season, and for leading England players abroad, is the principal feature of this popular soccer annual.

2084　**Encyclopedia of British football.**
　　Phil Soar.　London: Willow, 1987. 261p.
All Football League and Scottish League tables, every League club's Cup and League history season by season, the result of the major Cup competitions, and of all international matches played by the four home countries, plus a wealth of other facts and opinions on the modern game, are all to be found within this lavishly-illustrated encyclopedia which was first published by Marshall Cavendish in 1974.

2085　**The Hamlyn A-Z of British football records.**
　　Philip Soar.　London: Hamlyn, 1984. 2nd ed. 204p. bibliog.
First published in 1981 this compendium of facts and figures includes details of every game in the Football Association Challenge Cup from the fifth round onwards, of all the major league competitions since their beginning, of international matches, and of individual appearances and medals. Every conceivable 'who won what' question is quickly answered.

2086　**The football almanac.**
　　Peter Stewart.　Moffat, Scotland: Lochar, 1991. 158p.
Profiles of all Barclay's League and the B&Q Scottish League clubs are included in this pocket almanac. Club colours, records, post-war managers, some famous players of the past, and a brief history, are all clearly set out.

2087　**The Hillsborough Stadium disaster: final report.**
　　Rt. Hon. Lord Justice Taylor.　London: HMSO for the Home Office, 1990. 116p.
Ninety-five people were crushed to death at a FA Cup semi-final at Hillsborough Stadium, Sheffield, 15 April 1989. An official enquiry was armed with wide terms of reference to include crowd control and safety at all sporting events. Lord Justice Taylor's report examines the lessons to be learned from the disaster, looks generally at contemporary football, and proposes a series of measures to ensure it a better future.

2088 **Football and its fans: supporters and their relations with the game 1885-1985.**
Rogan Taylor. Leicester, England: Leicester University Press, 1992. 198p. (Sport, Politics and Culture Series).

Football supporters are increasingly coming under academic study especially when outbreaks of crowd violence and disorder at football matches rises to an intolerable level. This study reveals the extent to which organized supporters have contributed to ground developments and the provision of what amenities exist. The whole question of fundraising, the debate on football hooliganism, the relations of the supporters with the football authorities, the clubs, and the police, over the last century, is explored in this detailed scrutiny.

2089 **Barclays League club directory 1993.**
Edited by Tony Williams. Epping, England: Barclays, 1992. 680p.

Full club records, ground details, 1991-92 match statistics; the leading scorers, the 1991-92 players' details, and team group photographs, are featured in this directory of all ninety-three Premier and Barclay League clubs. Special sections on managers and referees complete a first class handbook.

2090 **The Guinness non-league football fact book.**
Tony Williams. Enfield, England: Guinness, 1991. 256p.

A historical sketch of the senior leagues and a club directory of the four pyramid leagues to the Football League, namely the GM Vauxhall Conference, the Isthmian League, Beazer Homes League, and the HFS Loans League, are the main features of this definitive survey. Other features include a complete record of the Home Counties' amateur international matches and players, a review of each season 1979 to 1991, and coverage of the Football Association's Trophy, the Challenge Trophy, the Challenge Vase, and former Amateur Cup.

Athletics

2091 **AAA/WAAA handbook 1991/92.**
London: H. D. M. Associates, 1991. 242p.

Directory information on the Amateur Athletics Association and the Women's Amateur Athletics Association, their laws and coaching schemes, facilities and equipment, competition rules, and English athletic records, are all included in this annual handbook. The AAA was founded in 1880 to co-ordinate and govern amateur athletics in England and Wales.

2092 **British Olympians: a hundred years of gold medallists.**
Ian Buchanan. Enfield, England: Guinness, 1991. 191p.

This illustrated volume provides detailed career records of all 406 Britons who have won an Olympic gold medal, and a complete listing of all British Olympic competitors. Great Britain is the only country which has taken part in every winter and summer Olympic Games since 1896 when the modern games began.

2093 **The official centenary history of the Amateur Athletic Association.**
Peter Lovesey. Enfield, England: Guinness Superlatives, 1979. 223p.
bibliog.

The AAA, or the 'three As' as it is known throughout the athletic world, is the world's oldest national governing body. This comprehensive official history demonstrates how the essentials of modern field and track events, rules, and records, were established. It is, in effect, a history of British athletics. A complete list of all senior, junior, and youth AAA championship results is included.

2094 **Who's who in British athletics.**
Peter Matthews. Runcorn, England: Archive Publications in conjunction with Express Newspapers, 1989. 128p.

Features on Sebastian Coe, Daley Thompson, and Liz McColgan, precede summaries of achievements by outstanding track and field athletes of recent years. The British Athletics Writers Association's 'Athlete of the Year' award-winners, 1963-1989, and United Kingdom Record holders, are listed to complete the story.

Boxing

2095 **Hugman's British boxing yearbook.**
Compiled by Barry J. Hugman. Marlborough, England: Crowood, 1991. 8th ed. 319p.

Prepared in association with the British Boxing Board of Control, this yearbook outlines the structure of amateur and professional boxing in Britain. It gives a summary of the previous season's boxing scene, a tournament diary; the careers of the current professional title holders, a list of outright winners of the Lord Lonsdale Challenge Belts, the results of British title bouts 1891-1991, the Amateur Boxing Association's national champions, and the names of licensed promoters, managers, matchmakers, referees, timekeepers, inspectors, and ringwhips.

2096 **England's boxing heroes.**
Frank McGhee. London: Bloomsbury, 1988. 191p.

Forty English boxers, at all fighting weights, and their greatest contests, are portrayed in this personal record of English boxing. First into the ring is Bob Fitzsimmons, still the only English heavyweight champion of the world.

Camping and caravanning

2097　**Good camps guide 1992: British Isles.**
Edited by Lois Broughton-Edwards, Clive Edwards, Sue Smart.
Dorchester, England: Deneway Guides & Travel, 1991. 25th ed. 160p.
6 maps.

Thoughtfully arranged within the official Tourist Board regions this selective guide concentrates on especially good camping sites, and reviews the strengths and weaknesses of their facilities and services besides providing factual information on how to find them, their charges, opening periods, and reservation procedures.

2098　**RAC camping and caravanning guide Great Britain and Ireland 1992.**
Abingdon, England: RAC, 1992.

Fully revised and updated this annually-published guide provides information on over 2,000 campsites, their locations and facilities, arranged alphabetically by the nearest town. Additional information includes notes on caravanning for beginners, buying a tent or caravan, and a section on sites close to the main routes and ferry ports.

Climbing

2099　**Classic rock climbs in Great Britain.**
Bill Birkett.　Yeovil, England: Oxford Illustrated Press, 1986. 171p.

Over sixty first-class climbs in Southwest England, Northern England, the Lake District, and other areas in Britain, are described in ascending order of difficulty in this guidebook, which was published to coincide with the centenary of W. P. Haskett-Smith's first solo climb of Napes Needle, in the Lake District, 27th June 1886.

2100　**The mountains of England and Wales: tables of mountains of two thousand feet and more in altitude.**
George Bridge.　Reading, England: Gastons Alpine Books and West Col, 1973. 199p. 18 maps. bibliog.

Information on the whereabouts, heights, nomenclature, and accessibility of 400 mountains is presented in this geographical directory. There are two subsidiary sequences: a list in order of altitude, and a series of county highests.

2101　**The crag guide to England and Wales.**
David Jones.　Marlborough, England: Crowood, 1989. 224p.
25 maps. bibliog.

All English crags of interest to climbers are described in this regionally-arranged gazetteer which gives locations, heights, routes and difficulties, and bouldering potentials, conveying an overall impression on what climbing is available.

2102 **The mountains of England and Wales: vol. 2: England.**
John Nuttall, Anne Nuttall. Milnthorpe, England: Cicerone Press, 1990. 320p. maps.
Based on the latest Ordnance Survey data, supplemented by on the spot surveys, this definitive volume describes how to best climb all English mountains over 2,000 feet in a series of day- and half-day long walks each linking a number of summits.

2103 **Where to climb in the British Isles.**
Edward C. Pyatt. London: Faber, 1960. 287p. 17 maps. bibliog.
British climbing as a sport began in 1881. This gazetteer of all the principal mountain precipices, sea cliffs, and other rock exposures used for climbing, enables the beginner to assess the climbing potential of any part of the country including eighteen English counties and regions. It indicates the location of each crag pinpointed by Ordnance Survey grid references, its distance and bearing from a local landmark, its rock type, and standard of climbing required. It also serves as a comprehensive reference work to all specialized local climbers' guide-books published since organized climbing began.

Cricket

2104 **Who's who of cricketers: a complete who's who of all cricketers who have played first-class cricket in England with full career records.**
Philip Bailey, Philip Thorn, Peter Wynne-Thomas. Feltham, Middlesex: Newnes Books in association with the Association of Cricket Statisticians, 1984. 1,144p.
Career information on about 12,000 cricketers who played first class cricket in England, 1864-1983, is given in this mammoth work. The compilers, all prominent members of the Association of Cricket Statisticians, have included a consolidated list of all first-class teams which took the field in that period, information not readily available elsewhere.

2105 **The Collins who's who of English first-class cricket 1945-1984.**
Compiled by Robert Brooke. London: Collins, 1985. 411p.
This is the first of a series of volumes giving details of every player to appear in first-class cricket in England since 1744. The information provided includes dates of birth and death, type of player, education, debut, teams played for, Test Matches, best batting and bowling performances, and full career first-class and Test Match records. Robert Brooke founded the Association of Cricket Statisticians in 1973.

2106 **A history of the County Championship.**
Robert Brooke. Enfield, England: Guinness Publishing, 1991. 192p.
Now a hundred years old the County Championship remains the senior cricket competition and the yardstick by which the counties measure the success of their season. This statistical survey gives its early history, championship milestones, the

records of each season from its beginning in 1890, championship and county records, and a final section on such matters as its regulations, points, and qualifications.

2107 **England Test Cricketers: the complete record from 1877.**
Bill Frindall. London: Willow, 1989. 518p.

Profiles and accounts of their notable performances of each of the 536 players selected for England since the first Test Match in March 1877 are given in this comprehensive work. Batting, bowling, wicketkeeping and fielding statistics are given for each individual Test Match.

2108 **The illustrated history of county cricket.**
Eric Midwinter. London: Kingswood in association with Bass Brewers, 1992. 256p.

Midwinter's narrative history examines the origins, early development, and progress of county cricket, relating each stage to the cultural and social values of the times. A second section analyses the seventeen first-class counties (not including Durham), giving an account both of their high days of celebration and their despondent days, whilst the third section deals with county records and individual performances.

2109 **The Wisden guide to cricket grounds.**
William Powell. London: Stanley Paul, 1992. 2nd ed. 624p. map. bibliog.

Descriptions of eighty-nine grounds, including all first-class grounds, along with League Cricket Conference, Minor Counties Cricket Association, Combined Services, and National Cricket Association grounds, are contained in this authoritative work. Information for each ground includes the history of the club to which it belongs, access directions, accommodation close by, ground records, and ground facilities. For the cricket enthusiast this is a work of true delight.

2110 **The cricketers' who's who 1992.**
Compiled by Iain Sproat. Harpenden, England: Lennard, 1992. 13th ed. 608p.

All those who played first-class county cricket at least once during the previous season, along with those who retired at the end of the season, and the umpires on the first-class list, are featured in this annual 'who's who'. Their county debuts, career performances, Test Match appearance, season's averages, and much else conceived to be of interest, are fully recorded.

2111 **Wisden cricketers' almanack 1992.**
Edited by Graeme Wright. Guildford, England: Wisden, 1992. 1,344p. bibliog.

A 'household' name, *Wisden* is incontestably one of the most famous of all sports handbooks. First published in 1864, and sometimes described as the cricketer's *Bible*, it remains essentially English in scope and coverage although it includes a section on overseas cricket. Each issue contains a regular feature, in-depth profiles of 'Five cricketers of the year', a complete list of Test Match cricketers, a county-by-county review of the previous season, including the Test Matches, the County Championship, the one-day competitions, and the Minor Counties championships.

Cycling

2112 **British Cycling Federation Handbook and Diary.**
Kettering, England: BCF, 320p + diary. annual.

Formed in 1959 as the result of a merger of the National Cyclists Union and the British League of Racing Cyclists, the British Cycling Federation is the controlling administrative body for road racing and track events in Britain. This handbook is essential for all club cyclists and provides directory and general information on the law and cyclists, the racing calendar, cycle racing rules, and on a host of other topics. Competition records also find a place. The governing body for time trialling is the RTTC (Road Time Trials Council), who publish an annual handbook (Ashford, England: Geerings) listing all time trials held nationally throughout the year, rules and regulations, competition record holders at the set distances of ten, twenty-five, fifty, 100 miles and twelve and twenty-four hours, and information on how to join a club and enter your first time trial.

2113 **Great cycle tours of Britain.**
Tim Hughes. London: Ward Lock, 1988. 176p. 15 maps. bibliog.

Ten week-end routes, sixty to 100 miles in length, and five routes of 200 miles in length for week long tours, are described and superbly illustrated in this guidebook which also includes information on road and rail connections, accommodation *en route*, and the whereabouts of cycle repair shops.

Equestrianism

2114 **British equestrian directory 1992-93.**
Wetherby, England: Equestrian Management Consultants, 1992.
14th ed. 846p.

The main section of this directory is an A to Z classified list of all things equestrian e.g. accommodation, breeders, business and publicity services, clubs, dealers, employment services, farriers, feed and corn merchants, holidays and trekking centres, livery yards, racehorse trainers, riding schools, show and event secretaries, vetinary laboratories etc. An introductory chapter reports on important equestrian developments. No horseperson could survive without it.

2115 **Where to ride 1992-93: a guide to BHS-approved establishments in the UK and Ireland.**
Buckingham, England: Kenilworth, in association with the British Horse Society, 1992. 169p.

For over twenty years the BHS has run an approval scheme for riding schools based on sound riding instruction, good facilities, and properly maintained safety equipment and facilities. This directory, arranged by region, provides the address and proprietor of each of 600 riding establishments, their staffing, standard of schooling, and details of evening classes and other courses offered.

2116   **The riding handbook.**
        Edited by Anne Wood.   Windsor, England: Burlington, 1991. 5th ed.
        389p.

This comprehensive guide to the world of horses and riding in Britain is arranged in six
sections: where to ride (including a directory of riding establishments, auctions, and
auctioneers); hints for responsible riders (riding wear, safety, public rights of way); the
healthy horse (feeding, stabling, grooming, clipping); the world of horsemanship (Pony
Club and other equine organizations); careers with horses; and tables of suppliers.

Golf

2117   **AA/Securicor guide to golf courses in Britain and Ireland.**
        Basingstoke, England: Automobile Association, 1992. New ed. 376p.
        10 maps.

This county arranged gazetteer of 2,000 golf clubs that welcome visitors contains
details of course lengths and par scores, green fees, membership numbers, facilities,
and of nearby AA inspected hotels.

2118   **The golfers almanac.**
        Malcolm Campbell.   Moffat, Scotland: Lochar, 1991. 144p.

Championship venues and hidden golfing gems off the beaten track are included in this
directory of British golf courses. Information is given on senior club personnel, the
name of the club professional, on holes and lengths, ladies and visitors facilities, green
fees, etc. Malcolm Campbell was for ten years editor of *Golf Monthly*.

2119   **Golf in Britain: a social history from the beginnings to the present day.**
        Geoffrey Cousins.   London: Routledge, 1975. 176p.

Golf has been peculiarly subject to social and economic change. This book traces its
development from a folk game in Scotland into a pastime dominated by the wealthy,
leisured classes, until it finally became a sport enjoyed by all sections of the
community. Other topics considered at length include the growth of the women's
game, clothes and equipment, the status of professional golfers, and golfing facilities.

2120   **RAC golf guide.**
        Edited by Mitchell Platts.   Croydon, England: RAC, 1991. 248p.
        10 maps.

A hole-by-hole analysis of the top fourteen tournament courses, and a county-by-
county directory of 2,500 courses in Britain and Ireland, together with nearby RAC
recommended hotels, comprise the principal sections of this attractive guide. A
complete listing of the winners of all the major tournaments in Europe and America is
also included.

2121 **The Royal and Ancient golfers handbook.**
London: Macmillan, 1992. 911p.

Now in its eighty-ninth year of publication this authoritative handbook includes the major championship and tournament results of the previous season, the schedule of events for the current season, past tournament results, a gazetteer of clubs and courses in Britain and Ireland, a 'who's who' in golf, a golfing hotel compendium, and sections on the government and history of golf, including the evolution of the rules, and a miscellany of interesting facts and record scores.

2122 **Royal and Ancient championship records 1860-1980.**
Edited by Peter Ryde. St. Andrews, Scotland: Royal and Ancient Golf Club, 1987. 535p.

This record book contains the results of the major competitions in Britain controlled by the Royal and Ancient Golf Club.

2123 **Sunday Telegraph golf-course guide to Britain and Ireland.**
Donald Steel. London: Telegraph Books, 1992. 10th ed. maps.

Over 2,500 courses, and their facilities, are featured in this regionally-arranged guide, including more than 300 new courses opened since 1989. Originally published as *The golf course guide to the British Isles*.

2124 **The official history of the Ryder Cup 1927-1989.**
Michael Williams. London: Stanley Paul, 1989. 200p.

First contested in 1927 the Ryder Cup competition for professional golfers was first played for by the United States and Great Britain. In 1979, perhaps to make a more even match of it, it became a contest between the United States and Europe although the European team still includes a high percentage of British and Irish players. This official history by the Golf Correspondent of the *Daily Telegraph* describes all the matches up to 1989 and includes an analysis of Ryder Cup appearances.

Greyhound racing

2125 **The Sporting Life greyhound annual.**
Compiled by Bob Betts. London: Sporting Life. 144p.

A guide to British greyhound tracks is the principal feature of this annual publication. The date of each track's opening, the names of its racing and general managers, race days and trial days, the number of bookmakers attending, direction to the tracks, track records, and a plan of the track, are all to be found here.

2126 **The NGRC book of greyhound racing: a history of the sport completely revised and updated by the National Greyhound Racing Club.**
NGRC, Roy Genders.   London: Pelham, 1990. new ed. 342p. bibliog.

Based on Genders' *The encyclopaedia of greyhound racing* (1981) this history presents in dictionary order famous greyhounds, trainers and owners, the classic events, the courses, and winners of the main events and track record holders since the first meeting at Belle Vue, Manchester, in 1926. The National Greyhound Racing Club is the judicious, disciplinary and regulatory body which controls the major group of greyhound racecourses in Britain.

Horse-racing

2127 **Over the sticks: the sport of National Hunt racing.**
Michael Ayres, Gary Newbon.   Newton Abbot, England: David & Charles, 1971. 216p. map. bibliog.

The stormy history of racing over the sticks, from the first ever event at Leicester in 1792, is well chronicled in this authoritative study which goes behind the scenes to report on the duties of stewards, clerks of the course, handicappers, and starters. Other topics discussed include how courses are laid out, how fences are built, and methods of training. Brief descriptions of National Hunt racecourses, a glossary of racing terms, a directory of National Hunt racing organizations, and a list of the winners of the Grand National, the Cheltenham Gold Cup, and the Champion Hurdle Challenge Cup, are also included.

2128 **Horses in training 1990.**
Edited by Len Bell.   Newbury, England: Raceform, 1990. 97th ed. 856p.

Features of this longstanding annual publication include a directory of 679 trainers, the horses in their care, a list of jockeys and apprentices, the dates of the forthcoming season's principal races, and a guide to British Flat and National Hunt racecourses.

2129 **The Benson and Hedges book of racing colours.**
Birmingham: The Jockey's Association of Great Britain, 1973. 340p.

The registered racing colours of nearly 10,000 owners are illustrated in this substantial work which also includes a three-page essay on their history.

2130 **The Guinness book of flat racing.**
Gerry Cranham, Christopher Poole.   Enfield, England: Guinness Publishing, 1990. 240p. bibliog.

Every possible aspect of British flat racing is covered in this pictorial overview of the sport. Famous horses and jockeys, the production of thoroughbreds and the obsession with bloodlines, the top trainers and owners, racecourses, the administrative bodies, and the overall design of racing to establish the best horses of each age and sex over the various distances, all come under professional scrutiny to make it an indispensable companion to 'the sport of kings'. Results of the 1,000 guineas, 2,000 guineas, the Derby, St. Leger, and the Oaks, along with the winners of the top Irish and French races are listed from 1946.

2131 **Racecourses of Great Britain.**
James Gill. London: Barrie & Jenkins, 1975. 256p. map. bibliog.
The past, present and future of sixty-one racecourses in England, Scotland, and Wales are discussed in this comprehensive guide which gives the setting of each course, a plan, meetings held and distances of each race, hints on how best to tackle the course, and accounts of some memorable and outstanding races.

2132 **Grand National: the official celebration of 150 years.**
Anne Holland. London: Macdonald Queen Anne Press, 1988. 223p. bibliog.
An air of informality pervades this celebratory history of what is unquestionably the most famous, and most formidable, steeplechase in the world. Held at Aintree, over a decidedly awe-inspiring course, its sheer unpredictability and danger always attracts a large measure of public attention. Anedotes of famous owners, trainers, riders, and horses add entertainment value.

2133 **Royal Ascot.**
Dorothy Laird. London: Hodder & Stoughton, 1976. 288p.
Tracing the history of the Royal Ascot race meeting from its founding by Queen Anne early in the eighteenth century to modern times, this study provides detailed profiles of trainers, jockeys, and punters as they mingle on the course. An outline of the form of the meeting, including the race order; winners of the King George VI and Queen Elizabeth Stakes; record times at Ascot; and specialist horses and jockeys for the course, are all included in a series of appendices.

2134 **The Channel Four book of the racing year.**
Sean Magee. London: Sidgwick & Jackson in association with Channel Four Television Company, 1990. 192p.
This sumptuously-illustrated volume describes the major races of both the Flat and National Hunt seasons, chronicling their history, the courses where they are run, and what is required of the horses running in them. Other features include the winners since 1980 and their price, age and sex, and the annual cycle of breeding and training.

2135 **Horse racing: records, facts and champions.**
Tony Morris, John Randall. Enfield, England: Guinness Publishing, 1990. 3rd ed. 160p.
Milestones in the history of the Turf, triple crown winners, horses of the year, horses with the longest winning sequences, the records of top owners, breeders, trainers and jockeys, and the results of the English 'classics' and other major national and international races, are all contained in this comprehensive single-volume reference work.

Sport and Recreation. Horse-racing

2136 **Biographical encyclopaedia of British flat racing.**
Roger Mortimer, Richard Onslow, Peter Willett.   London:
Macdonald & Janes, 1978. 699p.

Covering British racing from the later Stuart period onwards, although preference is given to the history of the Turf since 1900, this authoritative and knowledgeable work contains some 2,000 entries relating to jockeys, owners, trainers, famous racehorses, racecourses in regular use, and to the major racing organizations.

2137 **The flat: flat racing in Britain since 1939.**
Roger Mortimer.   London: Allen & Unwin, 1979. 406p.

Since 1939 flat racing in Britain has irreversibly changed from a sport to a big business industry. Concentrating on the classic races and on horses of household fame, this narrative history is encyclopedic in scope.

2138 **The history of the Derby Stakes.**
Roger Mortimer.   London: Cassell, 1962. 695p.

The Derby is undoubtedly the most exacting test for three-year-olds in the racing calendar. This history gives a complete record of each year's race, the circumstances of the race, all the runners, the first three in the frame, prize money, the winning distance, and the on-course betting odds. A plan of the past and present courses is also included.

2139 **Ruff's guide to the Turf and Sporting Life annual 1989.**
Edited by Ken Oliver.   London: Sporting Life, 1988. 855p.

The largest section in this directory is devoted to the previous season's Flat Racing results. Other features include lists of owners, trainers, jockeys and apprentices, horses, breeders, and bloodstock sales.

2140 **Directory of the Turf 1989.**
Edited by Martin Pickering.   London: Pacemaker, 1989. 13th ed.
621p.

First published in 1961 – annually since 1985 – this illustrated directory contains a review of leading horses; and information on racing authorities and their officials (including the Jockey Club, the Horserace Betting Board, and owners', breeders', trainers', jockeys', and veterinary organizations); a guide to British racecourses; and sections on owners, trainers, jockeys, the racing press, bloodstock agencies, studs, and pedigree research.

2141 **The history of steeplechasing.**
Michael Seth-Smith, Peter Willett, Roger Mortimer,
John Lawrence.   London: Michael Joseph, 1966. 272p.

Compiled to commemorate the centenary of the National Hunt Committee which was founded in 1866, this history highlights the famous personalities and the outstanding horses that have contributed to steeplechasing's rich heritage.

2142 **Encyclopaedia of steeplechasing.**
Compiled by Patricia Smyly. London: Robert Hale, 1979. 303p.

Included in this encyclopedia are entries for all winners of the steeplechase 'classics', the Cheltenham Gold Cup, the Grand National, and Champion Hurdle, together with their trainers and jockeys; all champion and champion amateur jockeys extending as far back as reliable records allow; leading jockeys in pattern races; leading sires and broodmares; and current racecourses. There is also an outline history of betting and its influence on the sport.

2143 **The Champion Hurdle.**
Michael Tanner. London: Pelham, 1989. 192p. bibliog.

Published to coincide with the sixtieth running of the Champion Hurdle, this illustrated history gives full rein to the human and equine celebrities associated with this famous steeplechase. A full list of the results, giving the runners' names, weights, and distances, is appended.

2144 **The Guinness book of great jockeys of the flat: a celebration of two centuries of jockeyship.**
Michael Tanner, Gerry Cranham. Enfield, England: Guinness Publishing, 1992. 256p.

Over forty of the greatest names in flat racing, including Steve Donoghue, Gordon Richards, Lester Piggott, and Pat Eddery, are portrayed in this luxuriously illustrated celebration.

2145 **Chasing around Britain.**
John Tyrrel. Marlborough, England: Crowood, 1990. 242p. map. bibliog.

This beautifully illustrated, stylishly presented, and alphabetically arranged gazetteer to the steeplechasing courses of Britain captures steeplechasing's unique thrills and changing social pattern.

2146 **Thoroughbred studs of Great Britain.**
Alan Yuill Walker. London: Weidenfeld & Nicolson, 1991. 240p.

An essential reference book for serious racegoers, this work examines the most important studs in both an historical and contemporary context. It undoubtedly rescues individual breeders from relative obscurity.

2147 **Julian Wilson's 100 greatest racehorses.**
Julian Wilson. London: Macdonald Queen Anne Press, 1987. 255p.

Most horses profiled here, chosen from the truly great horses of the last 200 years, are either British or Irish, reflecting Britain's acknowledged status as 'the cradle of the thoroughbred'. All profiles include a descriptive career record, a photograph or other illustration, and a factbox of big races won by the horse.

2148 The encyclopaedia of flat racing.
Howard Wright. London: Robert Hale, 1986. 2nd ed. 430p.

Confined to flat racing in Britain this encyclopedia includes the most renowned trainers, jockeys, breeders, and horses, past and present, in the history of British racing. Winners of the Classics and other major races are given automatic entry. Racing terminology is also included, and there is a long list of appendices giving the leading amateur riders, breeders, the racehorse of the year winners, the trainer of 100 winners in a season since 1945, classics' winners, and much else besides.

Motoring sports

2149 The Motor Cycling Club: Britain's oldest sporting club for motor cycles and cars.
Peter Garnier. Newton Abbot, England: David & Charles, 1989. 221p. map.

Despite its name the Motor Cycling Club which was founded in 1901 is a club for car enthusiasts as well as motor cycle owners. It holds long distance trials for both types of vehicle. This illustrated history tells the full story of these and other events and of the exploits of the most celebrated riders and drivers. Peter Garnier was Sports Editor of *Autocar* for thirteen years and Editor for a further eight.

2150 British Grand Prix.
Maurice Hamilton. Marlborough, England: Crowood, 1989. 254p. bibliog.

From the first British Grand Prix at Brooklands in 1926, via Donington Park, Aintree, and Brands Hatch, to Silverstone in 1988, the full story of grand prix motor racing in Britain is recorded in words and pictures. The cars, the drivers, the races, are all featured in an exciting text which is supported by a statistical section giving the results, the starting grid, and the fastest lap of each race.

2151 Grand Prix British winners.
Maurice Hamilton. Enfield, England: Guinness Publishing, 1991. 224p.

This tribute to the British drivers who have ever won a race in the Formula One World Championship includes detailed career biographies and descriptions of the major world Grand Prix circuits.

2152 RAC Motor Sports Association yearbook 1991.
Slough, England: RAC Motor Sports Association, 1991. 473p.

The major part of this yearbook is given over to the general and technical regulations in the control of British motor sport. Other features include the procedures for applying for a licence, national records, and a directory of British motor clubs.

Rugby League

2153 **Rugby League who's who.**
Jeff Connor. Enfield, England: Guinness Publishing, 1991. 224p.
This definitive statistical annual gives the career records and scoring performances of every player currently engaged in the Stones Bitter Championship. Full directory information is provided for all the thirty-five professional Rugby League clubs.

2154 **The grounds of Rugby League.**
Trevor Delaney. [n.p.], 208p. bibliog.
Everything it is possible to know about the grounds at which professional Rugby League is played, or has been played, is recorded in this definitive study.

2155 **Rothmans Rugby League yearbook 1992-93.**
Raymond Fletcher, David Howes. London: Headline, 1992. 12th ed. 416p.
A gold mine of historical and current information on every conceivable aspect of Rugby League, this yearbook contains brief club histories, individual scoring records, milestones of the previous season, coverage of all cup competitions, Great Britain 'Test' matches, teams, and scorers, and, in this edition, career profiles of all Home Countries Rugby Union international players who signed Rugby League forms over the past twenty years.

2156 **The Guinness Rugby League fact book.**
Robert Gate. Enfield, England: Guinness Publishing, 1991. 224p.
This complete reference guide to the professional code includes a milestone chronology of significant events 1871-1992; a club directory and record; the history and results of all current and defunct competitions; match, season, and career individual records; Great Britain Test Match results; and career profiles of thirteen all-time Rugby League 'greats'.

2157 **The Rugby League Challenge Cup.**
John Huxley. Enfield, England: Guinness Publishing, 1992. 224p.
Now one of England top sporting occasions, the RL Challenge Cup final at Wembley has transcended the north-south divide in English sport. This work is a complete history of the competition from its modest beginnings, the move to Wembley in 1929, to the huge television coverage it enjoys today.

2158 **The Stones Bitter Rugby League directory 1991-92.**
Ian Proctor, Andrew Varley. London: Kingswood, 1991. 2nd ed. 256p.
Concentrating on the thirty-six professional clubs, this illustrated directory provides a historical sketch of each club, its honours and achievements since the Second World War, and the records of individual players. Player profiles, accounts of matches to remember drawn from contemporary newspaper accounts, ground travel directions, team colours, record attendances, biggest victory and heaviest defeat, are also included.

Rugby Union

2159   **The International Rugby Championship 1883-1983.**
      Terry Goodwin.   London: Willow Books, 1984. 498p. bibliog.

The first Rugby Union international, Scotland v. England, took place at Raeburn Place, Edinburgh, 27 March 1871 while Ireland first played England in 1875 and Wales in 1883 – this 1882-83 season is now accepted as the starting point for the International Championship. The Four Nations Championship became the Five Nations Championship in 1910 when France first participated. This comprehensive history provides a complete set of match reports and team lists.

2160   **Rothmans Rugby Union yearbook 1992-93.**
      Edited by Stephen Jones.   London: Headline, 1992. 21st ed. 447p.

A review of the previous season, the results of the Five Nations Championship, lists of international players, a directory of the senior clubs, coverage of the Pilkington Cup, the Courage leagues, the ADT County Championship, the 'Varsity Match, school Rugby, and fixtures for the new season, provide the bedrock of this indispensable publication. Five players of the year are chosen.

2161   **The complete who's who of England Rugby Union Internationals.**
      Raymond Maule.   Derby, England: Breedon, 1992.

Contains biographical sketches of all 'capped' players who have worn the white jersey in senior international matches.

2162   **Centenary history of the Rugby Football Union.**
      U. A. Titley, R. McWhirter.   London: Rugby Football Union, 1970. 312p.

All aspects of English rugby football are covered in this celebratory history: its origins, the university clubs, the Services, county rugby, the International Board, Twickenham, and brief biographies of the RFU's Patrons, Presidents and Vice-presidents, Secretaries, Treasurers, and England 'capped' players.

2163   **Official Rugby Union club directory 1990-91.**
      Edited by Tony Williams, Bill Mitchell.   Windsor, England: Burlington, 1990. 3rd ed. 729p. (A Daily Mail Publication).

A complete guide to all clubs which compete in the Courage Club championships, this directory provides extended information on National Division club's date of foundation, its ground, club colours, and its previous season's record, its players and officials, and a ground plan. Fixtures for the coming season, the championship regulations, and a list of national media contacts are also included.

Tennis

2164 **100 Wimbledon championships: a celebration.**
John Barrett. London: Willow, 1986. 287p. bibliog.
An advertisement placed in *The Field* magazine for 9th June 1877 read: 'The All-England Croquet and Lawn Tennis Club, Wimbledon, propose to hold a lawn tennis meeting, open to all amateurs, on Monday July 9th and following days'. This celebratory history, which includes a short biography of every Wimbledon champion, traces how a croquet club in Surrey became the home of the world's greatest tennis championships.

2165 **Lawn Tennis Association official handbook: incorporating the LTA club manual. 1991.**
London: LTA, 1991. 300 + 56p.
This official yearbook contains facts and records relating to the previous summer's Wimbledon Championships; British senior and junior rankings; the Prudential Northern Championships; the inter-County Championships; the junior championships; and features on the Wimbledon Lawn Tennis Museum and the LTA's badges, colours and awards.

2166 **Wimbledon 1877-1977.**
Max Robertson. London: Arthur Barker, 1977. 180p.
This illustrated volume celebrates the centenary of the All England Croquet and Lawn Tennis Club's championships. A chronological narrative explains how Wimbledon has retained its position as the most glamorous event on the tennis circuit and remembers the illustrious players and the great matches they participated in. The results of all championship finals are recorded in a series of appendices.

Walking

2167 **Great walks: great walks of the national parks of Britain.**
Frank Duerden. London: Ward Lock, 1991. 352p. 60 maps.
Local experts describe fifty classic walks in the Yorkshire Dales, the Lake District, on Dartmoor, and along the South Downs, in this celebration of the National Parks.

2168 **John Hillaby's walking in Britain.**
Edited by John Hillaby. London: Collins, 1988. 256p.
Nearly twenty distinguished authors and journalists contribute to this splendid comprehensive guide to the great walks and finest walking country in Britain. Among the lavish colour illustrations is a selection of watercolours by David Bellamy. Strangely there are no maps.

2169 **The National Trust book of long walks.**
Adam Nicolson. London: National Trust/Weidenfeld & Nicolson, 1981. 287p. 11 maps. bibliog.

The author describes at length ten walks he completed, ranging from eighty to 500 miles in distance, incorporating geological, archaeological, historical and literary discussions into the thread of his topographical narrative.

2170 **Rambler's yearbook and accommodation guide 1992.**
London: Rambler's Association, 1991. 254p.

Included in this all-encompassing guide is information on access to the countryside, a summary of legal rights to public footpaths and open country; on the best use of Ordnance Survey maps; on forty-six long distance paths; and on local authorities providing details of walks in their areas. An accommodation guide includes independent hostels and bunkhouses as well as guesthouses and hotels.

2171 **Walking canals.**
Edited by Ronald Russell. Newton Abbot, England: David & Charles, 1984. 160p. 16 maps. bibliog.

Two thousand miles of urban and rural pathway are opened up in this book of walks along English canal banks and towpaths. After introductory chapters on the historical and legal background of towpaths, canal boats and their crews, abandoned and derelict canals, and canal natural history, sixteen canal walks, between four and twelve miles in length, are described by local enthusiasts, each knowledgeable about both the district and the history of the canal in question.

2172 **YHA walking in Britain.**
Sue Seddon. London: Ward Lock, 1989. 208p.

The Youth Hostels Association claims 270,000 members, a network of 260 hostels throughout England and Wales, and a well-deserved reputation for taking care of serious and casual walkers. This colourfully-illustrated guide contains detailed instructions for fifteen seven-day walks and ten weekend routes from hostel to hostel. There is also a YHA hostel directory and practical information on vital preparations for long walks such as booking the hostel, safety and equipment, and maps and map reading.

Other

2173 **Baily's hunting directory 1991/92.**
Windsor, England: Burlington, 1991. 85th ed. 429p.

Essentially this is a directory of hunts arranged by county and type of hounds followed: foxhounds, beaglehounds, bassethounds, staghounds, draghounds, and bloodhounds, giving details of the Master, secretary, days of meets, history, and former Masters. There are also lists of Masters on the active list and Masters in office. An introductory section reviews the previous season's foxhunting scene.

2174 **Guinness book of darts.**

Derek Brown. Enfield, England: Guinness Publishing, 1981. 159p.

During the 1970s darts developed into a newsworthy mainline sport, far exceeding its previous status. This encyclopedic work examines its equipment, players and records, tournaments, and the role of the British Darts Organisation.

2175 **Flashing blades: the story of British ice-hockey.**

Phil Drackett. Marlborough, England: Crowood, 1987. 192p. bibliog.

British ice-hockey reached its peak in 1936 when the national team pulled off an unlikely treble becoming European, World, and Olympic champions. This illustrated narrative traces British ice-hockey from its infancy in the 1880s to its revival as a fast-moving spectator sport 100 years later.

2176 **English Bowling Association 1992 official yearbook.**

Worthing, England: English Bowling Association, 1992. 335p.

This yearbook contains directory information of the EBA's rules and constitution, its officers and committee members, county associations, and the laws of the game. British Isles championship records, county statistics, the results of international matches, and a list of all players who have represented England since 1903 when the EBA was founded, are also included.

2177 **Rothmans snooker yearbook 1990-91.**

Edited by Janice Hale. London: Rothmans Queen Anne Press, 1990. 6th ed. 383p.

The results of every major home and overseas tournament, an up-to-date record of every professional player, a review of the previous season, a complete ranking list, details of prize money earnings, and sections on professional billiards, women's snooker, and on the amateur game, are all regular features of this indispensable yearbook.

2178 **The British leisure and swimming pool directory 1990/91.**

Edited by Judy Richardson. Cambridge, England: John S. Turner, 1990. 550p.

This management guide to some 1,300 community swimming and leisure pools gives their location, hours, admission control and charges, together with details of their main facilities, changing room systems, special features, and events. A buyer's guide ranges through the whole gamut of services and suppliers.

2179 **The Squash Rackets Association annual 1990-91.**

Edited by Kate Scott. London: SRA, 1990. 290p.

Included in this SRA directory are the results of international and other major tournaments, the senior and junior national rankings, and a county section listing registered coaches, referees, and markers, county championship results, affiliated clubs, and current leading players.

2180 **British white water: a guide to the 100 best canoeing rivers.**
Terry Storry.   London: Constable, 1991. maps.

Eminently suitable for planning serious expeditions in unknown waters, this expertly researched guide for experienced canoeists contains directions to, and rigorous examinations of all problem stretches of water. Its convenient pocket size means that it can be taken along for on-the-spot reference when hazards are anticipated.

Libraries, Museums and Galleries

Libraries

2181 **Treasures of the British Library.**
Compiled by Nicolas Barker and the Curatorial Staff of the British
Library. London: British Library, 1988. 272p. bibliog.
Never before has the wealth and variety of the British Library's holdings been so fully
presented. The treasures preserved there include some of the most famous and finest
items not only from the British Isles, but also from all parts of the globe. The
Lindisfarne Gospels, *Magna Carta*, Shakespeare's First Folio edition, and the
manuscripts of the earliest extant versions of the best-known works of English
literature, from *Beowulf* onwards, are among the unsurpassed heritage items to be
discovered at the British Library in the heart of London. The history and progress of
Britain's national library are also narrated with great skill in this handsome volume.

2182 **The Library Association Yearbook.**
Edited by Kathryn Beecroft, Bob Palmer. London: Library
Association, 1992. 416p.
Essentially a directory of chartered librarians, this yearbook also contains details of the
Association's structure, its Branches and Groups, and its headquarters' staff.

2183 **British librarianship and information work 1986-1990: volume one:
General libraries and the profession: volume two: Special libraries,
materials and processes.**
Edited by David W. Bromley, Angela M. Allott. London: Library
Association, 1992.
British librarianship and information work continues a series which began in 1928 as
Year's work in librarianship, changing to *Five years' work in librarianship* from 1951,
and to its present title with the volume for 1966-1970. The successive volumes, the
work of numerous contributors, constitute an important record of professional activity

493

as exemplified in major events and publications in every area of library and information work.

2184　**The libraries directory 1991-93.**
　　　　Edited by Richard S. Burnell.　Cambridge, England: Clarke, 1992.
　　　　240p.

English entries in this directory, formerly known as *The libraries, museums and art galleries year book*, are arranged in three sections: British Library; public libraries listed alphabetically by local authorities; and special libraries, including museums, galleries, stately homes, and cathedral and diocesan libraries, with significant collections, listed by location. Information is provided on stock, issues, subject coverage and special collections, opening hours and access, and the librarian and governing body of each library.

2185　**The Aslib directory of information sources in the United Kingdom.**
　　　　Edited by Ellen M. Codlin, Keith W. Reynard.　London: Aslib,
　　　　1992. 2 vols. 7th ed.

Two thousand organizations worldwide are members of Aslib, the Association for Information Management. Volume one of this directory, which was first published in 1928, contains 6,000 entries, and is an invaluable reference and research tool in business development and marketing in all sectors of the economy, science and technology, commerce and finance, the social sciences, medicine, and the humanities. The range of institutions represented varies from the very large to the very small, and includes commercial, scientific, government, negotiating, standardizing, qualifying, academic and professional bodies, producers of data, statistics and abstracts, experts in specific areas, and repositories of vast document collections. Volume two is a subject index covering more than 3,000 topics. New to this edition is a special feature on European Community Single Market information sources.

2186　**Copyright: interpreting the law for libraries and archives.**
　　　　Graham P. Cornish.　London: Library Association, 1990. 114p.
　　　　bibliog.

'Written by a librarian trying to understand the law, not a lawyer trying to understand libraries', this question and answer guide explains the implications of the 1988 Copyright Design and Patents Act. It covers printed material, manuscripts, audio-visual works, photographs, maps, databases, broadcasts, and works of art. The author is responsible for copyright interpretation throughout the British Library.

2187　**Corpus of British medieval library catalogues.**
　　　　London: British Library in association with the British Academy,
　　　　1990- . 3 vols. (vol. 1. *The Friars' libraries*. Edited by K. W.
　　　　Humphreys. 1990. 320p.; vol. 2. *The Registrum Anglie*. Edited by
　　　　R. A. B. Mynors, R. H. Rouse, M. A. Rouse, 1991. 520p.; vol. 3.
　　　　The libraries of the Cistercians, Gilbertines and Premonstratensians.
　　　　Edited by David N. Bell. 1992. 372p.).

Monastic and cathedral library holdings are among the most important extant written records of medieval intellectual life. The *Corpus* comprises a comprehensive and systematic edition on surviving medieval catalogues relating to libraries in Britain.

Each volume is either dedicated to an individual library, to a religious order, or, as in the case of number two in the series, a union catalogue. Twenty volumes are planned, to be published at the rate of two *per annum*.

2188 **Guide to libraries and information units in government departments and other organisations.**
Edited by Peter Dale. London: British Library, 1992. 30th ed. 164p.

First published in 1948 and formerly known as *Guide to government department and other libraries*, this biennial directory to over 600 UK government libraries, and libraries with collections on current affairs and subjects of topical concern, provides full address and contact details, information on stock coverage, services and opening hours, and on the availability of services to outside enquirers. One hundred entries are new to this edition.

2189 **Guide to libraries in key UK companies.**
Peter Dale. London: British Library, 1992. 120p.

This is a guide to the specialist resources available in the UK's top business and industrial libraries. The information provided includes full address and contact details; stock, services, and access details, and the availability of services to outside researchers.

2190 **The British Library: a guide to its structure, publications, collections and services.**
Alan Day. London: Library Association, 1988. 190p.

Formed in 1973 under the terms of the British Library Act, the Library now comprises six previously independent national collections: the British Museum Library; National Central Library; National Lending Library for Science and Technology; Library Association Library; India Office Library and Records; and the National Sound Archive. It also encompasses the *British National Bibliography*. This guide follows British Library's own framework, as revised in 1985, and is intended for potential users of its collections.

2191 **Who's who in the UK information world 1992.**
Edited by Matthew Finlay. London: TFPL, 1991. 3rd ed. 459p.

This biographical index provides details of the qualifications and memberships, length of experience, where biographees were educated, their previous posts, present work, professional involvement, and of the personal interests of some 3,700 individuals in the library and information profession.

2192 **The library of the British Museum: retrospective essays on the Department of Printed Books.**
Edited by P. R. Harris. London: British Library, 1991. 305p.

These commemorative essays capture various aspects of the history and working practices of the former Department of Printed Books of the British Museum Library on the eve of its departure to the new British Library buildings at St. Pancras. Among the episodes recounted are the story of a previous move between 1838 and 1842, the enforcing of the legal deposit regulations (1850-53), and the history of the

Department's pornographic material which was separated from the general collections in 1841. Personal reminiscences of more recent times complete a very attractive work.

2193 **Academic libraries in the United Kingdom and Republic of Ireland.**
Edited by Ann Harrold. London: Library Association, 1992. 112p.
'Provides information on over 700 libraries, giving addresses, telephone, fax and telex numbers. It also lists hours of opening, number of staff, size of stock, controlling authorities and the relationship of each with other departments and institutions.' (Advance notice).

2194 **Libraries in the United Kingdom and the Republic of Ireland 1993.**
Edited by Ann Harrold. London: Library Association, 1992.
19th ed. 192p.
This annual directory lists all public, university, higher education, and selected government, national and special libraries.

2195 **Out of the dinosaurs: the evolution of the National Lending Library for Science and Technology.**
Bernard Houghton. London: Clive Bingley, 1972. 127p.
In the years following the Second World War the need for industry and industrial research organizations to have rapid access to scientific and technical literature became ever more apparent. This book describes the circumstances leading up to the establishment of a specialist national library to meet this need, and traces its development up to its amalgamation with the National Central Library to form the British Library Lending Division in 1973.

2196 **Medieval libraries of Great Britain: a list of surviving books.**
Edited by N. R. Ker. London: Royal Historical Society, 1964.
2nd ed. 424p. (RHS Guides and Handbooks, no. 3).
About 6,000 books and service books from some 500 college, cathedral, and religious houses' libraries are referred to in this descriptive list which provides information on the library in which the book is now deposited, its present shelfmark, the language in which it was written if that was not Latin, and a provenance record from the evidence of library bindings and *ex libris* and other inscriptions. The *Supplement to the second edition* (Edited by Andrew G. Watson. London: RHS, 1987. 149p. [RHS Guides and Handbooks, no. 15]) adds details of books, previously in private hands, which have subsequently come to light.

2197 **Libraries and information in Britain.**
London: British Library, 1992. 2nd ed. [n.p.]. (British Library Information Guide).
'The United Kingdom possesses a rich variety of library and information facilities and services. Researchers, business and the public have unrestricted, free access to the world's published resources of knowledge and culture, to a greater degree than in most other countries. Universal, uncensored access is provided through locally-controlled public libraries, academic libraries and special libraries, backed up by the extensive resources of the British Library' (Introduction to first edition). Originally issued in connection with the International Federation of Library Associations' conference in

Brighton in 1987, this glossy publication is intended primarily for library and information professionals. This edition was prepared for the British Library Research and Development Department by the Information Partnership.

2198 **Information UK 2000.**
Edited by John Martyn, Peter Vickers, Mary Feeney. London:
Bowker Saur, 1990. 301p.

Various groups consisting of librarians, publishers, journalists, and computer, telecommunications, conservation and broadcasting experts, investigated the likely trends in information handling storage and use up to the year 2,000 in eleven crucial areas: social trends; technology; archives, libraries and information services; recording; communications; publishing; the domestic use of information; manpower, education and training; the organizational use of information; policy issues for information users; and policy issues from the policy maker's viewpoint. This is their report; it identifies the crucial developments, and peers into the future.

2199 **The House of Commons library: a history.**
David Menhennet. London: HMSO, 1991. 162p. bibliog.

Formerly resembling a gentlemen's club library of the nineteenth century, the House of Commons library now offers MPs a vital research and information service on economic affairs, education and social services, science, the environment, defence, and international affairs. This illustrated history concludes with examples of research papers compiled for MPs in the 1989-90 session. David Menhennet was Librarian of the House for fifteen years until 1991.

2200 **Prince of librarians: the life and times of Antonio Panizzi of the British Museum.**
Edward Miller. London: British Library, 1988. 356p. bibliog.

Antonio Panizzi arrived penniless in England in 1823, a political refugee from the Duchy of Modena. Eight years later he was appointed as Extra Assistant Librarian in the British Museum Library. He reached the summit of British librarianship as Keeper of Printed Books 1837-56 and Principal Librarian 1856-66. The author, himself on the Library staff for forty years, was ideally placed to write this biography, enjoying unrivalled access to previously unpublished source material. *Prince of librarians* was originally published by Andre Deutsch in 1967.

2201 **That noble cabinet: a history of the British Museum.**
Edward Miller. London: André Deutsch, 1973. 400p. bibliog.

The British Museum, established by Act of Parliament which received the Royal Assent 7 June 1753, opened its doors to the public in January 1759. Its foundation collections embraced the 50,000 books belonging to Sir Hans Sloane (1661-1753) along with his entire natural history collection, his coins and medals, and ancient, medieval and oriental antiquities; the Harleian manuscripts collected in the early years of the eighteenth-century by Robert and Edward Harley, first and second Earls of Oxford; and the Cottonian collection of manuscripts assembled by Sir Richard Cotton (1571-1631). To these were added the 'Old Royal Library', some 9,000 books and 2,000 manuscripts presented by George II in 1757. Since that time its international reputation as one of the world's leading museums and libraries has steadily grown, although not without controversy or the occasional setback. The library collections were merged into the British Library in 1973. Edward Miller joined the British

Museum staff in 1934, retiring forty years later, and was admirably placed to write this spectacular history, having access to a mass of previously unpublished documentary source material.

2202 **Directory of law libraries in the British Isles.**
C. Miskin. Hebden Bridge, England: Legal Information Resources, 1988. 3rd ed. 120p.

Published for the British and Irish Association of Law Libraries, this directory contains 317 entries based on replies to a postal questionnaire. These provide information on opening hours, terms of admission, loan facilities and services, and subject coverage.

2203 **History of the Library Association 1877-1977.**
W. A. Munford. London: Library Association, 1977. 360p. bibliog.

Published to mark the Library Association's centenary, this official historical includes biographical sketches of many prominent figures who helped to shape its development and progress.

2204 **The parochial libraries of the Church of England: report of a committee appointed by the Central Council for the Care of Churches to investigate the number and condition of parochial libraries belonging to the Church of England.**
London: Faith Press, 1959. 135p.

The Central Council for the Care of Churches was established in 1923 to advise on the protection and conservation of ancient churches and the treasures they guard. In 1949 it was asked by the Archbishop of Canterbury to prepare a report on the condition of parochial libraries in England. Issued in this format in a limited edition of 500 copies, the report includes a historical introduction; the recommendations of the Council's Parochial Library Committee; an alphabetical list of past and present parochial libraries, including notes on the history of their collections, and published references; and county tables of parochial libraries founded before 1800 and still existing in 1959.

2205 **Old English libraries: the making, collection, and use of books during the Middle Ages.**
Ernest A. Savage. London: Methuen, 1970. 298p. bibliog. (Methuen Library Reprints).

First published in the illustrious Antiquaries Books series in 1911, this classic work describes how manuscript books were produced and traded during the medieval period, explores the range of English libraries then available, and gives an account of the books that were most in demand.

2206 **Rude words: a discursive history of the London Library.**
John Wells. London: Macmillan, 1991. 240p.

Today the London Library can rejoice in some 8,000 members, each paying an annual subscription of £80, a million volumes on its shelves, and disposable funds in excess of £5 million. A computerized catalogue, and plans for a new wing at an advanced stage, testify to its determined up-to-date approach. This anecdotal and discursive history, based on some excellent dipping into the Library's archives, is published to mark the 150th anniversary of its foundation by Thomas Carlyle who was incensed at his inability to borrow books from the British Museum Library. It captures very pleasantly the highlights of this unique institution's progress.

Archives and records

2207 **The Public Record Office 1838-1958.**
John D. Cantwell.   London: HMSO for Public Record Office, 1991.
644p.

Created in 1838 to house the public records of England and Wales, the Public Record Office at first dealt mainly with legal records but in 1852 its work was extended to government departments and in 1854 it absorbed the State Paper Office. This authoritative history stresses the impact of successive deputy keepers and Masters of the Rolls in shaping the PRO's progress.

2208 **The nation's memory: a pictorial guide to the Public Record Office.**
Edited by Jane Cox.   London: HMSO, 1988. 64p. maps on
endpapers.

The Public Record Office at Chancery Lane houses ninety shelf-miles of documentary records, from the eleventh-century *Domesday Book*, to present-day official government papers. Parchment rolls, registers, diaries, private letters, maps, are among the types of records that may be inspected and used by interested members of the public. This popular guide to the PRO's building and services indicates the types of material available. Of particular use is an identification of the different groups of records located at the PRO's new buildings at Kew.

2209 **British archives: a guide to archive resources in the United Kingdom.**
Janet Foster, Julia Sheppard.   London: Macmillan, 1989. 2nd ed.
834p.

Extensive archives in almost all areas of scholarship are available to United Kingdom research workers. This directory of archive repositories, first published in 1982, aims 'to consolidate information for the historian and archivist and provide a starting point for the first-time user of archives'. Data given on over 1,000 repositories include parent institution, address, hours of opening, historical background, acquisitions policy, major collections, significant non-manuscript material, finding aids, facilities, and publications.

2210 **The records of the nation: the Public Record Office 1838-1988: the British Record Society 1888-1988.**
Edited by G. H. Martin, Peter Spufford.   Woodbridge, England:
Boydell/British Record Society, 1990. 312p.

Twenty-one conference papers given at the conference called to mark the PRO's 150th anniversary and the British Record Society's centenary are included in this collection. Among the principal topics are the PRO's history and development, its calendars and indexes, and the national probate records.

Museums and art galleries

2211 The art galleries of Britain and Ireland: a guide to their collections.
Joan Abse.   London: Robson, 1985. rev. ed. 383p.

First published by Sidgwick & Jackson in 1974, this revised edition is an up-to-date guide to the works of art held in the permanent collections of British and Irish art galleries. Arranged alphabetically by location, it describes the history of the collections and lists their outstanding individual items.

2212 Museums yearbook 1991-1992 including a directory of museums and galleries of the British Isles.
Edited by Sheena Barbour.   London: Museums Association, 1991. 439p.

First published in 1955, the main section of this annual publication comprises an alphabetical town-by-town directory of museums and galleries open to the public giving additional information on their collections, scheduled exhibitions, staffing, and their published reports and catalogues. Almost 100 new museums are included in this edition and there are supplementary directories of related organizations, of museum suppliers and services, and a guide to the Museums Association's functions.

2213 The story of the British Museum.
Marjorie Caygill.   London: British Museum, 1992. new ed. 72p.

Drawing upon contemporary newspapers, journals and diaries, and the British Museum's own rich archives, Marjorie Caygill, who is Assistant to the Museum's Director, outlines the Museum's development and the growth of its world-famous collections. Originally published in 1981, this new edition looks at the Museum's collecting policies over the last ten years. The same author's *Treasures of the British Museum* (1992. 240p) is a lavishly illustrated record of some of its more imposing items.

2214 Exploring Museums.
London: HMSO, 1989-90. 8 vols. (*East Anglia* (Alf Hatton); *The Home Counties* (Geoff Marsh, Nell Hoare, Karen Hull); *London* (Simon Holding); *The Midlands* (Tim Schadle-Hall); *North East England* (David Fleming); *South West England* (Arnold Wilson); *Southern England and the Channel Islands* (Kenneth James Barton)).

Sponsored by *The Times* newspaper, this series of well-illustrated regional guides, commissioned to mark Museums Year, highlights the best museums, giving location and access details, together with descriptions of their most interesting holdings. In each volume a gazetteer lists other museums not described in detail.

2215 **Treasures of the British Museum.**

Edited by Sir Frank Francis. London: Thames & Hudson, 1971. 360p.

Included in this authoritative and superbly-illustrated book, containing thirteen essays by senior members of staff, each describing the work and chief treasurers of their Departments, is a fascinating glimpse into the methods and techniques of the Research Laboratory. Sir Frank Francis, Director and Principal Librarian 1959-68, provides a magisterial historical introduction.

2216 **A guide to the transport museums of Great Britain.**

Jude Garvey. London: Pelham, 1982. 238p. map on endpaper.

Detailed descriptions of the exhibits and themes of fifty-two major transport museums are followed in this guide by a comprehensive gazetteer of all 106 such museums in Britain.

2217 **The Cambridge guide to the museums of Britain and Ireland.**

Kenneth Hudson, Ann Nicholls. Cambridge, England: Cambridge University Press, 1989. rev. ed. 452p. + 16p. of maps.

First published in 1987, this handbook contains over 2,000 detailed and informative entries on museums, art galleries, and historic houses. Providing a complete guide on what to see and do, and with 400 illustrations, and a sixteen-page section giving information on Britain and Ireland's newest museums, it is the most comprehensive museum guide yet published.

2218 **The good museums guide.**

Kenneth Hudson. London: Macmillan, 1982. 2nd ed. 282p. 8 maps.

Described as the first consumer guide to museums and art galleries in Britain, this work selects 400 museums and galleries which measured up to the stringent standards set by the author and his team of over 250 volunteers who, between them, reported on the scope and contents of all 1,600 museums and galleries in the British Isles, noting their good and bad features, their facilities for visitors, their shops and publications, etc. The main text consists of a descriptive gazetteer arranged alphabetically by location supplemented by a list of museums with outstanding special-interest collections and eight regional maps.

2219 **The Shell book of country museums.**

Kenneth Hudson. London: Heinemann, 1980. 241p. 3 maps.

Over 100 country museums (i.e. small, with a local rather than a national flavour), accessible and hospitable to the public, feature in this descriptive regional gazetteer.

2220 **Local authorities and museums: report by a working party 1991.**

London: HMSO for Museums and Galleries Commission, 1991. 146p. bibliog.

Set up 'to consider the role and responsibilities of local authorities in relation to museums and galleries in the United Kingdom now and in the future, to instance ways in which local authorities may best provide support . . . and to make recommenda-tions', the Museum and Galleries Commission's Working Party reviewed all the relevant factors leading to significant changes in the way local authorities support museums and galleries. Their report highlights the educational, social, and economic importance of museums and suggests ways in which their role and performance can be further improved and extended.

2221 **Museums and galleries.**
London: HMSO, 1990. rev. ed. 32p. (Sectional List, no. 73).

This sectional list covers in print publications from the museums and galleries of the United Kingdom and other bodies with similar or relevant interests available from Her Majesty's Stationery Office. A selection of appropriate Parliamentary publications is also included. This list replaces List 55 (*Victoria and Albert Museum*) and parts of List 24 (*British National Archives*) and List 50 (*Miscellaneous*) which are now discontinued.

2222 **Museums and galleries in Great Britain and Ireland. 1992.**
East Grinstead, England: British Leisure, 1991. 180p.

Published annually since 1955, this is a detailed guide to over 1,300 museums and art galleries whose collections are open to the public listed in county order and in alphabetical order within counties. A separate section is devoted to museums of the armed services. All entries give details of opening hours, facilities, admission charges, and brief descriptions of the principal collections.

2223 **The national museums and galleries of the United Kingdom.**
London: HMSO for the Museums and Galleries Commission, 1988. 64p.

This official report, the first for nearly sixty years, critically examines the characteristics, importance, and duties of the national museums. It explains how they are funded, governed, controlled, directed and staffed, and it also includes some observations on their collections.

2224 **British aviation museums and collections.**
Bob Ogden. Stamford, England: Key Publishing, 1986. 2nd ed. 121p. (Fly Past Reference Library).

An illustrated guide giving the address, situation, admission hours, and descriptions of the aircraft on view of Britain's various aircraft museums.

2225 **The treasury of London's past: an historical account of the Museum of London and its predecessors: Guildhall Museum and the London Museum.**
Francis Sheppard. London: HMSO for the Museum of London, 1990. 224p.

The Museum of London's formidable collections owe much to the work of its two rival predecessors. This work tells the full story of these two disparate but complementary institutions, not least their mutual distrust and rivalry, to their eventual amalgamation.

2226 **The other museum guide.**
D. Shipley, M. Peplow. London: Grafton, 1988. 331p.
About 300 regional and specialist museums are entered in this selective guide for tourists. Each entry includes a short description and a note on the museum's special features.

2227 **The Natural History Museum at South Kensington: A history of the British Museum (Natural History) 1753-1980.**
William T. Stearn. London: Heinemann in association with the British Museum (Natural History), 1981. 414p.
Based on research in the unpublished minutes, confidential reports, and memoranda of the Museum's Trustees, and drawing upon the memories of senior Museum staff, this authoritative history looks at the original collections housed in the British Museum, recounts the detailed story of the new purpose-built buildings in Kensington, and traces the development of what is now one of the world's finest scientific research institutions.

2228 **Victoria and Albert Museum.**
London: HMSO, 1986. rev. ed. 18p. (Sectional List, no. 55).
This catalogue of V & A publications divides them under a number of subject headings: art of the book, ceramics; costume, dolls and toys; exhibitions; furniture and woodwork; metalwork; oriental art; paintings and watercolours; prints and drawings; sculpture, textiles; and the Theatre Museum.

2229 **Britain's railway museums.**
Peter Williams. London: Ian Allan, 1974. 176p.
This pictorial volume presents the treasures of the Museum of British Transport (Clapham); the Railway Museum (York); the Museum of Transport (Glasgow); the Great Western Railway Museum (Swindon); the Science Museum (South Kensington); the Museum of Technology for the East Midlands (Leicester); and the Museum of Science and Industry (Birmingham). Soon after publication the museum at Clapham was closed and its exhibits were combined with those at York in new premises as the National Railway Museum.

2230 **The British Museum: purpose and politics.**
David M. Wilson. London: British Museum, 1989. 126p.
Written by the Museum's Director, this book is an attempt to unravel 'the complicated practicalities of running the British Museum, and the philosophy upon which it was founded'. The Museum's perennial problems include the horrendous costs of conservation, the thorny question of public funding and public charging, and the controversy over the restitution of objects to their country of origin.

2231   **The collections of the British Museum.**
Edited by David M. Wilson.   London: British Museum, 1989. 304p.
bibliog.

In a good year the vast artistic, archaeological and numismatic collections of the British Museum attract nearly four million visitors, half of them from overseas. This superbly-illustrated handbook to the most interesting of its antiquities also includes a study of the Museum's conservation and scientific research work which is continually in progress.

Guide to military museums.
See item no. 1134.

Book Trade

2232 British literary publishing houses 1820-1880.
Edited by Patricia J. Anderson, Jonathan Rose.   Detroit, Michigan:
Gale, 1991. 412p.

Both well-known and obscure firms are included in this comprehensive reference work
which contains sixty-eight expert essays on the history and development of literary
publishing houses which flourished at the height of the Victorian period. In some cases,
although by no means all, there is an indication of where a firm's archives and records
may be located.

**2233 Her Majesty's Stationery Office: the story of the first 200 years
1786-1986.**
Hugh Barty-King.   London: HMSO, 1986. 160p. bibliog.

With an establishment of fifteen men, two women, two horses, and a cart, the
Stationery Office was created in April 1786 to reduce the cost of government
stationery, which was becoming enormously inflated by the excessive profits and the
corrupt purchasing system of the times. Two hundred years later it is one of the top
British publishers, in the forefront of new technology developments, with huge
government and Parliament printing and publishing commitments, and a large business
in office supplies. This detailed history, which includes a ten-page chronology, extends
over the whole range of HMSO's activities.

2234 **English books and readers.**
H. S. Bennett. Cambridge, England: Cambridge University Press, 1952-70. 3 vols. (vol. 1. *1475-1557: being a study in the history of the book trade from Caxton to the incorporation of the Stationers Company.* 1969. 2nd ed. 338p.; vol. 2. *1558-1603: being a study of the book trade in the reign of Elizabeth I.* 1965. 320p.; vol. 3. *1605-1640: being a study of the book trade in the reigns of James I and Charles I.* 1970. 254p.).

The basic purpose of these three volumes is to give an account of the total output of books and pamphlets from the time William Caxton set up his printing press at Westminster in 1476 to the English Civil War. In doing so Bennett also encompasses the making of books from the printer's reception of the author's manuscript to the appearance of the printed book on the bookseller's stalls, the relationship of author and reader, the history and control of the early book trade, and the part it played in the cultural and intellectual life of the age.

2235 **Cambridge University Press 1584-1984.**
M. H. Black. Cambridge, England: Cambridge University Press, 1984. 343p.

The royal charter by which the University's right to print and publish was founded, a commitment to Bible printing from the beginning, the development of an equal commitment to learned printing and publishing, and a struggle with the London book trade drawn out over centuries, are prominent features in the history of Cambridge University Press. This quatercentennial history celebrates a unique English institution.

2236 **Cole's register of British antiquarian and secondhand bookdealers 1991.**
York, England: The Clique, 1991. 313p.

First published in 1983 this annual directory of British and Irish bookdealers contains three main sections: an alphabetical name and address list; an index of specialist bookdealers; and a geographic listing A to Z by county. *The Clique* is the weekly organ of the antiquarian book trade.

2237 **The comprehensive British publishers' directory.**
Andover, England: Gale Research, 1993. (forthcoming).

Over 3,000 firms are listed in this directory along with their key personnel, affiliations, imprints, areas of activity, and distribution arrangements. A biennial cycle of publication is planned.

2238 **Directory of book publishers and wholesalers.**
London: Booksellers' Associations, 1991. 20th ed. 677p.

First published in 1954 this alphabetical listing of publishers and distributors provides the names of the principal personnel, and their responsibilities, for each company. Other information includes the text of the Net Book Agreement, trade terms, and a list of the major conglomerates and their imprints.

2239   Directory of publishing.
London: Cassell, 1992. 2 vols. 17th ed.

Volume one *UK, Commonwealth and Overseas* gives detailed profiles of publishers, authors' agents, trade associations and agencies, and UK packagers. Cross-referenced indexes allow rapid access to companies, imprints, named key personnel, who owns whom information, publishers' areas of activity, ISBN prefixes, and overseas representation. Volume two *Continental Europe* was first published in 1992.

2240   drif's guide to the secondhand and antiquarian book shops of Britain.
drif field.   London: drif field, 1991. no pagination.

drif's irreverent, some would say scandalous, comments on bookshops he has visited (and there's not many he has missed), are eminently readable by anyone who possesses an efficient magnifying glass. His round Britain tour of secondhand bookshops begins reasonably enough in London, following the tube and rail lines round the capital in a clockwise direction. For some unfathomable reason the tour of the rest of the country starts at Newcastle.

2241   The private presses.
Colin Franklin, John R. Turner.   Aldershot, England: Scolar Press, 1991. 2nd ed. 378p. bibliog.

Concentrating on the period 1891-1914 this review, which was first published by Studio Vista in 1969, includes an 175-page bibliography of books issued by the Daniel, Kelmscott, Ashendene, Vale, Doves, Golden Cockerel, and Shakespeare Head Presses, thus listing some of the finest ever examples of English printed books.

2242   Harold Munro and the Poetry Bookshop.
Joy Grant.   London: Routledge & Kegan Paul, 1967. 286p. bibliog.

Formally opened by Henry Newbolt, 8 January 1913, the Poetry Bookshop at 35 Devonshire Street, five minutes' walk from the British Museum, was devoted to the sale of poetry, and of all books, pamphlets and periodicals connected with poetry. It was the brainchild of Harold Munro, editor of *The Poetry Review*, and together with the popular *Georgian Poetry* series issued under its auspices, it served as a reading room, poetry reading centre, and as a club and home for indigent poets, in fact as 'an academy for poetry on the Alexandrian model, where the Muses should find an actual substantial home'. It survived at another address in Great Russell Street until 1935, three years after Munro's death. No appreciation of the literary and cultural scene between the wars is complete without a deep understanding of the part played by the Poetry Bookshop. This work provides it.

2243   Gollancz: the story of a publishing house 1928-1978.
Sheila Hodges.   London: Gollancz. 1978. 256p.

Victor Gollancz's yellow and magenta dustwrappers were a noted feature of a strong list in the half-century of publishing recorded here. This account is especially valuable for its inside story of the foundation of the Left Book Club which undoubtedly helped pave the way for Labour's victory in the 1945 general election.

2244 **The House of Dent 1888-1938.**
London: J. M. Dent, 1938. 334p.

Essentially this is a reprint of *The memoirs of J. M. Dent 1849-1926* first issued in 1928, with four additional chapters by his son, Hugh R. Dent, published to mark the firm's jubilee. One episode related at length tells the story of the concept, planning, and launch of the world-famous Everyman's Library, one thousand best books made up of out of copyright 'classics' and translations of foreign literature, later leavened by a number of modern works.

2245 **The House of Warne: one hundred years of publishing.**
Arthur King, A. F. Stuart. London: Frederick Warne, 1965. 107p.

Largely sustained by the picture books of Kate Greenaway and Ralph Caldecott, the works of Beatrix Potter, and latterly by the Observer's series, the firm of Frederick Warne still retains its own individual niche in British publishing. This illustrated history is superbly produced.

2246 **The Bodley Head 1887-1987.**
J. W. Lambert, Michael Ratcliffe. London: Bodley Head, 1987. 365p.

Undoubtedly one of the most readable and entertaining company histories, this book begins with the early life of John Lane, Bodley Head's founder, and ends with the firm's federation with Chatto & Windus and Jonathan Cape, two other independent firms, who shared Bodley Head's vision and philosophy of book publishing. Good stories and sketches of some of the celebrated authors associated with Bodley Head are in abundant supply.

2247 **An author's guide to publishing.**
Michael Legat. London: Robert Hale, 1982. 191p.

The world of books (the British, American and open markets), how to submit work to a publisher, a discussion on what publishers are looking for, a description of the publishing process, contracts, author-publisher relationships, reasons for complaint, and author organizations (e.g. The Society of Authors), are the topics treated in this guide. It is required reading for all those intending to take on the perils of authorship.

2248 **Antiquarian books: an insider's account.**
Roy Harley Lewis. Newton Abbot, England: David & Charles, 1978. 200p. bibliog.

An anecdotal guided tour of the English antiquarian book trade including features on booksellers and collectors, book hunting, book thieves, and book auctions.

2249 **Popular reading and publishing in Britain 1914-1950.**
Joseph McAleer. Oxford: Clarendon, 1992. 310p.

Based on research in the archives of Mass Observation, and in previously inaccessible publishers' archives, this study examines the size and nature of the reading public in the first half of the twentieth century. The successful editorial policies of Mills & Boon, and D. C. Thompson, which allowed them to corner large slices of the popular fiction market, are described and closely analysed. The decline of the Religious Tract Society as an influential popular publisher is also outlined.

2250 **The House of Macmillan (1843-1943).**
Charles Morgan. London: Macmillan, 1943. 248p.

Lewis Carroll, Thomas Hardy and Rudyard Kipling, Edith Sitwell, Hugh Walpole, and W. B. Yeats, were all Macmillan authors. So too was Charles Morgan who writes this official centenary history of the firm. The Net Book Agreement of 1899 and the 1906-08 'Book War', along with The Times Book Club versus the publishers and booksellers, are two important episodes in the history of British publishing which are related in detail.

2251 **The republic of letters: working class writing and local publishing.**
Edited by Dave Morley, Ken Worpole. London: Comedia
Publishing Group, 1982. 155p.

In recent years working-class people, including women and the black community, have explored new forms of creative writing, and new local publishing and distribution outlets. This analysis of the problems faced, the successes achieved, and of possible future developments, ends with a descriptive list of writers' workshops, community publishers, and members' groups.

2252 **Mumby's publishing and bookselling in the twentieth century.**
Edited by Ian Norrie. London: Bell & Hyman, 1982. 6th ed. 253p.
bibliog.

First published by Jonathan Cape in 1930, this standard text on the history of the British book trade has been substantially restructured to include not only traditional Mumby features but all the major issues confronting the trade in the last two decades of the twentieth century: the Net Book Agreement, export markets, international copyright, book clubs and the paperback revolution, and the growing influence of information technology. This is essential reading for all those who wish to comprehend a major industry which faces its own unique problems in a period of economic recession.

2253 **Blackwell's 1879-1979: the history of a family firm.**
A. L. P. Norrington. Oxford: Blackwell, 1983. 191p.

'There, in the Broad, within whose booky house Half England's scholars nibble books or browse. Where'er they wander blessed fortune theirs: Books to the ceiling, other books upstairs; Books, doubtless, in the cellar, and behind Romantic bays, where iron ladders wind.' (John Masefield). Benjamin Harris Blackwell's first second-hand bookshop opened in 1845 and closed nine years later on his death. In 1879 his son, Benjamin Henry Blackwell, opened a similar business in Broad Street in premises still occupied by the family firm, with a stock of 700 second-hand volumes relating to ancient and modern literature, conservatively valued at £110,00. From these modest beginnings there developed today's modern bookselling operations and Basil Blackwell Publications and Blackwell Scientific Publications. This scholarly history traces the firm's fortunes in fine detail.

2254 **The radical bookseller directory 1992.**

Compiled by Einde O'Callaghan. London: Radical Bookseller, 1992. 127p.

Listing those radical publishers and alternative bookshops which have a strong commitment to left-wing and community concerns such as gay and lesbian politics, green issues, equal opportunities, women's rights, civil liberties, and ethnic minority rights, this directory also includes a descriptive guide to some 500 publishers and details of 350 radical newspapers, magazines and journals.

2255 **Skoob directory of second-hand bookshops in the British Isles.**

Edited by Mai P. Ong. London: Skoob Books, 1991. 4th ed. 277p. maps.

Previously known as *Skoob's directory of bookshops in the United Kingdom*, this directory is arranged first by region and then alphabetically by town. Its well-ordered entries provide addresses, opening hours, telephone numbers, size of stock, and a brief stock description. Other information includes the number of catalogues issues, credit card facilities, the shop's policy on buying books directly from the public, the nearest railway station, and the proprietor's name.

2256 **Publishers in the UK and their addresses.**

London: J. Whitaker, 1992. 80p.

This is an annual listing of over 2,500 of the most active publishers and their distributors with their addresses, telephone, fax and telex numbers, and their International Standard Book Number prefixes. Also listed are trade organizations and service companies, wholesalers, library suppliers, and export booksellers.

2257 **British literary publishing houses 1881-1965.**

Edited by Jonathan Rose, Patricia J. Anderson. Detroit, Michigan: Gale, 1991. 420p. (Dictionary of Literary Biography, no. 112).

Essays on eighty-three publishers are contained in this encyclopedic work. Although they vary in length they all examine each firm's history, prominent writers, commercial book successes, and business affiliations. They are invaluable in tracing the various takeovers and changes in ownership which have afflicted British publishers in recent years.

2258 **William Heinemann: a century of publishing 1890-1990.**

John St. John. London: Heinemann, 1990. 689p. bibliog.

The complete experience of British publishing over the last hundred years is captured in this history of Heinemann. Founded by William Heinemann, a young Londoner of German and British Jewish extraction, his firm would have in all probability folded on his death in 1920 had it not been for the rescue operation mounted by the American publishing giant, Doubleday. After expansion in the period between the wars, a further takeover in the 1950s, and more recent changes, amalgamation, and the bewildering redeployment of publishers' assets, reflect the volatile trends in contemporary British publishing. The author of this meticulously researched publishing history was himself employed at Heinemann for over thirty years and built up the specialized non-fiction list still flourishing under the imprint of Heinemann Professional Publishing.

2259   **Sheppard's book dealers in the British Isles: a directory of antiquarian and secondhand book dealers in the United Kingdom, the Channel Islands, the Isle of Man and the Republic of Ireland.**
London: Europa, 1987. 12th ed. 458p. 3 maps.
Beginning with miscellaneous information on the book trade, this directory's main section is a geographically-arranged list of book dealers which outlines their type of business (shop, private house accommodation, or mail order only), their size of stock, and their special interests. A supplementary alphabetical list and a specialism index are also included.

2260   **The Oxford University Press: an informal history.**
Peter Sutcliffe.   Oxford: Clarendon Press, 1978. 303p.
Dealing for the most part with the period after 1860, when the Delegates of the University Press reasoned that they were not an appropriate body to administer a mainstream publisher, this history tells the story of the transformation of a lucrative Bible publishing house into an international publishing giant. Among the many distinguished works whose origins and progress are narrated are the massive *Dictionary of national biography*, the *Oxford book of English verse*, the *Oxford companion to English literature*, and the long saga of the *Oxford English dictionary*.

2261   **Bookselling in Britain: a comprehensive assessment of bookselling in the UK.**
Martin Whitaker, Charles Tongue.   London: Jordans, with The Bookseller, 1991.
Combining hard statistical data with anecdotal evidence, this impressive overview of the book trade covers the specialist multiple booksellers; the impact of shop design on bookselling; the increasing levels of staff skills and training; analyses of bookbuyers by age and usage; the application of computer technology and central purchasing on retail margins, and the relationship of the mainstream book trade with the book clubs in terms of the Net Book Agreement. Profiles of leading companies and their prospects for the 1990s are also included.

2262   **Who owns whom: book publishing and retailing: 1980-1989.**
London: The Bookseller, 1990. 38p.
A guide to ownership changes affecting the book trade, this supplement to *The Bookseller* lists publishers alphabetically, noting whom they bought and sold, or who bought them. Also present is a list of paperback imprints and who owns them.

2263   **Allen Lane: a personal portrait.**
W. E. Williams.   London: Bodley Head, 1973. 96p.
Sir Allen Lane (1902-70) pioneered the paperback revolution in Britain when he launched the first ten Penguin books in 1935. These personal memoirs by a close collaborator (who first suggested and then supervised the publication of the Pelican list) provide an authoritative insight into the unorthodox Penguin style of work. *Fifty Penguin years* (Harmondsworth, England: Penguin, 1985. 142p.) was published to accompany the exhibition commemorating Penguin Books' first half-century. It comprises two essays: Linda Lloyd Jones' 'Fifty years of Penguin Books' and Jeremy Aynsley's 'Fifty years of Penguin design'.

Book Trade

2264   **First with the news: the history of W. H. Smith 1792-1972.**
Charles Wilson.   London: Cape, 1985. 510p. bibliog.
Based on the firm's business archives and on newspaper and early railway records, this
study outlines W. H. Smith's obscure origins, its significant role in nineteenth-century
newspaper and magazine distribution, and the formation of its railway bookstall
empire, the true foundation of its future success. Book wholesaling and retailing, its
popular circulating libraries, and its development of Book Club Associates, now by far
the most large-scale book club operation in Britain, are other themes explored.

Religious books in print.
See item no. 625.

The Press

2265   **A-Z of Britain's free newspapers and magazines.**
Gloucester, England: Association of Free Newspapers, 1989. 261p.
3 maps.
Published annually since 1985 this directory lists every free newspaper issued in Britain
arranged first by commercial television area and then by town. The information
provided for each newspaper includes its circulation figures, page size, average number
of pages, a map of its distribution area, and its post-code district.

2266   **Guardian: biography of a newspaper.**
David Ayerst.   London: Collins, 1971. 702p. bibliog.
Famed for its independent radical stance, and for its staunch indifference to current
popular opinions, *The Manchester Guardian*, a national rather than a provincial
newspaper, dropped Manchester from its masthead, 24 August 1959, and began
simultaneous printing in London and Manchester 11,September 1960. This definitive
history from its first appearance, 5 May 1821, less than two years after the 'Peterloo'
massacre, to its part in opposing the government's disastrous Suez adventure in 1956, is
based on the newspaper's own files and archives.

2267   **Women's worlds: ideology, feminity and the women's magazines.**
Ros Ballaster, Margaret Beetham, Elizabeth Frazer, Sandra
Hebron.   London: Macmillan, 1991. 196p. bibliog. (Women in
Society).
From their beginnings women's magazines have had a dual purpose. One, to offer their
readers support and encouragement in responding and, if possible, in transforming
their experiences as women. And, secondly, to enhance their everyday life by means of
pleasure, fantasy, and escape. This penetrating study presents an historical approach to
what are described as 'the pleasures and dangers' of the popular magazine since its first
appearance in the late seventeenth century. Concentrating on the mass market
publications, it ends with an analysis of their social function in 'a patriarchal and
capitalist culture'.

2268 **Benn's media directory 1993: volume one: United Kingdom.**
Tonbridge, England: Benn Business Information Services, 1993.
141st ed. 992p.

Formerly known as *Newspaper press directory* and as *Benn's press directory* from 1978 to 1985, this annually-published comprehensive guide to the UK mass media of communications is in eleven sections: publishers; national and regional newspapers; consumer, business and professional periodicals; reference publications; broadcasting; other advertising media, media organizations and services, and a master index. Separate volumes are published for Europe and the world.

2269 **The essential Fleet Street: its history and influence.**
Ray Boston.   London: Blandford, 1990. 192p. bibliog.

With its evacuation by the contemporary giants of the newspaper press to Wapping and elsewhere in London's docklands, Fleet Street will no doubt lose its magical force which reached its peak in the later nineteenth century. In its heyday Fleet Street could rock governments but its influence gradually waned as tabloid journalism replaced the more sober and thoughtful journals of opinion. This meticulously researched history traces its story from the fifteenth century and explains why it emerged as the traditional location of the daily press.

2270 **BRAD publishing groups portfolio: a guide to corporate structures in print media.**
Barnet, England: British Rate and Data, 1991. 90p.

An A to Z list of UK publishing companies and their subsidiaries, giving their business interests, and the newspapers, magazines, and directories they publish, takes up the major portion of this directory. An index of all the publications appearing in the portfolio occupies the remainder.

2271 **British Humanities Index.**
London: Bowker Saur, 1963- . quarterly, with separate annual cumulation.

An invaluable reference book for locating periodical literature in the arts, economics, history, philosophy, politics, and contemporary society, *BHI* indexes some 325 British journals and newspapers.

2272 **Peterborough Court: the story of the Daily Telegraph.**
Lord Burnham.   London: Cassell, 1955. 225p.

Renowned today for its solid support of the Conservative Party, it comes as some surprise to learn that the *Daily Telegraph* was started in 1855 to pursue a private vendetta against the Duke of Cambridge and was for a short time a Liberal journal. The author, a member of the Lawson family who owned the *Telegraph* until the sale to Lord Camrose in 1927, describes his book as an 'impressionist sketch' as opposed to a formal history which is impossible to write because of a distinct lack of research of its early days.

2273   **The story of street literature: forerunner of the popular press.**
Robert Collison.   London: Dent, 1973. 182p. bibliog.
Chapbooks of up to 7,000 words of text cheaply gathered in twenty-four pages and
crudely illustrated, and single-sheet broadsides printed on primitive back-street
presses, featuring ballads, humorous verse, patriotic songs, election propaganda, and
satires on the Royal Family, the government and local councils, were a popular form of
sensation, news, and entertainment at the end of the eighteenth and the first half of the
nineteenth century. This detailed study of an early stage in British journalism is largely
based on the activities of James Catsnatch (1792-1841), the founder of the Catsnatch
Press, off Seven Dials, in London.

2274   **The making of The Independent.**
Michael Crozier.   London: Gordon Fraser, 1988. 128p. bibliog.
The Independent, a new quality newspaper, first hit the streets on Monday 6th October
1986. Written by an experienced journalist who joined the project at an early stage,
this is the story of its conception in the mind of a *Daily Telegraph* financial editor, the
search for the launch capital, the investment in modern technology, and the planning
and the countdown to a successful launch.

2275   **A world of women: an illustrated history of women's magazines.**
Irene Dancyger.   Dublin: Gill & Macmillan, 1978. 181p. bibliog.
Focusing particularly on the period 1600-1900, Dancyger explains how women's
magazines carried features on the social problems of the day. Their influence extended
beyond traditional women's interests such as home-making, cooking, and child rearing,
to social issues like slums, labour exploitation, homelessness and unemployment. In
the field of widening women's career opportunities their support was unflagging.

2276   **The Mirror: a political history.**
Maurice Edelman.   London: Hamish Hamilton, 1966. 221p. bibliog.
This account by a former Labour MP tells the story of the *Mirror's* transformation
from a run of-the-mill picture paper to a powerful voice of working-class Britain and a
perhaps decisive influence in the Labour Party's victory in the 1945 general election.

2277   **What news, the market, politics and the local press.**
Bob Franklin, David Murphy.   London: Routledge, 1991. 240p.
Independently owned in the past, English local newspapers are now largely in the
hands of monopolistic national (in some instances multinational) corporations. In this
study Franklin and Murphy, who are both university lecturers in mass media, chart the
transformation of the local press brought about by new technology, the appearance of
the alternative press in the 1970s, and the increasing circulation of free newspapers.

2278   **Freelance directory 1991/92.**
London: National Union of Journalists, 1991. 366p.
Freelance journalists are listed in this directory which gives their specialized skills,
their subject expertise, and the type of work which they undertake.

The Press

2279　**The Yorkshire Post: two centuries.**
Mildred A. Gibb, Frank Beckwith.　Leeds, England: Yorkshire Conservative Newspaper Co., 1954. 112p.
The *Leeds Intelligencer*, the *Post's* direct ancestor, first saw the light of day 2 July 1754. Its transformation from a city newspaper into a provincial daily of high national reputation is well told in this authoritative history.

2280　**The encyclopedia of the British press.**
Edited by Denis Griffiths.　London: Macmillan, 1992. 700p. bibliog.
Six chapters relating the history of British newspapers from the early Stuart period to the death of Robert Maxwell are followed in this encyclopedia by more than 2,500 biographies of newspaper personalities and over 100 histories of the leading UK national and provincial papers. Nearly all the entries for living newspaper people are provided by the individuals themselves. Some sixty famous newspaper front pages reproduced in full, lend an air of immediacy and authenticity to this attractive and informative volume. A detailed chronology, circulation figures, group ownerships, and a thematic bibliography, are among thirty appendices.

2281　**Editor-in-chief.**
Denis Hamilton.　London: Hamish Hamilton, 1989. 208p.
From personal assistant to Lord Kemsley the author proceeded to become editor of the *Sunday Times* and editor-in-chief of both *The Times* and the *Sunday Times*. This inside account of Times Newspapers' bitter struggle with the print unions, culminating in their year-long shutdown, is a forceful reminder of Fleet Street's death throes.

2282　**The house the Berry's built.**
Duff Hart-Davis.　London: Hodder & Stoughton, 1990. 368p. bibliog.
After sixty years of rising circulation the *Daily Telegraph* found to its consternation that the economic climate of the 1980s was harsh and unprofitable. New and expensive print technology was urgently needed when union over-manning was rife and industrial malpractice was common. Enormous sums of money were demanded which the *Daily Telegraph* and *Sunday Telegraph* could not easily provide and eventually Conrad Black, a Canadian entrepreneur, gained control from the Berry family which had acquired the Telegraph in 1928. The author was closely involved with the *Sunday Telegraph* from its launching in 1961 and this is very much an inside story.

2283　**News in the regions: Plymouth Sound to Moray Firth.**
Alastair Hetherington.　London: Macmillan, 1989. 263p. map.
Examining news priorities, decision making, sources, and the differences between newspapers, radio and television news, this pioneering study gives an inside view of journalists at work in the Midlands, Yorkshire, in the southeast and southwest, and in central Scotland. Twenty-four provincial newspapers and regional broadcasting units allowed the author to observe their operations at first hand. Some surprising omissions in national coverage of regional events are brought to light.

2284   **News, newspapers and television.**
Alastair Hetherington.   London: Macmillan, 1985. 329p. bibliog.
With access to the newsroom and staff of the BBC, ITN, Scottish TV, BBC Scotland, the *Guardian*, *Times*, *Daily Mirror*, and *Daily Mail*, the author analyses how working journalists judge what is 'hot news' and how this is presented. The problems of covering the national coal strike of 1984-85, the South Atlantic War, and terrorism in Northern Ireland, are especially brought into close focus. He finds much to criticize but concludes that British audiences are fortunate to have high quality newspapers and reliable news broadcasts.

2285   **The history of The Times.**
London: The Times, 1935-84. 5 vols in 6.
Of a length and depth commensurate with *The Times*' prestige and influence, this comprehensive history is in five chronological volumes: *1785-1841* (1935); *1841-84* (1939); *1884-1912* (1947); *1912-1948* (in two parts, 1919-20 and 1921-48); and *1939-46* (1984). Volume four includes an appendix listing the proprietors, editors, policy, and price of London daily newspapers contemporary with *The Times*. The apparent overlap between volumes four and five was due to a desire to flesh out coverage of an 'abbreviated nature' for the period 1939-48 in volume four. The fifth volume was published on the occasion of *The Times*' bicentenary. A variety on indexes to *The Times* gives complete coverage: *The Times index 1785-1790* (Reading, England: Newspaper Archive Developments, 1978-83. 5 vols.); *Palmer's Index to The Times newspaper, October 1790 – June 1941* (London: Palmers, annual volumes); *Index to The Times* (*The Times*, 1906-72) and *The Times Index* (Newspaper Archive Developments, 1973- . monthly, with annual cumulation) which is compiled from *The Times*' final edition.

2286   **Picture Post 1938-50.**
Edited by Tom Hopkinson.   London: Allen Lane with The Penguin Press, 1970. 288p.
Tom Hopkinson helped to launch *Picture Post*, Britain's only really successful pictorial news-magazine and later became its editor. Reproduced from the original weekly issues, this selection of features also includes a number of 'hindsight' articles written by the original subjects or contributors. Hopkinson pens a long analytical introduction tracing *Picture Post's* history and examining the reasons for its decline and eventual demise in 1957.

2287   **Wellesley index to Victorian periodicals 1824-1900: tables of contents and identification of contributors with bibliographies of their articles and stories and an index of initials and pseudonyms.**
Edited by W. E. Houghton.   Toronto: University of Toronto Press; London: Routledge & Kegan Paul, 1966-89. 5 vols.
It was the practice in the nineteenth century for contributors to the monthlies and quarterlies, which then proliferated, to be either anonymous or identified only by initials or pseudonyms. The overriding virtue of this incomparable and monumental work derives not only from its contents lists of forty-three British journals of the period but also from its identifying the writings of nearly 12,000 authors.

2288 **The market for glory: Fleet Street ownership in the twentieth century.**
Simon Jenkins. London: Faber, 1986. 247p. bibliog.

Culminating in Eddie Shah's launch of *Today* newspaper, the move of Rupert Murdoch's newspapers to Wapping, and the strong rumours of new national newspapers, this lively study attempts to explain the attraction of owning newspapers. In turn the spotlight falls on the press barons of the earlier part of the century, the struggles their sons experienced in retaining their family empires, and on the new proprietors who, from 1970 onwards, sought to restructure Fleet Street.

2289 **The rise and fall of the political press in Britain: vol. 1: The nineteenth century: vol. 2: The twentieth century.**
Stephen Koss. London: Hamish Hamilton, 1981-84. 2 vols. bibliog.

After the repeal of the Stamp Act in 1855, when they were freed from government control, the numbers of London and provincial daily newspapers burgeoned. Politicians of all parties were quick to seize the opportunity to appeal to a widening electorate. To gain their support newspaper proprietors were rewarded with financial support and, eventually, peerages. This monumental work surveys the close and continuing relationship between journalism and party politics as it has evolved over the last 150 years.

2290 **The origins of the popular press 1855-1914.**
Alan J. Lee. London: Croom Helm, 1980. 310p. 7 maps. bibliog.

This study examines the changes in society at large, and in the newspaper industry, in the sixty years following the repeal of the Newspaper Stamp Act, with special reference to the organization, working, and development of the London and provincial press, and especially to its board room control. The profession of journalism, the press and party politics, and the place of the press in an emerging democratic society, are also closely investigated.

2291 **The newspaper press in Britain: an annotated bibliography.**
Edited by D. Linton, Ray Boston. London: Mansell, 1987. 361p.

Comprising 2,900 critically annotated items relating to books, articles, and theses on printed news journalism from the origins of the press in Britain to the present day, this important bibliography covers photojournalism, cartoons, and news agencies. A chronology of British newspapers 1476-1986 and a note on the archival sources of over 150 newspapers are also included in this major reference work.

2292 **In the chair: Barrington-Ward of The Times, 1927-1948.**
Donald McLachlan. London: Weidenfeld & Nicolson, 1971. 304p.

Robin Barrington-Ward was deputy-editor of *The Times* in the decade leading up to the Second World War when that newspaper's apparent appeasement policy towards Nazi Germany is rated by some to have contributed to its outbreak. Making extensive use of Barrington-Ward's unpublished diaries, and the newspaper's archives, this work is a much-needed counterweight to the final volume of Morison's *History of The Times* for any complete understanding of *The Times'* policy and influence in the 1930s.

2293 **NEWSPLAN: report of the NEWSPLAN project in the Northern Region October 1987-September 1988.**
David Parry. London: British Library, 1989. 352p.

NEWSPLAN is the name given to the programme by which the British Library and regional library systems finance the preservation and microfilming of UK local newspapers. The ultimate aim is for all newspapers published in the UK to be preserved on microfilm, with film for all major titles to be available both locally and in the British Library Newspaper Library. These regional volumes provide a definitive record of local and British Library holdings of local newspapers either in their original form or on microfilm. Also of interest are NEWSPLANS for the East Midlands (1989), Yorkshire and Humberside (1990), and the North Western region (1990).

2294 **The directory of British alternative periodicals 1965-1974.**
John Noyce. Hassocks, England: Harvester, 1979. 359p.

Very few of the 1,250 titles recorded in this substantial list of British alternative and underground press publications are held in public or academic libraries and it is feared that copies of many of the 1960s titles have entirely disappeared. Information for each title includes the date of its first and last issue; its frequency; the place of publication; a description which includes a brief history, an assessment of its influence using contemporary quotations, the names of its editors or editorial collectives, and its links with other periodicals; the number of copies printed; its format and available indexes; its availability in microform; and library holdings (if any). Poetry and traditional politics periodicals are excluded.

2295 **The power of news: the history of Reuters.**
Donald Read. Oxford: Oxford University Press, 1992. 450p.

Julius Reuter set up his news agency in London in 1851 and for the next half-century it enjoyed semi-official status as the news agency of the British Empire. In the post-war years Reuters has concentrated on selling business information, maintaining its leading position in the forefront of communications technology. Based on unrestricted access to the Reuters' archives this authoritative history tells Reuters' own story from its pigeon post days to its public flotation in the 1980s.

2296 **The British press and broadcasting since 1945.**
Colin Seymour-Ure. Oxford: Blackwell, 1991. 269p. bibliog.
(Making Contemporary Britain).

Supported by detailed tables, this study traces the changes in size and ownership of the national and provincial press, the growth in television services, especially the advent and impact of commercial television not within the BBC's orbit, and the fluctuating fortunes of radio. It also enquires into the uneasy and volatile relations between the government and the news media and the whole question of the media's accountability. An appendix lists those provincial evening newspapers existing in 1945 and those founded subsequently.

2297 **Small press yearbook 1991.**
London: Small Press Group of Britain, 1991. 3rd ed. 248p.

The Small Press Group is an independent body composed chiefly of autonomous publishers whose brief is to increase public awareness of the valuable role of small press publications. Hundreds of small press publishers are listed in this yearbook which also includes an index of their vast array of titles currently in print.

2298   **The British press since the war.**
        Edited by Anthony Smith.   Newton Abbot, England: David &
        Charles, 1974. 320p. bibliog. (David & Charles Sources for
        Contemporary Issues).

Designed for students of the mass media of communications ('the media'), this
compendium of documents covers the finance, ownership and structure of newspapers;
the press and the law, the social and governmental curbs on its freedom ranging from
the libel laws to the Official Secrets Act; the vexed question of the relationships
between press and public; and industrial relations. Although compiled before the
'Wapping revolution', it remains an essential text for any clear understanding of the
role of the press in modern British society.

2299   **The Times Index.**
        Reading, England: Research Publications, 1973- . monthly, with
        annual cumulation.

The London daily newspaper, *The Times*, first published as *The Daily Universal
Register* in 1785, is universally regarded as an authoritative journal of contemporary
record. This index is compiled from each day's final edition with entries arranged
under some 350 main subject headings. It also covers *The Sunday Times*, *The Times
Literary Supplement*, *The Times Educational Supplement*, and *The Times Higher
Education Supplement*. *Palmer's index to The Times newspaper October 1790 – June
1941* (London: Palmer, 1863-1943. quarterly) is generally considered to be less
accurate than *The Times index to The Times* (1906-1972).

2300   **Bibliography of British Newspapers.**
        Edited by Charles A. Toase.   London: British Library Newspaper
        Library, 1975- . irregular.

Originally a Library Association Reference Special and Information Section project,
this bibliography will eventually cover all British newspapers in a series of historical
county or counties volumes. Each newspaper is listed under its current title if still
published and, unless specifically stated otherwise, all entries represent weekly
publications. The information provided includes publishers' names and addresses, and
details of library locations for complete files. Microfilm holdings are also registered. So
far the volumes for Kent, Durham and Northumberland, Derbyshire, and Nottinghamshire, have been published.

2301   **Current British journals 1992.**
        Edited by Mary Toase.   Boston Spa, England: British Library
        Document Supply Centre and United Kingdom Serials Group, 1992.
        6th ed.

Indispensable for verifying titles or discovering further titles in a particular area of
study, this authoritative subject guide to some 10,000 periodicals published in Britain
was first published in 1970. Entries for each title listed give basic information on the
date of the first issue, previous title(s), publishers, an indication of subject content,
indexes, International Standard Serials Number, price, and frequency. New to this
edition is an index of organizations sponsoring periodicals and an index of ceased titles.

2302　**Walford's guide to current British periodicals in the humanities and social sciences.**
A. J. Walford, Joan M. Harvey.　London: Library Association, 1985. 473p.

This meticulous and thorough guide provides coverage of over 3,000 titles in librarianship and bibliography, philosophy and psychology, religion, the arts, language and literature, county magazines, biography and genealogy, architecture and history. The information given for each title includes foundation date, frequency, publisher, and price, and a list of representative articles from a recent issue.

2303　**Dangerous estate: the anatomy of newspapers.**
Francis Williams.　London: Longmans Green, 1957. 304p.

The British appetite for daily newspapers, although perhaps declining under the onslaught of television, is still far greater than that of any other people. Yet the number of newspapers has steadily diminished and their ownership resides in fewer and fewer hands as the circulation wars continue. This classic study and history of the press in Britain seeks to examine its eternal dilemma: how to inform an enlightened public opinion whilst entertaining the greatest possible number of paying customers.

2304　**Willings press guide 1992: volume one: United Kingdom.**
London: Reed Information Services, 1992. 118th ed. 1,830p.

For Willings purposes, the press includes newspapers, free sheets, magazines, journals, and any other publication appearing on a regular basis at least once a year. This guide, which was first published in 1874, is arranged in six sequences: a classified index, i.e. a list of subject headings under which periodicals are listed; a classified index to periodicals listed in the main section arranged according to their principal area of subject matter; an alphabetical list of almost 13,500 newspapers and periodicals published at least once a year in the United Kingdom, giving information on their date of foundation, frequency, former titles, circulation, publisher, and editor; a list of newly launched and ceased publications; a list of publishers and their newspapers and periodicals; and a list of services and suppliers (e.g. advertisement space contractors, cartoon features, picture libraries, subscription agents). A second volume covers the principal publications of Europe, the Americas, Australasia, the Far East, Africa and the Middle East.

2305　**The rise and fall of Fleet Street.**
Charles Wintour.　London: Hutchinson, 1989. 271p.

Starting at the turn of the century with Alfred Harmsworth, Lord Northcliffe, the author charts the rise and fall of Fleet Street's heyday in a series of bibliographical portraits of the press barons and proprietors.

Radio and Television

2306 **The listener speaks: the radio audience and the future of radio.**
Steven Barnett, David Morrison.   London: HMSO for Broadcasting
Research Unit, 1989. 140p.

Following the Government's 1987 Green Paper, *Radio: choices and opportunities*, the
Broadcasting Research Unit was commissioned to examine the role of local, national,
and commercial radio on the national scene. The demands and needs of the radio
audience, the adequacy of provision, the contrasting appeal of national and local
services, and attitudes towards commercial radio, are some of the topics discussed in
this report.

2307 **The history of broadcasting in the United Kingdom.**
Asa Briggs.   London: Oxford University Press, 1961-79. 4 vols.
(vol. 1. *The birth of broadcasting*. 1961. 425p. bibliog.; vol. 2. *The
golden age of wireless*. 1965. 688p. bibliog.; vol. 3. *The war of words*.
1970. 766p. bibliog.; vol. 4. *Sound and vision*. 1979. 1082p. bibliog.).

This monumental history is an authoritative account of the development of
broadcasting in Britain from its beginnings to the Independent Television Act of 1955
which ended the BBC's monopoly. *The birth of broadcasting* covers the early
experiments in America and England, the beginnings of organized broadcasting, and
its rapid growth in the British Broadcasting Company's first four years until it became a
public corporation in 1927. The main theme of *The golden age of wireless* is the
expansion and enrichment of BBC programmes in the twelve years before the
outbreak of war whilst *The war of words* is solely concerned with the War's impact on
the BBC's structure, organization and programmes, and the BBC's role in fighting the
War. *Sound and vision* relates the rise of television to its dominant role as an
entertainment and news medium and the advent of the commercial television channels.

2308 **British television: the formative years.**
R. W. Burns. London: Peter Peregrinus/Science Museum, 1986. 488p.

This well-researched historical study opens with the experimental work of James Logie Baird and other pioneers and ends with the closure of the BBC's television service at the beginning of the Second World War. It provides a full account of the early developments, tests, and trial public transmissions, leading up to the launch of the world's first high-definition television service by the BBC in 1936.

2309 **Selling the sixties: the pirates and pop music radio.**
Robert Chapman. London: Unwin Hyman, 1991. 224p.

Arguably the definitive work on pirate radio, this study provides a lively history of light entertainment in the off-shore radio era 1964-68. It includes a comparative analysis of Radio Caroline and Radio London as two contrasting models of pop radio; a discussion of the early days of Radio One, gauging the extent to which the BBC assumed the pirates' mantle in establishing its own pop service; and interviews with the personalities involved.

2310 **The British CB book.**
Peter Chippindale, illustrated by Steve Bell. London: Kona, 1981. 226p.

Citizen Band radio was authorized in Britain in 1981 only after a strenuous campaign against Home Office prejudice and indifference. Everything the CB enthusiast needs to know – and more – is included in this comprehensive but compact guide: how to speak on CB, AMv FM technical terms and details, buying equipment, slang, and Home Office regulations, etc.

2311 **Dished: the rise and fall of British Satellite Broadcasting.**
Peter Chippindale, Suzanne Franks. London: Simon & Schuster, 1991. 327p.

Undoubtedly one of the most memorable commercial disasters in British history – and certainly the greatest in the history of the British mass news and entertainment media – the failure of BSB to establish itself on a secure footing can be attributed to its failure to comprehend that a satellite with the capacity for only a few extra television channels would not prevail over a system that could potentially offer many more. This book chronicles the story of the war between BSB and Rupert Murdoch's Sky TV, underlines what was at stake, and why BSB was remorselessly taken to the cleaners.

2312 **A code of practice.**
London: Broadcasting Standards Council, 1989. 56p.

Established in 1988, the Broadcasting Standards Council was given the tasks of drawing up a code on the portrayal of violence and sex and standards of taste and decency on radio and television. It was also charged with monitoring and reporting the contents of radio and television programmes received in the United Kingdom. This Code gives guidelines on the portrayal of violence in news bulletins, current affairs programmes, drama and entertainment; and on taste and decency with regard to the use of language, to religious sensibilities, to preserving dignity, and to smoking, alcohol and drug abuse. It is expected that the Code will be modified in the light of experience over the next few years as new channels beamed from outside Britain come into existence and an inevitable shift in public attitudes occurs.

Radio and Television

2313 **Under the hammer: the ITV franchise battle.**
Andrew Davidson.   London: Heinemann, 1992. 318p.
Concentrating on the large Independent Television companies, this study of the deep
and widespread bloodletting that occurred when the franchises were reallocated in the
early 1990s offers perhaps an object lesson on how not to conduct an auction for
licences to print money by mixing quality programme and commercial acumen criteria.

2314 **The radio companion.**
Paul Donovan.   London: Harper Collins, 1991. 301p.
Nine out of ten people, it is estimated, listen to the radio more than twice a week.
Commemorating radio's importance in British culture this encyclopedic companion
contains in one alphabetical sequence biographical sketches of over 400 past and
present personalities and the stories of hundreds of celebrated services and
programmes.

2315 **The future of the BBC: a consultation document.**
London: HMSO for Department of National Heritage, 1992. 44p.
Although this government Green Paper, which is issued for wide discussion, poses a
number of serious questions as to the future role and shape of the BBC, it actually
provides very few firm opinions on their respective merits and demerits. It indicates
that the government is prepared 'to contemplate radical changes in the way the BBC
operates'. The questions raised include the BBC's role in public service broadcasting,
its editorial independence, the types of radio and television programmes it should
broadcast, its structure and organization, and those old perennials how it should be
financed and be made accountable to public opinion. The BBC's present charter runs
out in 1996.

2316 **The golden age of radio: an illustrated companion.**
Denis Gifford.   London: Batsford, 1985. 319p.
Concentrating mainly on the 1930s, 1940s, and 1950s, this reference guide contains
1,600 alphabetically arranged entries relating to radio shows, the star performers, the
series and serials, the personalities, dance bands, comedy characters, and their
catchphrases, news announcers, and others, who flourished in radio's halcyon days.

2317 **BBC Children's Hour: a celebration of those magical years.**
Wallace Grevatt.   Lewes, England: Book Guild, 1988. 524p.
Surely one of the most treasured radio programmes ever broadcast Children's Hour,
which had its origins in the BBC's earliest days, was brutally snuffed out in March 1964
because of the widening appeal of television. This detailed record of the programme –
perhaps a touch too detailed, Wallace Grevatt was an unabashed enthusiast – is
crammed with nostalgia for the over-forties. It is, too, a significant piece of social
history but is marred by the unpardonable lack of a badly-needed index.

2318   **Guide to the BBC 1990.**

London: British Broadcasting Corporation, 1990. 48p. 8 maps.

This official guide and directory outlines the BBC's constitution, Board of Governors, Board of Management, senior staff, councils and committees, regions and addresses, financial information, an analysis of its output, public serves, and commercial services. A chronology and lists of its Chairmen and Directors General also appear.

2319   **British television advertising: the first thirty years.**

Edited by Brian Henry.   London: Century Bentham, 1986. 528p. 2 maps.

A year-by-year chronicle describing the development of television advertising in Britain, 1955-1985, is accompanied by a series of essays from different hands exploring various social, planning and marketing aspects of this novel medium.

2320   **British broadcasting 1922-82: a selected and annotated bibliography.**

Edited by Gavin Higgens.   London: BBC Data, 1983. 279p.

Over 1,200 items are registered in this bibliography relating to books and pamphlets concerned with all aspects of British broadcasting in its first sixty years: education broadcasting, engineering, external broadcasting, the fourth television channel, organization policy, pirate broadcasting, programme making techniques, regional, local and community broadcasting, and relations with government.

2321   **Questions of broadcasting.**

Stuart Hood, Garret O'Leary.   London: Methuen, 1990. 237p.

Proposals in the Government's 1988 White Paper on the future of British television broadcasting to abolish the Independent Broadcasting Authority, and to replace it with an emasculated Independent Television Commission, to provide for a fifth commercial television channel, to require Channel 4 to compete for its own advertising revenue, and for all commercial television franchises to be auctioned, prompted an immediate public debate. Two crucial questions that emerged were: 'Is broadcasting essentially an adjunct to the advertising industry?' and 'Are programmes simply a bait to get viewers to watch the commercials?'. This book first examines the history of British broadcasting and then provides the views of decision makers in the communications industry, terrestrial television, satellite broadcasting, and cable. Among the specific topics discussed are the future shape of broadcasting in the United Kingdom, the concept of public service television, finance, the contribution of the independent producer, the effect of the new technologies, the impact of satellites, and the prospects for cable television.

2322   **Inside BBC television: a year behind the camera.**

Rosalie Horner, introduction by Richard Baker.   Exeter, England: Webb & Bower in collaboration with BBC TV, 1983. 224p.

A celebration of fifty years of BBC television since its first experimental transmissions in 1932, this book goes behind the scenes to examine the skills, techniques, and complex organization required to present over 6,000 programmes every year. In turn the spotlight falls on outside broadcasts like Wimbledon and the open Golf Championship, on location work for programmes such as *Last of the summer wine*, on studio productions, and on the technology which brings them to the screen.

Radio and Television

2323 **Teletalk: a dictionary of broadcasting terms.**
Compiled by Peter Jarvis, illustrated by Nick Skelton.
Borehamwood, England: BBC Television Training, 1991. 332p.
Originally conceived as a ten-page pamphlet, this glossary outlines the basic terminology of the television industry: the jargon employed by transmitter engineers; film sound recordists; actors; newsroom journalists; graphic designers; and others.

2324 **Box of delights.**
Hilary Kingsley, Geoff Tibballs.   London: Macmillan, 1989. 314p.
bibliog.
This anecdotal, illustrated, year-by-year review of British television programmes, including those produced abroad, runs from the year of the Coronation (1953), when many people saw television for the first time, to the end of the 1980s. A final 'where are they now?' section investigates the subsequent career of some television 'personalities' who disappeared from view.

2325 **Broadcasting in the United Kingdom: a guide to information sources.**
Barrie MacDonald.   London: Mansell, 1992. 288p. bibliog.
In this comprehensive work a narrative history of British broadcasting, an outline of its structure and of the legislative and constitutional framework that governs it, and a description of a wide range of organizations relevant to broadcasting, are followed by a guide to appropriate reference and research materials. Also included is a directory of archives, libraries, and museums that hold information on broadcasting.

2326 **The Blue Book of British broadcasting.**
Edited by Bevis O'Neill.   London: Tellex Monitors, 1991. 18th ed.
620p.
This directory of UK broadcasting encompasses the BBC, the Independent Television Commission, all the Independent Television companies, the new franchises, the radio authorities, cable and satellite operators and the Open College.

2327 **Television and radio in the United Kingdom.**
Burton Paulu.   London: Macmillan, 1981. 476p. bibliog.
The legal structure of broadcasting in the United Kingdom; the development of television; technical facilities; finance; personnel; news programmes; current affairs, opinion and controversy; talk features and documentaries; educational and religious broadcasting; drama, film, and light entertainment; music programmes; outside broadcasting and sport, all feature in this wide ranging survey. The author regards British broadcasting as the best in the world and attributes this to the present system of controlled competition.

2328 **Desert island lists.**
Roy Plomley, Derek Drescher.   London: Hutchinson, 1984. 301p.
Vic Oliver, the radio comedian, was the first to accept Roy Plomley's invitation to join him in the BBC's studio and there, to the strains of Eric Coates's *Blue Lagoon*, and the cries of sea-birds, confide to the microphone the gramophone records he would choose to have with him if he were to be marooned on a desert island. Compiled from BBC Programme-as-Broadcast archives, this catalogue lists 1,700 guests, and 14,000

records broadcast since 29 January 1942. In the meantime, of course, the programme continues.

2329 The ITV encyclopedia of adventure.

Dave Rogers. London: TV Times, 1988. 593p.

Largely based on information supplied by the television companies responsible for producing the original programmes, this illustrated encyclopedia provides a complete reference guide to every thriller, cops and robbers, private eye, secret agent, spy, and science fiction adventure series, transmitted on the Independent Television network from 22 September 1955 to the end of 1987. Details are given of the cast lists, seasons transmitted, the number of episodes, in colour or monochrome, story synopses, etc. of 5,400 episodes of nearly 200 series.

2330 A social history of British broadcasting vol. 1. 1922-1939 serving the nation.

Paddy Scannell, David Cardiff. Oxford: Blackwell, 1991. 400p.

Although covering much the same ground as Asa Briggs' *The history of broadcasting in the United Kingdom* (q.v.), this first volume concentrates on various aspects of BBC programmes, news, talks, varieties, and their impact on national life before the Second World War, rather than on the institutional progress of the Corporation, stressing once again that the programmes are ultimately more important than the organization and that the key person in the organization is the programme producer. Three further volumes are expected.

2331 Independent television in Britain.

Bernard Sendall, Jeremy Potter. London: Macmillan, 1982-90.

4 vols.

After the BBC had enjoyed a thirty-year monopoly of public broadcasting, the 1954 Television Act established a rival network deriving its income from advertising. The first volume of this authoritative work (*Origin and foundation 1946-62*. Bernard Sendall. 1982. 418p. bibliog.) describes the campaign to end the BBC's monopoly and shows how ITV immediately captured a major share of the television audience. A detailed review of the Pilkington Report and the passing of the 1963 Television Act takes up a large part of volume two (*Expansions and change 1958-68*. Bernard Sendall. 1983. 420p. bibliog.) whilst volume three (*Politics and control 1968-80*. Jeremy Potter. 1989. 352p. bibliog.) tells of the profusion of committees and reports on the future of broadcasting in the 1970s. Pervasive themes include the concern at the excessive profits the independent companies enjoyed, the possibility of television usurping the functions of Parliament, the campaigns against undue sex, violence and bad language on the screen, and the coverage of events in Northern Ireland. The final volume (*Companies and programmes 1968-80*. Jeremy Potter. 1990. 440p. bibliog.) concentrates on the diversity of programmes broadcast and on the television companies which contributed to ITV's overall service in the 1980s.

2332   **UK media yearbook 1992/1993.**

London: Zenith Media and Campaign, 1992.

A comprehensive analysis of the mass-media advertising market, radio and television, the regional and national press, consumer and business magazines, the cinema, outdoor advertising, and direct mail, this edition also contains a number of features covering the trends and outlook for the UK economy with particular emphasis on the advertising sector. These include forecasts for each media market, the growth of satellite television, cable television, and the end of the free newspaper boom.

Directories

2333 The directories of London 1677-1977.
Peter J. Adkins.   London: Mansell, 1980. 736p. maps.
This record of three hundred years of London directories describes the various types of directory published, traces their evolution, remarks on their research value, and locates copies in a number of libraries.

2334 BRAD directories and annuals: a guide to rates and data in the annual print media: Autumn 1991.
Barnet, England: Maclean Hunter. 1991. 70p.
Directories are defined here as publications arranged either alphabetically or classified by trade name which contain information on companies, goods, services, individuals, organizations, or membership lists. This annual guide considers three different types of directories: consumer and special interest publications; telephone directories; and business and professional directories. The data supplied include the price, advertising rate, mechanical information, the names of executive personnel, print order, and, at times, circulation figures.

2335 Directories and other reference works.
In: *Benn's media directory 1992*.   Tonbridge, England: Benn Business Information Services, 1992. 140th ed., p. 613-71.
Most of the titles listed here under various subject headings are annual publications but certain other standard works are included.

2336 Directory Publishers Association.
London: DPA, 1992. 4th ed. 64p.
The Directory Publishers Association was established in 1970 to promote the interest of *bona fide* directory publishers, and to protect the public against disreputable and fraudulent practices which were causing concern at the time. Directories now published by firms belonging to the Association number some 700 titles including many which

Directories

have become household names and standard works in their field. This handbook lists publishers alphabetically with brief background company information and an indication of the titles they publish.

2337   **Current British directories: a guide to directories published in the British Isles.**
Edited by Crispin Alastair Poland Henderson.   Beckenham, England: CBD Research, 1988. 11th ed. 355p.

Intended to facilitate the selection, acquisition, and the use of directories, this guide contains buyers' guides, financial yearbooks, membership lists, registers of ships and aircraft, and 'who's who' volumes. Data for each directory includes title, organization and publisher, dates of publication, and its principal contents. In this edition 600 new titles are included for the first time and a similar number deleted from the previous edition.

2338   **Directory of British associations and associations in Ireland.**
G. P. Henderson, S. P. A. Henderson.   Beckenham, England: CBD Research, 1992. 11th ed. 610p.

About 8,000 organizations are listed alphabetically in this major British directory of associations which covers national associations, societies and institutions. Regional and local organizations connected with industry and trade, local chambers of commerce, and county archaeological, architectural, and natural history societies, are also included. Each entry gives the permanent headquarters of the organization, the name of its chief executive, its sphere of interest, its activities and publications, and membership data.

2339   **The women's directory.**
Compiled by Fiona Macdonald.   London: NCVO, 1991. 124p.

Nearly 400 specialist organizations for women are entered in this directory whose purpose is to allow women to locate and identify suitable groups and organizations for social, cultural, sporting, political, and self-help shared interests. A long series of appendices encompasses umbrella organizations, women's centres and crisis groups, and organizations which can offer advice and help in setting up new groups.

2340   **British national directories 1781-1819: an index to places in the British Isles included in trade directories with general provincial coverage.**
Compiled by Ian Maxted.   Exeter, England: Maxted, 1989. 34p. map.

'Before the series of county based directories introduced by Pigot in 1820 there was a series of national directories, normally issued as supplements to London directories, which covered over one thousand places throughout the British Isles. the majority of which had no directory of their own. This index records the coverage in two tables, one in a single alphabetical sequence of places and the other arranged by county' (Introduction).

2341   **Guide to the national and provincial directories of England and Wales excluding London published before 1856.**
J. E. Norton.   London: Royal Historical Society, 1984. 241p.
Although excluding directories of particular trades and professions, this guide which was first published in 1950, does include a number of histories and guide books which have directories added to them. Library locations are given for each of the 878 directories entered and there is a useful introduction dealing with the origins and development of directories, their authorship and methods of compilation, and of their general reliability.

2342   **British directories: a bibliography and guide to directories published in England and Wales (1850-1950) and Scotland (1773-1950).**
Gareth Shaw, Alison Tipper.   Leicester, England: Leicester University Press, 1989. 440p. bibliog.
Extending the coverage of C. W. F. Goss' *The London directories 1677-1955* (1932) and J. E. Norton's *Guide to the national and provincial directories of England and Wales* (1984), this bibliography first provides a detailed account of the evolution of directories, explains the different types of commercial and industrial directories that were published, and indicates the scope of their contents. The bibliography consists of some 2,200 titles arranged by county and region.

2343   **The top 3,000 directories and annuals.**
Folkestone, England: Dawson, 1992. 10th ed. 374p.
Titled *The top 1000* when first published in 1980, this publication includes a main section of directories and annuals listed alphabetically by title giving details of publisher, the current edition, its International Standard Book Number, and an indication of its contents. This is followed by lists of directories and annuals available on microfiche, online, or CD-ROM, of publishers and their directories and annuals, and of publishers' addresses. Over 400 new entries have been added to this edition.

2344   **Books of the Month and Books to Come.**
London: J. Whitaker. 1970- . monthly.
Published monthly since 1970, and based principally on the titles included in the 'Publications of the Week' section of *The Bookseller*, and on publishers' announcements of their books to appear in the following two months, this monthly record lists all titles under author, title, and keyword in a single alphabetical sequence.

Bibliography

2345 **The Bookseller.**

London: J. Whitaker. 1858- . weekly.

Published weekly, *The Bookseller* is the recognized organ of the book trade, printing reports, news items, and feature articles of interest to booksellers, publishers and librarians in addition to 'Publications of the Week', a classified list of new titles. Two special issues published in February and August provide details of books scheduled to appear in the following six months. The Spring 1992 issue (14th February) listed 8,602 advertised titles.

2346 **British Library general catalogue of printed books to 1975.**

London: K. G. Saur, 1980-87. 362 vols.

The British Library, formed in 1973, is the successor to the British Museum Library which was first opened to the public in 1759. From its beginning, copyright law has required one copy of every new book published in the United Kingdom to be deposited within the Library. Consequently the Library's catalogue is an unparalleled record of British publishing including periodicals, serials, and government publications. Entries in the catalogue are listed in a single alphabetical author sequence. But, of course, the catalogue represents far more than a record of British publishing: it has been estimated that only fifty-one per cent of the Library's holdings are in the English language, reflecting the immense wealth and spread of its scholarly resources. A six volume *Supplement* was published 1987-1988 incorporating pre-1971 titles accessioned too late to be included in the main sequence. Sadly one catalogue can never achieve full coverage of a rapidly growing collection and updating supplements become necessary: *1976-1982* (50 vols, 1983); *1982-1985* (26 vols, 1986); *1986-1987* (22 vols, 1988); *1988-1989* (28 vols, 1990). The historical background of this monumental work can be followed in A. H. Chaplin's *GK: 150 years of the general catalogue of printed books in the British Museum* (Aldershot, England: Scolar Press, 1987. 177p.).

2347 **British Library general subject catalogue 1975-1985.**
London: K. G. Saur, 1986. 75 vols.
A continuation of the *British Museum subject index of modern books* series which
provided coverage from 1880-1978, this catalogue is arranged in an alphabetical subject
sequence according to subject headings as used in the *British National Bibliography*. It
includes some material from the British Library's Map Library, Music Library and
India Office Library.

2348 **British National Bibliography.**
London: British Library National Bibliographic Service, 1950- .
weekly.
Under the terms of the 1911 Copyright Act, as amended by the British Library Act of
1972, the publisher of every new book published in the United Kingdom is obliged
within one month of publication to deliver a copy of the book to the British Library
Board. *BNB* lists new books and the first issues of periodical titles received at the
British Library's Legal Deposit Office. Detailed entries are arranged in a classified
subject sequence according to the twentieth edition of the *Dewey Decimal
Classification*. There are author/title and subject indexes. It also includes advance
details of forthcoming books under the Cataloguing-in-Publication (CiP) Programme.
The weekly lists are cumulated January-April, May-August, and annually.

2349 **Official publications in Britain.**
David Butcher. London: Library Association Publishing, 1991.
2nd ed. 192p. bibliog.
Although Her Majesty's Stationery Office is the largest single general publisher of
government material its publications represent only a small proportion of the total.
This overview not only examines the nature and organization, the range and extent, of
official publishing at local, regional and national levels, but also its complicated
bibliographical control. It encompasses parliamentary, government department, and
local government publications.

2350 **Catalogue of British official publications not published by HMSO.**
Cambridge, England: Chadwyck-Healey, 1991. 540p.
Published bi-monthly with annual cumulations since 1980, this catalogue covers 'the
publications of over 500 organizations financed or controlled completely or partially by
the British Government which are not published by HMSO'. These organizations
break down into government departments, nationalized industries, research institutes,
government quangos, and other non-official bodies. Arranged alphabetically by
organization the entries include periodicals, newspapers, single-sheet updates, give-
away leaflets, publicity material (if of permanent value), maps and atlases, posters, and
audio-visual aids. A total of 11,462 titles is listed in this 1990 edition, compared to
3,542 in 1980.

2351 **Catalogue of cartographic materials in the British Library 1975-1988.**
London: K. G. Saur, 1989. 3 vols. 1,500p.
Not only material received in the British Library's Map Library from United Kingdom
publishers under the legal deposit regulations, but also worldwide material acquired by
donation, exchange, and purchase is included in this monumental catalogue which
extends coverage in *Catalogue of printed maps, charts and plans* (London: British

Museum, 1967. 15 vols.) and *The British Library catalogue of printed maps, charts and plans ten year supplement 1965-1974* (1978). Nearly 50,000 entries relating to atlases, single-sheet maps, maritime charts, plans, and globes are included in three sequences: geographical names, authors and titles, and a subject index. Also included are details of some 260 digital cartographic and remote sensing United Kingdom databases located as a result of a British Library sponsored project carried out by Birkbeck College.

2352 Children's Books in Print.
London: J. Whitaker. 1972- . annual.

Published annually since 1972 this bibliography lists about 30,000 titles in print in alphabetical order with a classified index arranged in ninety-eight subject categories. It ends with a directory of over 1,000 publishers.

2353 Picture sources UK.
Edited by Rosemary Eakins.   London: MacDonald, 1985. 474p.

This definitive reference work contains directory information on over, 1,140 general and specialized collections of photographs, prints, drawings, and other visual material presented in fourteen thematic sections. All entries include a detailed listing of the subjects covered.

2354 An English library.
Edited by Nigel Farrow, Brian Last, Vernon Pratt.   Aldershot, England: Gower in association with Book Trust, 1990. 6th ed. 385p.

This is an extremely reader-friendly 'good book' guide to over 2,500 of the best books in the English language. Coverage is limited to the humanities and ranges over fiction, poetry and drama, biography and autobiography, essays, travel writing, literary criticism, and reference works. For the first time the works of living writers are included in this edition. Each section has a short introduction explaining the selection criteria.

2355 HMSO Annual Catalogue.
London: HMSO 1922- . annual.

Cumulated from *HMSO Daily List*, and *HMSO Monthly Catalogue*, this publication lists the 8-9,000 items which are published by HMSO during the calendar year. These include House of Lords and House of Commons Command Papers, Public General Acts and Local Acts of Parliament. A classified section lists publications under the Government Department responsible for them. *Catalogues and indexes of British government publications 1920-1970* (Bishops Stortford, England: Chadwyck-Healey, 1974. 5 vols.) is a reduced size reprint of the annual catalogues and their considated indexes.

2356 British sources of information: a subject guide and bibliography.
Paul Jackson.   London: Routledge, 1987. 526p.

Aiming 'to provide assistance to the general reader, the student, and the teacher in locating texts, information and teaching resources for work on major aspects of British life, society and culture', this subject guide is arranged in four parts. The first comprises a select bibliography of relevant and accessible publications covering forty key areas which includes introductory material, textbooks, comprehensive studies, and reference works. Periodicals, journals and magazines are listed in the second part whilst directory-type information sources occupy the third. The final part consists of a teaching resources listing of publishers, film distributors, video workshops, and audio-visual suppliers.

2357   **A London bibliography of the social sciences.**
London: British Library of Political and Economic Science (to 1970) and Mansell (from 1970), 1931-1989. 47 vols.

Essentially, this massive bibliography records the holdings of the London School of Economics' British Library of Political and Economic Science although in its early days in the 1930s it also included the holdings of eight other libraries. BLPES's collections are especially rich in economics, commerce and business administration, law, and social and economic history. After the publication of the twenty-fourth annual supplement in 1989 the *London bibliography* was incorporated in the *International bibliography of the social sciences*.

2358   **A short-title catalogue of books printed in England, Scotland and Ireland: and of English books printed abroad 1475-1640.**
A. W. Pollard, G. R. Redgrave.   London: Bibliographical Society, 1976-91. 3 vols. 2nd ed.

Without question this compilation is the primary source for bibliographical information on early English books. It lists 37,000 items listed by author with nearly 500 library locations. Volume three is titled *A printers and publishers index, other indexes and appendices, cumulative addenda and corrigenda with a chronological index*.

2359   **British government publications: an index to chairmen and authors.**
Stephen Richard.   London: Library Association, 1982-84. 4 vols. (vol. 1. *1800-1899*. 1982. 196p.; vol. 2. *1900-1940*. 1982. 174p.; vol. 3. *1941-1978*. 1982. 162p.; vol. 4. *1979-1982*. 1984. 95p.).

'A government committee report is frequently referred to by its chairman's name. This series links Chairmen to report name. In the compilation of the last volume a new definition of official organizations has been used which extends its coverage to the whole range of British official publications, including those from quangos'.

2360   **A guide to British government publications.**
Frank Rodgers.   New York: H. W. Wilson, 1980. 750p.

The main purpose of this guide is 'to present a broad though necessarily selective view of the publications released by British government departments and related agencies'. To prepare the ground it first outlines the British constitution and system of government, the organization of government publications, the evolution of official printing and publishing, and various general catalogues and indexes. A review of parliamentary publications (journals, reports of debates, sessional papers, etc.) is then followed by a discussion of the most important publications of each department and agency.

Bibliography

2361 Whitaker's Book List.
London: J. Whitaker. 1967- . annual.

Known until 1987 as *Whitakers Cumulative Booklist*, this annual compilation of books published in the calendar year represents an accumulation of the monthly lists in *Books of the Month and Books to Come*. Over 60,000 titles appeared in the 1991 edition.

2362 Whitaker's books in print.
London: J. Whitaker, 1992. 4 vols.

Subtitled *The reference catalogue of current literature: the national inclusive book-reference index of books in print and on sale in the United Kingdom with details as to author, title, editor, translator, reviser, year of publication or year of latest edition. number of edition, size, number of pages, illustrations, series, binding – where not cloth – price, whether net or non-net, publisher's name, and international standard book number*, this is now an annual publication. The 1992 edition includes 550,000 titles, a separate listing of series and their publishers, and a directory of 18,000 publishers.

2363 A directory of rare book and special collections in the United Kingdom and the Republic of Ireland.
Edited by Moelwyn I. Williams.   London: Library Association, 1985. 664p.

Initiated by the Rare Books Group of the Library Association, this directory of over 5,000 collections of rare books (i.e. books printed before 1851, first and limited editions, and ephemera) was compiled by a network of regional contributors who scoured the holdings of large national, university, and public libraries, colleges and schools, churches and cathedrals, societies and institutes, National Trust properties and private houses in their own region. Its aim is 'to bring to the notice of scholars and researchers the location of rare book collections . . . and to provide such information about their nature, size and importance as will enable them to assess whether or not further investigation is likely to be to their benefit' (Introduction). To that end entries give admission conditions, a brief history and a detailed description of the collection including its contents, and published catalogues and references.

2364 Short-title catalogue of books printed in England, Scotland, Ireland, Wales and British America and of English books printed in other countries 1641-1700.
Compiled by D. G. Wing.   New York: Index Committee of the Modern Language Association, 1972-88. 3 vols.

Now containing 120,000 entries, these vastly expanded volumes which continue Pollard and Redgrave's *A short-title catalogue. . . 1475-1640* were first published between 1945 and 1951. P. G. Morrison's *Index of printers, publishers, and booksellers in Donald Wing's 'Short-title catalogue'* (Charlottesville, Virginia: Bibliographical Society of the University of Virginia, 1955. 217p.) further enhances their considerable bibliographical value.

British catalogue of music.
See item no. 1691.

Index

The index is a single alphabetical sequence of authors (personal and corporate), titles of publications and subjects. Index entries refer both to the main items and to other works mentioned in the note to each item. Title entries are in italics. Numbers refer to bibliographical entries.

Architecture 1818, 1823, 1825, 1827, 1829, 1838, 1840, 1876, 1878, 1884, 1886
architects 1817, 1836, 1843, 1846, 1868 1889, 1892, 1895
domestic and vernacular 1816, 1819-1820, 1824, 1826, 1839, 1867, 1870, 1873, 1883, 1885, 1888
history and historic architecture 1842, 1845, 1847-1848, 1851-1857, 1859, 1861, 1863, 1865-1877, 1890, 1893-1894, 1896
industrial 1862
see also Industrial archaeology
materials 1834
official 1837, 1841
religious 1821-1822, 1828, 1830-1833, 1835, 1849, 1858, 1860, 1864, 1866, 1871, 1874-1875, 1881-1882, 1887, 1891
styles 1844, 1850, 1869, 1872, 1879-1880
Architecture in Britain 1530-1830 1889
Architecture in Norman Britain 1865
Architecture of Northern England 1886
Architecture of Southern England 1876
Architecture of the Anglo-Saxons 1847
Architecture of Wren 1843
Archives 2207-2210 *see also* History
Archives and local history 498
Archives of the British chemical industry 1750-1914 1264
Argles, M. 766
Aristocracy of labour in the nineteenth century 1451

Arlidge, A. J. 932
Armes, R. 1799
Armorial bearings of the sovereigns of England 564
Armstrong, W. A. 808
Army 1060-1081, 1129
Army list 1061
Arnold, B. 1586
Arnold, C. J. 360
Arnold, E. N. 160
Arnold, G. 648
Arnold, H. R. 224
Arnold, J. 1427
Arnott, J. F. 1761
Arnstein, W. L. 530
Arsenal: a complete record 2080
Art 1586-1593, 1595-1600
Art and architecture of London 346
Art atlas of Great Britain and Ireland 1586
Art galleries *see* Museums and art galleries
Art galleries of Britain and Ireland 2211
Arthurian encyclopedia 895
Arthurian history and legends 357, 870-874, 879, 892, 895, 909
Arthur's Britain 357
Artistic directory 1597
Arts Council of Great Britain 1598
Arts funding guide 1592
Arundel, D. 1762
Acoli, D. 1062
Ash, D. 1640
Ashe, G. 870-874
Ashley, M. 637
Ashton, T. S. 1591
Ashworth, W. 1261
Asian who's who international 586
Aslet, C. 1818, 1831
Aslib directory of informnation sources in the UK 2185
Aspinall, A. 419
Aster, S. 1038
Atheism 593

Atkinson-Willes, G. L. 161
Atlas of Anglo-Saxon England 449
Atlas of breeding birds in Britain and Ireland 198
Atlas of Britain and Northern Ireland 74
Atlas of British bird life 197
Atlas of British politics 1014
Atlas of British social and economic history 645
Atlas of butterflies in Britain and ireland 180
Atlas of ferns of the British Isles 224
Atlas of industrializing Britain 1253
Atlas of magical Britain 877
Atlas of prehistoric Britain 394
Atlas of renewable energy sources in the UK and North America 1536
Atlas of Roman Britain 443
Atlas of the British flora 230
Atlas of the seas round the British Isles 1442
Atlases 73-102
Atterbury, P. 270, 1605
Aubrey, J. 361
Audit Commission performance review in local government 1018
Author's guide to publishing 2247
Aviation archaeology 1390
Awards for business excellence 1161
Awdry, C. 1348
Ayerst, D. 2266
Ayre, L. 1763
Ayres, J. 1819
Ayres, M. 2127
Ayto, J. 1903, 1912

B

BBC Children's Hour 2317

Benn's press directory 2268
Benson, J. 650
Benson and Hedges book
 of racing colours 2129
Bentley, J. 626
Bentley-Cranch, D. 543
Benyon, J. 671
Beresford, M. W. 133, 492
Beresford, P. 573
Berg, D. L. 1973
Berman, D. 593
Berries 227
Berthoud, R. 672
Best buildings in Britain
 1831
Best buildings of England
 1878
Best years of their lives
 1131
Betjeman, J. 317, 1821
Bett, W. H. 1351
Bettley, J. H. 493
Betts, B. 2125
Bevan, V. 673
Bibliographical account of
 English theatre
 literature 1761
Bibliographical account of
 the principal works
 relating to English
 topography 526
Bibliographies 2344-2364
 see also individual
 topics by name e.g.
 History
Bibliography of British
 business histories 1180
Bibliography of British
 economic and social
 history 1144
Bibliography of British
 geomorphology 114
Bibliography of British
 history 409
Bibliography of British
 industrial relations
 1446
Bibliography of British
 literary bibliographies
 1995
Bibliography of British
 newspapers 2300

Bibliography of British
 railway history 1376
Bibliography of Domesday
 Book 36
Bibliography of the
 Chartist movement 993
Bickmore, D. P. 74
Bicknell, E. J. 594
Biddle, G. 1352-1353
Bienkowski, M. 1163
Bindman, D. 1588
Biogeography of the British
 Isles 158
Biographical dictionary of
 British architects 1660-
 1840 1836
Biographical dictionary of
 British feminists 572
Biographical dictionary of
 English architects
 1660-1840 1836
Biographical dictionary of
 modern British
 radicals 966
Biographical encyclopaedia
 of British flat racing
 2136
Biographical study of the
 Father of Railways
 George Stephenson
 1359
Biography 572-587
Birch, A. H. 967
Birds 161-162, 164, 167,
 170, 179, 184, 193,
 197, 199, 205, 207
Birds of prey of Britain and
 Europe 205
Birds of the British Isles
 162
Birkett, B. 2099
Birkinshaw, P. 914
Birth statistics (historical
 series) 804
Birth statistics. Review of
 the Registrar General
 805
Black, J. 1042
Black, J. B. 414
Black, M. H. 2235
Black British, white British
 848

Black's guide to England
 and Wales 56
Blackstone, G. V. 1019
Blackwell biographical
 dictionary of British
 political life in the
 twentieth century 1006
Blackwell encyclopedia of
 industrial archaeology
 1295
Blackwell history of music
 in Britain 1688
Blackwell's 1879-1979 2253
Blair, C. 542
Blair, J. 1225
Blair, P. H. 447
Blair, S. 1767
Blake, N. F. 1903
Blake, R. 2
Bland, A. 1768
Blandford, P. W. 1395
Blatch, M. 318
Bloomsbury dictionary of
 contemporary slang
 1931
Bloomsbury dictionary of
 word origins 1912
Bloomsbury guide to
 English literature 2028
Blue Book of British
 broadcasting 2326
Blue Guide cathedrals and
 abbeys of England and
 Wales 1887
Blue guide churches and
 chapels 1858
Blue guide England 297
Blue guide literary Britain
 and Ireland 2006
Blue Guide museums and
 galleries of London
 345
Blue Guide Victorian
 architecture in Britain
 1877
Blue Plaque guide to
 London 322
Blue Plaques of London
 322
Blues the British
 connection 1694
Blunden, J. 1506
Blyth, J. 1428

British government
publications 2355
Catalogus plantarum
Angliae et insularum
adjacentium 210
Cathedrals 286, 1833,
1835, 1875, 1878,
1887, 1891 see also
Architecture
Cathedrals of England 1833
Catholic churches since
1623 1866
Catholic directory of
England and Wales
602
Catterall, P. 483-484
Catuvellauni, The 364
Caught in the web of
worlds 1970
Cavendish, R. 270
Cawley, A. C. 1789
Caygill, M. 2213
Celtic Britain 296, 385
Census 1991 reports 807
Census user's handbook
827
Centenary history of the
Rugby Football Union
2162
Centipedes of the British
Isles 172
Century of diplomatic Blue
Books 1814-1914 1054
Chadwick, O. 613
Chaffers, W. 1625
Challinor, J. 113
Chaloner, W. H. 1144
Chamberlain, M. E. 1044
Chamberlain, P. 1068
Chamberlain, R. 268, 270
Chamberlain and
appeasement 1049
Chambers, E. 1996
Chambers, E. K. 2026
Chambers, J. D. 808, 1400
Chambers, M. 918
Chambers 20th century
thesaurus 1943
Champion, A. G. 58
Champion Hurdle 2143
Chandler, J. 52
Changing anatomy of
Britain 24

Changing English language
1902
Changing geography of the
United Kingdom 67
Changing population of
Britain 817
Changing secondary school
782
Channel Four book of the
racing year 2134
Channel Tunnel 1362-1363,
1367, 1384 see also
Transport
Channel Tunnel – Le
Tunnel sous la Manche
1362
Chant, C. 1064
Chapel, J. 1590
Chaplin, A. H. 2346
Chapman, A. 167
Chapman, C. 1169
Chapman, R. 2309
Character of England 1
Charities 712-713, 715, 752
Charities by counties and
regions 712
Charities Digest 713
Charles-Edwards, D. 722
Charleston, R. J. 1641
Charlesworth, G. 1327
Charlesworth, P. E. 1976
Chasing round Britain 2145
Chatset directory of Lloyds
of London 1216
Checkland, S. G. 639
Checklist of the birds of
Great Britain and
Ireland 178
Checklist of women writers
1801-1900 1977
Cheney, C. R. 413
Cherry. B. 1878
Cherry, G. E. 1509
Cherry, J. 393
Chester, T. R. 2059
Chevalier, T. 2035
Chibnall, M. 456
Chichester, H. M. 1065
Chief Constables 694
Chief elements used in
English place-names
524

Chiefs: the story of the
United Kingdom
Chiefs of Staff 1126
Child, F. J. 1980
Child abuse 669, 689 see
also Society
Child and the book 2058
Child sexual abuse; the
search for healing
669
Children as readers 2053
Children's annual 2036
Children's books in print
2352
Childrens' comics
2041-2042 see also
Literature
Children's fiction
sourcebook 2045
Children's games in street
and playground 901
Childrens verse 2050
Chinery, M. 168
Chippindale, P. 2310-2311
Chippingdale, C. 373
Choosing a state school
770
Christian England 598
Christie, J. R. 409
Christie, R. 1315
Chronicle of the Royal
Family 561
Chronicles of England 41
Chronology of English
literature 1990
Chronology of post war
British politics 987
Chronology of the
construction of
Britain's railways
1366
Church, R. A. 1261
Church and parish 493
Church builders of the
nineteenth century
1832
Church furnishing and
decoration in England
and Wales 1881
Church of England in crisis
592
Church of England year
book 603

Deane, P. 1149
Deane, T. 900
Dearlove, J. 983
Death 890, 897
Death, ritual and bereavement 890
Debrett's bibliography of business history 1221
Debrett's distinguished people of today 579
Debrett's handbook 579
Debrett's Kings and Queens of Britain 571
Debrett's people of Kent 579
Decade of discontent: the changing British economy since 1973 1152
Decline and fall of the British aristocracy 652
Decline of British seapower 1104
Defence 1123-1134
Definitive guide to working offshore 1234
Defoe, D. 40
Delaney, T. 2154
Delderfield, E. R. 547
Delieb, E. 1629
The deluge: British society and the First World War 656
Demography *see* Population
Dench, L. 1358
Dennis, G. 1493
Dennis, R. 61
Dent, A. 171
Dent, E. J. 1771
Department of Prints and Drawings in the British Museum user's guide 1681
Derbyshire, J. 984
Derbyshire, J. D. 984
De Salis, H. R. 1338
Description of England 41
Descriptive catalogue of materials relating to the history of Great Britain and Ireland 436

Desert island discs 2328
Design and British industry 1282
Design directory 1237
Desmond, R. 213
Detsicas, A. 364
Development of the British economy 1914-1980 1156
Development of the welfare state 1939-1951 739
Devlin, K. 932
Dialects of England 1920
Dickens, A. G. 608
Dickie, J. 1046
Dickins, I. 1548
Dictionaries *see* Language
Dictionary of American and British euphemisms 1925
Dictionary of anonymous and pseudonymous English literature 1991
Dictionary of anonymous and pseudonymous publications in English 1991
Dictionary of archaic and provincial words 1908
Dictionary of artists of the English school 1595
Dictionary of artists who have exhibited works in the principal London exhibitions 1660
Dictionary of British and Irish botanists and horticulturists 213
Dictionary of British antique glass 1640
Dictionary of British art Series 1591
Dictionary of British artists 1880-1940 1591
Dictionary of British artists working 1900-1950 1675
Dictionary of British book illustrators and caricaturists 1800-1914 1682
Dictionary of British book illustrators: the twentieth century 1684
Dictionary of British children's fiction 2044
Dictionary of British educationalists 765
Dictionary of British equestrian artists 1668
Dictionary of British folk tales in the English language 878
Dictionary of British history 429
Dictionary of British portraiture 1670
Dictionary of British qualifications 769
Dictionary of British sculptors from the XIIIth century to the XXth century 1602
Dictionary of British sculptors 1660-1851 1603
Dictionary of British ships and seamen 1103
Dictionary of British steel engravers 1636
Dictionary of British studio potters 1607
Dictionary of British surnames 585
Dictionary of British twentieth century painters and sculptors 1591
Dictionary of British watercolour artists up to 1920 1667
Dictionary of British woman writers 2023
Dictionary of business biography 1191
Dictionary of catch phrases 1933
Dictionary of changes in meaning 1916
Dictionary of clichés 1934
Dictionary of contemporary British artists 1591
Dictionary of diseased English 1926

560

Guide to medieval sites in Britain 391

Guide to military museums 1134

Guide to official statistics 1495

Guide to Old English 1910

Guide to prehistoric England 405

Guide to Royal Britain 551

Guide to stained glass in Britain 1642

Guide to the abbeys of England and Wales 1874

Guide to the antique shops of Britain 1585

Guide to the archaeological sites of the British Isles 370

Guide to the architecture of London 336

Guide to the BBC 2318

Guide to the British food manufacturing industry 1278

Guide to the castles of England and Wales 1848

Guide to the cathedrals of Britain 1875

Guide to the Data Protection Act 1215

Guide to the local administrative units of England 1037

Guide to the national and provincial directories of England and Wales 2341

Guide to the national curriculum 787

Guide to the Oxford English Dictionary 1973

Guide to the prehistoric and Roman monuments in England and Wales 387

Guide to the Roman remains in Britain 407

Guide to the sources of

British military history 1125

Guide to the transport museums of Great Britain 2216

Guide to zoos and specialist collections 192

Guidebook to Arthurian Britain 870

Guinness book of British hit albums 1706

Guinness book of British hit singles 1705

Guinness book of darts 2174

Guinness book of flat racing 2130

Guinness book of great jockeys of the flat 2144

Guinness book of top forty charts 1706

Guinness guide to superlative Britain 273

Guinness non-league football fact book 2090

Guinness Rugby League fact book 2156

Gummett, P. 1567

Gunnis, R. 1603

Guth, D. G. 415

Gypsies 847, 859, 867

Gypsies: waggon-time and after 847

Gypsy-travellers in nineteenth-century society 859

H

HM Treasury and allied departments 991

HMSO annual catalogue 2355

HMSO daily list 2355

HMSO monthly catalogue 2355

Hadfield C. 1342

Hadfield, J. 274

Hadfield, M. 221

Hadrian's Wall 396

Hague, D. B. 1315

Haigh, C. 426

Hailstone, A. 1710

Haining, P. 684, 1115, 1363

Hale, J. 2177

Hale, J. R. 535

Halkett, S. 1991

Hall, A. R. 1565

Hall, D. J. 612

Hall, P. 552

Hall, S. J. G. 1409

Hallam, E. 460

Hallam, H. E. 1421

Hallam, J. 887

Hallé 1858-1983: a history of the orchestra 1718

Hallé tradition 1718

Hallgarten, E. 329

Halliwell-Phillips, J. D. 1908

Hallmarks on gold and silver plate 1625

Hallows, J. S. 1071

Halsbury's laws of England 928

Halsbury's statutes of England and Wales 929

Halsey, A. 653

Hambro company guide 1183

Hamid Ghodse 675, 932

Hamilton, D. 2281

Hamilton, J. 1664

Hamilton, K. A. 1048

Hamilton, M. 2150-2151

Hamlyn A-Z of British football 2085

Hammond, P. W. 1568

Hampshire, D. 11

Handbook of British archaeology 356

Handbook of British architectural styles 1844

Handbook of British birds 207

Handbook of British chronology 423

Handbook of British mammals 169

Handbook of British pottery and porcelain marks 1613

Hill, B. 119
Hill, D. 449
Hill, F. 654
Hill, P. 439
Hill-forts of Britain 389
Hillaby, J. 2168
Hillier, P. 1712
Hillman, E. 350
*Hillsborough Stadium
    disaster* 2087
Hilton, A. 1186
Hinde, T. 13
Hindley, G. 471
Hinton, J. 1464
Hiro, D. 848
Hirst, A. 1440
Hirst, M. 932
*Historic architecture of the
    Royal Navy* 1087
*Historic houses castles and
    gardens open to the
    public* 261
Historic houses handbook
    1829
*Historic railway sites in
    Britain* 1355
Historic towns 81
Historical atlas of Britain
    421
*Historical directory of trade
    unions* 1474
*Historical geography of
    England and Wales* 62
*Historical geography of
    England before AD
    1800* 60
*Historical writing in
    England* 534
Histories of old schools 799
*Histories of the First and
    Second World Wars*
    427
History
    pre-1485 409, 414-415,
        439, 539
    18th century 409-410,
        414-415, 417, 432, 439
    19th century 409-410,
        414-415, 417, 432, 439,
        477-479, 480-481, 532
    20th century 409-410,
        414-415, 417, 432,
        482-489

Anglo Saxon 414, 432,
    439, 444, 447-454
Anglo-Saxon Chronicle
    454, 539
Archives 411, 422, 427,
    430, 435, 498-499, 504,
    512, 1038
Atlas 416, 421, 425, 443,
    449, 520
bibliographies 409, 427,
    433-434, 437, 440-441,
    445, 448, 483, 506
Celts 448
Civil War 470, 472-473,
    476
county history 496,
    506-507, 509, 527
date guide 413
dictionary 429, 431, 438,
    489
economic 1140-1142,
    1145, 1149, 1153
Edwardian 488
feudalism 468
foreign relations 1038,
    1041-1042, 1044, 1050,
    1054, 1058, 1059
general and reference
    works 409-440
heraldry 502
historiography 530-540
Industrial Revolution
    829, 1255, 1258, 1562
industrialization 477
inter-war 485
local 490-529
Middle Ages 415, 432
    455-468
military 531
monarchy 455, 457, 465,
    474
Norman 415, 432, 456,
    458
overview 412, 420, 423,
    426, 428, 431, 447, 484
place names 424, 494,
    497, 500, 511, 515,
    519, 521, 524
prehistory 418
political 416-417
post-War 486, 530
primary sources 419,

430, 436, 461, 523,
    525, 528-529
Restoration 415
Roman 414, 439,
    441-446
Social 637-640, 642-647,
    657, 659, 663, 1144
Stuart 409-410, 414, 432,
    439
topography 490-491, 526
Tudor 409-410, 414-415,
    432, 469-476
World War One 531
World War Two 482
see also Architecture,
    Industrial
    Archaeology, Music,
    Politics, Prehistory,
    Religion, Society
History in print 427
*History men: the historical
    profession in England
    since the Renaissance*
    537
History of adult education
    780
*History of agricultural
    science in Great
    Britain* 1417
History of Anglican liturgy
    606
*History of atheism in
    Britain* 593
History of Britain Series
    432
History of Britain's trees
    240
*History of British bus
    services* 1331
History of British geology
    113
*History of British industrial
    relations* 1492
*History of British livestock
    husbandry* 1422
*History of British
    motorways* 1327
History of British music
    1760
*History of British space
    science* 1576
History of British surnames
    582

Jamieson, A. 781
Japanization of British industry 1211
Jarvis, P. 2323
Jasper, T. 1700, 1717
Jazz 1708
Jefferson, A. 1782
Jenkins, D. T. 1249
Jenkins, E. 892
Jenkins, J. G. 1412
Jenkins, R. 855
Jenkins, S. 2288
Jenner, M. 280
Jennings, I. 935
Jennings, P. 185
Jensen, M. 419
Jeremy, D. J. 1191
Jerman, B. 281
Jermy, A. C. 224
Jermy, C. 225
Jerome, J. A. 1316
Jervoise, E. 1318
Jewels of Queen Elizabeth II 548
Jewish year book 618
Jewry 833, 838, 858, 862, 868 *see also* Ethnic minorities, Religion
Jews of Britain 858
Job book 1483
Jobfile 92 1468
Jodrell Bank telescopes 1573
John Aubrey and the realms of learning 361
John Bull's island 851
John Hillaby's walking in Britain 2168
Johns, E. A. 655
Johnson, A. W. 212
Johnson, H. 932
Johnson, J. 1591
Johnson, N. 736
Johnson, P. 689, 1861
Johnson, S. 282, 1966
Johnson's England 480
Johnston, R. C. 67, 996
Johnstone, H. D. 1688
Jones, B. 364, 390, 443, 1367
Jones, B. L. 1522
Jones, C. 335
Jones, D. K. C. 110, 133

Jones, Edgar 1250, 1862
Jones, Edward 336
Jones, Emrys 1996
Jones, G. 1251
Jones, M. 736
Jones, P. F. 858
Jones, R. 1469
Jones, S. 1192, 2160
Jones-Baker, D. 900
Jordan, G. 1125
Joshi, H. 817
Joslin, E. C. 1137
Jourdain, F. C. R. 207
Journeys in England 51
Journeys into medieval England 280
Jowett, A. 1368
Jowett's railway atlas of Great Britain and Ireland 1368
Jowitt, W. A. 936
Joyce, J. 1319
Judicial statistics annual report 937
Julian Wilson's 100 great race horses 2147

K

Kadish, F. 337
Kain, R. J. P. 80
Kamen, R. H. 1863
Kavanagh, D. 997
Kavanagh, P. J. 1997
Kaye, D. 1193
Kaye, H. J. 536
Kearney, H. 428
Keen, M. H. 462
Keeping score 1502
Keir, D. K. 938
Keith, B. 410
Kelly's business directory 1194
Kelly's business links 1195
Kelly's export services 1302
Kelsall, R. K. 818
Kemp, I. 1727
Kemp, P. 714, 1091
Kempson, E. 939
Kennedy, C. 1252
Kennedy, M. 1718
Kennedy, P. 1719
Kennedy, R. 1531

Kenyon, J. P. 429, 472, 537
Kenyon, N. 1720
Ker, N. R. 2196
Kerney, M. P. 186
Kerr, M. 391
Kerr, N. 391
Kettle, M. 1470
Kew gardens 222, 238
Key British enterprises 1196
Key business ratios 1197
Key data: UK social and business statistics 1198
Kibby, G. 226
Kids' Britain 281
Kidson, F. 1714
Kightly, C. 893-894, 1127
Kilmurray, E. 1670
King, A. 2245
King, A. H. 1721
King, C. A. M. 110
King, E. 463
King, H. L. 1073
King, K. 669
King Arthur's Avalon 871
Kingdom, J. 1026
Kingfisher guide to the mammals of Britain and Europe 165
Kings and Queens of England and Great Britain 547
King's England Series 47
King's English 1949
King's peace 1637-1641 476
King's war 1641-1647 476
Kingsford, C. L. 338
Kingsley, H. 2324
Kinrade, D. 718
Kipling, A. L. 1073
Kiralfy, A. K. R. 940
Kirby, J. L. 578
Kirkpatrick, D. L. 1999
Kitchener's army 1077
Klapper, C. F. 1332
Knight, C. 163
Knight, D. 1572
Knights, E. 737
Knowles, A. 1369
Knowles, D. 436, 617
Korea 1950-1951 1048
Kosmin, B. 868
Koss, S. 2289

Kunitz, S. J. 2000-2001

L

LSO at 70 1741
Labour 1447, 1449-1451,
1463-1464, 1466-1467,
1477, 1487, 1489-1490,
1492 *see also*
Employment, Trades
Unions
*Labour and socialism: a
history of the British
labour movement* 1464
*Labour force survey 1990
and 1991* 1471
*Labour law in Great
Britain and Ireland*
1479
Labour party *see* Politics
Labour people 1001
Labour's grass routes 1487
Lacy, N. J. 895
Laing, J. 392, 1991
Laing, L. 392
Laing, W. 738
*Laing's review of private
health care* 738
Laird. D. 2133
Lake, C. 1528
Lake District 285, 306
Lamb, H. H. 133
Lambert, A. J. 547
Lambert, J. W. 2246
Lambourn, L. 1664
Lamming, D. 2079
Land, A. 739
*Land and water bugs of the
British Isles* 203
Land fit for heroin? 677
*Land of Britain: its use and
misuse* 1419
Landowners 1420
Landscape 108, 111, 115,
118, 120, 121, 128,
131, 133
Landscape of Britain 128
Landscape of King Arthur
872
Lane, A. 1048
Lang, D. C. 227
Langford, P. 644

Langton, J. 1253
Language 1900-1902, 1904,
1906
bad language 1923-1931
bibliography 1897
dialect 1917-1922
dictionary 1908,
1911-1914, 1916, 1918,
1922-1923, 1925-1926,
1928, 1930, 1933-1938,
1940, 1945, 1948,
1951, 1959, 1962-1976
English usage 1946-1952,
1954-1955, 1959-1960
etymology and word
origins 1912-1916
grammar 1909, 1953,
1958, 1961
history 1898-1899,
1903-1905, 1907
idioms 1932-1936
Old and Middle English
1908-1911
pronunciation 1956-1957
synonyms 1937-1945
thesaurus 1939,
1942-1944, 1968
Lapidge, M. 452
La Roche, N. 1941
Larkin, E. J. 1370
Larkin, J. G. 1370
Laslett, P. 811
Lass, R. 1903
Last, B. 2354
*Late Georgian and
Regency England
1760-1837* 415
*Late-medieval England
1377-1485* 415
*Later English broadside
ballads* 1994
*Later Middle Ages in
England* 432
Later Stuarts 1660-1714 414
Latin for local history 503
*Latin glossary for family
and local historians*
503
Laundy, P. 941
Law 914, 919, 928-929,
932-934, 936-937, 942,
947-949, 951, 954-955,
962-963

legal system 924-925, 940
legal profession 917-918,
939, 943
Parliament 915-917,
920-923, 926-927, 935,
941, 944-946, 952-953,
956-961, 964
periodicals 913
see also Customs
Law 942
Law for the travel industry
243
*Law Society's directory of
solicitors and barristers*
943
Lawless, P. 690
*Lawn Tennis Association
official handbook*
2165
Lawrence, J. 2141
Lawrence, N. 1199
Lawton, D. 776
Laybourn, K. 485
Layman, R. 1979
*Layman's dictionary of
English law* 947
Layton-Henry, Z. 856-857
Layzell, R. 1597
Leach, R. 896
*Leaders of the Church of
England 1828-1978*
610
Leafe, D. 1807
Leapman, M. 340
Lebrecht, N. 1722
Ledger, P. 1723
Lee, A. J. 1442, 2290
Lees, N. 1532
Lees, S. 1015
Lees-Spalding, J. 768
Legal advice and assistance
939
Legal profession 1990 918
Legat, M. 2247
Legget, J. 283
Leighton, P. 1472
Leland, J. 52
Leman, J. 1665
Leman, M. 1665
Lenman, B. P. 944
Leonard, E. M. 740
Leslie, N. B. 1074

570

Rights guide to non-means-
    tested benefits 749
Riley, N. D. 182
Riley, T. 1748
Rimmer, A. 301
Rise and decline of the
    English working
    classes 11918-1990
    1466
Rise and fall of Fleet Street
    2305
Rise and fall of the political
    press in Britain 2289
Rise of English nationalism
    20
Rise of industrial society in
    England 639
Rise of professional society
    641
Rise of the British coal
    industry 1261
Rise of the cinema in Great
    Britain 1801
Rise of the English actress
    1790
Ritchie, L. A. 1273
River quality in England
    and Wales 1542
Rivers 122, 125, 275, 290,
    352, 1339, 1542 see
    also Canals, Transport
Rivet, A. L. F. 398
Roach, J. 790
Road Time Trials Council
    (RTTC) 2112
Roads 404, 1323,
    1327-1328
Roads and their traffic
    1750-1850 1328
Roads and tracks of Britain
    404
Roaf, S. 1885
Robbins, C. 1543
Robbins, K. 1006
Roberts, E. 1451
Roberts, M. J. 196
Robertson, B. 1390
Robertson, M. 386, 2166
Robin Hood 889
Robins, L. 979
Robins, M. O. 1576
Robinson, A. 129
Robinson, A. H. 98
Robinson, B. 566

Robinson, E. 1577
Robinson, F. C. 1910
Robinson, J. M. 1886
Robinson, K. 752
Robinson, M. 1544
Rodale, J. I. 1941
Rodgers, D. 2360
Rodwell, J. S. 234
Rodwell, W. 399-400, 626
Rogers, D. 2329
Rogers, J. E. T. 1484
Rogers, M. 345, 580, 1670
Rogers, P. 40, 2014
Rogers, R. 1545
Roget, P. M. 1942
Roget's thesaurus of
    English words and
    phrases 1942
Rolles, S. I. 210
Rollin, J. 2082-2083
Rollings, N. 1138
Rolls Series 436
Rolt, L. T. C. 1274, 1345,
    1378-1379
Romaine, S. 1903
Roman and Anglian York
    396
Roman and medieval Bath
    396
Roman and medieval
    Canterbury 396
Roman Britain 296, 364,
    367, 369, 376-378, 387,
    396, 398, 407-408, 414,
    439, 441-446 see also
    History
Roman Britain 396
Roman Britain and the
    English settlements 414
Roman Catholicism 602,
    617, 622-623 see also
    Religion
Roman Catholicism in
    England 623
Roman England 270, 367
Roman forts 408
Roman London 396
Roman villa in Britain 398
Romano-British
    bibliography 441
Ronan, C. A. 1580
Rook, P. 932
Room, A. 519, 1916
Roose-Evans, J. 1791

Roots of urban unrest 671
Rose, C. 1546
Rose, J. 2257
Rose, R. 1007
Rose, T. 567
Ross, A. 296
Roth, A. 1008
Rotha, P. 1812
Rothenstein, J. 1673
Rothman's Football League
    players records 2077
Rothmans football
    yearbook 2082
Rothmans Rugby League
    yearbook 2155
Rothmans Rugby Union
    yearbook 2160
Rothmans snooker
    yearbook 2177
Rothwell, H. 419
Rouse, M. A. 2187
Rouse, R. H. 2187
Routh, C. R. N. 439
Routh, G. 1485
Routledge dictionary of
    historical slang 1928
Rowell, G. 1792
Rowley, C. K. 1309
Rowley, T. 296
Rowling, M. 900
Royal Academy exhibitors
    1905-1907 1661
Royal Academy of Arts
    1661
Royal Air Force (RAF)
    1105-1122, 1129
Royal air force and two
    World Wars 1108
Royal Air Force retired list
    1105
Royal and Ancient
    championship records
    2122
Royal and Ancient golfer's
    handbook 2121
Royal Ascot 2133
Royal Ballet: the first fifty
    years 1768
Royal Botanic Gardens
    Kew (Hepper) 222
Royal botanic Gardens
    Kew (Turrill) 238
Royal Britain 544

Royal Commission on
  Historical Manuscripts
  434
*Royal Commission on the
  Ancient and Historical
  Monuments of
  England* 401
*Royal Commissions
  1937-1981* 427, 1009
Royal Doulton 1815-1965
  1608
*Royal Doulton figures
  produced at Burslem
  c1890-1978* 1609
Royal encyclopedia 541
Royal faces 543
*Royal fortune: tax, money
  and the monarchy* 552
Royal heritage 565
*Royal Historical Society
  annual bibliography of
  British and Irish
  history* 437
Royal House of Windsor
  560
*Royal Institute of British
  Architects* 1868
Royal line of succession
  563
*Royal Mail. The Post
  Office since 1840* 1314
Royal Marines 1082, 1100
Royal Marines 1100
Royal Maundy 566
Royal mistresses 546
Royal National Life-boat
  Institution 1335
Royal Navy 1082-1099,
  1104, 1129
*Royal Navy aircraft carriers
  1945-1990* 1094
*Royal Opera House in the
  twentieth century* 1772
Royal palaces 556
Royal river highway 1339
*Royal Shakespeare
  Company* 1766
*Royal Society of Musicians
  of Great Britain. List
  of members 1738-1984*
  1728
Royal Worcester Porcelain
  1623

Royle, T. 1131
Rude words 2206
Ruff's guide to the turf 2139
*Rugby League Challenge
  Cup* 2157
Rugby League who's who
  2153
Rule, J. 639, 1486
Rundell, M. 1972
Runnymede Trust 837
Ruoff, J. E. 2015
Rupp, G. 607, 627
*Rural life in Victorian
  England* 657
Rural rides 39
Rushbridge, B. J. 1032
Russell, A. 628
Russell, C. 474
Russell, E. J. 1417
Russell, R. 1685, 2171
Russell, T. 1749
Rust, B. 1750
Rutherford simple genius
  1584
Ryall, W. 1388
Ryan, V. 1474
Ryde, P. 2122
Ryle, M. 927

S

Sachar, J. S. 586
Sachse, W. L. 415
Sacred sites 262, 286, 301,
  588, 612 *see also*
  Archaeology
Sadie, S. 1727
St. John, J. 2258
Saint, A. 330, 386
Salvation Army yearbook
  629
Salway, P. 414
Salzman, L. F. 1225
Sampson, A. 24
Samuel, R. 25
Sandall, R. 630
Sanderman, S. 1921
Sandon, H. 1623
Sangster, P. 631
Saturday night soldiers
  1076
Saul, N. 467

Saunders, A. 346, 386
Saunders, D. 170
Saunders, G. 16
Saunders, P. 983
Savage, A. 454
Savage, E. A. 2205
Savage, N. 1215
Saville, J. 1447
Savoy operas 1778
Saxon shore 444
Scannell, P. 2330
Scaping, P. 1275
Schlueter, J. 2017
Schlueter, P. 2017
Schofield, B. 904
Schofield, R. S. 832
Schomberg, G. 159
*School effect: a study of
  multi-racial
  comprehensives* 792
School Librarian 2031
School now 786
Schouvloff, A. 1793
Schroder, T. 1639
*Schumann Plan, Council of
  Europe and Western
  European integration
  1950-1952* 1048
Schwarz, C. M. 1943
Science and technology
  1555-1584
*Science and technology in
  the Industrial
  Revolution* 1577
*Science and technology in
  the United Kingdom*
  1578
*Science and Technology
  Policy* 1581
Science Park directory 1263
*Scientific names of the
  lepidoptera* 173
Scientists in Whitehall 1567
*Scientists of the Industrial
  Revolution* 1561
Scott, A. 302
Scott, B. 197
Scott, J. 1276
Scott, K. 2179
Scott-Kilvert, I. 2018
*Scottish Geographical
  Magazine* 30
Sculpture 1601-1604

Map of England

This map shows the more important towns and other features.

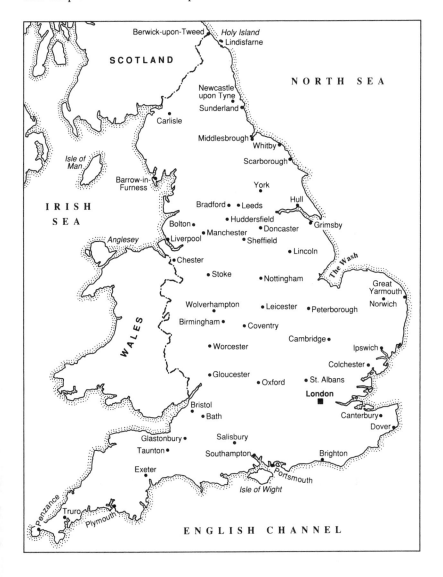